Practical WPF Charts and Graphics

Advanced Chart and Graphics Programming with the Windows Presentation Foundation

Jack Xu

Practical WPF Charts and Graphics

ISBN-13 (pbk): 978-1-4302-2481-5

ISBN-13 (electronic): 978-1-4302-2482-2

Printed and bound in the United States of America 9 8 7 6 5 4 3 2 1

Lead Editor: Ewan Buckingham
Technical Reviewer: Todd Meister
Editorial Board: Clay Andres, Steve Anglin, Mark Beckner, Ewan Buckingham, Tony Campbell, Gary Cornell, Jonathan Gennick, Michelle Lowman, Matthew Moodie, Jeffrey Pepper, Frank Pohlmann, Ben Renow-Clarke, Dominic Shakeshaft, Matt Wade, Tom Welsh
Copy Editor: Elliot Simon
Compositor: MacPS, LLC
Indexer: BIM Indexing and Proofreading Services
Artist: April Milne

Distributed to the book trade worldwide by Springer-Verlag New York, Inc., 233 Spring Street, 6th Floor, New York, NY 10013. Phone 1-800-SPRINGER, fax 201-348-4505, e-mail orders-ny@springer-sbm.com, or visit http://www.springeronline.com.

For information on translations, please e-mail info@apress.com, or visit http://www.apress.com.

Apress and friends of ED books may be purchased in bulk for academic, corporate, or promotional use. eBook versions and licenses are also available for most titles. For more information, reference our Special Bulk Sales–eBook Licensing web page at http://www.apress.com/info/bulksales.

The source code for this book is available to readers at http://www.apress.com. You will need to answer questions pertaining to this book in order to successfully download the code.

For my family, Ruth, Anna, Betty, and Tyler

Contents at a Glance

Contents

About the Author

 **Jack Xu** has a Ph.D in theoretical physics and has over 15 years of programming experience in Basic, Fortran, C, C++, Matlab, and C#. He specializes in numerical computation methods, algorithms, physical modeling, computer-aided design (CAD) tool development, graphical user interfaces, and 3D graphics. He is the author of several books about .NET programming, including *Practical C# Charts and Graphics*, *Practical WPF Graphics Programming*, *Practical Silverlight Programming*, and *Practical Numerical Methods with C#*

Technical Reviewer

 **Todd Meister** has been developing using Microsoft technologies for over ten years. He's been a Technical Editor on over 50 titles ranging from SQL Server to the .NET Framework. Besides technical editing titles he is an Assistant Director for Computing Services at Ball State University in Muncie, Indiana. He lives in central Indiana with his wife, Kimberly, and their four charismatic children.

Acknowledgments

First, I want to thank the whole Apress team, especially my editor, Ewan Buckingham, for giving me the opportunity to write this book. His trust, comments, questions, and patience helped me greatly as I was writing. I would also like to thank my copy editor, Elliot Simon, for ensuring that all the text flowed clearly and fit Apress' book style; and my coordinating editor, Anita Castro, for holding my feet to the fire to meet aggressive deadlines.

This book would not have been possible without my technical editor, Todd Meister, who deserves my sincere thanks for his excellent and insightful technical review comments. His suggestions helped me to improve the overall quality of the book. He also double-checked all code examples and technical instructions to ensure that you, the readers, would be able to follow them completely.

As always, I'm grateful to my wife, Dr. Ruth Zhang, and my lovely children Anna, Betty, and Tyler, for their patience, understanding, and encouragement.

Introduction

Overview

Welcome to *Practical WPF Charts and Graphics*. This book will provide all the tools you need to develop professional chart and graphics applications using the Windows Presentation Foundation (WPF) and C# based on the .NET Framework. I hope this book will be useful for WPF and C# programmers of all skill levels.

We've all heard the saying "A picture's worth a thousand words." Charts and graphics play a very important role in every Windows application. They make data easier to understand, add interest to reports, and have wide applications in our daily life. The scientific, engineering, and mathematics community always has a need to present data and results graphically. Microsoft's .NET platform with C# and WPF is one of the few and best development tools available for providing the computational capabilities both to generate data as a simulation engine and to display it in a variety of graphical representations based on the WPF graphics capability.

As a C# programmer, you are probably already familiar with Windows Forms, the mature and full-featured development tool. Windows Forms is built on top of the .NET Framework and uses the Windows Application Programming Interface (API) to create the visual appearance of standard user interface elements. It provides all kinds of tools for laying out windows, menus, dialogs, and controls. You can also develop graphics applications based on Windows Forms using the Graphical Device Interface (GDI+). However, creating a feature-rich graphics application using Windows Forms can be a difficult and tedious task. For example, Windows Forms provides no tools for creating three-dimensional (3D) graphics applications. Even a 3D point, the simplest of 3D graphics objects, must be defined first in a suitable 3D coordinate system before it can be used as a 3D graphics object.

WPF changes the landscape of graphics programming completely. At first, you might think that WPF just provides another way to create windows, menus, dialogs, and controls. However, WPF has much more to offer than any other Windows programming framework. It integrates three basic Windows elements — text, controls, and graphics — into a single programming model and puts these three elements in the same element tree in the same manner.

Without WPF, developing a graphics application would involve a number of different technologies, ranging from GDI/GDI+ for 2D graphics to Direct3D or OpenGL for 3D graphics. WPF, on the contrary, is designed as a single model for graphics application development, providing seamless integration between such services within an application. Similar constructs can be used for creating animations, data binding, and 3D models.

To take further advantage of new, powerful graphics hardware technologies, WPF implements a vector-based graphics model. This allows for graphics to be scaled based on screen-specific resolution without the loss of image quality, something impossible to do with fixed-size raster graphics. In addition, WPF leverages Direct3D for vector-based rendering and makes use of the graphics processing unit on any video card that implements DirectX in hardware.

With WPF, graphics elements can easily be integrated into any part of your user interface. For example, WPF provides 2D shape elements that can be involved in the user interface (UI) tree like other elements can. You are free to mix these shapes with any other kind of element, such as a button. The WPF 3D model is based on Direct3D technology and allows you to create a custom 3D shape library that can be reused in your projects. The main benefits that WPF offers in creating 3D graphics are its ease of use and its ability to integrate 3D content anywhere in applications.

As you may have already noticed, a plethora of WPF programming books are currently available in bookstores. The vast majority of these books are general-purpose user guides and tutorials that explain the basics of WPF and how to use it in implementing simple WPF applications. To help users take full advantage of WPF graphics features, however, requires a book that provides an in-depth introduction specifically to WPF chart and graphics programming.

This book is written with the intention of providing a complete and comprehensive explanation of WPF chart and graphics capability, and it pays special attention to creating various charts that can be used directly in real-world WPF applications. Much of this book contains original work based on my own programming experience when I was developing commercial computer-aided design (CAD) packages. Without WPF and the .NET Framework, developing advanced charts and graphics is a difficult and time-consuming task. To add even simple charts or graphs to your applications, you might often have to waste effort creating a chart program or buy commercial graphics and chart add-on packages.

Using third-party graphics and chart add-on products in your applications has several drawbacks, however:

- It isn't cost effective — it might cost hundreds or thousands of dollars for a sophisticated graphics and chart package.

- Compatibility is an issue — these third-party graphics and chart add-on tools are usually provided as DLL or COM components, which often lead to unexpected interface exceptions and unstable operations.

- There is little flexibility — from users' point of view, these packages appear to be black boxes because the source code is usually not provided, making it hard for users to add or modify any functionalities. You might find that these third-party products lack the special features you want in your applications, even though these products often provide an excess of extraneous functionalities you will never use.

- The coding is inefficient — these third-party add-on tools are often very large packages that contain far more functionalities than you will ever need in your applications. Even for a simple program, the final release tends to be huge due to the use of third-party add-ons. This is very inefficient for both coding management and distribution.

- License royalty is another issue — some third-party add-ons require not only the developing license, but also the distributed license royalty, resulting in an unnecessary increase in the development cost.

- Finally, maintenance is a problem — in most cases, third-party tools use a different programming language than the one you use in developing your applications, so you have to maintain the codes in an unmanaged manner.

Practical WPF Charts and Graphics provides everything you need to create your own advanced charts and graphics in your WPF applications. It shows you how to use C# and WPF to create a variety of graphics and charts that range from simple two-dimensional (2D) X-Y plots to complicated three-dimensional (3D) surface graphs. I will try my best to introduce you to C# and WPF chart and graphics programming in a simple way — simple enough to be easily followed by a beginner who has no prior experience developing WPF chart and graphics applications. You can learn from this book how to create a full range of 2D and 3D color graphics applications and how to use custom chart controls to create impressive graphic and chart effects without having to buy expensive third-party add-on products.

What This Book Includes

This book and its sample code listings, which are available for download from the Apress web site or my own web site, www.DrXuDotNet.com, provide you with:

- A complete, in-depth instruction on practical chart and graphics programming with C# and WPF. After reading this book and running the example programs, you will be able to add various sophisticated charts and graphics to your WPF applications.
- Ready-to-run example programs that allow you to explore the chart and graphics techniques described in the book. You can use these examples to understand better how the chart and graphics algorithms work. You can modify the code examples or add new features to them to form the basis of your own projects. Some of the example code listings provided in this book are already sophisticated chart and graphics packages that you can use directly in your own real-world WPF applications.
- Many classes in the sample code listings that you will find useful in your WPF chart and graphics programming. These classes include matrix manipulation, coordinate transformation, colormaps, chart controls, and the other useful utility classes. You can extract these classes and plug them into your own applications.

Is This Book for You?

You don't have to be an experienced WPF developer or an expert to use this book. I designed this book to be useful to people of all levels of WPF programming experience. In fact, I believe that if you have some experience with the programming language C#, Windows Forms, HTML, and the .NET Framework, you will be able to sit down in front of your computer, start up Microsoft Visual Studio 2008 and .NET 3.5, follow the examples provided in this book, and quickly become proficient with WPF chart and graphics programming. For those of you who are already experienced WPF developers, I believe this book has much to offer as well. A great deal of the information in this book about chart and graphics programming is not available in other WPF tutorial and reference books. In addition, you can use most of the example programs in this book directly in your own real-world application development. This book will provide you with a level of detail, explanation, instruction, and sample program code that will enable you to do just about anything related to WPF charts and graphics.

Perhaps you are a scientist, an engineer, a mathematician, a student, or a teacher rather than a professional programmer; nevertheless, this book is still a good bet for you. In fact, my own background is in theoretical physics, a field involving extensive numerical calculations as well as graphical representations of calculated data. I devoted my efforts to this field for many years, starting from undergraduate up to Ph.D. My first computer experience was with FORTRAN. Later on, I had programming experience with Basic, C, C++, and MATLAB. I still remember how hard it was in the early days to present computational results graphically. I often spent hours creating a publication-quality chart by hand, using a ruler, graph paper, and rub-off lettering. A year later, our group bought a chart-and-graphics package; however, I still needed to prepare my data in a proper format in order to process it with this package. During that time, I started paying attention to various development tools I could use to create integrated applications. I tried to find an ideal development tool that would allow me not only to generate data easily (computation capability) but also to represent data graphically (graphics and chart power). The C# and WPF development environment made it possible to develop such integrated applications. Ever since Microsoft .NET 1.0 came out, I have been in love with the C# language, and I have been able to use this tool successfully to create powerful graphics and chart applications, including commercial CAD packages.

WPF developers and technical professionals can use the majority of the example programs in this book routinely. Throughout the book, I'll emphasize the usefulness of WPF chart and graphics programming to real-world applications. If you follow closely the instructions presented in this book, you'll easily be able to develop various practical WPF chart and graphics applications, from 2D graphics and charts to sophisticated 3D surface chart packages. At the same time, I won't spend too much time discussing programming style, execution speed, or code optimization, because a plethora of books out there already deal with these topics. Most of the example programs you'll find in this book omit error handling. This makes the code easier to understand by focusing only on the key concepts and practical applications.

What Do You Need to Use This Book?

You'll need no special equipment to make the best use of this book and understand the algorithms. To run and modify the sample programs, you'll need a computer capable of running either Windows Vista or Windows XP. The software installed on your computer should include Visual Studio 2008 and .NET 3.5 standard edition or higher. If you have Visual Studio 2005 and .NET 3.0, you can also run most of the sample code with few modifications. Please remember, however, that this book is intended for Visual Studio 2008 and .NET 3.5 and that all of the example programs were created and tested on this platform, so it is best to run the sample code on the same platform.

How the Book Is Organized

This book is organized into 16 chapters, each of which covers a different topic about WPF chart and graphics programming. The following summaries of each chapter should give you an overview of the book's content.

Chapter 1, Overview of WPF Programming, introduces the basics of WPF and reviews some of the general aspects of WPF programming, including the XAML files you need to define user interfaces.

Chapter 2, 2D Transformations, covers the mathematical basics of 2D graphics programming. It discusses 2D vectors, matrices, and transformations in the homogeneous coordinate system, including translation, scaling, reflection, and rotation. These 2D matrices and transformations allow WPF applications to perform a wide variety of graphical operations on graphics objects in a simple and consistent manner.

Chapter 3, WPF Graphics Basics in 2D, reviews some fundamental concepts of 2D graphics and the 2D drawing model in WPF. It introduces coordinate systems and basic 2D shapes.

Chapter 4, Colors and Brushes, covers the color system and brushes that WPF uses to paint graphics objects. It introduces a variety of brushes and their transformations. You'll learn how to create exotic visual effects using different brushes, including gradient and drawing brushes.

Chapter 5, 2D Line Charts, contains instructions on how to create elementary 2D X-Y line charts. It introduces basic chart elements, including chart area, plot area, axes, title, labels, ticks, symbols, and legend. These basic chart elements are common in the other types of charts as well.

Chapter 6, Specialized 2D Charts, covers the specialized charts often found in commercial chart packages and spreadsheet applications. These specialized charts include bar charts, stair-step charts, stem charts, charts with error bars, pie charts, area charts, and polar charts.

Chapter 7, Stock Charts, shows how to create a variety of stock charts in WPF, including the standard Hi-Lo Open-Close stock charts, Candlestick stock charts, and moving averages. In addition, it discusses embedding Yahoo stock charts into WPF applications.

Chapter 8, Interactive 2D Charts, demonstrates how to implement interactive charts, which allow the user to interact with them by using a mouse to zoom, pan, and retrieve data from the chart.

Chapter 9, 2D Chart Controls, shows how to put 2D chart applications into a custom user control and how to use such a control in WPF applications.

Chapter 10, Data Interpolations, explains the implementation of several interpolation methods, which can be used to construct new data points within the range of a discrete set of known data points.

Chapter 11, Curve Fitting, explains a variety of curve-fitting approaches that you can apply to data containing noise, usually due to measuring errors. Curve fitting tries to find the best fit to a given set of data.

Chapter 12, 3D Transformations, extends the concepts described in Chapter 2 into the third dimension. It explains how to define 3D graphics objects and how to translate, scale, reflect, and rotate these 3D objects. It also describes transformation matrices that represent projection and transformations, which allow you to view 3D graphics objects on a 2D screen. You'll also learn how WPF defines 3D vectors, matrices, and projections.

Chapter 13, WPF Graphics Basics in 3D, explores the basics of 3D models in WPF. It introduces Viewport3D, the 3D geometry and the mesh model, lighting, and camera, among other topics. You'll also learn how to create basic 3D shapes directly in WPF.

Chapter 14, 3D Charts with the WPF 3D Engine, explains how to create various 3D surface charts, from simple surfaces to complex surfaces, using rectangular meshes and a variety of techniques, including parameterization, extrusion, and revolution. It also describes how to add lighting and shading effects to these surfaces.

Chapter 15, 3D Charts Without the WPF 3D Engine, begins with a description of the coordinate system used in 3D charts and graphics and shows you how to create 3D coordinate axes, tick marks, axis labels, and gridlines without using the WPF 3D engine. It then explains techniques for creating simple 3D surface charts.

Chapter 16, Specialized 3D Charts, shows how to create a wide variety of 3D charts, including contour charts, 3D bar charts, and 3D combination charts. In creating these charts, you will use a few specialized techniques, including Z-order, to manipulate the data displayed on your 2D computer screen.

Using Code Examples

You may use the code in this book in your own applications and documentation. You don't need to contact the author or the publisher for permission, unless you are reproducing a significant portion of the code. For example, writing a program that uses several chunks of code from this book doesn't require permission. Selling or distributing the example code listings does require permission. Incorporating a significant amount of example code from this book into your applications and documentation also requires permission. Integrating the example code from this book into commercial products is not allowed without written permission of the author and publisher.

Customer Support

I am always interested in hearing from readers and would enjoy learning of your thoughts on this book. You can send me comments by e-mail to jxu@DrXuDotNet.com. I also provide updates, bug fixes, and ongoing support via the Apress web site

www.apress.com

and my own web site:

www.DrXuDotNet.com

You can also obtain the complete source code for all of the examples in this book from the foregoing web sites.

■ ■ ■

CHAPTER 1

Overview of WPF Programming

Windows Presentation Foundation (WPF) is a next-generation graphics platform included in Microsoft .NET Framework 3.0 and 3.5. It allows you to build advanced user interfaces (UIs) that incorporate documents, media, two-dimensional (2D) and three-dimensional (3D) graphics, animations, and weblike characteristics. Built on the .NET Framework 3.0 and 3.5, WPF provides a managed environment for developing applications using the Windows operating system. Like other features of the .NET Framework 3.0 and 3.5, WPF is available for Windows Vista, Windows XP, Windows Server 2003, and Windows Server 2008.

In a pre-WPF world, developing a Windows application would have required the use of several different technologies. For instance, in order to add forms and user controls to your application, you needed to use the Windows Forms included in the .NET Framework. You had to use GDI+ to create images and 2D graphics. To add 3D graphics, you would have needed to use Direct3D or OpenGL.

WPF is designed to be a unified solution for application development, providing a seamless integration of different technologies. With WPF, you can create vector graphics or complex animations and incorporate media into your applications to address all of the areas just listed.

New features in WPF

WPF introduces several new features that you can take advantage of when you develop your WPF applications. To utilize powerful new graphics hardware, WPF implements a vector graphics model based on Direct3D technology. This allows graphics to scale according to screen-specific resolution without losing image quality, something impossible to do with fixed-size raster graphics. WPF leverages Direct3D for vector-based rendering, using the graphics-processing unit on any video card with built-in DirectX implemented. In anticipation of future technology, such as high-resolution display, WPF uses a floating-point logical pixel system and supports 32-bit ARGB colors.

Furthermore, to easily represent UI and user interaction, WPF introduces a new XML-based language called Extensible Application Markup Language (XAML). XAML allows applications to dynamically parse and manipulate user interface elements at either design time or runtime. It uses the code-behind model, similar to ASP.NET programming, allowing designers and developers to work in parallel and to seamlessly combine their work into a compelling user experience. Of course, WPF also allows you to opt out of using XAML files when you develop WPF applications, meaning you can still develop your applications entirely in code, such as C#, C++, or Visual Basic.

Another new feature is the resolution-independent layout. All WPF layout dimensions are specified using device-independent pixels. A device-independent pixel is one ninety-sixth of an inch in size and resolution-independent, so your results will be similar regardless of whether you render to a 72-DPI (dots per inch) monitor or a 19,200-DPI printer.

WPF is also based on a dynamic layout. This means that a UI element arranges itself on a window or page according to its content, its parent layout container, and the available screen area. Dynamic layout facilitates localization by automatically adjusting the size and position of UI elements when the strings they contain change length. By contrast, the layout in Windows Forms is device-dependent and more likely to be static. Typically, Windows Forms controls are positioned absolutely on a form using dimensions specified in hardware pixels.

XAML Basics

As mentioned previously, using XAML to create a UI is a new feature in WPF. In this section, I'll present an introduction to XAML and consider its structure and syntax. Once you understand the basics of XAML, you can easily create a UI and layout in WPF applications.

Why Is XAML Needed?

Since WPF applications can be developed entirely in code, it is perfectly natural to ask, "Why do I even need XAML in the first place?" The reason can be traced back to the issue of efficient implementation of complex, graphically rich applications. A long time ago, developers realized that the most efficient way to develop such applications was to separate the graphics portion from the underlying code. This way, designers could work on the graphics while developers could work on the code behind the graphics. Both parts could be separately designed and refined, without any versioning headaches.

Before WPF, it was impossible to separate the graphics content from the code. For example, when you work with Windows Forms, you define every form entirely in C# code or any other language. As you add controls to the UI and configure them, the program needs to adjust the code in corresponding form classes. If you want to decorate your forms, buttons, and other controls with graphics that designers have developed, you have to extract the graphic content and export it to a bitmap format. This approach works for simple applications, but it is very limited for complex, dynamic applications. In addition, graphics in bitmap format can lose their quality when they are resized.

The XAML technology introduced in WPF resolves these issues. When you develop a WPF application in Visual Studio, the window you create isn't translated into code. Instead, it is serialized into a set of XAML tags. When you run the application, these tags are used to generate the objects that compose the UI.

XAML isn't a must in order to develop WPF applications. You can implement your WPF applications entirely in code; however, the windows and controls created in code will be locked into the Visual Studio environment and only available to programmers. There is no way to separate the graphics portion from the code.

In other words, WPF doesn't require XAML. However, XAML opens up a world of possibilities for collaboration, because many design tools understand the XAML format.

Creating XAML Files

There are some standard rules for creating an XAML file. First, every element in an XAML file must relate to an instance of a .NET class. The name of the element must match the name of the class exactly. For example, <TextBlock> tells WPF to create a TextBlock object.

In an XAML file, you can nest one element inside another. This way, you can place an element as a child of another element. For example, if you have a Button inside a Canvas, this means that your UI contains a Canvas that has a Button as its child. You can also set the properties of each element through attributes.

Let's look at a simple XAML structure:

```
<Window x:Class="WPFOverview.FirstWPFProgram"
    xmlns="http://schemas.micro.softcom/winfx/2006/xaml/presentation"
    xmlns:x="http://schemas.microsoft.com/winfx/2006/xaml"
    Title=" FirstWPFProgram" Height="300" Width="300">
    <Grid>
        <TextBlock>Hello, WPF!</TextBlock>
    </Grid>
</Window>
```

This file includes three elements: a top-level Window element, which represents the entire window; a *Grid*; and a *TextBlock* that is placed inside the *Grid* as a child. You can use either a Window or a Page as the top-level element in WPF. A Page is similar to a Window, but it is used for navigable applications. WPF also involves an Application file that defines application resources and startup settings. If you start with a new WPF Window (or Page) project, Visual Studio will automatically generate an Application file called *App.xaml*. In this book, I'll use Window as the top-level WPF element, though you can just as easily use Page.

The starting tag for the Window element includes a class name and two XML namespaces. The *xmlns* attribute is a specialized attribute in XML that is reserved for declaring namespaces. The two namespaces in the preceding code snippet will appear in every WPF XAML file. You only need to know that these namespaces simply allow the XAML parser to find the right classes. Also notice the three properties inside the tag: *Title*, *Height*, and *Width*. Each attribute corresponds to a property of the Window class. These attributes tells WPF to create a 300-by-300 window with the title *FirstWPFProgram*.

Inside the Window tag is a *Grid* control that in turn contains a *TextBlock* with its *Text* property set to "Hello, WPF!" You can also create the same *TextBlock* using the following snippet:

```
<TextBlock Text="Hello, WPF!"/>
```

Code-Behind Files

XAML is used to create the UI for your application; but in order to make your application function, you need to attach event handlers to the UI. XAML makes this easy using the class attribute:

```
<Window x:Class="WPFOverview.FirstWPFProgram"… … >
```

The *x* namespace prefix places the class attribute in the XAML namespace, which means that this is a more general part of the XAML language. This example creates a new class named *WPFOverview.FirstWPFProgram*, which derives from the base Window class.

When you create a WPF Windows application, Visual Studio will automatically create a partial class where you can place your event-handling code. Previously, we discussed the simple XAML file *WPFOverview.xaml*. If you create a WPF Windows application named *FirstWPFProgram*, Visual Studio will automatically generate the following code-behind file:

```
using System;
using System.Windows;
using System.Windows.Controls;
using System.Windows.Media;

namespace FristWPFProgam
{
    /// <summary>
    /// Interaction logic for FirstWPFProgram.xaml
    /// </summary>

    public partial class FirstWPFProgram : Window
```

```
    {
        public FirstWPFProgram()
        {
            InitializeComponent();
        }
    }
}
```

When you compile this application, XAML is translated into a CLR-type declaration that is merged with the logic in the code-behind class file (*FirstWPFProgram.xaml.cs* in this example) to form one single unit.

The foregoing code-behind file contains only a default constructor, which calls the *InitializeComponent* method when you create an instance of the class. This is similar to the C# class in Windows Forms.

Your First WPF Program

Let's consider a simple WPF example. Open Visual Studio 2008 and create a new WPF Windows Application project called *WPFOverview*. Remove the default *window1.xaml* and *window1.xaml.cs* files from the project and add a new WPF Window to the project. Name it *StartMenu*, which will add two files, *StartMenu.xaml* and *StartMenu.xaml.cs*, to the project. Open the *App.xaml* file and change its *StartupUri* property from *window1.xaml* to *StartMenu.xaml*. By doing this, you make the *StartMenu* window the main menu window, from which you can access all of the examples in the project. You can examine the source code for these two files to see how you implement them. This file structure will be used for accessing code examples in each chapter throughout this book. Add another new WPF Window to the project and name it *FirstWPFProgram*. Figure 1-1 shows the results of running this example. It includes several controls: a *Grid*, which is the most common control for arranging layouts in WPF, a *StackPanel* inside the *Grid* used to hold other controls, including a *TextBlock*, a *TextBox*, and two *Button* controls. The goal of this example is to change the text in the *TextBlock* accordingly when the user enters text in the *TextBox*. At the same time, the text color or font size of the text in the *TextBlock* control can be changed when the user clicks the *Change Text Color* or *Change Text Size* button.

Figure1-1. *Your first WPF program example.*

Properties in XAML

Open the default *FirstWPFProgrm.xaml* file and add the following code to the file:

```
<Window x:Class="WPFOverview.FirstWPFProgram"
    xmlns="http://schemas.microsoft.com/winfx/2006/xaml/presentation"
    xmlns:x="http://schemas.microsoft.com/winfx/2006/xaml"
    Title=" FirstWPFProgram" Height="300" Width="300">
    <Grid>
        <StackPanel>
            <TextBlock Name="textBlock" Margin="5"
                TextAlignment="Center"
                Text="Hello WPF!"/>
            <TextBox Name="textBox" Margin="5" Width="200"
                TextAlignment="Center"
                TextChanged="OnTextChanged"/>
            <Button Margin="5" Width="200"
                Content="Change Text Color"
                Click="btnChangeColor_Click"/>
            <Button Margin="5" Width="200"
                Content="Change Text Size"
                Click="btnChangeSize_Click"/>
        </StackPanel>
    </Grid>
</Window>
```

You can see that the attributes of an element set properties of the corresponding object. For example, the *TextBlock* control in the preceding XAML file configures the name, margin, text alignment, and text:

```
<TextBlock Name="textBlock" Margin="5"
        TextAlignment="Center" Text="Hello WPF!"/>
```

In order for this to work, the *TextBlock* class in WPF must provide corresponding properties. You specify various properties for other controls that affect your layout and UI in a similar fashion.

To achieve the goal of this example, you will need to manipulate the *TextBlock*, *TextBox*, and *Button* controls programmatically in the code-behind file. First, you need to name the *TextBlock* and *TextBox* controls in your XAML file. In this example, these controls are named *textBlock* and *textBox*. Although in a traditional Windows Forms application every control must have a name, in a WPF application you only need to name the elements that are manipulated programmatically. Here, for example, you don't need to name the *Grid*, *StackPanel*, and *Button* controls.

Event Handlers in Code-Behind Files

In the previous section, you learned how to map attributes to corresponding properties. However, to make controls function you may sometimes need to attach attributes with event handlers. In the foregoing XAML file, you must attach an *OnTextChanged* event handler to the *TextChanged* property of the *TextBox*. You must also define the *Click* property of the two buttons using two click event handlers: *btnChangeColor_Click* and *btnChangeSize_Click*.

This assumes that there should be methods associated with names *OnTextChanged*, *btnChangeColor_Click*, and *btnChangeSize_Click* in the code-behind file. Here is the corresponding code-behind file for this example:

```csharp
using System;
using System.Windows;
using System.Windows.Controls;
using System.Windows.Media;

namespace WPFOverview
{
    public partial class FirstWPFProgram : Window
    {
        public FirstWPFProgram ()
        {
            InitializeComponent();
        }

        private void OnTextChanged(object sender,
                TextChangedEventArgs e)
        {
            textBlock.Text = textBox.Text;
        }

        private void btnChangeColor_Click(object sender,
                RoutedEventArgs e)
        {
            if (textBlock.Foreground == Brushes.Black)
                textBlock.Foreground = Brushes.Red;
            else
                textBlock.Foreground = Brushes.Black;
        }

        private void btnChangeSize_Click(object sender,
                RoutedEventArgs e)
        {
            if (textBlock.FontSize == 11)
                textBlock.FontSize = 24;
            else
                textBlock.FontSize = 11;
        }
    }
}
```

Note that event handlers must have the correct signature. The event model in WPF is slightly different than that in earlier versions of .NET. WPF supports a new model based on event routing. The rest of the preceding code-behind file is very similar to that used in Windows Forms applications with which you are already familiar.

Running this example produces the results shown in Figure 1-1. If you type any text in the text box field, the same text as in the text block will appear. In addition, the color or font size will change depending on which button is clicked.

Code-Only Example

As mentioned previously, XAML is not necessary for creating WPF applications. WPF fully supports code-only implementation, although the use of this approach is less common. There are pros and cons with the code-only approach. An advantage of the code-only method is that it gives you full control over customization. For example, when you want to conditionally add or substitute controls depending on the user's input, you can easily implement condition logic in code. This is hard to do in XAML because controls in XAML are embedded in your assembly as fixed, unchanging resources. A disadvantage is that since WPF controls do not include constructors with parameters, developing a code-only application in WPF is sometimes tedious. Even adding a simple control, such as a button, to your application takes several lines of code.

In the following example, we'll convert the previous example, *FirstWPFProgram*, into a code-only application. Open the *WPFOverview* project, add a new WPF Window, and name it *CodeOnly*. Open the *CodeOnly.xaml* file and remove the *Grid* control from the Window. The file should look as follows:

```
<Window x:Class="WPFOverview.CodeOnly"
    xmlns="http://schemas.microsoft.com/winfx/2006/xaml/presentation"
    xmlns:x="http://schemas.microsoft.com/winfx/2006/xaml">
</Window>
```

Open the code-behind file, *CodeOnly.xaml.cs*, and add the following code to the file:

```
using System;
using System.Windows;
using System.Windows.Controls;
using System.Windows.Media;

namespace WPFOverview
{
    public partial class CodeOnly : Window
    {
        private TextBlock textBlock;
        private TextBox textBox;

        public CodeOnly()
        {
            InitializeComponent();
            Initialization();
        }

        private void Initialization()
        {
            // Configure the window:
            this.Height = 300;
            this.Width = 300;
            this.Title = "Code Only Example";

            // Create Grid and StackPanel and add them to window:
            Grid grid = new Grid();
            StackPanel stackPanel = new StackPanel();
            grid.Children.Add(stackPanel);
            this.AddChild(grid);

            // Add a text block to stackPanel:
```

7

```
        textBlock = new TextBlock();
        textBlock.Margin = new Thickness(5);
        textBlock.Height = 30;
        textBlock.TextAlignment = TextAlignment.Center;
        textBlock.Text = "Hello WPF!";
        stackPanel.Children.Add(textBlock);

        // Add a text box to stackPanel:
        textBox = new TextBox();
        textBox.Margin = new Thickness(5);
        textBox.Width = 200;
        textBox.TextAlignment = TextAlignment.Center;
        textBox.TextChanged += OnTextChanged;
        stackPanel.Children.Add(textBox);

        // Add button to stackPanel used to change text color:
        Button btnColor = new Button();
        btnColor.Margin = new Thickness(5);
        btnColor.Width = 200;
        btnColor.Content = "Change Text Color";
        btnColor.Click += btnChangeColor_Click;
        stackPanel.Children.Add(btnColor);

        // Add button to stackPanel used to change text font size:
        Button btnSize = new Button();
        btnSize.Margin = new Thickness(5);
        btnSize.Width = 200;
        btnSize.Content = "Change Text Color";
        btnSize.Click += btnChangeSize_Click;
        stackPanel.Children.Add(btnSize);
    }

    private void OnTextChanged(object sender,
        TextChangedEventArgs e)
    {
        textBlock.Text = textBox.Text;
    }

    private void btnChangeColor_Click(object sender,
        RoutedEventArgs e)
    {
        if (textBlock.Foreground == Brushes.Black)
            textBlock.Foreground = Brushes.Red;
        else
            textBlock.Foreground = Brushes.Black;
    }

    private void btnChangeSize_Click(object sender,
        RoutedEventArgs e)
    {
        if (textBlock.FontSize == 11)
            textBlock.FontSize = 24;
        else
```

```
                textBlock.FontSize = 11;
        }
    }
}
```

This code listing will reproduce the same results as shown in Figure 1-1.

You can see that the *CodeOnly* class is similar to a form class in a traditional Windows Forms application. It derives from the base Window class and adds private member variables for *TextBlock* and *TextBox*. Pay close attention to how controls are added to their parents and how event handlers are attached.

XAML-Only Example

In the previous sections, you learned how to create the same WPF application using the XAML plus code and the code-only techniques. The standard approach for developing WPF applications is to use both XAML and a code-behind file. Namely, you use XAML to lay out your UI, and then you use code to implement event handlers. For applications with a dynamic UI, you may want to go with the code-only method.

However, for simple applications, it is also possible to use an XAML-only file without writing any C# code. This is called a *loose* XAML file. At first glance, a loose XAML file appears useless — after all, what's the point of a UI with no code to drive it? However, XAML provides several features that allow you to perform certain functions without using code-behind files. For example, you can develop an XAML-only application including features such as animation, event trigger, and data binding.

Here we'll create a loose XAML application that mimics the *FirstWPFProgram* example. Even though it can't reproduce perfectly the results shown in Figure 1-1, the XAML-only application still generates a much more impressive result than static HTML would.

Add a new WPF Window to the *WPFOverview* project and name it *XAMLOnly*. Here is the markup for this example:

```
<Window x:Class="WPFOverview.XAMLOnly"
    xmlns="http://schemas.microsoft.com/winfx/2006/xaml/presentation"
    xmlns:x="http://schemas.microsoft.com/winfx/2006/xaml"
    Title="Window1" Height="300" Width="300">
    <Grid>
        <StackPanel>
            <TextBlock Name="textBlock" Margin="5"
                TextAlignment="Center" Height="30"
                Text="{Binding ElementName=textBox,Path=Text}"/>
            <TextBox Name="textBox" Margin="5" Width="200"
                TextAlignment="Center" Text="Hello, WPF!"/>
            <Button Margin="5" Width="200"
                Content="Change Text Color">
                <Button.Triggers>
                    <EventTrigger RoutedEvent="Button.Click">
                        <BeginStoryboard>
                            <Storyboard>
                                <ColorAnimation
Storyboard.TargetName="textBlock"
Storyboard.TargetProperty= "(TextBlock.Foreground).(SolidColorBrush.Color)"
From="Black" To="Red" Duration="0:0:1"/>
                            </Storyboard>
                        </BeginStoryboard>
                    </EventTrigger>
```

```
                    </EventTrigger>
                </Button.Triggers>
            </Button>

            <Button Margin="5" Width="200"
                Content="Change Text Size">
                <Button.Triggers>
                    <EventTrigger RoutedEvent="Button.Click">
                        <BeginStoryboard>
                            <Storyboard>
                                <DoubleAnimation
                                    Storyboard.TargetName="textBlock"
                                    Storyboard.TargetProperty="FontSize"
                                    From="11" To="24" Duration="0:0:0.2"/>
                            </Storyboard>
                        </BeginStoryboard>
                    </EventTrigger>
                </Button.Triggers>
            </Button>
        </StackPanel>
    </Grid>
</Window>
```

This XAML file first binds the *Text* property of the *TextBlock* to the *Text* property of the *TextBox*. This data binding allows you to change the text of the *TextBlock* by typing text in the *TextBox* field. Then two buttons are created, which function to change text color and font size. This can be done by using the buttons' event triggers, which start a color animation or a double animation, depending on which button is clicked.

Even though this application lacks a code-behind file, the buttons can still function. Of course, this XAML-only example cannot replicate the previous example involving a code-behind file. The reason is that although the event triggers in XAML files can start an animation, they cannot involve if-statements, for-loops, methods, and any other computation algorithm.

CHAPTER 2

■■■

2D Transformations

In the previous chapter, you learned about basic WPF programming using both XAML and code-behind files. To create graphics and charts in real-world WPF applications, you need to understand transformation operations on graphics objects.

In a graphics application, operations can be performed in different coordinate systems. Moving from one coordinate space to another requires the use of transformation matrices. In this chapter, we review the mathematic basis of vectors, matrices, and transformations in 2D space. Here, I'll acknowledge the importance of matrices and transforms in chart and graphics applications by presenting you with a more formal exposition of their properties. We concern ourselves with linear transformations among different coordinate systems. Such transforms include simple scaling, reflection, translation, and rotations. You'll learn how to perform matrix operations and graphics object transformations in WPF. More complicated transformations in 3D will be covered in Chapter 12.

Basics of Matrices and Transformations

Vectors and matrices play an important role in the transformation process. WPF uses a row-major definition for both vectors and matrices. Thus, in WPF a vector is a row array and a matrix is a multidimensional array. This section explains the basics of 2D matrices and 2D transformations. By changing the coordinates of a graphics object in the world coordinate system, such as zooming or panning, you can easily move the graphics object to another region of the screen. However, if your graphic contains more than one object, you may want to move one of the objects without affecting the others. In this case, you can't use simple zooming and panning to move the object because doing so would move the other objects as well.

Instead, you can apply a transformation to the object you want to move. Here we'll discuss transformations that scale, rotate, and translate an object.

Vectors and Points

In a row-major representation, a vector is a row array that represents a displacement in a 2D space. A point, on the other hand, is defined by its X and Y coordinates at a fixed position, as shown in Figure 2-1.

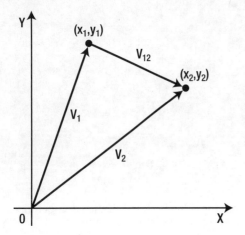

Figure 2-1. *Points and vectors.*

The difference between a vector and a point is that a point represents a fixed position, whereas a vector represents a direction and a magnitude. Thus, the end points (x_1, y_1) and (x_2, y_2) of a line segment are points, but their difference, V_{12}, is a vector that represents the direction and length of that line segment. In WPF, the following code snippet is a valid statement:

```
Vector v12 = new Point(x2, y2) - new Point(x1, y1);
```

Mathematically, you should keep in mind that $V_{12} = V_2 - V_1$, where V_2 and V_1 are vectors from the origin to the point (x_1, y_1) and the point (x_2, y_2), respectively.

In WPF, you can apply a transform matrix directly to either a vector or a point.

Scaling

To scale or stretch an object in the X direction, you simply multiply the X coordinates of each of the object's points by a scaling factor s_x. Similarly, you can also scale an object in the Y direction. The scaling process can be described by the following equation:

$$(x_1 \ y_1) = (x \ y) \begin{pmatrix} s_x & 0 \\ 0 & s_y \end{pmatrix} = (s_x x \ s_y y)$$

(2.1)

For example, a scaling matrix that shrinks X and Y uniformly by a factor of 2 as well as a matrix that halves in the Y direction and increases by three-halves in the X direction are, respectively,

$$\begin{pmatrix} 0.5 & 0 \\ 0 & 0.5 \end{pmatrix} \text{ and } \begin{pmatrix} 1.5 & 0 \\ 0 & 0.5 \end{pmatrix}$$

These two scaling matrix operations have very different effects on objects, as shown in Figure 2-2.

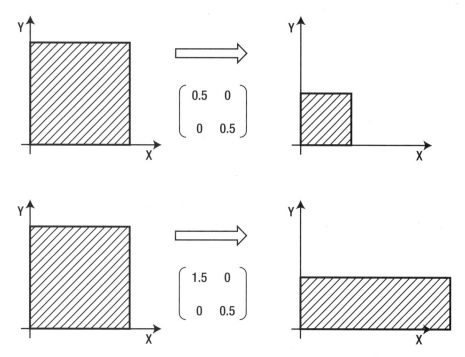

Figure 2-2. Uniform scaling by half in the x and y directions (top) and nonuniform scaling in the X and Y directions (bottom).

Reflection

By reflecting an object across the X and Y axes, you can create a mirror image of the object. Reflecting an object across an axis is equivalent to scaling it with a negative scaling factor. The transform matrices across either of the coordinate axes can be written in the following forms:

Reflection across the X axis: $\begin{pmatrix} -1 & 0 \\ 0 & 1 \end{pmatrix}$

Reflection across the Y axis: $\begin{pmatrix} 1 & 0 \\ 0 & -1 \end{pmatrix}$

As you might expect, a matrix with –1 in both elements of the diagonal is a reflection that is simply a rotation by 180 degrees.

Rotation

Suppose you want to rotate an object by an angle θ counterclockwise. First, suppose you have a point (x_1, y_1) that you want to rotate by an angle θ to get to the point (x_2, y_2), as shown in Figure 2-3.

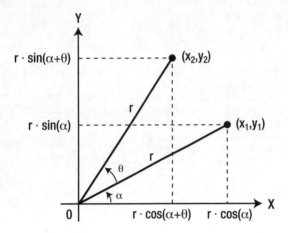

Figure 2-3. *Rotation from point (x_1, y_1) to (x_2, y_2).*

The distance from the point to the origin is assumed to be r. We then have the following relations:

$$x_1 = r\cos\alpha$$

$$y_1 = r\sin\alpha$$

The point (x_2, y_2) is the same point rotated by an additional angle of θ. Since this point also has a distance r from the origin, its coordinates are given by

$$x_2 = r\cos(\alpha + \theta) = r\cos\alpha\cos\theta - r\sin\alpha\sin\theta$$

$$y_2 = r\sin(\alpha + \theta) = r\sin\alpha\cos\theta + r\cos\alpha\sin\theta$$

Substituting the components of $x_1 = r\cos\alpha$ and $y_1 = r\sin\alpha$ into the preceding equations gives

$$x_2 = x_1\cos\theta - y_1\sin\theta$$

$$y_2 = x_1\sin\theta + y_1\cos\theta$$

In matrix form, the equivalent rotation transformation that takes point (x_1, y_1) to (x_2, y_2) is given by the following rotation matrix:

$$R(\theta) = \begin{pmatrix} \cos\theta & \sin\theta \\ -\sin\theta & \cos\theta \end{pmatrix} \qquad (2.2)$$

Translation

To translate an object, you simply add an offset to the original X and Y coordinates of the points that make up the object:

$$x_1 = x + dx$$
$$y_1 = y + dy \qquad \text{(2.3)}$$

Although translations look simple, they can't be expressed in terms of a transform matrix. It would be feasible to keep track of scales, reflections, and rotations as matrices while keeping track of translations separately. However, doing so would involve fairly painful bookkeeping, particularly in an application that includes many different transformations. Instead, you can use a technique that moves the computation into a higher dimension. This technique allows you to treat each different transformation in a uniform or homogeneous way. This approach, called *homogeneous coordinates*, has become standard in almost every graphics program. In the following section, I'll introduce homogeneous coordinates, which allow you to manipulate all of these transformations with matrices.

Homogeneous Coordinates

We expect that all transformations in 2D space, including scaling, reflection, rotation, and translation, can be treated equally if points are expressed in homogeneous coordinates. Homogeneous coordinates were first introduced in geometry and have been applied subsequently to graphics representation.

In homogeneous coordinates, you add a third coordinate to a point. Instead of being represented by a pair of (X, Y) numbers, each point is represented by a triple (X, Y, W). If the W coordinate is nonzero, you can divide through by it; (X, Y, W) represents the same point as $(X/W, Y/W, 1)$. When W is nonzero, you normally perform this division, and the numbers X/W and Y/W are usually called the *point coordinates* in the homogeneous coordinate system. The points where $W = 0$ are called *points at infinity*.

Since vectors and points in 2D space are now three-element row arrays, transform matrices, which multiply a vector to produce another vector, should be 3 by 3.

Translation in Homogeneous Coordinates

In homogeneous coordinates, a translation can be expressed in the form

$$(x_1 \ y_1 \ 1) = (x \ y \ 1) \begin{pmatrix} 1 & 0 & 0 \\ 0 & 1 & 0 \\ dx & dy & 1 \end{pmatrix} \qquad \text{(2.4)}$$

This transform can be expressed differently as

$$P_1 = P \cdot T(dx, dy) \qquad \text{(2.5)}$$

Here P and P_1 represent point (x, y) and point (x_1, y_1), respectively, and $T(dx, dy)$ is the following translation matrix:

$$T(dy, dy) = \begin{pmatrix} 1 & 0 & 0 \\ 0 & 1 & 0 \\ dy & dy & 1 \end{pmatrix} \qquad \text{(2.6)}$$

What happens if a point P is translated by $T(dx_1, dy_1)$ to P_1 and then translated by $T(dx_2, dy_2)$ to P_2? The result, as you might expect, is a net translation of $T(dx_1 + dx_2, dy_1 + dy_2)$. This can be confirmed by the following definitions:

$$P_1 = P \cdot T(dx_1, dy_1)$$
$$P_2 = P_1 \cdot T(dx_2, dy_2)$$

From the foregoing equations we have

$$P_2 = P \cdot T(dx_1, dy_1) \cdot T(dx_2, dy_2)$$

The matrix product $T(dx_1, dy_1)\ T(dx_2, dy_2)$ is

$$\begin{pmatrix} 1 & 0 & 0 \\ 0 & 1 & 0 \\ dx_1 & dy_1 & 1 \end{pmatrix} \begin{pmatrix} 1 & 0 & 0 \\ 0 & 1 & 0 \\ dx_2 & dy_2 & 1 \end{pmatrix} = \begin{pmatrix} 1 & 0 & 0 \\ 0 & 1 & 0 \\ dx_1 + dx_2 & dy_1 + dy_2 & 1 \end{pmatrix} \quad (2.7)$$

The net translation is indeed $T(dx1 + dx2, dy1 + dy2)$.

Scaling in Homogeneous Coordinates

Similarly, the scaling Equation (2.1) can be represented in matrix form in homogeneous coordinates as

$$(x_1\ y_1\ 1) = (x\ y\ 1)\begin{pmatrix} s_x & 0 & 0 \\ 0 & s_y & 0 \\ 0 & 0 & 1 \end{pmatrix}$$

It can also be expressed in the following form:

$$P_1 = P \cdot S(s_x, s_y) \quad (2.8)$$

Just as successive translations are additive, we expect that successive scaling should be multiplicative. Given

$$P_1 = P \cdot S(s_{x1}, s_{y1}) \quad (2.9)$$
$$P_2 = P_1 \cdot S(s_{x2}, s_{y2}) \quad (2.10)$$

and substituting Equation (2.9) into Equation (2.10) yields

$$P_2 = [P \cdot S(s_{x1}, s_{y1})] \cdot S(s_{x2}, s_{y2}) = P \cdot [S(s_{x1}, s_{y1}) \cdot S(s_{x2}, s_{y2})]$$

The matrix product in the preceding equation is

$$\begin{pmatrix} s_{x1} & 0 & 0 \\ 0 & s_{y1} & 0 \\ 0 & 0 & 1 \end{pmatrix} \begin{pmatrix} s_{x2} & 0 & 0 \\ 0 & s_{y2} & 0 \\ 0 & 0 & 1 \end{pmatrix} = \begin{pmatrix} s_{x1}s_{x2} & 0 & 0 \\ 0 & s_{y1}s_{y2} & 0 \\ 0 & 0 & 1 \end{pmatrix}$$

Thus, scaling is indeed multiplicative.

Reflection is a special case of scaling with a scaling factor of –1. You can represent a reflection in the same way as scaling.

Rotation in Homogeneous Coordinates

A rotation in homogeneous coordinates can be represented as

$$(x_1 \ y_1 \ 1) = (x \ y \ 1) \begin{pmatrix} \cos\theta & \sin\theta & 0 \\ -\sin\theta & \cos\theta & 0 \\ 0 & 0 & 1 \end{pmatrix} \quad (2.11)$$

We can also write Equation (2.11) as

$$P_1 = P \cdot R(\theta)$$

where $R(\theta)$ is the rotation matrix in homogeneous coordinates. You may expect that two successive rotations should be additive. Given

$$P_1 = P \cdot R(\theta_1) \quad (2.12)$$
$$P_2 = P_1 \cdot R(\theta_2) \quad (2.13)$$

and substituting Equation (2.12) into Equation (2.13) yields

$$P_2 = [P \cdot R(\theta_1)] \cdot R(\theta_2) = P \cdot [R(\theta_1) \cdot R(\theta_2)]$$

The matrix product $R(\theta_1) \ R(\theta_2)$ is

$$\begin{pmatrix} \cos\theta_1 & \sin\theta_1 & 0 \\ -\sin\theta_1 & \cos\theta_1 & 0 \\ 0 & 0 & 1 \end{pmatrix} \begin{pmatrix} \cos\theta_2 & \sin\theta_2 & 0 \\ -\sin\theta_2 & \cos\theta_2 & 0 \\ 0 & 0 & 1 \end{pmatrix}$$

$$= \begin{pmatrix} \cos\theta_1\cos\theta_2 - \sin\theta_1\sin\theta_2 & \cos\theta_1\sin\theta_2 + \sin\theta_1\cos\theta_2 & 0 \\ -\sin\theta_1\cos\theta_2 - \cos\theta_1\sin\theta_2 & \cos\theta_1\cos\theta_2 - \sin\theta_1\sin\theta_2 & 0 \\ 0 & 0 & 1 \end{pmatrix}$$

$$= \begin{pmatrix} \cos(\theta_1+\theta_2) & \sin(\theta_1+\theta_2) & 0 \\ -\sin(\theta_1+\theta_2) & \cos(\theta_1+\theta_2) & 0 \\ 0 & 0 & 1 \end{pmatrix}$$

Thus, rotations are indeed additive.

Combining Transforms

It is common for graphics applications to apply more than one transform to a graphics object. For example, you might want to apply first a scaling transform S and then a rotation transform R. You can combine the fundamental S, T, and R matrices to produce desired general transform results. The basic purpose of combining transforms is to gain efficiency by applying a single composed transform to a point, rather than applying a series of transforms, one after another.

Consider the rotation of an object about an arbitrary point P_1. Since you only know how to rotate about the origin, you need to convert the original problem into several separate problems. Thus, to rotate about P_1, you need to perform a sequence of several fundamental transformations:

- Translate it so that the point is at the origin.

- Rotate it to the desired angle.

- Translate so that the point at the origin returns back to P_1.

This sequence is illustrated in Figure 2-4, in which a rectangle is rotated about P_1 (x_1, y_1). The first translation is by $(-x_1, -y_1)$, whereas the later translation is by the inverse (x_1, y_1). The result is quite different than that of applying just the rotation. The net transformation is

$$
T(-x1,-y1) \cdot R(\theta) \cdot T(x1,y1) = \begin{pmatrix} 1 & 0 & 0 \\ 0 & 1 & 0 \\ -x1 & -y1 & 1 \end{pmatrix} \begin{pmatrix} \cos\theta & \sin\theta & 0 \\ -\sin\theta & \cos\theta & 0 \\ 0 & 0 & 1 \end{pmatrix} \begin{pmatrix} 1 & 0 & 0 \\ 0 & 1 & 0 \\ x1 & y1 & 1 \end{pmatrix}
$$

$$
= \begin{pmatrix} \cos\theta & -\sin\theta & 0 \\ \sin\theta & \cos\theta & 0 \\ x1 \cdot (1-\cos\theta) + y1 \cdot \sin\theta & y1 \cdot (1-\cos\theta) - x1 \cdot \sin\theta & 1 \end{pmatrix}
$$

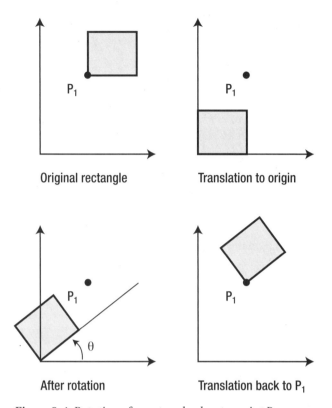

Original rectangle   Translation to origin

After rotation   Translation back to P$_1$

Figure 2-4. Rotation of a rectangle about a point P$_1$.

Vectors and Matrices in WPF

WPF implements a *Vector* and a *Matrix* structure in homogeneous coordinates in 2D space. It uses a convention of premultiplying matrices by row vectors. A point or a vector in homogeneous coordinates is defined using three double values (X, Y, 1). In WPF, these coordinates can also be expressed in terms of two doubles (X, Y), since the third double is always equal to 1.

Vector Structure

A vector in WPF is defined using a *structure*. A structure is similar in nature to a class. Both a class and a structure can contain data members and function members. One major difference between a structure and a class is that a structure is a value type and therefore is stored in the stack. A class, on the other hand, is a reference type that stores a reference to a dynamically allocated object. Usually, structures have a performance advantage over classes because structures are allocated in the stack and are immediately deallocated when out of scope. Note that a structure can't inherit from another class or structure; that is, a structure can't be a base class, due to its implicitly sealed nature. Structures are not permitted to have a constructor without a parameter. Many simple math functions, including vectors and matrices, are defined in WPF using structures because of the performance advantage.

A *Vector* object is a row array with three elements in homogeneous coordinates. Since the last element is always equal to 1, only the first two elements need to be specified. For instance:

```
Vector v = new Vector(10, 20);
```

Note that a vector and a point in WPF are two different objects. The following statement is invalid in WPF:

```
Vector v = new Point(10,20);
```

However, you can define a *Vector* using *Points*, or vice versa, in the following manner:

```
Vector v1 = new Point(10, 20) - new Point(20, 30);
Vector v2 = (Vector)new Point(10, 20);
Point pt1 = (Point)new Vector(10, 20);
```

A *Vector* has four public properties:

- *Length* – Gets the length of the vector.

- *LengthSquared* – Gets the square of the length of the vector.

- *X* – Gets or sets the *X* component of the vector.

- *Y* – Gets or sets the *Y* component of the vector.

In addition, there are methods associated with vectors that allow you to perform various mathematical operations on them. The following are some frequently used methods:

- *Add* – Adds a vector to a point or another vector.

- *Subtract* – Subtracts one vector from another vector.

- *Multiply* – Multiplies a vector by a specified double, matrix, or vector and returns the result as a vector.

- *Divide* – Divides a vector by a scalar and returns a vector.

- *CrossProduct* – Calculates the cross product of two vectors.

- *AngleBetween* – Retrieves the angle, expressed in degrees, between two vectors.

- *Normalize* – Normalizes the vector.

For example:

```
Vector v1 = new Vector(20, 10);
Vector v2 = new Vector(10, 20);
double cross = Vector.CrossProduct(v1, v2);
double angle = Vector.AngleBetween(v1, v2);
v1.Normalize();
double length2 = v1.LengthSquared;
```

This generates the magnitude of the cross product *cross* = 300 with a direction along the *Z* axis, which can easily be confirmed by the formula

$$result = v1.X \cdot v2.Y - v1.Y \cdot v2.X = 20 \cdot 20 - 10 \cdot 10 = 300$$

The *angle* = 36.87 degrees. This can be confirmed by the following formula, which calculates the angle between the two vectors:

$$\theta = \arctan\left(\frac{v2.Y}{v2.X}\right) - \arctan\left(\frac{v1.Y}{v1.X}\right) = \arctan(10/20) - \arctan(20/10) = 36.87 \deg$$

The normalized result of $v1$ is stored in $v1$ again. In this case, $v1$ becomes (0.894, 0.447), which is confirmed by its length squared: $length2 = 1$.

Matrix Structure

We have demonstrated that the transform matrices in homogeneous coordinates always have a last column of (0 0 1). It can be shown that any combined transform matrix using these fundamental transforms has the same last column. Based on this fact, WPF defines the transform in terms of a 3×2 matrix. Thus, the matrix structure in WPF takes six elements arranged in three rows and two columns. In methods and properties, the *Matrix* object is usually specified as an array with six elements, as follows: (*M11, M12, M21, M22, OffsetX, OffsetY*). The *OffsetX* and *OffsetY* represent translation values.

For example, the default identity matrix constructed by the default constructor has a value of (1, 0, 0, 1, 0, 0). In matrix representation, this means $\begin{pmatrix} 1 & 0 \\ 0 & 1 \\ 0 & 0 \end{pmatrix}$. This is a simplification of $\begin{pmatrix} 1 & 0 & 0 \\ 0 & 1 & 0 \\ 0 & 0 & 1 \end{pmatrix}$. The last column is always $\begin{pmatrix} 0 \\ 0 \\ 1 \end{pmatrix}$.

Thus a translation of 3 units in the X direction and 2 units in the Y direction would be represented as (1, 0, 0, 1, 3, 2). In matrix form, we should have $\begin{pmatrix} 1 & 0 \\ 0 & 1 \\ 3 & 2 \end{pmatrix}$. This is a simplification of $\begin{pmatrix} 1 & 0 & 0 \\ 0 & 1 & 0 \\ 3 & 2 & 1 \end{pmatrix}$.

You can create a matrix object in WPF by using overloaded constructors. These take an array of double values, which hold the matrix items, as arguments. The following code snippet creates three matrix objects for translation, scaling, and rotation in code:

```
double dx = 3;
double dy = 2;
double sx = 0.5;
double sy = 1.5;
double theta = Math.PI / 4;
double sin = Math.Sin(theta);
double cos = Math.Cos(theta);
Matrix tm = new Matrix(1, 0, 0, 1, dx, dy);
Matrix sm = new Matrix(sx, 0, 0, sy, 0, 0);
Matrix rm = new Matrix(cos, sin, -sin, cos, 0, 0);
```

The matrix *tm* is a translation matrix that moves an object by 3 units in the *X* direction and by 2 units in the *Y* direction. The scaling matrix *sm* scales an object by a factor of 0.5 in the *X* direction and by a factor of 1.5 in the *Y* direction. The final matrix *rm* is a rotation matrix that rotates an object 45 degrees about the origin.

In addition to the properties of these six matrix elements, there are four other public properties associated with matrices:

- *Determinant* – Gets the determinant of the *Matrix* structure.

- *HasInverse* – Gets a value that indicates whether the *Matrix* structure is invertible.

- *Identity* – Gets an identity matrix.

- *IsIdentity* – Gets a value that indicates whether the *Matrix* structure is an identity matrix.

There are many public methods associated with the *Matrix* structure that allow you to perform various matrix operations.

Matrix Operations

The *Matrix* structure in WPF provides methods for performing rotation, scaling, and translation. It also implements several methods for performing matrix operations. For example, you can use the *Invert* method to take the inverse of an invertible matrix. This method takes no parameters. The *multiply* method multiplies two matrices and returns the result in a new matrix. The following are some frequently used methods for matrix operations:

- *Scale* – Appends the specified scale vector to the *Matrix* structure.

- *ScaleAt* – Scales the matrix by the specified amount about the specified point.

- *Translate* – Appends a translation of the specified offsets to the *Matrix* structure.

- *Rotate* – Applies a rotation of the specified angle about the origin to the *Matrix* structure.

- *RotateAt* – Rotates the matrix about a specified point.

- *Skew* – Appends a skew of the specified angles in the *X* and *Y* directions to the *Matrix* structure.

- *Invert* – Inverts the *Matrix* structure.

- *Multiply* – Multiplies a *Matrix* structure by another *Matrix* structure.

- *Transform* – Transforms the specified point, array of points, vector, or array of vectors by the *Matrix* structure.

There are also corresponding *Prepend* methods associated with *Scale, Translation, Rotation*, and *Skew*. The default method is *Append*. Both *Append* and *Prepend* determine the matrix order. *Append* specifies that the new operation is applied after the preceding operation; *Prepend* specifies that the new operation is applied before the preceding operation.

Let's consider an example demonstrating matrix operations in WPF. Start with a new WPF Windows application project, and name it *Transformation2D*. Add a new WPF Window called *MatrixOperations* to the project. Here is the XAML file for this example:

```xml
<Window x:Class="Transformation2D.MatrixOperations"
    xmlns="http://schemas.microsoft.com/winfx/2006/xaml/presentation"
    xmlns:x="http://schemas.microsoft.com/winfx/2006/xaml"
    Title="Matrix Operations" Height="250" Width="250">
    <Grid>
        <StackPanel>
            <TextBlock Margin="10,10,5,5" Text="Original Matrix:"/>
            <TextBlock x:Name="tbOriginal" Margin="20,0,5,5"/>
            <TextBlock Margin="10,0,5,5" Text="Inverted Matrix:"/>
            <TextBlock x:Name="tbInvert" Margin="20,0,5,5"/>
            <TextBlock Margin="10,0,5,5" Text="Original Matrices:"/>
            <TextBlock x:Name="tbM1M2" Margin="20,0,5,5"/>
            <TextBlock Margin="10,0,5,5" Text="M1 x M2:"/>
            <TextBlock x:Name="tbM12" Margin="20,0,5,5"/>
            <TextBlock Margin="10,0,5,5" Text="M2 x M1:"/>
            <TextBlock x:Name="tbM21" Margin="20,0,5,5"/>
        </StackPanel>
    </Grid>
</Window>
```

This markup creates a layout that displays results using *TextBlocks*. The matrix operations are performed in the corresponding code-behind file, as listed here:

```csharp
using System;
using System.Windows;
using System.Windows.Media;

namespace Transformation2D
{
    public partial class MatrixOperations : Window
    {
        public MatrixOperations()
        {
            InitializeComponent();

            // Invert matrix:
            Matrix m = new Matrix(1, 2, 3, 4, 0, 0);
            tbOriginal.Text = "(" +  m.ToString() +")";
            m.Invert();
            tbInvert.Text = "(" + m.ToString() + ")";

            // Matrix multiplication:
            Matrix m1 = new Matrix(1, 2, 3, 4, 0, 1);
            Matrix m2 = new Matrix(0, 1, 2, 1, 0, 1);
            Matrix m12 = Matrix.Multiply(m1, m2);
            Matrix m21 = Matrix.Multiply(m2, m1);

            tbM1M2.Text = "M1 = (" + m1.ToString() + "), " +
                        " M2 = (" + m2.ToString() + ")";
            tbM12.Text = "(" + m12.ToString() + ")";
            tbM21.Text = "(" + m21.ToString() + ")";
        }
    }
}
```

This code-behind file performs matrix inversion and multiplications. In particular, it shows how the results of the matrix multiplication depend on the order of the matrix operations. Executing this example generates the output shown in Figure 2-5.

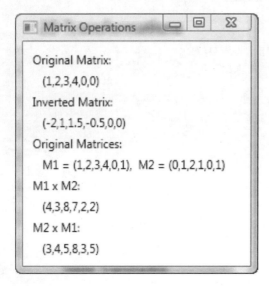

Figure 2-5. *Results of matric operations in WPF.*

First, let's examine the matrix invert method, which inverts a matrix (1, 2, 3, 4, 0, 0). The *Matrix.Invert* method gives the result (–2, 1, 1.5, –0.5, 0, 0). This can easily be confirmed by multiplying the matrix (1, 2, 3, 4, 0, 0) by (–2, 1, 1.5, –0.5, 0, 0), which should be equal to an identity matrix (1, 0, 0, 1, 0, 0). In fact:

$$\begin{pmatrix} 1 & 2 & 0 \\ 3 & 4 & 0 \\ 0 & 0 & 1 \end{pmatrix} \begin{pmatrix} -2 & 1 & 0 \\ 1.5 & -0.5 & 0 \\ 0 & 0 & 1 \end{pmatrix} = \begin{pmatrix} -2+2\times1.5 & 1-2\times0.5 & 0 \\ -2\times3+4\times1.5 & 3-4\times0.5 & 0 \\ 0 & 0 & 1 \end{pmatrix} = \begin{pmatrix} 1 & 0 & 0 \\ 0 & 1 & 0 \\ 0 & 0 & 1 \end{pmatrix}$$

This is indeed an identity matrix, as expected.

Next, let's consider matrix multiplication. In the code, you create two matrices $m1$ = (1, 2, 3, 4, 0, 1) and $m2$ = (0, 1, 2, 1, 0, 1). You first multiply $m1$ by $m2$ and return the result in $m12$; then you multiply $m2$ by $m1$ and store the result in $m21$. Note that the result is stored in $m1$ if the matrix $m1$ is multiplied by $m2$. You can see from Figure 2-5 that $M12$ = (4, 3, 8, 7, 2, 2). In fact:

$$\begin{pmatrix} 1 & 2 & 0 \\ 3 & 4 & 0 \\ 0 & 1 & 1 \end{pmatrix} \begin{pmatrix} 0 & 1 & 0 \\ 2 & 1 & 0 \\ 0 & 1 & 1 \end{pmatrix} = \begin{pmatrix} 4 & 3 & 0 \\ 8 & 7 & 0 \\ 2 & 2 & 1 \end{pmatrix}$$

For $M21 = m2 \times m1$, you would expect the following result:

$$\begin{pmatrix} 0 & 1 & 0 \\ 2 & 1 & 0 \\ 0 & 1 & 1 \end{pmatrix}\begin{pmatrix} 1 & 2 & 0 \\ 3 & 4 & 0 \\ 0 & 1 & 1 \end{pmatrix} = \begin{pmatrix} 3 & 4 & 0 \\ 5 & 8 & 0 \\ 3 & 5 & 1 \end{pmatrix}$$

This is consistent with (3, 4, 5, 8, 3, 5) shown in the figure.

Matrix Transforms

As mentioned in the previous section, the *Matrix* structure in WPF also provides methods for rotating, scaling, and translating matrices.

You can use both the *Rotate* and *RotateAt* methods to rotate matrices. The *Rotate* method rotates a matrix at a specified angle. This method takes a single argument: a double value specifying the angle. The *RotateAt* method is useful when you need to change the center of rotation. Its first parameter is the angle; its second and third parameters (both double types) specify the center of rotation.

Let's illustrate the basic matrix transforms (translation, scaling, rotation, and skew) in WPF through an example. Add a new WPF Window to the project *Transformation2D* and name it *MatrixTransforms*. The following is the XAML file for this example:

```
<Window x:Class="Transformation2D.MatrixTransforms"
    xmlns="http://schemas.microsoft.com/winfx/2006/xaml/presentation"
    xmlns:x="http://schemas.microsoft.com/winfx/2006/xaml"
    Title="Matrix Transforms" Height="450" Width="270">
    <StackPanel>
        <TextBlock Margin="10,10,5,5" Text="Original Matrix:"/>
        <TextBlock Name="tbOriginal" Margin="20,0,5,5"/>
        <TextBlock Margin="10,0,5,5" Text="Scale:"/>
        <TextBlock Name="tbScale" Margin="20,0,5,5"/>
        <TextBlock Margin="10,0,5,5" Text="Scale - Prepend:"/>
        <TextBlock Name="tbScalePrepend" Margin="20,0,5,5"/>
        <TextBlock Margin="10,0,5,5" Text="Translation:"/>
        <TextBlock Name="tbTranslate" Margin="20,0,5,5"/>
        <TextBlock Margin="10,0,5,5" Text="Translation - Prepend:"/>
        <TextBlock Name="tbTranslatePrepend" Margin="20,0,5,5"/>
        <TextBlock Margin="10,0,5,5" Text="Rotation:"/>
        <TextBlock Name="tbRotate" Margin="20,0,5,5" TextWrapping="Wrap"/>
        <TextBlock Margin="10,0,5,5" Text="Rotation - Prepend:"/>
        <TextBlock Name="tbRotatePrepend" Margin="20,0,5,5" TextWrapping="Wrap"/>
        <TextBlock Margin="10,0,5,5" Text="RotationAt:"/>
        <TextBlock x:Name="tbRotateAt" Margin="20,0,5,5" TextWrapping="Wrap"/>
        <TextBlock Margin="10,0,5,5" Text="RotationAt - Prepend:"/>
        <TextBlock x:Name="tbRotateAtPrepend" Margin="20,0,5,5"
                    TextWrapping="Wrap"/>
        <TextBlock Margin="10,0,5,5" Text="Skew:"/>
        <TextBlock Name="tbSkew" Margin="20,0,5,5"/>
        <TextBlock Margin="10,0,5,5" Text="Skew - Prepend:"/>
        <TextBlock Name="tbSkewPrepend" Margin="20,0,5,5"/>
    </StackPanel>
</Window>
```

This markup creates the layout for displaying results using *TextBlocks*, which are embedded into a *StackPanel* control. The corresponding code-behind file is given by the following code:

```
using System;
using System.Windows;
using System.Windows.Media;

namespace Transformation2D
{
    public partial class MatrixTransforms : Window
    {
        public MatrixTransform()
        {
            InitializeComponent();

            // Original matrix:
            Matrix m = new Matrix(1, 2, 3, 4, 0, 1);
            tbOriginal.Text = "(" + m.ToString() + ")";

            //Scale:
            m.Scale(1, 0.5);
            tbScale.Text = "(" + m.ToString() + ")";

            // Scale - Prepend:
            m = new Matrix(1, 2, 3, 4, 0, 1);
            m.ScalePrepend(1, 0.5);
            tbScalePrepend.Text = "(" + m.ToString() + ")";

            //Translation:
            m = new Matrix(1, 2, 3, 4, 0, 1);
            m.Translate(1, 0.5);
            tbTranslate.Text = "(" + m.ToString() + ")";

            // Translation - Prepend:
            m = new Matrix(1, 2, 3, 4, 0, 1);
            m.TranslatePrepend(1, 0.5);
            tbTranslatePrepend.Text =
                    "(" + m.ToString() + ")";

            //Rotation:
            m = new Matrix(1, 2, 3, 4, 0, 1);
            m.Rotate(45);
            tbRotate.Text = "(" + MatrixRound(m).ToString()
                           + ")";

            // Rotation - Prepend:
            m = new Matrix(1, 2, 3, 4, 0, 1);
            m.RotatePrepend(45);
            tbRotatePrepend.Text = "(" + MatrixRound(m).ToString() + ")";

            //Rotation at (x = 1, y = 2):
            m = new Matrix(1, 2, 3, 4, 0, 1);
            m.RotateAt(45, 1, 2);
            tbRotateAt.Text = "(" + MatrixRound(m).ToString() + ")";
```

```
        // Rotation at (x = 1, y = 2) - Prepend:
        m = new Matrix(1, 2, 3, 4, 0, 1);
        m.RotateAtPrepend(45, 1, 2);
        tbRotateAtPrepend.Text = "(" + MatrixRound(m).ToString() + ")";

        // Skew:
        m = new Matrix(1, 2, 3, 4, 0, 1);
        m.Skew(45, 30);
        tbSkew.Text = "(" + MatrixRound(m).ToString() + ")";

        // Skew - Prepend:
        m = new Matrix(1, 2, 3, 4, 0, 1);
        m.SkewPrepend(45, 30);
        tbSkewPrepend.Text = "(" + MatrixRound(m).ToString() + ")";
    }

    private Matrix MatrixRound(Matrix m)
    {
        m.M11 = Math.Round(m.M11, 3);
        m.M12 = Math.Round(m.M12, 3);
        m.M21 = Math.Round(m.M21, 3);
        m.M22 = Math.Round(m.M22, 3);
        m.OffsetX = Math.Round(m.OffsetX, 3);
        m.OffsetY = Math.Round(m.OffsetY, 3);
        return m;
    }
}
}
```

Building and running this application generates the output shown in Figure 2-6.

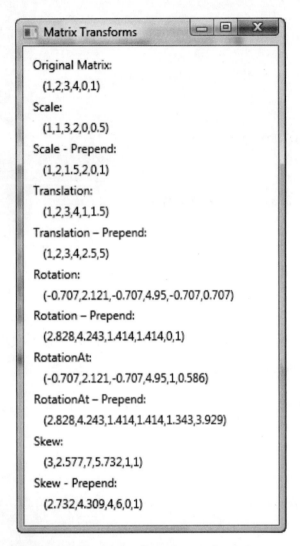

Figure 2-6. *The results of matrix transformations.*

The original matrix, $m = (1, 2, 3, 4, 0, 1)$, is operated on by various transforms. First, let's examine the scale transform, which sets a scaling factor of 1 in the X direction and 0.5 in the Y direction. For the *Apppend* scaling (the default setting), we have

$$\begin{pmatrix} 1 & 2 & 0 \\ 3 & 4 & 0 \\ 0 & 1 & 1 \end{pmatrix} \begin{pmatrix} 1 & 0 & 0 \\ 0 & 0.5 & 0 \\ 0 & 0 & 1 \end{pmatrix} = \begin{pmatrix} 1 & 1 & 0 \\ 3 & 2 & 0 \\ 0 & 0.5 & 1 \end{pmatrix}$$

This gives the same result (1, 1, 3, 2, 0, 0.5) shown in Figure 2-6. On the other hand, for the *Prepend* scaling, we have

$$\begin{pmatrix} 1 & 0 & 0 \\ 0 & 0.5 & 0 \\ 0 & 0 & 1 \end{pmatrix}\begin{pmatrix} 1 & 2 & 0 \\ 3 & 4 & 0 \\ 0 & 1 & 1 \end{pmatrix} = \begin{pmatrix} 1 & 2 & 0 \\ 1.5 & 2 & 0 \\ 0 & 1 & 1 \end{pmatrix}$$

This confirms the result (1, 2, 1.5, 2, 0, 1) shown in Figure 2-6.

We then translate the matrix *m* one unit in the *X* direction and one-half unit in the *Y* direction. For the *Append* (the default setting) translation, we have

$$\begin{pmatrix} 1 & 2 & 0 \\ 3 & 4 & 0 \\ 0 & 1 & 1 \end{pmatrix}\begin{pmatrix} 1 & 0 & 0 \\ 0 & 1 & 0 \\ 1 & 0.5 & 1 \end{pmatrix} = \begin{pmatrix} 1 & 2 & 0 \\ 3 & 4 & 0 \\ 1 & 1.5 & 1 \end{pmatrix}$$

This is consistent with the result (1, 2, 3, 4, 1, 1.5) shown in Figure 2-6.

For the *Prepend* translation, we perform the following transformation:

$$\begin{pmatrix} 1 & 0 & 0 \\ 0 & 1 & 0 \\ 1 & 0.5 & 1 \end{pmatrix}\begin{pmatrix} 1 & 2 & 0 \\ 3 & 4 & 0 \\ 0 & 1 & 1 \end{pmatrix} = \begin{pmatrix} 1 & 2 & 0 \\ 3 & 4 & 0 \\ 2.5 & 5 & 1 \end{pmatrix}$$

This confirms the result (1, 2, 3, 4, 2.5, 5) shown in Figure 2-6.

For the rotation transformation, the original *m* matrix is rotated by 45 degrees. In the case of the *Append* rotation, we have

$$\begin{pmatrix} 1 & 2 & 0 \\ 3 & 4 & 0 \\ 0 & 1 & 1 \end{pmatrix}\begin{pmatrix} \cos(\pi/4) & \sin(\pi/4) & 0 \\ -\sin(\pi/4) & \cos(\pi/4) & 0 \\ 0 & 0 & 1 \end{pmatrix} = \begin{pmatrix} -0.707 & 2.121 & 0 \\ -0.707 & 4.949 & 0 \\ -0.707 & 0.707 & 1 \end{pmatrix}$$

Note that in the foregoing calculation, we used the fact that $\cos(\pi/4) = \sin(\pi/4) = 0.707$. This gives the same result (–0.707, 2.121, –0.707, 4.95, –0.707, 0.707) as that given in Figure 2-6.

For the *Prepend* rotation, we have

$$\begin{pmatrix} \cos(\pi/4) & \sin(\pi/4) & 0 \\ -\sin(\pi/4) & \cos(\pi/4) & 0 \\ 0 & 0 & 1 \end{pmatrix}\begin{pmatrix} 1 & 2 & 0 \\ 3 & 4 & 0 \\ 0 & 1 & 1 \end{pmatrix} = \begin{pmatrix} 2.828 & 4.243 & 0 \\ 1.414 & 1.414 & 0 \\ 0 & 1 & 1 \end{pmatrix}$$

This result is the same as (2.828, 4.243, 1.414, 1.414, 0, 1) shown in Figure 2-6.

The *RotateAt* method is designed for cases in which you need to change the center of rotation. In fact, the *Rotate* method is a special case of *RotateAt*, with the rotation center at (0, 0). In this example, the matrix *m* is rotated by 45 degrees at the point (1, 2). As discussed previously in this chapter, the rotation of an object about an arbitrary point P_1 must be performed according to the following procedures:

- Translate $P1$ to the origin.

- Rotate it to the desired angle.

- Translate so that the point at the origin returns to $P1$.

Considering the matrix transformations in WPF, the rotation matrix at point (1, 2) should be expressed in the following form:

$$T(-dx,-dy) \cdot R(\theta) \cdot T(dx,dy)$$

$$= \begin{pmatrix} 1 & 0 & 0 \\ 0 & 1 & 0 \\ -1 & -2 & 1 \end{pmatrix} \begin{pmatrix} \cos(\pi/4) & \sin(\pi/4) & 0 \\ -\sin(\pi/4) & \cos(\pi/4) & 0 \\ 0 & 0 & 1 \end{pmatrix} \begin{pmatrix} 1 & 0 & 0 \\ 0 & 1 & 0 \\ 1 & 2 & 1 \end{pmatrix} = \begin{pmatrix} 0.707 & 0.707 & 0 \\ -0.707 & 0.707 & 0 \\ 1.707 & -0.121 & 1 \end{pmatrix}$$

Thus, the *Append* rotation of *Matrix m* by 45 degrees at *Point*(1, 2) becomes

$$\begin{pmatrix} 1 & 2 & 0 \\ 3 & 4 & 0 \\ 0 & 1 & 1 \end{pmatrix} \begin{pmatrix} 0.707 & 0.707 & 0 \\ -0.707 & 0.707 & 0 \\ 1.707 & -0.121 & 1 \end{pmatrix} = \begin{pmatrix} -0.707 & 2.121 & 0 \\ -0.707 & 4.949 & 0 \\ 1 & 0.586 & 1 \end{pmatrix}$$

This gives the same result of (–0.707, 2.121, –0.707, 4.949, 1, 0.586) shown in Figure 2-6. The minor difference is due to decimal rounding.

Similarly, the *Prepend* rotation of *Matrix m* by 45 degrees at *Point*(1, 2) should give

$$\begin{pmatrix} 0.707 & 0.707 & 0 \\ -0.707 & 0.707 & 0 \\ 1.707 & -0.121 & 1 \end{pmatrix} \begin{pmatrix} 1 & 2 & 0 \\ 3 & 4 & 0 \\ 0 & 0 & 1 \end{pmatrix} = \begin{pmatrix} 2.828 & 4.242 & 0 \\ 1.414 & 1.414 & 0 \\ 1.344 & 3.93 & 1 \end{pmatrix}$$

Again, the result is the same as the one shown in Figure 2-6.

Finally, we'll examine the *Skew* method, which creates a shearing transform. This method takes two double arguments, *AngleX* and *AngleY*, which represent, respectively, the horizontal and vertical skew factors. The skew transformation in homogeneous coordinates can be expressed in the form

$$(x1 \quad y1 \quad 1) = (x \quad y \quad 1) \begin{pmatrix} 1 & \tan(AngleY) & 0 \\ \tan(AngleX) & 1 & 0 \\ 0 & 0 & 1 \end{pmatrix}$$

$$= (x + y\tan(AngleX) \quad y + x\tan(AngleY) \quad 1)$$

where $\tan(AngleX)$ and $\tan(AngleY)$ are the skew transform factors in the X and Y directions, respectively. Take a look at the *Skew* transform in this example. The skew angles are *AngleX* = 45 degrees and *AngleY* = 30 degrees. In this case, the *Skew* matrix is given by

$$
\begin{pmatrix} 1 & \tan(30^o) & 0 \\ \tan(45^o) & 1 & 0 \\ 0 & 0 & 1 \end{pmatrix} = \begin{pmatrix} 1 & 0.577 & 0 \\ 1 & 1 & 0 \\ 0 & 0 & 1 \end{pmatrix}
$$

Thus, for the *Append Skew* transformation, we have

$$
\begin{pmatrix} 1 & 2 & 0 \\ 3 & 4 & 0 \\ 0 & 1 & 1 \end{pmatrix} \begin{pmatrix} 1 & 0.577 & 0 \\ 1 & 1 & 0 \\ 0 & 0 & 1 \end{pmatrix} = \begin{pmatrix} 3 & 2.577 & 0 \\ 7 & 5.732 & 0 \\ 1 & 1 & 1 \end{pmatrix}
$$

This confirms the result shown in Figure 2-6.

For the *Prepend Skew* transformation, we have

$$
\begin{pmatrix} 1 & 0.577 & 0 \\ 1 & 1 & 0 \\ 0 & 0 & 1 \end{pmatrix} \begin{pmatrix} 1 & 2 & 0 \\ 3 & 4 & 0 \\ 0 & 1 & 1 \end{pmatrix} = \begin{pmatrix} 2.732 & 4.308 & 0 \\ 4 & 6 & 0 \\ 0 & 1 & 1 \end{pmatrix}
$$

This result is again the same as the one given in Figure 2-6.

Here, I have presented detailed explanations of matrix transformations in WPF. This information is useful for understanding the definitions and internal representations of matrices in WPF and for applying matrices to WPF applications correctly.

Creating Perpendicular Lines

Remember that the matrix transformations discussed in the previous sections can't be applied directly to graphics objects. Instead, they can be applied only to points and vectors. If these transforms aren't related to objects, you might ask why we need them in the first place. But here I'll show you that matrix transformations are often necessary in real-world applications.

I'll use an example to demonstrate how to use matrix transformations in WPF applications. The example application is very simple. As shown in Figure 2-7, for a given line segment (the solid line) specified by two end points, (x_1, y_1) and (x_2, y_2), we want to find a perpendicular line segment (the dashed line) at one end (for example, at $Point(x_2, y_2)$) of the original line segment.

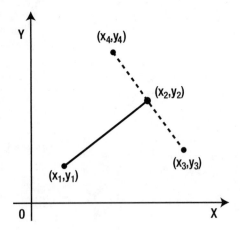

Figure 2-7. *Creating a perpendicular line for a given line segment.*

Open the project *Transformation2D* and add a new WPF Window to the project. Name this new Window *PerpendicularLine*. Create a user interface by means of the following XAML code:

```
<Window x:Class="Transformation2D.PerpendicularLine"
    xmlns="http://schemas.microsoft.com/winfx/2006/xaml/presentation"
    xmlns:x="http://schemas.microsoft.com/winfx/2006/xaml"
    Title="Perpendicular Line" Height="300" Width="400">

    <Viewbox Stretch="Uniform">
        <Grid Width="430" Height="300" HorizontalAlignment="Left"
              VerticalAlignment="Top">
            <Grid.ColumnDefinitions>
                <ColumnDefinition Width="150" />
                <ColumnDefinition Width="280" />
            </Grid.ColumnDefinitions>
            <Grid Width="140" Height="300" Margin="5,10,5,5">
                <Grid.ColumnDefinitions>
                    <ColumnDefinition Width="60" />
                    <ColumnDefinition Width="70" />
                </Grid.ColumnDefinitions>
                <Grid.RowDefinitions>
                    <RowDefinition Height="Auto" />
                    <RowDefinition Height="Auto" />
                    <RowDefinition Height="Auto" />
                    <RowDefinition Height="Auto" />
                    <RowDefinition Height="Auto" />
                    <RowDefinition Height="Auto" />
                    <RowDefinition Height="Auto" />
                </Grid.RowDefinitions>

                <TextBlock HorizontalAlignment="Right" Grid.Column="0"
                        Grid.Row="0" Margin="5,5,10,5">X1</TextBlock>
                <TextBox Name="tbX1" Grid.Column="1" Grid.Row="0"
                        TextAlignment="Center">50</TextBox>
```

```
                    <TextBlock HorizontalAlignment="Right" Grid.Column="0"
                            Grid.Row="1" Margin="5,5,10,5">Y1</TextBlock>
                    <TextBox Name="tbY1" Grid.Column="1" Grid.Row="1"
                            TextAlignment="Center">200</TextBox>
                    <TextBlock HorizontalAlignment="Right" Grid.Column="0"
                            Grid.Row="2" Margin="5,5,10,5">X2</TextBlock>
                    <TextBox Name="tbX2" Grid.Column="1" Grid.Row="2"
                            TextAlignment="Center">150</TextBox>
                    <TextBlock HorizontalAlignment="Right" Grid.Column="0"
                            Grid.Row="3" Margin="5,5,10,5">Y2</TextBlock>
                    <TextBox Name="tbY2" Grid.Column="1" Grid.Row="3"
                            TextAlignment="Center">100</TextBox>
                    <TextBlock HorizontalAlignment="Right" Grid.Column="0"
                            Grid.Row="4" Margin="5,5,10,5">Length</TextBlock>
                    <TextBox Name="tbLength" Grid.Column="1" Grid.Row="4"
                            TextAlignment="Center">100</TextBox>
                    <Button Click="BtnApply_Click" Margin="15,20,15,5" Grid.Row="5"
                            Height="25" Grid.ColumnSpan="2"
                            Grid.Column="0">Apply</Button>
                    <Button Click="BtnClose_Click" Margin="15,0,15,5"
                            Grid.Row="6" Height="25" Grid.ColumnSpan="2"
                            Grid.Column="0">Close</Button>
                </Grid>

                <Canvas Name="canvas1" Grid.Column="1" Margin="10"
                        ClipToBounds="True" Width="270" Height="280">
                    <TextBlock Name="tbPoint1" Canvas.Top="10">Point1</TextBlock>
                    <TextBlock Name="tbPoint2" Canvas.Top="25">Point2</TextBlock>
                    <TextBlock Name="tbPoint3" Canvas.Top="40">Point3</TextBlock>
                    <TextBlock Name="tbPoint4" Canvas.Top="55">Point4</TextBlock>
                </Canvas>
            </Grid>
        </Viewbox>
</Window>
```

This XAML code creates a user interface that allows you to specify the end points of the line and the length of the perpendicular line segment. The corresponding code-behind file of this example is as follows:

```
using System;
using System.Windows;
using System.Windows.Controls;
using System.Windows.Media;
using System.Windows.Shapes;

namespace Transformation2D
{
    public partial class PerpendicularLine : Window
    {
        private Line line1;
        private Line line2;
        public PerpendicularLine()
        {
            InitializeComponent();
```

33

```
        Rectangle rect = new Rectangle();
        rect.Stroke = Brushes.Black;
        rect.Width = canvas1.Width;
        rect.Height = canvas1.Height;
        canvas1.Children.Add(rect);
        line1 = new Line();
        line2 = new Line();
        AddLines();
    }

    private void AddLines()
    {
        Point pt1 = new Point();
        Point pt2 = new Point();

        pt1.X = Convert.ToDouble(tbX1.Text);
        pt1.Y = Convert.ToDouble(tbY1.Text);
        pt2.X = Convert.ToDouble(tbX2.Text);
        pt2.Y = Convert.ToDouble(tbY2.Text);
        double length = 0.5 * Convert.ToDouble(tbLength.Text);

        line1 = new Line();
        line1.X1 = pt1.X;
        line1.Y1 = pt1.Y;
        line1.X2 = pt2.X;
        line1.Y2 = pt2.Y;
        line1.Stroke = Brushes.Gray;
        line1.StrokeThickness = 4;
        canvas1.Children.Add(line1);
        Canvas.SetLeft(tbPoint1, pt1.X);
        Canvas.SetTop(tbPoint1, pt1.Y);
        Canvas.SetLeft(tbPoint2, pt2.X);
        Canvas.SetTop(tbPoint2, pt2.Y);
        tbPoint1.Text = "Pt1(" + pt1.ToString() + ")";
        tbPoint2.Text = "Pt2(" + pt2.ToString() + ")";

        Vector v1 = pt1 - pt2;
        Matrix m1 = new Matrix();
        Point pt3 = new Point();
        Point pt4 = new Point();
        m1.Rotate(-90);
        v1.Normalize();
        v1 *= length;
        line2 = new Line();
        line2.Stroke = Brushes.Gray;
        line2.StrokeThickness = 4;
        line2.StrokeDashArray = DoubleCollection.Parse("3, 1");
        pt3 = pt2 + v1 * m1;
        m1 = new Matrix();
        m1.Rotate(90);
        pt4 = pt2 + v1 * m1;
        line2.X1 = pt3.X;
        line2.Y1 = pt3.Y;
```

```
            line2.X2 = pt4.X;
            line2.Y2 = pt4.Y;
            canvas1.Children.Add(line2);
            Canvas.SetLeft(tbPoint3, pt3.X);
            Canvas.SetTop(tbPoint3, pt3.Y);
            Canvas.SetLeft(tbPoint4, pt4.X);
            Canvas.SetTop(tbPoint4, pt4.Y);
            pt3.X = Math.Round(pt3.X, 0);
            pt3.Y = Math.Round(pt3.Y, 0);
            pt4.X = Math.Round(pt4.X, 0);
            pt4.Y = Math.Round(pt4.Y, 0);
            tbPoint3.Text = "Pt3(" + pt3.ToString() + ")";
            tbPoint4.Text = "Pt4(" + pt4.ToString() + ")";
        }

        public void BtnApply_Click(object sender, EventArgs e)
        {
            if (line1 != null)
                canvas1.Children.Remove(line1);
            if (line2 != null)
                canvas1.Children.Remove(line2);
            AddLines();
        }

        public void BtnClose_Click(object sender, EventArgs e)
        {
            this.Close();
        }
    }
}
```

Here, we first create a *Line* segment (*line*1) using two end points specified by the user and then create a vector using these two end points:

```
            Vector v1 = pt1 - pt2;
```

This gives the direction of *line*1. The perpendicular line you want to create will have a length specified by the user. We want the vector to have the same length as the perpendicular line (*line*2), so we use the following statements:

```
            v1.Normalize();
            v1 *= length;
```

This vector is first normalized to a unit vector and then multiplied by the length of the perpendicular line. Now the vector has the proper length and direction along $Point(x_2, y_2)$ to $Point(x_1, y_1)$. If we rotate this vector by 90 or –90 degrees at $Point(x_2, y_2)$, we'll obtain a perpendicular line. We can achieve this via the following code snippet:

```
            Matrix m1 = new Matrix();
            m1.Rotate(-90);
            pt3 = pt2 + v1 * m1;
            m1 = new Matrix();
            m1.Rotate(90);
            pt4 = pt2 + v1 * m1;
```

Here a rotation matrix $m1$ is used to rotate the vector by 90 or –90 degrees to find two end points that define the perpendicular line.

Executing this project produces the results shown in Figure 2-8. The user interface allows the user to specify arbitrary points and length, and the program automatically draws the perpendicular line on the screen.

If you change the rotation angle and make a few modifications to the program, you can easily use it to draw a line with an arrowhead.

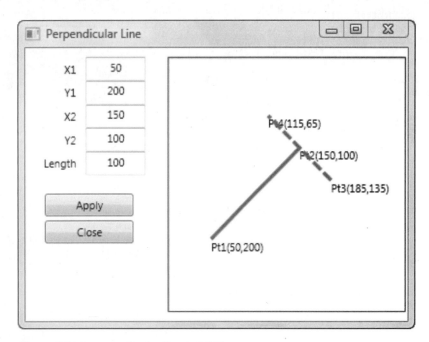

Figure 2-8. A perpendicular line in WPF.

Object Transformations in WPF

In the previous sections, we discussed the *Vector* and *Matrix* structures as well as their operations in WPF. The *Matrix* structure can be applied to a *Point* or a *Vector* object. However, if you want to apply 2D transforms to objects or coordinate systems, you need to use the *Transform* classes. In WPF, there are five derived classes that can be used to perform specific transforms on objects:

- *ScaleTransform* – Scales an object in both the *X* and *Y* directions. The *ScaleX* property specifies how much you stretch or shrink an object along the *X* direction, and the *ScaleY* property specifies how much to stretch or shrink an object along the *Y* direction. *Scale* operations are centered at the point specified by the *CenterX* and *CenterY* properties.

- *TranslateTransform* – Defines a translation along the *X* and *Y* directions. You specify the amount by which the object is translated using the *X* and *Y* properties.

- *RotateTransform* – Rotates an object in 2D space by specifying an angle using the *Angle* property and a center point specified by the *CenterX* and *CenterY* properties.

- *SkewTransform* – Defines a 2D skew that stretches the coordinate space in a nonuniform manner. Use the *CenterX* and *CenterY* properties to specify the center point of the transform. Use the *AngleX* and *AngleY* properties to specify the skew angle along the *X* and *Y* directions.

- *MatrixTransform* – Creates an affine matrix transform to manipulate an object in 2D space using a custom transform not provided by other *Transform* classes. You can multiply affine transform matrices to form any number of linear transforms; for example, you can rotate or skew an object and then translate it to a new location.

The structure of the *TransformMatrix* is the same as that of the *Matrix* structure in WPF. In the homogeneous coordinate system, the *TransformMatrix* always has a last column of (0, 0, 1). Based on this fact, WPF defines the *TransformMatrix* in terms of a 3 × 2 matrix. This means the *TransformMatrix* classes in WPF take six elements arranged in three rows and two columns. In methods and properties, the transform matrix is usually specified as an array with six members as follows: (*M11*, *M12*, *M21*, *M22*, *OffsetX*, *OffsetY*). *OffsetX* and *OffsetY* represent translation values.

By manipulating matrix values directly using the *MatrixTransform* class, you can rotate, scale, skew, and move an object. For example, if you change the value in the first column of the third row (the *OffsetX* value) to 100, you can use it to move an object 100 units along the *X* axis. If you change the value in the second column of the second row to 3, you can use it to stretch an object to three times its current height. If you change both values, you move the object 100 units along the *X* axis and stretch its height by a factor of 3. Since WPF only supports affine transforms in 2D, the values in the third column are always (0, 0, 1).

Although WPF allows you to manipulate matrix values in the *MatrixTransform* class directly, it also provides several *Transform* classes that enable you to transform an object without knowing how the underlying matrix structure is configured. For example, the *ScaleTransform* class enables you to scale an object by setting its *ScaleX* and *ScaleY* properties instead of manipulating a transform matrix. Likewise, the *RotateTransfrom* class enables you to rotate an object simply by setting its *Angle* property. WPF will use the underlying structure of the *TransformMatrix* to perform the corresponding operation on the object. For instance, when you specify a *RotateTransform* with an angle of 45 degrees, the corresponding underlying *TransformMatrix* takes the following form:

$$\begin{pmatrix} \cos\theta & \sin\theta & 0 \\ -\sin\theta & \cos\theta & 0 \\ 0 & 0 & 1 \end{pmatrix} = \begin{pmatrix} 0.707 & 0.707 & 0 \\ -0.707 & 0.707 & 0 \\ 0 & 0 & 1 \end{pmatrix}$$

One way to transform an object is to declare the appropriate *Transform* type and to apply it to the transform property of the object. Different types of objects have different types of transform properties. The following table lists several commonly used WPF types and their transform properties.

Type	Transform Properties
FrameworkElement	RenderTransform, LayoutTransform
UIElement	RenderTransform
Geometry	Transform
TextEffect	Transform
Brush	Transform, RelativeTransform
ContainerVisual	Transform
DrawingGroup	Transform

When you transform an object, you don't just transform the object itself; you transform the coordinate space in which that object exists. By default, a transform is centered at the origin of the target object's coordinate system: (0, 0). You can change the transform center by specifying the *CenterX* and *CenterY* properties of the transform matrix. The only exception is the *TranslateTransform*, which has no center properties to set, because the translation effect is the same regardless of where it is centered.

In the following few sections, you will apply various transforms to a *Rectangle* shape, a type of *FrameworkElement* that derives from the *UIElement* class.

MatrixTransform Class

You can create a custom transform using the *MatrixTransform* class. And you can apply the custom transform to any *FrameworkElement* or *UIElement* object, including graphics shapes, user controls, and panels.

Here I'll use an example to show you how to perform transforms on a *Rectangle* shape using the *MatrixTransform* class. Open the *Transformation2D* project, and add a new WPF Window named *ObjectMatrixTransforms*. This application will allow the user to enter matrix elements for the transform matrix and interactively view the transformed *Rectangle* shape on the screen. Here is the XAML file for this example:

```
<Window x:Class="Transformation2D.ObjectMatrixTransforms"
    xmlns="http://schemas.microsoft.com/winfx/2006/xaml/presentation"
    xmlns:x="http://schemas.microsoft.com/winfx/2006/xaml"
    Title="Object Matrix Transforms" Height="300" Width="400">

    <Viewbox Stretch="Uniform">
        <Grid Width="430" Height="300" HorizontalAlignment="Left"
            VerticalAlignment="Top">
            <Grid.ColumnDefinitions>
                <ColumnDefinition Width="150"/>
                <ColumnDefinition Width="280"/>
            </Grid.ColumnDefinitions>
            <Grid Width="140" Height="300" Margin="5,10,5,5">
```

```xml
        <Grid.ColumnDefinitions>
            <ColumnDefinition Width="60"/>
            <ColumnDefinition Width="70"/>
        </Grid.ColumnDefinitions>
        <Grid.RowDefinitions>
            <RowDefinition Height="Auto"/>
            <RowDefinition Height="Auto"/>
            <RowDefinition Height="Auto"/>
            <RowDefinition Height="Auto"/>
            <RowDefinition Height="Auto"/>
            <RowDefinition Height="Auto"/>
            <RowDefinition Height="Auto"/>
            <RowDefinition Height="Auto"/>
        </Grid.RowDefinitions>

        <TextBlock HorizontalAlignment="Right" Grid.Column="0"
                Grid.Row="0" Margin="5,5,10,5">M11</TextBlock>
        <TextBox Name="tbM11" Grid.Column="1" Grid.Row="0"
                TextAlignment="Center">1</TextBox>
        <TextBlock HorizontalAlignment="Right"
                Grid.Column="0" Grid.Row="1"
                Margin="5,5,10,5">M12</TextBlock>
        <TextBox Name="tbM12" Grid.Column="1" Grid.Row="1"
                TextAlignment="Center">0</TextBox>
        <TextBlock HorizontalAlignment="Right" Grid.Column="0" Grid.Row="2"
                Margin="5,5,10,5">M21</TextBlock>
        <TextBox Name="tbM21" Grid.Column="1" Grid.Row="2"
                TextAlignment="Center">0</TextBox>
        <TextBlock HorizontalAlignment="Right"
                Grid.Column="0" Grid.Row="3"
                Margin="5,5,10,5">M22</TextBlock>
        <TextBox Name="tbM22" Grid.Column="1" Grid.Row="3"
                TextAlignment="Center">1</TextBox>
        <TextBlock HorizontalAlignment="Right"
                Grid.Column="0" Grid.Row="4" Margin="5,5,10,5">
                OffsetX</TextBlock>
        <TextBox Name="tbOffsetX" Grid.Column="1" Grid.Row="4"
                TextAlignment="Center">0</TextBox>
        <TextBlock HorizontalAlignment="Right" Grid.Column="0" Grid.Row="5"
                Margin="5,5,10,5">OffsetY</TextBlock>
        <TextBox Name="tbOffsetY" Grid.Column="1" Grid.Row="5"
                TextAlignment="Center">0</TextBox>
        <Button Click="BtnApply_Click" Margin="15,20,15,5" Grid.Row="6"
                Height="25" Grid.ColumnSpan="2" Column="0">Apply</Button>
        <Button Click="BtnClose_Click" Margin="15,0,15,5" Grid.Row="7"
                Height="25" Grid.ColumnSpan="2"
                Grid.Column="0">Close</Button>
    </Grid>

    <Border Margin="10" Grid.Column="1" BorderBrush="Black"
            BorderThickness="1" HorizontalAlignment="Left"
            Background="{StaticResource MyGrayGridBrush}">
        <Canvas Name="canvas1" Grid.Column="1" ClipToBounds="True"
```

```
                        Width="270" Height="280">
                    <TextBlock Canvas.Top="53" Canvas.Left="90">
                            Original shape</TextBlock>
                    <Rectangle Canvas.Top="70" Canvas.Left="100" Width="50"
                            Height="70" Stroke="Black" StrokeThickness="2"
                            StrokeDashArray="3,1"/>
                    <Rectangle Name="rect" Canvas.Top="70" Canvas.Left="100"
                            Width="50" Height="70" Fill="LightCoral"
                            Opacity="0.5" Stroke="Black" StrokeThickness="2">
                        <Rectangle.RenderTransform>
                            <MatrixTransform x:Name="matrixTransform"/>
                        </Rectangle.RenderTransform>
                    </Rectangle>
                </Canvas>
            </Border>
        </Grid>
    </Viewbox>
</Window>
```

This markup creates a user interface that contains *TextBoxes*, *Buttons*, and a *Canvas*, which allows the user to interactively manipulate the elements of the *TransformMatrix* and to display the transformed *Rectangle* shape on the screen. In order to monitor the transformed shape precisely, we also add gridlines to the *Canvas* (*canvas*1). These gridlines, called *MyGrayGridBrush*, are defined in the *Application.Resource* of the *App.xaml* file, as listed here:

```
<Application x:Class="Transformation2D.App"
    xmlns="http://schemas.microsoft.com/winfx/2006/xaml/presentation"
    xmlns:x="http://schemas.microsoft.com/winfx/2006/xaml"
    StartupUri="StartMenu.xaml">
    <Application.Resources>
        <DrawingBrush x:Key="MyGrayGridBrush" Viewport="0,0,10,10"
                    ViewportUnits="Absolute" TileMode="Tile">
            <DrawingBrush.Drawing>
                <DrawingGroup>
                    <DrawingGroup.Children>
                        <GeometryDrawing Brush="White">
                            <GeometryDrawing.Geometry>
                                <RectangleGeometry Rect="0,0,1,1" />
                            </GeometryDrawing.Geometry>
                        </GeometryDrawing>
                        <GeometryDrawing Geometry="M0,0 L1,0 1,0.1, 0,0.1Z"
                                    Brush="#EEEEEE" />
                        <GeometryDrawing Geometry="M0,0 L0,1 0.1,1, 0.1,0Z"
                                    Brush="#EEEEEE" />
                    </DrawingGroup.Children>
                </DrawingGroup>
            </DrawingBrush.Drawing>
        </DrawingBrush>
    </Application.Resources>
</Application>
```

This resource is available at the application level.

The transform on the rectangle is specified with the following XAML snippet:

```
<Rectangle.RenderTransform>
    <MatrixTransform x:Name="matrixTransform"/>
</Rectangle.RenderTransform>
```

In this snippet, you can see that to apply transforms to a *FrameworkElement*, you need to create a *Transform* matrix and apply it to one of the two properties that the *FrameworkElement* class provides:

- *LayoutTransform* – A transform that is applied before the layout pass. After the transform is applied, the layout system processes the transformed size and position of the element.

- *RenderTransform* – A transform that modifies the appearance of the element but is applied after the layout pass is completed. By using the *RenderTransform* property instead of the *LayoutTransform*, you can gain performance benefits.

You may ask which property to use. Because of the performance benefits that it provides, use the *RenderTransform* property whenever possible, especially when you involve animated *Transform* objects. Use the *LayoutTransform* property when you are scaling, rotating, or skewing and you need the parent of the element to adjust to the transformed size of the element. Note that when they are used with the *LayoutTransform* property, *TranslateTransform* objects appear to have no effect on elements. This is because the layout system returns the translated element to its original position as part of its processing.

This example uses the *RenderTransform* property of the rectangle. The following is the corresponding C# code responsible for the event handlers:

```csharp
using System;
using System.Windows;
using System.Windows.Controls;
using System.Windows.Media;
using System.Windows.Shapes;

namespace Transformation2D
{
public partial class ObjectMatrixTransforms : Window
    {
        public ObjectMatrixTransforms()
        {
            InitializeComponent();
        }

        public void BtnApply_Click(object sender, EventArgs e)
        {
            Matrix m = new Matrix();
            m.M11 = Double.Parse(tbM11.Text);
            m.M12 = Double.Parse(tbM12.Text);
            m.M21 = Double.Parse(tbM21.Text);
            m.M22 = Double.Parse(tbM22.Text);
            m.OffsetX = Double.Parse(tbOffsetX.Text);
            m.OffsetY = Double.Parse(tbOffsetY.Text);
            matrixTransform.Matrix = m;
        }

        public void BtnClose_Click(object sender, EventArgs e)
        {
```

```
            this.Close();
        }
    }
}
```

The main part of this code-behind file is the *Apply* button's click event handler. We create a new *Matrix* instance *m* and specify its elements using the text content of the corresponding *TextBoxes*. The matrix *m* is then passed to the transform matrix *matrixTransform*, which is defined in the XAML file.

Building and running this project produces the output shown in Figure 2-9. In the left pane, you can change all six elements of a custom transform matrix by entering values of the double type in the *TextBoxes*. The entered values take effect after you click the *Apply* button. The original location of the *Rectangle* is obtained by an identity matrix (1, 0, 0, 1, 0, 0) in homogeneous coordinates. The results shown in the figure are obtained by moving the rectangle –50 units in the *X* direction and 100 units in the *Y* direction.

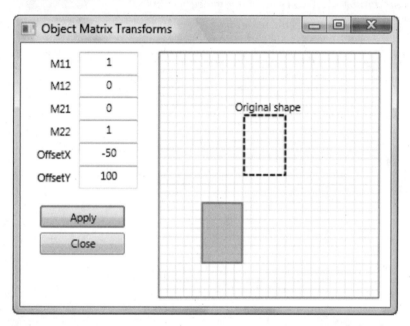

Figure 2-9. *Transform on a rectangle using the MatrixTransform class.*

By changing the other elements, you can obtain a variety of transforms, including translation, scale, rotation, and skew.

ScaleTransform Class

In the previous section, we discussed how to perform transforms on *UIElement* or *FrameworkElement* objects by manipulating transform matrix values directly. However, WPF also provides several *Transform* classes that allow you to transform an object without knowing how the underlying matrix structure is configured. For example, the *ScaleTransform* class enables you to scale an object by setting its *ScaleX* and *ScaleY* properties instead of manipulating a transform matrix directly.

Let's look at an example. Open the *Transformation2D* project, add a WPF Window, and name it *ScaleTransforms*. In this example, you create two *Canvas* panels. The left *Canvas* is used to animate a scale transform on a rectangle shape; the right *Canvas* is used for an interactive transform that allows you to change the *ScaleX* and *ScaleY* properties on the screen. The animation gives you the real sense of how the scaling transformation works. The following is the XAML file for this example:

```
<Window x:Class="Transformation2D.ScaleTransforms"
    xmlns="http://schemas.microsoft.com/winfx/2006/xaml/presentation"
    xmlns:x="http://schemas.microsoft.com/winfx/2006/xaml"
    Title="Scale Transforms" Height="330" Width="480">

    <Viewbox Stretch="Uniform">
        <Grid Width="525" Height="330" HorizontalAlignment="Left"
            VerticalAlignment="Top" ShowGridLines="True">
            <Grid.ColumnDefinitions>
                <ColumnDefinition Width="260" />
                <ColumnDefinition Width="260" />
            </Grid.ColumnDefinitions>

            <StackPanel Grid.Column="0">
                <TextBlock HorizontalAlignment="Center" Margin="10,10,10,0"
                        TextWrapping="Wrap" FontSize="14" FontWeight="Bold"
                        Text="Scaling Animation"/>
                <TextBlock Margin="10,10,10,0" TextWrapping="Wrap"
                        Text="The scaling parameters ScaleX
                            and ScaleY are animated from 0 to 4."/>
                <Border Margin="10" BorderBrush="Black" BorderThickness="1"
                        Background="{StaticResource MyGrayGridBrush}"
                        HorizontalAlignment="Left">
                  <Canvas ClipToBounds="True" Width="240" Height="250">
                    <Rectangle Canvas.Left="100" Canvas.Top="80" Width="50"
                            Height="70" Fill="LightCoral" Opacity="0.5"
                            Stroke="Black" StrokeThickness="2">
                        <Rectangle.RenderTransform>
                            <ScaleTransform x:Name="rectScale"
                                CenterX="25" CenterY="35" />
                        </Rectangle.RenderTransform>
                    </Rectangle>

                    <!-- Animate the rectangle: -->
                    <Canvas.Triggers>
                        <EventTrigger RoutedEvent="Canvas.Loaded">
                            <BeginStoryboard>
                                <Storyboard RepeatBehavior="Forever"
                                        AutoReverse="True">
                                    <DoubleAnimation
                                        Storyboard.TargetName="rectScale"
                                        Storyboard.TargetProperty="ScaleX"
                                        From="0" To="4" Duration="0:0:5"/>
                                    <DoubleAnimation
                                        Storyboard.TargetName="rectScale"
                                        Storyboard.TargetProperty="ScaleY"
                                        From="0" To="4" Duration="0:0:5"/>
                                </Storyboard>
```

```
                        </BeginStoryboard>
                    </EventTrigger>
                </Canvas.Triggers>
            </Canvas>
        </Border>
    </StackPanel>

    <StackPanel Grid.Column="1">
        <TextBlock  HorizontalAlignment="Center" Margin="10,10,10,10"
                    TextWrapping="Wrap" FontSize="14" FontWeight="Bold"
                    Text="Interactive Scaling"/>
        <Grid Width="260" Height="26" HorizontalAlignment="Left"
              VerticalAlignment="Top">
            <Grid.ColumnDefinitions>
                <ColumnDefinition Width="70" />
                <ColumnDefinition Width="50" />
                <ColumnDefinition Width="70" />
                <ColumnDefinition Width="50" />
            </Grid.ColumnDefinitions>

            <TextBlock Margin="2,2,10,2" TextAlignment="Right"
                    Text="ScaleX"/>
            <TextBox Name="tbScaleX" Width="50" Height="20" Grid.Column="1"
                    TextAlignment="Center" Text="1"/>
            <TextBlock Margin="2,2,10,2" Grid.Column="2"
                    TextAlignment="Right" Text="ScaleY"/>
            <TextBox Name="tbScaleY" Width="50" Height="20" Grid.Column="3"
                    TextAlignment="Center" Text="1"/>
        </Grid>

        <Border Margin="10" BorderBrush="Black" BorderThickness="1"
                Background="{StaticResource MyGrayGridBrush}"
                HorizontalAlignment="Left">
            <Canvas ClipToBounds="True" Width="240" Height="250">
                <TextBlock Canvas.Left="90" Canvas.Top="63"
                        Text="Original shape"/>
                <Rectangle Canvas.Top="80" Canvas.Left="100" Width="50"
                        Height="70" Stroke="Black" StrokeThickness="1"
                        StrokeDashArray="3,1"/>
                <Rectangle Canvas.Top="80" Canvas.Left="100" Width="50"
                        Height="70" Fill="LightCoral" Opacity="0.5"
                        Stroke="Black" StrokeThickness="2">
                    <!-- Set interactive scale: -->
                    <Rectangle.RenderTransform>
                        <ScaleTransform ScaleX="{Binding
                            ElementName=tbScaleX,Path=Text}"
                            ScaleY="{Binding ElementName=tbScaleY,Path=Text}"
                            CenterX="25" CenterY="35"/>
                    </Rectangle.RenderTransform>
                </Rectangle>
            </Canvas>
        </Border>
    </StackPanel>
```

```
        </Grid>
    </Viewbox>
</Window>
```

This XAML file creates a complete WPF application that includes not only a layout and user interface, but also the animation and interactive scale transform on the rectangle shape.

The animation for the rectangle object is started by varying its *ScaleX* and *ScaleY* dependency properties from 0 to 4.

For the interactive scale transform on the rectangle on the right pane, the *ScaleX* and *ScaleY* properties of the transform are bound to the *Text* properties of the corresponding *TextBoxes*, which can be specified by the user's input. This allows you to interactively examine the scaling transform directly on the screen. Figure 2-10 shows a snapshot of this example.

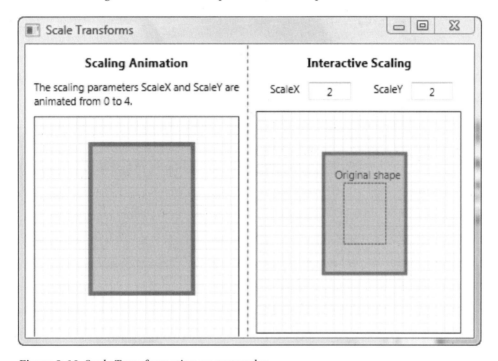

Figure 2-10. *Scale Transformation on rectangles.*

TranslateTransform Class

The *TranslateTransform* class enables you to move an object by setting its *X* and *Y* properties. This transform has no center properties to set because the translation effect is the same regardless of where it is centered.

Let's consider an example of a translation on a *Rectangle* object with the same layout as that used in the previous example. Add a WPF Window to the project *Transformation2D* and call it *TranslateTransforms*. The XAML file is similar to the previous *ScaleTransformations* example, except for the *RenderTransform* property of the rectangle. Here is the XAML file for this example:

```
<Window x:Class="Transformation2D.TranslateTransforms"
```

45

```xml
    xmlns="http://schemas.microsoft.com/winfx/2006/xaml/presentation"
    xmlns:x="http://schemas.microsoft.com/winfx/2006/xaml"
    Title="Translation Transforms" Height="330" Width="480">

<Viewbox Stretch="Uniform">
    <Grid Width="525" Height="330" HorizontalAlignment="Left"
            VerticalAlignment="Top" ShowGridLines="True">
        <Grid.ColumnDefinitions>
            <ColumnDefinition Width="260" />
            <ColumnDefinition Width="260" />
        </Grid.ColumnDefinitions>

        <StackPanel Grid.Column="0">
            <TextBlock HorizontalAlignment="Center" Margin="10,10,10,0"
                        TextWrapping="Wrap" FontSize="14" FontWeight="Bold"
                        Text="Translation Animation"/>
            <TextBlock Margin="10,10,10,0" TextWrapping="Wrap"
                        Text="The translation properties X and Y
                            are animated from -90 to 90."/>
            <Border Margin="10" BorderBrush="Black" BorderThickness="1"
                    Background="{StaticResource MyGrayGridBrush}"
                    HorizontalAlignment="Left">
                <Canvas ClipToBounds="True" Width="240" Height="250">
                    <Rectangle Name="rect" Canvas.Left="100" Canvas.Top="80"
                                Width="50" Height="70" Fill="LightCoral"
                                Opacity="0.5" Stroke="Black" StrokeThickness="2">
                        <Rectangle.RenderTransform>
                            <TranslateTransform x:Name="translate"/>
                        </Rectangle.RenderTransform>
                    </Rectangle>

                    <!-- Animate the rectangle: -->
                    <Canvas.Triggers>
                        <EventTrigger RoutedEvent="Canvas.Loaded">
                            <BeginStoryboard>
                                <Storyboard RepeatBehavior="Forever"
                                        AutoReverse="True">
                                    <DoubleAnimation
                                        Storyboard.TargetName="translate"
                                        Storyboard.TargetProperty="X"
                                        From="-90" To="90" Duration="0:0:5"/>
                                    <DoubleAnimation
                                        Storyboard.TargetName="translate"
                                        Storyboard.TargetProperty="Y"
                                        From="-90" To="90" Duration="0:0:5"/>
                                </Storyboard>
                            </BeginStoryboard>
                        </EventTrigger>
                    </Canvas.Triggers>
                </Canvas>
            </Border>
        </StackPanel>
```

```
    <StackPanel Grid.Column="1">
        <TextBlock  HorizontalAlignment="Center" Margin="10,10,10,10"
                    TextWrapping="Wrap" FontSize="14" FontWeight="Bold"
                    Text="Interactive Translation"/>
        <Grid Width="260" Height="26" HorizontalAlignment="Left"
                VerticalAlignment="Top">
            <Grid.ColumnDefinitions>
                <ColumnDefinition Width="70" />
                <ColumnDefinition Width="50" />
                <ColumnDefinition Width="70" />
                <ColumnDefinition Width="50" />
            </Grid.ColumnDefinitions>

            <TextBlock Margin="2,2,10,2" TextAlignment="Right" Text="X"/>
            <TextBox Name="tbX" Width="50" Height="20" Grid.Column="1"
                    TextAlignment="Center" Text="0"/>
            <TextBlock Margin="2,2,10,2" Grid.Column="2"
                        TextAlignment="Right" Text="Y"/>
            <TextBox Name="tbY" Width="50" Height="20" Grid.Column="3"
                    TextAlignment="Center" Text="0"/>
        </Grid>

        <Border Margin="10" BorderBrush="Black" BorderThickness="1"
                Background="{StaticResource MyGrayGridBrush}"
                HorizontalAlignment="Left">
            <Canvas ClipToBounds="True" Width="240" Height="250">
                <TextBlock Canvas.Left="90" Canvas.Top="63"
                        Text="Original shape"/>
                <Rectangle Canvas.Top="80" Canvas.Left="100"
                        Width="50" Height="70" Stroke="Black"
                        StrokeThickness="1" StrokeDashArray="3,1"/>

                <Rectangle Name="rect1" Canvas.Top="80" Canvas.Left="100"
                        Width="50" Height="70" Fill="LightCoral"
                        Opacity="0.5" Stroke="Black" StrokeThickness="2">
                    <!-- Set interactive translation: -->
                    <Rectangle.RenderTransform>
                        <TranslateTransform
                            X="{Binding ElementName=tbX,Path=Text}"
                            Y="{Binding ElementName=tbY,Path=Text}"/>
                    </Rectangle.RenderTransform>
                </Rectangle>
            </Canvas>
        </Border>
    </StackPanel>
    </Grid>
    </Viewbox>
</Window>
```

You can see that the animation is performed using a storyboard that animates the *X* and *Y* properties of the translation. For the interactive translation of the rectangle on the right pane, the following XAML snippet defines its *RenderTransform* property:

47

```
<!-- Set interactive translation: -->
<Rectangle.RenderTransform>
    <TranslateTransform X="{Binding ElementName=tbX,Path=Text}"
                        Y="{Binding ElementName=tbY,Path=Text}"/>
</Rectangle.RenderTransform>
```

Here the *X* and *Y* properties of the translation are attached to the text fields of the corresponding *TextBoxes* with data binding. This allows you to interactively manipulate the translation of the rectangle by changing the text fields of the *TextBoxes*. Figure 2-11 shows a snapshot of this example.

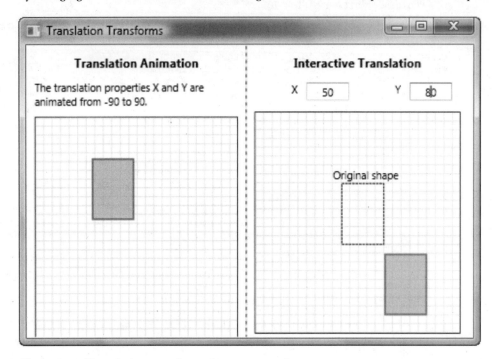

Figure 2-11. *Translation transformation on rectangles.*

RotateTransform Class

The *RotateTransform* class allows you to rotate an object by setting its *Angle, CenterX,* and *CenterY* properties. In the next example, we'll animate the rotation of a *Rectangle* object about its center. However, the origin of this rectangle will be moved from 0 to 180 units. For the interactive rotation, the *Angle, CenterX,* and *CenterY* properties of the transform take values directly from the user's inputs.

Open the *Transformation2D* project, add a new WPF Window, and name it *RotateTransforms*. The XAML file is similar to the one used in the previous example, except for the *RenderTransform* property of the rectangle. Here is the code listing for the XAML file:

```
<Window x:Class="Transformation2D.RotateTransforms"
    xmlns="http://schemas.microsoft.com/winfx/2006/xaml/presentation"
    xmlns:x="http://schemas.microsoft.com/winfx/2006/xaml"
```

```
Title="Rotation Transforms" Height="350" Width="480">

<Viewbox Stretch="Uniform">
    <Grid Width="525" Height="340" HorizontalAlignment="Left"
        VerticalAlignment="Top" ShowGridLines="True">
        <Grid.ColumnDefinitions>
            <ColumnDefinition Width="260" />
            <ColumnDefinition Width="260" />
        </Grid.ColumnDefinitions>

        <StackPanel Grid.Column="0">
            <TextBlock HorizontalAlignment="Center" Margin="10,10,10,0"
                    TextWrapping="Wrap" FontSize="14" FontWeight="Bold"
                    Text="Rotation Animation"/>
            <TextBlock Margin="10,10,10,0" TextWrapping="Wrap"
                    Text="The rotation angle is animated from 0 to 360,
                    and the center property is animated from (-20,-50) to
                    (120,90)."/>
            <Border Margin="10" BorderBrush="Black" BorderThickness="1"
                    Background="{StaticResource MyGrayGridBrush}"
                    HorizontalAlignment="Left">
                <Canvas ClipToBounds="True" Width="240" Height="250">
                    <Rectangle Name="rect" Canvas.Left="100" Canvas.Top="80"
                            Width="50" Height="70" Fill="LightCoral"
                            Opacity="0.5" Stroke="Black" StrokeThickness="2">
                        <Rectangle.RenderTransform>
                            <RotateTransform x:Name="rotate"/>
                        </Rectangle.RenderTransform>
                    </Rectangle>

                    <!-- Animate the rectangle: -->
                    <Canvas.Triggers>
                        <EventTrigger RoutedEvent="Canvas.Loaded">
                            <BeginStoryboard>
                                <Storyboard RepeatBehavior="Forever">
                                    <DoubleAnimation
                                        Storyboard.TargetName="rotate"
                                        Storyboard.TargetProperty="Angle"
                                        From="0" To="360" Duration="0:0:5"/>
                                    <DoubleAnimation
                                        Storyboard.TargetName="rotate"
                                        Storyboard.TargetProperty="CenterX"
                                        From="-20" To="120" Duration="0:0:5"/>
                                    <DoubleAnimation
                                        Storyboard.TargetName="rotate"
                                        Storyboard.TargetProperty="CenterY"
                                        From="-50" To="90" Duration="0:0:5"/>
                                </Storyboard>
                            </BeginStoryboard>
                        </EventTrigger>
                    </Canvas.Triggers>
                </Canvas>
            </Border>
```

```
    </StackPanel>

    <StackPanel Grid.Column="1">
        <TextBlock  HorizontalAlignment="Center" Margin="10,10,10,10"
                    TextWrapping="Wrap" FontSize="14" FontWeight="Bold"
                    Text="Interactive Translation"/>
        <Grid Width="260" Height="26" HorizontalAlignment="Left"
              VerticalAlignment="Top" Margin="0 0 0 15">
            <Grid.ColumnDefinitions>
                <ColumnDefinition Width="55" />
                <ColumnDefinition Width="30" />
                <ColumnDefinition Width="55" />
                <ColumnDefinition Width="30" />
                <ColumnDefinition Width="55" />
                <ColumnDefinition Width="30" />
            </Grid.ColumnDefinitions>

            <TextBlock Margin="2,2,10,2" TextAlignment="Right"
                       Text="CenterX"/>
            <TextBox Name="tbCenterX" Width="30" Height="20" Grid.Column="1"
                     TextAlignment="Center" Text="0"/>
            <TextBlock Margin="2,2,10,2" Grid.Column="2"
                       TextAlignment="Right" Text="CenterY"/>
            <TextBox Name="tbCenterY" Width="30" Height="20" Grid.Column="3"
                     TextAlignment="Center" Text="0"/>
            <TextBlock Margin="2,2,10,2" Grid.Column="4"
                       TextAlignment="Right" Text="Angle"/>
            <TextBox Name="tbAngle" Width="30" Height="20" Grid.Column="5"
                     TextAlignment="Center" Text="0"/>
        </Grid>

        <Border Margin="10" BorderBrush="Black" BorderThickness="1"
                Background="{StaticResource MyGrayGridBrush}"
                HorizontalAlignment="Left">
            <Canvas ClipToBounds="True" Width="240" Height="250">
                <TextBlock Canvas.Left="90" Canvas.Top="63"
                           Text="Original shape"/>
                <Rectangle Canvas.Top="80" Canvas.Left="100" Width="50"
                           Height="70" Stroke="Black" StrokeThickness="1"
                           StrokeDashArray="3,1"/>
                <Rectangle Name="rect1" Canvas.Top="80" Canvas.Left="100"
                           Width="50" Height="70" Fill="LightCoral"
                           Opacity="0.5" Stroke="Black" StrokeThickness="2">
                    <!-- Set interactive rotation: -->
                    <Rectangle.RenderTransform>
                        <RotateTransform
                         CenterX="{Binding ElementName=tbCenterX,Path=Text}"
                         CenterY="{Binding ElementName=tbCenterY,Path=Text}"
                         Angle="{Binding ElementName=tbAngle,Path=Text}"/>
                    </Rectangle.RenderTransform>
                </Rectangle>
            </Canvas>
        </Border>
```

```
            </StackPanel>
        </Grid>
    </Viewbox>
</Window>
```

You can see that the animation is performed using a storyboard that animates the *CenterX*, *CenterY*, and *Angle* properties of the rotation transform. For the interactive rotation transform on the rectangle in the right pane, the following XAML snippet defines its *RenderTransform* property:

```
<!-- Set interactive rotation: -->
<Rectangle.RenderTransform>
    <RotateTransform CenterX="{Binding ElementName=tbCenterX,Path=Text}"
                     CenterY="{Binding ElementName=tbCenterY,Path=Text}"
                     Angle="{Binding ElementName=tbAngle,Path=Text}"/>
</Rectangle.RenderTransform>
```

Here the *Angle*, *CenterX*, and *CenterY* properties of the rotation transform are attached to the text fields of the corresponding *TextBoxes* with data binding. This allows you to interactively manipulate the rotation transform on the rectangle by changing the text fields of the *TextBoxes*.

Figure 2-12 shows the result of running this application.

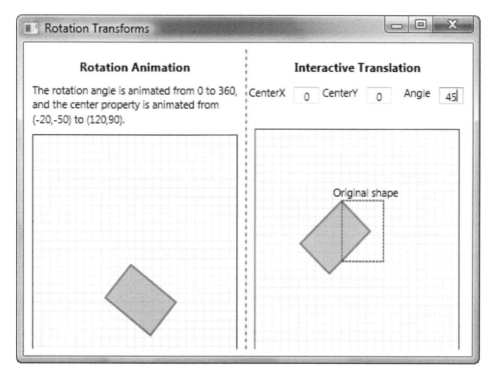

Figure 2-12. Rotation transform on rectangles.

SkewTransform Class

The *SkewTransform* class defines a 2D skew that stretches the coordinate space of a *FrameworkElement* or a *UIElement* object in a nonuniform manner. You can use the *CenterX* and *CenterY* properties to specify the center point of the transform and use the *AngleX* and *AngleY* properties to specify the skew angle along the *X* and *Y* directions.

In this example, we'll animate the skew transform of a *Rectangle* object about its center by varying its *AngleX* and *AngleY* properties. For the interactive skew transformation, the *AngleX* and *AngleY* properties of the transform take values directly from the user's input.

Open the *Transformation2D* project, add a new WPF Window, and name it *SkewTransforms*. The XAML file is similar to that of the previous example, except for the *RenderTransform* property of the rectangle. Here is the code listing:

```
<Window x:Class="Transformation2D.SkewTransforms"
    xmlns="http://schemas.microsoft.com/winfx/2006/xaml/presentation"
    xmlns:x="http://schemas.microsoft.com/winfx/2006/xaml"
    Title="Skew Transforms" Height="350" Width="480">

    <Viewbox Stretch="Uniform">
        <Grid Width="525" Height="340" HorizontalAlignment="Left"
            VerticalAlignment="Top" ShowGridLines="True">
            <Grid.ColumnDefinitions>
                <ColumnDefinition Width="260" />
                <ColumnDefinition Width="260" />
            </Grid.ColumnDefinitions>

            <StackPanel Grid.Column="0">
                <TextBlock HorizontalAlignment="Center" Margin="10,10,10,0"
                        TextWrapping="Wrap" FontSize="14" FontWeight="Bold"
                        Text="Skew Animation"/>
                <TextBlock Margin="10,10,10,0" TextWrapping="Wrap"
                        Text="The skew properties AngleX and AngleY are animated
                        from 0 to 360."/>
                <Border Margin="10" BorderBrush="Black" BorderThickness="1"
                        Background="{StaticResource MyGrayGridBrush}"
                        HorizontalAlignment="Left">
                    <Canvas ClipToBounds="True" Width="240" Height="250">
                        <Rectangle Name="rect" Canvas.Left="100" Canvas.Top="80"
                                Width="50" Height="70" Fill="LightCoral"
                                Opacity="0.5" Stroke="Black" StrokeThickness="2">
                            <Rectangle.RenderTransform>
                                <SkewTransform x:Name="skew" CenterX="25"
                                        CenterY="35"/>
                            </Rectangle.RenderTransform>
                        </Rectangle>

                        <!-- Animate the rectangle: -->
                        <Canvas.Triggers>
                            <EventTrigger RoutedEvent="Canvas.Loaded">
                                <BeginStoryboard>
                                    <Storyboard RepeatBehavior="Forever">
                                        <DoubleAnimation
                                            Storyboard.TargetName="skew"
```

```
                            Storyboard.TargetProperty="AngleX"
                            From="0" To="360" Duration="0:0:10"/>
                        <DoubleAnimation
                            Storyboard.TargetName="skew"
                            Storyboard.TargetProperty="AngleY"
                            From="0" To="360" Duration="0:0:10"/>
                    </Storyboard>
                </BeginStoryboard>
            </EventTrigger>
        </Canvas.Triggers>
    </Canvas>
  </Border>
</StackPanel>

<StackPanel Grid.Column="1">
    <TextBlock HorizontalAlignment="Center" Margin="10,10,10,10"
            TextWrapping="Wrap"
            FontSize="14" FontWeight="Bold"
            Text="Interactive Translation"/>
    <Grid Width="260" Height="26" HorizontalAlignment="Left"
        VerticalAlignment="Top">
        <Grid.ColumnDefinitions>
            <ColumnDefinition Width="70" />
            <ColumnDefinition Width="50" />
            <ColumnDefinition Width="60" />
            <ColumnDefinition Width="50" />
        </Grid.ColumnDefinitions>

        <TextBlock Margin="2,2,10,2" TextAlignment="Right"
                Text="AngleX"/>
        <TextBox Name="tbAngleX" Width="50" Height="20"
                Grid.Column="1" TextAlignment="Center" Text="0"/>
        <TextBlock Margin="2,2,10,2" Grid.Column="2"
                TextAlignment="Right" Text="AngleY"/>
        <TextBox Name="tbAngleY" Width="50" Height="20" Grid.Column="3"
                TextAlignment="Center" Text="0"/>
    </Grid>

    <Border Margin="10" BorderBrush="Black" BorderThickness="1"
            Background="{StaticResource MyGrayGridBrush}"
            HorizontalAlignment="Left">
        <Canvas ClipToBounds="True" Width="240" Height="250">
            <TextBlock Canvas.Left="90" Canvas.Top="63"
                    Text="Original shape"/>
            <Rectangle Canvas.Top="80" Canvas.Left="100" Width="50"
                    Height="70" Stroke="Black" StrokeThickness="1"
                    StrokeDashArray="3,1"/>
            <Rectangle Name="rect1" Canvas.Top="80" Canvas.Left="100"
                    Width="50" Height="70" Fill="LightCoral"
                    Opacity="0.5" Stroke="Black" StrokeThickness="2">
                <!-- Set interactive skew: -->
                <Rectangle.RenderTransform>
                    <SkewTransform CenterX="25" CenterY="35"
```

```
                            AngleX="{Binding ElementName=tbAngleX,Path=Text}"
                            AngleY="{Binding ElementName=tbAngleY,Path=Text}"/>
                    </Rectangle.RenderTransform>
                </Rectangle>
            </Canvas>
        </Border>
    </StackPanel>
</Grid>
</Viewbox>
</Window>
```

Here, the animation is performed using a storyboard that animates the *AngleX* and *AngleY* properties of the skew transform. For the interactive skew transform on the rectangle in the right pane, the following XAML snippet defines its *RenderTransform* property:

```
<!-- Set interactive skew: -->
<Rectangle.RenderTransform>
    <SkewTransform CenterX="25" CenterY="35"
        AngleX="{Binding ElementName=tbAngleX,Path=Text}"
        AngleY="{Binding ElementName=tbAngleY,Path=Text}"/>
</Rectangle.RenderTransform>
```

Here the *AngleX* and *AngleY* properties of the skew transform are attached to the text fields of the corresponding *TextBoxes* with data binding. This allows you to interactively manipulate the skew transform on the rectangle by changing the text fields of the *TextBoxes*.

Figure 2-13 shows a snapshot of this example.

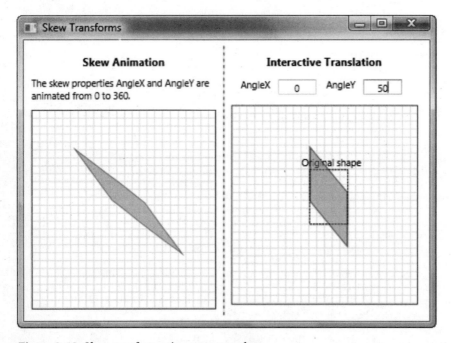

Figure 2-13. *Skew tranformation on rectangles.*

Composite Transforms

You can apply the *TransformGroup* class, which allows you to combine any of the preceding transforms, to any *UIElement* or *FrameworkElement* object. In other words, you can apply to a graphics object a composite transform that consists of any number of transforms. The *TransformGroup* class derived from the *Transform* base class represents a combining transform that contains a collection of *Transforms*.

You can represent various transforms using a simple C# code snippet. For example, to scale a rectangle two times in the *X* direction and three times in the *Y* direction, you can use a *ScaleTransform* object:

```
Rectangle.RenderTransformation = new ScaleTransformation(2, 3);
```

To move the rectangle 100 units in the *X* direction and –100 units in the *Y* direction, you can simply write:

```
Rectangle.RenderTransform = new TranslateTransform(100, - 100);
```

To rotate the rectangle 45 degrees, you can create a new *RotateTransform* object and set the angle to 45:

```
Rectangle.RenderTransform = new RotateTransform(45);
```

To skew an element 30 degrees in the *X* direction and 45 degrees in the *Y* direction, you can use a *SkewTransform*:

```
Rectangle.RenderTransform = new SkewTransform(30, 45);
```

Finally, if you want to apply all of these transforms to this rectangle, you can use a *TransformGroup*:

```
TransformGroup tg = new TransformGroup();
tg.Children.Add(ScaleTransform(2, 3));
tg.Children.Add(TranslateTransform(100, -100));
tg.Children.Add(RotateTransform(45));
tg.Children.Add(SkewTransform(30, 45));
Rectangle.RenderTransform = tg;
```

Let's consider an example that illustrates how to use the *TransformGroup* class in a WPF application. In this example, you'll use a composite transform that contains a scale transform and a rotation transform. You'll apply this composite transform to a rectangle object (a square in this case) about its center. You'll animate the dependency properties of both the scale and rotation transformations.

Open the *Transformation2D* project, add a new WPF Window, and name it *CombineTransforms*. Here, we'll only consider the animation of the combined transform. The following is the XAML file for this example:

```
<Window x:Class="Transformation2D.CombineTransforms"
    xmlns="http://schemas.microsoft.com/winfx/2006/xaml/presentation"
    xmlns:x="http://schemas.microsoft.com/winfx/2006/xaml"
    Title="Combining Transforms" Height="330" Width="300">

    <Viewbox Stretch="Uniform">
        <StackPanel>
            <TextBlock HorizontalAlignment="Center" Margin="10,10,10,0"
                    TextWrapping="Wrap" FontSize="14" FontWeight="Bold"
                    Text="Animation of Combining Transform"/>
            <Border Margin="10" BorderBrush="Black" BorderThickness="1"
                    Background="{StaticResource MyGrayGridBrush}"
```

55

```
                    HorizontalAlignment="Left">
        <Canvas ClipToBounds="True" Width="340" Height="320">
            <Ellipse Canvas.Left="165" Canvas.Top="145" Width="10"
                    Height="10" Fill="Red"/>

            <Rectangle Canvas.Left="120" Canvas.Top="100" Width="100"
                    Height="100" Fill="LightCoral" Opacity="0.5"
                    Stroke="Black" StrokeThickness="2">
                <Rectangle.RenderTransform>
                    <TransformGroup>
                        <ScaleTransform  x:Name="scale" CenterX="50"
                                        CenterY="50" />
                        <RotateTransform x:Name="rotate" CenterX="50"
                                        CenterY="50"/>
                    </TransformGroup>
                </Rectangle.RenderTransform>
            </Rectangle>

            <!-- Animate the shape: -->
            <Canvas.Triggers>
                <EventTrigger RoutedEvent="Canvas.Loaded">
                    <BeginStoryboard>
                        <Storyboard RepeatBehavior="Forever"
                                    AutoReverse="True">
                            <DoubleAnimation Storyboard.TargetName="scale"
                                Storyboard.TargetProperty="ScaleX"
                                From="0" To="3" Duration="0:0:5"/>
                            <DoubleAnimation Storyboard.TargetName="scale"
                                Storyboard.TargetProperty="ScaleY"
                                From="0" To="3" Duration="0:0:5"/>
                            <DoubleAnimation Storyboard.TargetName="rotate"
                                Storyboard.TargetProperty="Angle"
                                From="0" To="360" Duration="0:0:5"/>
                        </Storyboard>
                    </BeginStoryboard>
                </EventTrigger>
            </Canvas.Triggers>
        </Canvas>
    </Border>
</StackPanel>
    </Viewbox>
</Window>
```

Here, we specify the rectangle's *RenderTransform* property using a *TransformGroup*. Within this *TransformGroup*, we define two transforms: a *ScaleTransform* named "*scale*" and a *RotateTransform* named "*rotate*." Both transforms are animated using a *StoryBoard*. Within the *StoryBoard*, we first animate the *ScaleX* and *ScaleY* dependency properties of the *ScaleTransform*. Then we perform the rotation animation on the rectangle by animating the Angle property from 0 to 360 degrees.

This example produces the results shown in Figure 2-14.

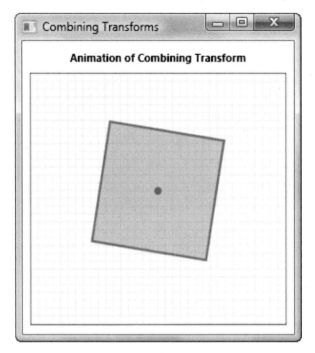

Figure 2-14. Combining transform on a square.

CHAPTER 3

■ ■ ■

WPF Graphics Basics in 2D

As mentioned in Chapter 1, WPF provides a unified graphics platform that allows you to easily create a variety of user interfaces and graphics objects in your applications. In the previous chapter, we discussed various transformation operations on graphics objects in WPF. This chapter begins by describing graphics coordinate systems used in WPF and shows you several different coordinate systems you can use to make graphics programming easier. Then I'll show you how to create basic 2D shapes in WPF applications using WPF's built-in *Shape* class and your own custom shapes.

2D Coordinate Systems in WPF

When you create graphic object in WPF, you must determine where the graphics object or drawing will be displayed. To do this, you need to understand how WPF measures coordinates of the graphics object. Each point on a WPF window or page has an *X* and a *Y* coordinate. In the following sections, we'll discuss various coordinate systems and their relationships.

Default Coordinates

For 2D graphics, the WPF coordinate system places the origin in the upper-left corner of the rendering area. In the 2D space, the positive *X* axis points to the right, and the positive *Y* axis points downward, as shown in Figure 3-1.

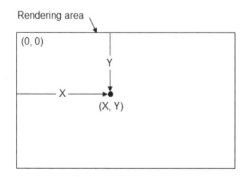

Figure 3-1. *Default coordinate system in WPF*

All coordinates and sizes in the default WPF system are measured in units of 96 dots per inch (DPI), called *device-independent pixels*. In this system, you can create adaptive layouts to deal with different resolutions, which make sure your controls and graphics objects stretch accordingly when the window is stretched.

You can define the rendering area in WPF using layout elements that derive from the *Panel* class, such as *Canvas, DockPanel, Grid, StackPanel, VirtualizingStatckPanel*, and *WrapPanel*. However, it is also possible to use a custom layout component for the rendering area by overriding the default behavior of any of these layout elements.

Let's look at an example and see how this can be achieved. Start up Microsoft Visual Studio 2008, create a new WPF Windows project, and name it *GraphicsBasics*. Add a new WPF Window to the project and name it *LineInDefaultSystem*. Add a *Canvas* element to the application. The *Canvas* control is particularly useful when you need to place graphics and other drawing elements at absolute positions. What's interesting is that *Canvas* elements can be nested. This means you can prepare part of a drawing in a canvas and then insert that entire drawing as a single element into another canvas. You can also apply various transformations, such as scaling and rotation, directly to the canvas.

Now you can draw a line from *Point* (0, 0) to *Point* (100, 100) on the canvas, using the default units of device-independent pixels, with the following XAML file:

```
<Window x:Class="GraphicsBasics.LineInDefaultSystem"
    xmlns="http://schemas.microsoft.com/winfx/2006/xaml/presentation"
    xmlns:x="http://schemas.microsoft.com/winfx/2006/xaml"
    Title="Line in Default System" Height="300" Width="300">
    <Canvas Height="300" Width="300">
        <Line X1="0" Y1="0" X2="100" Y2="100" Stroke="Black" StrokeThickness="2" />
    </Canvas>
</Window>
```

Figure 3-2 shows the results of running this example.

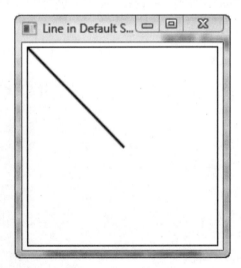

Figure 3-2. Drawing a line from (0, 0) to (100, 100) on a canvas

It is also possible to use other units to create graphics objects. WPF provides four different units of measure:

- *px*: is the default device-independent unit (1/96 inch per unit).

- *in*: is inches; $1in = 96\,px$.

- *cm*: is centimeters; $1cm = (96/2.54)\,px$.

- *pt*: is points; $1pt = (96/72)\,px$.

You can create graphics objects and UIs using either one of the units of measure just listed or mixed units. For example, the coordinates for the starting and ending points of the line can be specified in pixels (*px*), centimeters (*cm*), inches (*in*), or points (*pt*). If you omit the unit (such as in the *StrokeThickness* attribute), the default device-independent pixels will be used.

Replacing the code inside the canvas of the previous example with the following piece of XAML code generates the output shown in Figure 3-3:

```
<Canvas Height="300" Width="300">
    <Line X1="0.5in" Y1="2.0cm" X2="150" Y2="80pt" Stroke="Blue"
          StrokeThickness="0.1cm"/>
</Canvas>
```

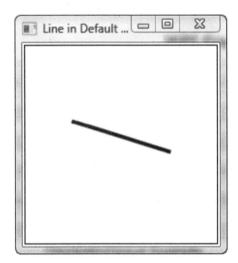

Figure 3-3. Drawing a line on a canvas using different units of measure

Also note the decimal values in the preceding XAML code. All coordinates in WPF are double precision values. This allows you to create device-independent applications easily by using real-world units; the WPF rendering engine will make sure that everything is rendered in the correct size, regardless of whether you are drawing to the screen or the printer.

Custom Coordinates

In addition to the default WPF coordinate system discussed in the previous section, a WPF application can define its own coordinate system. For example, 2D charting applications usually use a coordinate system in which the *Y* axis points from bottom to top, as illustrated in Figure 3-4.

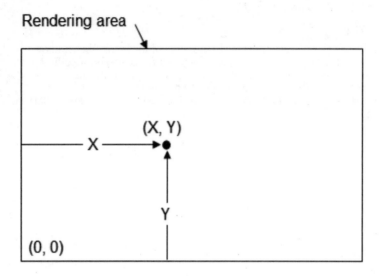

Figure 3-4. *A custom coordinate system*

This system can easily be created in WPF by performing corresponding transformations directly to the canvas, as discussed in the previous chapter. Let's consider an example.

Add a new WPF Window to the project *GraphicsBasics* and name it *LineInCustomSystem*. Here is the XAML file for this example:

```
<Window x:Class=" GraphicsBasics.LineInCustomSystem"
    xmlns="http://schemas.microsoft.com/winfx/2006/xaml/presentation"
    xmlns:x="http://schemas.microsoft.com/winfx/2006/xaml"
    Title="Line in Custom System" Height="240" Width="220">
    <Border BorderBrush="Black" BorderThickness="1" Height="200" Width="200">
        <Canvas Height="200" Width="200">
            <Canvas.RenderTransform>
                <TransformGroup>
                    <ScaleTransform ScaleY="-1" />
                    <TranslateTransform Y="200" />
                </TransformGroup>
            </Canvas.RenderTransform>
            <Line X1="0" Y1="0" X2="100" Y2="100" Stroke="Black"
                StrokeThickness="2" />
        </Canvas>
    </Border>
</Window>
```

In this example, you perform two successive transforms on the canvas. The scale transform reverses the *Y* axis, and the translation transform translates 200 *px* (the height of the canvas) in the *Y* direction. These transforms move the origin from the top-left corner to the bottom-left corner.

Figure 3-5 shows the result produced by this example. The line from (0, 0) to (100, 100) is now measured relative to the origin of the new custom coordinate system. You can compare this line with that drawn in the default system of Figure 3-2.

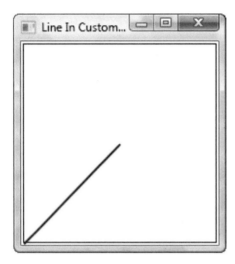

Figure 3-5. *Drawing a line from (0, 0) to (100, 100) in a custom coordinate system*

You may notice an issue with this custom coordinate system: Everything inside the *Canvas* will be transformed the same way the canvas is. For instance, when you add a button control and a text block to the canvas using the following XAML code, the content of the button and the text block will be upside down, as shown in Figure 3-6:

```
<Button Canvas.Top="50" Canvas.Left="80" FontSize="15"
        Foreground="Red" Name="label1" Content="My Button"/>
<TextBlock Canvas.Top="120" Canvas.Left="20" FontSize="12pt"
           Foreground="Blue"> <Bold>My Text Block</Bold>
</TextBlock>
```

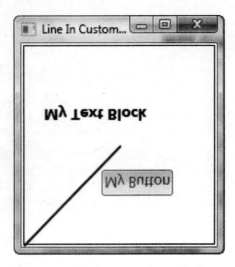

Figure 3-6. *The button and text block are upside down in the custom coordinate system.*

In order to view text normally in this custom coordinate system, you have to perform a reflective transform on the corresponding controls using the following XAML code:

```
<Button Canvas.Top="50" Canvas.Left="80" FontSize="15"
        Foreground="Red" Content="My Button">
    <Button.RenderTransform>
        <ScaleTransform ScaleY="-1"/>
    </Button.RenderTransform>
</Button>
<TextBlock Canvas.Top="120" Canvas.Left="20" FontSize="12pt" Foreground="Blue">
        <Bold>My Text Block</Bold>
    <TextBlock.RenderTransform>
        <ScaleTransform ScaleY="-1"/>
    </TextBlock.RenderTransform>
</TextBlock>
```

The boldface text statements in this code snippet perform a reflection transform in the *Y* direction (corresponding to a scale transform with a scaling factor of –1). Running this application now produces the result shown in Figure 3-7.

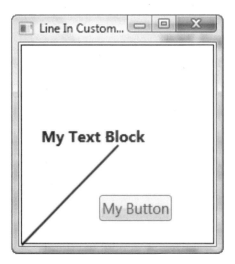

Figure 3-7. *The button and text block in the custom coordinate system after reflection*

You can change the apparent size and location of the graphics objects and user controls on a screen using this custom coordinate system, through a process called *Zooming* or *Panning*. You can achieve Zooming and Panning via scaling and translation transforms.

Add a new WPF Window to the project *GraphicsBasics* and call it *ScaleInCustomSystem*. Add a *StackPanel* element to the application, add a *Slider* control and a *Border* control to the content of the *StackPanel*, and add a canvas to the *Border* control. Finally, create a line and a rectangle object on the canvas control. Here is the XAML file for this example:

```
<Window x:Class=" GraphicsBasics.ScaleInCustomSystem"
    xmlns="http://schemas.microsoft.com/winfx/2006/xaml/presentation"
    xmlns:x="http://schemas.microsoft.com/winfx/2006/xaml"
    Title="Scale In Custom System" Height="310" Width="260">
    <StackPanel Height="280" Width="250">
        <Border BorderBrush="Black" BorderThickness="1" Height="200" Width="200"
                Margin="20">
            <Canvas Height="200" Width="200">
                <Canvas.RenderTransform>
                    <TransformGroup>
                        <ScaleTransform ScaleY="-1" />
                        <TranslateTransform Y="200" />
                    </TransformGroup>
                </Canvas.RenderTransform>

                <Line X1="0" Y1="0" X2="80" Y2="80" Stroke="Black"
                    StrokeThickness="2">
                    <Line.RenderTransform>
                        <ScaleTransform
                            ScaleX="{Binding ElementName=slider,Path=Value}"
                            ScaleY="{Binding ElementName=slider,Path=Value}"/>
                    </Line.RenderTransform>
                </Line>
```

```
            <Rectangle Canvas.Top="100" Canvas.Left="30" Width="80" Height="40"
                    Stroke="DarkRed" StrokeThickness="3">
                <Rectangle.RenderTransform>
                    <ScaleTransform
                        ScaleX="{Binding ElementName=slider,Path=Value}"
                        ScaleY="{Binding ElementName=slider,Path=Value}"/>
                </Rectangle.RenderTransform>
            </Rectangle>
        </Canvas>
    </Border>

    <Slider Name="slider" Minimum="0" Maximum="3" Value="1"
            TickPlacement="BottomRight" TickFrequency="0.2"
            IsSnapToTickEnabled="True"/>
</StackPanel>
</Window>
```

Here, you bind the scaling factors *ScaleX* and *ScaleY* of the line and rectangle to the value of the slider. The value of the slider varies from 0 to 3, meaning that the scaling factor for both the line and the rectangle changes in a range of [0, 3]. When the user moves the slider with the mouse, the dimension of the line and the rectangle will change accordingly.

Figure 3-8 shows the results of running this example. You can zoom in or zoom out by moving the slider with your mouse. When you increase the scaling factor, however, you might obtain unexpected results, such as those shown in the figure. Namely, the graphics objects are extended outside of the *canvas*1 control.

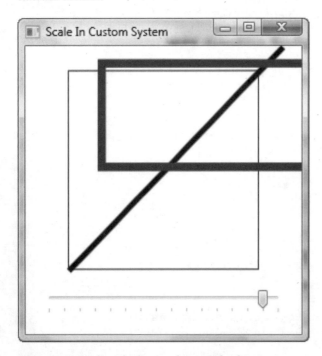

Figure 3-8. *Scaling the line and rectangle objects*

This can easily be fixed by specifying the *ClipToBounds* property of the canvas to true:

```
<Canvas Height="200" Width="200" ClipToBounds="True">
```

This will produce the results shown in Figure 3-9. You can clearly see the difference between Figure 3-8 and Figure 3-9.

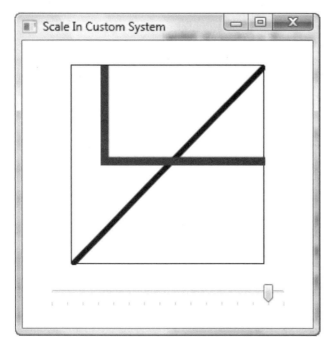

Figure 3-9. Drawing line and rectangle objects inside of the canvas control

There are still issues associated with this custom coordinate system. First, the scaling affects not only the shape of the graphics objects but also the *StrokeThickness*, which may be undesirable for some applications. For example, for charting applications, we want only the shape of the graphics or the line length to vary with the scaling factor, not the *StrokeThickness* itself.

Another issue is the unit of the measure used in the coordinate system, in which the default units are utilized. In real-world applications, real-world units are usually involved. For example, it is impossible to draw a line with a length of 100 miles on the screen in the current coordinate system. In the following section, we'll develop a new custom coordinate system that can be used in 2D chart applications.

Custom Coordinates for 2D Charts

The custom coordinate system used in 2D chart applications must satisfy the following conditions: It must be independent of the unit of the real-world graphics objects, and its *Y* axis must point from bottom to top, as it does in most chart applications. This custom coordinate system is illustrated in Figure 3-10.

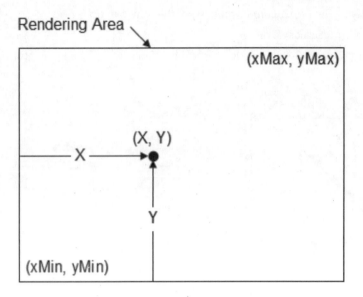

Figure 3-10. *Custom coordinate system for 2D chart applications*

The real-world *X-Y* coordinate system is defined within a rendering area. You can create such a coordinate system using a custom panel control by overriding its *MeasureOverride* and *ArrangeOverride* methods. Each method returns the size data needed to position and render child elements. This is a standard method for creating custom coordinate systems. Instead of creating a custom panel control, here we'll construct this coordinate system using a different approach, based on direct coding.

Add a new WPF Window to the project *GraphicsBasics* and name it *Chart2DSystem*. The following is the XAML file for this example:

```
<Window x:Class="GraphicsBasics.Chart2DSystem"
    xmlns="http://schemas.microsoft.com/winfx/2006/xaml/presentation"
    xmlns:x="http://schemas.microsoft.com/winfx/2006/xaml"
    Title="Chart2D Coordinate System" Height="420" Width="360">
    <Viewbox Stretch="Uniform">
        <StackPanel Height="420" Width="360" Margin="0,10,0,10">
            <Border BorderBrush="Gray" BorderThickness="1">
                <Canvas x:Name="chartCanvas" ClipToBounds="True" Width="300"
                        Height="250" Margin="30,30,30,30"/>
            </Border>
            <Grid Width="340" Height="100" HorizontalAlignment="Left"
                VerticalAlignment="Top" Margin="0,10,0,0">
                <Grid.ColumnDefinitions>
                    <ColumnDefinition Width="60*" />
                    <ColumnDefinition Width="110*" />
                    <ColumnDefinition Width="60*"/>
                    <ColumnDefinition Width="110*" />
                </Grid.ColumnDefinitions>
                <Grid.RowDefinitions>
                    <RowDefinition Height="Auto" />
```

```
            <RowDefinition Height="Auto" />
            <RowDefinition Height="Auto" />
        </Grid.RowDefinitions>

        <TextBlock Grid.Column="0" Grid.Row="0"
                Margin="20,5,10,5">XMin</TextBlock>
        <TextBox Name="tbXMin" Grid.Column="1" Grid.Row="0"
                TextAlignment="Center">0</TextBox>
        <TextBlock Grid.Column="2" Grid.Row="0"
                Margin="20,5,10,5">XMax</TextBlock>
        <TextBox Name="tbXMax" Grid.Column="3" Grid.Row="0"
                TextAlignment="Center">10</TextBox>
        <TextBlock Grid.Column="0" Grid.Row="1"
                Margin="20,5,10,5">YMin</TextBlock>
        <TextBox Name="tbYMin" Grid.Column="1" Grid.Row="1"
                TextAlignment="Center" >0</TextBox>
        <TextBlock Grid.Column="2" Grid.Row="1"
                Margin="20,5,10,5">YMax</TextBlock>
        <TextBox Name="tbYMax" Grid.Column="3" Grid.Row="1"
                TextAlignment="Center">10</TextBox>
        <Button Click="btnApply_Click" Margin="40,20,20,0"
                Height="25" Grid.ColumnSpan="2"
                Grid.Column="0" Grid.Row="2">Apply
        </Button>
        <Button Click="btnClose_Click"  Margin="40,20,20,0"
                Height="25" Grid.ColumnSpan="2"
                Grid.Column="2" Grid.Row="2" >Close
        </Button>
    </Grid>
  </StackPanel>
 </Viewbox>
</Window>
```

This XAML file places a *Viewbox* control as the topmost element and sets its *Stretch* property to *UniForm*, which will preserve the aspect ratio of the child elements when the window gets resized. Otherwise, the *Stretch* property can be set to *Fill*, which disregards the aspect ratio. A great advantage of the *Viewbox* object is that everything inside of it is scalable.

The graphics objects or drawings will be created on a *Canvas* control, called *chartCanvas*. The *Border* element as the parent of the *chartCanvas* serves as the border of the rendering area. The other UI elements will be used to control the appearance of the graphics.

Here is the corresponding C# code-behind file:

```
using System;
using System.Collections.Generic;
using System.Windows;
using System.Windows.Controls;
using System.Windows.Media;
using System.Windows.Shapes;

namespace GraphicsBasics
{
    public partial class Chart2DSystem : Window
    {
        private double xMin = 0.0;
```

```
private double xMax = 10.0;
private double yMin = 0.0;
private double yMax = 10.0;
private Line line1;
private Polyline polyline1;

public Chart2DSystem()
{
    InitializeComponent();
    AddGraphics();
}

private void AddGraphics()
{
    line1 = new Line();
    line1.X1 = XNormalize(2.0);
    line1.Y1 = YNormalize(4.0);
    line1.X2 = XNormalize(8.0);
    line1.Y2 = YNormalize(10.0);
    line1.Stroke = Brushes.Blue;
    line1.StrokeThickness = 2;
    chartCanvas.Children.Add(line1);

    polyline1 = new Polyline();
    polyline1.Points.Add(new Point(XNormalize(8), YNormalize(8)));
    polyline1.Points.Add(new Point(XNormalize(6), YNormalize(6)));
    polyline1.Points.Add(new Point(XNormalize(6), YNormalize(4)));
    polyline1.Points.Add(new Point(XNormalize(4), YNormalize(4)));
    polyline1.Points.Add(new Point(XNormalize(4), YNormalize(6)));
    polyline1.Points.Add(new Point(XNormalize(6), YNormalize(6)));
    polyline1.Stroke = Brushes.Red;
    polyline1.StrokeThickness = 5;
    chartCanvas.Children.Add(polyline1);
}

private double XNormalize(double x)
{
    double result = (x - xMin) * chartCanvas.Width / (xMax - xMin);
    return result;
}

private double YNormalize(double y)
{
    double result = chartCanvas.Height - (y - yMin)*
                    chartCanvas.Height / (yMax - yMin);
    return result;
}

private void btnClose_Click(object sender, EventArgs e)
{
    this.Close();
}
```

```
        private void btnApply_Click(object sender, EventArgs e)
        {
            chartCanvas.Children.Clear();
            xMin = Convert.ToDouble(tbXMin.Text);
            xMax = Convert.ToDouble(tbXMax.Text);
            yMin = Convert.ToDouble(tbYMin.Text);
            yMax = Convert.ToDouble(tbYMax.Text);
            AddGraphics();
        }
    }
}
```

In this code-behind file, we begin by defining private members to hold the minimum and maximum values of the custom coordinate axes. Note that by changing the values of *xMin*, *xMax*, *yMin*, and *yMax*, you can define the size of the rendering area you like, depending on the requirements of your applications. Make sure that the units of these quantities are in real-world units defined in the real-world coordinate system.

You may notice an issue over how to draw graphics objects inside the rendering area, which should be independent of the units of the world coordinate system. Here we use the *XNormalize* and *YNormalize* methods to convert the *X* and *Y* coordinates in the real-world coordinate system to the default device-independent coordinate system. After this conversion, the units for all graphics objects are in device-independent pixels. This can easily be done by passing the *X* and *Y* coordinates of any unit in the world coordinate system to the *XNormalize* and *YNormalize* methods, which will perform the unit conversion automatically and always return the *X* and *Y* coordinates in device-independent pixels in the default WPF coordinate system.

Let's examine what we do inside the *XNormalize* method. We convert the *X* coordinate in the real-world coordinate system via the following formula:

```
double result = (x - xMin) * chartCanvas.Width / (xMax - xMin);
```

Here, we simply perform a scaling operation. Both terms of $(x - xMin)$ and $(xMax - xMin)$ have the same unit in the world coordinate system, which is cancelled out by division. This means that the unit of this scaling term is determined solely by the unit of *chartCanvas.Width*, whose unit is in device-independent pixels. You can easily examine that the foregoing conversion provides not only the correct unit but also the correct position in the default WPF coordinate system.

For the *Y* coordinate conversion, the situation is a bit different. Not only do you need to perform a scaling operation, but you also must reverse the direction of the *Y* axis in the default coordinate system. The following formula is used for the *Y* coordinate conversion:

```
double result = chartCanvas.Height - (y - yMin) *
                chartCanvas.Height / (yMax - yMin);
```

Next, you add a straight line (*line1*) and a polyline (*polyline1*) to the *chartCanvas* using the *AddGraphics* method. You draw the straight line from *point* (2, 4) to *point* (8, 10). The end points of this line are in the unit (which can be any unit!) defined in the world coordinate system. These points aren't used directly in drawing the line, but their converted *X* and *Y* coordinates are used instead. You create the *Polyline* object by means of the same procedure.

The click event of the *Apply* button allows you to redraw the straight line and the polyline using new values for axis limits specified in corresponding *TextBox* elements. Notice that this requires the following statement inside the *Apply* button's event handler:

```
chartCanvas.Children.Clear();
```

Otherwise, both the original and the newly created graphics objects will remain on the screen. The foregoing statement ensures that original objects are removed when new graphics objects are created.

Figure 3-11 shows the result of running this example. From this window, you can change the appearance of the graphics objects by changing the values of *xMin*, *XMax*, *Ymin*, and *yMax* and then clicking the *Apply* button.

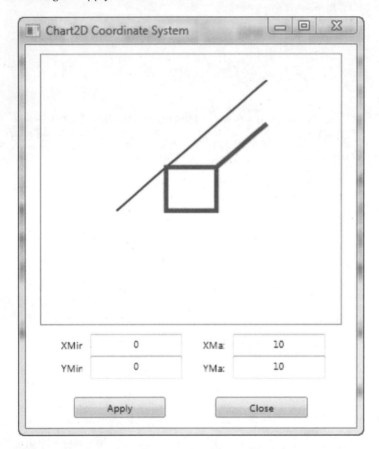

Figure 3-11. Drawing a line and a polyline in the custom coordinate system

2D Viewport

A graphics object can be considered to be defined in its own coordinate system, which is some abstract place with boundaries. For example, suppose you want to create a simple X-Y chart that plots Y values from 50 to 100 over an X-data range from 0 to 10. You can work in a coordinate system space with $0 \leq X \leq 10$ and $50 \leq Y \leq 100$. This space is called the *world coordinate system*.

In practice, you usually aren't interested in the entire graphic, but only a portion of it. Thus, you can define the portion of interest as a specific area in the world coordinate system. This area of interest is called the "Window." In order to draw graphics objects on the screen, you need to map this "Window" to the default WPF coordinate system. We call this mapped "Window" in the default coordinate system a *2D viewport*. The concept of the window and viewport in 2D space is illustrated in Figure 3-12.

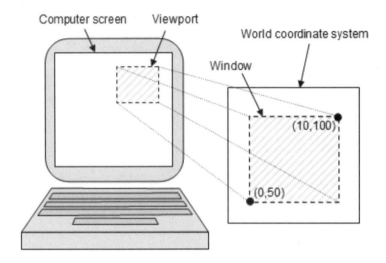

Figure 3-12. Window and viewport in 2D space

In the previous section, we defined the default limits for the X and Y axes in the custom (world) coordinate system. For example:

```
private double xMin = 0.0;
private double xMax = 10.0;
private double yMin = 0.0;
private double yMax = 10.0;
```

This defines a portion of interest in the custom coordinate system. This area of interest is called the "Window." Once you know what you want to view, you need to decide where on the computer screen to display it. In the previous example of *Chart2DSystem*, we defined a rendering area (the *chartCanvas*) in the default WPF coordinate system, which creates a screen area to display the graphics objects. This rendering area is called the *viewport*.

You can use this viewport to change the apparent size and location of the graphics objects on the screen. Changing the viewport affects the display of the graphics objects on the screen. These effects are called *Zooming* and *Panning*.

Zooming and Panning

The size and position of the "Window" determine which part of the graphics object is drawn. The relative size of the Window and the viewport determine the scale at which the graphics object is displayed on the screen. For a given viewport or rendering area, a relatively large Window produces a small graphics object, because you are drawing a large piece of the custom coordinate space into a small viewport (rendering area). On the other hand, a relatively small Window produces a large graphics object. Therefore, by increasing the size of the Window (specified by the X axis and Y axis limits), you'll see a "zooming out" effect. This can be done by changing the values of the parameters, such as *xMin*, *xMax*, *yMin*, and *yMax* in the *Chart2DSystem* example discussed in the previous section. For instance, setting

```
xMin = -10;
xMax = 20;
yMin = 0;
yMax = 20;
```

and clicking the *Apply* button will generate the results shown in Figure 3-13.

Figure 3-13. *Changing both the size and the location of the graphics objects by increasing the size of the window, resulting in a "zoom out" effect*

On the other hand, if you decrease the Window size, the objects will appear larger on the screen; you would then have a "zoom in" effect. Change the parameters of your axis limits to the following:

```
xMin = 2;
xMax = 7;
yMin = 2;
yMax = 7;
```

You will get the result shown in Figure 3-14 when you click the *Apply* button.

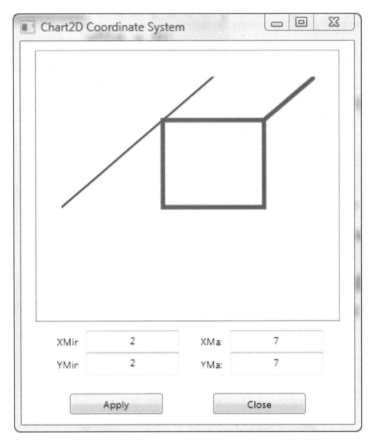

Figure 3-14. Changing both the size and the location of the graphics objects by decreasing the size of the window, resulting in a "zoom in" effect

Panning is defined as the moving of all graphics objects in the scene by shifting the Window. In a panning process, the Window size is kept unchanged. For example, you can move the Window to the left by changing the following parameters:

```
xMin = -3;
xMax = 7;
yMin = 0;
yMax = 10;
```

This is equivalent to moving graphics objects toward the right side of the rendering area.

Please note that when you increase or decrease the size of graphics objects by zooming in or zooming out, the stroke thickness remains unchanged. This differs from performing a scaling operation directly to the *chartCanvas*, because in a scaling operation both the shape and stroke thickness change correspondingly with the scaling factor. In 2D chart applications, you usually want to change the size of only the graphics and to keep the stroke thickness unchanged.

Resizable Canvas

In the previous example, we used a *Viewbox* control as the topmost element. This way, every object inside the *Viewbox* element will scale when the application window is resized. This scalable behavior affects all sizable properties of the elements inside the *Viewbox*, including, for example, label font and stroke thickness of the graphics shapes and lines. However, this behavior may not be suitable for real-world chart applications, because chart applications usually require graphics and line themselves to be scalable, but not label fonts and stroke thicknesses. To achieve this, here we'll implement a resizable *Canvas* to replace the *Viewbox* used in the previous example.

As mentioned previously, the *Canvas* element allows you to place graphics objects at absolute positions. An issue associated with the default WPF *Canvas* element is that unlike the *Grid* control, the size of the *Canvas* is usually fixed when the application window is resized. For chart applications, we want to have a resizable *Canvas* element. We want this element to adjust its size automatically with the application window's actual size. At the same time, we want the resizable *Canvas* to allow us to place graphics objects at absolute positions.

We can easily create such a resizable canvas by combining a *Grid* with a *Canvas* control. Here, I'll use an example to show you how to create this resizable canvas in WPF. Add a new WPF Window to the project *GraphicsBasics* and name it *ResizableCanvas*. The following is the XAML file for this example:

```xml
<Window x:Class="GraphicsBasics.ResizableCanvas"
    xmlns="http://schemas.microsoft.com/winfx/2006/xaml/presentation"
    xmlns:x="http://schemas.microsoft.com/winfx/2006/xaml"
    Title="ResizableCanvas" Height="420" Width="360">

    <Grid>
        <Grid.RowDefinitions>
            <RowDefinition Height="*"/>
            <RowDefinition Height="120"/>
        </Grid.RowDefinitions>
        <Grid x:Name="chartGrid" SizeChanged="chartGrid_SizeChanged">
            <Border x:Name="chartBorder" BorderBrush="Gray"
                    BorderThickness="1" Margin="10">
                <Canvas x:Name="chartCanvas" ClipToBounds="True"/>
            </Border>
        </Grid>
        <StackPanel Grid.Row="1" Margin="0,10,0,0">
            <Grid HorizontalAlignment="Center"
                  VerticalAlignment="Top">
                <Grid.ColumnDefinitions>
                    <ColumnDefinition Width="60*" />
                    <ColumnDefinition Width="110*" />
                    <ColumnDefinition Width="60*"/>
                    <ColumnDefinition Width="110*" />
                </Grid.ColumnDefinitions>
                <Grid.RowDefinitions>
                    <RowDefinition Height="Auto" />
                    <RowDefinition Height="Auto" />
                    <RowDefinition Height="Auto" />
                </Grid.RowDefinitions>

                <TextBlock Grid.Column="0" Grid.Row="0"
                           Margin="25,5,10,5">XMin</TextBlock>
                <TextBox Name="tbXMin" Grid.Column="1" Grid.Row="0"
```

```xml
                          TextAlignment="Center">0</TextBox>
            <TextBlock Grid.Column="2" Grid.Row="0"
                    Margin="25,5,10,5">XMax</TextBlock>
            <TextBox Name="tbXMax" Grid.Column="3" Grid.Row="0"
                    TextAlignment="Center">10</TextBox>
            <TextBlock Grid.Column="0" Grid.Row="1"
                    Margin="25,5,10,5">YMin</TextBlock>
            <TextBox Name="tbYMin" Grid.Column="1" Grid.Row="1"
                    TextAlignment="Center" >0</TextBox>
            <TextBlock Grid.Column="2" Grid.Row="1"
                    Margin="25,5,10,5">YMax</TextBlock>
            <TextBox Name="tbYMax" Grid.Column="3" Grid.Row="1"
                    TextAlignment="Center">10</TextBox>
            <Button Click="btnApply_Click" Margin="40,20,20,0"
                    Height="25" Grid.ColumnSpan="2"
                    Grid.Column="0" Grid.Row="2">Apply
            </Button>
            <Button Click="btnClose_Click"  Margin="40,20,20,0"
                    Height="25" Grid.ColumnSpan="2"
                    Grid.Column="2" Grid.Row="2" >Close
            </Button>
        </Grid>
    </StackPanel>
  </Grid>
</Window>
```

This XAML file is basically similar to that used in the previous example, except for the addition of a *Grid* element called *chartGrid*, which is attached to a *SizeChanged* event. The *chartGrid* contains a child *Canvas* control named *chartCanvas*. Note that we don't specify the size of the *chartCanvas;* instead, we'll determine its size according to the *chartGrid*'s actual size in the code-behind file.

Here is the code-behind file for this example:

```csharp
using System;
using System.Collections.Generic;
using System.Windows;
using System.Windows.Controls;
using System.Windows.Media;
using System.Windows.Shapes;

namespace GraphicsBasics
{
    /// <summary>
    /// Interaction logic for ResizableCanvas.xaml
    /// </summary>
    public partial class ResizableCanvas : Window
    {
        private double xMin = 0.0;
        private double xMax = 10.0;
        private double yMin = 0.0;
        private double yMax = 10.0;
        private Line line1;
        private Polyline polyline1;

        public ResizableCanvas()
```

```
{
    InitializeComponent();
}

private void AddGraphics()
{
    chartCanvas.Children.Clear();
    xMin = Convert.ToDouble(tbXMin.Text);
    xMax = Convert.ToDouble(tbXMax.Text);
    yMin = Convert.ToDouble(tbXMin.Text);
    yMax = Convert.ToDouble(tbYMax.Text);

    line1 = new Line();
    line1.X1 = XNormalize(2.0);
    line1.Y1 = YNormalize(4.0);
    line1.X2 = XNormalize(8.0);
    line1.Y2 = YNormalize(10.0);
    line1.Stroke = Brushes.Blue;
    line1.StrokeThickness = 2;
    chartCanvas.Children.Add(line1);

    polyline1 = new Polyline();
    polyline1.Points.Add(new Point(XNormalize(8), YNormalize(8)));
    polyline1.Points.Add(new Point(XNormalize(6), YNormalize(6)));
    polyline1.Points.Add(new Point(XNormalize(6), YNormalize(4)));
    polyline1.Points.Add(new Point(XNormalize(4), YNormalize(4)));
    polyline1.Points.Add(new Point(XNormalize(4), YNormalize(6)));
    polyline1.Points.Add(new Point(XNormalize(6), YNormalize(6)));
    polyline1.Stroke = Brushes.Red;
    polyline1.StrokeThickness = 5;
    chartCanvas.Children.Add(polyline1);
}

private double XNormalize(double x)
{
    double result = (x - xMin) * chartCanvas.Width / (xMax - xMin);
    return result;
}

private double YNormalize(double y)
{
    double result = chartCanvas.Height
                    - (y - yMin) * chartCanvas.Height / (yMax - yMin);
    return result;
}

private void btnClose_Click(object sender, EventArgs e)
{
    this.Close();
}

private void btnApply_Click(object sender, EventArgs e)
{
```

```
        AddGraphics();
    }

    private void chartGrid_SizeChanged(object sender,
                                    SizeChangedEventArgs e)
    {
        chartCanvas.Width =  chartGrid.ActualWidth
                           - chartBorder.Margin.Left
                           - chartBorder.Margin.Right
                           - chartBorder.BorderThickness.Left
                           - chartBorder.BorderThickness.Right;
        chartCanvas.Height = chartGrid.ActualHeight
                           - chartBorder.Margin.Top
                           - chartBorder.Margin.Bottom
                           - chartBorder.BorderThickness.Top
                           - chartBorder.BorderThickness.Bottom;
        AddGraphics();
    }
  }
}
```

Pay special attention to what happens inside the *chartGrid_SizeChanged* event handler, where we relate the *Width* and *Height* properties of the *chartCanvas* to the *ActualWidth* and *ActualHeight* properties of the *chartGrid*. This way, the *chatCanvas* will adjust its size automatically when the application window is resized. Furthermore, we put the *AddGraphics* method inside this event handler to ensure that the coordinates of the graphics elements on the *chartCanvas* are recalculated when the application window is resized.

Figure 3-15 shows the result of running this example, which is basically similar to the previous example. However, only the graphics elements, *Line* and *Polyline* in this example, change size when you resize the application window. The label fonts and stroke thickness remain unchanged.

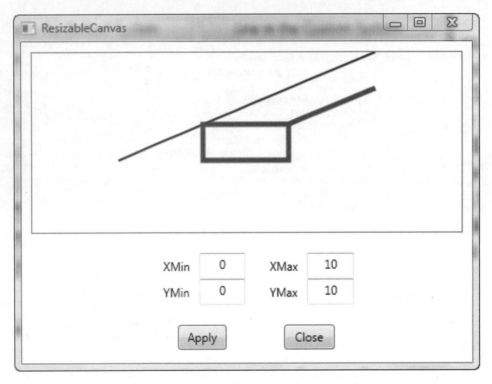

Figure 3-15. Drawing a line and a polyline in the resizable Canvas

Basic 2D Graphics Shapes in WPF

The simplest way to create 2D graphics objects in a WPF application is to use the *Shape* class, which represents a number of ready-to-use graphics shape objects. Available shape objects in WPF include *Line, Polyline, Path, Rectangle*, and *Ellipse*. These shapes are drawing primitives, which can be combined to generate more complex graphics. In the following sections, we'll consider these basic WPF shapes.

Lines

You can use the *Line* class in WPF to create straight lines between two end points. The *X1* and *Y1* properties specify the start point; the *X2* and *Y2* properties represent the end point. The following XAML code snippet creates a blue line from point (30, 30) to point (180, 30):

```
<Line X1="30" Y1="30" X2 ="180" Y2="30" Stroke="Blue" StrokeThickness="2"/>
```

This code snippet produces a solid line. However, lines can have many different styles. For example, you can draw a dashed line with line caps, as shown in Figure 3-16. This means that a line is made up of three parts: the line body, the starting cap, and the ending cap.

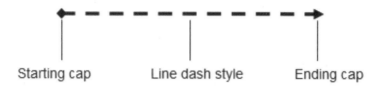

Figure 3-16. A line with starting cap, ending cap, and dash style

The starting and ending caps can be specified by the *StrokeStartLineCap* and *StrokeEndLineCap* properties, respectively. Both properties get or set a *PenLineCap* enumeration value that describes the shape at the ends of the line. Available values in the *PenLineCap* enumeration include *Flat*, *Round*, *Square*, and *Triangle*. Unfortunately, the size of the line cap is the same as the *StrokeThickness* of the line. Thus, these caps aren't very useful in practical applications. If you want to create a line with an end anchor or an arrowhead, you'll need to create a custom shape, which is discussed later in this chapter.

The dash style of a line is specified by the *StrokeDashArray* property that gets or sets a collection of double variables, which specify the pattern of dashes and gaps of the line. Let's consider an example that shows how to create lines with different dash styles. Add a new WPF Window to the project *GraphicsBasics* and name it *LineDashStyles*. Here is the XAML for this example:

```
<Window x:Class="GraphicsBasics.LineDashStyles"
    xmlns="http://schemas.microsoft.com/winfx/2006/xaml/presentation"
    xmlns:x="http://schemas.microsoft.com/winfx/2006/xaml"
    Title="Line Dash Styles" Height="150" Width="350">
    <Grid Margin="0,10,0,0">
        <Grid.RowDefinitions>
            <RowDefinition/>
            <RowDefinition/>
            <RowDefinition/>
        </Grid.RowDefinitions>
        <Grid.ColumnDefinitions>
            <ColumnDefinition/>
            <ColumnDefinition/>
        </Grid.ColumnDefinitions>
            <Line X1="0" Y1="5" X2 ="150" Y2="5" Margin="5" Grid.Column="0"
                Grid.Row="0" Stroke="Blue" StrokeThickness="2"
                StrokeDashArray="5,3"/>
            <TextBlock Grid.Column="1" Grid.Row="0"
                    Text="StrokeDashArray = '5,3'" />
        <Line X1="0" Y1="5" X2 ="150" Y2="5" Margin="5" Grid.Column="0"
            Grid.Row="1" Stroke="Blue" StrokeThickness="2"
            StrokeDashArray="5,1,3,2" StrokeStartLineCap="Round"
            StrokeEndLineCap="Triangle"/>
        <TextBlock Grid.Column="1" Grid.Row="1"
                Text="StrokeDashArray = '5,1,3,2'" />
        <Line X1="0" Y1="5" X2 ="150" Y2="5" Margin="5" Grid.Column="0" Grid.Row="2"
            Stroke="Blue" StrokeThickness="2" StrokeDashArray="5,1,3"/>
        <TextBlock Grid.Column="1" Grid.Row="2" Text="StrokeDashArray = '5,1,3'" />
    </Grid>
</Window>
```

This code creates three dashed lines, each with a different dash style, which are shown in Figure 3-17.

Figure 3-17. *Dashed lines with different styles*

The first line in the figure is a dashed line that is specified by a *StrokeDashArray*="5,3". These values mean that the line has a value of 5 and a gap of 3, interpreted relative to the *StrokeThickness* of the line. So if your line is 2 units thick (as it is in this example), the solid portion is 5 × 2 = 10 units, followed by a gap portion of 3 × 2 = 6 units. The line then repeats this pattern for its entire length.

You can create a line with more complex dash pattern by varying the values of the *StrokeDashArray*. For example, you can specify the *StrokeDashArray* to be the following:

```
StrokeDashArray="5,1,3,2"
```

This creates the second line with a more complex sequence: a solid portion of 10-unit length, then a 1 × 2 = 2-unit break, followed by a solid portion of 3 × 2 = 6 units, and another gap of 2 × 2 = 4 units. At the end of this sequence, the line repeats the pattern from the beginning.

A funny thing happens if you use an odd number of values for the *StrokeDashArray*. Take this one, for example:

```
StrokeDashArray="5,1,3"
```

When you draw this line, you begin with a 10-unit solid line, followed by a 2-unit gap, followed by a 6-unit line. But when the line repeats the pattern it starts with a gap, meaning you get a 10-unit space, followed by a 2-unit line, and so on. The dashed line simply alternates its pattern between solid portions and gaps, as shown in Figure 3-16.

Note from the code that the second line has a round starting cap and a triangle ending cap. However, it is difficult to see the line caps in Figure 3-16, making them not very useful in real-world applications

Rectangles and Ellipses

The rectangle and the ellipse are the two simplest shapes. To create either one, set the *Height* and *Width* properties, which define the size of the shape, and then set the *Fill* and *Stroke* properties to make the shape visible.

The *Rectangle* class has two extra properties: *RadiusX* and *RadiusY*. When set to nonzero values, these two properties allow you to create rectangles with rounded corners.

Let's consider an example that demonstrates how to create rectangles in WPF. Add a new WPF Window to the project *GraphicsBasics* and name it *RectangleShape*. Here is the XAML file for this example:

```
<Window x:Class="GraphicsBasics.RectangleShape"
    xmlns="http://schemas.microsoft.com/winfx/2006/xaml/presentation"
```

```
    xmlns:x="http://schemas.microsoft.com/winfx/2006/xaml"
    Title="Rectangles" Height="340" Width="200">
    <Grid>
        <StackPanel>
            <TextBlock Text="RadiusX = 0, RadiusY = 0:" Margin="10 10 10 5"/>
            <Rectangle Width="150" Height="70" Fill="LightGray" Stroke="Black"/>
            <TextBlock Text="RadiusX = 20, RadiusY = 10:" Margin="10 10 10 5"/>
            <Rectangle Width="150" Height="70" RadiusX="20" RadiusY="10"
                       Fill="LightGray" Stroke="Black"/>
            <TextBlock Text="RadiusX = 75, RadiusY = 35:" Margin="10 10 10 5"/>
            <Rectangle Width="150" Height="70" RadiusX="75" RadiusY="35"
                       Fill="LightGray" Stroke="Black"/>
        </StackPanel>
    </Grid>
</Window>
```

Figure 3-18 shows the results of running this example. You can easily create rectangles with rounded corners by specifying *RadiusX* and *RadiusY* properties to nonzero values. You can even create an ellipse by setting *RadiusX* and *RadiusY* to large values (larger than the half of the respective side length).

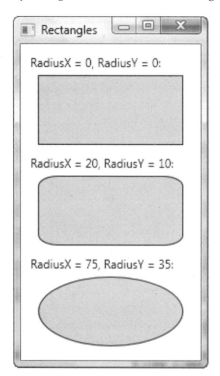

Figure 3-18. Rectangles in WPF

You can create ellipses with properties similar to those used in creating rectangles. You can also create a circle by setting *RadiusX = RadiusY*.

83

Add a new WPF Window to the project *GraphicsBasics* and name it *EllipseShape*. Here is the XAML file for this example:

```
<Window x:Class=" GraphicsBasics.EllipseShape"
    xmlns="http://schemas.microsoft.com/winfx/2006/xaml/presentation"
    xmlns:x="http://schemas.microsoft.com/winfx/2006/xaml"
    Title="Ellipses" Height="280" Width="200">
    <Grid>
      <StackPanel>
            <TextBlock Text="Ellipse:" Margin="10 10 10 5"/>
            <Ellipse Width="150" Height="70" Fill="LightGray" Stroke="Black"/>
            <TextBlock Text="Circle:" Margin="10 10 10 5"/>
            <Ellipse Width="100" Height="100" Fill="LightGray" Stroke="Black"/>
      </StackPanel>
    </Grid>
</Window>
```

This example produces the results shown in Figure 3-19.

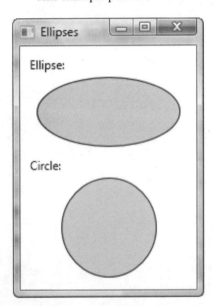

Figure 3-19. *Ellipses in WPF*

Both the rectangle and the ellipse have the ability to resize themselves to fill the available space. If the *Height* and *Width* properties aren't specified, the shape is sized based on its container. The sizing behavior of a shape depends on the value of its stretch property. The default value is set to *Fill*, which stretches a shape to fill its container if an explicit size is not specified.

Let's consider another example, one that illustrates placing and sizing rectangles and ellipses in *Grid* cells. Add a new WPF Window to the project *GraphicsBasics* and name it *PlaceShapes*. Here is the markup for this example:

```
<Window x:Class="GraphicsBasics.PlaceShapes"
    xmlns="http://schemas.microsoft.com/winfx/2006/xaml/presentation"
```

```
        xmlns:x="http://schemas.microsoft.com/winfx/2006/xaml"
        Title="Place Shapes" Height="300" Width="360">

        <Grid ShowGridLines="True">
            <Grid.RowDefinitions>
                <RowDefinition Height="Auto"/>
                <RowDefinition/>
                <RowDefinition/>
            </Grid.RowDefinitions>
            <Grid.ColumnDefinitions>
                <ColumnDefinition Width="Auto"/>
                <ColumnDefinition/>
                <ColumnDefinition/>
                <ColumnDefinition/>
            </Grid.ColumnDefinitions>

            <TextBlock Grid.Column="0" Grid.Row="1" Text="Rectagle" Margin="5"/>
            <TextBlock Grid.Column="0" Grid.Row="2" Text="Ellipse" Margin="5"/>
            <TextBlock Grid.Column="1" Grid.Row="0" Text="Fill"
                    TextAlignment="Center" Margin="5"/>
            <TextBlock Grid.Column="2" Grid.Row="0" Text="Uniform"
                    TextAlignment="Center" Margin="5"/>
            <TextBlock Grid.Column="3" Grid.Row="0" Text="UniformToFill"
                    TextAlignment="Center" Margin="5"/>

            <Rectangle Grid.Column="1" Grid.Row="1" Fill="LightGray" Stroke="Black"
                    Stretch="Fill" Margin="5"/>
            <Rectangle Grid.Column="2" Grid.Row="1" Fill="LightGray" Stroke="Black"
                    Stretch="Uniform" Margin="5"/>
            <Rectangle Grid.Column="3" Grid.Row="1" Fill="LightGray" Stroke="Black"
                    Stretch="UniformToFill" Margin="5"/>

            <Ellipse Grid.Column="1" Grid.Row="2" Fill="LightGray"
                    Stroke="Black" Stretch="Fill" Margin="5"/>
            <Ellipse Grid.Column="2" Grid.Row="2" Fill="LightGray"
                    Stroke="Black" Stretch="Uniform" Margin="5"/>
            <Ellipse Grid.Column="3" Grid.Row="2" Fill="LightGray"
                    Stroke="Black" Stretch="UniformToFill" Margin="5"/>
        </Grid>
</Window>
```

In this example, you create three rectangles and three ellipses, each with different *Stretch* property. Figure 3-20 shows the result of running this application. You can see how the different *Stretch* properties affect the appearances of shapes.

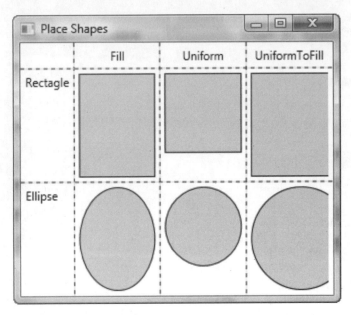

Figure 3-20. Shapes with different Stretch properties

You can see from the figure that the sizing behavior depends on the *Stretch* property. As mentioned previously, by default it is set to *Fill*, which stretches the shapes to fill their container if an explicit size isn't specified. If you set the *Stretch* property to *Uniform*, the width and height of the shapes are sized up proportionately until the shape reaches the edge of the container. Finally, if you set it to *UniformToFill*, the width and height of the shapes are sized proportionately until the shapes fill all the available area.

Polylines

The *Polyline* class allows you to draw a series of connected straight lines. You simply provide a list of points using its *Points* property, which requires a *PointCollection* object if you create a polyline using code. However, you can fill this collection in XAML by means of a *lean string-based syntax*. That is, you simply need to supply a list of points and add a space or a comma between the coordinates.

Let's consider an example that demonstrates how to create a simple polyline, a closed polyline, and a Sine curve in code. Add a new WPF Window to the project *GraphicsBasics* and name it *Polylines*. Here is the XAML file for this example:

```
<Window x:Class="GraphicsBasics.Polylines"
    xmlns="http://schemas.microsoft.com/winfx/2006/xaml/presentation"
    xmlns:x="http://schemas.microsoft.com/winfx/2006/xaml"
    Title="Polylines" Height="340" Width="250">
    <Grid>
        <StackPanel Name="stackPanel1" Margin="10">
            <TextBlock Text="Polyline:"/>
            <Polyline Stroke="Black" StrokeThickness="3"
                    Points="0 70,60 10,110 60,160 10,210 70"/>
            <TextBlock Text="Closed polyline:" Margin="0 10 0 0"/>
            <Polyline Stroke="Black" StrokeThickness="3"
```

```
                   Points="0 70,60 10,110 60,160 10,210 70, 0 70"/>
            <TextBlock Text="Sine curve:" Margin="0 10 0 0"/>
            <Polyline Name="polyline1" Stroke="Red" StrokeThickness="2"/>
        </StackPanel>
    </Grid>
</Window>
```

Here you create two polylines directly in the XAML file. You also define another polyline, called *polyline1*, which needs to be created in code. Here is the code-behind file used to generate the Sine curve:

```
using System;
using System.Windows;
using System.Windows.Media;
using System.Windows.Shapes;

namespace GraphicsBasics
{
    public partial class Polylines : Window
    {
        public Polylines()
        {
            InitializeComponent();

            for (int i = 0; i < 70; i++)
            {
                double x = i * Math.PI;
                double y = 40 + 30 * Math.Sin(x/10);
                polyline1.Points.Add(new Point(x, y));
            }
        }
    }
}
```

Here, you simply add points to *polyline1*'s *Points* collection using a Sine function with a for-loop. Running this application produces the results shown in Figure 3-21.

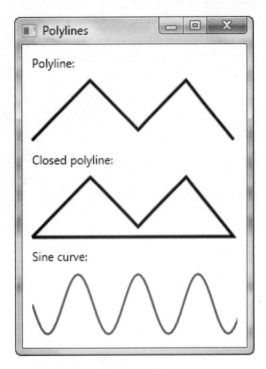

Figure 3-21. *Polylines in WPF*

Polygons

The polygon is very similar to the polyline. Like the *Polyline* class, the *Polygon* class has a *Points* collection that takes a list of *X* and *Y* coordinates. The only difference is that the polygon adds a final line segment that connects the final point to the starting point. You can fill the interior of this shape using the *Fill* property.

Add a new WPF Window to the project *GraphicsBasics* and name it *Polygons*. This example fills the polylines in the previous example with a light gray color. Here is the XAML file for this example:

```
<Window x:Class="GraphicsBasics.Polygons"
    xmlns="http://schemas.microsoft.com/winfx/2006/xaml/presentation"
    xmlns:x="http://schemas.microsoft.com/winfx/2006/xaml"
    Title="Polygons" Height="300" Width="300">
    <Grid>
        <StackPanel Name="stackPanel1" Margin="10">
            <TextBlock Text="Polygon:"/>
            <Polygon Stroke="Black" StrokeThickness="3" Fill="LightGray"
                    Points="0 70,60 10,110 60,160 10,210 70"/>
            <TextBlock Text="Filled sine curve:" Margin="0 10 0 0"/>
            <Polygon Name="polygon1" Stroke="Red"
                    StrokeThickness="2" Fill="LightCoral"/>
        </StackPanel>
    </Grid>
</Window>
```

The *polygon1* is created using a Sine function in the code-behind file:

```
using System;
using System.Windows;
using System.Windows.Media;
using System.Windows.Shapes;

namespace GraphicsBasics
{
    public partial class Polygons : Window
    {
        public Polygons()
        {
            InitializeComponent();
            for (int i = 0; i < 71; i++)
            {
                double x = i * Math.PI;
                double y = 40 + 30 * Math.Sin(x / 10);
                polygon1.Points.Add(new Point(x, y));
            }
        }
    }
}
```

Running this application produces the results shown in Figure 3-22.

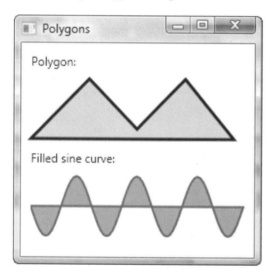

Figure 3-22. Polygons in WPF

In a simple shape whose lines never cross, it is easy to fill the interior. Sometimes, however, you'll have a more complex polygon in which it isn't necessarily obvious which portions should be filled and which portions should not.

Let's consider another example, one that shows a line crossing more than one other line, leaving an irregular region at the center that may or may not be filled. Add a new WPF Window to the project *GraphicsBasics* and name it *PolygonFillRule*. Here is the XAML file for this example:

```
<Window x:Class=" GraphicsBasics.PolygonFillRule"
    xmlns="http://schemas.microsoft.com/winfx/2006/xaml/presentation"
    xmlns:x="http://schemas.microsoft.com/winfx/2006/xaml"
    Title="PolygonFillRule" Height="600" Width="300">
    <Grid>
        <StackPanel Margin="10">
            <TextBlock Text="FillRule = EvenOdd:" Margin="0 0 0 5"/>
            <Polygon Stroke="Black" Fill="LightGray" FillRule="EvenOdd"
                    Points="0 0,0 150,100 150,100 50,50 50,50 100,150 100,150 0"/>
            <TextBlock Text="FillRule = NonZero:" Margin="0 10 0 5"/>
            <Polygon Stroke="Black" Fill="LightGray" FillRule="Nonzero"
                    Points="0 0,0 150,100 150,100 50,50 50,50 100,150 100,150 0"/>
            <TextBlock Text="FillRule = NonZero:" Margin="0 10 0 5"/>
            <Polygon Stroke="Black" Fill="LightGray" FillRule="Nonzero"
                    Points="0 0,0 150,100 150,100 100,50 100,50 50,
                            100 50,100 100,150 100,150 0"/>
        </StackPanel>
    </Grid>
</Window>
```

Here, you use the *FillRule* property to control the filled regions. Every polygon has a *FillRule* property that allows you to choose between two different methods for filling in regions, *EvenOdd* (the default value) and *NonZero*. In the *EvenOdd* case, in order to determine which region will be filled, WPF counts the number of lines that must be crossed to reach the outside of the shape. If this number is odd, the region is filled; if it is even, the region is left empty, as shown in Figure 3-23.

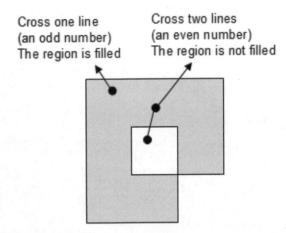

Figure 3-23. Determining filled regions when FillRule is set to EvenOdd

When *FillRule* is set to *NonZero*, determining which region will be filled becomes trickier. In this case, WPF follows the same line-counting process as *EvenOdd* but takes into account the line direction. If the number of lines going in one direction is equal to the number of lines going in the opposite direction, the region isn't filled; if the difference between these two counts isn't zero, the region is filled. Figure 3-24 shows the results of running this example.

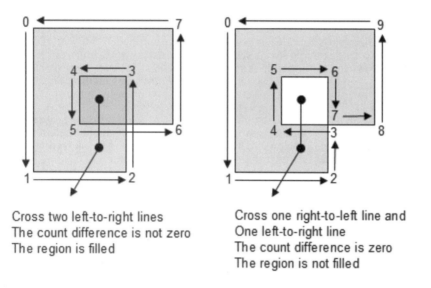

Cross two left-to-right lines
The count difference is not zero
The region is filled

Cross one right-to-left line and
One left-to-right line
The count difference is zero
The region is not filled

Figure 3-24. Determining filled regions when FillRule is set to NonZero

The difference between the two shapes in the figure is that the order of points in the *Points* collection is different, leading to different line directions. This means that in the *NonZero* case, whether a region is filled or not depends on how you draw the shape, not on what the shape itself looks like. Figure 3-24 clearly demonstrates this conclusion.

Paths and Geometries

In previous sections, you learned how to create simple 2D graphics using shapes that derive from the *Shape* class, including *Line*, *Rectangle*, *Ellipse*, and *Polygon*. However, we haven't considered a more powerful *Shape*-derived class, the *Path* class. The *Path* class has the ability to draw curves and complex shapes, which are described using *Geometry* objects. To use a *Path* element, you create a *Geometry* object, which is used to set the *Path*'s *Data* property. You can't draw a *Geometry* object directly on your screen because it is an abstract class. Instead, you need to use one of the following seven derived classes:

- *LineGeometry* – Represents the geometry of a straight line.

- *RectangleGeometry* – Represents the geometry of a 2D rectangle.

- *EllipseGeometry* – Represents the geometry of an ellipse.

- *GeometryGroup* – Represents a composite geometry, which can be added to a single path.

91

- *CombinedGeometry* – Represents a 2D geometry shape defined by the combination of two *Geometry* objects.

- *PathGeometry* – Represents a complex geometry shape that may be composed of arcs, curves, ellipses, lines, and rectangles.

- *StreamGeometry* – Defines a geometric shape described using *StreamGeometryContext*. This geometry is a read-only lightweight alternative to *PathGeometry;* it doesn't support data binding, animation, or modification.

The *LineGeometry*, *RectangleGeometry*, and *EllipseGeometry* classes describe relatively simple geometry shapes. To create more complex shapes or curves, you need to use a *PathGeometry* object.

There is a critical difference between the *Shape* class and the *Geometry* class. The *Geometry* class inherits from the *Freezable* class, whereas the *Shape* class inherits from *FrameworkElement*. Because *Shape* objects are elements, they can render themselves and participate in the layout system, but *Geometry* objects can't.

Although *Shape* objects are more readily usable than *Geometry* objects, *Geometry* objects are more versatile. Whereas a *Shape* object is used to render 2D graphics, a *Geometry* object can be used to define the geometric region for 2D graphics, define a region for clipping, or define a region for hit testing, for example. *Geometry* objects can't render themselves, and they must be drawn by another element, such as a *Drawing* or *Path* element. The attributes common to shapes, such as the *Fill*, *Stroke*, and *StrokeThickness* properties, are attached to the *Path* or *Drawing*, which can be used to draw *Geometry* objects.

You can see from the foregoing discussion that the *Geometry* object defines a shape, whereas a *Path* object allows you to draw the *Geometry* shape on your screen. In the following sections, I'll show you how to create shapes using the objects derived from the *Geometry* class.

Line, Rectangle, and Ellipse Geometries

The *LineGeometry*, *RectangleGeometry*, and *EllipseGeometry* classes correspond directly to the *Line*, *Rectangle*, and *Ellipse* shapes used previously. For example, you can convert the following XAML snippet, which uses the *Line* element

```
<Line X1="30" Y1="30" X2 ="180" Y2="30" Stroke="Blue" StrokeThickness="2"/>
```

into the following markup, which uses the *Path* element and *LineGeometry*:

```
<Path Stroke="Blue" StrokeThickness="2">
    <Path.Data>
        <LineGeometry StartPoint="30 30" EndPoint="180 30"/>
    </Path.Data>
</Path>
```

The only difference is that the *Line* shape takes *X1*, *Y1*, *X2*, and *Y2* values, whereas the *LineGeometry* object takes *StartPoint* and *EndPoint*.

Similarly, you can convert the code snippet

```
<Rectangle Fill="Gray" Stroke="Blue" StrokeThickness="2" Width="10" Height="20"/>
```

into this *RectangleGeometry*:

```
<Path Fill="Gray" Stroke="Blue" StrokeThickness="2">
    <Path.Data>
        <RectangleGeometry Rect="0,0,10,20"/>
    </Path.Data>
</Path>
```

You can see that the *Rectangle* shape takes *Height* and *Width* values, whereas the *RectangleGeometry* element takes four numbers describing the location and size of the rectangle. The first two numbers represent the *X* and *Y* coordinates where the top-left corner will be placed; the last two numbers define the width and height of the rectangle.

You can also convert an Ellipse shape such as

```
<Ellipse Fill="Gray" Stroke="Blue" StrokeThickness="2" Width="10" Height="20"/>
```

into an *EllipseGeometry*:

```
<Path Fill="Gray" Stroke="Blue" StrokeThickness="2">
    <Path.Data>
        <EllipseGeometry RadiusX="5" RadiusY="10" Center="5,10"/>
    </Path.Data>
</Path>
```

Notice that the two radius values are simply half of the width and height values. You can also use the *Center* property to offset the location of the ellipse.

It is clear from the foregoing discussion that these simple geometries work in exactly the same way as the corresponding shapes. *Geometry* objects allow you to offset rectangles and ellipses, but this isn't necessary if you draw the shapes on a *Canvas*, which already gives you the ability to position your shapes at a specific position using the *Canvas.Top* and *Canvas.Left* properties. The real difference between the *Shape* and *Geometry* classes appears when you decide to combine more than one *Geometry* object in a single path, as described in the next section.

GeometryGroup Class

The simplest way to combine geometries is to use the *GeometryGroup* object. Here is an example that creates two circles:

```
<Path Fill="LightGray" Stroke="Blue" StrokeThickness="2">
    <Path.Data>
        <GeometryGroup FillRule="Nonzero">
            <EllipseGeometry RadiusX="50" RadiusY="50" Center="120,120"/>
            <EllipseGeometry RadiusX="30" RadiusY="30" Center="120,120"/>
        </GeometryGroup>
    </Path.Data>
</Path>
```

This code snippet creates a similar effect as if you had used two *Path* elements, each one with an *EllipseGeometry* object of a different radius. However, the advantage to using the *GeometryGroup* object is that you replace two elements with one, which means you reduce the overhead of your user interface. In general, an application that uses a smaller number of elements with more complex geometries will perform faster than an application that uses a large number of elements with simple geometries. This will become significant when you create complicated computer-aided design (CAD) applications.

Another advantage of the *Geometry* class is that the same geometry can be reused in separate *Path* elements. You can simply define the geometry in a *Resources* collection and refer to it in your path.

I'll now present an example to illustrate how you can create 2D shapes using *GeometryGroup*. Add a new WPF Window to the *GraphicsBasics* project and call it *GeometryGroupExample*. Here is the XAML file for this example:

```
<Window x:Class=" GraphicsBasics.GeometryGroupExample"
    xmlns="http://schemas.microsoft.com/winfx/2006/xaml/presentation"
    xmlns:x="http://schemas.microsoft.com/winfx/2006/xaml"
    Title="Geometry Group" Height="310" Width="300">
```

```
<Window.Resources>
    <GeometryGroup x:Key="GeometryNonzero" FillRule="Nonzero">
        <EllipseGeometry RadiusX="50" RadiusY="50" Center="65,60"/>
        <EllipseGeometry RadiusX="30" RadiusY="30" Center="65,60"/>
    </GeometryGroup>

    <GeometryGroup x:Key="GeometryEvenOdd" FillRule="EvenOdd">
        <EllipseGeometry RadiusX="50" RadiusY="50" Center="65,60"/>
        <EllipseGeometry RadiusX="30" RadiusY="30" Center="65,60"/>
    </GeometryGroup>
</Window.Resources>

<Border Margin="5" BorderBrush="Black" BorderThickness="1"
        Background="{StaticResource MyGrayGridBrush}">
    <Canvas Height="310" Width="300">
        <Grid ShowGridLines="True" Height="265">
            <Grid.ColumnDefinitions>
                <ColumnDefinition Width="140"/>
                <ColumnDefinition Width="140"/>
            </Grid.ColumnDefinitions>

            <StackPanel Margin="5" Grid.Column="0">
                <TextBlock Text="FillRule = Nonzero" Margin="15,5,5,5"/>
                <Path Fill="LightBlue" Stroke="Blue" StrokeThickness="2"
                    Data="{StaticResource GeometryNonzero}"/>
                <Path Fill="LightCoral" Stroke="Red"
                    StrokeThickness="2" Canvas.Left="150"
                    Data="{StaticResource GeometryNonzero}"/>
            </StackPanel>

            <StackPanel Margin="5" Grid.Column="1">
                <TextBlock Text="FillRule = EvenOdd" Margin="15,5,5,5"/>
                <Path Fill="LightBlue" Stroke="Blue" StrokeThickness="2"
                    Data="{StaticResource GeometryEvenOdd}"/>
                <Path Fill="LightCoral" Stroke="Red" StrokeThickness="2"
                    Canvas.Left="150"
                    Data="{StaticResource GeometryEvenOdd}"/>
            </StackPanel>
        </Grid>
    </Canvas>
</Border>
</Window>
```

In the *Resources*, we define two *GeometryGroup* objects: *GeometryNonzero* and *GeometryEvenOdd*. Each includes two circles with different radii but the same center. The main difference lies in their *FillRule* properties: one is set to *Nonzero* and the other to *EvenOdd*. Like the *Polygon* shape, the *GeometryGroup* also has a *FillRule* property that specifies which shapes will be filled. You can then use these *Resources* to create multiple shapes at different locations on a *Canvas* with different *Fill* colors and *Strokes*.

This markup generates the results shown in Figure 3-25. The two solid circles are created at each of two different locations. The left images show results when the *FillRule* of the *GeometryGroup* is set to *Nonzero*. Two solid circles with the same center location are created. If you change the *FillRule* property to *EvenOdd*, you'll obtain the results shown in the right pane. Here, you create two rings, each made up of a solid circle with a blank hole.

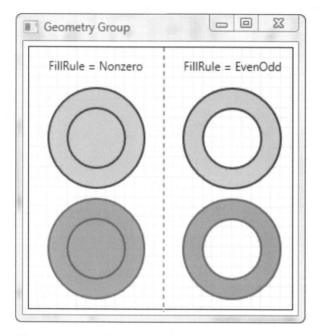

Figure 3-25. 2D shapes created using GeometryGroup

CombinedGeometry Class

The *GeometryGroup* class has many advantages in creating complex shapes. However, it still has some limitations when it comes to developing CAD-like applications. For example, although the *GeometryGroup* allows you to create a shape by drawing one shape and subtracting other shapes from its interior by changing its *FillRule* property, it doesn't allow you to perform real logic operations on shapes. To address this issue, WPF implements another class, the *CombinedGeometry* class, that takes two geometries specified using the *Geometry1* and *Geometry2* properties.

This class doesn't include the *FillRule* property; instead, it has a much more powerful *GeometryCombineMode* property that takes one of four values:

- *Union* – Creates a shape that includes all the areas of the two geometries.

- *Intersect* – Creates a shape that contains the shared area between the two geometries.

- *Xor* – Creates a shape that contains the area that isn't shared between the two geometries.

- *Exclude* – Creates a shape that includes all the area from the first geometry, but doesn't include the area that falls in the second geometry.

Note that *CombinedGeometry* combines only the *Area* specified by two geometries, so geometries that don't have area, such as *LineGeometry,* disappear when combined.

Let's consider an example that demonstrates how you can combine two circles into one shape using *CombinedGeometry.* Add a new WPF Window to the project *GraphicsBasics* and name it *CombinedGeometryExample.* Here is the XAML file for this example:

```xml
<Window x:Class=" GraphicsBasics.CombinedGeometryExample"
    xmlns="http://schemas.microsoft.com/winfx/2006/xaml/presentation"
    xmlns:x="http://schemas.microsoft.com/winfx/2006/xaml"
    Title="Combined Geometry" Height="340" Width="300">

    <Border Margin="5" BorderBrush="Black" BorderThickness="1"
            Background="{StaticResource MyGrayGridBrush}">
        <Canvas Width="300" Height="340" Margin="5">
            <Grid>
                <Grid.ColumnDefinitions>
                    <ColumnDefinition />
                    <ColumnDefinition />
                </Grid.ColumnDefinitions>

                <StackPanel Grid.Column="0" Margin="5 0 0 10">
                    <TextBlock FontSize="12pt" Text="Union" Margin="40,5,5,10"/>
                    <Path Fill ="LightBlue" Stroke="Blue">
                        <Path.Data>
                            <CombinedGeometry GeometryCombineMode="Union">
                                <CombinedGeometry.Geometry1>
                                    <EllipseGeometry Center="50,50"
                                        RadiusX="50" RadiusY="50"/>
                                </CombinedGeometry.Geometry1>
                                <CombinedGeometry.Geometry2>
                                    <EllipseGeometry Center="80,50"
                                        RadiusX="50" RadiusY="50"/>
                                </CombinedGeometry.Geometry2>
                            </CombinedGeometry>
                        </Path.Data>
                    </Path>

                    <TextBlock FontSize="12pt" Text="Xor" Margin="45,15,5,10"/>
                    <Path Fill ="LightBlue" Stroke="Blue">
                        <Path.Data>
                            <CombinedGeometry
                                GeometryCombineMode="Xor">
                                <CombinedGeometry.Geometry1>
                                    <EllipseGeometry Center="50,50"
                                        RadiusX="50" RadiusY="50"/>
                                </CombinedGeometry.Geometry1>
                                <CombinedGeometry.Geometry2>
                                    <EllipseGeometry Center="80,50"
                                        RadiusX="50" RadiusY="50"/>
                                </CombinedGeometry.Geometry2>
                            </CombinedGeometry>
                        </Path.Data>
                    </Path>
                </StackPanel>
```

```xml
<StackPanel Grid.Column="1" Margin="20 0 0 0">
    <TextBlock FontSize="12pt" Text="Intersect" Margin="30,5,5,10"/>
    <Path Fill ="LightBlue" Stroke="Blue" Margin="5,0,0,0">
        <Path.Data>
            <CombinedGeometry
                GeometryCombineMode="Intersect">
                <CombinedGeometry.Geometry1>
                    <EllipseGeometry Center="50,50"
                        RadiusX="50" RadiusY="50"/>
                </CombinedGeometry.Geometry1>
                <CombinedGeometry.Geometry2>
                    <EllipseGeometry Center="80,50"
                        RadiusX="50" RadiusY="50"/>
                </CombinedGeometry.Geometry2>
            </CombinedGeometry>
        </Path.Data>
    </Path>

    <TextBlock FontSize="12pt" Text="Exclude" Margin="35,15,5,10"/>
    <Path Fill ="LightBlue" Stroke="Blue" Margin="10,0,0,0">
        <Path.Data>
            <CombinedGeometry GeometryCombineMode="Exclude">
                <CombinedGeometry.Geometry1>
                    <EllipseGeometry Center="50,50"
                        RadiusX="50" RadiusY="50"/>
                </CombinedGeometry.Geometry1>
                <CombinedGeometry.Geometry2>
                    <EllipseGeometry Center="80,50"
                        RadiusX="50" RadiusY="50"/>
                </CombinedGeometry.Geometry2>
            </CombinedGeometry>
        </Path.Data>
    </Path>
</StackPanel>
            </Grid>
        </Canvas>
    </Border>
</Window>
```

Figure 3-26 shows the results of running this example. You can clearly see how the *CombinedGeometryMode* property affects the combined area. Although the *CombinedGeometry* object takes only two geometries, you can actually combine any number of shapes by using *CombinedGeometry* objects successively.

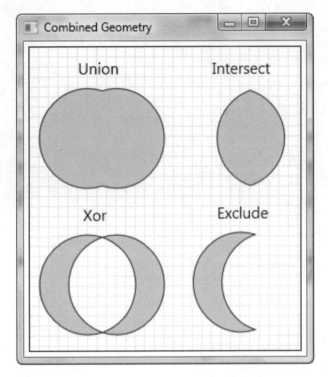

Figure 3-26. *2D shapes created using CombinedGeometry*

PathGeometry Class

The *PathGeometry* class is more powerful than the derived geometry classes discussed previously. With it you can create any of the shapes that the other geometries can and much more. A *PathGeometry* object is built out of one or more *PathFigure* objects. Each *PathFigure* object is a continuous set of connected lines and curves that can be closed or open. The *PathFigure* object is closed if the end point of the last line in the object connects to the starting point of the first line.

The *PathFigure* class has four key properties:

- *StartPoint* – A point that indicates where the line or figure begins.

- *Segments* – A collection of *PathSegment* objects that are used to draw the figure.

- *IsClosed* – If true, WPF adds a straight line connecting the starting and end points.

- *IsFilled* – If true, the area inside the figure is filled using the *Path.Fill* property.

Note that the *PathFigure* is a shape that is drawn using an unbroken line consisting of a number of segments. There are several types of segments, all of which derive from the *PathSegment* class. You can use different types of segments freely to build your figure. These are the segment classes in WPF:

- *LineSegment* – Creates a straight line between two points.

- *ArcSegment* – Creates an elliptical arc between two points.

- *PolyLineSegment* – Creates a series of straight lines.

- *BezierSegment* – Creates a Bezier curve between two points.

- *QuadraticBezierSegment* – Creates a Bezier curve that has one point instead of two.

- *PolyBezierSegment* – Creates a series of Bezier curves.

- *PolyQuadraticBezierSegment* – Creates a series of simpler quadratic Bezier curves.

The *Line*, *Arc*, and *PolyLine* segments may be more familiar to you than the Bezier-related segments. However, Bezier lines are one of the most important mathematical representations of curves and surfaces used in computer graphics and CAD applications. Bezier curves are polynomial curves based on a complicated mathematical representation. Fortunately, no mathematical knowledge is required in order to use the Bezier curves in WPF.

Lines and Polylines

It is easy to create a simple line using the *LineSegment* and *PathGeometry* classes. For example, the following XAML snippet begins at (10, 10), draws a straight line to (150, 150), and then draws a line from (150, 150) to (150, 200):

```
<Path Stroke="Black">
    <Path.Data>
        <PathGeometry>
            <PathFigure StartPoint="10,10">
                <LineSegment Point="150,150"/>
                <LineSegment Point="150,200"/>
            </PathFigure>
        </PathGeometry>
    </Path.Data>
</Path>
```

The *PolyLineSegment* creates a series of straight lines. You can get the same effect using multiple *LineSegment* objects, but a single *PolyLineSegment* is simpler. The following code creates a polyline:

```
<Path Stroke="Blue">
    <Path.Data>
        <PathGeometry>
            <PathFigure StartPoint="100,120">
                <PolyLineSegment Points="200,120,200,220,100,170"/>
            </PathFigure>
        </PathGeometry>
    </Path.Data>
</Path>
```

Note that the number of *PathFigure* objects in a *PathGeometry* element is unlimited. This means that you can create several separate open or closed figures that are all considered part of the same path.

Arcs

An *ArcSegment* object is defined by its start and end points; its *X* and *Y* radii specified by the *Size* property; its *X* axis rotation factor, a value indicating whether the arc should be greater than 180 degrees;

and a value describing the direction in which the arc is drawn. Like the *LineSegment*, the *ArcSegment* class doesn't contain a property for the starting point of the arc; it only defines the destination point of the arc it represents. The beginning point of the arc is the current point of the *PathFigure* to which the *ArcSegment* is added.

The following markup creates an ellipse shape using two *ArcSegment* objects:

```
<Path Stroke="Blue">
    <Path.Data>
        <PathGeometry>
            <PathFigure StartPoint="100,50">
                <ArcSegment Point="200,50" Size="50,30"
                    SweepDirection="Counterclockwise"/>
            </PathFigure>
            <PathFigure StartPoint="100,50">
                <ArcSegment Point="200,50" Size="50,30"
                    SweepDirection="Clockwise"/>
            </PathFigure>
        </PathGeometry>
    </Path.Data>
</Path>
```

The complete markup file for *Lines*, *PolyLines*, and *Arcs* is given in the *LineCurveExample.xaml* file in the project *GraphicsBasics*.

Bezier Curves

It is also easy to create a Bezier curve using the *BezierSegment* object. Note that a Bezier curve is defined by four points: a start point, an end point, and two control points. The *BezierSegment* class doesn't contain a property for the starting point of the curve; it only defines the end point. The beginning point of the curve is the current point of the *PathFigure* to which the *BezierSegment* is added.

The two control points of a cubic Bezier curve behave like magnets, attracting portions of what would otherwise be a straight line toward themselves and producing a curve. The first control point affects the beginning portion of the curve; the second control point affects the ending portion of the curve. The curve doesn't necessarily pass through either of the control points; each control point moves its portion of the line toward itself, not through itself.

The following example shows a Bezier curve whose two control points are animated. The *X* coordinate of the first control point and the *Y* coordinate of the second control point vary in the range [50, 250]. You can clearly see how the Bezier curve changes shape when the control points are animated.

Add a new WPF Window to the project *GraphicsBasics* and name it *AnimateBezierCurve*. Here is the markup for this example:

```
<Window x:Class="GraphicsBasics.AnimateBezierCurve"
    xmlns="http://schemas.microsoft.com/winfx/2006/xaml/presentation"
    xmlns:x="http://schemas.microsoft.com/winfx/2006/xaml"
    Title="Bezier Curve" Height="300" Width="300">

    <Viewbox Stretch="Fill">
        <Border Margin="5" BorderBrush="Black" BorderThickness="1"
                Background="{StaticResource MyGrayGridBrush}"
                HorizontalAlignment="Left">
            <Canvas x:Name="canvas1" Width="300" Height="270">
                <Path Stroke="Black" StrokeThickness="5">
                    <Path.Data>
```

```xml
        <PathGeometry>
            <PathFigure StartPoint="20,20">
                <BezierSegment x:Name="bezierSegment"
                                    Point1="150,50" Point2="60,160"
                                    Point3="250,230"/>
            </PathFigure>
        </PathGeometry>
    </Path.Data>
</Path>
<Path x:Name="path1" Fill="Red" Stroke="Red">
    <Path.Data>
        <GeometryGroup>
            <LineGeometry x:Name="line1" StartPoint="20,20"
                            EndPoint="150,50"/>
            <EllipseGeometry x:Name="ellipse1" Center="150,50"
                            RadiusX="5" RadiusY="5" />
            <LineGeometry x:Name="line2" StartPoint="60,160"
                            EndPoint="250,230"/>
            <EllipseGeometry x:Name="ellipse2" Center="60,160"
                            RadiusX="5" RadiusY="5" />
        </GeometryGroup>
    </Path.Data>
</Path>

<!-- Set animation: -->
<Canvas.Triggers>
    <EventTrigger RoutedEvent="Canvas.Loaded">
        <BeginStoryboard>
            <Storyboard RepeatBehavior="Forever" AutoReverse="True">
                <PointAnimation
                    Storyboard.TargetName="bezierSegment"
                    Storyboard.TargetProperty="Point1"
                    From="50 20" To="250 20" Duration="0:0:5"/>

                <PointAnimation Storyboard.TargetName="line1"
                    Storyboard.TargetProperty="EndPoint"
                    From="50 20" To="250 20" Duration="0:0:5"/>

                <PointAnimation Storyboard.TargetName="ellipse1"
                    Storyboard.TargetProperty="Center"
                    From="50 20" To="250 20" Duration="0:0:5"/>

                <PointAnimation
                    Storyboard.TargetName="bezierSegment"
                    Storyboard.TargetProperty="Point2"
                    From="60 50" To="60 250" Duration="0:0:5"/>

                <PointAnimation Storyboard.TargetName="line2"
                    Storyboard.TargetProperty="StartPoint"
                    From="60 50" To="60 250" Duration="0:0:5"/>

                <PointAnimation Storyboard.TargetName="ellipse2"
                    Storyboard.TargetProperty="Center"
```

```
                          From="60 50" To="60 250" Duration="0:0:5"/>
                    </Storyboard>
                  </BeginStoryboard>
                </EventTrigger>
              </Canvas.Triggers>
            </Canvas>
          </Border>
        </Viewbox>
      </Window>
```

This XAML file creates a Bezier curve using *BezierSegment*. The two control points, *Point1* and *Point2*, of the Bezier curve are marked specifically by two ellipse shapes. At the same time, two line segments are created to guide your eye during the animation. The first line segment connects the starting point and *Point1*; the second segment connects the end point and *Point2*.

The animation is performed within a *Storyboard* element using *PointAnimation*. Here, you animate not only the control points of the Bezier curve but also the red dots (ellipses) and the guide lines.

This example produces the result shown in Figure 3-27, where you can see how the Bezier curve changes when the control points move.

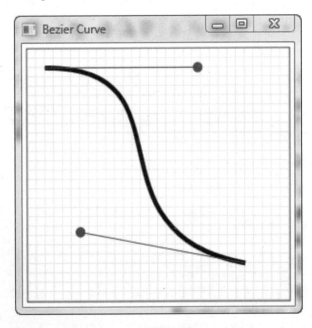

Figure 3-27. *A Bezier curve in WPF*

Geometry and Mini-Language

StreamGeometry is a light-weight alternative to the *PathGeometry* class for creating complex geometric shapes. You can use *StreamGeometry* when you need to describe a complex geometry but don't want the overhead of supporting data binding, animation, and modification. WPF supports a powerful mini-language that you can use to describe geometric paths.

There are two classes in WPF that provide the mini-language for describing geometric paths: *StreamGeometry* and *PathFigureCollection*. You need to use the *StreamGeometry* mini-language when you set a property of the *Geometry* type, such as the *Data* property of a *Path* element. On the other hand, you use the *PathFigureCollection* mini-language when you set the *Figures* property of a *PathGeometry*.

To understand the mini-language, you need to realize that it is simply a long string holding a series of commands. These commands are used by WPF to create corresponding geometries. Each command is a single letter followed by numeric information separated by spaces or commas.

For example, in the earlier section, you created a polyline with a *PathGeometry* using the following XAML snippet:

```
<Path Stroke="Blue">
    <Path.Data>
        <PathGeometry>
            <PathFigure StartPoint="100,120">
                <PolyLineSegment Points="200,120,200,220,100,170"/>
            </PathFigure>
        </PathGeometry>
    </Path.Data>
</Path>
```

You can use the *StreamGeometry* mini-language to duplicate this polyline:

```
<Path Stroke="Blue" Data="M 100 120 L 200 120 L 200 220 L 100 170"/>
```

This path uses a sequence of four commands. The first command, *M*, creates the *PathFigure* and sets the starting point to (100, 120). The following three commands (*L*) create line segments.

When you create a *StreamGeometry* object using the *StreamGeometry* mini-language, you can't modify the geometry later on in your code. If this isn't acceptable, you can create a *PathGeometry* using the *PathFigureCollection* mini-language. The following example uses attribute syntax to create a *PathFigure* collection for a *PathGeometry*:

```
<Path Stroke="Blue">
    <Path.Data>
        <PathGeometry Figures="M 100 120 L 200 120 L 200 220 L 100 170"/>
    </Path.Data>
</Path>
```

As you can see from the preceding examples, the two mini-languages are very similar. It is always possible to use *PathGeometry* in any situation where you could use *StreamGeometry*; so which one should you use? Use *StreamGeometry* when you don't need to modify the path after creating it; use *PathGeometry* if you do need to modify the path in your code.

It is easy to use the mini-language to create complex geometry shapes. The mini-language involves a fairly small set of commands, which are listed for your reference in Table 3-1.

Table 3-1. Commands for the Geometry Mini-Language

Name	Command	Description
Fill rule	F0 or F1	Specifies geometry's FillRule property. F0 for EvenOdd, F1 for NonZero. This command must appear at beginning of the string.
Move	M startPt or m startPt	Creates a new PathFigure and sets its start point. This command must be used before any other commands except for F0 or F1.
Line	L endPt or l endPt	Creates a LineSegment from the current point to the specified end point.
Horizontal line	H x or h x	Creates a horizontal line between the current point and the specified X-coordinate.
Vertical line	V y or v y	Creates a vertical line between the current point and the specified Y-coordinate.
Cubic Bezier curve	C pt1, pt2, endPt or c pt1, pt2, endPt	Creates a cubic Bezier curve between the current point and the specified end point by using the two specified control points (pt1 and pt2).
Quadratic Bezier curve	Q pt, endPt or q pt, endPt	Creates a quadratic Bezier curve between the current point and the specified end point using the specified control point (pt).
Smooth cubic Bezier curve	S pt2, endPt or s pt2, endPt	Creates a cubic Bezier curve between the current point and specified end point. The first control point is assumed to be the reflection of the second control point of the previous command relative to the current point.
Smooth Quadratic Bezier curve	T pt, endPt or t pt, endPt	Creates a quadratic Bezier curve between the current point and the specified end point. The control point is assumed to be the reflection of the control point of the previous command relative to the current point.
Elliptical Arc	A size, angle, isLargeArc, Direction, endPt or a size, angle, ...	Creates an elliptical arc between the current point and the specified end point. You specify the size of the ellipse, the rotation angle, and Boolean flags that set the *IsLargeArc* and *SweepDirection* properties.
Close	Z, z	Ends the current figure and creates a line that connects the current point to the starting point of the figure. You don't need to use this command if you don't want to close the path.
Point	X, Y or x, y	Describe the X and Y coordinates of a point.
Special values	Infinity or -Infinity or NaN	Instead of a standard numerical value, you can use these special values, which are case-sensitive.

The commands with uppercase letters use absolute coordinates; the commands with lowercase letters evaluate parameters relative to the previous point.

Hit Testing

When you create interactive 2D drawing applications in WPF, you can deal directly with the user's interaction with the graphics objects using mouse event handlers. However, WPF provides powerful hit-testing for graphics objects through the static *VisualTreeHelper.HitTest* method. When you develop interactive 2D drawing applications, you can perform tasks such as dragging, moving, dropping, and deleting shapes more efficiently using the *HitTest* method. In particular, when you design a complex application that contains overlapped visuals, the *HitTest* method allow you to retrieve all the visuals (not just the topmost visual) at a specified point, even the visuals obscured underneath other visuals. You can also find all the visuals that fall within a given geometry.

In order to use this advanced hit-testing feature, you need to create a callback. The *VisualTreeHelper* will then walk through your visuals from top to bottom. Whenever it finds a match, it calls the callback with the details. You can then choose to stop the search or to continue until no more visuals remain.

The following example shows how to use this advanced hit-testing feature. Add a new WPF Window to the project *GraphicsBasics* and name it *HitTestExample*. In this example, you'll create several rectangle shapes on a *Canvas*, some of which overlap each other. The program will tell you how many rectangles are hit when the user clicks a point on the rectangles. Here is the XAML file for this example:

```xml
<Window x:Class="GraphicsBasics.HitTestExample"
    xmlns="http://schemas.microsoft.com/winfx/2006/xaml/presentation"
    xmlns:x="http://schemas.microsoft.com/winfx/2006/xaml"
    Title="Chapter04" Height="300" Width="300">

    <Canvas x:Name="canvas1"
        MouseLeftButtonDown="OnMouseLeftButtonDown">
        <Rectangle Canvas.Left="20" Canvas.Top="20" Width="100" Height="60"
                Stroke="Black" Fill="LightBlue" Opacity="0.7"/>
        <Rectangle Canvas.Left="70" Canvas.Top="50" Width="100" Height="60"
                Stroke="Black" Fill="LightBlue" Opacity="0.7"/>
        <Rectangle Canvas.Left="150" Canvas.Top="80" Width="100" Height="60"
                Stroke="Black" Fill="LightBlue" Opacity="0.7"/>
        <Rectangle Canvas.Left="20" Canvas.Top="100" Width="50" Height="50"
                Stroke="Black" Fill="LightBlue" Opacity="0.7"/>
        <Rectangle Canvas.Left="40" Canvas.Top="60" Width="50" Height="50"
                Stroke="Black" Fill="LightBlue" Opacity="0.7"/>
        <Rectangle Canvas.Left="30" Canvas.Top="130" Width="50" Height="50"
                Stroke="Black" Fill="LightBlue" Opacity="0.7"/>
    </Canvas>
</Window>
```

This XAML file adds six rectangles to the *Canvas*. The hit-testing is performed in code:

```csharp
using System;
using System.Collections.Generic;
using System.Windows;
using System.Windows.Controls;
using System.Windows.Input;
using System.Windows.Media;
using System.Windows.Shapes;

namespace GraphicsBasics
{
    public partial class HitTestExample : Window
    {
```

```
private List<Rectangle> hitList = new List<Rectangle>();
private EllipseGeometry hitArea = new EllipseGeometry();

public HitTestExample()
{
    InitializeComponent();
    Initialize();
}

private void Initialize()
{
    foreach (Rectangle rect in canvas1.Children)
    {
        rect.Fill = Brushes.LightBlue;
    }
}

private void OnMouseLeftButtonDown(
    object sender, MouseButtonEventArgs e)
{
    // Initialization:
    Initialize();

    // Get mouse click point:
    Point pt = e.GetPosition(canvas1);

    // Define hit-testing area:
    hitArea = new EllipseGeometry(pt, 1.0, 1.0);
    hitList.Clear();

    // Call HitTest method:
    VisualTreeHelper.HitTest(canvas1, null,
        new HitTestResultCallback(HitTestCallback),
        new GeometryHitTestParameters(hitArea));

    if (hitList.Count > 0)
    {
        foreach (Rectangle rect in hitList)
        {
        // Change rectangle fill color if it is hit:
            rect.Fill = Brushes.LightCoral;
        }
        MessageBox.Show("You hit " + hitList.Count.ToString() +
                        "rectangles.");
    }
}

public HitTestResultBehavior HitTestCallback(
    HitTestResult result)
{
    // Retrieve the results of the hit test.
    IntersectionDetail intersectionDetail =
        ((GeometryHitTestResult)result).IntersectionDetail;
```

```
switch (intersectionDetail)
{
    case IntersectionDetail.FullyContains:
        // Add the hit test result to the list:
        hitList.Add((Rectangle)result.VisualHit);
        return HitTestResultBehavior.Continue;

    case IntersectionDetail.Intersects:
        // Set the behavior to return visuals at all z-order levels:
        return HitTestResultBehavior.Continue;

    case IntersectionDetail.FullyInside:
        // Set the behavior to return visuals at all z-order levels:
        return HitTestResultBehavior.Continue;

    default:
        return HitTestResultBehavior.Stop;
        }
    }
  }
}
```

In this code-behind file, you expand the hit-test area using an *EllipseGeometry*. When the user clicks on the *Canvas*, the program starts the hit-testing process by calling the *HitTestCallback* method. If it hits any rectangle, that rectangle will be added to the *hitList*. When the process is finished, the program gives a collection in the *hitList* with all of the rectangles it found.

Note that the *HitTestCallback* method implements the hit-testing behavior. Usually, the *HitTestResult* object provides just a single property (*VisualHit*), but you can cast it to one of two derived types, depending on the type of hit-test you're performing.

If you're hit-testing a point, you can cast *HitTestResult* to *PointHitTestResult*, which provides a *PointHit* property that returns the original point you used to perform the hit-test. If you are hit-testing a *Geometry* object (or shape), as you are in this example, you can cast *HitTestResult* to *GeometryHitTestResult* and get access to the *IntersectionDetail* property. This property tells you whether your geometry (*hitArea*) completely wraps your rectangle (*FullyInside*), overlaps it (*Intersect*), or is fully inside of it (*FullyContains*). In this example, you implement all these options in the *HitTestCallback*. You can choose any of these options, depending on the requirements of your application. In this example, hits are counted only if the geometry (*hitArea*) is completely inside the rectangle (*FullyContains*). Finally, at the end of the callback, you can return one of two values from the *HitTestResultBehavior* enumeration: Either continue looking for hits, or stop the hit-testing process.

Figure 3-28 shows results of running this example.

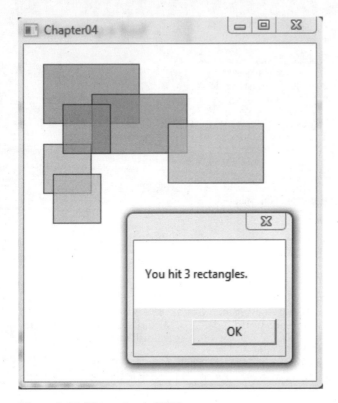

Figure 3-28. *Hit-testing in WPF.*

Custom Shapes

Sometimes, you may find that the simple shapes defined in WPF aren't enough for advanced graphics applications. In these cases, you can create custom shapes that derive from the *Shape* class. The custom shapes you create in this way inherit all of the properties and methods of the *Shape* class and become *FrameworkElement* objects. Therefore, you can use them in your applications just like standard WPF shapes such as *Line*, *Rectangle*, *Ellipse*, and *Polygon*.

In this section, I'll show you how to create some commonly used custom shapes, including a *Star*, *ArrowLine*, and *USFlag*. By following the procedure presented here, you can easily develop your own custom-shape library.

Star Class

Creating a custom shape is relatively easy. You simply need to inherit the custom shape that you want to create from the abstract *Shape* class and provide an override for the getter of the *DefiningGeometry* property. This returns the *Geometry* object, which defines the geometry of your shape.

Let's consider an example that shows how to create a custom *Star* shape. Open the project *GraphicsBasics* and add a new class, called *Star*, to the project. I first list the code and then explain how it works.

```
using System;
using System.Windows;
using System.Windows.Media;
using System.Windows.Shapes;

namespace GraphicsBasics
{
    public class Star : Shape
    {
        protected PathGeometry pg;
        PathFigure pf;
        PolyLineSegment pls;

        public Star()
        {
            pg = new PathGeometry();
            pf = new PathFigure();
            pls = new PolyLineSegment();
            pg.Figures.Add(pf);
        }

        // Specify the center of the star
        public static readonly DependencyProperty CenterProperty =
            DependencyProperty.Register("Center", typeof(Point), typeof(Star),
            new FrameworkPropertyMetadata(new Point(20.0, 20.0),
            FrameworkPropertyMetadataOptions.AffectsMeasure));

        public Point Center
        {
            set { SetValue(CenterProperty, value); }
            get { return (Point)GetValue(CenterProperty); }
        }

        // Specify the size of the star:
        public static readonly DependencyProperty SizeRProperty =
            DependencyProperty.Register("SizeR", typeof(double), typeof(Star),
            new FrameworkPropertyMetadata(10.0,
            FrameworkPropertyMetadataOptions.AffectsMeasure));

        public double SizeR
        {
            set { SetValue(SizeRProperty, value); }
            get { return (double)GetValue(SizeRProperty); }
        }

        protected override Geometry DefiningGeometry
        {
            get
            {
                double r = SizeR;
```

```
        double x = Center.X;
        double y = Center.Y;
        double sn36 = Math.Sin(36.0 * Math.PI / 180.0);
        double sn72 = Math.Sin(72.0 * Math.PI / 180.0);
        double cs36 = Math.Cos(36.0 * Math.PI / 180.0);
        double cs72 = Math.Cos(72.0 * Math.PI / 180.0);

        pf.StartPoint = new Point(x, y - r);
        pls.Points.Add(new Point(x + r * sn36, y + r * cs36));
        pls.Points.Add(new Point(x - r * sn72, y - r * cs72));
        pls.Points.Add(new Point(x + r * sn72, y - r * cs72));
        pls.Points.Add(new Point(x - r * sn36, y + r * cs36));
        pls.Points.Add(new Point(x, y - r));
        pf.Segments.Add(pls);
        pf.IsClosed = true;
        pg.FillRule = FillRule.Nonzero;
        return pg;
    }
  }
 }
}
```

In order to draw a *Star* shape, you need to have a reference to two parameters. One is the *Center* (a *Point* object) of the *Star*; the other is the size of the *Star,* named *SizeR* (a *double* object). However, you need to add two dependency properties in the preceding code for these two parameters. You may notice that these two properties are passed into the *DependencyProperty.Register* method. This registration process is necessary in order to expose these properties to the user.

Next, you override the getter of the *DefiningGeometry* property. Here the *Star* shape is created using the *PolyLineSegment* object. First, you need to define the coordinates of the *Star*. As illustrated in Figure 3-29, we assume that the center coordinates of the star are at (x, y) and that r is the radius of the circle around the star shape. In this notation, r is the same as *SizeR*. The angle α is equal to 72 degrees and β is equal to 36 degrees. From this figure, you can easily determine the coordinates of points 0 to 4, as shown in Table 3-2.

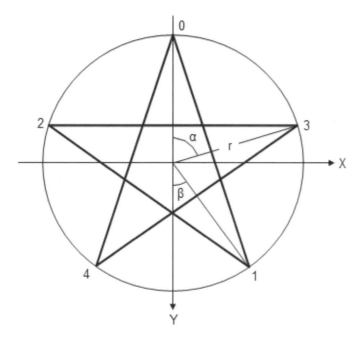

Figure 3-29. *Coordinates of the Star shape*

Table 3-2. *Coordinates of the Star*

Point	X Coordinate	Y Coordinate
0	x	$y - r$
1	$x + r * \sin \beta$	$y + r * \cos \beta$
2	$x - r * \sin \alpha$	$y - r * \cos \alpha$
3	$x + r * \sin \alpha$	$y - r * \cos \alpha$
4	$x - r * \sin \beta$	$y + r * \cos \beta$

Note that the *NonZero* fill rule is used here. As discussed previously in this chapter, with *Nonzero*, WPF follows the same line-counting process as the default *EvenOdd* fill rule, but it takes into account the direction that each line flows. If the number of lines going in one direction is equal to the number going in the opposite direction, the region is not filled. Otherwise, the region will be filled. You can see from Figure 3-29 that the pentagon at the center will be filled because the difference between these two counts is not zero. If you had set the fill rule to *EvenOdd*, the pentagon at the center would not be filled because you must cross two lines to get out of the pentagon.

Using this information and the *Star* class, you can easily create a custom *Star* shape (see the U.S. flag example in the upcoming section "Testing Custom Shapes").

ArrowLine Class

As mentioned previously in this chapter, you can specify the end caps of a line shape through its *StrokeStartLineCap* and *StrokeEndLineCap* properties. However, the size of these caps is always the same as the *StrokeThickness*. Thus, it is impossible to create a line with an arrowhead using these properties.

Instead, you can create an arrowhead line using a custom shape class. In this class, in addition to the standard line properties, such as $X1$, $Y1$, $X2$, and $Y2$, you need to add four more dependency properties that are used to control the arrowhead: *ArrowheadSizeX*, *ArrowheadSizeY*, *ArrowheadEnd*, and *IsArrowheadClosed*. The *ArrowheadSizeX* and *ArrowheadSizeY* properties are used to specify the size of the arrowhead, as defined in Figure 3-30. The *ArrowheadEnd* property allows you to select whether the arrowhead should be at the start point, the end point, both ends, or neither end of the line. The *IsArrowheadClosed* property lets you set the arrowhead type as open or closed, as illustrated in Figure 3-30.

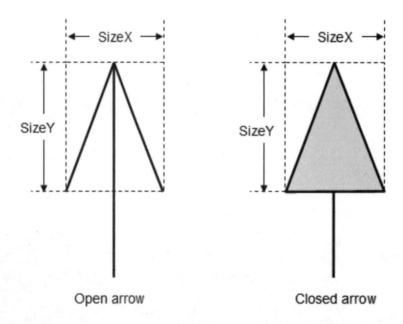

Figure 3-30. Arrowheads to be used in the ArrowLine class

Open the project *GraphicsBasics* and add a class named *ArrowLine* to the project. This class also inherits from the *Shape* class. Here is the C# code for this class:

```
using System;
using System.Windows;
using System.Windows.Media;
using System.Windows.Shapes;
```

```
namespace GraphicsBasics
{
    public class ArrowLine : Shape
    {
        protected PathGeometry pg;
        protected PathFigure pf;
        protected PolyLineSegment pls;

        PathFigure pfStartArrow;
        PolyLineSegment plsStartArrow;
        PathFigure pfEndArrow;
        PolyLineSegment plsEndArrow;

        public ArrowLine()
        {
            pg = new PathGeometry();
            pf = new PathFigure();
            pls = new PolyLineSegment();
            pf.Segments.Add(pls);
            pfStartArrow = new PathFigure();
            plsStartArrow = new PolyLineSegment();
            pfStartArrow.Segments.Add(plsStartArrow);
            pfEndArrow = new PathFigure();
            plsEndArrow = new PolyLineSegment();
            pfEndArrow.Segments.Add(plsEndArrow);
        }

        // Specify the X1 dependency property:
        public static readonly DependencyProperty X1Property =
            DependencyProperty.Register("X1", typeof(double), typeof(ArrowLine),
            new FrameworkPropertyMetadata(0.0,
            FrameworkPropertyMetadataOptions.AffectsMeasure));

        public double X1
        {
            set { SetValue(X1Property, value); }
            get { return (double)GetValue(X1Property); }
        }

        // Specify the Y1 dependency property:
        public static readonly DependencyProperty Y1Property =
            DependencyProperty.Register("Y1", typeof(double), typeof(ArrowLine),
            new FrameworkPropertyMetadata(0.0,
            FrameworkPropertyMetadataOptions.AffectsMeasure));

        public double Y1
        {
            set { SetValue(Y1Property, value); }
            get { return (double)GetValue(Y1Property); }
        }

        // Specify the X2 dependency property:
```

```
public static readonly DependencyProperty X2Property =
    DependencyProperty.Register("X2", typeof(double), typeof(ArrowLine),
    new FrameworkPropertyMetadata(0.0,
    FrameworkPropertyMetadataOptions.AffectsMeasure));

public double X2
{
    set { SetValue(X2Property, value); }
    get { return (double)GetValue(X2Property); }
}

// Specify the Y2 dependency property:
public static readonly DependencyProperty Y2Property =
    DependencyProperty.Register("Y2", typeof(double), typeof(ArrowLine),
    new FrameworkPropertyMetadata(0.0,
    FrameworkPropertyMetadataOptions.AffectsMeasure));

public double Y2
{
    set { SetValue(Y2Property, value); }
    get { return (double)GetValue(Y2Property); }
}

// Specify the arrowhead size in the x direction:
public static readonly DependencyProperty ArrowheadSizeXProperty =
    DependencyProperty.Register("ArrowheadSizeX",
    typeof(double), typeof(ArrowLine),
    new FrameworkPropertyMetadata(10.0,
    FrameworkPropertyMetadataOptions.AffectsMeasure));

public double ArrowheadSizeX
{
    set { SetValue(ArrowheadSizeXProperty, value); }
    get { return
        (double)GetValue(ArrowheadSizeXProperty); }
}

// Specify the arrowhead size in the y direction:
public static readonly DependencyProperty ArrowheadSizeYProperty =
    DependencyProperty.Register("ArrowheadSizeY",
    typeof(double), typeof(ArrowLine),
    new FrameworkPropertyMetadata(10.0,
    FrameworkPropertyMetadataOptions.AffectsMeasure));

public double ArrowheadSizeY
{
    set { SetValue(ArrowheadSizeYProperty, value); }
    get { return
        (double)GetValue(ArrowheadSizeYProperty); }
}

// Specify arrowhead ends:
public static readonly DependencyProperty ArrowheadEndProperty =
```

```
        DependencyProperty.Register("ArrowheadEnd",
        typeof(ArrowheadEndEnum), typeof(ArrowLine),
        new FrameworkPropertyMetadata(ArrowheadEndEnum.End,
        FrameworkPropertyMetadataOptions.AffectsMeasure));

    public ArrowheadEndEnum ArrowheadEnd
    {
        set { SetValue(ArrowheadEndProperty, value); }
        get { return
        (ArrowheadEndEnum)GetValue(ArrowheadEndProperty);}
    }

    // Specify IsArrowheadClosed property
    public static readonly DependencyProperty IsArrowheadClosedProperty =
        DependencyProperty.Register("IsArrowheadClosed",
        typeof(bool), typeof(ArrowLine),
        new FrameworkPropertyMetadata(false,
        FrameworkPropertyMetadataOptions.AffectsMeasure));

    public bool IsArrowheadClosed
    {
        set { SetValue(IsArrowheadClosedProperty,
            value); }
        get { return
          (bool)GetValue(IsArrowheadClosedProperty); }
    }

    protected override Geometry DefiningGeometry
    {
        get
        {
            pg.Figures.Clear();
            pf.StartPoint = new Point(X1, Y1);
            pls.Points.Clear();
            pls.Points.Add(new Point(X2, Y2));
            pg.Figures.Add(pf);

            if (pls.Points.Count > 0)
            {
                Point pt1 = new Point();
                Point pt2 = new Point();

                if ((ArrowheadEnd & ArrowheadEndEnum.Start)
                    == ArrowheadEndEnum.Start)
                {
                    pt1 = pf.StartPoint;
                    pt2 = pls.Points[0];
                    pg.Figures.Add(CreateArrowhead(pfStartArrow, pt2, pt1));
                }

                if ((ArrowheadEnd & ArrowheadEndEnum.End)
                    == ArrowheadEndEnum.End)
                {
```

```
                    pt1 = pls.Points.Count == 1 ? pf.StartPoint :
                        pls.Points[pls.Points.Count - 2];
                    pt2 = pls.Points[pls.Points.Count - 1];
                    pg.Figures.Add(CreateArrowhead(pfEndArrow, pt1, pt2));
                }
            }
            return pg;
        }
    }

    PathFigure CreateArrowhead(PathFigure pathFigure, Point pt1, Point pt2)
    {
        Point pt = new Point();
        Vector v = new Vector();

        Matrix m = ArrowheadTransform(pt1, pt2);
        PolyLineSegment pls1 = pathFigure.Segments[0] as PolyLineSegment;

        pls1.Points.Clear();
        if (!IsArrowheadClosed)
        {
            v = new Point(0, 0) - new Point(ArrowheadSizeX / 2, ArrowheadSizeY);
            pt = pt2 + v * m;
            pathFigure.StartPoint = pt;
            pls1.Points.Add(pt2);
            v = new Point(0, 0) - new Point(-ArrowheadSizeX / 2,
                                            ArrowheadSizeY);
            pt = pt2 + v * m;
            pls1.Points.Add(pt);
        }
        else if (IsArrowheadClosed)
        {
            v = new Point(0, 0) - new Point(ArrowheadSizeX / 2, 0);
            pt = pt2 + v * m;
            pathFigure.StartPoint = pt;
            v = new Point(0, 0) - new Point(0, -ArrowheadSizeY);
            pt = pt2 + v * m;
            pls1.Points.Add(pt);
            v = new Point(0, 0) - new Point(-ArrowheadSizeX / 2, 0);
            pt = pt2 + v * m;
            pls1.Points.Add(pt);
        }
        pathFigure.IsClosed = IsArrowheadClosed;
        return pathFigure;
    }

    private Matrix ArrowheadTransform(Point pt1, Point pt2)
    {
        Matrix m = new Matrix();
        double theta = 180 * (Math.Atan((pt2.X - pt1.X) /
            (pt2.Y - pt1.Y))) / Math.PI;
        double dx = pt2.X - pt1.X;
        double dy = pt2.Y - pt1.Y;
```

```
                if (dx >= 0 && dy >= 0)
                    theta = -theta;
                else if (dx < 0 && dy >= 0)
                    theta = -theta;
                else if (dx < 0 && dy < 0)
                    theta = 180 - theta;
                else if (dx >= 0 && dy < 0)
                    theta = 180 - theta;
                m.Rotate(theta);
                return m;
            }
        }

        public enum ArrowheadEndEnum
        {
            None = 0,
            Start = 1,
            End = 2,
            Both = 3
        }
    }
```

In this class, you add eight dependency properties and pass them to the
DependencyProperty.Register method. This registration process is necessary in order to expose these
properties to the user.

Next, you override the getter of the *DefiningGeometry* property. The arrowhead line is created using
PolyLineSegment. The arrowhead is first created in the absolute coordinate system and then placed at
the starting or end point of the line using matrix transforms.

Following the procedures presented here, you can create more custom shapes and build you own
custom-2D-shape library.

Testing Custom Shapes

The custom shapes *Star* and *ArrowLine* created in the preceding sections can be used the same way as
the standard shapes in WPF and in both XAML and code-behind files. In order to use custom shapes in
XAML files, you need to add the project in which the custom shape classes reside to the *xmlns*
namespace. This way, the markup code can find the location of your custom classes. In our case, you
need to add the following line:

```
xmlns:local="clr-namespace:GraphicsBasics"
```

Let's consider an example in which you first create a U.S. flag in code using the custom *Star* shape,
then create a *Star* and two arrowhead lines in the XAML file, and finally perform various transforms and
animations to the star and arrowhead lines.

Add a new WPF Window to the project *GraphicsBasics* and name it *CustomShape*. Here is the
markup for this example:

```
<Window x:Class="GraphicsBasics.CustomShape"
    xmlns="http://schemas.microsoft.com/winfx/2006/xaml/presentation"
    xmlns:x="http://schemas.microsoft.com/winfx/2006/xaml"
    xmlns:local="clr-namespace:GraphicsBasics"
    Title="Custom Shapes" Height="400" Width="300">
```

```xml
        <Viewbox Stretch="Uniform">
            <Border Margin="5" BorderBrush="Black" BorderThickness="1"
                    Background="LightCyan" HorizontalAlignment="Left">
                <Canvas x:Name="canvas1" Width="300" Height="375" ClipToBounds="True">
                    <local:Star x:Name="star1"  Canvas.Top="190" Canvas.Left ="50"
                                Fill="Red" Stroke="Blue" SizeR="30" Center="0,20">
                        <local:Star.RenderTransform>
                            <TransformGroup>
                                <ScaleTransform x:Name="starScale"
                                    CenterX="0" CenterY="20" />
                                <TranslateTransform x:Name="starTranslate"/>
                            </TransformGroup>
                        </local:Star.RenderTransform>
                    </local:Star>

                    <local:ArrowLine x:Name="arrowLine1" Canvas.Top="280" X1="50"
                                     Y1="20" X2="100" Y2="20" Stroke="Blue" Fill="Red"
                                     IsArrowheadClosed="True" ArrowheadEnd="Both">
                        <local:ArrowLine.RenderTransform>
                            <ScaleTransform x:Name="line1Scale"/>
                        </local:ArrowLine.RenderTransform>
                    </local:ArrowLine>
                    <local:ArrowLine x:Name="arrowLine2" Canvas.Top="250" X1="150"
                                     Y1="20" X2="230" Y2="20" Stroke="Blue"
                                     StrokeThickness="3">
                        <local:ArrowLine.RenderTransform>
                            <RotateTransform x:Name="line2Rotate"
                                CenterX="150" CenterY="20"/>
                        </local:ArrowLine.RenderTransform>
                    </local:ArrowLine>
                </Canvas>
            </Border>
        </Viewbox>
</Window>
```

Here is the corresponding code-behind file:

```csharp
using System;
using System.Windows;
using System.Windows.Controls;
using System.Windows.Media;
using System.Windows.Media.Animation;
using System.Windows.Shapes;

namespace GraphicsBasics
{
    public partial class CustomShape : Window
    {
        public CustomShape()
        {
            InitializeComponent();
            AddUSFlag(10, 10, 280);
            StartAnimation();
        }
```

```
private void AddUSFlag(double x0, double y0, double width)
{
    SolidColorBrush whiteBrush = new SolidColorBrush(Colors.White);
    SolidColorBrush blueBrush = new SolidColorBrush(Colors.DarkBlue);
    SolidColorBrush redBrush = new SolidColorBrush(Colors.Red);
    Rectangle rect = new Rectangle();
    double height = 10 * width / 19;

    //Draw white rectangle background:
    rect.Fill = whiteBrush;
    rect.Width = width;
    rect.Height = height;
    Canvas.SetLeft(rect, x0);
    Canvas.SetTop(rect, y0);
    canvas1.Children.Add(rect);

    // Draw seven red stripes:
    for (int i = 0; i < 7; i++)
    {
        rect = new Rectangle();
        rect.Fill = redBrush;
        rect.Width = width;
        rect.Height = height / 13;
        Canvas.SetLeft(rect, x0);
        Canvas.SetTop(rect, y0 + 2 * i * height / 13);
        canvas1.Children.Add(rect);
    }

    // Draw blue box:
    rect = new Rectangle();
    rect.Fill = blueBrush;
    rect.Width = 2 * width / 5;
    rect.Height = 7 * height / 13;
    Canvas.SetLeft(rect, x0);
    Canvas.SetTop(rect, y0);
    canvas1.Children.Add(rect);

    // Draw fifty stars:
    double offset = rect.Width / 40;
    double dx = (rect.Width - 2 * offset) / 11;
    double dy = (rect.Height - 2 * offset) / 9;
    for (int j = 0; j < 9; j++)
    {
        double y = y0 + offset + j * dy + dy / 2;
        for (int i = 0; i < 11; i++)
        {
            double x = x0 + offset + i * dx + dx / 2;
            if ((i + j) % 2 == 0)
            {
                Star star = new Star();
                star.Fill = whiteBrush;
                star.SizeR = width / 55;
```

```
                        star.Center = new Point(x, y);
                        canvas1.Children.Add(star);
                    }
                }
            }
        }

        private void StartAnimation()
        {
            // Animating the star:
            AnimationTimeline at =
                new DoubleAnimation(0.1, 1.2, new Duration(new TimeSpan(0, 0, 5)));
            at.RepeatBehavior = RepeatBehavior.Forever;
            at.AutoReverse = true;
            starScale.BeginAnimation(ScaleTransform.ScaleXProperty, at);
            starScale.BeginAnimation(ScaleTransform.ScaleYProperty, at);
            at = new DoubleAnimation(0, 200, new Duration(new TimeSpan(0, 0, 3)));
            at.RepeatBehavior = RepeatBehavior.Forever;
            at.AutoReverse = true;
            starTranslate.BeginAnimation(TranslateTransform.XProperty, at);

            // Animating arrowline1:
            at = new DoubleAnimation(0, 2.5, new Duration(new TimeSpan(0, 0, 4)));
            at.RepeatBehavior = RepeatBehavior.Forever;
            at.AutoReverse = true;
            line1Scale.BeginAnimation(ScaleTransform.ScaleXProperty, at);
            line1Scale.BeginAnimation(ScaleTransform.ScaleYProperty, at);

            // Animating arrowline2:
            at = new DoubleAnimation(0, 50, new Duration(new TimeSpan(0, 0, 5)));
            at.RepeatBehavior = RepeatBehavior.Forever;
            at.AutoReverse = true;
            arrowLine2.BeginAnimation(ArrowLine.ArrowheadSizeXProperty, at);
            arrowLine2.BeginAnimation(ArrowLine.ArrowheadSizeYProperty, at);
            at = new DoubleAnimation(0, 360, new Duration(new TimeSpan(0, 0, 5)));
            at.RepeatBehavior = RepeatBehavior.Forever;
            line2Rotate.BeginAnimation(RotateTransform.AngleProperty, at);
        }
    }
}
```

In the foregoing code, the *AddUSFlag* method creates a U.S. flag. You can specify the location and width of the flag. Inside this method, the 50 stars on the U.S. flag are drawn using the custom *Star* class. Next, you perform the animations for a star and arrow lines using various transforms. Note here that the animation is implemented in code instead of the *Storyboard* approach in XAML, which was used in earlier sections of this chapter.

Running this example produces the output shown in Figure 3-31.

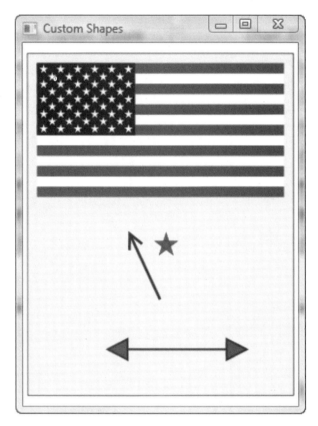

Figure 3-31. Graphics objects created using custom-shape classes

CHAPTER 4

■ ■ ■

Colors and Brushes

Almost everything visible on your computer screen is somehow related to colors and brushes. For example, you use a brush with a specified color to paint the background of a button, the foreground of text, and the fill of a shape. We have used colors and brushes throughout this book, but so far we have done most of the work with the simple *SolidColorBrush* object. In fact, you can use colors and brushes to paint user interface and graphics objects with anything from simple solid colors to complex sets of patterns and images. This chapter covers the color system and some of the brushes defined in WPF. It also discusses custom colormap brushes and color shading, which will be useful in 3D surface chart applications. Some more advanced brushes, such as *Image* and *Visual* brushes, and brush transformations are beyond the scope of this book.

Colors

In WPF, a color is specified as a *Color* structure from the *System.Windows.Media* namespace. This *Color* structure describes a color in terms of alpha (A), red (R), green (G), and blue (B) channels. WPF uses two color systems, sRGB and ScRGB. You can specify a color using either system.

sRGB is a standard RGB color space created cooperatively by HP and Microsoft for use in monitors, printers, and the Internet. It is designed to match typical home and office viewing conditions. sRGB has found wide applications. Software, LCD displays, digital cameras, printers, and scanners all follow the sRGB standard. For this reason, you can assume that any 8-bit image file or device interface falls in the sRGB color space.

ScRGB system is the latest color space developed by Microsoft. This system offers 64-bit encoding with 16 bits per channel, which allows you to specify over 65,000 steps for each color instead of the 256 steps available with sRGB's 8 bits per channel.

Unlike sRGB, ScRGB allows negative values and values above 1.0, which significantly improves color processing. In manipulating color information based on sRGB, most applications have to cut off anything below 0 (black) and anything above 1 (white), resulting in the discarding of some of the color information.

Microsoft's goal for ScRGB is to give it the ease of use and simplicity of sRGB. This means that it should require little or no extra work to take advantage of it. However, there is a trade-off involved: ScRGB will make more demands on performance and bandwidth, which makes it unacceptable for low-end systems. Since no ScRGB devices are available yet, it isn't clear how the system will translate into real-world applications.

WPF allows you to specify a color using both sRGB and ScRGB. Several ways to create color are available in WPF, including:

- *An ARGB color value.* You specify each value as an integer in the range [0, 255].

- *A ScRGB value.* The current version of the ScRGB system in WPF has a value range of [0, 1].

- *A predefined color name.* You choose the correspondingly named property from the *System.Windows.Media.Colors* class. The *Colors* class has 141 predefined color names.

In addition, you may find the *ColorConverter* class useful. This class allows you to convert a color from a string, or vice versa.

System Colors

In WPF, as mentioned previously, a color is represented by a 32-bit structure made of four components: A, R, G, and B, referred to as sRGB. Color can also be represented by a 64-bit structure made up of four components: ScA, ScR, ScG, ScB, referred to as ScRGB. In the sRGB system, the components' values range from 0 to 255; in the ScRGB system, this range becomes [0, 1] in the current WPF implementation. The alpha component of the color represents transparency, which determines how much a color is blended with the background. An alpha value of zero represents a fully transparent color; a value of 255 in sRGB or 1 in ScRGB represents a fully opaque color.

The following code snippet shows several ways to specify a color:

```
Color color = new Color();
//Create a color from a RGB value:
color = Color.FromRgb(255, 0, 0);
// Create a color from an ARGB value:
color = Color.FromArgb(100, 255, 0, 0);
// Create a color from a ScRGB value:
color = Color.FromScRgb(0.5f, 1.0f, 0.0f, 0.0f);
// Create a color using predefined color names:
color = Colors.Red;
// Create a color using ColorConverter:
color = (Color)ColorConverter.ConvertFromString("#FFFF0000");
```

Pay attention to the ScRGB value. It requires a *Float* value rather than a *Double* value. You can also use a few methods on any *Color* structure to retrieve color information. For example, you can use a predefined color name from the *Colors* class to obtain corresponding color information, including sRGB and ScRGB values.

Let's look at an example that puts all of these techniques to work. Start with a new WPF Windows project and name it *ColorsAndBrushes*. Add a *StartMenu* Window as you did in the projects presented in the previous chapters. Then add a new WPF Window called *SystemColors* to the project.

This example allows you to select a color from a *ListBox* loaded with all of the predefined color names in the *Colors* class. When you type the *Opacity* in a *TextBox* and select an item from the *ListBox*, the *Fill* color of a rectangle is changed accordingly.

Here is the markup for this example:

```
<Window x:Class="ColorsAndBrushes.SystemColors"
    xmlns="http://schemas.microsoft.com/winfx/2006/xaml/presentation"
    xmlns:x="http://schemas.microsoft.com/winfx/2006/xaml"
    Title="System Colors" Height="350" Width="350">
    <Grid>
        <Grid.ColumnDefinitions>
```

```xml
            <ColumnDefinition Width="145"/>
            <ColumnDefinition Width="145"/>
        </Grid.ColumnDefinitions>
        <StackPanel Grid.Column="0" Margin="5">
            <TextBlock Text ="Select Color" Margin="5,5,5,0"/>
            <ListBox x:Name="listBox1" SelectionChanged="listBox1SelectionChanged"
                Height="100" Margin="5"/>
            <TextBlock Text="Show selected color:" Margin="5,5,5,0"/>
            <Rectangle x:Name="rect1" Stroke="Blue" Fill="AliceBlue"
                   Height="100" Width="122" Margin="5"/>
        </StackPanel>

        <StackPanel Grid.Column="1" Margin="5">
            <TextBlock Text="Opacity:" Margin="5,5,5,0"/>
            <TextBox Name="textBox" HorizontalAlignment="Left"
                    TextAlignment="Center" Text="1" Width="50" Margin ="5,5,5,8"/>
            <Separator></Separator>
            <TextBlock FontWeight="Bold" Text="sRGB Information:" Margin="5,5,5,2"/>
            <TextBlock Name="tbAlpha" Text="Alpha =" Margin="5,0,5,2"/>
            <TextBlock Name="tbRed" Text="Red =" Margin="5,0,5,2"/>
            <TextBlock Name="tbGreen" Text="Green =" Margin="5,0,5,2"/>
            <TextBlock Name="tbBlue" Text="Blue =" Margin="5,0,5,2"/>
            <TextBlock Name="tbRGB" Text="ARGB Hex =" Margin="5,0,5,5"/>
            <Separator/>
            <TextBlock FontWeight="Bold" Text="ScRGB Information:"
                        Margin="5,5,5,2"/>
            <TextBlock Name="tbScA" Text="ScA =" Margin="5,0,5,2"/>
            <TextBlock Name="tbScR" Text="ScR =" Margin="5,0,5,2"/>
            <TextBlock Name="tbScG" Text="ScG =" Margin="5,0,5,2" />
            <TextBlock Name="tbScB" Text="ScB =" Margin="5,0,5,2"/>
        </StackPanel>
    </Grid>
</Window>
```

Here is the corresponding code-behind file for this example:

```csharp
using System;
using System.Windows;
using System.Windows.Controls;
using System.Windows.Input;
using System.Windows.Media;
using System.Windows.Shapes;
using System.Reflection;
using System.Collections.Generic;

namespace ColorsAndBrushes
{
    public partial class SystemColors : System.Windows.Window
    {
        private Color color;
        SolidColorBrush colorBrush = new SolidColorBrush();

        public SystemColors()
        {
```

```
            InitializeComponent();
            Type colorsType = typeof(Colors);
            foreach (PropertyInfo property in colorsType.GetProperties())
            {
                listBox1.Items.Add(property.Name);
                color = Colors.AliceBlue;
                listBox1.SelectedIndex = 0;
                ColorInfo();
            }
        }

        private void listBox1SelectionChanged(object sender, EventArgs e)
        {
            string colorString = listBox1.SelectedItem.ToString();
            color = (Color)ColorConverter.ConvertFromString(colorString);
            float opacity = Convert.ToSingle(textBox.Text);
            if (opacity > 1)
                opacity = 1.0f;
            else if (opacity < 0)
                opacity = 0.0f;
            color.ScA = opacity;
            ColorInfo();
        }

        private void ColorInfo()
        {
            rect1.Fill = new SolidColorBrush(color);
            // sRGB color info :
            tbAlpha.Text = "Alpha = " + color.A.ToString();
            tbRed.Text = "Red = " + color.R.ToString();
            tbGreen.Text = "Green = " + color.G.ToString();
            tbBlue.Text = "Blue = " + color.B.ToString();
            string rgbHex = string.Format("{0:X2}{1:X2}{2:X2}{3:X2}",
                            color.A, color.R, color.G,color.B);
            tbRGB.Text = "ARGB = #" + rgbHex;

            // ScRGB color info:
            tbScA.Text = "ScA = " + color.ScA.ToString();
            tbScR.Text = "ScR = " + color.ScR.ToString();
            tbScG.Text = "ScG = " + color.ScG.ToString();
            tbScB.Text = "ScB = " + color.ScB.ToString();
        }
    }
}
```

To put all of the predefined color names from the *Colors* class into the *ListBox*, you use the following *foreach* loop:

```
Type colorsType = typeof(Colors);
foreach (PropertyInfo property in colorsType.GetProperties())
{
    listBox1.Items.Add(property.Name);
    ......
}
```

You also need a *using System.Reflection* statement to make this loop work. You simply retrieve the *PropertyInfo* of the *Colors* class and place its name into the *ListBox*. Now change the *Opacity* (within the range of 0 to 1) in the *TextBox* and select the item from the *ListBox*. The rectangle's fill color will change correspondingly, and the color information will also display on your screen. Note that if you change the opacity after selecting a color from the list box, you have to click the color again in the list box in order to update the opacity. Figure 4-1 shows the result of running this example.

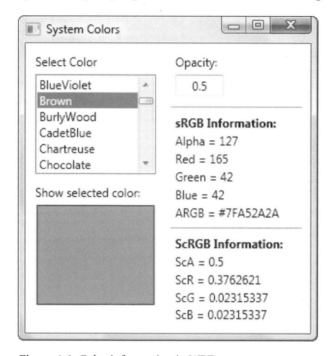

Figure 4-1. Color information in WPF

Color Picker

You might have noticed that unlike GDI+ and Window Forms, WPF unfortunately lacks a few standard common dialogs. For example, WPF doesn't implement a *ColorDialog*. If you want to have a color picker-like functionality, you need to create a custom *ColorDialog* control by yourself.

Fortunately, the WPF team did create several sample custom dialogs, including a *ColorPickerDialog*. I don't want to reinvent the wheel, so instead I'll show you how to use this *ColorPickerDialog* in your own WPF applications.

The *ColorPickerDialog* control is packed in a *ColorPicker.dll*. You can download this package from the following link:

```
http://blogs.msdn.com/wpfsdk/archive/2006/10/26/Uncommon-Dialogs--Font-Chooser-and-Color-
Picker-Dialogs.aspx
```

If you want to use this control in a WPF application, you can simply add the DLL file to the References for your project. You also need to add a using statement such as this:

```
using Microsoft.Samples.CustomControls;
```

Then you can create an instance of the color dialog:

```
ColorPickerDialog cPicker = new ColorPickerDialog();
```

Here, I'll present an example that shows you how to use this color dialog in a simple 2D drawing application. In this application, you can draw *Rectangle* and *Ellipse* shapes with your mouse. You can then change the fill color of a selected shape using the *ColorPickerDialog*.

Open the project *ColorsAndBrushes* and add a new WPF Window called *ColorPicker* to the project. Here is the markup for this example:

```
<Window x:Class="ColorsAndBrushes.ColorPicker"
    xmlns="http://schemas.microsoft.com/winfx/2006/xaml/presentation"
    xmlns:x="http://schemas.microsoft.com/winfx/2006/xaml"
    Title="Color Picker" Height="300" Width="300">

<DockPanel>
    <ToolBarTray DockPanel.Dock="Left" Orientation="Vertical" IsLocked="True">
        <ToolBar Padding="2">
            <RadioButton x:Name="rbRectangle" IsChecked="True"
                        ToolTip="Add Rectangle" Margin="3">
                <Rectangle Width="20" Height="12" Stroke="Blue"
                        Fill="LightBlue"/>
            </RadioButton>
            <RadioButton x:Name="rbEllipse" IsChecked="False"
                        ToolTip="Add Ellipse" Margin="3">
                <Ellipse Width="22" Height="15" Stroke="Blue" Fill="LightBlue"/>
            </RadioButton>
            <RadioButton x:Name="rbSelect" IsChecked="False"
                        ToolTip="Select" Margin="3">
                <Path Stroke="Blue" Fill="LightBlue" Width="20" Height="20">
                    <Path.Data>
                        <PathGeometry Figures="M5,15
                                    L 10,0 15,15 12,15 12,20 8,20 8,15Z">
                            <PathGeometry.Transform>
                                <RotateTransform CenterX="10"
                                                CenterY="10" Angle="45"/>
                            </PathGeometry.Transform>
                        </PathGeometry>
                    </Path.Data>
                </Path>
            </RadioButton>

            <RadioButton x:Name="rbDelete" IsChecked="False"
                        ToolTip="Delete Shape" Margin="3">
                <Path Stroke="Blue" Fill="LightBlue" Width="20" Height="20">
                    <Path.Data>
                        <CombinedGeometry>
                            <CombinedGeometry.Geometry1>
                                <PathGeometry
                                    Figures="M0,0 L 15,20 15,15 20,15Z"/>
                            </CombinedGeometry.Geometry1>
                            <CombinedGeometry.Geometry2>
                                <PathGeometry
                                    Figures="M20,0 L 0,15 5,15 5,20Z"/>
```

```
                        </CombinedGeometry.Geometry2>
                    </CombinedGeometry>
                </Path.Data>
            </Path>
        </RadioButton>

        <Separator Margin="0,10,0,10"></Separator>

        <TextBlock Margin="10,3,0,0">Fill</TextBlock>
        <Button Click="btnFill_Click" Background="Transparent">
            <Rectangle x:Name="rectFill" Width="20" Height="20"
                       Stroke="Black" Fill="LightBlue"/>
        </Button>
    </ToolBar>
</ToolBarTray>

<Border BorderThickness="2" BorderBrush="LightBlue" Margin="5">
    <Canvas Name="canvas1" Background="Transparent"
            MouseLeftButtonDown="OnMouseLeftButtonDown"
            MouseMove="OnMouseMove"
            MouseLeftButtonUp="OnMouseLeftButtonUp">
    </Canvas>
</Border>
</DockPanel>
</Window>
```

The foregoing XAML file creates a user interface and layout for this example. Here is the corresponding code-behind file:

```csharp
using System;
using System.Windows;
using System.Windows.Controls;
using System.Windows.Input;
using System.Windows.Media;
using System.Windows.Shapes;
using Microsoft.Samples.CustomControls;

namespace ColorsAndBrushes
{
    public partial class ColorPicker : System.Windows.Window
    {
        private Rectangle rubberBand;
        private Point startPoint;
        private Point currentPoint;
        private Path selectedShape;
        private double selectedStrokeThickness = 5;
        private double originalStrokeThickness = 1;
        private SolidColorBrush strokeBrush = new SolidColorBrush(Colors.Blue);
        private SolidColorBrush fillBrush = new SolidColorBrush(Colors.LightBlue);

        public ColorPicker()
        {
            InitializeComponent();
        }
```

```
private void OnMouseLeftButtonDown(object sender, MouseButtonEventArgs e)
{
    if (!canvas1.IsMouseCaptured)
    {
        startPoint = e.GetPosition(canvas1);
        canvas1.CaptureMouse();

        if (rbSelect.IsChecked == true)
        {
            if (canvas1 == e.Source)
                return;

            foreach (Path path in canvas1.Children)
                path.StrokeThickness = originalStrokeThickness;

            selectedShape = (Path)e.Source;
            selectedShape.StrokeThickness = selectedStrokeThickness;
            fillBrush = (SolidColorBrush)selectedShape.Fill;
            e.Handled = true;
        }
        else if (rbDelete.IsChecked == true)
        {
            if (canvas1 == e.Source)
                return;
            selectedShape = (Path)e.Source;
            DeleteShape(selectedShape);
        }
    }
}

private void DeleteShape(Path path)
{
    path.StrokeThickness = selectedStrokeThickness;
    string msg = "Do you really want to delete this shape?";
    string title = "Delete Shape?";
    MessageBoxButton buttons = MessageBoxButton.YesNo;
    MessageBoxImage icon = MessageBoxImage.Warning;
    MessageBoxResult result = MessageBox.Show(msg, title, buttons, icon);
    if (result == MessageBoxResult.Yes)
        canvas1.Children.Remove(path);
    else
    {
        path.StrokeThickness = originalStrokeThickness;
        return;
    }
}

private void OnMouseMove(object sender, MouseEventArgs e)
{
    if (canvas1.IsMouseCaptured)
    {
        currentPoint = e.GetPosition(canvas1);
```

```
        if (rubberBand == null)
        {
            rubberBand = new Rectangle();
            rubberBand.Stroke = Brushes.LightCoral;
            rubberBand.StrokeDashArray =
                    new DoubleCollection(new double[] { 4, 2 });
            if (rbRectangle.IsChecked == true ||
                rbEllipse.IsChecked == true)
            {
                canvas1.Children.Add(rubberBand);
            }
        }

        double width = Math.Abs(startPoint.X - currentPoint.X);
        double height = Math.Abs(startPoint.Y - currentPoint.Y);
        double left = Math.Min(startPoint.X, currentPoint.X);
        double top = Math.Min(startPoint.Y, currentPoint.Y);
        rubberBand.Width = width;
        rubberBand.Height = height;
        Canvas.SetLeft(rubberBand, left);
        Canvas.SetTop(rubberBand, top);
    }
}

private void OnMouseLeftButtonUp(object sender, MouseButtonEventArgs e)
{
    if (rbRectangle.IsChecked == true)
        AddShape(startPoint, currentPoint, "rectangle");
    else if (rbEllipse.IsChecked == true)
        AddShape(startPoint, currentPoint, "ellipse");
    if (rubberBand != null)
    {
        canvas1.Children.Remove(rubberBand);
        rubberBand = null;
        canvas1.ReleaseMouseCapture();
    }
}

private void AddShape(Point pt1, Point pt2, string s)
{
    Path path = new Path();
    path.Fill = fillBrush;
    path.Stroke = strokeBrush;
    path.StrokeThickness = originalStrokeThickness;
    if (s == "rectangle")
    {
        RectangleGeometry geometry = new RectangleGeometry();
        double width = Math.Abs(pt1.X - pt2.X);
        double height = Math.Abs(pt1.Y - pt2.Y);
        double left = Math.Min(pt1.X, pt2.X);
        double top = Math.Min(pt1.Y, pt2.Y);
        geometry.Rect = new Rect(left, top, width, height);
        path.Data = geometry;
```

```
        }
        else if (s == "ellipse")
        {
            EllipseGeometry geometry = new EllipseGeometry();
            double width = Math.Abs(pt1.X - pt2.X);
            double height = Math.Abs(pt1.Y - pt2.Y);
            double left = Math.Min(pt1.X, pt2.X);
            double top = Math.Min(pt1.Y, pt2.Y);
            geometry.Center = new Point(left + width / 2, top + height / 2);
            geometry.RadiusX = width / 2;
            geometry.RadiusY = height / 2;
            path.Data = geometry;
        }
        canvas1.Children.Add(path);
    }

    private void btnFill_Click(object sender, RoutedEventArgs e)
    {
        ColorPickerDialog cPicker = new ColorPickerDialog();
        cPicker.StartingColor = fillBrush.Color;
        cPicker.Owner = this;
        rectFill.Fill = fillBrush;

        bool? dialogResult = cPicker.ShowDialog();
        if (dialogResult != null && (bool)dialogResult == true)
        {
            if (selectedShape != null)
            {
                if (selectedShape.StrokeThickness == selectedStrokeThickness)
                {
                    selectedShape.Fill =
                        new SolidColorBrush(cPicker.SelectedColor);
                    selectedShape.StrokeThickness = originalStrokeThickness;
                }
            }
            fillBrush = new SolidColorBrush(cPicker.SelectedColor);
            rectFill.Fill = fillBrush;
        }
    }
  }
}
```

This application allows you to add *Rectangle* and *Ellipse* shapes and lets you change the color of a selected shape using the *ColorPickerDialog* control. The *btnFill_Click* handler is responsible for the color changes made using the color picker control. Figure 4-2 shows a snapshot of this example.

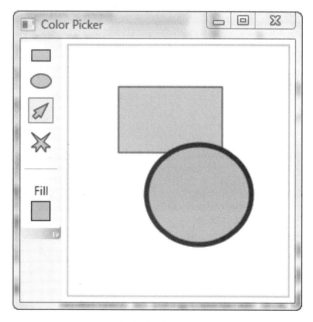

Figure 4-2. Change the fill color of a selected shape using the ColorPickerDialog

In this application, you draw shapes by selecting the *Add Rectangle* or *Add Ellipse* button. You can then change a shape's fill color by clicking the *Select* button and then clicking on a shape, which will highlight the selected shape and increase its *StrokeThickness* (see Figure 4-2, in which the ellipse shape is selected). Then select the *Fill* button (the square beneath the word *Fill*), which brings up the *ColorPickerDialog*, as shown in Figure 4-3.

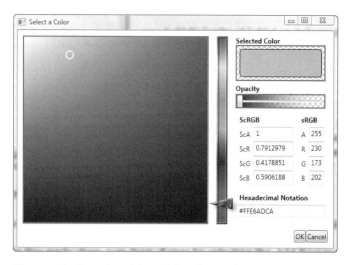

Figure 4-3. The color picker dialog, from which you can specify whatever color you like

133

To use this color picker, you select a color by clicking the left color pane with your mouse and changing the R, G, and B components using the slider. The dialog also allows you to change the opacity of the color. You can preview the selected color in the *Selected Color* view window. If you're satisfied with the selected color, click the *OK* button. The fill color of the selected shape will be changed.

The *ColorPicker.dll* file is located in the *ColorsAndBrushes* project's */bin/Debug* directory. You can use it in your application by adding it to the References for your project.

Brushes

Brushes aren't new to you. You have used brushes throughout this book, but so far you have done most of your work with the simple *SolidColorBrush* object. However, WPF provides a variety of brushes you can use to create graphically rich applications. A brush is much more than a means of applying color to pixels; it also allows you to paint with color, gradients, images, drawings, etc. A gradient brush lets you create glass effects or the illusion of depth. Painting with an *ImageBrush* object provides a means to stretch, tile, or fill an area with a specified bitmap. A *VisualBrush* allows you to fill an area with a visual from another part of the application's visual tree. You can use this brush to create the illusion of reflection or magnification in your user interfaces.

In WPF, a brush paints an area with its output. Different brushes have different types of output:

- *SolidColorBrush* – Paints an area with a solid color. The color's opacity can be changed.

- *LinearGradientBrush* – Paints an area with a linear *gradient* fill, that is a gradually shaded fill that changes from one color to another.

- *RadialGradientBrush* – Paints an area with a radial gradient fill, which is similar to a linear gradient except that the fill radiates out in a circular pattern from a center point.

- *ImageBrush* – Paints an area with an image that can be stretched, scaled, or tiled.

- *DrawingBrush* – Paints an area with a *Drawing* object. This object can be a shape or a bitmap.

- *VisualBrush* – Paints an area with a *Visual* object. A *VisualBrush* enables you to project content from one portion of your application to another area. It is useful for creating reflection effects and magnifying portions of the screen.

From this list, you can see that a brush can indeed provide output other than simple solid colors. By using the different brushes available in WPF, you can create interesting effects such as gradient, reflection, and lighting effects, among others.

In the following sections, you will explore some of these brushes, including *SolidColorBrush*, *LinearGradientBrush*, *RadialGradientBrush*, and *DrawingBrush*, and learn how to use them in your WPF applications.

SolidColorBrush

The most common brush, and the simplest to use, is the *SolidColorBrush*. This brush simply paints an area with a solid color. Please note that a brush is different from a color. A brush is an object that tells the system to paint specific pixels with a specified output defined by the brush. A *SolidColorBrush* paints a color in a specific area of your screen. The output of a *SolidColorBrush* is the color.

A *SolidColorBrush* can be defined by simply providing a value for its *Color* property. As mentioned previously, there are several ways to specify a color, including declaring sRGB or ScRGB values, using hexadecimal strings, using the predefined color names in the *Colors* class, and even using the *ColorPickerDialog* discussed in the preceding section. You can also specify the opacity of a *SolidColorBrush*.

As with the *Colors* class for colors, WPF provides some handy classes for brushes. The *Brushes* class, for example, exposes a set of predefined brushes based on solid colors. This provides a shortcut you can use for creating common solid color brushes.

Let's consider an example, *SolidColorBrushExample*, in which you define a *SolidColorBrush* using different methods. Here, you create the interface and layout using XAML, while you fill the color of the *Rectangle* shapes using C# code. Of course, you can obtain the same results using either XAML or C# code only. The following is the XAML file for this example:

```
<Window x:Class="ColorsAndBrushes.SolidColorBrushExample"
    xmlns="http://schemas.microsoft.com/winfx/2006/xaml/presentation"
    xmlns:x="http://schemas.microsoft.com/winfx/2006/xaml"
    Title="Solid Color Brushes" Height="450" Width="300">

    <Canvas Margin="5">
        <StackPanel>
            <TextBlock Margin="0,0,0,5">Predefined Brush in the Brushes
                        class:</TextBlock>
            <Rectangle x:Name="rect1" Width="100" Height="30" Stroke="Blue"/>
            <TextBlock Margin="0,10,0,5">From predefined color name in
                        the Colors class:</TextBlock>
            <Rectangle x:Name="rect2" Width="100" Height="30" Stroke="Blue"/>
            <TextBlock Margin="0,10,0,5">From sRGB value in the Color
                        structure:</TextBlock>
            <Rectangle x:Name="rect3" Width="100" Height="30" Stroke="Blue"/>
            <TextBlock Margin="0,10,0,5">From ScRGB value in the Color
                        structure:</TextBlock>
            <Rectangle x:Name="rect4" Width="100" Height="30" Stroke="Blue"/>
            <TextBlock Margin="0,10,0,5">From Hex string using
                        ColorConverter:</TextBlock>
            <Rectangle x:Name="rect5" Width="100" Height="30" Stroke="Blue"/>
            <TextBlock Margin="0,10,0,5">From ColorPickerDialog:</TextBlock>
            <Rectangle x:Name="rect6" Width="100" Height="30" Stroke="Blue"
                        Fill="LightBlue"/>
            <Button Click="ChangeColor_Click" Width="100" Height="25"
                Content="Change Color" Margin="10"/>
        </StackPanel>
    </Canvas>
</Window>
```

Here is the corresponding code-behind file for this example:

```
using System;
using System.Windows;
using System.Windows.Controls;
using System.Windows.Input;
using System.Windows.Media;
using System.Windows.Shapes;
using Microsoft.Samples.CustomControls;
```

```
namespace ColorsAndBrushes
{
    public partial class SolidColorBrushExample : System.Windows.Window
    {
        public SolidColorBrushes()
        {
            InitializeComponent();
            SolidColorBrush brush = new SolidColorBrush();

            // Predefined brush in Brushes Class:
            brush = Brushes.Red;
            rect1.Fill = brush;

            // From predefined color name in the Colors class:
            brush = new SolidColorBrush(Colors.Green);
            rect2.Fill = brush;

            // From sRGB values in the Color strutcure:
            brush = new SolidColorBrush(Color.FromArgb(100, 0, 0, 255));
            rect3.Fill = brush;

            // From ScRGB values in the Color structure:
            brush = new SolidColorBrush(Color.FromScRgb(0.5f, 0.7f, 0.0f, 0.5f));
            rect4.Fill = brush;

            // From a Hex string using ColorConverter:
            brush = new
              SolidColorBrush((Color)ColorConverter.ConvertFromString("#CBFFFFAA"));
            rect5.Fill = brush;
        }

        // From ColorPickerDialog:
        private void ChangeColor_Click(object sender, RoutedEventArgs e)
        {
            ColorPickerDialog cPicker = new ColorPickerDialog();
            cPicker.StartingColor = Colors.LightBlue;
            cPicker.Owner = this;
            bool? dialogResult = cPicker.ShowDialog();
            if (dialogResult != null && (bool)dialogResult == true)
            {
                rect6.Fill = new SolidColorBrush(cPicker.SelectedColor);
            }
        }
    }
}
```

In this example, you create six *Rectangle* shapes and specify their *Fill* properties using a different *SolidColorBrush* for each of them. In particular, for *rect*6, you use the *ColorPickerDialog* to specify the color of the brush. You need to click the *Change Color* button to bring up the Color Picker window, from which you can select any color you like.

Figure 4-4 shows the results of executing this sample application.

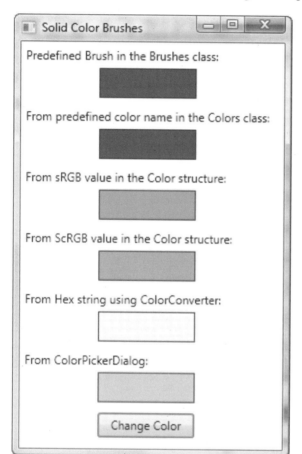

Figure 4-4. *Shapes painted using SolidColorBrush*

LinearGradientBrush

The *LinearGradientBrush* allows you to paint an area with multiple colors and to create a blended fill effect that changes from one color to another.

The *LinearGradientBrush* follows a linear gradient axis. You can define the direction of the axis to obtain vertical, horizontal, or diagonal gradient effects. The gradient axis is defined by two points, *StartPoint* and *EndPoint*, which map to a 1 × 1 matrix. For example, a *StartPoint* of (0, 0) and an *EndPoint* of (0, 1) would produce a vertical gradient, whereas a *StartPoint* of (0, 0) and an *EndPoint* of (1, 1) would generate a diagonal gradient. The *StartPoint* and *EndPoint* properties of a *LinearGradientBrush* let you choose the point at which the first color begins to change and the point at which the color change ends with the final color. Remember that the coordinates you use for the *StartPoint* and *EndPoint* aren't real coordinates. Instead, the *LinearGradientBrush* assigns the point (0, 0) to the top-left corner and (1, 1) to the bottom-right corner of the area you want to fill, no matter how high and wide it actually is.

Along the axis you specify a series of *GradientStop* objects, which are points on the axis at which you want the colors to blend and transition to other colors. You can define as many *GradientStop* objects as you need. A *GradientStop* object has two properties of interest, *Color* and *Offset*. The *Offset* property defines a distance, ranging from 0 to 1, from the start point of the axis at which the color specified in the *Color* property should begin.

Now let's look at an example that uses the *LinearGradientBrush*. Add a new WPF Window, called *LinearGradientBrushExample*, to the project *ColorsAndBrushes*. Here is the markup for this example:

```
<Window x:Class="ColorsAndBrushes.LinearGradientBrushExample"
    xmlns="http://schemas.microsoft.com/winfx/2006/xaml/presentation"
    xmlns:x="http://schemas.microsoft.com/winfx/2006/xaml"
    Title="Linear Gradient Brushes" Height="400" Width="350">
    <Grid>
        <Grid.ColumnDefinitions>
            <ColumnDefinition/>
            <ColumnDefinition/>
        </Grid.ColumnDefinitions>
        <Grid.RowDefinitions>
            <RowDefinition Height="Auto"/>
            <RowDefinition Height="Auto"/>
            <RowDefinition Height="Auto"/>
        </Grid.RowDefinitions>

        <StackPanel Grid.Column="0" Grid.Row="0">
            <TextBlock Margin="5" Text="Vertical linear gradient:"/>
            <Rectangle Width="100" Height="75" Stroke="Blue">
                <Rectangle.Fill>
                    <LinearGradientBrush StartPoint="0,0" EndPoint="1,0">
                        <GradientStop Color="Blue" Offset="0"/>
                        <GradientStop Color="Yellow" Offset="1"/>
                    </LinearGradientBrush>
                </Rectangle.Fill>
            </Rectangle>
        </StackPanel>

        <StackPanel Grid.Column="1" Grid.Row="0">
            <TextBlock Margin="5" Text="Horizontal linear gradient:"/>
            <Rectangle Width="100" Height="75" Stroke="Blue">
                <Rectangle.Fill>
                    <LinearGradientBrush StartPoint="0,0" EndPoint="0,1">
                        <GradientStop Color="Red" Offset="0"/>
                        <GradientStop Color="White" Offset="1"/>
                    </LinearGradientBrush>
                </Rectangle.Fill>
            </Rectangle>
        </StackPanel>

        <StackPanel Grid.Column="0" Grid.Row="1">
            <TextBlock Margin="5,10,5,0" Text="Diagonal linear gradient"/>
            <TextBlock Margin="5,0,5,5" Text="- with 1 Offset for White"/>
            <Rectangle Width="100" Height="75" Stroke="Blue">
                <Rectangle.Fill>
```

```xml
                        <LinearGradientBrush StartPoint="0,0" EndPoint="1,1">
                            <GradientStop Color="Green" Offset="0"/>
                            <GradientStop Color="White" Offset="1"/>
                        </LinearGradientBrush>
                    </Rectangle.Fill>
                </Rectangle>
            </StackPanel>

            <StackPanel Grid.Column="1" Grid.Row="1">
                <TextBlock Margin="5,10,5,0" Text="Diagonal linear gradient"/>
                <TextBlock Margin="5,0,5,5" Text="- with 0.5 Offset for White"/>
                <Rectangle Width="100" Height="75" Stroke="Blue">
                    <Rectangle.Fill>
                        <LinearGradientBrush StartPoint="0,0" EndPoint="1,1">
                            <GradientStop Color="Green" Offset="0"/>
                            <GradientStop Color="White" Offset="0.5"/>
                        </LinearGradientBrush>
                    </Rectangle.Fill>
                </Rectangle>
            </StackPanel>

            <StackPanel Grid.Column="0" Grid.Row="2">
                <TextBlock Margin="5,10,5,0" Text="Vertical linear gradient"/>
                <TextBlock Margin="5,0,5,5" Text="- multiple colors"/>
                <Rectangle Width="100" Height="75" Stroke="Blue">
                    <Rectangle.Fill>
                        <LinearGradientBrush StartPoint="0,0" EndPoint="1,0">
                            <GradientStop Color="Red" Offset="0.3"/>
                            <GradientStop Color="Yellow" Offset="0.5"/>
                            <GradientStop Color="Blue" Offset="0.8"/>
                        </LinearGradientBrush>
                    </Rectangle.Fill>
                </Rectangle>
            </StackPanel>

            <StackPanel Grid.Column="1" Grid.Row="2">
                <TextBlock Margin="5,10,5,0" Text="Diagonal linear gradient"/>
                <TextBlock Margin="5,0,5,5" Text="- multiple colors"/>
                <Rectangle Width="100" Height="75" Stroke="Blue">
                    <Rectangle.Fill>
                        <LinearGradientBrush StartPoint="0,0" EndPoint="1,1">
                            <GradientStop Color="Red" Offset="0.2"/>
                            <GradientStop Color="Yellow" Offset="0.3"/>
                            <GradientStop Color="Coral" Offset="0.4"/>
                            <GradientStop Color="Blue" Offset="0.5"/>
                            <GradientStop Color="White" Offset="0.6"/>
                            <GradientStop Color="Green" Offset="0.7"/>
                            <GradientStop Color="Purple" Offset="0.8"/>
                        </LinearGradientBrush>
                    </Rectangle.Fill>
                </Rectangle>
            </StackPanel>
        </Grid>
</Window>
```

Figure 4-5 illustrates the results of this example.

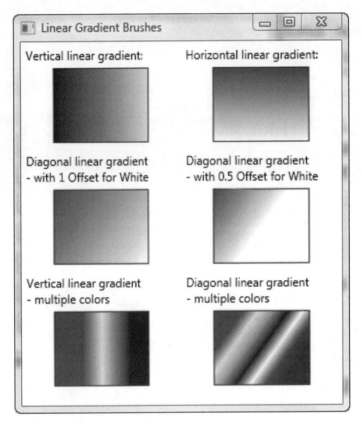

Figure 4-5. *Rectangles filled with different linear gradients*

The first rectangle is filled by a *LinearGradientBrush* with a blue and yellow gradient along a vertical axis. The second rectangle is filled by a horizontal gradient brush with red and white colors. Now look at *rect*3 and *rect*4. Both rectangles are filled by a diagonal gradient brush with green and white colors. The *GradientStop* for the green color has an offset of 0, which means that the green color is placed at the very beginning of the gradient. The *GradientStop* for the white has an offset of 1 for *rect*3, which places the white color at the end. For *rect*4, however, the *GradientStop* offset of the white color is set to 0.5, resulting in the much quicker color blend from green (in the top-left corner) to white in the middle (the point between the two corners). It can be seen from Figure 4-5 that the right side of *rect*4 is almost completely white. The last two rectangles, *rect*5 and *rect*6, are filled by a multicolor *GradientBrush*, the first along a vertical gradient axis and the second along a diagonal gradient axis.

The *LinearGradientBrush* example presented here is intended to demonstrate the use of the brush's basic features in WPF applications. In real-world applications, you may need to create a custom colormap in order to achieve specific visual effects. I'll show you how to create custom colormap brushes later in this chapter.

RadialGradientBrush

The *RadialGradientBrush* works in a similar way to the *LinearGradientBrush*. Like the *LinearGradientBrush*, it takes a sequence of colors with different offsets, but blends the colors in a radial pattern. A radial gradient is defined as a circle. The axis of *RadialGradientBrush* starts from the origin, which is specified by its *GradientOrigin*, and runs to the outer edge of the circle.

You can set the edge of the gradient circle using three properties: *Center*, *RadiusX*, and *RadiusY*. By default, the *Center* property is set at (0.5, 0.5), which places the center of the circle in the middle of the fill region and in the same position as the gradient origin.

Let's take a look at an example to see how the *RadialGradientBrush* works. Add a new WPF Window to the project *ColorsAndBrushes* and name it *RadialGradientBrushExample*. Here is the XAML file for this example:

```
<Window x:Class="ColorsAndBrushes.RadialGradientBrushExample"
    xmlns="http://schemas.microsoft.com/winfx/2006/xaml/presentation"
    xmlns:x="http://schemas.microsoft.com/winfx/2006/xaml"
    Title="Radial Gradient Brushes" Height="330" Width="380">
    <Canvas>
        <Grid>
            <Grid.ColumnDefinitions>
                <ColumnDefinition/>
                <ColumnDefinition/>
                <ColumnDefinition/>
            </Grid.ColumnDefinitions>
            <Grid.RowDefinitions>
                <RowDefinition/>
                <RowDefinition/>
            </Grid.RowDefinitions>

            <StackPanel Grid.Column="0" Grid.Row="0" Margin="5">
                <TextBlock Text="ellipse1" Margin="35,5,5,5"/>
                <Ellipse x:Name="ellipse1" Stroke="Blue" Width="100"
                        Height="100" Margin="5">
                    <Ellipse.Fill>
                        <RadialGradientBrush
                            GradientOrigin="0.5,0.5" Center="0.5,0.5"
                                RadiusX="1" RadiusY="1">
                            <GradientStop Color="Red" Offset="0" />
                            <GradientStop Color="Yellow" Offset="0.3" />
                            <GradientStop Color="Green" Offset="0.6" />
                        </RadialGradientBrush>
                    </Ellipse.Fill>
                </Ellipse>
            </StackPanel>

            <StackPanel Grid.Column="1" Grid.Row="0" Margin="5">
                <TextBlock Text="ellipse2" Margin="35,5,5,5"/>
                <Ellipse x:Name="ellipse2" Stroke="Blue" Width="100"
                        Height="100" Margin="5">
                    <Ellipse.Fill>
                        <RadialGradientBrush GradientOrigin="0.5,0.5" Center="0,0"
                                    RadiusX="1" RadiusY="1">
                            <GradientStop Color="Red" Offset="0" />
```

```xml
                        <GradientStop Color="Yellow" Offset="0.3" />
                        <GradientStop Color="Green" Offset="0.6" />
                    </RadialGradientBrush>
                </Ellipse.Fill>
            </Ellipse>
        </StackPanel>

        <StackPanel Grid.Column="2" Grid.Row="0" Margin="5">
            <TextBlock Text="ellipse3" Margin="35,5,5,5"/>
            <Ellipse x:Name="ellipse3" Stroke="Blue" Width="100"
                    Height="100" Margin="5">
                <Ellipse.Fill>
                    <RadialGradientBrush GradientOrigin="0.5,0.5"
                        Center="0.5,0.5" RadiusX="0.5" RadiusY="0.5">
                        <GradientStop Color="Red" Offset="0" />
                        <GradientStop Color="Yellow" Offset="0.3" />
                        <GradientStop Color="Green" Offset="0.6" />
                    </RadialGradientBrush>
                </Ellipse.Fill>
            </Ellipse>
        </StackPanel>

        <StackPanel Grid.Column="0" Grid.Row="1" Margin="5">
            <TextBlock Text="ellipse4" Margin="35,5,5,5"/>
            <Ellipse x:Name="ellipse4" Stroke="Blue" Width="100"
                    Height="100" Margin="5">
                <Ellipse.Fill>
                    <RadialGradientBrush GradientOrigin="0.5,0.5" Center="0,0"
                                        RadiusX="0.5" RadiusY="0.5">
                        <GradientStop Color="Red" Offset="0" />
                        <GradientStop Color="Yellow" Offset="0.3" />
                        <GradientStop Color="Green" Offset="0.6" />
                    </RadialGradientBrush>
                </Ellipse.Fill>
            </Ellipse>
        </StackPanel>

        <StackPanel Grid.Column="1" Grid.Row="1" Margin="5">
            <TextBlock Text="ellipse5" Margin="35,5,5,5"/>
            <Ellipse x:Name="ellipse5" Stroke="Blue" Width="100"
                    Height="100" Margin="5">
                <Ellipse.Fill>
                    <RadialGradientBrush GradientOrigin="0.5,0.5"
                                        Center="0.5,0.5" RadiusX="1"
                                        RadiusY="0.5">
                        <GradientStop Color="Red" Offset="0" />
                        <GradientStop Color="Yellow" Offset="0.3" />
                        <GradientStop Color="Green" Offset="0.6" />
                    </RadialGradientBrush>
                </Ellipse.Fill>
            </Ellipse>
        </StackPanel>
```

```
            <StackPanel Grid.Column="2" Grid.Row="1" Margin="5">
                <TextBlock Text="ellipse6" Margin="35,5,5,5"/>
                <Ellipse x:Name="ellipse6" Stroke="Blue" Width="100"
                        Height="100" Margin="5">
                    <Ellipse.Fill>
                        <RadialGradientBrush GradientOrigin="0.5,0.5"
                                             Center="0.5,0.5"
                                             RadiusX="0.5" RadiusY="1">
                            <GradientStop Color="Red" Offset="0" />
                            <GradientStop Color="Yellow" Offset="0.3" />
                            <GradientStop Color="Green" Offset="0.6" />
                        </RadialGradientBrush>
                    </Ellipse.Fill>
                </Ellipse>
            </StackPanel>
        </Grid>
    </Canvas>
</Window>
```

This XAML file creates six circles using the *Ellipse* shape class. The first two circles are filled using a *RadialGradientBrush* with *RadiusX* = 1 and *RadiusY* = 1. The difference is that the brush for the first circle has a *Center* at (0.5, 0.5), which is the same as its *GradientOrigin* of (0.5, 0.5), whereas the brush for the second circle has a *Center* at (0, 0), which does not line up with its *GradientOrigin* of (0.5, 0.5). *ellipse*3 and *ellipse*4 have *Fill* properties similar to the first two shapes, but they have smaller *RadiusX* and *RadiusY* values. The final two circles have *RadiusX* and *RadiusY* properties that are not identical, which turns the gradient into an ellipse instead of a circle.

Figure 4-6 illustrates the results of running this example.

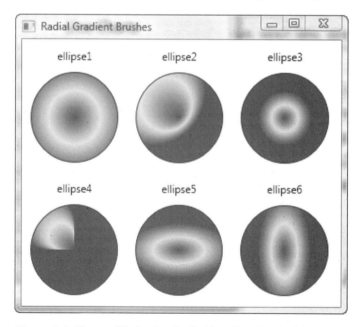

Figure 4-6. Shapes filled using RadialGradientBrush objects

DrawingBrush

DrawingBrush fills an area using a *Drawing* object. It can paint shapes, text, images, and video. The *Drawing* class represents a 2D drawing and is the base class for other drawing objects, including *GeometryDrawing*, *GlyphRunDrawing*, *ImageDrawing*, and *VideoDrawing*. The *GeometryDrawing* class allows you to define and render shapes using a specified *Fill* and *Stroke*. The *GlyphRunDrawing* class provides text operations.

The *GeometryDrawing* class adds the stroke and fill details that determine the way the geometry should be painted. There is another class that derives from *Drawing* class, the *DrawingGroup*, that allows you to group multiple *Drawing* objects together to create a single complex *Drawing* object.

The following example applies a *DrawingBrush* and *DrawingGroup* in order to draw gridlines for the background of a *Grid* control. Add a new WPF Window to the project *ColorsAndBrushes* and name it *DrawingBrushes*. Here is the XAML file for this example:

```
<Window x:Class="ColorsAndBrushes.DrawingBrushes"
    xmlns="http://schemas.microsoft.com/winfx/2006/xaml/presentation"
    xmlns:x="http://schemas.microsoft.com/winfx/2006/xaml"
    Title="Drawing Brushes - Gridline" Height="300" Width="300">
    <Grid>
        <Grid.Background>
            <DrawingBrush Viewport="0,0,50,50" ViewportUnits="Absolute"
                        TileMode="Tile">
                <DrawingBrush.Drawing>
                    <DrawingGroup>
                        <DrawingGroup.Children>
                            <GeometryDrawing Geometry="M0,0 L50,0">
                                <GeometryDrawing.Pen>
                                    <Pen Thickness="2" Brush="LightGreen"/>
                                </GeometryDrawing.Pen>
                            </GeometryDrawing>
                            <GeometryDrawing Geometry="M0,10 L50,10">
                                <GeometryDrawing.Pen>
                                    <Pen Thickness="1" Brush="LightGreen"/>
                                </GeometryDrawing.Pen>
                            </GeometryDrawing>
                            <GeometryDrawing Geometry="M0,20 L50,20">
                                <GeometryDrawing.Pen>
                                    <Pen Thickness="1" Brush="LightGreen"/>
                                </GeometryDrawing.Pen>
                            </GeometryDrawing>
                            <GeometryDrawing Geometry="M0,30 L50,30">
                                <GeometryDrawing.Pen>
                                    <Pen Thickness="1" Brush="LightGreen"/>
                                </GeometryDrawing.Pen>
                            </GeometryDrawing>
                            <GeometryDrawing Geometry="M0,40 L50,40">
                                <GeometryDrawing.Pen>
                                    <Pen Thickness="1" Brush="LightGreen"/>
                                </GeometryDrawing.Pen>
                            </GeometryDrawing>
```

```
                    <GeometryDrawing Geometry="M0,0 L0,50">
                        <GeometryDrawing.Pen>
                            <Pen Thickness="2" Brush="LightGreen"/>
                        </GeometryDrawing.Pen>
                    </GeometryDrawing>
                    <GeometryDrawing Geometry="M10,0 L10,50">
                        <GeometryDrawing.Pen>
                            <Pen Thickness="1" Brush="LightGreen"/>
                        </GeometryDrawing.Pen>
                    </GeometryDrawing>
                    <GeometryDrawing Geometry="M20,0 L20,50">
                        <GeometryDrawing.Pen>
                            <Pen Thickness="1" Brush="LightGreen"/>
                        </GeometryDrawing.Pen>
                    </GeometryDrawing>
                    <GeometryDrawing Geometry="M30,0 L30,50">
                        <GeometryDrawing.Pen>
                            <Pen Thickness="1" Brush="LightGreen"/>
                        </GeometryDrawing.Pen>
                    </GeometryDrawing>
                    <GeometryDrawing Geometry="M40,0 L40,50">
                        <GeometryDrawing.Pen>
                            <Pen Thickness="1" Brush="LightGreen"/>
                        </GeometryDrawing.Pen>
                    </GeometryDrawing>
                </DrawingGroup.Children>
            </DrawingGroup>
        </DrawingBrush.Drawing>
      </DrawingBrush>
    </Grid.Background>
  </Grid>
</Window>
```

This example uses *DrawingBrush* to define the background of a *Grid* control. The *Viewport* and *TileMode* properties of *DrawingBrush* are specified so that the drawing repeats. Furthermore, the *ViewportUnits* are set to *Absolute* to make sure that the size of the gridlines doesn't change when the *Grid* control is resized. Then the *Drawing* objects are created for the *DrawingBrush* using a *DrawingGroup* object. Next, we create five horizontal and five vertical line segments using *GeometryDrawing* with the *Pen* object. Notice that the topmost and leftmost line segments use a thick pen, which provides us with a better view of the gridlines. The *Drawing* element created using *DrawingGroup* is illustrated in Figure 4-7.

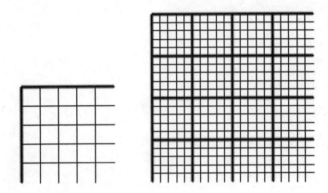

Figure 4-7. Drawing Element (left) used to create gridlines (right)

If you repeat this *Drawing* element in both the *X* and *Y* directions by specifying the *TileMode* property of *DrawingBrush*, you'll create gridlines that fill the entire *Grid* control, as shown in Figure 4.7. Figure 4-8 shows the results of running this example.

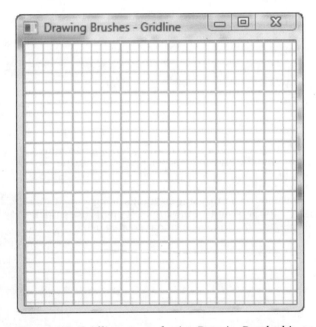

Figure 4-8. Gridlines created using DrawingBrush objects

Remember that since the drawing-derived classes aren't elements, they can't be placed directly in your user interface. Instead, in order to display a drawing object, you need to paint it using *DrawingBrush*, as illustrated in the preceding example. The *DrawingBrush* allows you to wrap a drawing with a brush, and you can use it to paint any surface. There are several other ways you can display

Drawing objects, including the *DrawingImage* and *DrawingVisual* classes. The *DrawingImage* class allows you to host a drawing inside an *Image* element; the *DrawingVisual* class lets you place a drawing in a lower-level visual object.

   DrawingBrush is very flexible and powerful. It allows you to paint many low-level objects from the WPF framework. These objects don't derive from the *UIElement* or *FrameworkElement*, so they don't participate in the layout system, which makes them conveniently lightweight.

Custom Colormap and Shading

Although WPF implements a variety of brushes that allow you to paint graphics objects with a wide range of visual effects, you may sometimes need to create your own custom brushes to meet the requirements of your specific applications, such as 3D surface charts. In this section, I'll show you how to create brushes with custom colormaps and how to achieve a special shading effect with a bilinear interpolation.

Custom Colormap Brushes

WPF includes a *ColorMap* class in the *System.Windows.Media.Imaging* namespace. This class defines a map between the existing colors and the new colors to which they are converted. When the map is applied, any pixel of the old color is converted into the new color. This class is useful for image processing applications.

   However, in some charting applications, you may need custom colormaps to achieve specific visual effects, such as in pie and 3D surface charts. These colormaps are simply tables or lists of colors that are organized in some desired fashion, which cannot be created using the *ColorMap* class. The shape, surface, and image objects can be associated with a custom colormap. You can easily create a custom colormap brush using an $m \times 4$ colormap matrix. Each row of this matrix represents an ARGB value. The row index can represent the Y data of a 2D chart or the height (the Z data) of a 3D surface graph. For a given colormap matrix with m rows, the color data values can be linearly scaled to the colormap.

   For example, if you want to use the colormap to represent the Y coordinates of a 2D graphics object, you can use the Y_{min} and Y_{max} values to transform the Y data values linearly into indices, where each index identifies an ARGB row (i.e., a color) in the colormap matrix. The mathematical transformation of the color index values is described by the following formula:

$$color\ Index = \begin{cases} 1 & y < Y_{min} \\ (int)\left[\dfrac{m(y - Y_{min})}{Y_{max} - Y_{min}}\right] & Y_{min} \leq y < Y_{max} \\ m & y \geq Y_{max} \end{cases} \quad (4.1)$$

Here y is the individual value of Y data and m is the length of the colormap matrix. This allows you to use the entire range of colors in the colormap over the plotted data. For 3D surface charts, replace the Y data with the Z data.

   In some existing CAD and software development tools, many commonly used colormaps have already been defined. Here, I'll show you how to create these colormaps in WPF applications. These colormaps will be used extensively in 3D chart applications in later chapters of this book.

   Add a new class to the project *ColorsAndBrushes* and name it *ColormapBrush*. The following is the code listing for this class:

```
using System;
using System.Collections.Generic;
using System.Windows;
using System.Windows.Media;
using System.Windows.Controls;

namespace ColorsAndBrushes
{
    public class ColormapBrush
    {
        private int colormapLength = 64;
        private byte alphaValue = 255;
        private double ymin = 0;
        private double ymax = 10;
        private int ydivisions = 10;
        private ColormapBrushEnum colormapBrushType = ColormapBrushEnum.Jet;

        public ColormapBrushEnum ColormapBrushType
        {
            get { return colormapBrushType; }
            set { colormapBrushType = value; }
        }

        public int ColormapLength
        {
            get { return colormapLength; }
            set { colormapLength = value; }
        }

        public byte AlphaValue
        {
            get { return alphaValue; }
            set { alphaValue = value; }
        }

        public double Ymin
        {
            get { return ymin; }
            set { ymin = value; }
        }

        public double Ymax
        {
            get { return ymax; }
            set { ymax = value; }
        }

        public int Ydivisions
        {
            get { return ydivisions; }
            set { ydivisions = value; }
        }
```

```
public SolidColorBrush[] ColormapBrushes()
{
    byte[,] cmap = new byte[ColormapLength, 4];
    double[] array = new double[ColormapLength];

    switch (ColormapBrushType)
    {
        case ColormapBrushEnum.Spring:
            for (int i = 0; i < ColormapLength; i++)
            {
                array[i] = 1.0 * i / (ColormapLength - 1);
                cmap[i, 0] = AlphaValue;
                cmap[i, 1] = 255;
                cmap[i, 2] = (byte)(255 * array[i]);
                cmap[i, 3] = (byte)(255 - cmap[i, 2]);
            }
            break;

        case ColormapBrushEnum.Summer:
            for (int i = 0; i < ColormapLength; i++)
            {
                array[i] = 1.0 * i / (ColormapLength - 1);
                cmap[i, 0] = AlphaValue;
                cmap[i, 1] = (byte)(255 * array[i]);
                cmap[i, 2] = (byte)(255 * 0.5 * (1 + array[i]));
                cmap[i, 3] = (byte)(255 * 0.4);
            }
            break;

        case ColormapBrushEnum.Autumn:
            for (int i = 0; i < ColormapLength; i++)
            {
                array[i] = 1.0 * i / (ColormapLength - 1);
                cmap[i, 0] = AlphaValue;
                cmap[i, 1] = 255;
                cmap[i, 2] = (byte)(255 * array[i]);
                cmap[i, 3] = 0;
            }
            break;

        case ColormapBrushEnum.Winter:
            for (int i = 0; i < ColormapLength; i++)
            {
                array[i] = 1.0 * i / (ColormapLength - 1);
                cmap[i, 0] = AlphaValue;
                cmap[i, 1] = 0;
                cmap[i, 2] = (byte)(255 * array[i]);
                cmap[i, 3] = (byte)(255 * (1.0 - 0.5 * array[i]));
            }
            break;

        case ColormapBrushEnum.Gray:
            for (int i = 0; i < ColormapLength; i++)
```

```
        {
            array[i] = 1.0 * i / (ColormapLength - 1);
            cmap[i, 0] = AlphaValue;
            cmap[i, 1] = (byte)(255 * array[i]);
            cmap[i, 2] = (byte)(255 * array[i]);
            cmap[i, 3] = (byte)(255 * array[i]);
        }
        break;

    case ColormapBrushEnum.Jet:
        int n = (int)Math.Ceiling(ColormapLength / 4.0);
        double[,] cMatrix = new double[ColormapLength, 3];
        int nMod = 0;
        double[] array1 = new double[3 * n - 1];
        int[] red = new int[array1.Length];
        int[] green = new int[array1.Length];
        int[] blue = new int[array1.Length];

        if (ColormapLength % 4 == 1)
            nMod = 1;

        for (int i = 0; i < array1.Length; i++)
        {
            if (i < n)
                array1[i] = (i + 1.0) / n;
            else if (i >= n && i < 2 * n - 1)
                array1[i] = 1.0;
            else if (i >= 2 * n - 1)
                array1[i] = (3.0 * n - 1.0 - i) / n;
            green[i] = (int)Math.Ceiling(n / 2.0) - nMod + i;
            red[i] = green[i] + n;
            blue[i] = green[i] - n;
        }

        int nb = 0;
        for (int i = 0; i < blue.Length; i++)
        {
            if (blue[i] > 0)
                nb++;
        }

        for (int i = 0; i < ColormapLength; i++)
        {
            for (int j = 0; j < red.Length; j++)
            {
                if (i == red[j] && red[j] < ColormapLength)
                    cMatrix[i, 0] = array1[i - red[0]];
            }
            for (int j = 0; j < green.Length; j++)
            {
                if (i == green[j] && green[j] < ColormapLength)
                    cMatrix[i, 1] = array1[i - green[0]];
            }
```

```
        for (int j = 0; j < blue.Length; j++)
        {
            if (i == blue[j] && blue[j] >= 0)
                cMatrix[i, 2] = array1[array1.Length - 1 - nb + i];
        }
    }

    for (int i = 0; i < ColormapLength; i++)
    {
        cmap[i, 0] = AlphaValue;
        for (int j = 0; j < 3; j++)
            cmap[i, j + 1] = (byte)(cMatrix[i, j] * 255);
    }
    break;

case ColormapBrushEnum.Hot:
    int n1 = (int)3 * ColormapLength / 8;
    double[] red1 = new double[ColormapLength];
    double[] green1 = new double[ColormapLength];
    double[] blue1 = new double[ColormapLength];
    for (int i = 0; i < ColormapLength; i++)
    {
        if (i < n1)
            red1[i] = 1.0 * (i + 1.0) / n1;
        else
            red1[i] = 1.0;
        if (i < n1)
            green1[i] = 0.0;
        else if (i >= n1 && i < 2 * n1)
            green1[i] = 1.0 * (i + 1 - n1) / n1;
        else
            green1[i] = 1.0;
        if (i < 2 * n1)
            blue1[i] = 0.0;
        else
            blue1[i] = 1.0 * (i + 1 - 2 * n1) /
                      (ColormapLength - 2 * n1);

        cmap[i, 0] = AlphaValue;
        cmap[i, 1] = (byte)(255 * red1[i]);
        cmap[i, 2] = (byte)(255 * green1[i]);
        cmap[i, 3] = (byte)(255 * blue1[i]);
    }
    break;

case ColormapBrushEnum.Cool:
    for (int i = 0; i < ColormapLength; i++)
    {
        array[i] = 1.0 * i / (ColormapLength - 1);
        cmap[i, 0] = AlphaValue;
        cmap[i, 1] = (byte)(255 * array[i]);
        cmap[i, 2] = (byte)(255 * (1 - array[i]));
        cmap[i, 3] = 255;
    }
```

```
                }
                break;
        }
        return SetBrush(cmap);
    }


    public enum ColormapBrushEnum
    {
        Spring = 0,
        Summer = 1,
        Autumn = 2,
        Winter = 3,
        Gray = 4,
        Jet = 5,
        Hot = 6,
        Cool = 7
    }

    private SolidColorBrush[] SetBrush(byte[,] cmap)
    {
        SolidColorBrush[] brushes = new SolidColorBrush[Ydivisions];
        double dy = (Ymax - Ymin) / (Ydivisions - 1);
        for (int i = 0; i < Ydivisions; i++)
        {
            int colorIndex =
                (int)((ColormapLength - 1) * i * dy / (Ymax - Ymin));
            brushes[i] = new SolidColorBrush(Color.FromArgb(
                            cmap[colorIndex, 0],
                            cmap[colorIndex, 1],
                            cmap[colorIndex, 2],
                            cmap[colorIndex, 3]));
        }
        return brushes;
    }

    public SolidColorBrush GetBrush(double y)
    {
        SolidColorBrush brush = new SolidColorBrush();
        double dy = (Ymax - Ymin) / (Ydivisions - 1);
        for (int i = 0; i < ColormapBrushes().Length; i++)
        {
            double y1 = Ymin + i * dy;
            if (y >= y1 && y < y1 + dy)
                brush = ColormapBrushes()[i];
        }
        return brush;
    }
    }
}
```

This class defines *a ColormapBrush* object, which is actually a *SolidColorBrush* array. Each *SolidColorBrush* element in the array represents a different color specified by the corresponding elements of an $m \times 4$ colormap matrix and is associated with a *Y* data value according to Equation (4.1), which is implemented in the *SetBrushes* method. Thus, a *ColormapBrush* allows you to use the entire range of colors in the colormap matrix over the plotted data. For 3D surface charts, replace the *Y* data with the *Z* data.

This class contains several public properties, including the *ColormapLength*, *AlphaValue*, *Y* data range, and number of *Y* data points. The *ColormapLength* property specifies how many individual colors a *ColormapBrush* object contains, and the *AlphaValue* property represents the color opacity.

The *ColormapBrushEnum* in the class allows you to select one of eight predefined *ColormapBrush* objects by their names: *Spring, Summer, Autumn, Winter, Gray, Jet, Hot,* and *Cool.* These names are commonly used in graphics and chart applications.

This class also implements a *GetBrush* method, which returns a *SolidColorBrush* element in the *ColormapBrush* object for a given *Y* data value. This method is especially useful in chart and graphics shading applications.

Testing Colormap Brushes

Here, I'll show you how to use the *ColormapBrush* class in your applications. Add a new WPF Window to the project *ColorsAndBrushes* and name it *CustomColormapBrushes*. Here is the XAML file for this example:

```
<Window x:Class="ColorsAndBrushes.CustomColormapBrushes"
    xmlns="http://schemas.microsoft.com/winfx/2006/xaml/presentation"
    xmlns:x="http://schemas.microsoft.com/winfx/2006/xaml"
    Title="Custom Colormap Brushes" Width="365" Height="300">
    <Grid  Margin="0" x:Name ="chartGrid" ClipToBounds="False"
            Background="Transparent" SizeChanged="chartGrid_SizeChanged">
        <Canvas Margin="10" Name="chartCanvas" ClipToBounds="False"
                Background="#66CCCCCC"/>
    </Grid>
</Window>
```

This XAML creates a resizable canvas element. The *ColormapBrush* objects used to fill the rectangles will be implemented in the following code-behind file:

```
using System;
using System.Windows;
using System.Windows.Controls;
using System.Windows.Media;
using System.Windows.Media.Imaging;
using System.Windows.Shapes;

namespace ColorsAndBrushes
{
    public partial class CustomColormapBrushes : Window
    {
        public CustomColormapBrushes()
        {
            InitializeComponent();
        }
```

```
    private void chartGrid_SizeChanged(object sender, SizeChangedEventArgs e)
    {
        chartCanvas.Width = chartGrid.ActualWidth -20 ;
        chartCanvas.Height = chartGrid.ActualHeight - 20;
        chartCanvas.Children.Clear();
        AddColormap();
    }

    private void AddColormap()
    {
        DrawColorbar(ColormapBrush.ColormapBrushEnum.Spring, 0);
        DrawColorbar(ColormapBrush.ColormapBrushEnum.Summer, 1);
        DrawColorbar(ColormapBrush.ColormapBrushEnum.Autumn, 2);
        DrawColorbar(ColormapBrush.ColormapBrushEnum.Winter, 3);
        DrawColorbar(ColormapBrush.ColormapBrushEnum.Gray, 4);
        DrawColorbar(ColormapBrush.ColormapBrushEnum.Jet, 5);
        DrawColorbar(ColormapBrush.ColormapBrushEnum.Hot, 6);
        DrawColorbar(ColormapBrush.ColormapBrushEnum.Cool, 7);
    }

    private void DrawColorbar(ColormapBrush.ColormapBrushEnum brushType,
                             double offset)
    {
        double width = 30.0;
        double height = 20.0;
        ColormapBrush cb = new ColormapBrush();
        cb.Ydivisions = 10;
        cb.ColormapBrushType = brushType;
        SolidColorBrush[] brush = cb.ColormapBrushes();
        Rectangle rect;

        for (int i = 0; i < 10; i++)
        {
            rect = new Rectangle();
            rect.Width = width;
            rect.Height = height;
            Canvas.SetTop(rect, 10 + i * 23);
            Canvas.SetLeft(rect, 10 + 40 * offset);
            rect.Fill = brush[i];
            chartCanvas.Children.Add(rect);
        }
    }
}
}
```

Inside the *DrawColorbar* method, we divide each color bar into 10 rectangles. Each rectangle is filled with a *SolidColorBrush* element that belongs to a specified *ColormapBrush* object. In this example we use the default values for the *ColormapLength, AlphaValue,* and *Y* data range properties.

The *AddColormap* method creates eight different color bars, each painted with a different *ColormapBrush* object.

Running this example produces the output displayed in Figure 4-9.

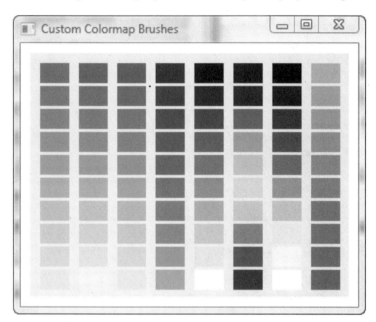

Figure 4-9. *Color map created using custom ColormapBrush objects*

Color Shading

In the previous sections, we drew color bars by associating each Y data value with a SolidColorBrush element of the ColormapBrush object. In some graphics applications, you may want to map the color of a surface object directly according to a given set of color data. Consider a situation involving a *ColormapBrush* object with the name *Jet*, as defined in the *ColormapBrush* class.

Suppose we have a 3 × 3 color data matrix

$$Color\ Data = \begin{pmatrix} 3 & 0 & 4 \\ -2 & 3 & 1 \\ -1 & 2 & -3 \end{pmatrix}$$

In this case, the maximum and minimum of the color data are 4 and –3, respectively. Using Equation (4.1), we can easily determine the color map numbers to be

$$Color\ Index = \begin{pmatrix} 54 & 27 & 63 \\ 9 & 54 & 36 \\ 18 & 45 & 0 \end{pmatrix}$$

Here the default value of *ColormapLength* (= 64) is used. Up to this point, we have not supplied the *X* coordinate and *Y* coordinate data. We have assumed that the color data values along the row (*x* data) and the column (*y* data) specify nine vertices where each neighboring set of four elements is connected by means of a quadrilateral. As shown in Figure 4-10, in terms of the elements within the color data matrix, there are four quadrilaterals. You may wonder why we need nine indices in the colormap when there are only four quadrilaterals. With surface objects, each vertex can be assigned a color. This allows you to perform a bilinear interpolation among four vertex colors to determine the color at any point within the quadrilateral.

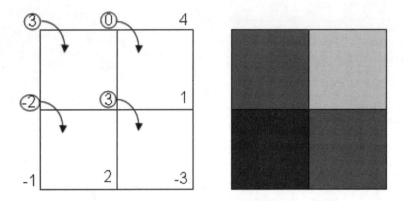

Figure 4-10. Color matrix and colormap. The top-left vertex color data (circled elements on the left) are used to fill the corresponding quadrilaterals, leading to the result shown on the right.

If you do not want to use color interpolation, the color data can also be represented by a 2 × 2 matrix, as shown by the circled elements in Figure 4-10. In this case, you can use the top-left vertex color data to fill the corresponding quadrilateral. By combining this with the color indices, you can obtain the direct color map for these four quadrilaterals, as shown in the figure.

You can see from Figure 4-10 that the color changes very abruptly from one quadrilateral to another. To obtain a smoother color-shading effect, you need to perform a bilinear color interpolation. Bilinear interpolation uses four vertex values surrounding each quadrilateral to obtain any value inside the quadrilateral. Suppose you want to get the value at (x, y) and that the vertices of the quadrilateral are located at (x_0, y_0), (x_1, y_0), (x_0, y_1), and (x_1, y_1), which have the color data values C_{00}, C_{10}, C_{01}, and C_{11}, respectively, as shown in Figure 4-11.

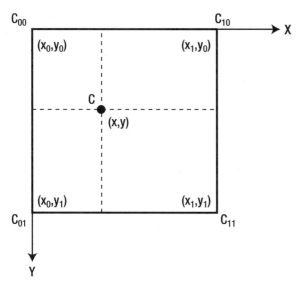

Figure 4-11. Coordinates used for bilinear interpolation

Linear interpolation on the top row of neighbors, between (x_0, y_0) and (x_1, y_0), estimates the value C_0 at (x, y_0) as

$$C_0 = \frac{x_1 - x}{x_1 - x_0} C_{00} + \frac{x - x_0}{x_1 - x_0} C_{10}$$

(4.2)

Likewise, linear interpolation on the bottom row of neighbors, between (x_0, y_1) and (x_1, y_1), estimates the value C_1 at (x, y_1) as

$$C_1 = \frac{x_1 - x}{x_1 - x_0} C_{01} + \frac{x - x_0}{x_1 - x_0} C_{11}$$

(4.3)

Finally, linear interpolation between C_0 and C_1 estimates the value C at (x, y) as

$$C = \frac{y_1 - y}{y_1 - y_0} C_0 + \frac{y - y_0}{y_1 - y_0} C_1$$

(4.4)

By substituting the expressions for C_0 in Equation (4.2) and C_1 in Equation (4.3) into Equation (4.4), we obtain

$$C = \frac{y_1 - y}{y_1 - y_0} \left(\frac{x_1 - x}{x_1 - x_0} C_{00} + \frac{x - x_0}{x_1 - x_0} C_{10} \right) + \frac{y - y_0}{y_1 - y_0} \left(\frac{x_1 - x}{x_1 - x_0} C_{01} + \frac{x - x_0}{x_1 - x_0} C_{11} \right)$$

(4.5)

You can see that the equation for C is a polynomial involving powers of x and y no greater than 1, with four coefficients: $C = a_1 + a_2 *x + a_3 *y + a_4 *x*y$. Because these four coefficients are determined by four values (C_{00}, C_{01}, C_{10}, and C_{11}), they are usually uniquely determined by the data. This immediately implies that the comparable procedure of first interpolating along the columns (in the *Y* direction) and then interpolating the results in the *X* direction will give the same result, because it, too, will have a similar formula with a unique solution.

Note that the term *bilinear* derives from the process of linear interpolation (twice in one direction, then once in the perpendicular direction), *not* from the formula for *C*. The formula involves a term with $x * y$, which is not linear.

We can easily implement this bilinear interpolation in WPF. Add a new class, *BilinearInterpolation*, to the project *ColorsAndBrushes*. Here is the code listing for this class:

```
using System;
using System.Windows;
using System.Windows.Media;
using System.Windows.Controls;
using System.Collections.Generic;
using System.Windows.Shapes;

namespace ColorsAndBrushes
{
    class BilinearInterpolation
    {
        public double Cmin { get; set; }
        public double Cmax { get; set; }
        public int Cdivisions { get; set; }
        public int NInterps { get; set; }
        public Canvas ChartCanvas { get; set; }

        private double BilinearCoeff(double x, double y, double X0, double Y0,
                            double X1, double Y1, double C00, double C10,
                            double C01, double C11)
        {
            return (Y1 - y) * ((X1 - x) * C00 +
                   (x - X0) * C10) / (X1 - X0) / (Y1 - Y0) +
                   (y - Y0) * ((X1 - x) * C01 +
                   (x - X0) * C11) / (X1 - X0) / (Y1 - Y0);
        }

        public void SetInterpShading(double X0, double Y0, double X1, double Y1,
                            double C00, double C10, double C01, double C11)
        {
            ColormapBrush cb = new ColormapBrush();
            cb.ColormapBrushType = ColormapBrush.ColormapBrushEnum.Jet;
            cb.Ymin = Cmin;
            cb.Ymax = Cmax;
            cb.Ydivisions = Cdivisions;
            double dx = (X1 - X0) / NInterps;
            double dy = (Y1 - Y0) / NInterps;

            for (int i = 0; i < NInterps; i++)
            {
                double x = X0 + i * dx;
                for (int j = 0; j < NInterps; j++)
                {
                    double y = Y0 + j * dy;
                    double C =
```

```
                    BilinearCoeff(x, y, X0, Y0, X1, Y1, C00, C10, C01, C11);
                Polygon plg = new Polygon();
                plg.Points.Add(new Point(x, y));
                plg.Points.Add(new Point(x, y + dy));
                plg.Points.Add(new Point(x + dx, y + dy));
                plg.Points.Add(new Point(x + dx, y));
                plg.Fill = cb.GetBrush(C);
                ChartCanvas.Children.Add(plg);
            }
        }
    }

    public void SetOriginalShading(double C, double X0, double Y0,
                                   double X1, double Y1)
    {
        ColormapBrush cb = new ColormapBrush();
        cb.ColormapBrushType = ColormapBrush.ColormapBrushEnum.Jet;
        Polygon plg = new Polygon();
        cb.Ymin = Cmin;
        cb.Ymax = Cmax;
        cb.Ydivisions = Cdivisions;
        double dx = X1 - X0;
        double dy = Y1 - Y0;
        plg.Points.Add(new Point(X0, Y0));
        plg.Points.Add(new Point(X0, Y0 + dy));
        plg.Points.Add(new Point(X0 + dx, Y0 + dy));
        plg.Points.Add(new Point(X0 + dx, Y0));
        plg.Fill = cb.GetBrush(C);
        ChartCanvas.Children.Add(plg);
    }
}
}
```

This class first defines several public properties using the new C# automatic property feature. The properties *Cmin*, *Cmax*, and *Cdivisions* are equivalent to the properties *Ymin*, *Ymax*, and *Ydivisions* defined in the *ColormapBrush* class. The property *NInterps* represents how many interpolation points you'll need in each direction, and the *ChartCanvas* property provides a host canvas in which you can draw the quadrilateral with interpolated color shading.

The *BilinearCoeff* method calculates the color data value at a given point (x, y) in the quadrilateral. The *SetInterpShading* method allows you to create color shading for a quadrilateral using bilinear interpolation, and the *SetOriginalShading* method can be used to create color shading without interpolation.

Testing Color Shading

Here, I'll show you how to create color shading using the *BilinearInterpolation* class implemented in the previous section. Add a new WPF Window to the project *ColorsAndBrushes* and name it *CustomColorShading*. Here is the XAML file for this example:

```
<Window x:Class="ColorsAndBrushes.CustomColorShading"
    xmlns="http://schemas.microsoft.com/winfx/2006/xaml/presentation"
    xmlns:x="http://schemas.microsoft.com/winfx/2006/xaml"
    Title="CustomColorShading" Height="180" Width="300">
```

```
    <Canvas x:Name="chartCanvas" Width="290" Height="140"
            Background="Transparent"/>
</Window>
```

This markup is very simple and includes only a Canvas element. Here is the code-behind file for this example:

```
using System;
using System.Windows;
using System.Windows.Controls;
using System.Windows.Media;
using System.Windows.Media.Imaging;
using System.Windows.Shapes;

namespace ColorsAndBrushes
{
    public partial class CustomColorShading : Window
    {
        public CustomColorShading()
        {
            InitializeComponent();
            AddShading();
        }

        public void AddShading()
        {
            chartCanvas.Children.Clear();
            double width = chartCanvas.Width / 2 - 20;
            double height = chartCanvas.Height - 20;

            BilinearInterpolation bi = new BilinearInterpolation();
            bi.Cdivisions = 32;
            bi.NInterps = 30;
            bi.Cmin = -3;
            bi.Cmax = 4;
            bi.ChartCanvas = chartCanvas;

            // Original color map:
            double x0 = 10;
            double y0 = 10;
            bi.SetOriginalShading(3, x0, y0, x0+width/2, y0+height/2);

            x0 = 10 + width / 2;
            bi.SetOriginalShading(0, x0, y0, x0+width/2, y0+height/2);

            x0 = 10;
            y0 = 10 + height / 2;
            bi.SetOriginalShading(-2, x0, y0, x0 + width / 2, y0 + height / 2);

            x0 = 10 + width / 2;
            y0 = 10 + height / 2;
            bi.SetOriginalShading(3, x0, y0, x0 + width / 2, y0 + height / 2);

            // Bilinear interpolation:
```

```
        x0 = 20 + width;
        y0 = 10;
        bi.SetInterpShading(x0, y0, x0 + width / 2,
                            y0 + height / 2, 3, 0, -2, 3);

        x0 = x0 + width / 2;
        bi.SetInterpShading(x0, y0, x0 + width / 2,
                            y0 + height / 2, 0, 4, 3, 1);

        x0 = 20 + width;
        y0 = 10 + height / 2;
        bi.SetInterpShading(x0, y0, x0 + width / 2,
                            y0 + height / 2, -2, 3, -1, 2);

        x0 = x0 + width / 2;
        y0 = 10 + height / 2;
        bi.SetInterpShading(x0, y0, x0 + width / 2,
                            y0 + height / 2, 3, 1, 2, -3);
        }
    }
}
```

In this example, we want to create color shading using the color data listed in Figure 4-10. For comparison, we will first create an example of color shading without bilinear interpolation, in which each quadrilateral is filled with a *SolidColorBrush* corresponding to the color data value at the top-left corner. We will then create an example of interpolated color shading using the *BilinearInterpolation* class.

Running this example generates the result shown in Figure 4-12. Notice that for very fine color shading (large *NInterps*), the program runs very slowly. Thus, you have a trade-off between color shading quality and performance speed. The bilinearly interpolated colormap has found wide applications in image processing and 3D surface chart applications.

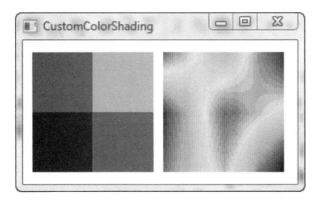

Figure 4-12. Direct colormap (left) and interpolated colormap (right)

CHAPTER 5

■ ■ ■

2D Line charts

In the previous chapters, we discussed graphics basics, matrix transformations in 2D space, and color and brush systems in WPF. This chapter will show you how to apply the knowledge and approaches from previous chapters to create real-world chart applications. We'll discuss the common charting elements and how to implement them in a simple 2D *X-Y* line plot.

Simple Line Charts

The most basic and useful type of chart you can create with WPF is a simple 2D line chart of numerical data. WPF provides a set of commands and methods you can use to create these charts. Even the most elementary 2D chart consists of several basic elements, including lines, symbols, axes, tick marks, labels, a title, and a legend. The following list quickly overviews the most basic chart elements without getting into detail. These elements will often be referred to in this chapter.

- Axes – a graphics object that defines a region of the chart in which the chart is drawn.

- Line – a graphics object that represents the data you have plotted.

- Text – a graphics object comprising a string of characters.

- Title – the text string object located directly above an axis object.

- Label – the text string object associated with the axis object (*X* or *Y* axis).

- Legend – the text string array object that represents the color and values of the lines.

The *X-Y* line chart uses two values to represent each data point. This type of chart is very useful for describing relationships between data and is often involved in the statistical analysis of data, with wide applications in the scientific, mathematics, engineering, and finance communities as well as in daily life.

Creating Simple Line Charts

It is easy to create a 2D *X-Y* line chart in WPF. Let's use an example to illustrate the procedure. Start with a new WPF Windows project and name it *LineCharts*. Add a new WPF Window to the project and name it *SimpleLineChart*. We'll create the user interface and layout using XAML and perform the computations and generate the data in code. The XAML file for this example is very simple:

```
<Window x:Class="LineCharts.SimpleLineChart"
    xmlns="http://schemas.microsoft.com/winfx/2006/xaml/presentation"
    xmlns:x="http://schemas.microsoft.com/winfx/2006/xaml"
    Title="Simple Line Chart" Height="300" Width="300">
    <Grid  Margin="0" x:Name ="chartGrid" ClipToBounds="True"
            Background="Transparent" SizeChanged="chartGrid_SizeChanged">
        <Border HorizontalAlignment="Center" VerticalAlignment="Center"
                BorderBrush="Gray" BorderThickness="1"
                Background="White" Margin="0">
            <Canvas  Margin="0" x:Name ="chartCanvas" ClipToBounds="True"
                    Background="Transparent"/>
        </Border>
    </Grid>
</Window>
```

Here we implement a resizable *Canvas* element, *chartCanvas*, on which we want to create the simple line chart. Here is the corresponding code-behind file, which creates the line chart, for this example:

```
using System;
using System.Collections.Generic;
using System.Windows;
using System.Windows.Controls;
using System.Windows.Input;
using System.Windows.Media;
using System.Windows.Shapes;

namespace LineCharts
{
    public partial class SimpleLineChart : System.Windows.Window
    {
        private double xmin = 0;
        private double xmax = 6.5;
        private double ymin = -1.1;
        private double ymax = 1.1;
        private Polyline pl;

        public SimpleLineChart()
        {
            InitializeComponent();
        }

        private void AddChart()
        {
            // Draw sine curve:
            pl = new Polyline();
            pl.Stroke = Brushes.Black;
            for (int i = 0; i < 70; i++)
            {
                double x = i/5.0;
                double y = Math.Sin(x);
                pl.Points.Add(NormalizePoint(new Point(x, y)));
            }
            chartCanvas.Children.Add(pl);
```

```
        // Draw cosine curve:
        pl = new Polyline();
        pl.Stroke = Brushes.Black;
        pl.StrokeDashArray = new DoubleCollection(new double[] { 4, 3 });

        for (int i = 0; i < 70; i++)
        {
            double x = i / 5.0;
            double y = Math.Cos(x);
            pl.Points.Add(NormalizePoint(new Point(x, y)));
        }
        chartCanvas.Children.Add(pl);
    }

    private Point NormalizePoint(Point pt)
    {
        Point result = new Point();
        result.X = (pt.X - xmin) * chartCanvas.Width / (xmax - xmin);
        result.Y = chartCanvas.Height -
                   (pt.Y - ymin) * chartCanvas.Height / (ymax - ymin);
        return result;
    }

    private void chartGrid_SizeChanged(object sender, SizeChangedEventArgs e)
    {
        chartCanvas.Width = chartGrid.ActualWidth;
        chartCanvas.Height = chartGrid.ActualHeight;
        chartCanvas.Children.Clear();
        AddChart();
    }
}
}
```

Figure 5-1 shows the result of running this example.

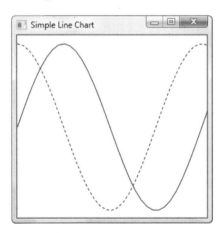

Figure 5-1. *2D chart for Sine and Cosine functions*

How It Works

Note that the axis limits *xmin*, *xmax*, *ymin*, and *ymax* are defined in the real-world coordinate system. The sine and cosine functions are represented using *Polyline* objects that are added to the *chartCanvas*'s children collection.

A key step in creating this line chart is to transform the original data points in the world coordinate system into points in the units of device-independent pixels using the *NormalizePoint* method. The *NormalizePoint* method converts points of any unit in the world coordinate system into points with a unit of device-independent pixel in the device coordinate system.

Another point I'd like to make here is that we defined the chart area as a resizable *Canvas* control, *chartCanvas*, which occupies the entire area of the application window. In some cases, you may want the chart to occupy only a portion of the application window; in other situations, you may want to move the chart to a particular position in the window. This can be achieved by redefining the *Width* and *Height* properties of the *chartCanvas* without touching the rest of the code. For example, replace the following code in the preceding example:

```
chartCanvas.Width = chartGrid.ActualWidth;
chartCanvas.Height = chartGrid.ActualHeight;
```

with the following code snippet:

```
chartCanvas.Width = chartGrid.ActualWidth / 2;
chartCanvas.Height = chartGrid.ActualHeight / 2;
```

In this case, the chart area is reduced compared to the application window. In addition, if you combine the resizable canvas with another *Grid* control, you can also place your chart anywhere you like.

Line Charts with Data Collection

The preceding example demonstrated how easy it is to create a simple 2D line chart in WPF, but it didn't pay much attention to the program structure. In order for the chart program to be more object-oriented and to extend easily to add new features, you need to define three new classes: *ChartStyle*, *DataCollection*, and *DataSeries*. The *ChartStyle* class defines all chart layout–related information. The *DataCollection* class holds the *DataSeries* objects, each of which represents one curve on the chart. The *DataSeries* class holds the chart data and line styles, including the line color, thickness, dash style, etc.

Chart Style

Now add a public class, *ChartStyle*, to the project *LineCharts*. The following is the code listing for this class:

```
using System;
using System.Windows.Controls;
using System.Windows;

namespace LineCharts
{
    public class ChartStyle
    {
        private Canvas chartCanvas;
        private double xmin = 0;
        private double xmax = 10;
```

```
    private double ymin = 0;
    private double ymax = 10;

    public Canvas ChartCanvas
    {
        get { return chartCanvas; }
        set { chartCanvas = value; }
    }

    public double Xmin
    {
        get { return xmin; }
        set { xmin = value; }
    }

    public double Xmax
    {
        get { return xmax; }
        set { xmax = value; }
    }

    public double Ymin
    {
        get { return ymin; }
        set { ymin = value; }
    }

    public double Ymax
    {
        get { return ymax; }
        set { ymax = value; }
    }

    public Point NormalizePoint(Point pt)
    {
        if (ChartCanvas.Width.ToString() == "NaN")
            ChartCanvas.Width = 270;
        if (ChartCanvas.Height.ToString() == "NaN")
            ChartCanvas.Height = 250;
        Point result = new Point();
        result.X = (pt.X - Xmin) * ChartCanvas.Width / (Xmax - Xmin);
        result.Y = ChartCanvas.Height -
                    (pt.Y - Ymin) * ChartCanvas.Height / (Ymax - Ymin);
        return result;
    }
}
}
```

In this class, we first define a public property *ChartCanvas*, which is needed to specify the chart area. In addition, the *NormalizePoint* method requires the *Width* and *Height* of this *ChartCanvas* to obtain the point conversion from the real-world coordinate system to device-independent pixels. We then create member fields and corresponding public properties for the axis limits. You can override the default values of these properties according to your application requirements.

Data Series

Now add the *DataSeries* class to the current project. The following is the code listing for this class:

```
using System;
using System.Windows;
using System.Windows.Media;
using System.Windows.Shapes;

namespace LineCharts
{
    public class DataSeries
    {
        private Polyline lineSeries = new Polyline();
        private Brush lineColor;
        private double lineThickness = 1;
        private LinePatternEnum linePattern;
        private string seriesName = "Default Name";
        private Symbols symbols;

        public DataSeries()
        {
            LineColor = Brushes.Black;
            symbols = new Symbols();
        }

        /*public Symbols Symbols
        {
            get { return symbols; }
            set { symbols = value; }
        }*/

        public Brush LineColor
        {
            get { return lineColor; }
            set { lineColor = value; }
        }

        public Polyline LineSeries
        {
            get { return lineSeries; }
            set { lineSeries = value; }
        }

        public double LineThickness
        {
            get { return lineThickness; }
            set { lineThickness = value; }
        }

        public LinePatternEnum LinePattern
        {
            get { return linePattern; }
```

```
            set { linePattern = value; }
        }

        public string SeriesName
        {
            get { return seriesName; }
            set { seriesName = value; }
        }

        public void AddLinePattern()
        {
            LineSeries.Stroke = LineColor;
            LineSeries.StrokeThickness = LineThickness;

            switch (LinePattern)
            {
                case LinePatternEnum.Dash:
                    LineSeries.StrokeDashArray =
                        new DoubleCollection(new double[2] { 4, 3 });
                    break;
                case LinePatternEnum.Dot:
                    LineSeries.StrokeDashArray =
                        new DoubleCollection(new double[2] { 1, 2 });
                    break;
                case LinePatternEnum.DashDot:
                    LineSeries.StrokeDashArray =
                        new DoubleCollection(new double[4] { 4, 2, 1, 2 });
                    break;
                case LinePatternEnum.None:
                    LineSeries.Stroke = Brushes.Transparent;
                    break;
            }
        }

        public enum LinePatternEnum
        {
            Solid = 1,
            Dash = 2,
            Dot = 3,
            DashDot = 4,
            None = 5
        }
    }
}
```

This class creates a *Polyline* object for a given *DataSeries*. It then defines the line style for the line object, including the line color, thickness, line pattern, and series name. The *SeriesName* property will be used in creating the legend for the chart. The line pattern is defined by a public enumeration called *LinePatternEnum*, in which five line patterns are defined, including *Solid* (default), *Dash*, *Dot*, *DashDot*, and *None*. The *None* enumeration member means there will be no line drawn on the chart canvas.

You create the line pattern via the *AddLinePattern* method. There is no need to create the solid line pattern because it is the default setting of the *Polyline* object. You create the dashed or dotted line patterns using the *StrokeDashArray* property of the *Polyline*. You define the invisible line (corresponding to the *None* type of line pattern) by setting the stroke's color to transparent.

Data Collection

Finally, we need to add another public class, *DataCollection*, to the current project. The following is the code listing for this class:

```
using System;
using System.Collections.Generic;
using System.Windows.Controls;
using System.Windows.Media;
using System.Windows.Shapes;

namespace LineCharts
{
    public class DataCollection
    {
        private List<DataSeries> dataList;

        public DataCollection()
        {
            dataList = new List<DataSeries>();
        }

        public List<DataSeries> DataList
        {
            get { return dataList; }
            set { dataList = value; }
        }

        public void AddLines(ChartStyle cs)
        {
            int j = 0;
            foreach (DataSeries ds in DataList)
            {
                if (ds.SeriesName == "Default Name")
                {
                    ds.SeriesName = "DataSeries" + j.ToString();
                }
                ds.AddLinePattern();
                for (int i = 0; i < ds.LineSeries.Points.Count; i++)
                {
                    ds.LineSeries.Points[i] =
                        cs.NormalizePoint(ds.LineSeries.Points[i]);
                }
                cs.ChartCanvas.Children.Add(ds.LineSeries);
                j++;
            }
        }
    }
}
```

This class holds the *DataSeries* objects. We begin with a member field *DataSeries* list and its corresponding public property, *DataList*. The *DataList* property holds the *DataSeries*. We then implement an *AddLines* method, which draws lines using the *DataSeries* objects in the *DataCollection* class. For each *DataSeries*, a line is added to the chart canvas using the specified line style for that *DataSeries*. Notice how all data points from the world coordinate system are transformed to the device coordinate system using the *NormalizePoint* method defined in the *ChartStyle* class.

Creating Line Charts

Now you can create line charts using the *ChartStyle*, *DataCollection*, and *DataSeries* classes. Again I'll present an example to illustrate how to create a line chart using these classes. Let's add a new WPF Window, named *LineChartExample*, to the project *LineCharts*. The layout of this example is created via the following XAML file:

```
<Window x:Class="LineCharts.LineChartExample"
    xmlns="http://schemas.microsoft.com/winfx/2006/xaml/presentation"
    xmlns:x="http://schemas.microsoft.com/winfx/2006/xaml"
    Title="Line Chart Example" Height="300" Width="300">
    <Grid  x:Name ="chartGrid" ClipToBounds="False" Background="Transparent"
            SizeChanged="chartGrid_SizeChanged" >
        <Border HorizontalAlignment="Center" VerticalAlignment="Center"
                BorderBrush="Gray" BorderThickness="1" Background="White"
                Margin="10" >
            <Canvas  Margin="0" x:Name ="chartCanvas" ClipToBounds="True"
                    Background="Transparent"/>
        </Border>
    </Grid>
</Window>
```

This markup defines a resizable *Canvas* named *chartCanvas*, which you will use to hold the line chart. Here is the corresponding code-behind file for this example:

```
using System;
using System.Windows;
using System.Collections.Generic;
using System.Windows.Controls;
using System.Windows.Media;
using System.Windows.Media.Imaging;
using System.Windows.Shapes;

namespace LineCharts
{
    public partial class LineChartExample : Window
    {
        private ChartStyle cs;
        private DataCollection dc;
        private DataSeries ds;

        public LineChartExample()
        {
            InitializeComponent();
        }
```

```
private void AddChart()
{
    cs = new ChartStyle();
    cs.ChartCanvas = chartCanvas;
    dc = new DataCollection();
    cs.Xmin = 0;
    cs.Xmax = 7;
    cs.Ymin = -1.1;
    cs.Ymax = 1.1;

    // Draw Sine curve:
    ds = new DataSeries();
    ds.LineColor = Brushes.Blue;
    ds.LineThickness = 2;
    for (int i = 0; i < 50; i++)
    {
        double x = i / 5.0;
        double y = Math.Sin(x);
        ds.LineSeries.Points.Add(new Point(x, y));
    }
    dc.DataList.Add(ds);

    // Draw cosine curve:
    ds = new DataSeries();
    ds.LineColor = Brushes.Red;
    ds.LinePattern = DataSeries.LinePatternEnum.DashDot;
    ds.LineThickness = 2;

    for (int i = 0; i < 50; i++)
    {
        double x = i / 5.0;
        double y = Math.Cos(x);
        ds.LineSeries.Points.Add(new Point(x, y));
    }
    dc.DataList.Add(ds);
    dc.AddLines(cs);
}

private void chartGrid_SizeChanged(object sender, SizeChangedEventArgs e)
{
    chartCanvas.Width = chartGrid.ActualWidth - 20;
    chartCanvas.Height = chartGrid.ActualHeight - 20;
    chartCanvas.Children.Clear();
    AddChart();
}
        }
    }
}
```

In this code-behind file, you begin by defining instances for the *ChartStyle*, *DataCollection*, and *DataSeries* classes. Inside the *AddChart* method, you override the axis limit properties that were originally defined in the *ChartStyle* class to meet the requirements of your current application.

Pay attention to how the *DataSeries* objects are added to the *DataCollection* class:

```
// Draw Sine curve:
ds = new DataSeries();
ds.LineColor = Brushes.Blue;
ds.LineThickness = 2;
for (int i = 0; i < 50; i++)
{
    double x = i / 5.0;
    double y = Math.Sin(x);
    ds.LineSeries.Points.Add(new Point(x, y));
}
dc.DataList.Add(ds);
```

Here you first create a new *DataSeries* object and define its line style, including the line color and thickness. Notice here that you didn't specify the line pattern, so the default line pattern, *Solid*, is used. You then add the data points to the *ds.LineSeries* object's point collection. Finally, you add the data series "*ds*" to the *DataCollection* using the *dc.DataList.Add* method. This way, you can add any number of *DataSeries* objects to the *DataCollection*. Finally, the *AddLines* method in the *DataCollection* class draws curves on the chart for all the *DataSeries* objects contained in the *DataCollection*.

Figure 5-2 shows the results of running this example.

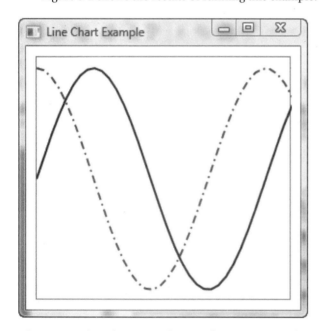

Figure 5-2. Chart for sine and cosine functions created using the DataCollection class

Gridlines and Labels

In the previous sections, only the lines for the sine and cosine functions were drawn on the chart. In this section, you will add more features to the 2D line chart, including gridlines, a title, tick marks, and labels for axes.

Chart Style with Gridlines

Here, we'll implement the gridlines and labels in a new class, *ChartStyleGridlines*. This new class can derive from the original *ChartStyle* class used in previous sections. Here is the code listing for this class:

```
using System;
using System.Windows.Controls;
using System.Windows;
using System.Windows.Media;
using System.Windows.Shapes;

namespace LineCharts
{
    public class ChartStyleGridlines : ChartStyle
    {
        private string title;
        private string xLabel;
        private string yLabel;
        private Canvas textCanvas;
        private bool isXGrid = true;
        private bool isYGrid = true;
        private Brush gridlineColor = Brushes.LightGray;
        private double xTick = 1;
        private double yTick = 0.5;
        private GridlinePatternEnum gridlinePattern;
        private double leftOffset = 20;
        private double bottomOffset = 15;
        private double rightOffset = 10;
        private Line gridline = new Line();

        public ChartStyleGridlines()
        {
            title = "Title";
            xLabel = "X Axis";
            yLabel = "Y Axis";
        }

        public string Title
        {
            get { return title; }
            set { title = value; }
        }

        public string XLabel
        {
            get { return xLabel; }
```

```csharp
        set { xLabel = value; }
    }

    public string YLabel
    {
        get { return yLabel; }
        set { yLabel = value; }
    }

    public GridlinePatternEnum GridlinePattern
    {
        get { return gridlinePattern; }
        set { gridlinePattern = value; }
    }

    public double XTick
    {
        get { return xTick; }
        set { xTick = value; }
    }

    public double YTick
    {
        get { return yTick; }
        set { yTick = value; }
    }

    public Brush GridlineColor
    {
        get { return gridlineColor; }
        set { gridlineColor = value; }
    }

    public Canvas TextCanvas
    {
        get { return textCanvas; }
        set { textCanvas = value; }
    }

    public bool IsXGrid
    {
        get { return isXGrid; }
        set { isXGrid = value; }
    }

    public bool IsYGrid
    {
        get { return isYGrid; }
        set { isYGrid = value; }
    }

    public void AddChartStyle(TextBlock tbTitle, TextBlock tbXLabel,
                              TextBlock tbYLabel)
```

```
        {
            Point pt = new Point();
            Line tick = new Line();
            double offset = 0;
            double dx, dy;
            TextBlock tb = new TextBlock();

            //  determine right offset:
            tb.Text = Xmax.ToString();
            tb.Measure(new Size(Double.PositiveInfinity, Double.PositiveInfinity));
            Size size = tb.DesiredSize;
            rightOffset = size.Width / 2 + 2;

            // Determine left offset:
            for (dy = Ymin; dy <= Ymax; dy += YTick)
            {
                pt = NormalizePoint(new Point(Xmin, dy));
                tb = new TextBlock();
                tb.Text = dy.ToString();
                tb.TextAlignment = TextAlignment.Right;
                tb.Measure(new Size(Double.PositiveInfinity,
                                    Double.PositiveInfinity));
                size = tb.DesiredSize;
                if (offset < size.Width)
                    offset = size.Width;
            }
            leftOffset = offset + 5;

            Canvas.SetLeft(ChartCanvas, leftOffset);
            Canvas.SetBottom(ChartCanvas, bottomOffset);
            ChartCanvas.Width = Math.Abs(TextCanvas.Width -
                            leftOffset - rightOffset);
            ChartCanvas.Height = Math.Abs(TextCanvas.Height -
                             bottomOffset - size.Height / 2);
            Rectangle chartRect = new Rectangle();
            chartRect.Stroke = Brushes.Black;
            chartRect.Width = ChartCanvas.Width;
            chartRect.Height = ChartCanvas.Height;
            ChartCanvas.Children.Add(chartRect);

            // Create vertical gridlines:
            if (IsYGrid == true)
            {
                for (dx = Xmin + XTick; dx < Xmax; dx += XTick)
                {
                    gridline = new Line();
                    AddLinePattern();
                    gridline.X1 = NormalizePoint(new Point(dx, Ymin)).X;
                    gridline.Y1 = NormalizePoint(new Point(dx, Ymin)).Y;
                    gridline.X2 = NormalizePoint(new Point(dx, Ymax)).X;
                    gridline.Y2 = NormalizePoint(new Point(dx, Ymax)).Y;
                    ChartCanvas.Children.Add(gridline);
                }
```

```
    }

    // Create horizontal gridlines:
    if (IsXGrid == true)
    {
        for (dy = Ymin + YTick; dy < Ymax; dy += YTick)
        {
            gridline = new Line();
            AddLinePattern();
            gridline.X1 = NormalizePoint(new Point(Xmin, dy)).X;
            gridline.Y1 = NormalizePoint(new Point(Xmin, dy)).Y;
            gridline.X2 = NormalizePoint(new Point(Xmax, dy)).X;
            gridline.Y2 = NormalizePoint(new Point(Xmax, dy)).Y;
            ChartCanvas.Children.Add(gridline);
        }
    }

    // Create x-axis tick marks:
    for (dx = Xmin; dx <= Xmax; dx += xTick)
    {
        pt = NormalizePoint(new Point(dx, Ymin));
        tick = new Line();
        tick.Stroke = Brushes.Black;
        tick.X1 = pt.X;
        tick.Y1 = pt.Y;
        tick.X2 = pt.X;
        tick.Y2 = pt.Y - 5;
        ChartCanvas.Children.Add(tick);

        tb = new TextBlock();
        tb.Text = dx.ToString();
        tb.Measure(new Size(Double.PositiveInfinity,
                            Double.PositiveInfinity));
        size = tb.DesiredSize;
        TextCanvas.Children.Add(tb);
        Canvas.SetLeft(tb, leftOffset + pt.X - size.Width / 2);
        Canvas.SetTop(tb, pt.Y + 2 + size.Height / 2);
    }

    // Create y-axis tick marks:
    for (dy = Ymin; dy <= Ymax; dy += YTick)
    {
        pt = NormalizePoint(new Point(Xmin, dy));
        tick = new Line();
        tick.Stroke = Brushes.Black;
        tick.X1 = pt.X;
        tick.Y1 = pt.Y;
        tick.X2 = pt.X + 5;
        tick.Y2 = pt.Y;
        ChartCanvas.Children.Add(tick);

        tb = new TextBlock();
        tb.Text = dy.ToString();
```

```
            tb.Measure(new Size(Double.PositiveInfinity,
                              Double.PositiveInfinity));
            size = tb.DesiredSize;
            TextCanvas.Children.Add(tb);
            Canvas.SetRight(tb, ChartCanvas.Width + 10);
            Canvas.SetTop(tb, pt.Y);
        }

        // Add title and labels:
        tbTitle.Text = Title;
        tbXLabel.Text = XLabel;
        tbYLabel.Text = YLabel;
        tbXLabel.Margin = new Thickness(leftOffset + 2, 2, 2, 2);
        tbTitle.Margin = new Thickness(leftOffset + 2, 2, 2, 2);
    }

    public void AddLinePattern()
    {
        gridline.Stroke = GridlineColor;
        gridline.StrokeThickness = 1;

        switch (GridlinePattern)
        {
            case GridlinePatternEnum.Dash:
                gridline.StrokeDashArray =
                        new DoubleCollection(new double[2] { 4, 3 });
                break;
            case GridlinePatternEnum.Dot:
                gridline.StrokeDashArray =
                        new DoubleCollection(new double[2] { 1, 2 });
                break;
            case GridlinePatternEnum.DashDot:
                gridline.StrokeDashArray =
                        new DoubleCollection(new double[4] { 4, 2, 1, 2 });
                break;
        }
    }

    public enum GridlinePatternEnum
    {
        Solid = 1,
        Dash = 2,
        Dot = 3,
        DashDot = 4
    }
    }
}
```

In this class, we add more member fields and corresponding properties, which you use to manipulate the chart's layout and appearance. You can easily understand the meaning of each field and property from its name. Notice that we add another *Canvas* property, *TextCanvas*, which you use to hold the tick mark labels, while the *ChartCanvas* in the original *ChartStyle* class holds the chart itself.

In addition, we add the following member fields to define the gridlines for your chart:

```
private bool isXGrid = true;
private bool isYGrid = true;
private Brush gridlineColor = Brushes.LightGray;
private GridlinePatternEnum gridlinePattern;
```

These fields and their corresponding properties provide a great deal of flexibility in customizing the appearance of the gridlines. The *GridlinePattern* property allows you to choose various line dash styles, including solid, dash, dot, and dash-dot. You can change the gridlines' color using the *GridlineColor* property. In addition, we define two *bool* properties, *IsXGrid* and *IsYGrid*, which allow you to turn horizontal or vertical gridlines on or off.

We then define member fields and corresponding properties for the *X* and *Y* labels, title, and tick marks so that we can change them to our liking. If you like, you can easily add more member fields to control the appearance of your charts; for example, you can change the font and text color of the labels and title.

The *AddChartStyle* method seems quite complicated in this class; however, it is actually reasonably easy to follow. First, we define the size of the *ChartCanvas* by considering the suitable offset relative to the *TextCanvas*. Next, we draw gridlines with a specified color and line pattern. Please note that all of the end points of the gridlines have been transformed from the world coordinate system to device-independent pixels using the *NormalizePoint* method.

We then draw the tick marks for the *X* and *Y* axes of the chart. For each tick mark, we find the points in the device coordinate system at which the tick mark joins the axes and draw a black line, 5 pixels long, from this point toward the inside of the *ChartCanvas*.

The title and labels for the *X* and *Y* axes are attached to the corresponding *TextBlock* names in code. We can also create data bindings that bind the *Title*, *XLabel*, and *YLabel* properties to the corresponding *TextBlock* directly in the XAML file.

Creating a Chart with Gridlines

Here, we'll create the chart layout using XAML and put the title and the labels for the *X* and *Y* axes into different cells of a *Grid* control. Add a new WPF Window to the project *LineCharts* and name it *LineChartWithGridlines*. The following is the XAML file for this example:

```
<Window x:Class="LineCharts.LineChartWithGridlines"
    xmlns="http://schemas.microsoft.com/winfx/2006/xaml/presentation"
    xmlns:x="http://schemas.microsoft.com/winfx/2006/xaml"
    Title="Line Chart with Gridlines and Labels" Height="400" Width="400">

    <Grid Name="grid1" Margin="10">
        <Grid.ColumnDefinitions>
            <ColumnDefinition Width="Auto"/>
            <ColumnDefinition Name="column1" Width="*"/>
        </Grid.ColumnDefinitions>
        <Grid.RowDefinitions>
            <RowDefinition Height="Auto"/>
            <RowDefinition Name="row1" Height="*"/>
            <RowDefinition Height="Auto"/>
        </Grid.RowDefinitions>
        <TextBlock Margin="2" x:Name="tbTitle" Grid.Column="1" Grid.Row="0"
                    RenderTransformOrigin="0.5,0.5" FontSize="14" FontWeight="Bold"
                    HorizontalAlignment="Stretch" VerticalAlignment="Stretch"
                    TextAlignment="Center" Text="Title"/>
```

```
        <TextBlock Margin="2" x:Name="tbXLabel" Grid.Column="1" Grid.Row="2"
                   RenderTransformOrigin="0.5,0.5" TextAlignment="Center"
                   Text="X Axis"/>

        <TextBlock Margin="2" Name="tbYLabel" Grid.Column="0" Grid.Row="1"
                   RenderTransformOrigin="0.5,0.5" TextAlignment="Center"
                   Text="Y Axis">
            <TextBlock.LayoutTransform>
                <RotateTransform Angle="-90"/>
            </TextBlock.LayoutTransform>
        </TextBlock>

        <Grid  Margin="0,0,0,0" x:Name ="chartGrid" Grid.Column="1" Grid.Row="1"
               ClipToBounds="False" Background="Transparent"
               SizeChanged="chartGrid_SizeChanged" >
        </Grid>
        <Canvas Margin="2" Name="textCanvas" Grid.Column="1" Grid.Row="1"
                ClipToBounds="True">
            <Canvas Name="chartCanvas" ClipToBounds="True"/>
        </Canvas>
    </Grid>
</Window>
```

Here, we create two canvas controls, *textCanvas* and *chartCanvas*. The *textCanvas* becomes a resizable *Canvas* control when its size combines with the *SizeChanged* property of the *Grid* control named *chartGrid*. We use the *textCanvas* control, as a parent of the *chartCanvas*, to hold the tick mark labels; the *chartCanvas* control will hold the chart itself. We can also use the *DataCollection* and *DataSeries* classes from the previous example. We use the *ChartStyleGridlines* class, inherited from the *ChartStyle* class, to create gridlines, labels, and tick marks.

Open the code-behind file of *LineChartWithGridlines* and add the following code to it:

```
using System;
using System.Windows;
using System.Windows.Controls;
using System.Windows.Media;
using System.Windows.Shapes;

namespace LineCharts
{
    public partial class LineChartWithGridlines : Window
    {
        private ChartStyleGridlines cs;
        private DataCollection dc;
        private DataSeries ds;

        public LineChartWithGridlines()
        {
            InitializeComponent();
        }

        private void AddChart()
        {
            cs = new ChartStyleGridlines();
            dc = new DataCollection();
```

```
        ds = new DataSeries();

        cs.ChartCanvas = chartCanvas;
        cs.TextCanvas = textCanvas;
        cs.Title = "Sine and Cosine Chart";
        cs.Xmin = 0;
        cs.Xmax = 7;
        cs.Ymin = -1.5;
        cs.Ymax = 1.5;
        cs.YTick = 0.5;
        cs.GridlinePattern = ChartStyleGridlines.GridlinePatternEnum.Dot;
        cs.GridlineColor = Brushes.Black;
        cs.AddChartStyle(tbTitle,tbXLabel,tbYLabel);

        // Draw Sine curve:
        ds.LineColor = Brushes.Blue;
        ds.LineThickness = 2;
        for (int i = 0; i < 50; i++)
        {
            double x = i / 5.0;
            double y = Math.Sin(x);
            ds.LineSeries.Points.Add(new Point(x, y));
        }
        dc.DataList.Add(ds);

        // Draw cosine curve:
        ds = new DataSeries();
        ds.LineColor = Brushes.Red;
        ds.LinePattern = DataSeries.LinePatternEnum.DashDot;
        ds.LineThickness = 2;

        for (int i = 0; i < 50; i++)
        {
            double x = i / 5.0;
            double y = Math.Cos(x);
            ds.LineSeries.Points.Add(new Point(x, y));
        }
        dc.DataList.Add(ds);
        dc.AddLines(cs);
    }

    private void chartGrid_SizeChanged(object sender, SizeChangedEventArgs e)
    {
        textCanvas.Width = chartGrid.ActualWidth;
        textCanvas.Height = chartGrid.ActualHeight;
        chartCanvas.Children.Clear();
        textCanvas.Children.RemoveRange(1, textCanvas.Children.Count - 1);
        AddChart();
    }
  }
}
```

This code is similar to the code used in the previous example, except that we now specify the gridlines' properties. Here we set the *TextCanvas* and *ChartCanvas* properties of the *ChartStyleGridlines* object using the *textCanvas* and *chartCanvas* defined in XAML:

```
cs.ChartCanvas = chartCanvas;
cs.TextCanvas = textCanvas;
```

We also pass the text blocks *tbTitle*, *tbXLabel*, and *tbYLabel* to the *AddChartStyle* method using the following code snippet:

```
cs.AddChartStyle(tbTitle,tbXLabel,tbYLabel);
```

Pay attention to the *chartGrid_SizeChanged* event handler:

```
private void chartGrid_SizeChanged(object sender, SizeChangedEventArgs e)
{
    textCanvas.Width = chartGrid.ActualWidth;
    textCanvas.Height = chartGrid.ActualHeight;
    chartCanvas.Children.Clear();
    textCanvas.Children.RemoveRange(1, textCanvas.Children.Count - 1);
    AddChart();
}
```

Here we make the *textCanvas* into a resizable *Canvas* control by specifying its *Width* and *Height* properties using the *chartGrid*'s *ActualWidth* and *ActualHeight* properties. In order to redraw the chart when the application window is resized, we need to remove all of the children elements of the *textCanvas* but the *chartCanvas* element, which is achieved by means of the bolded code statement in the foregoing event handler.

The rest of the code is similar to the code used in the previous example. Figure 5-3 illustrates the results of running this application. You can see that the chart has a title, labels, gridlines, and tick marks. Obviously, there is still no chart legend. I'll show you how to add a legend in the next section.

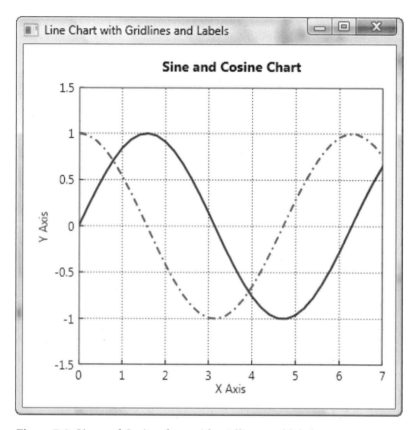

Figure 5-3. *Sine and Cosine chart with gridlines and labels*

Legends

For a 2D line chart with multiple curves, you may want to use a legend to identify each curve plotted on your chart. The legend will show a sample of the curve type, marker symbol, color, and text label you specify.

Legend Class

Add a new *Legend* class to the project *LineCharts*. The following is its code listing:

```
using System;
using System.Windows.Controls;
using System.Windows;
using System.Windows.Media;
using System.Windows.Shapes;
```

```
namespace LineCharts
{
    public class Legend
    {
        private bool isLegend;
        private bool isBorder;
        private Canvas legendCanvas;
        private LegendPositionEnum legendPosition;

        public Legend()
        {
            isLegend = false;
            isBorder = true;
            legendPosition = LegendPositionEnum.NorthEast;
        }

        public LegendPositionEnum LegendPosition
        {
            get { return legendPosition; }
            set { legendPosition = value; }
        }

        public Canvas LegendCanvas
        {
            get { return legendCanvas; }
            set { legendCanvas = value; }
        }

        public bool IsLegend
        {
            get { return isLegend; }
            set { isLegend = value; }
        }

        public bool IsBorder
        {
            get { return isBorder; }
            set { isBorder = value; }
        }

        public enum LegendPositionEnum
        {
            North,
            NorthWest,
            West,
            SouthWest,
            South,
            SouthEast,
            East,
            NorthEast
        }
```

```
public void AddLegend(Canvas canvas, DataCollection dc)
{
    TextBlock tb = new TextBlock();
    if (dc.DataList.Count < 1 || !IsLegend)
        return;
    int n = 0;
    string[] legendLabels = new string[dc.DataList.Count];
    foreach (DataSeries ds in dc.DataList)
    {
        legendLabels[n] = ds.SeriesName;
        n++;
    }

    double legendWidth = 0;
    Size size = new Size(0, 0);
    for (int i = 0; i < legendLabels.Length; i++)
    {
        tb = new TextBlock();
        tb.Text = legendLabels[i];
        tb.Measure(new Size(Double.PositiveInfinity,
                            Double.PositiveInfinity));
        size = tb.DesiredSize;
        if (legendWidth < size.Width)
            legendWidth = size.Width;
    }

    legendWidth += 50;
    legendCanvas.Width = legendWidth + 5;
    double legendHeight = 17 * dc.DataList.Count;
    double sx = 6;
    double sy = 0;
    double textHeight = size.Height;
    double lineLength = 34;
    Rectangle legendRect = new Rectangle();
    legendRect.Stroke = Brushes.Black;
    legendRect.Fill = Brushes.White;
    legendRect.Width = legendWidth;
    legendRect.Height = legendHeight;

    if (IsLegend && IsBorder)
        LegendCanvas.Children.Add(legendRect);
    Canvas.SetZIndex(LegendCanvas, 10);

    n = 1;
    foreach (DataSeries ds in dc.DataList)
    {
        double xSymbol = sx + lineLength / 2;
        double xText = 2 * sx + lineLength;
        double yText = n * sy + (2 * n - 1) * textHeight / 2;
        Line line = new Line();
        AddLinePattern(line, ds);
        line.X1 = sx;
        line.Y1 = yText;
```

```
        line.X2 = sx + lineLength;
        line.Y2 = yText;
        LegendCanvas.Children.Add(line);
        ds.Symbols.AddSymbol(legendCanvas,
                    new Point(0.5 * (line.X2 - line.X1 +
                            ds.Symbols.SymbolSize) + 1, line.Y1));
        tb = new TextBlock();
        tb.Text = ds.SeriesName;
        LegendCanvas.Children.Add(tb);
        Canvas.SetTop(tb, yText - size.Height / 2);
        Canvas.SetLeft(tb, xText);
        n++;
    }
    legendCanvas.Width = legendRect.Width;
    legendCanvas.Height = legendRect.Height;

    double offSet = 7.0;
    switch (LegendPosition)
    {
        case LegendPositionEnum.East:
            Canvas.SetRight(legendCanvas, offSet);
            Canvas.SetTop(legendCanvas,
                    canvas.Height / 2 - legendRect.Height / 2);
            break;
        case LegendPositionEnum.NorthEast:
            Canvas.SetTop(legendCanvas, offSet);
            Canvas.SetRight(legendCanvas, offSet);
            break;
        case LegendPositionEnum.North:
            Canvas.SetTop(legendCanvas, offSet);
            Canvas.SetLeft(legendCanvas,
                    canvas.Width / 2 - legendRect.Width / 2);
            break;
        case LegendPositionEnum.NorthWest:
            Canvas.SetTop(legendCanvas, offSet);
            Canvas.SetLeft(legendCanvas, offSet);
            break;
        case LegendPositionEnum.West:
            Canvas.SetTop(legendCanvas,
                    canvas.Height / 2 - legendRect.Height / 2);
            Canvas.SetLeft(legendCanvas, offSet);
            break;
        case LegendPositionEnum.SouthWest:
            Canvas.SetBottom(legendCanvas, offSet);
            Canvas.SetLeft(legendCanvas, offSet);
            break;
        case LegendPositionEnum.South:
            Canvas.SetBottom(legendCanvas, offSet);
            Canvas.SetLeft(legendCanvas,
                canvas.Width / 2 - legendRect.Width / 2);
            break;
        case LegendPositionEnum.SouthEast:
            Canvas.SetBottom(legendCanvas, offSet);
```

```
                Canvas.SetRight(legendCanvas, offSet);
                break;
        }
    }

    private void AddLinePattern(Line line, DataSeries ds)
    {
        line.Stroke = ds.LineColor;
        line.StrokeThickness = ds.LineThickness;

        switch (ds.LinePattern)
        {
            case DataSeries.LinePatternEnum.Dash:
                line.StrokeDashArray =
                    new DoubleCollection(new double[2] { 4, 3 });
                break;
            case DataSeries.LinePatternEnum.Dot:
                line.StrokeDashArray =
                    new DoubleCollection(new double[2] { 1, 2 });
                break;
            case DataSeries.LinePatternEnum.DashDot:
                line.StrokeDashArray =
                    new DoubleCollection(new double[4] { 4, 2, 1, 2 });
                break;
            case DataSeries.LinePatternEnum.None:
                line.Stroke = Brushes.Transparent;
                break;
        }
    }
  }
}
```

At first glance, this class looks quite complicated. However, if you read through it carefully, you'll actually find it quite easy to follow what is happening. It begins with the following member fields, which describe the legend behavior:

```
private bool isLegend;
private bool isBorder;
private Canvas legendCanvas;
private LegendPositionEnum legendPosition;
```

The *isLegend* allows you to turn the legend on or off. The default setting for this field is false. Therefore, you'll need to change this default value to true if you want to display the legend on your chart. The *isBorder* field allows you to add a border to the legend. You use the *legendCanvas* to hold the legend and the *LegendPosition* to control the location of the legend in your chart. You can add more member fields if you want more control over the legend. For example, you can add corresponding field members and properties for changing the legend's text color, font, background color, etc. Here, I simply want to show you the basic steps of creating a legend, without adding these extra features.

Note that the *Legend* class uses the *DataSeries* class that contains the *Symbols*, which we will implement in the next section.

In this class, we use the legend layout shown in Figure 5-4. The placement of the legend in the chart is controlled by the *LegendPosition* property, which you specify in the enumeration *LegendPositionEnum*. You have eight positions from which to choose: *North, South, West, East, NorthWest, NorthEast, SouthWest,* and *SouthEast*. The default setting is *NorthEast*, corresponding to the upper-right corner of the chart.

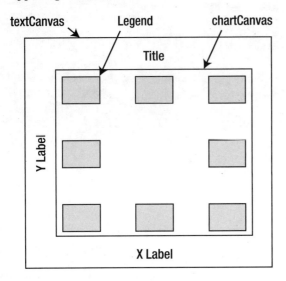

Figure 5-4. Legend layout on the chart

You can also add more positions to the *LegendPositionEnum*. For example, you may add positions such as the right side or the bottom of the chart. Next, we implement the properties for all of these member fields using the *get* and *set* statements.

Finally, we use the *AddLegend* method to create the legend. It defines the contents of a single legend, including the line type, marker symbol, color, and text label. It is also responsible for placing the legend in the suitable position through a *switch* statement by setting the position of the *legendCanvas*.

Creating a Chart with a Legend

Here, we'll use an example to demonstrate how to create a line chart with a legend. Add a new WPF Window to the project *LineCharts* and name it *LineChartWithLegend*. The following is the XAML file for this example:

```
<Window x:Class="LineCharts.LineChartWithLegend"
    xmlns="http://schemas.microsoft.com/winfx/2006/xaml/presentation"
    xmlns:x="http://schemas.microsoft.com/winfx/2006/xaml"
    Title="Line Chart with Legend" Height="400" Width="500">

    <Grid Name="grid1" Margin="10">
        <Grid.ColumnDefinitions>
            <ColumnDefinition Width="Auto"/>
            <ColumnDefinition Name="column1" Width="*"/>
        </Grid.ColumnDefinitions>
```

```
    <Grid.RowDefinitions>
        <RowDefinition Height="Auto"/>
        <RowDefinition Name="row1" Height="*"/>
        <RowDefinition Height="Auto"/>
    </Grid.RowDefinitions>
    <TextBlock Margin="2" x:Name="tbTitle" Grid.Column="1" Grid.Row="0"
            RenderTransformOrigin="0.5,0.5" FontSize="14"
            FontWeight="Bold" HorizontalAlignment="Stretch"
            VerticalAlignment="Stretch" TextAlignment="Center"
            Text="Title"/>

    <TextBlock Margin="2" x:Name="tbXLabel" Grid.Column="1" Grid.Row="2"
            RenderTransformOrigin="0.5,0.5" TextAlignment="Center"
            Text="X Axis"/>

    <TextBlock Margin="2" Name="tbYLabel" Grid.Column="0" Grid.Row="1"
            RenderTransformOrigin="0.5,0.5" TextAlignment="Center"
            Text="Y Axis">
        <TextBlock.LayoutTransform>
            <RotateTransform Angle="-90"/>
        </TextBlock.LayoutTransform>
    </TextBlock>

    <Grid  Margin="0" x:Name ="chartGrid" Grid.Column="1" Grid.Row="1"
                    ClipToBounds="True" Background="Transparent"
                    SizeChanged="chartGrid_SizeChanged" />
    <Canvas Margin="2" Name="textCanvas" ClipToBounds="True"
            Grid.Column="1" Grid.Row="1">
        <Canvas Name="chartCanvas" ClipToBounds="True">
            <Canvas Name="legendCanvas" Background="Transparent" />
        </Canvas>
    </Canvas>
    </Grid>
</Window>
```

This markup is basically similar to that used in the previous example. Here we create two canvas controls, *textCanvas* and *chartCanvas*. The *textCanvas* becomes a resizable *Canvas* control when its size combines with the *SizeChanged* property of the Grid control, named *chartGrid*. The *textCanvas* control, as a parent of the *chartCanvas*, will hold the tick mark labels, and the *chartCanvas* control will hold the chart itself.

Open the code-behind file of the *LineChartWithLegend* and add the following code to it:

```
using System;
using System.Windows;
using System.Windows.Controls;
using System.Windows.Media;
using System.Windows.Shapes;

namespace LineCharts
{
    public partial class LineChartWithLegend : Window
    {
        private ChartStyleGridlines cs;
        private Legend lg;
```

```
private DataCollection dc;
private DataSeries ds;

public LineChartWithLegend()
{
    InitializeComponent();
    AddChart();
}

private void AddChart()
{
    cs = new ChartStyleGridlines();
    lg = new Legend();
    dc = new DataCollection();
    ds = new DataSeries();

    cs.ChartCanvas = chartCanvas;
    cs.TextCanvas = textCanvas;
    cs.Title = "Sine and Cosine Chart";
    cs.Xmin = 0;
    cs.Xmax = 7;
    cs.Ymin = -1.5;
    cs.Ymax = 1.5;
    cs.YTick = 0.5;
    cs.GridlinePattern = ChartStyleGridlines.GridlinePatternEnum.Dot;
    cs.GridlineColor = Brushes.Black;
    cs.AddChartStyle(tbTitle, tbXLabel, tbYLabel);

    // Draw Sine curve:
    ds.LineColor = Brushes.Blue;
    ds.LineThickness = 1;
    ds.SeriesName = "Sine";
    for (int i = 0; i < 70; i++)
    {
        double x = i / 5.0;
        double y = Math.Sin(x);
        ds.LineSeries.Points.Add(new Point(x, y));
    }
    dc.DataList.Add(ds);

    // Draw cosine curve:
    ds = new DataSeries();
    ds.LineColor = Brushes.Red;
    ds.SeriesName = "Cosine";
    ds.LinePattern = DataSeries.LinePatternEnum.DashDot;
    ds.LineThickness = 2;
    for (int i = 0; i < 70; i++)
    {
        double x = i / 5.0;
        double y = Math.Cos(x);
        ds.LineSeries.Points.Add(new Point(x, y));
    }
    dc.DataList.Add(ds);
```

190

```
            // Draw sine^2 curve:
            ds = new DataSeries();
            ds.LineColor = Brushes.DarkGreen;
            ds.SeriesName = "Sine^2";
            ds.LinePattern = DataSeries.LinePatternEnum.Dot;
            ds.LineThickness = 2;
            for (int i = 0; i < 70; i++)
            {
                double x = i / 5.0;
                double y = Math.Sin(x) * Math.Sin(x);
                ds.LineSeries.Points.Add(new Point(x, y));
            }
            dc.DataList.Add(ds);

            dc.AddLines(cs);

            lg.LegendCanvas = legendCanvas;
            lg.IsLegend = true;
            lg.IsBorder = true;
            lg.LegendPosition = Legend.LegendPositionEnum.NorthWest;
            lg.AddLegend(cs.ChartCanvas, dc);
        }

        private void chartGrid_SizeChanged(object sender, SizeChangedEventArgs e)
        {
            textCanvas.Width = chartGrid.ActualWidth;
            textCanvas.Height = chartGrid.ActualHeight;
            legendCanvas.Children.Clear();
            chartCanvas.Children.RemoveRange(1, chartCanvas.Children.Count - 1);
            textCanvas.Children.RemoveRange(1, textCanvas.Children.Count - 1);
            AddChart();
        }
    }
}
```

This code-behind file also looks similar to that of the previous example. The bolded code is specifically required in order to add the legend. Here, you add one more curve to the chart for demonstration purposes. Notice that you need to specify the *SeriesName* property for each *DataSeries* because the legend uses the *SeriesName* as the legend labels. Otherwise, the legend will use the default *SeriesName* (*DataSeries0, DataSeries1, DataSeries2*, etc.) as the legend labels.

In order to have the legend appear on your chart, you need to call the *AddLegend* method. First, add a new member field to this class:

```
private Legend lg = new Legend();
```

Then set the *Legend*'s *IsLegend* property to true. Please note that you must place the *AddLegend* method after the *AddLines* method of the *DataCollection* object because the legend needs to know how many curves are on your chart.

Figure 5-5 shows the results of running this example.

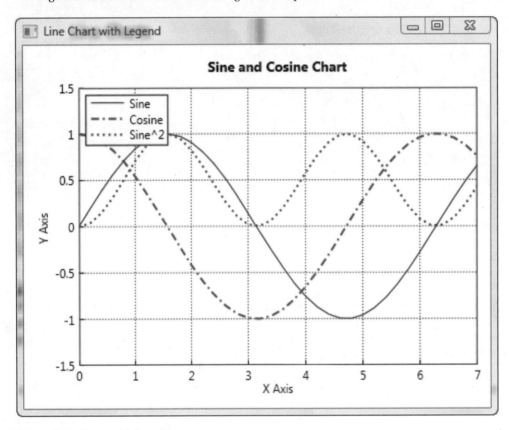

Figure 5-5. *Chart with legend*

Symbols

Sometimes, you may want a chart to display not only lines but symbols as well at the data points. Sometimes you may want to have a chart with only symbols and no lines. In this section, I'll show you how to create such a chart in WPF.

Defining Symbols

Let's first look at two symbols, the diamond and the triangle, as shown in Figure 5-6. The surrounding dotted-line square outlines the size of the symbol; (x_c, y_c) represent the center coordinates of the symbol in the device coordinate system. Suppose the length of each side of the dotted-line square is *SymbolSize* and that we define *halfsize*= *SymbolSize*/2. We can then easily determine the coordinates of the points at the vertices of each symbol.

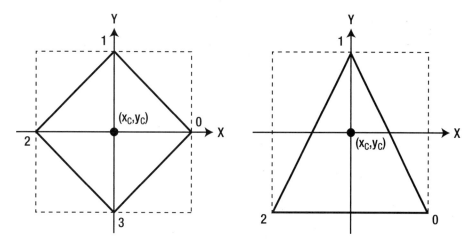

Figure 5-6. *Definitions of the diamond symbol (left) and the triangle symbol (right)*

For the diamond symbol, we have the following coordinates:

```
Point0: (xc + halfsize, yc)
Point1: (xc, yc + halfsize)
Point2: (xc - halfsize, yc)
Point3: (xc, yc - halfsize)
```

We can then use the *Polygon* object to create either an open or a solid diamond symbol by controlling the *Polygon*'s *Fill* property. For the triangle symbol, the corresponding point coordinates are:

```
Point0: (xc + halfsize, yc - halfsize)
Point1: (xc, yc + halfsize)
Point2: (xc - halfsize, yc - halfsize)
```

Again, we can use the *Polygon* object's *Fill* property to create either an open or a solid triangle symbol. By following the procedure presented here, you can create any symbol you want to use in your chart applications.

Symbols Class

Now add a public class, *Symbols*, to the project *LineCharts*. The following is the code listing for this class:

```
using System;
using System.Collections.Generic;
using System.Windows.Controls;
using System.Windows;
using System.Windows.Media;
using System.Windows.Shapes;

namespace LineCharts
{
    public class Symbols
    {
        private SymbolTypeEnum symbolType;
```

```
        private double symbolSize;
        private Brush borderColor;
        private Brush fillColor;
        private double borderThickness;

        public Symbols()
        {
            symbolType = SymbolTypeEnum.None;
            symbolSize = 8.0;
            borderColor = Brushes.Black;
            fillColor = Brushes.Black;
            borderThickness = 1.0;
        }

        public double BorderThickness
        {
            get { return borderThickness; }
            set { borderThickness = value; }
        }

        public Brush BorderColor
        {
            get { return borderColor; }
            set { borderColor = value; }
        }

        public Brush FillColor
        {
            get { return fillColor; }
            set { fillColor = value; }
        }

        public double SymbolSize
        {
            get { return symbolSize; }
            set { symbolSize = value; }
        }

        public SymbolTypeEnum SymbolType
        {
            get { return symbolType; }
            set { symbolType = value; }
        }


        public enum SymbolTypeEnum
        {
            Box = 0,
            Circle = 1,
            Cross = 2,
            Diamond = 3,
            Dot = 4,
            InvertedTriangle = 5,
```

```
        None = 6,
        OpenDiamond = 7,
        OpenInvertedTriangle = 8,
        OpenTriangle = 9,
        Square = 10,
        Star = 11,
        Triangle = 12,
        Plus = 13
}

public void AddSymbol(Canvas canvas, Point pt)
{
    Polygon plg = new Polygon();
    plg.Stroke = BorderColor;
    plg.StrokeThickness = BorderThickness;
    Ellipse ellipse = new Ellipse();
    ellipse.Stroke = BorderColor;
    ellipse.StrokeThickness = BorderThickness;
    Line line = new Line();
    double halfSize = 0.5 * SymbolSize;

    Canvas.SetZIndex(plg, 5);
    Canvas.SetZIndex(ellipse, 5);

    switch (SymbolType)
    {
        case SymbolTypeEnum.Square:
            plg.Fill = Brushes.White;
            plg.Points.Add(new Point(pt.X - halfSize, pt.Y - halfSize));
            plg.Points.Add(new Point(pt.X + halfSize, pt.Y - halfSize));
            plg.Points.Add(new Point(pt.X + halfSize, pt.Y + halfSize));
            plg.Points.Add(new Point(pt.X - halfSize, pt.Y + halfSize));
            canvas.Children.Add(plg);
            break;
        case SymbolTypeEnum.OpenDiamond:
            plg.Fill = Brushes.White;
            plg.Points.Add(new Point(pt.X - halfSize, pt.Y));
            plg.Points.Add(new Point(pt.X, pt.Y - halfSize));
            plg.Points.Add(new Point(pt.X + halfSize, pt.Y));
            plg.Points.Add(new Point(pt.X, pt.Y + halfSize));
            canvas.Children.Add(plg);
            break;
        case SymbolTypeEnum.Circle:
            ellipse.Fill = Brushes.White;
            ellipse.Width = SymbolSize;
            ellipse.Height = SymbolSize;
            Canvas.SetLeft(ellipse, pt.X - halfSize);
            Canvas.SetTop(ellipse, pt.Y - halfSize);
            canvas.Children.Add(ellipse);
            break;
        case SymbolTypeEnum.OpenTriangle:
            plg.Fill = Brushes.White;
            plg.Points.Add(new Point(pt.X - halfSize, pt.Y + halfSize));
```

```
        plg.Points.Add(new Point(pt.X, pt.Y - halfSize));
        plg.Points.Add(new Point(pt.X + halfSize, pt.Y + halfSize));
        canvas.Children.Add(plg);
        break;
    case SymbolTypeEnum.None:
        break;
    case SymbolTypeEnum.Cross:
        line = new Line();
        Canvas.SetZIndex(line, 5);
        line.Stroke = BorderColor;
        line.StrokeThickness = BorderThickness;
        line.X1 = pt.X - halfSize;
        line.Y1 = pt.Y + halfSize;
        line.X2 = pt.X + halfSize;
        line.Y2 = pt.Y - halfSize;
        canvas.Children.Add(line);
        line = new Line();
        Canvas.SetZIndex(line, 5);
        line.Stroke = BorderColor;
        line.StrokeThickness = BorderThickness;
        line.X1 = pt.X - halfSize;
        line.Y1 = pt.Y - halfSize;
        line.X2 = pt.X + halfSize;
        line.Y2 = pt.Y + halfSize;
        canvas.Children.Add(line);
        Canvas.SetZIndex(line, 5);
        break;
    case SymbolTypeEnum.Star:
        line = new Line();
        Canvas.SetZIndex(line, 5);
        line.Stroke = BorderColor;
        line.StrokeThickness = BorderThickness;
        line.X1 = pt.X - halfSize;
        line.Y1 = pt.Y + halfSize;
        line.X2 = pt.X + halfSize;
        line.Y2 = pt.Y - halfSize;
        canvas.Children.Add(line);
        line = new Line();
        Canvas.SetZIndex(line, 5);
        line.Stroke = BorderColor;
        line.StrokeThickness = BorderThickness;
        line.X1 = pt.X - halfSize;
        line.Y1 = pt.Y - halfSize;
        line.X2 = pt.X + halfSize;
        line.Y2 = pt.Y + halfSize;
        canvas.Children.Add(line);
        line = new Line();
        Canvas.SetZIndex(line, 5);
        line.Stroke = BorderColor;
        line.StrokeThickness = BorderThickness;
        line.X1 = pt.X - halfSize;
        line.Y1 = pt.Y;
        line.X2 = pt.X + halfSize;
```

```
            line.Y2 = pt.Y;
            canvas.Children.Add(line);
            line = new Line();
            Canvas.SetZIndex(line, 5);
            line.Stroke = BorderColor;
            line.StrokeThickness = BorderThickness;
            line.X1 = pt.X;
            line.Y1 = pt.Y - halfSize;
            line.X2 = pt.X;
            line.Y2 = pt.Y + halfSize;
            canvas.Children.Add(line);
            break;
        case SymbolTypeEnum.OpenInvertedTriangle:
            plg.Fill = Brushes.White;
            plg.Points.Add(new Point(pt.X, pt.Y + halfSize));
            plg.Points.Add(new Point(pt.X - halfSize, pt.Y - halfSize));
            plg.Points.Add(new Point(pt.X + halfSize, pt.Y - halfSize));
            canvas.Children.Add(plg);
            break;
        case SymbolTypeEnum.Plus:
            line = new Line();
            Canvas.SetZIndex(line, 5);
            line.Stroke = BorderColor;
            line.StrokeThickness = BorderThickness;
            line.X1 = pt.X - halfSize;
            line.Y1 = pt.Y;
            line.X2 = pt.X + halfSize;
            line.Y2 = pt.Y;
            canvas.Children.Add(line);
            line = new Line();
            Canvas.SetZIndex(line, 5);
            line.Stroke = BorderColor;
            line.StrokeThickness = BorderThickness;
            line.X1 = pt.X;
            line.Y1 = pt.Y - halfSize;
            line.X2 = pt.X;
            line.Y2 = pt.Y + halfSize;
            canvas.Children.Add(line);
            break;
        case SymbolTypeEnum.Dot:
            ellipse.Fill = FillColor;
            ellipse.Width = SymbolSize;
            ellipse.Height = SymbolSize;
            Canvas.SetLeft(ellipse, pt.X - halfSize);
            Canvas.SetTop(ellipse, pt.Y - halfSize);
            canvas.Children.Add(ellipse);
            break;
        case SymbolTypeEnum.Box:
            plg.Fill = FillColor;
            plg.Points.Add(new Point(pt.X - halfSize, pt.Y - halfSize));
            plg.Points.Add(new Point(pt.X + halfSize, pt.Y - halfSize));
            plg.Points.Add(new Point(pt.X + halfSize, pt.Y + halfSize));
            plg.Points.Add(new Point(pt.X - halfSize, pt.Y + halfSize));
```

```
                    canvas.Children.Add(plg);
                    break;
                case SymbolTypeEnum.Diamond:
                    plg.Fill = FillColor;
                    plg.Points.Add(new Point(pt.X - halfSize, pt.Y));
                    plg.Points.Add(new Point(pt.X, pt.Y - halfSize));
                    plg.Points.Add(new Point(pt.X + halfSize, pt.Y));
                    plg.Points.Add(new Point(pt.X, pt.Y + halfSize));
                    canvas.Children.Add(plg);
                    break;
                case SymbolTypeEnum.InvertedTriangle:
                    plg.Fill = FillColor;
                    plg.Points.Add(new Point(pt.X, pt.Y + halfSize));
                    plg.Points.Add(new Point(pt.X - halfSize, pt.Y - halfSize));
                    plg.Points.Add(new Point(pt.X + halfSize, pt.Y - halfSize));
                    canvas.Children.Add(plg);
                    break;
                case SymbolTypeEnum.Triangle:
                    plg.Fill = FillColor;
                    plg.Points.Add(new Point(pt.X - halfSize, pt.Y + halfSize));
                    plg.Points.Add(new Point(pt.X, pt.Y - halfSize));
                    plg.Points.Add(new Point(pt.X + halfSize, pt.Y + halfSize));
                    canvas.Children.Add(plg);
                    break;
            }
        }
    }
}
```

In this class, we define five private fields and their corresponding public properties. You can select the type of symbol from the *SymbolTypeEnum* enumeration using the *SymbolType* property. The *SymbolTypeEnum* contains 13 different symbols as well as a *None* type, which means that no symbols will be drawn on your chart. This type is the default value, which means you must choose a symbol type other than *None* if you want to draw symbols on your chart applications. You can easily add your own symbols to this enumeration as you like.

The *BorderColor* property allows you to specify the border color of a symbol. For the *Star*, *Plus*, and open symbols, the *BorderColor* property is the only property you need to define. The default color for this property is black. The *FillColor* property, with a default color of white, is defined for solid symbols, such as the diamond, triangle, box, and dot. This means that it is possible for a solid symbol to have a border of a different color than its fill by specifying different colors for the *BorderColor* and *FillColor* properties.

The *BorderThickess* property allows you to specify the border line thickness for a symbol. The default value of this property is 1 pixel. The *SymbolSize* property, which has a default value of 8 pixels, controls the symbol size,

There is a public method in this class called *AddSymbol*, which takes *Canvas* and *Point* objects as input. The *Canvas* object should be the *ChartCanvas* you defined in the *ChartStyle* class, and the *Point* object represents the center location of the symbol. Note that you must define this input *Point* in the device coordinate system. Namely, a *Point* in the world coordinate system must undergo a transformation from the world system to the device system using the *NormalizePoint* method implemented in the *ChartStyle* class.

Notice that the symbols must be associated with a *DataSeries* because each *DataSeries* can have different symbols. Thus, we need to add the *Symbols* object to the *DataSeries* class. Open the *DataSeries* class and add the following private field and corresponding public property to it:

```
using System;
using System.Windows;
using System.Windows.Media;
using System.Windows.Shapes;

namespace LineCharts
{
    public class DataSeries
    {
        private Polyline lineSeries = new Polyline();
        private Brush lineColor;
        private double lineThickness = 1;
        private LinePatternEnum linePattern;
        private string seriesName = "Default Name";
        private Symbols symbols;

        public DataSeries()
        {
            LineColor = Brushes.Black;
            symbols = new Symbols();
        }

        public Symbols Symbols
        {
            get { return symbols; }
            set { symbols = value; }
        }
        ......
    }
}
```

In order to add the symbols to your chart, you will also need to add the corresponding code snippet to the *AddLines* method in the *DataCollection* class:

```
using System;
using System.Collections.Generic;
using System.Windows.Controls;
using System.Windows.Media;
using System.Windows.Shapes;

namespace LineCharts
{
    public class DataCollection
    {
        ......
        public void AddLines(ChartStyle cs)
        {
            int j = 0;
            foreach (DataSeries ds in DataList)
            {
                if (ds.SeriesName == "Default Name")
                {
                    ds.SeriesName = "DataSeries" + j.ToString();
                }
```

```
            ds.AddLinePattern();
            for (int i = 0; i < ds.LineSeries.Points.Count; i++)
            {
                ds.LineSeries.Points[i] =
                    cs.NormalizePoint(ds.LineSeries.Points[i]);
                ds.Symbols.AddSymbol(cs.ChartCanvas,
                    ds.LineSeries.Points[i]);
            }
            cs.ChartCanvas.Children.Add(ds.LineSeries);
            j++;
        }
    }
  }
}
```

Creating a Chart with Symbols

Here, we'll use an example to demonstrate how to create a line chart with symbols. Add a new WPF Window to the project *LineCharts* and name it *LineChartWithSymbols*. The XAML file for this example is the same as that in the previous example. Here is the code-behind file:

```
using System;
using System.Collections.Generic;
using System.Windows;
using System.Windows.Controls;
using System.Windows.Media;
using System.Windows.Media.Imaging;
using System.Windows.Shapes;

namespace LineCharts
{
    public partial class LineChartWithSymbols : Window
    {
        private ChartStyleGridlines cs;
        private Legend lg;
        private DataCollection dc;
        private DataSeries ds;

        public LineChartWithSymbols()
        {
            InitializeComponent();
            AddChart();
        }

        private void AddChart()
        {
            cs = new ChartStyleGridlines();
            lg = new Legend();
            dc = new DataCollection();
            ds = new DataSeries();

            cs.ChartCanvas = chartCanvas;
            cs.TextCanvas = textCanvas;
```

```
cs.Title = "Sine and Cosine Chart";
cs.Xmin = 0;
cs.Xmax = 7;
cs.Ymin = -1.5;
cs.Ymax = 1.5;
cs.YTick = 0.5;
cs.GridlinePattern = ChartStyleGridlines.GridlinePatternEnum.Dot;
cs.GridlineColor = Brushes.Black;
cs.AddChartStyle(tbTitle, tbXLabel, tbYLabel);

// Draw Sine curve:
ds = new DataSeries();
ds.Symbols.BorderColor = Brushes.Blue;
ds.Symbols.SymbolType = Symbols.SymbolTypeEnum.OpenDiamond;
ds.LineColor = Brushes.Blue;
//ds.LineThickness = 1;
ds.SeriesName = "Sine";
for (int i = 0; i < 70; i++)
{
    double x = i / 5.0;
    double y = Math.Sin(x);
    ds.LineSeries.Points.Add(new Point(x, y));
}
dc.DataList.Add(ds);

// Draw cosine curve:
ds = new DataSeries();
ds.Symbols.BorderColor = Brushes.Red;
ds.Symbols.SymbolType = Symbols.SymbolTypeEnum.Dot;
ds.Symbols.FillColor = Brushes.Red;
ds.LineColor = Brushes.Red;
ds.SeriesName = "Cosine";
ds.LinePattern = DataSeries.LinePatternEnum.DashDot;
//ds.LineThickness = 2;
for (int i = 0; i < 70; i++)
{
    double x = i / 5.0;
    double y = Math.Cos(x);
    ds.LineSeries.Points.Add(new Point(x, y));
}
dc.DataList.Add(ds);

// Draw sine^2 curve:
ds = new DataSeries();
ds.Symbols.BorderColor = Brushes.DarkGreen;
ds.Symbols.SymbolType = Symbols.SymbolTypeEnum.OpenTriangle;
ds.LineColor = Brushes.DarkGreen;
ds.SeriesName = "Sine^2";
ds.LinePattern = DataSeries.LinePatternEnum.Dot;
//ds.LineThickness = 2;
for (int i = 0; i < 70; i++)
{
    double x = i / 5.0;
```

```
            double y = Math.Sin(x) * Math.Sin(x);
            ds.LineSeries.Points.Add(new Point(x, y));
        }
        dc.DataList.Add(ds);
        dc.AddLines(cs);

        lg.LegendCanvas = legendCanvas;
        lg.IsLegend = true;
        lg.IsBorder = true;
        lg.LegendPosition = Legend.LegendPositionEnum.NorthEast;
        lg.AddLegend(cs.ChartCanvas, dc);
    }

    private void chartGrid_SizeChanged(object sender, SizeChangedEventArgs e)
    {
        textCanvas.Width = chartGrid.ActualWidth;
        textCanvas.Height = chartGrid.ActualHeight;
        legendCanvas.Children.Clear();
        chartCanvas.Children.RemoveRange(1, chartCanvas.Children.Count - 1);
        textCanvas.Children.RemoveRange(1, textCanvas.Children.Count - 1);
        AddChart();
    }
}
}
```

Here, we specify the *Symbols'* properties for each *DataSeries*, which resembles the way we specified the line styles. Figure 5-7 shows the result of running this example.

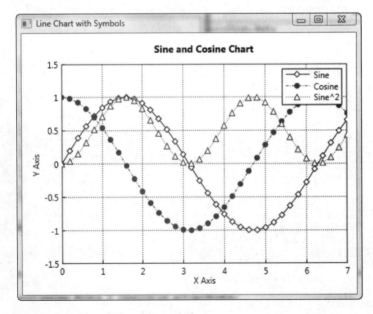

***Figure 5-7.** Line chart with symbols*

Line Charts with Two *Y* Axes

In the previous sections, we implemented a powerful 2D line chart program. There was no restriction in this program on the number of lines or curves you could add to a single chart. In this section, we'll add another feature, an additional *Y* axis, to the 2D line chart.

Why We Need Two *Y* Axes

In some instances, you may have multiple data sets you would like to display on the same chart. However, the Y axis data values for each data set are not within the same range. Let's say you implement the following code for the *AddData* method in the code-behind file for the example *LineChartWithLegend*:

```
private void AddChart1()
{
    cs = new ChartStyleGridlines();
    lg = new Legend();
    dc = new DataCollection();
    ds = new DataSeries();

    cs.ChartCanvas = chartCanvas;
    cs.TextCanvas = textCanvas;
    cs.Title = "x*cos(x) & 100+20*x";
    cs.Xmin = 0;
    cs.Xmax = 30;
    cs.Ymin = -100;
    cs.Ymax = 700;
    cs.XTick = 5;
    cs.YTick = 100;
    cs.XLabel = "X";
    cs.YLabel = "Y";
    cs.GridlinePattern = ChartStyleGridlines.GridlinePatternEnum.Dot;
    cs.GridlineColor = Brushes.Black;
    cs.AddChartStyle(tbTitle, tbXLabel, tbYLabel);

    // Draw x*cos(x) curve:
    ds.LineColor = Brushes.Blue;
    ds.LineThickness = 1;
    ds.SeriesName = "x*cos(x)";
    for (int i = 0; i < 20; i++)
    {
        double x = 1.0 * i;
        double y = x * Math.Cos(x);
        ds.LineSeries.Points.Add(new Point(x, y));
    }
    dc.DataList.Add(ds);

    // Draw 100+20*x curve:
    ds = new DataSeries();
    ds.LineColor = Brushes.Red;
    ds.SeriesName = "100+20*x";
    ds.LinePattern = DataSeries.LinePatternEnum.Dash;
```

203

```
    ds.LineThickness = 2;
    for (int i = 5; i < 30; i++)
    {
        double x = 1.0 * i;
        double y = 100 + 20 * x;
        ds.LineSeries.Points.Add(new Point(x, y));
    }
    dc.DataList.Add(ds);
    dc.AddLines(cs);

    lg.LegendCanvas = legendCanvas;
    lg.IsLegend = true;
    lg.IsBorder = true;
    lg.LegendPosition = Legend.LegendPositionEnum.NorthWest;
    lg.AddLegend(cs.ChartCanvas, dc);
}
```

This will produce the results shown in Figure 5-8. From the figure, we can see how difficult it is to view the values of the function $x*\cos(x)$ because the Y axis limits have been defined to display all of the data points on the same chart; however, the values of these two functions have very different data ranges. This problem can be solved by adding another $Y2$ axis to the chart program.

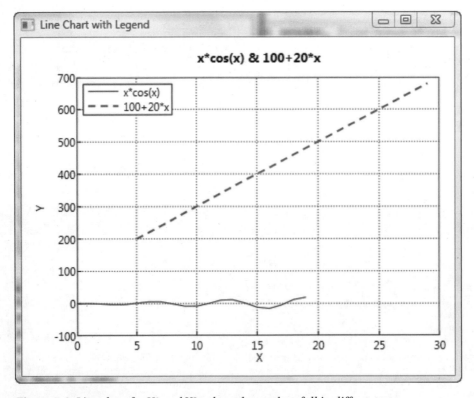

Figure 5-8. Line chart for Y1 and Y2, whose data values fall in different ranges

Chart Style with Two *Y* Axes

In order to add the *Y*2 axis to a chart, you need to modify the original *ChartStyle* class. Add a new class, *ChartStyle2Y*, to the project *LineCharts*. This new class is inherited from the *ChartStyle* class:

```
using System;
using System.Windows.Controls;
using System.Windows;

namespace LineCharts
{
    public class ChartStyle2Y : ChartStyle
    {
        private double y2min = 0;
        private double y2max = 10;
        private double y2Tick = 2;

        public double Y2min
        {
            get { return y2min; }
            set { y2min = value; }
        }

        public double Y2max
        {
            get { return y2max; }
            set { y2max = value; }
        }
        public double Y2Tick
        {
            get { return y2Tick; }
            set { y2Tick = value; }
        }

        public Point NormalizePoint2Y(Point pt)
        {
            if (ChartCanvas.Width.ToString() == "NaN")
                ChartCanvas.Width = 270;
            if (ChartCanvas.Height.ToString() == "NaN")
                ChartCanvas.Height = 250;
            Point result = new Point();
            result.X = (pt.X - Xmin) * ChartCanvas.Width / (Xmax - Xmin);
            result.Y = ChartCanvas.Height -
                     (pt.Y - Y2min) * ChartCanvas.Height / (Y2max - Y2min);
            return result;
        }
    }
}
```

In this class, you simply define fields and properties for the *Y*2 axis limits and add a method *NormalizePoint2Y* to convert the *Y*2 data points from the world coordinate system to the device-independent pixel system, just as you did for the *Y* data points using the *NormalizePoint* method.

For a chart that uses the *Y2* axis, you may also want to add additional gridlines, labels, and tick marks. You can achieve this by adding a new class, named *ChartStyleGridlines2Y,* to the current project. This class, inherited from *ChartStyle2Y,* is quite similar to the *ChartStyleGridlines* class, except it contains an additional *Y2* axis. Here, I'll list the code for this new class for your reference:

```
using System;
using System.Windows.Controls;
using System.Windows;
using System.Windows.Media;
using System.Windows.Shapes;

namespace LineCharts
{
    class ChartStyleGridlines2Y : ChartStyle2Y
    {
        private string title;
        private string xLabel;
        private string yLabel;
        private string y2Label;
        private Canvas textCanvas;
        private bool isXGrid = true;
        private bool isYGrid = true;
        private Brush gridlineColor = Brushes.LightGray;
        private double xTick = 1;
        private double yTick = 0.5;
        private GridlinePatternEnum gridlinePattern;
        private double leftOffset = 20;
        private double bottomOffset = 15;
        private double rightOffset = 10;
        private Line gridline = new Line();

        public ChartStyleGridlines2Y()
        {
            title = "Title";
            xLabel = "X Axis";
            yLabel = "Y Axis";
            y2Label = "Y2 Axis";
        }

        public string Title
        {
            get { return title; }
            set { title = value; }
        }

        public string XLabel
        {
            get { return xLabel; }
            set { xLabel = value; }
        }

        public string YLabel
        {
```

```csharp
    get { return yLabel; }
    set { yLabel = value; }
}

public string Y2Label
{
    get { return y2Label; }
    set { y2Label = value; }
}

public GridlinePatternEnum GridlinePattern
{
    get { return gridlinePattern; }
    set { gridlinePattern = value; }
}

public double XTick
{
    get { return xTick; }
    set { xTick = value; }
}

public double YTick
{
    get { return yTick; }
    set { yTick = value; }
}

public Brush GridlineColor
{
    get { return gridlineColor; }
    set { gridlineColor = value; }
}

public Canvas TextCanvas
{
    get { return textCanvas; }
    set { textCanvas = value; }
}

public bool IsXGrid
{
    get { return isXGrid; }
    set { isXGrid = value; }
}

public bool IsYGrid
{
    get { return isYGrid; }
    set { isYGrid = value; }
}
```

```
public void AddChartStyle(TextBlock tbTitle, TextBlock tbXLabel,
                          TextBlock tbYLabel, TextBlock tbY2Label)
{
    Point pt = new Point();
    Line tick = new Line();
    double offset = 0;
    double dx, dy;
    TextBlock tb = new TextBlock();
    Size size = new Size();

    // Determine right offset:
    for (dy = Y2min; dy <= Y2max; dy += Y2Tick)
    {
        pt = NormalizePoint2Y(new Point(Xmax, dy));
        tb = new TextBlock();
        tb.Text = dy.ToString();
        tb.TextAlignment = TextAlignment.Left;
        tb.Measure(new Size(Double.PositiveInfinity,
                            Double.PositiveInfinity));
        size = tb.DesiredSize;
        if (offset < size.Width)
            offset = size.Width;
    }
    rightOffset = offset + 10;

    // Determine left offset:
    for (dy = Ymin; dy <= Ymax; dy += YTick)
    {
        pt = NormalizePoint(new Point(Xmin, dy));
        tb = new TextBlock();
        tb.Text = dy.ToString();
        tb.TextAlignment = TextAlignment.Right;
        tb.Measure(new Size(Double.PositiveInfinity,
                            Double.PositiveInfinity));
        size = tb.DesiredSize;
        if (offset < size.Width)
            offset = size.Width;
    }
    leftOffset = offset + 5;

    Canvas.SetLeft(ChartCanvas, leftOffset);
    Canvas.SetBottom(ChartCanvas, bottomOffset);
    ChartCanvas.Width = TextCanvas.Width - leftOffset - rightOffset;
    ChartCanvas.Height = TextCanvas.Height - bottomOffset - size.Height / 2;
    Rectangle chartRect = new Rectangle();
    chartRect.Stroke = Brushes.Black;
    chartRect.Width = ChartCanvas.Width;
    chartRect.Height = ChartCanvas.Height;
    ChartCanvas.Children.Add(chartRect);

    // Create vertical gridlines:
    if (IsYGrid == true)
    {
```

```
        for (dx = Xmin + XTick; dx < Xmax; dx += XTick)
        {
            gridline = new Line();
            AddLinePattern();
            gridline.X1 = NormalizePoint(new Point(dx, Ymin)).X;
            gridline.Y1 = NormalizePoint(new Point(dx, Ymin)).Y;
            gridline.X2 = NormalizePoint(new Point(dx, Ymax)).X;
            gridline.Y2 = NormalizePoint(new Point(dx, Ymax)).Y;
            ChartCanvas.Children.Add(gridline);
        }
    }

    // Create horizontal gridlines:
    if (IsXGrid == true)
    {
        for (dy = Ymin + YTick; dy < Ymax; dy += YTick)
        {
            gridline = new Line();
            AddLinePattern();
            gridline.X1 = NormalizePoint(new Point(Xmin, dy)).X;
            gridline.Y1 = NormalizePoint(new Point(Xmin, dy)).Y;
            gridline.X2 = NormalizePoint(new Point(Xmax, dy)).X;
            gridline.Y2 = NormalizePoint(new Point(Xmax, dy)).Y;
            ChartCanvas.Children.Add(gridline);
        }
    }

    // Create x-axis tick marks:
    for (dx = Xmin; dx <= Xmax; dx += xTick)
    {
        pt = NormalizePoint(new Point(dx, Ymin));
        tick = new Line();
        tick.Stroke = Brushes.Black;
        tick.X1 = pt.X;
        tick.Y1 = pt.Y;
        tick.X2 = pt.X;
        tick.Y2 = pt.Y - 5;
        ChartCanvas.Children.Add(tick);

        tb = new TextBlock();
        tb.Text = dx.ToString();
        tb.Measure(new Size(Double.PositiveInfinity,
                            Double.PositiveInfinity));
        size = tb.DesiredSize;
        TextCanvas.Children.Add(tb);
        Canvas.SetLeft(tb, leftOffset + pt.X - size.Width / 2);
        Canvas.SetTop(tb, pt.Y + 2 + size.Height / 2);
    }

    // Create y-axis tick marks:
    for (dy = Ymin; dy <= Ymax; dy += YTick)
    {
        pt = NormalizePoint(new Point(Xmin, dy));
```

```
            tick = new Line();
            tick.Stroke = Brushes.Black;
            tick.X1 = pt.X;
            tick.Y1 = pt.Y;
            tick.X2 = pt.X + 5;
            tick.Y2 = pt.Y;
            ChartCanvas.Children.Add(tick);

            tb = new TextBlock();
            tb.Text = dy.ToString();
            tb.Measure(new Size(Double.PositiveInfinity,
                                Double.PositiveInfinity));
            size = tb.DesiredSize;
            TextCanvas.Children.Add(tb);
            Canvas.SetRight(tb, ChartCanvas.Width + 35);
            Canvas.SetTop(tb, pt.Y - 1);
        }

        // Create y2-axis tick marks:
        for (dy = Y2min; dy <= Y2max; dy += Y2Tick)
        {
            pt = NormalizePoint2Y(new Point(Xmax, dy));
            tick = new Line();
            tick.Stroke = Brushes.Black;
            tick.X1 = pt.X;
            tick.Y1 = pt.Y;
            tick.X2 = pt.X - 5;
            tick.Y2 = pt.Y;
            ChartCanvas.Children.Add(tick);

            tb = new TextBlock();
            tb.Text = dy.ToString();
            tb.Measure(new Size(Double.PositiveInfinity,
                                Double.PositiveInfinity));
            size = tb.DesiredSize;
            TextCanvas.Children.Add(tb);
            Canvas.SetLeft(tb, ChartCanvas.Width + 30);
            Canvas.SetTop(tb, pt.Y - 1);
        }

        // Add title and labels:
        tbTitle.Text = Title;
        tbXLabel.Text = XLabel;
        tbYLabel.Text = YLabel;
        tbY2Label.Text = Y2Label;
```

```
            tbXLabel.Margin = new Thickness(leftOffset - rightOffset + 2, 2, 2, 2);
            tbTitle.Margin = new Thickness(leftOffset - rightOffset + 2, 2, 2, 2);
        }

        public void AddLinePattern()
        {
            gridline.Stroke = GridlineColor;
            gridline.StrokeThickness = 1;

            switch (GridlinePattern)
            {
                case GridlinePatternEnum.Dash:
                    gridline.StrokeDashArray =
                        new DoubleCollection(new double[2] { 4, 3 });
                    break;
                case GridlinePatternEnum.Dot:
                    gridline.StrokeDashArray =
                        new DoubleCollection(new double[2] { 1, 2 });
                    break;
                case GridlinePatternEnum.DashDot:
                    gridline.StrokeDashArray =
                        new DoubleCollection(new double[4] { 4, 2, 1, 2 });
                    break;
            }
        }

        public enum GridlinePatternEnum
        {
            Solid = 1,
            Dash = 2,
            Dot = 3,
            DashDot = 4
        }
    }
}
```

In the foregoing code, the changes made to include the *Y2* axis have been highlighted.

DataSeries and *DataCollection* with Two *Y* Axes

We also need to make modifications to both the *DataSeries* and *DataCollection* classes. Add a new class, *DataSeries2Y,* to the current project. This class derives from the original *DataSeries* class. We only need to add one member field and corresponding property to this class:

```
using System;
using System.Windows;
using System.Windows.Media;
using System.Windows.Shapes;
```

```
namespace LineCharts
{
    public class DataSeries2Y : DataSeries
    {
        private bool isY2Data = false;

        public bool IsY2Data
        {
            get { return isY2Data; }
            set { isY2Data = value; }
        }
    }
}
```

The *IsY2Data* property allows you to associate a *DataSeries2Y* object with either the Y axis or the *Y2* axis. If it is false, the *DataSeries2Y* is associated with the original *Y* axis. On the other hand, the *DataSeries2Y* is associated with the *Y2* axis if this property is set to true.

You also need to make corresponding changes to the *DataCollection* class. Add a new class, *DataCollection2Y,* to the current project. Here is its code listing:

```
using System;
using System.Collections.Generic;
using System.Windows.Controls;
using System.Windows.Media;
using System.Windows.Shapes;

namespace LineCharts
{
    public class DataCollection2Y : DataCollection
    {
        public void AddLines2Y(ChartStyle2Y cs)
        {
            int j = 0;
            foreach (DataSeries2Y ds in DataList)
            {
                if (ds.SeriesName == "Default Name")
                {
                    ds.SeriesName = "DataSeries" + j.ToString();
                }
                ds.AddLinePattern();
                for (int i = 0; i < ds.LineSeries.Points.Count; i++)
                {
                    if (ds.IsY2Data)
                        ds.LineSeries.Points[i] =
                            cs.NormalizePoint2Y(ds.LineSeries.Points[i]);
                    else
                        ds.LineSeries.Points[i] =
                            cs.NormalizePoint(ds.LineSeries.Points[i]);

                    ds.Symbols.AddSymbol(cs.ChartCanvas, ds.LineSeries.Points[i]);
                }
                cs.ChartCanvas.Children.Add(ds.LineSeries);
                j++;
            }
```

```
        }
    }
}
```

This class, inherited from the *DataCollection* class, contains only one method, *AddLines2Y*, which allows you to create a line chart with two *Y* axes.

Creating a Chart with Two *Y* Axes

Here, I'll use an example to demonstrate how to create a line chart with two *Y* axes. Add a new WPF Window to the project *LineCharts* and name it *LineChartWith2YAxes*. Here is the XAML file for this example:

```xml
<Window x:Class="LineCharts.LineChartWith2YAxes"
    xmlns="http://schemas.microsoft.com/winfx/2006/xaml/presentation"
    xmlns:x="http://schemas.microsoft.com/winfx/2006/xaml"
    Title="LineChartWithTwoYAxes" Height="400" Width="500">
    <Grid Name="grid1" Margin="10">
        <Grid.ColumnDefinitions>
            <ColumnDefinition Width="auto"/>
            <ColumnDefinition Name="column1" Width="*"/>
            <ColumnDefinition Width="auto"/>
        </Grid.ColumnDefinitions>
        <Grid.RowDefinitions>
            <RowDefinition Height="auto"/>
            <RowDefinition Name="row1" Height="*"/>
            <RowDefinition Height="auto"/>
        </Grid.RowDefinitions>
        <TextBlock Margin="2" x:Name="tbTitle" Grid.Column="1" Grid.Row="0"
                RenderTransformOrigin="0.5,0.5" FontSize="14" FontWeight="Bold"
                HorizontalAlignment="Stretch" VerticalAlignment="Stretch"
                TextAlignment="Center"
                Text="Title"/>

        <TextBlock Margin="5" x:Name="tbXLabel" Grid.Column="1" Grid.Row="2"
                RenderTransformOrigin="0.5,0.5" TextAlignment="Center"
                Text="X Axis"/>

        <TextBlock Margin="5" Name="tbYLabel" Grid.Column="0" Grid.Row="1"
                RenderTransformOrigin="0.5,0.5" TextAlignment="Center"
                Text="Y Axis">
            <TextBlock.LayoutTransform>
                <RotateTransform Angle="-90"/>
            </TextBlock.LayoutTransform>
        </TextBlock>

        <TextBlock Margin="5" Name="tbY2Label" Grid.Column="2" Grid.Row="1"
                RenderTransformOrigin="0.5,0.5" TextAlignment="Center"
                Text="Y2 Axis">
            <TextBlock.LayoutTransform>
                <RotateTransform Angle="-90"/>
            </TextBlock.LayoutTransform>
        </TextBlock>
```

```
    <Grid  Margin="0" x:Name ="chartGrid" Grid.Column="1" Grid.Row="1"
                    ClipToBounds="True" Background="Transparent"
                 SizeChanged="chartGrid_SizeChanged" />
        <Canvas Margin="2" Name="textCanvas" ClipToBounds="True"
              Grid.Column="1" Grid.Row="1">
            <Canvas Name="chartCanvas" ClipToBounds="True">
                <Canvas Name="legendCanvas" Background="Transparent" />
            </Canvas>
        </Canvas>

    </Grid>
</Window>
```

This XAML code is similar to that used in the previous example, except for the addition of the Y2 label. Here is the code-behind file for this example:

```
using System;
using System.Collections.Generic;
using System.Windows;
using System.Windows.Controls;
using System.Windows.Media;
using System.Windows.Shapes;

namespace LineCharts
{
    public partial class LineChartWith2YAxes : Window
    {
        private ChartStyleGridlines2Y cs;
        private Legend lg;
        private DataCollection2Y dc;
        private DataSeries2Y ds;

        public LineChartWith2YAxes()
        {
            InitializeComponent();
            AddChart();
        }

        private void AddChart()
        {
            cs = new ChartStyleGridlines2Y();
            lg = new Legend();
            dc = new DataCollection2Y();
            ds = new DataSeries2Y();

            cs.ChartCanvas = chartCanvas;
            cs.TextCanvas = textCanvas;
            cs.Title = "Sine and Cosine Chart";
            cs.Xmin = 0;
            cs.Xmax = 30;
            cs.Ymin = -20;
            cs.Ymax = 20;
            cs.YTick = 5;
```

```
        cs.XTick = 5;
        cs.Y2min = 100;
        cs.Y2max = 700;
        cs.Y2Tick = 100;
        cs.XLabel = "X Axis";
        cs.YLabel = "Y Axis";
        cs.Y2Label = "Y2 Axis";
        cs.Title = "line Chart with Y2 Axis";
        cs.GridlinePattern = ChartStyleGridlines2Y.GridlinePatternEnum.Dot;
        cs.GridlineColor = Brushes.Transparent;
        cs.AddChartStyle(tbTitle, tbXLabel, tbYLabel, tbY2Label);

        // Draw Y curve:
        ds = new DataSeries2Y();
        ds.Symbols.BorderColor = Brushes.Blue;
        ds.Symbols.SymbolType = Symbols.SymbolTypeEnum.OpenDiamond;
        ds.LineColor = Brushes.Blue;
        ds.SeriesName = "x * cos (x)";
        for (int i = 0; i < 20; i++)
        {
            double x = 1.0 * i;
            double y = x*Math.Cos(x);
            ds.LineSeries.Points.Add(new Point(x, y));
        }
        dc.DataList.Add(ds);

        // Draw Y2 curve:
        ds = new DataSeries2Y();
        ds.IsY2Data = true;
        ds.Symbols.BorderColor = Brushes.Red;
        ds.Symbols.SymbolType = Symbols.SymbolTypeEnum.Dot;
        ds.Symbols.FillColor = Brushes.Red;
        ds.LineColor = Brushes.Red;
        ds.SeriesName = "100 + 20 * x";
        ds.LinePattern = DataSeries.LinePatternEnum.DashDot;
        for (int i = 5; i < 30; i++)
        {
            double x = 1.0 * i;
            double y = 100.0 + 20.0 * x;
            ds.LineSeries.Points.Add(new Point(x, y));
        }
        dc.DataList.Add(ds);
        dc.AddLines2Y(cs);

        lg.LegendCanvas = legendCanvas;
        lg.IsLegend = true;
        lg.IsBorder = true;
        lg.LegendPosition = Legend.LegendPositionEnum.NorthWest;
        lg.AddLegend(cs.ChartCanvas, dc);
    }

private void chartGrid_SizeChanged(object sender, SizeChangedEventArgs e)
{
```

```
            textCanvas.Width = chartGrid.ActualWidth;
            textCanvas.Height = chartGrid.ActualHeight;
            legendCanvas.Children.Clear();
            chartCanvas.Children.RemoveRange(1, chartCanvas.Children.Count - 1);
            textCanvas.Children.RemoveRange(1, textCanvas.Children.Count - 1);
            AddChart();
        }
    }
}
```

Here, we first set different limits for the *Y* and *Y2* axes. Also note how we associate the *Y2 DataSeries2Y* object with the *IsY2Data* property. A *DataSeries2Y* object with an *IsY2Data = true* property tells the program that this *DataSeries2Y* object should be drawn using the *Y2* axis.

By building and running this example, you should obtain the result shown in Figure 5-9. When you compare this result with the one shown in Figure 5-8, you can see that both sets of data are clearly displayed in Figure 5-9, even though these two sets of data have drastically different data ranges.

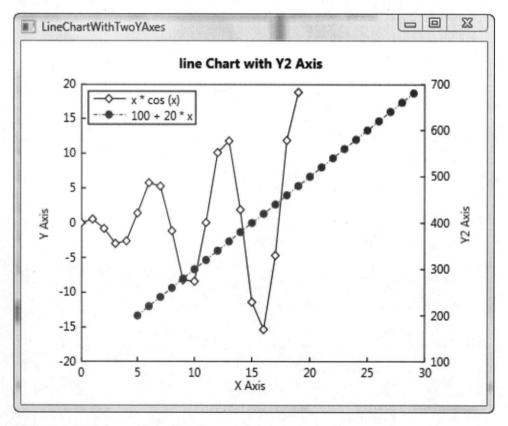

Figure 5-9. *Line chart with two Y axes*

■ ■ ■

CHAPTER 6

Specialized 2D Charts

In the previous chapter, we discussed 2D line charts, which you can use to visualize data in real-world WPF applications. In this chapter, I'll show you how to create certain special or application-specific charts in WPF. These charts are typically found in commercial charting packages or spreadsheet applications. I'll discuss a variety of special charts that display statistical distributions of data or discrete data, including bar, stair-step, stem, error bar, and area charts. You'll also learn how to create charts in other coordinate systems, such as pie and polar charts.

Bar Charts

The bar chart is useful for comparing classes or groups of data. In a bar chart, a class or group can contain a single category of data, or it can be broken down further into multiple categories for a greater depth of analysis. A bar chart is often used in exploratory data analysis to illustrate the major features of the distribution of the data in a convenient form. It displays the data using a number of rectangles of the same width, each of which represents a particular category. The length (and hence area) of each rectangle is proportional to the number of cases in the category it represents, for example, age group or religious affiliation.

DataSeries for Bar Charts

You can use the same *ChartStyle* class implemented in the previous chapter to create bar charts. However, you'll need to modify the *DataSeries* and *DataCollection* classes in order to create bar charts.

Let's start with a new WPF Window application project and name it *Specialized2DCharts*. Add to the current project the following files from the project *LineCharts* in Chapter 5: *ChartStyle.cs*, *ChartStyleGridlines.cs*, *DataSeries.cs*, *DataCollection.cs*, and *Symbols.cs*. Also add to the project the file *ColormapBrush.cs* from the project *ColorsAndBrushes* in Chapter 4. Change all of these classes' namespaces to *Specialized2DCharts*.

Now we want to implement a new *DataSeries* class for bar charts. Add a new class, *DataSeriesBar*, to the current project. This class is inherited from the original *DataSeries* class:

```
using System;
using System.Windows;
using System.Windows.Media;
using System.Windows.Shapes;
```

```
namespace Specialized2DCharts
{
    public class DataSeriesBar : DataSeries
    {
        private Brush fillColor = Brushes.Black;
        private Brush borderColor = Brushes.Black;
        private double borderThickness = 1.0;
        private double barWidth = 0.8;

        public Brush FillColor
        {
            get { return fillColor; }
            set { fillColor = value; }
        }

        public Brush BorderColor
        {
            get { return borderColor; }
            set { borderColor = value; }
        }

        public double BorderThickness
        {
            get { return borderThickness; }
            set { borderThickness = value; }
        }

        public double BarWidth
        {
            get { return barWidth; }
            set { barWidth = value; }
        }
    }
}
```

This class is very simple. We define several member fields and their corresponding properties, which will allow you to specify the bar width, fill color, and border style.

DataCollection for Bar Charts

The *DataCollection* class for bar charts is more complicated than that for line charts, because this class will be responsible for creating several different types of bar charts. Add a new class, *DataCollectionBar*, to the current project. Here is the code listing for this class:

```
using System;
using System.Collections.Generic;
using System.Windows;
using System.Windows.Controls;
using System.Windows.Media;
using System.Windows.Shapes;

namespace Specialized2DCharts
{
```

```
public class DataCollectionBar : DataCollection
{
    private BarTypeEnum barType = BarTypeEnum.Vertical;

    public BarTypeEnum BarType
    {
        get { return barType; }
        set { barType = value; }
    }

    public enum BarTypeEnum
    {
        Vertical = 0,
        Horizontal = 1,
        VerticalStack = 2,
        HorizontalStack = 3,
        VerticalOverlay = 4,
        HorizontalOverlay = 5
    }

    public void AddBars(ChartStyleGridlines csg)
    {
        int nSeries = DataList.Count;
        double width;

        switch (BarType)
        {
            case BarTypeEnum.Vertical:
                if (nSeries == 1)
                {
                    foreach (DataSeriesBar ds in DataList)
                    {
                        width = csg.XTick * ds.BarWidth;
                        for (int i = 0; i < ds.LineSeries.Points.Count; i++)
                        {
                            DrawVerticalBar(ds.LineSeries.Points[i],
                                        csg, ds, width, 0);
                        }
                    }
                }
                else
                {
                    int j = 0;
                    foreach (DataSeriesBar ds in DataList)
                    {
                        for (int i = 0; i < ds.LineSeries.Points.Count; i++)
                        {
                            DrawVerticalBar1(ds.LineSeries.Points[i],
                                        csg, ds, nSeries, j);
                        }
                        j++;
                    }
                }
```

```
            break;

        case BarTypeEnum.VerticalOverlay:
            if (nSeries > 1)
            {
                int j = 0;
                foreach (DataSeriesBar ds in DataList)
                {
                    width = csg.XTick * ds.BarWidth;
                    width = width / Math.Pow(2, j);
                    for (int i = 0; i < ds.LineSeries.Points.Count; i++)
                    {
                        DrawVerticalBar(ds.LineSeries.Points[i],
                                        csg, ds, width, 0);
                    }
                    j++;
                }
            }
            break;

        case BarTypeEnum.VerticalStack:
            if (nSeries > 1)
            {
                List<Point> temp = new List<Point>();
                double[] tempy =
                    new double[DataList[0].LineSeries.Points.Count];

                foreach (DataSeriesBar ds in DataList)
                {
                    width = csg.XTick * ds.BarWidth;

                    for (int i = 0; i < ds.LineSeries.Points.Count; i++)
                    {
                        if (temp.Count > 0)
                        {
                            tempy[i] += temp[i].Y;
                        }
                        DrawVerticalBar(ds.LineSeries.Points[i],
                                        csg, ds, width, tempy[i]);
                    }
                    temp.Clear();
                    temp.AddRange(ds.LineSeries.Points);
                }
            }
            break;

        case BarTypeEnum.Horizontal:
            if (nSeries == 1)
            {
                foreach (DataSeriesBar ds in DataList)
                {
                    width = csg.YTick * ds.BarWidth;
                    for (int i = 0; i < ds.LineSeries.Points.Count; i++)
```

```
            {
                DrawHorizontalBar(ds.LineSeries.Points[i],
                                csg, ds, width, 0);
            }
        }
    }
    else
    {
        int j = 0;
        foreach (DataSeriesBar ds in DataList)
        {
            for (int i = 0; i < ds.LineSeries.Points.Count; i++)
            {
                DrawHorizontalBar1(ds.LineSeries.Points[i],
                                csg, ds, nSeries, j);
            }
            j++;
        }
    }
    break;

case BarTypeEnum.HorizontalOverlay:
    if (nSeries > 1)
    {
        int j = 0;
        foreach (DataSeriesBar ds in DataList)
        {
            width = csg.YTick * ds.BarWidth;
            width = width / Math.Pow(2, j);
            for (int i = 0; i < ds.LineSeries.Points.Count; i++)
            {
                DrawHorizontalBar(ds.LineSeries.Points[i],
                                csg, ds, width, 0);
            }
            j++;
        }
    }
    break;

case BarTypeEnum.HorizontalStack:
    if (nSeries > 1)
    {
        List<Point> temp = new List<Point>();
        double[] tempy =
            new double[DataList[0].LineSeries.Points.Count];

        foreach (DataSeriesBar ds in DataList)
        {
            width = csg.YTick * ds.BarWidth;

            for (int i = 0; i < ds.LineSeries.Points.Count; i++)
            {
                if (temp.Count > 0)
```

```
                              {
                                  tempy[i] += temp[i].X;
                              }
                              DrawHorizontalBar(ds.LineSeries.Points[i],
                                                csg, ds, width, tempy[i]);
                          }
                          temp.Clear();
                          temp.AddRange(ds.LineSeries.Points);
                      }
                  }
                  break;
          }
}

private void DrawVerticalBar(Point pt, ChartStyleGridlines csg,
                            DataSeriesBar ds, double width, double y)
{
    Polygon plg = new Polygon();
    plg.Fill = ds.FillColor;
    plg.Stroke = ds.BorderColor;
    plg.StrokeThickness = ds.BorderThickness;

    double x = pt.X - 0.5 * csg.XTick;
    plg.Points.Add(csg.NormalizePoint(new Point(x - width / 2, y)));
    plg.Points.Add(csg.NormalizePoint(new Point(x + width / 2, y)));
    plg.Points.Add(csg.NormalizePoint(new Point(x + width / 2, y + pt.Y)));
    plg.Points.Add(csg.NormalizePoint(new Point(x - width / 2, y + pt.Y)));
    csg.ChartCanvas.Children.Add(plg);
}


private void DrawVerticalBar1(Point pt, ChartStyleGridlines csg,
                            DataSeriesBar ds, int nSeries, int n)
{
    Polygon plg = new Polygon();
    plg.Fill = ds.FillColor;
    plg.Stroke = ds.BorderColor;
    plg.StrokeThickness = ds.BorderThickness;

    double width = 0.7 * csg.XTick;
    double w1 = width / nSeries;
    double w = ds.BarWidth * w1;
    double space = (w1 - w) / 2;
    double x = pt.X - 0.5 * csg.XTick;
    plg.Points.Add(csg.NormalizePoint(
                new Point(x - width / 2 + space + n * w1, 0)));
    plg.Points.Add(csg.NormalizePoint(
                new Point(x - width / 2 + space + n * w1 + w, 0)));
    plg.Points.Add(csg.NormalizePoint(
                new Point(x - width / 2 + space + n * w1 + w, pt.Y)));
    plg.Points.Add(csg.NormalizePoint(
                new Point(x - width / 2 + space + n * w1, pt.Y)));
    csg.ChartCanvas.Children.Add(plg);
```

```
        }

        private void DrawHorizontalBar(Point pt, ChartStyleGridlines csg,
                                      DataSeriesBar ds, double width, double x)
        {
            Polygon plg = new Polygon();
            plg.Fill = ds.FillColor;
            plg.Stroke = ds.BorderColor;
            plg.StrokeThickness = ds.BorderThickness;

            double y = pt.Y - 0.5 * csg.YTick;
            plg.Points.Add(csg.NormalizePoint(new Point(x, y - width / 2)));
            plg.Points.Add(csg.NormalizePoint(new Point(x, y + width / 2)));
            plg.Points.Add(csg.NormalizePoint(new Point(x + pt.X, y + width / 2)));
            plg.Points.Add(csg.NormalizePoint(new Point(x + pt.X, y - width / 2)));
            csg.ChartCanvas.Children.Add(plg);
        }

        private void DrawHorizontalBar1(Point pt, ChartStyleGridlines csg,
                                       DataSeriesBar ds, int nSeries, int n)
        {
            Polygon plg = new Polygon();
            plg.Fill = ds.FillColor;
            plg.Stroke = ds.BorderColor;
            plg.StrokeThickness = ds.BorderThickness;

            double width = 0.7 * csg.YTick;
            double w1 = width / nSeries;
            double w = ds.BarWidth * w1;
            double space = (w1 - w) / 2;
            double y = pt.Y - 0.5 * csg.YTick;
            plg.Points.Add(csg.NormalizePoint(
                    new Point(0, y - width / 2 + space + n * w1)));
            plg.Points.Add(csg.NormalizePoint(
                    new Point(0, y - width / 2 + space + n * w1 + w)));
            plg.Points.Add(csg.NormalizePoint(
                    new Point(pt.X, y - width / 2 + space + n * w1 + w)));
            plg.Points.Add(csg.NormalizePoint(
                    new Point(pt.X, y - width / 2 + space + n * w1)));
            csg.ChartCanvas.Children.Add(plg);
        }
    }
}
```

This class is inherited from the original *DataCollection* class. Here, we first create a private field member named *barType* and its corresponding public property. Six types of bar charts are defined in the *BarTypeEnum*: vertical, horizontal, vertical stack, horizontal stack, vertical overlay, and horizontal overlay bar charts.

The main portion of this class is the *AddBars* method, within which we implement these six types of bar charts. The bar is defined by the point coordinates of its four corners; it is then created using a *Polygon* object. You can specify the fill color, border color, and border thickness for each bar set through the *DataSeriesBar* object. Notice that the original *ChartStyleGridlines* class is used for the bar chart style.

Creating Simple Bar Charts

In this section, I'll show you how to create two simple bar charts, vertical and horizontal. Add a new WPF Window to the current project and name it *BarCharts*. Here is the XAML file for this example:

```
<Window x:Class="Specialized2DCharts.BarCharts"
    xmlns="http://schemas.microsoft.com/winfx/2006/xaml/presentation"
    xmlns:x="http://schemas.microsoft.com/winfx/2006/xaml"
    Title="Bar Charts" Height="400" Width="500">
    <Grid Name="grid1" Margin="10">
        <Grid.ColumnDefinitions>
            <ColumnDefinition Width="Auto"/>
            <ColumnDefinition Name="column1" Width="*"/>
        </Grid.ColumnDefinitions>
        <Grid.RowDefinitions>
            <RowDefinition Height="Auto"/>
            <RowDefinition Name="row1" Height="*"/>
            <RowDefinition Height="Auto"/>
        </Grid.RowDefinitions>
        <TextBlock Margin="2" x:Name="tbTitle" Grid.Column="1" Grid.Row="0"
                   RenderTransformOrigin="0.5,0.5" FontSize="14" FontWeight="Bold"
                   HorizontalAlignment="Stretch" VerticalAlignment="Stretch"
                   TextAlignment="Center" Text="Title"/>

        <TextBlock Margin="2" x:Name="tbXLabel" Grid.Column="1" Grid.Row="2"
                   RenderTransformOrigin="0.5,0.5" TextAlignment="Center"
                   Text="X Axis"/>

        <TextBlock Margin="2" Name="tbYLabel" Grid.Column="0" Grid.Row="1"
                   RenderTransformOrigin="0.5,0.5" TextAlignment="Center"
                   Text="Y Axis">
            <TextBlock.LayoutTransform>
                <RotateTransform Angle="-90"/>
            </TextBlock.LayoutTransform>
        </TextBlock>

        <Grid  Margin="0" x:Name ="chartGrid" Grid.Column="1" Grid.Row="1"
               ClipToBounds="True" Background="Transparent"
               SizeChanged="chartGrid_SizeChanged" />
        <Canvas Margin="2" Name="textCanvas" ClipToBounds="True" Grid.Column="1"
                Grid.Row="1">
            <Canvas Name="chartCanvas" ClipToBounds="True"/>
        </Canvas>
    </Grid>
</Window>
```

This XAML is similar to that used in creating line charts in the previous chapter. Here is the code-behind file for this example:

```
using System;
using System.Collections.Generic;
using System.Windows;
using System.Windows.Controls;
using System.Windows.Media;
```

```csharp
using System.Windows.Media.Imaging;
using System.Windows.Shapes;

namespace Specialized2DCharts
{
    public partial class BarCharts : Window
    {
        private ChartStyleGridlines cs;
        private DataCollectionBar dc;
        private DataSeriesBar ds;

        public BarCharts()
        {
            InitializeComponent();
        }

        private void chartGrid_SizeChanged(object sender, SizeChangedEventArgs e)
        {
            textCanvas.Width = chartGrid.ActualWidth;
            textCanvas.Height = chartGrid.ActualHeight;
            chartCanvas.Children.Clear();
            textCanvas.Children.RemoveRange(1, textCanvas.Children.Count - 1);

            AddVerticalBarChart();
            //AddVerticalGroupBarChart();
            //AddHorizontalBarChart();
            //AddHorizontalGroupBarChart();
        }

        private void AddVerticalBarChart()
        {
            cs = new ChartStyleGridlines();
            dc = new DataCollectionBar();
            ds = new DataSeriesBar();

            dc.BarType = DataCollectionBar.BarTypeEnum.Vertical;
            cs.ChartCanvas = chartCanvas;
            cs.TextCanvas = textCanvas;
            cs.Title = "Bar Chart";
            cs.Xmin = 0;
            cs.Xmax = 5;
            cs.Ymin = 0;
            cs.Ymax = 10;
            cs.XTick = 1;
            cs.YTick = 2;
            cs.GridlinePattern = ChartStyleGridlines.GridlinePatternEnum.Dot;
            cs.GridlineColor = Brushes.Black;
            cs.AddChartStyle(tbTitle, tbXLabel, tbYLabel);

            // Draw the bar chart:
            dc.DataList.Clear();
            ds = new DataSeriesBar();
            ds.BorderColor = Brushes.Red;
```

```
        ds.FillColor = Brushes.Green;
        ds.BarWidth = 0.6;

        for (int i = 0; i < 5; i++)
        {
            double x = i + 1.0;
            double y = 2.0 * x;
            ds.LineSeries.Points.Add(new Point(x, y));
        }
        dc.DataList.Add(ds);
        dc.AddBars(cs);
    }
  }
}
```

Inside the *AddVerticalBarChart* method, we set the *BarType* property to *Vertical* (this is also the default value). The other parameters defined in this method are standard properties for all charts. We then associate bar style properties with the data series. Here, we set bar width to 0.6 (the default value is 0.8). This value must be in the range of [0, 1].

Running this example generates the result shown in Figure 6-1.

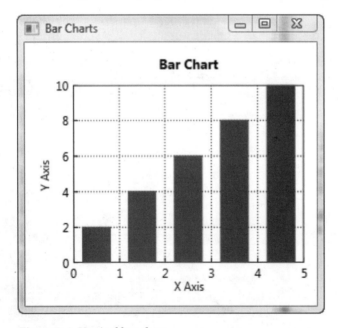

Figure 6-1. *Vertical bar chart*

In some cases, some of your points may be missing data. You can create a bar chart by assigning a zero value for the *Y* value at the missing data point. For example: You have a set of data: $X = [1, 2, 3, 4, 5]$ and $Y = [2, 0, 3, 8, 10]$. You can replace this code snippet in the preceding method:

```
for (int i = 0; i < 5; i++)
{
```

```
    double x = i + 1.0;
    double y = 2.0 * x;
    ds.LineSeries.Points.Add(new Point(x, y));
}
```

with the following code:

```
double[] x = new double[] { 1, 2, 3, 4, 5 };
double[] y = new double[] { 2, 0, 3, 8, 10 };
for (int i = 0; i < x.Length; i++)
{
    ds.LineSeries.Points.Add(new Point(x[i], y[i]));
}
```

This data set will create the result shown in Figure 6-2.

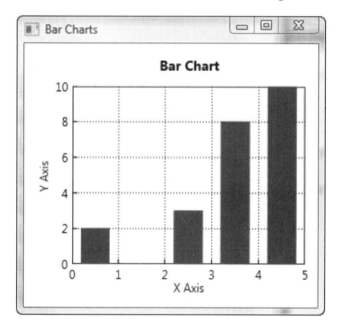

Figure 6-2. Vertical bar chart with a missing data point at x = 2

You can also create a horizontal bar chart just as easily by replacing the *AddVerticalBarChart* method with the following *AddHorizontalBarChart* method:

```
private void AddHorizontalBarChart()
{
    cs = new ChartStyleGridlines();
    dc = new DataCollectionBar();
    ds = new DataSeriesBar();

    dc.BarType = DataCollectionBar.BarTypeEnum.Horizontal;
    cs.ChartCanvas = chartCanvas;
    cs.TextCanvas = textCanvas;
```

227

```
    cs.Title = "Bar Chart";
    cs.Xmin = 0;
    cs.Xmax = 10;
    cs.Ymin = 0;
    cs.Ymax = 5;
    cs.XTick = 2;
    cs.YTick = 1;
    cs.GridlinePattern = ChartStyleGridlines.GridlinePatternEnum.Dot;
    cs.GridlineColor = Brushes.Black;
    cs.AddChartStyle(tbTitle, tbXLabel, tbYLabel);

    // Draw the bar chart:
    dc.DataList.Clear();
    ds = new DataSeriesBar();
    ds.BorderColor = Brushes.Red;
    ds.FillColor = Brushes.Green;
    ds.BarWidth = 0.6;

    for (int i = 0; i < 5; i++)
    {
    double x = i + 1.0;
    double y = 2.0 * x;
    ds.LineSeries.Points.Add(new Point(y, x));
    }
    dc.DataList.Add(ds);
    dc.AddBars(cs);
}
```

Note that I have already implemented the code for creating a variety of the bar charts inside the *chartGrid_SizeChanged* event handler. In order to obtain a desirable bar chart, you just need to uncomment and comment out the appropriate lines of code. Here, we specify the *BarType* as *Horizontal* and switch the *X* and *Y* axis limits. Build and run the project. You should obtain the horizontal bar chart shown in Figure 6-3.

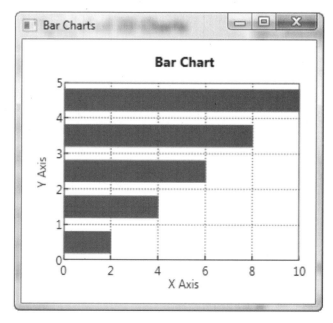

Figure 6-3. Horizontal bar chart

Creating Group Bar Charts

When you have multiple sets of data with the same X values, you can create a group bar chart using the current example program. The Y values are distributed along the X axis, with each Y at a different X drawn at a different location. All of the Y values at the same X are clustered around the same location on the X axis. In order to create such a bar chart, we use the following *AddVerticalGroupBarChart* method:

```
private void AddVerticalGroupBarChart()
{
    cs = new ChartStyleGridlines();
    dc = new DataCollectionBar();
    ds = new DataSeriesBar();

    dc.BarType = DataCollectionBar.BarTypeEnum.Vertical;
    cs.ChartCanvas = chartCanvas;
    cs.TextCanvas = textCanvas;
    cs.Title = dc.BarType.ToString();
    cs.Xmin = 0;
    cs.Xmax = 5;
    cs.Ymin = 0;
    cs.Ymax = 10;
    cs.XTick = 1;
    cs.YTick = 2;
    cs.GridlinePattern = ChartStyleGridlines.GridlinePatternEnum.Dot;
    cs.GridlineColor = Brushes.Black;
    cs.AddChartStyle(tbTitle, tbXLabel, tbYLabel);
```

```
    // Add the first bar series:
    dc.DataList.Clear();
    ds = new DataSeriesBar();
    ds.BorderColor = Brushes.Red;
    ds.FillColor = Brushes.Green;
    ds.BarWidth = 0.9;
    for (int i = 0; i < 5; i++)
    {
        double x = i + 1.0;
        double y = 2.0 * x;
        ds.LineSeries.Points.Add(new Point(x, y));
    }
    dc.DataList.Add(ds);

    // Add the second bar series:
    ds = new DataSeriesBar();
    ds.BorderColor = Brushes.Red;
    ds.FillColor = Brushes.Yellow;
    ds.BarWidth = 0.9;
    for (int i = 0; i < 5; i++)
    {
        double x = i + 1.0;
        double y = 1.5 * x;
        ds.LineSeries.Points.Add(new Point(x, y));
    }
    dc.DataList.Add(ds);

    // Add the third bar series:
    ds = new DataSeriesBar();
    ds.BorderColor = Brushes.Red;
    ds.FillColor = Brushes.Blue;
    ds.BarWidth = 0.9;
    for (int i = 0; i < 5; i++)
    {
        double x = i + 1.0;
        double y = 1.0 * x;
        ds.LineSeries.Points.Add(new Point(x, y));
    }
    dc.DataList.Add(ds);

    dc.AddBars(cs);
}
```

We add three sets of data series to the method, all with the same set of *X* values. The bar width is set to 0.9. The fill colors are green, yellow, and blue, respectively; the border color is red for all of the bars. Note that the bar type is still set to *Vertical*. The program will automatically create a grouped vertical bar chart if more than one set of data is provided. These data sets produce the results shown in Figure 6-4.

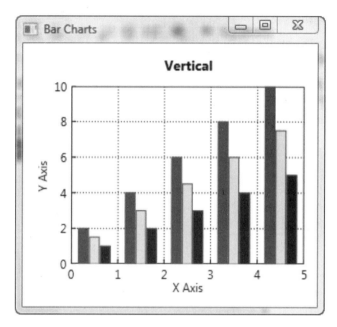

Figure 6-4. Grouped vertical bar chart

Similarly, you can easily create a grouped horizontal bar chart using the following *AddHorizontalGroupBarChart* method:

```
private void AddHorizontalGroupBarChart()
{
    cs = new ChartStyleGridlines();
    dc = new DataCollectionBar();
    ds = new DataSeriesBar();

    dc.BarType = DataCollectionBar.BarTypeEnum.Horizontal;
    cs.ChartCanvas = chartCanvas;
    cs.TextCanvas = textCanvas;
    cs.Title = dc.BarType.ToString();
    cs.Xmin = 0;
    cs.Xmax = 10;
    cs.Ymin = 0;
    cs.Ymax = 5;
    cs.XTick = 5;
    cs.YTick = 1;
    cs.GridlinePattern = ChartStyleGridlines.GridlinePatternEnum.Dot;
    cs.GridlineColor = Brushes.Black;
    cs.AddChartStyle(tbTitle, tbXLabel, tbYLabel);

    // Add the first bar series:
    dc.DataList.Clear();
    ds = new DataSeriesBar();
    ds.BorderColor = Brushes.Red;
```

231

```
    ds.FillColor = Brushes.Green;
    ds.BarWidth = 0.8;
    for (int i = 0; i < 5; i++)
    {
        double x = i + 1.0;
        double y = 2.0 * x;
        ds.LineSeries.Points.Add(new Point(y, x));
    }
    dc.DataList.Add(ds);

    // Add the second bar series:
    ds = new DataSeriesBar();
    ds.BorderColor = Brushes.Red;
    ds.FillColor = Brushes.Yellow;
    ds.BarWidth = 0.8;
    for (int i = 0; i < 5; i++)
    {
        double x = i + 1.0;
        double y = 1.5 * x;
        ds.LineSeries.Points.Add(new Point(y, x));
    }
    dc.DataList.Add(ds);

    // Add the third bar series:
    ds = new DataSeriesBar();
    ds.BorderColor = Brushes.Red;
    ds.FillColor = Brushes.Blue;
    ds.BarWidth = 0.8;
    for (int i = 0; i < 5; i++)
    {
        double x = i + 1.0;
        double y = 1.0 * x;
        ds.LineSeries.Points.Add(new Point(y, x));
    }
    dc.DataList.Add(ds);
    dc.AddBars(cs);
}
```

This produces the results of Figure 6-5.

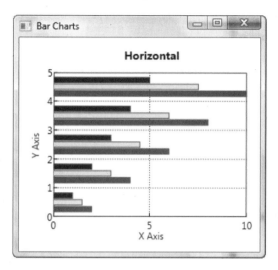

Figure 6-5. *Grouped Horizontal chart*

Creating Overlay Bar Charts

It is also easy to create an overlaid bar chart with the current example program. Use the code for the *AddVerticalGroupBarChart* method from the previous subsection, but change the *BarType* property to the *VerticalOverlay*:

```
dc.BarType = DataCollectionBar.BarTypeEnum.VerticalOverlay;
```

This will generate the output of Figure 6-6.

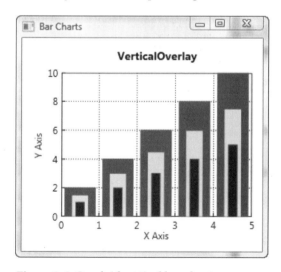

Figure 6-6. *Overlaid vertical bar chart*

Similarly, you can create an overlaid horizontal bar chart using the same code of the *AddHorizontalGroupBarChart* method, but with the following *BarType*:

```
dc.BarType = DataCollectionBar.BarTypeEnum.HorizontalOverlay;
```

This will produce the result shown in Figure 6-7.

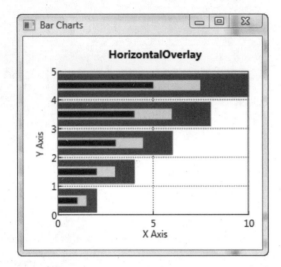

Figure 6-7. Overlaid horizontal bar chart

Creating Stacked Bar Charts

Bar charts can show how different *Y* values at the same *X* point contribute to the sum of all of the *Y* values at the point. These types of bar charts are referred to as *stacked* bar charts.

Stacked bar graphs display one bar per *X* value. The bars are divided into several fragments according to the number of *Y* values. For vertical stacked bar charts, the height of each bar equals the sum of all of the *Y* values at a given *X* value. Each fragment is equal to the value of its respective *Y* value.

You can create stacked bar charts with the current example program. Use the same code for the *AddVerticalGroupBarChart* method as in the previous subsection, but change the *BarType* property to the following:

```
dc.BarType = DataCollectionBar.BarTypeEnum.VerticalStack;
cs.Ymax = 25;
cs.YTick = 5;
```

This will generate the stacked vertical bar chart shown in Figure 6-8.

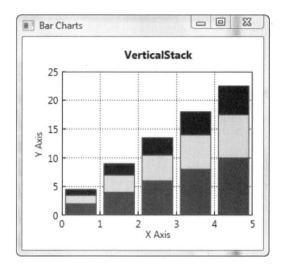

Figure 6-8. Stacked vertical bar chart

Similarly, you can create a stacked horizontal bar chart using the same code of the *AddHorizontalGroupBarChart* method, with the following changes:

```
dc.BarType = DataCollectionBar.BarTypeEnum.HorizontalStack;
cs.Xmax = 25;
cs.XTick = 5;
```

This will produce the result shown in Figure 6-9.

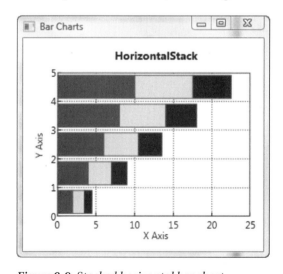

Figure 6-9. Stacked horizontal bar chart

235

Stair-Step Charts

In this section, I'll show you how to create a stair-step chart. Instead of creating lines that directly connect your data, you can choose to have your data plotted in a way that emphasizes the discrete nature of the data. Namely, stair-step charts draw horizontal lines at the level specified by the Y data. This level will be held constant over the period between the values specified by the X data values. Stair-step charts are similar to bar charts except for the fact that the vertical lines are not dropped all the way down to the zero-value point on the Y axis. This type of plot is useful for drawing time-history plots of digitally sampled data systems.

DataSeries for Stair-Step Charts

You can use the same *ChartStyle* class implemented in the previous chapter to create stair-step charts. However, you'll need to modify the *DataSeries* and *DataCollection* classes in order to create these charts.

Add a new class to the project *Specialized2DCharts* and name it *DataSeriesStairstep*. Here is the code listing for this new class:

```
using System;
using System.Windows;
using System.Windows.Media;
using System.Windows.Shapes;

namespace Specialized2DCharts
{
    public class DataSeriesStairstep : DataSeries
    {
        private Polyline stairstepLineSeries = new Polyline();
        private Brush stairstepLineColor;
        private double stairstepLineThickness = 1;
        private StairstepLinePatternEnum stairstepLinePattern;

        public Brush StairstepLineColor
        {
            get { return stairstepLineColor; }
            set { stairstepLineColor = value; }
        }

        public Polyline StairstepLineSeries
        {
            get { return stairstepLineSeries; }
            set { stairstepLineSeries = value; }
        }

        public double StairstepLineThickness
        {
            get { return stairstepLineThickness; }
            set { stairstepLineThickness = value; }
        }

        public StairstepLinePatternEnum StairstepLinePattern
        {
            get { return stairstepLinePattern; }
```

236

```
            set { stairstepLinePattern = value; }
        }

        public void AddStairstepLinePattern()
        {
            StairstepLineSeries.Stroke = StairstepLineColor;
            StairstepLineSeries.StrokeThickness = StairstepLineThickness;

            switch (StairstepLinePattern)
            {
                case StairstepLinePatternEnum.Dash:
                    StairstepLineSeries.StrokeDashArray =
                        new DoubleCollection(new double[2] { 4, 3 });
                    break;
                case StairstepLinePatternEnum.Dot:
                    StairstepLineSeries.StrokeDashArray =
                        new DoubleCollection(new double[2] { 1, 2 });
                    break;
                case StairstepLinePatternEnum.DashDot:
                    StairstepLineSeries.StrokeDashArray =
                        new DoubleCollection(new double[4] { 4, 2, 1, 2 });
                    break;
                case StairstepLinePatternEnum.None:
                    StairstepLineSeries.Stroke = Brushes.Transparent;
                    break;
            }
        }

        public enum StairstepLinePatternEnum
        {
            Solid = 1,
            Dash = 2,
            Dot = 3,
            DashDot = 4,
            None = 5
        }
    }
}
```

The class is inherited from the *DataSeries* class. It defines the style for the *Polyline* object, which is used to create the stair-step curve. This class is very similar to the original *DataSeries* class used for creating line charts.

DataCollection for Stair-Step Charts

Add a new class, *DataCollectionStairstep,* to the current project. Here is the code listing for this class:

```
using System;
using System.Collections.Generic;
using System.Windows;
using System.Windows.Controls;
using System.Windows.Media;
using System.Windows.Shapes;
```

```
namespace Specialized2DCharts
{
    public class DataCollectionStairstep : DataCollection
    {
        public void AddStairstep(ChartStyleGridlines csg)
        {
            foreach (DataSeriesStairstep ds in DataList)
            {
                List<Point> ptList = new List<Point>();
                Point[] pts = new Point[2];
                ds.AddStairstepLinePattern();

                // Create Stairstep data:
                for (int i = 0; i < ds.LineSeries.Points.Count - 1; i++)
                {
                    pts[0] = ds.LineSeries.Points[i];
                    pts[1] = ds.LineSeries.Points[i + 1];
                    ptList.Add(pts[0]);
                    ptList.Add(new Point(pts[1].X, pts[0].Y));
                }
                ptList.Add(new Point(pts[1].X, pts[0].Y));

                // Draw stairstep line:
                for (int i = 0; i < ptList.Count; i++)
                {
                    ds.StairstepLineSeries.Points.Add(
                        csg.NormalizePoint(ptList[i]));
                }
                csg.ChartCanvas.Children.Add(ds.StairstepLineSeries);
            }
        }
    }
}
```

This class simply implements an *AddStairstep* method. Note how we create the stair-step data — for two adjacent points, we regenerate two points with the same *Y* values, which provide the stair-step levels.

Creating Stair-Step Charts

In this section, I'll show you how to create stair-step charts using the *DataSeriesStairstep* and *DataCollectionStairstep* classes implemented in the previous sections. Add a new WPF Window to the current project and name it *StairstepCharts*. The XAML file for this example is the same as that used in the *BarCharts* example. Here I list only the code-behind file for this example:

```
using System;
using System.Windows;
using System.Windows.Controls;
using System.Windows.Media;
using System.Windows.Shapes;

namespace Specialized2DCharts
```

```
{
    public partial class StairstepCharts : Window
    {
        private ChartStyleGridlines cs;
        private DataCollectionStairstep dc;
        private DataSeriesStairstep ds;

        public StairstepCharts()
        {
            InitializeComponent();
        }

        private void chartGrid_SizeChanged(object sender, SizeChangedEventArgs e)
        {
            textCanvas.Width = chartGrid.ActualWidth;
            textCanvas.Height = chartGrid.ActualHeight;
            chartCanvas.Children.Clear();
            textCanvas.Children.RemoveRange(1, textCanvas.Children.Count - 1);
            AddChart();
        }

        private void AddChart()
        {
            cs = new ChartStyleGridlines();
            dc = new DataCollectionStairstep();
            ds = new DataSeriesStairstep();

            cs.ChartCanvas = chartCanvas;
            cs.TextCanvas = textCanvas;
            cs.Title = "Stair Step Chart";
            cs.Xmin = 0;
            cs.Xmax = 8;
            cs.Ymin = -1.5;
            cs.Ymax = 1.5;
            cs.XTick = 1;
            cs.YTick = 0.5;
            cs.GridlinePattern = ChartStyleGridlines.GridlinePatternEnum.Dot;
            cs.GridlineColor = Brushes.Black;
            cs.AddChartStyle(tbTitle, tbXLabel, tbYLabel);

            // Draw the stair step chart:
            dc.DataList.Clear();
            ds = new DataSeriesStairstep();
            ds.StairstepLineColor = Brushes.Red;
            for (int i = 0; i < 50; i++)
            {
                ds.LineSeries.Points.Add(new Point(0.4 * i, Math.Sin(0.4 * i)));
            }
            dc.DataList.Add(ds);
            dc.AddStairstep(cs);
        }
    }
}
```

Here we draw a red polyline for the stair-step chart by specifying the *StairstepLineColor* property within the *AddChart* method. Running this program generates the output shown in Figure 6-10.

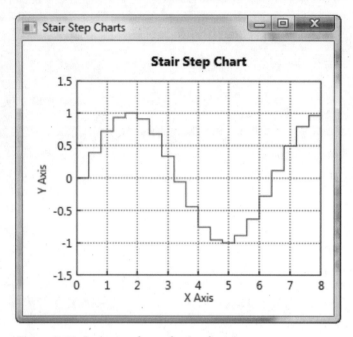

Figure 6-10. *Stair step chart of a sine function*

You can also overlap a stair-step chart with a line plot. You do this by adding the following boldface code snippet to the *AddChart* method:

```
private void AddChart()
{
    ... ...

    // Draw the stair step chart:
    dc.DataList.Clear();
    ds = new DataSeriesStairstep();
    ds.StairstepLineColor = Brushes.Red;
    for (int i = 0; i < 50; i++)
    {
        ds.LineSeries.Points.Add(new Point(0.4 * i, Math.Sin(0.4 * i)));
    }
    ds.LineColor = Brushes.Black;
    ds.LinePattern = DataSeries.LinePatternEnum.Dash;
    ds.Symbols.SymbolType = Symbols.SymbolTypeEnum.Circle;
    dc.DataList.Add(ds);
    dc.AddStairstep(cs);
    dc.AddLines(cs);
}
```

Here we specify both stair-step and line chart styles. We also add symbols to the line chart. Rebuilding this project yields the results shown in Figure 6-11.

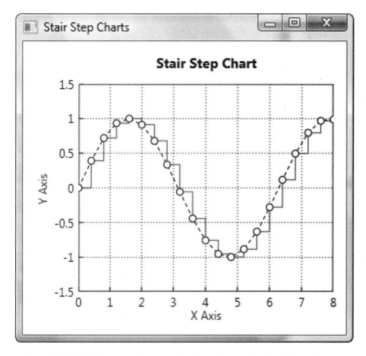

Figure 6-11. Stair-step chart and line chart of a sine function

Stem Charts

Stem charts provide another way to visualize discrete data sequences, such as digitally sampled time-series data. In this type of chart, vertical lines terminate with a marker symbol at each data value. In 2D stem charts, these stem lines extend from the *X* axis.

Creating stem charts is much easier because we can use the original *ChartStyle* and *DataSeries* classes. The only class that needs to be modified is the *DataCollection* class.

DataCollection for Stem Charts

Add a new class, *DataCollectionStem*, to the current project. This class derives from the original *DataCollection* class. Here is its code listing:

```
using System;
using System.Windows;
using System.Windows.Media;
using System.Windows.Shapes;
```

```
namespace Specialized2DCharts
{
    class DataCollectionStem : DataCollection
    {
        public void AddStems(ChartStyleGridlines csg)
        {
            foreach (DataSeries ds in DataList)
            {
                Point[] pts = new Point[2];
                for (int i = 0; i < ds.LineSeries.Points.Count; i++)
                {
                    pts[0] =
                        csg.NormalizePoint(new Point(ds.LineSeries.Points[i].X, 0));
                    pts[1] = csg.NormalizePoint(ds.LineSeries.Points[i]);

                    Line line = new Line();
                    line.Stroke = ds.LineColor;
                    line.StrokeThickness = ds.LineThickness;
                    line.X1 = pts[0].X;
                    line.Y1 = pts[0].Y;
                    line.X2 = pts[1].X;
                    line.Y2 = pts[1].Y;
                    csg.ChartCanvas.Children.Add(line);
                    ds.Symbols.AddSymbol(csg.ChartCanvas,
                        csg.NormalizePoint(ds.LineSeries.Points[i]));
                }
            }
        }
    }
}
```

This class looks quite simple, implementing only an *AddStem* method. Note that at a given point (x, y), we draw a straight line from $(x, 0)$ to (x, y), which defines the stem line at the point (x, y). You specify the stem line style, such as the *LineColor* and the *LineThickness*, using the line style defined in the original *DataSeries* class; you define the symbols at the data values of the stem line using the original *Symbols* class.

Creating Stem Charts

In this section, I'll show you how to create stem charts using the *DataCollectionStem* class implemented in the previous section. Add a new WPF Window to the current project and name it *StemCharts*. The XAML file for this example is the same as that used in the bar chart example. Here I only list the code-behind file for this example:

```
using System;
using System.Windows;
using System.Windows.Media;
using System.Windows.Shapes;

namespace Specialized2DCharts
{
    public partial class StemCharts : Window
    {
```

```
private ChartStyleGridlines cs;
private DataCollectionStem dc;
private DataSeries ds;

public StemCharts()
{
    InitializeComponent();
}

private void chartGrid_SizeChanged(object sender, SizeChangedEventArgs e)
{
    textCanvas.Width = chartGrid.ActualWidth;
    textCanvas.Height = chartGrid.ActualHeight;
    chartCanvas.Children.Clear();
    textCanvas.Children.RemoveRange(1, textCanvas.Children.Count - 1);
    AddChart();
}

private void AddChart()
{
    cs = new ChartStyleGridlines();
    dc = new DataCollectionStem();
    ds = new DataSeries();

    cs.ChartCanvas = chartCanvas;
    cs.TextCanvas = textCanvas;
    cs.Title = "Stem Chart";
    cs.Xmin = 0;
    cs.Xmax = 8;
    cs.Ymin = -1.5;
    cs.Ymax = 1.5;
    cs.XTick = 1;
    cs.YTick = 0.5;
    cs.GridlinePattern = ChartStyleGridlines.GridlinePatternEnum.Dot;
    cs.GridlineColor = Brushes.Black;
    cs.AddChartStyle(tbTitle, tbXLabel, tbYLabel);

    // Draw the stair step chart:
    dc.DataList.Clear();
    ds = new DataSeries();

    for (int i = 0; i < 50; i++)
    {
        ds.LineSeries.Points.Add(new Point(0.4 * i, Math.Sin(0.4 * i)));
    }

    ds.LineColor = Brushes.Red;
    ds.Symbols.SymbolType = Symbols.SymbolTypeEnum.Diamond;
    ds.Symbols.FillColor = Brushes.Yellow;
    ds.Symbols.BorderColor = Brushes.DarkGreen;
    dc.DataList.Add(ds);
    dc.AddStems(cs);
}
```

```
        }
}
```

This example produces the result shown in Figure 6-12. The current program has the ability to create a stem chart that terminates with any of the symbols defined in the *Symbols* class. In addition, these terminating symbols can be filled or unfilled.

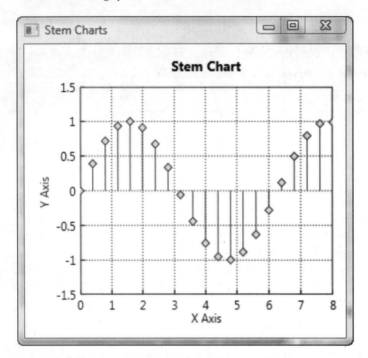

Figure 6-12. *Stem chart of a sine function*

Error Bar Charts

Error bars show the confidence level of data or the deviation along a curve. Error bar charts plot the *Y* data and draw an error bar at each *Y* data value. The error bar is the distance of the error function above and below the curve so that each bar is symmetric around the curve.

DataSeries for Error Bars

You can use the same *ChartStyle* class implemented in the previous chapter to create error bar charts. However, you'll need to modify the *DataSeries* and *DataCollection* classes.

Add a new class to the project *Specialized2DCharts* and name it *DataSeriesErrorbar*. Here is the code listing for this new class:

```
using System;
using System.Windows;
```

```
using System.Windows.Media;
using System.Windows.Shapes;

namespace Specialized2DCharts
{
    public class DataSeriesErrorbar : DataSeries
    {
        private Polyline errorLineSeries = new Polyline();
        private Brush errorLineColor;
        private double errorLineThickness = 1;
        private ErrorLinePatternEnum errorLinePattern;

        public Brush ErrorLineColor
        {
            get { return errorLineColor; }
            set { errorLineColor = value; }
        }

        public Polyline ErrorLineSeries
        {
            get { return errorLineSeries; }
            set { errorLineSeries = value; }
        }

        public double ErrorLineThickness
        {
            get { return errorLineThickness; }
            set { errorLineThickness = value; }
        }

        public ErrorLinePatternEnum ErrorLinePattern
        {
            get { return errorLinePattern; }
            set { errorLinePattern = value; }
        }

        public void AddErrorLinePattern()
        {
            ErrorLineSeries.Stroke = ErrorLineColor;
            ErrorLineSeries.StrokeThickness = ErrorLineThickness;

            switch (ErrorLinePattern)
            {
                case ErrorLinePatternEnum.Dash:
                    ErrorLineSeries.StrokeDashArray =
                        new DoubleCollection(new double[2] { 4, 3 });
                    break;
                case ErrorLinePatternEnum.Dot:
                    ErrorLineSeries.StrokeDashArray =
                        new DoubleCollection(new double[2] { 1, 2 });
                    break;
                case ErrorLinePatternEnum.DashDot:
                    ErrorLineSeries.StrokeDashArray =
```

```
                        new DoubleCollection(new double[4] { 4, 2, 1, 2 });
                    break;
                case ErrorLinePatternEnum.None:
                    ErrorLineSeries.Stroke = Brushes.Transparent;
                    break;
            }
        }

        public enum ErrorLinePatternEnum
        {
            Solid = 1,
            Dash = 2,
            Dot = 3,
            DashDot = 4,
            None = 5
        }
    }
}
```

The class is inherited from the *DataSeries* class. It defines the line style for error bars. This means you can specify the line styles for the original line curve and the error bars independently. This class is very similar to the original *DataSeries* class for line charts. Note also that the *ErrorLineSeries*'s *PointCollection* property holds the data of the error bars. In order to create an error bar chart, you need to provide two independent data sets, one for the original line curve and another for the error bars.

DataCollection for Error Bars

Add a new class, *DataCollectionErrorbar*, to the current project. Here is the code listing for this class:

```
using System;
using System.Windows;
using System.Collections.Generic;
using System.Windows.Media;
using System.Windows.Shapes;

namespace Specialized2DCharts
{
    public class DataCollectionErrorbar : DataCollection
    {
        private List<DataSeriesErrorbar> errorList;

        public DataCollectionErrorbar()
        {
            errorList = new List<DataSeriesErrorbar>();
        }

        public List<DataSeriesErrorbar> ErrorList
        {
            get { return errorList; }
            set { errorList = value; }
        }

        public void AddErrorbars(ChartStyleGridlines csg)
```

```
        {
            foreach (DataSeriesErrorbar ds in DataList)
            {
                double barLength = (csg.NormalizePoint(ds.LineSeries.Points[1]).X -
                    csg.NormalizePoint(ds.LineSeries.Points[0]).X) / 3;

                for (int i = 0; i < ds.ErrorLineSeries.Points.Count; i++)
                {
                    Point ep = ds.ErrorLineSeries.Points[i];
                    Point dp = ds.LineSeries.Points[i];
                    Point[] pts = new Point[2];
                    pts[0] = csg.NormalizePoint(new Point(dp.X, dp.Y - ep.Y / 2));
                    pts[1] = csg.NormalizePoint(new Point(dp.X, dp.Y + ep.Y / 2));
                    Line line = new Line();
                    line.Stroke = ds.ErrorLineColor;
                    line.StrokeThickness = ds.ErrorLineThickness;
                    ds.AddErrorLinePattern();
                    line.X1 = pts[0].X;
                    line.Y1 = pts[0].Y;
                    line.X2 = pts[1].X;
                    line.Y2 = pts[1].Y;
                    csg.ChartCanvas.Children.Add(line);
                    line = new Line();
                    line.Stroke = ds.ErrorLineColor;
                    line.StrokeThickness = ds.ErrorLineThickness;
                    ds.AddErrorLinePattern();
                    line.X1 = pts[0].X - barLength / 2;
                    line.Y1 = pts[0].Y;
                    line.X2 = pts[0].X + barLength / 2;
                    line.Y2 = pts[0].Y;
                    csg.ChartCanvas.Children.Add(line);
                    line = new Line();
                    line.Stroke = ds.ErrorLineColor;
                    line.StrokeThickness = ds.ErrorLineThickness;
                    ds.AddErrorLinePattern();
                    line.X1 = pts[1].X - barLength / 2;
                    line.Y1 = pts[1].Y;
                    line.X2 = pts[1].X + barLength / 2;
                    line.Y2 = pts[1].Y;
                    csg.ChartCanvas.Children.Add(line);
                }
            }
        }
    }
}
```

The *AddErrorbars* method in this class allows you to draw error bars. You must create the original line curve using the *AddLines* method in the original *DataCollection* class.

Creating Error Bar Charts

In this section, I'll show you how to create error bar charts using the *DataSeriesErrorbar* and *DataCollectionErrorbar* classes implemented in the previous sections. Add a new WPF Window to the current project and name it *ErrorBars*. The XAML file for this example is the same as that used in the bar chart example. Here I list only the code-behind file for this example:

```
using System;
using System.Windows;
using System.Windows.Media;
using System.Windows.Shapes;

namespace Specialized2DCharts
{
    public partial class ErrorBars : Window
    {
        private ChartStyleGridlines cs;
        private DataCollectionErrorbar dc;
        private DataSeriesErrorbar ds;

        public ErrorBars()
        {
            InitializeComponent();
        }

        private void chartGrid_SizeChanged(object sender, SizeChangedEventArgs e)
        {
            textCanvas.Width = chartGrid.ActualWidth;
            textCanvas.Height = chartGrid.ActualHeight;
            chartCanvas.Children.Clear();
            textCanvas.Children.RemoveRange(1, textCanvas.Children.Count - 1);
            AddChart();
        }

        private void AddChart()
        {
            cs = new ChartStyleGridlines();
            dc = new DataCollectionErrorbar();
            ds = new DataSeriesErrorbar();

            cs.ChartCanvas = chartCanvas;
            cs.TextCanvas = textCanvas;
            cs.Title = "Error Bar Chart";
            cs.Xmin = 0;
            cs.Xmax = 12;
            cs.Ymin = -1;
            cs.Ymax = 6;
            cs.XTick = 2;
            cs.YTick = 1;
            cs.GridlinePattern = ChartStyleGridlines.GridlinePatternEnum.Dot;
            cs.GridlineColor = Brushes.Black;
            cs.AddChartStyle(tbTitle, tbXLabel, tbYLabel);
```

```
        dc.DataList.Clear();
        dc.ErrorList.Clear();
        ds = new DataSeriesErrorbar();
        ds.LineColor = Brushes.Blue;
        ds.Symbols.SymbolType = Symbols.SymbolTypeEnum.Circle;
        ds.Symbols.BorderColor = Brushes.DarkGreen;
        ds.ErrorLineColor = Brushes.Red;

        for (int i = 2; i < 22; i++)
        {
            ds.LineSeries.Points.Add(
                new Point(0.5 * i, 10.0 * Math.Exp(-0.5 * i)));
            ds.ErrorLineSeries.Points.Add(new Point(0.5 * i, 3.0 / (0.5 * i)));
        }

        dc.DataList.Add(ds);
        dc.AddErrorbars(cs);
        dc.AddLines(cs);
    }
}
}
```

Inside the *AddChart* method, we assume that the error function is proportional to $1/x$. However, you can specify any error function you like, such as the standard deviation.

Run the application by pressing F5. You should obtain the results shown in Figure 6-13. The current program allows you to specify the style of the data line and the error bars separately.

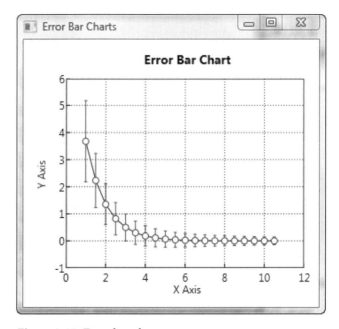

Figure 6-13. Error bar chart

Area Charts

An area chart displays Y data values as one or more curves and fills the area beneath each curve. When the *DataCollection* object has more than one data series, the curves are stacked, showing the relative contribution of each data series to the total height of the curve at each X value.

DataSeries for Area Charts

You can use the same *ChartStyle* class implemented in the previous chapter to create area charts. However, you need to modify the *DataSeries* and *DataCollection* classes.

Add a new class to the project *Specialized2DCharts* and name it *DataSeriesArea*. Here is the code listing for this new class:

```
using System;
using System.Windows;
using System.Windows.Media;
using System.Windows.Shapes;

namespace Specialized2DCharts
{
    public class DataSeriesArea : DataSeries
    {
        private Polygon areaSeries = new Polygon();
        private Brush borderColor = Brushes.Black;
        private double borderThickness = 1;
        private BorderPatternEnum borderPattern;
        private Brush fillColor = Brushes.White;

        public Brush FillColor
        {
            get { return fillColor; }
            set { fillColor = value; }
        }

        public Brush BorderColor
        {
            get { return borderColor; }
            set { borderColor = value; }
        }

        public Polygon AreaSeries
        {
            get { return areaSeries; }
            set { areaSeries = value; }
        }

        public double BorderThickness
        {
            get { return borderThickness; }
            set { borderThickness = value; }
        }
```

```
public BorderPatternEnum BorderPattern
{
    get { return borderPattern; }
    set { borderPattern = value; }
}

public void AddBorderPattern()
{
    AreaSeries.Stroke = BorderColor;
    AreaSeries.StrokeThickness = BorderThickness;
    AreaSeries.Fill = FillColor;

    switch (BorderPattern)
    {
        case BorderPatternEnum.Dash:
            AreaSeries.StrokeDashArray =
                new DoubleCollection(new double[2] { 4, 3 });
            break;
        case BorderPatternEnum.Dot:
            AreaSeries.StrokeDashArray =
                new DoubleCollection(new double[2] { 1, 2 });
            break;
        case BorderPatternEnum.DashDot:
            AreaSeries.StrokeDashArray =
                new DoubleCollection(new double[4] { 4, 2, 1, 2 });
            break;
        case BorderPatternEnum.None:
            AreaSeries.Stroke = Brushes.Transparent;
            break;
    }
}

public enum BorderPatternEnum
{
    Solid = 1,
    Dash = 2,
    Dot = 3,
    DashDot = 4,
    None = 5
}
    }
}
```

This class is inherited from the *DataSeries* class. It defines the style for area charts, including the *Border* style and the *Fill* property.

DataCollection for Area Charts

Add a new class, *DataCollectionArea*, to the current project. Here is the code listing for this class:

```
using System;
using System.Windows;
using System.Collections.Generic;
```

```csharp
using System.Windows.Media;
using System.Windows.Shapes;

namespace Specialized2DCharts
{
    class DataCollectionArea : DataCollection
    {
        private double areaAxis = 0;
        private List<DataSeriesArea> areaList;

        public DataCollectionArea()
        {
            areaList = new List<DataSeriesArea>();
        }

        public List<DataSeriesArea> AreaList
        {
            get { return areaList; }
            set { areaList = value; }
        }

        public double AreaAxis
        {
            get { return areaAxis; }
            set { areaAxis = value; }
        }

        public void AddAreas(ChartStyleGridlines csg)
        {
            int nSeries = AreaList.Count;
            int nPoints = AreaList[0].AreaSeries.Points.Count;
            double[] ySum = new double[nPoints];
            Point[] pts = new Point[2 * nPoints];
            Point[] pt0 = new Point[nPoints];
            Point[] pt1 = new Point[nPoints];

            for (int i = 0; i < nPoints; i++)
                ySum[i] = AreaAxis;

            foreach (DataSeriesArea area in AreaList)
            {
                area.AddBorderPattern();
                for (int i = 0; i < nPoints; i++)
                {
                    pt0[i] = new Point(area.AreaSeries.Points[i].X, ySum[i]);
                    ySum[i] += area.AreaSeries.Points[i].Y;
                    pt1[i] = new Point(area.AreaSeries.Points[i].X, ySum[i]);
                    pts[i] = csg.NormalizePoint(pt0[i]);
                    pts[2 * nPoints - 1 - i] = csg.NormalizePoint(pt1[i]);
                }
                area.AreaSeries.Points.Clear();
                for (int i = 0; i < pts.GetLength(0); i++)
                    area.AreaSeries.Points.Add(pts[i]);
```

```
            csg.ChartCanvas.Children.Add(area.AreaSeries);
        }
    }
}
}
```

In this class, we first define two properties, *AreaAxis* and *AreaList*. The *AreaAxis* property allows you to offset the *Y* value below which the area is filled. The *AreaList* property holds the *DataSeriesArea* objects. In the *AddAreas* method, we stack the *Y* data values from all of the different *DataSeriesArea* objects to show the relative contribution of each *DataSeriesArea* to the total height of the curve at each *X* value. Finally, we draw the area by filling the polygon with the specified colors.

Creating Area Charts

In this section, I'll show you how to create area charts using the *DataSeriesArea* and *DataCollectionArea* classes implemented in the previous sections. Add a new WPF Window to the current project and name it *AreaCharts*. The XAML file for this example is the same as that used in the *BarCharts* example. Here I list only the code-behind file for this example:

```
using System;
using System.Collections.Generic;
using System.Windows;
using System.Windows.Media;
using System.Windows.Shapes;

namespace Specialized2DCharts
{
    public partial class AreaCharts : Window
    {
        private ChartStyleGridlines cs;
        private DataCollectionArea dc;
        private DataSeriesArea area;

        public AreaCharts()
        {
            InitializeComponent();
        }

        private void chartGrid_SizeChanged(object sender, SizeChangedEventArgs e)
        {
            textCanvas.Width = chartGrid.ActualWidth;
            textCanvas.Height = chartGrid.ActualHeight;
            chartCanvas.Children.Clear();
            textCanvas.Children.RemoveRange(1, textCanvas.Children.Count - 1);
            AddChart();
        }

        private void AddChart()
        {
            cs = new ChartStyleGridlines();
            dc = new DataCollectionArea();
            area=new DataSeriesArea();
```

```
        cs.ChartCanvas = chartCanvas;
        cs.TextCanvas = textCanvas;
        cs.Title = "Area Chart";
        cs.Xmin = 0;
        cs.Xmax = 10;
        cs.Ymin = 0;
        cs.Ymax = 10;
        cs.XTick = 2;
        cs.YTick = 2;
        cs.GridlinePattern = ChartStyleGridlines.GridlinePatternEnum.Dot;
        cs.GridlineColor = Brushes.Black;
        cs.AddChartStyle(tbTitle, tbXLabel, tbYLabel);
        dc.AreaList.Clear();

        // Add sine data:
        area = new DataSeriesArea();
        area.BorderColor = Brushes.Black;
        area.FillColor = Brushes.LightPink;
        for (int i = 0; i < 41; i++)
        {
            area.AreaSeries.Points.Add(
                new Point(0.25 * i, 2.0 + Math.Sin(0.25 * i)));
        }
        dc.AreaList.Add(area);

        // Add cosine data:
        area = new DataSeriesArea();
        area.BorderColor = Brushes.Black;
        area.FillColor = Brushes.LightBlue;
        for (int i = 0; i < 41; i++)
        {
            area.AreaSeries.Points.Add(
                new Point(0.25 * i, 2.0 + Math.Cos(0.25 * i)));
        }
        dc.AreaList.Add(area);

        // Add another sine data:
        area = new DataSeriesArea();
        area.BorderColor = Brushes.Black;
        area.FillColor = Brushes.LightGreen;
        for (int i = 0; i < 41; i++)
        {
            area.AreaSeries.Points.Add(
                new Point(0.25 * i, 3.0 + Math.Sin(0.25 * i)));
        }
        dc.AreaList.Add(area);
        dc.AddAreas(cs);
    }
  }
}
```

Within the *AddChart* method, we add three sets of *DataSeriesArea* objects to the project. Running this application produces the result shown in Figure 6-14.

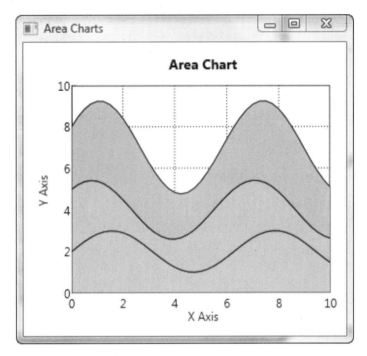

Figure 6-14. *Area chart*

Polar Charts

So far we have discussed various chart applications that make use of the Cartesian coordinate system. Now we'll plot data in polar coordinates (*r, theta*). Most polar charts, including commercial software packages, plot only positive *r* values; i.e., they plot absolute *r* values whether *r* is positive or negative. Here I'll show you how to create more generalized polar charts in WPF, in which *r* can have negative values. These polar charts will also allow you to specify the *r* range [*rMin, rMax*] and to draw multiple curves on a single polar chart.

Chart Style for Polar Charts

Unlike the charts created previously, where we used the original chart style class for line charts, we need to implement a new chart style class for polar charts. Add a new class to the current project and name it *ChartStylePolar*. Here is its code listing:

```
using System;
using System.Windows.Controls;
using System.Windows;
using System.Windows.Media;
using System.Windows.Shapes;
```

```csharp
namespace Specialized2DCharts
{
    public class ChartStylePolar
    {
        private double angleStep = 30;
        private AngleDirectionEnum angleDirection =
                AngleDirectionEnum.CounterClockWise;
        private double rmin = 0;
        private double rmax = 1;
        private int nTicks = 4;
        private Brush lineColor = Brushes.Black;
        private double lineThickness = 1;
        private LinePatternEnum linePattern = LinePatternEnum.Dash;

        public Canvas ChartCanvas { get; set; }

        public LinePatternEnum LinePattern
        {
            get { return linePattern; }
            set { linePattern = value; }
        }

        public double LineThickness
        {
            get { return lineThickness; }
            set { lineThickness = value; }
        }

        public Brush LineColor
        {
            get { return lineColor; }
            set { lineColor = value; }
        }

        public int NTicks
        {
            get { return nTicks; }
            set { nTicks = value; }
        }

        public double Rmax
        {
            get { return rmax; }
            set { rmax = value; }
        }

        public double Rmin
        {
            get { return rmin; }
            set { rmin = value; }
        }

        public AngleDirectionEnum AngleDirection
```

```
{
    get { return angleDirection; }
    set { angleDirection = value; }
}

public double AngleStep
{
    get { return angleStep; }
    set { angleStep = value; }
}

public enum AngleDirectionEnum
{
    CounterClockWise = 0,
    ClockWise = 1
}

public DoubleCollection SetLinePattern()
{
    DoubleCollection collection = new DoubleCollection();
    switch (LinePattern)
    {
        case LinePatternEnum.Dash:
            collection = new DoubleCollection(new double[2] { 4, 3 });
            break;
        case LinePatternEnum.Dot:
            collection = new DoubleCollection(new double[2] { 1, 2 });
            break;
        case LinePatternEnum.DashDot:
            collection = new DoubleCollection(new double[4] { 4, 2, 1, 2 });
            break;
    }
    return collection;
}

public double RNormalize(double r)
{
    double result = new double();
    if (r < Rmin || r > Rmax)
        result = double.NaN;
    double width = Math.Min(ChartCanvas.Width, ChartCanvas.Height);
    result = (r - Rmin) * width / 2 / (Rmax - Rmin);
    return result;
}

public enum LinePatternEnum
{
    Solid = 1,
    Dash = 2,
    Dot = 3,
    DashDot = 4
}
```

```
public void SetPolarAxes()
{
    double xc = ChartCanvas.Width / 2;
    double yc = ChartCanvas.Height / 2;

    // Draw circles:
    double dr = RNormalize(Rmax / NTicks) - RNormalize(Rmin / NTicks);
    for (int i = 0; i < NTicks; i++)
    {
        Ellipse circle = CircleLine();
        Canvas.SetLeft(circle, xc - (i + 1) * dr);
        Canvas.SetTop(circle, yc - (i + 1) * dr);
        circle.Width = 2.0 * (i + 1) * dr;
        circle.Height = 2.0 * (i + 1) * dr;
        ChartCanvas.Children.Add(circle);
    }

    //Draw radius lines:
    for (int i = 0; i < (int)360 / AngleStep; i++)
    {
        Line line = RadiusLine();
        line.X1 = RNormalize(Rmax) *
                  Math.Cos(i * AngleStep * Math.PI / 180) + xc;
        line.Y1 = RNormalize(Rmax) *
                  Math.Sin(i * AngleStep * Math.PI / 180) + yc;
        line.X2 = xc;
        line.Y2 = yc;
        ChartCanvas.Children.Add(line);
    }

    // Add radius labels:
    for (int i = 1; i <= NTicks; i++)
    {
        double rlabel = Rmin + i * (Rmax - Rmin) / NTicks;
        TextBlock tb = new TextBlock();
        tb.Text = rlabel.ToString();
        Canvas.SetLeft(tb, xc + 3);
        Canvas.SetTop(tb, yc - i * dr + 2);
        ChartCanvas.Children.Add(tb);
    }

    // Add angle Labels:
    double anglelabel = 0;
    for (int i = 0; i < (int)360 / AngleStep; i++)
    {
        if (AngleDirection == AngleDirectionEnum.ClockWise)
            anglelabel = i * AngleStep;
        else if (AngleDirection == AngleDirectionEnum.CounterClockWise)
        {
            anglelabel = 360 - i * AngleStep;
            if (i == 0)
                anglelabel = 0;
        }
```

```
            TextBlock tb = new TextBlock();
            tb.Text = anglelabel.ToString();
            tb.TextAlignment = TextAlignment.Center;
            tb.Measure(new Size(Double.PositiveInfinity,
                               Double.PositiveInfinity));
            Size size = tb.DesiredSize;

            double x = (RNormalize(Rmax) + 1.5 * size.Width / 2) *
                       Math.Cos(i * AngleStep * Math.PI / 180) + xc;
            double y = (RNormalize(Rmax) + 1.5 * size.Width / 2) *
                       Math.Sin(i * AngleStep * Math.PI / 180) + yc;
            Canvas.SetLeft(tb, x - size.Width / 2);
            Canvas.SetTop(tb, y - 1.2 * size.Height / 2);
            ChartCanvas.Children.Add(tb);
        }
    }

    private Ellipse CircleLine()
    {
        Ellipse ellipse = new Ellipse();
        ellipse.Stroke = LineColor;
        ellipse.StrokeThickness = LineThickness;
        ellipse.StrokeDashArray = SetLinePattern();
        ellipse.Fill = Brushes.Transparent;
        return ellipse;
    }

    private Line RadiusLine()
    {
        Line line = new Line();
        line.Stroke = LineColor;
        line.StrokeThickness = LineThickness;
        line.StrokeDashArray = SetLinePattern();
        return line;
    }
  }
}
```

In this class, the *AngleStep* property controls the number of *r* gridlines, and the *AngleDirection* property allows you to draw the polar chart in a counterclockwise (default) or clockwise manner. The other field members and their corresponding properties allow you to specify the *r* range and the gridline color, dash style, thickness, etc. In particular, you can specify the line styles of the *r* and *theta* gridlines separately to achieve a better visual effect.

The *SetPolarAxes* method in this class draws the *r* and *theta* gridlines as well as the *r* and *theta* labels. Pay special attention to the *RNormalize* method, which transforms the *r* value in the world coordinate system to an *r* value in the device coordinate system. A point in the polar coordinate system is represented by *Point(r, theta)*. The *theta* has the same unit, degrees, in both the world and device coordinate systems, so we need to perform the transformation on *r* only.

DataCollection for Polar Charts

We can still use the original *DataSeries* class for polar charts, but we will need to make some modifications to the *DataCollection* class. Add a new *DataCollectionPolar* class to the current project. Here is its code listing:

```
using System;
using System.Windows;
using System.Collections.Generic;
using System.Windows.Media;
using System.Windows.Shapes;

namespace Specialized2DCharts
{
    public class DataCollectionPolar : DataCollection
    {
        public void AddPolar(ChartStylePolar csp)
        {
            double xc = csp.ChartCanvas.Width/ 2;
            double yc = csp.ChartCanvas.Height / 2;

            int j = 0;
            foreach (DataSeries ds in DataList)
            {
                if (ds.SeriesName == "Default Name")
                {
                    ds.SeriesName = "DataSeries" + j.ToString();
                }
                ds.AddLinePattern();
                for (int i = 0; i < ds.LineSeries.Points.Count; i++)
                {

                    double r = ds.LineSeries.Points[i].Y;
                    double theta = ds.LineSeries.Points[i].X * Math.PI / 180;
                    if (csp.AngleDirection ==
                        ChartStylePolar.AngleDirectionEnum.CounterClockWise)
                        theta = -theta;
                    double x = xc + csp.RNormalize(r) * Math.Cos(theta);
                    double y = yc + csp.RNormalize(r) * Math.Sin(theta);
                    ds.LineSeries.Points[i] = new Point(x, y);
                }
                csp.ChartCanvas.Children.Add(ds.LineSeries);
                j++;
            }
        }
    }
}
```

This class implements an *AddPolar* method. Inside this method, we transform the polar points (*r*, *theta*) in the world coordinate system to the points (*x*, *y*) (the Cartesian coordinates) in the device system using the following relationships:

```
double x = xc + csp.RNormalize(r) * Math.Cos(theta);
double y = yc + csp.RNormalize(r) * Math.Sin(theta);
```

These equations indicate that the origin is located at (*xc*, *yc*) and that the *RNormalize* method transforms the polar points (*r*, *theta*) from the world to the device coordinate system. In this method, the polar chart direction is controlled by setting the angle variable *theta* to be positive (clockwise) or negative (counterclockwise).

Creating Polar Charts

In this section, I'll show you how to create polar charts using the *ChartStylePolar* and *DataCollectionPolar* classes implemented in the previous sections. Add a new WPF Window to the current project and name it *PolarCharts*. Here is the XAML file for this example:

```
<Window x:Class="Specialized2DCharts.PolarCharts"
    xmlns="http://schemas.microsoft.com/winfx/2006/xaml/presentation"
    xmlns:x="http://schemas.microsoft.com/winfx/2006/xaml"
    Title="Polar Charts" Height="330" Width="350">
    <Grid Name="grid1" Margin="10">
        <Grid.ColumnDefinitions>
            <ColumnDefinition Width="30"/>
            <ColumnDefinition Width="*"/>
            <ColumnDefinition Width="30"/>
        </Grid.ColumnDefinitions>
        <Grid.RowDefinitions>
            <RowDefinition Height="30"/>
            <RowDefinition Height="*"/>
            <RowDefinition Height="30"/>
        </Grid.RowDefinitions>
        <Grid  Margin="0" x:Name ="chartGrid" Grid.Column="1" Grid.Row="1"
               ClipToBounds="False" Background="Transparent"
               SizeChanged="chartGrid_SizeChanged" />
        <Canvas Margin="2" Name="chartCanvas" ClipToBounds="False"
               Grid.Column="1" Grid.Row="1"/>
    </Grid>
</Window>
```

This XAML creates a resizable canvas. Here is the corresponding code-behind file for this example:

```
using System;
using System.Windows;
using System.Windows.Media;
using System.Windows.Shapes;

namespace Specialized2DCharts
{
    public partial class PolarCharts : Window
    {
        private ChartStylePolar cs;
        private DataCollectionPolar dc;
        private DataSeries ds;

        public PolarCharts()
        {
            InitializeComponent();
        }
```

```
private void chartGrid_SizeChanged(object sender, SizeChangedEventArgs e)
{
    double width = chartGrid.ActualWidth;
    double height = chartGrid.ActualHeight;
    double side = width;
    if (width > height)
        side = height;
    chartCanvas.Width = side;
    chartCanvas.Height = side;
    chartCanvas.Children.Clear();
    AddChart();
}

private void AddChart()
{
    cs = new ChartStylePolar();
    dc = new DataCollectionPolar();
    cs.ChartCanvas = chartCanvas;
    cs.Rmax = 0.5;
    cs.Rmin = 0;
    cs.NTicks = 4;
    cs.AngleStep = 30;
    cs.AngleDirection = ChartStylePolar.AngleDirectionEnum.CounterClockWise;
    cs.LinePattern = ChartStylePolar.LinePatternEnum.Dot;
    cs.LineColor = Brushes.Black;
    cs.SetPolarAxes();
    dc.DataList.Clear();
    ds = new DataSeries();
    ds.LineColor = Brushes.Red;
    for (int i = 0; i < 360; i++)
    {
        double theta = 1.0 * i;
        double r = Math.Abs(Math.Cos(2.0 * theta * Math.PI / 180) *
                   Math.Sin(2.0 * theta * Math.PI / 180));
        ds.LineSeries.Points.Add(new Point(theta, r));
    }
    dc.DataList.Add(ds);
    dc.AddPolar(cs);
}
}
}
```

This application generates the output shown in Figure 6-15.

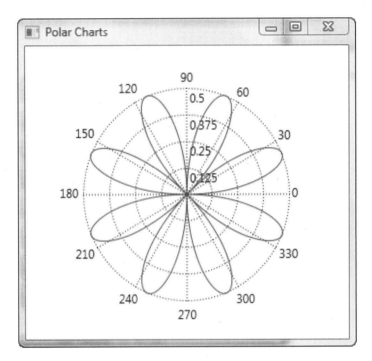

Figure 6-15. A polar plot in WPF

You can also create multiple curves with both positive and negative *r* values on a single polar chart. To test these features, we will draw two logarithm functions on the same polar chart. Change the *AddChart* method to the *AddChart1* method according to the following code snippet:

```
private void AddChart1()
{
    cs = new ChartStylePolar();
    dc = new DataCollectionPolar();
    cs.ChartCanvas = chartCanvas;
    cs.Rmax = 1.0;
    cs.Rmin = -7.0;
    cs.NTicks = 4;
    cs.AngleStep = 30;
    cs.AngleDirection = ChartStylePolar.AngleDirectionEnum.CounterClockWise;
    cs.LinePattern = ChartStylePolar.LinePatternEnum.Dot;
    cs.LineColor = Brushes.Black;
    cs.SetPolarAxes();
    dc.DataList.Clear();
    ds = new DataSeries();
    ds.LineColor = Brushes.Red;
    for (int i = 0; i < 360; i++)
    {
        double theta = 1.0 * i;
        double r = Math.Log(1.001 + Math.Sin(2 * theta * Math.PI / 180));
        ds.LineSeries.Points.Add(new Point(theta, r));
```

263

```
    }
    dc.DataList.Add(ds);

    ds = new DataSeries();
    ds.LineColor = Brushes.Blue;
    for (int i = 0; i < 360; i++)
    {
        double theta = 1.0 * i;
        double r = Math.Log(1.001 + Math.Cos(2 * theta * Math.PI / 180));
        ds.LineSeries.Points.Add(new Point(theta, r));
    }
    dc.DataList.Add(ds);
    dc.AddPolar(cs);
}
```

By running this project, you should obtain the results shown in Figure 6-16.

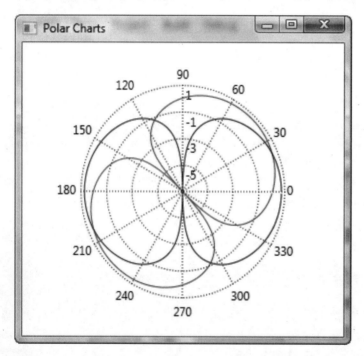

Figure 6-16. A polar plot with negative r value

Pie Charts

Creating a pie chart in WPF is quite simple, since there is an *ArcSegment* class available. The *ArcSegment* object is defined by its start and end points; its *X* and *Y* radii specified by the *Size* property; its *X*-axis rotation factor, a value indicating whether the arc should be greater than 180 degrees; and a value describing the direction in which the arc is drawn. You can use the *ArcSegment* to build the *PathFigure*, which in turn you use to build the *PathGeometry*. Finally, you can create a pie chart using the *Path* object with a specified *Fill* property.

Pie Chart Style

For a pie chart, we cannot use the *ChartStyle* or *ChartStyleGridlines* classes. We'll have to create a new pie chart style. Add a new class to the current project and name it *PieStyle*. Here is the code listing for this class:

```
using System;
using System.Windows;
using System.Windows.Controls;
using System.Windows.Media;
using System.Windows.Shapes;
using System.Collections.Generic;

namespace Specialized2DCharts
{
    public class PieStyle
    {
        private List<double> dataList = new List<double>();
        private List<string> labelList = new List<string>();
        private List<int> explodeList = new List<int>();
        private ColormapBrush colormapBrushes = new ColormapBrush();
        private Brush borderColor = Brushes.Black;
        private double borderThickness = 1.0;

        public List<double> DataList
        {
            get { return dataList; }
            set { dataList = value; }
        }

        public List<string> LabelList
        {
            get { return labelList; }
            set { labelList = value; }
        }

        public List<int> ExplodeList
        {
            get { return explodeList; }
            set { explodeList = value; }
        }
```

265

```csharp
public ColormapBrush ColormapBrushes
{
    get { return colormapBrushes; }
    set { colormapBrushes = value; }
}

public Brush BorderColor
{
    get { return borderColor; }
    set { borderColor = value; }
}

public double BorderThickness
{
    get { return borderThickness; }
    set { borderThickness = value; }
}

public void AddPie(Canvas canvas)
{
    int nData = DataList.Count;
    colormapBrushes.Ydivisions = nData;
    if (ExplodeList.Count == 0)
    {
        for (int i = 0; i < nData; i++)
            ExplodeList.Add(0);
    }

    double sum = 0.0;
    for (int i = 0; i < nData; i++)
    {
        sum += DataList[i];
    }
    double startAngle = 0;
    double sweepAngle = 0;

    for (int i = 0; i < nData; i++)
    {
        Brush brush = ColormapBrushes.ColormapBrushes()[i];
        int explode = ExplodeList[i];

        if (sum < 1)
        {
            startAngle += sweepAngle;
            sweepAngle = 2 * Math.PI * DataList[i];
        }

        else if (sum >= 1)
        {
            startAngle += sweepAngle;
            sweepAngle = 2 * Math.PI * DataList[i] / sum;
        }
```

```
            double dx = explode * Math.Cos(startAngle + sweepAngle / 2);
            double dy = explode * Math.Sin(startAngle + sweepAngle / 2);
            DrawArc(canvas, brush, startAngle, startAngle + sweepAngle, dx, dy);
        }
    }

    private void DrawArc(Canvas canvas, Brush fillColor, double startAngle,
                         double endAngle, double dx, double dy)
    {
        Path path = new Path();
        path.Stroke = BorderColor;
        path.StrokeThickness = BorderThickness;
        path.Fill = fillColor;
        PathGeometry pg = new PathGeometry();
        PathFigure pf = new PathFigure();
        LineSegment ls1 = new LineSegment();
        LineSegment ls2 = new LineSegment();
        ArcSegment arc = new ArcSegment();
        double xc = canvas.Width / 2 + dx;
        double yc = canvas.Height / 2 + dy;
        double r = 0.8 * xc;

        pf.IsClosed = true;
        pf.StartPoint = new Point(xc, yc);
        pf.Segments.Add(ls1);
        pf.Segments.Add(arc);
        pf.Segments.Add(ls2);
        pg.Figures.Add(pf);
        path.Data = pg;

        ls1.Point = new Point( xc + r * Math.Cos(startAngle),
                               yc + r * Math.Sin(startAngle));
        arc.SweepDirection = SweepDirection.Clockwise;
        arc.Point = new Point(xc + r * Math.Cos(endAngle),
                              yc + r * Math.Sin(endAngle));
        arc.Size = new Size(r, r);
        ls2.Point = new Point(xc + r * Math.Cos(endAngle),
                              yc + r * Math.Sin(endAngle));
        canvas.Children.Add(path);
    }
  }
}
```

In this class, we first define three generic collection list properties: *DataList*, *LabelList*, and *ExplodeList*. These lists hold the data with which to create the pie chart, the labels in the legend for the data values, and the data needed to highlight a particular pie slice by exploding the piece out from the rest of the pie, respectively. We also use the *ColormapBrush* object to fill the pie slices of the pie chart.

Inside the *AddPie* method, we first calculate the summation of the data values. Each value in the *DataList* is normalized via $1/sum$ to determine the area of each slice of the pie. If $sum \geq 1$, the values in the *DataList* specify the area of the pie slices directly. However, if $sum < 1$, the current program draws only a partial pie and the data values are not normalized by $1/sum$.

Note that the pie chart does not need the *DataSeries* and *DataCollection* classes, because these two classes are already incorporated in the *PieStyle* class.

Legend for Pie Charts

The *Legend* class used in pie charts is slightly different than that used in line charts. For completeness, I'll present here the code listing for the modified *Legend* class. Add a new class to the current project and name it *PieLegend*. Here is the code for this class:

```
using System;
using System.Windows;
using System.Windows.Controls;
using System.Windows.Media;
using System.Windows.Shapes;
using System.Collections.Generic;

namespace Specialized2DCharts
{
    public class PieLegend
    {
        private bool isLegendVisible = false;

        public bool IsLegendVisible
        {
            get { return isLegendVisible; }
            set { isLegendVisible = value; }
        }

        public void AddLegend(Canvas canvas, PieStyle ps)
        {
            TextBlock tb = new TextBlock();
            if (ps.DataList.Count < 1 || !IsLegendVisible)
                return;

            double legendWidth = 0;
            Size size = new Size(0, 0);
            for (int i = 0; i < ps.LabelList.Count; i++)
            {
                tb = new TextBlock();
                tb.Text = ps.LabelList[i];
                tb.Measure(new Size(Double.PositiveInfinity,
                                    Double.PositiveInfinity));
                size = tb.DesiredSize;
                if (legendWidth < size.Width)
                    legendWidth = size.Width;
            }

            legendWidth += 20;
            canvas.Width = legendWidth + 5;
            double legendHeight = 17 * ps.DataList.Count;
            double sx = 6;
            double sy = 0;
            double textHeight = size.Height;
            double lineLength = 34;
            Rectangle legendRect = new Rectangle();
            legendRect.Stroke = Brushes.Black;
```

```
        legendRect.Fill = Brushes.White;
        legendRect.Width = legendWidth + 18;
        legendRect.Height = legendHeight;

        if (IsLegendVisible)
            canvas.Children.Add(legendRect);

        Rectangle rect;
        int n = 1;
        foreach (double data in ps.DataList)
        {
            double xText = 2 * sx + lineLength;
            double yText = n * sy + (2 * n - 1) * textHeight / 2;

            rect = new Rectangle();
            rect.Stroke = ps.BorderColor;
            rect.StrokeThickness = ps.BorderThickness;
            rect.Fill = ps.ColormapBrushes.ColormapBrushes()[n - 1];
            rect.Width = 10;
            rect.Height = 10;
            Canvas.SetLeft(rect, sx + lineLength / 2 - 15);
            Canvas.SetTop(rect, yText - 2);
            canvas.Children.Add(rect);

            tb = new TextBlock();
            tb.Text = ps.LabelList[n - 1];
            canvas.Children.Add(tb);
            Canvas.SetTop(tb, yText - size.Height / 2 + 2);
            Canvas.SetLeft(tb, xText - 15);
            n++;
        }
        canvas.Width = legendRect.Width;
        canvas.Height = legendRect.Height;
    }
  }
}
```

Here the legend is always located on the right side of the pie chart.

Creating Pie Charts

In this section, I'll show you how to create pie charts using the *PieStyle* and *PieLegend* classes implemented in the previous sections. Add a new WPF Window to the current project and name it *PieCharts*. Here is the XAML file for this example:

```
<Window x:Class="Specialized2DCharts.PieCharts"
    xmlns="http://schemas.microsoft.com/winfx/2006/xaml/presentation"
    xmlns:x="http://schemas.microsoft.com/winfx/2006/xaml"
    Title="Pie Charts" Height="400" Width="500">
    <Grid Name="grid1" Margin="10">
        <Grid.ColumnDefinitions>
            <ColumnDefinition Width="30"/>
            <ColumnDefinition Width="*"/>
```

```
        <ColumnDefinition Width="auto"/>
        <ColumnDefinition Width="30"/>
    </Grid.ColumnDefinitions>
    <Grid.RowDefinitions>
        <RowDefinition Height="30"/>
        <RowDefinition Height="*"/>
        <RowDefinition Height="30"/>
    </Grid.RowDefinitions>

    <Grid  Margin="0" x:Name ="chartGrid" Grid.Column="1" Grid.Row="1"
           ClipToBounds="False" Background="Transparent"
           SizeChanged="chartGrid_SizeChanged" />
    <Canvas Margin="2" Name="chartCanvas" ClipToBounds="False"
            Grid.Column="1" Grid.Row="1"/>
    <Canvas Margin="2" Name="legendCanvas" Grid.Column="2" Grid.Row="1"/>
    </Grid>
</Window>
```

Here we create two *Canvas* elements, the *chartCanvas* and *legendCanvas*, which are used to host the pie chart and the legend, respectively. Here is the code-behind file for this example:

```
using System;
using System.Windows;
using System.Windows.Media;
using System.Windows.Shapes;

namespace Specialized2DCharts
{
    public partial class PieCharts : Window
    {
        private PieStyle ps;
        private PieLegend pl;

        public PieCharts()
        {
            InitializeComponent();
        }

        private void chartGrid_SizeChanged(object sender, SizeChangedEventArgs e)
        {
            double width = chartGrid.ActualWidth;
            double height = chartGrid.ActualHeight;
            double side = width;
            if (width > height)
                side = height;
            chartCanvas.Width = side;
            chartCanvas.Height = side;
            chartCanvas.Children.Clear();
            legendCanvas.Children.Clear();
            AddChart();
        }

        private void AddChart()
        {
```

```
        ps = new PieStyle();
        pl = new PieLegend();
        double[] data = new double[] { 30, 35, 15, 10, 8 };
        string[] labels = new string[] { "Soc. Sec. Tax", "Income Tax",
                                "Borrowing", "Corp. Tax", "Misc." };
        for (int i = 0; i < data.Length; i++)
        {
            ps.DataList.Add(data[i]);
            ps.LabelList.Add(labels[i]);
        }
        ps.ColormapBrushes.ColormapBrushType =
            ColormapBrush.ColormapBrushEnum.Summer;
        ps.AddPie(chartCanvas);
        pl.IsLegendVisible = true;
        pl.AddLegend(legendCanvas, ps);
    }
  }
}
```

Pay special attention to the *AddChart* method, which shows you how to add data values to the *DataList,* how to create labels for each data value, and how to specify the colormap for each pie slice.

Build and run this application by pressing F5. You should obtain the output shown in Figure 6-17.

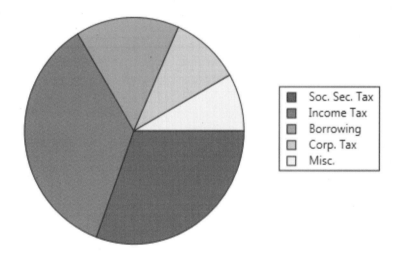

Figure 6-17. A pie chart of revenue data

The current project also gives you the option of highlighting particular pie slices by exploding the pieces out from the rest of the pie. To do this, you simply need to specify the *ExplodeList* property. For example, if you want to highlight the pie slices for the Social Security Tax and Corp. Tax data, you can use the following *AddChart* method:

```
private void AddChart()
{
    ps = new PieStyle();
    pl = new PieLegend();
    double[] data = new double[] { 30, 35, 15, 10, 8 };
    int[] explode = new int[] { 20, 0, 0, 20, 0 };
    string[] labels = new string[] { "Soc. Sec. Tax", "Income Tax",
                                     "Borrowing", "Corp. Tax", "Misc." };
    for (int i = 0; i < data.Length; i++)
    {
        ps.DataList.Add(data[i]);
        ps.ExplodeList.Add(explode[i]);
        ps.LabelList.Add(labels[i]);
    }
    ps.ColormapBrushes.ColormapBrushType = ColormapBrush.ColormapBrushEnum.Summer;
    ps.AddPie(chartCanvas);
    pl.IsLegendVisible = true;
    pl.AddLegend(legendCanvas, ps);
}
```

Here we specify that the first and fourth elements in the *ExplodeList* should be exploded out 20 pixels (the default value is always zero) from the center of the pie chart, since the Social Security Tax and the Corp. Tax are the first and fourth elements in the *DataList*. This produces the results shown in Figure 6-18.

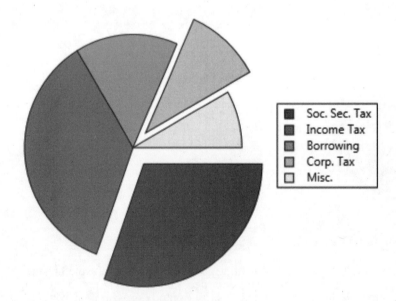

Figure 6-18. A pie chart with exploded pieces

Note also that the program draws a partial pie if the summation of the data values is less than 1. To demonstrate this effect, replace the *AddChart* method with the following code snippet:

```
private void AddChart()
{
    ps = new PieStyle();
    pl = new PieLegend();
    double[] data = new double[] { 0.3, 0.1, 0.25 };
    string[] labels = new string[] { "0.3 - 30%", "0.1 - 10%", "0.25 - 25%"};
    for (int i = 0; i < data.Length; i++)
    {
        ps.DataList.Add(data[i]);
        ps.LabelList.Add(labels[i]);
    }
    ps.ColormapBrushes.ColormapBrushType = ColormapBrush.ColormapBrushEnum.Summer;
    ps.AddPie(chartCanvas);
    pl.IsLegendVisible = true;
    pl.AddLegend(legendCanvas, ps);
}
```

You can see that the summation of the data values is 0.65, which is less than 1. This will generate a partial pie chart, as shown in Figure 6-19.

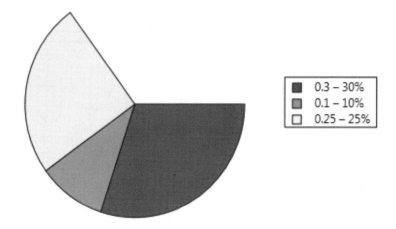

Figure 6-19. A partial pie chart

CHAPTER 7

■■■

Stock Charts

Stock charts and technical analysis play an important role in stock market research and analysis. Technical analysis, unlike fundamental analysis, usually ignores the actual nature of the company, market, currency, or commodity. It is based solely on stock charts, namely, the price and volume information. Stock charts usually show high, low, open, close, and volume data of a security. These charts allow you to plot the change of a stock price over time, analyze the history of stock price changes, and predict the future price of a stock based on prior price history.

In this chapter, I'll show you how to create a variety of stock charts in WPF, including the standard Hi-Lo Open-Close stock charts, Candlestick stock charts, and moving averages. In addition, I'll also discuss how to embed Yahoo stock charts into your own WPF applications.

Static Stock Charts

In this section, we'll implement various static stock charts.

Text File Reader

In order to import stock data (assuming ASCII text file format) into your WPF applications, you need to have a text file reader. Start with a new WPF project and name it *StockCharts*. Add the *DataSeries* class from the *LineCharts* project in Chapter 5 to the current project, and change its namespace to *StockCharts*. In addition, we need to comment out the code segments related to the *Symbols* object from this class since we don't need the *Symbols* object in the current project. Add a new class named *ChartStyle* to the project. Most of this class is a copy from both the *ChartStyle* and *ChartStyleGridlines* classes in the *LineCharts* project, by means of a simple cut-and-paste method, except several new methods are added. I'll not present the complete code listing here, only the new methods added to the class:

```
public double TimeSpanToDouble(TimeSpan ts)
{
    DateTime dt = DateTime.Parse("1 Jan");
    double d1 = BitConverter.ToDouble(BitConverter.GetBytes(dt.Ticks), 0);
    dt += ts;
    double d2 = BitConverter.ToDouble(BitConverter.GetBytes(dt.Ticks), 0);
    return d2 - d1;
}

public double DateToDouble(string date)
```

```
{
    DateTime dt = DateTime.Parse(date);
    return BitConverter.ToDouble(BitConverter.GetBytes(dt.Ticks), 0);
}

public DateTime DoubleToDate(double d)
{
    return new DateTime(BitConverter.ToInt64(BitConverter.GetBytes(d), 0));
}
```

These methods are related to the date-time and double type conversions. In addition, we make a little modification to the *AddChartStyle* method in order to display the date ticks correctly along the *X* axis. Here, I only list the code segment that is different from that used in the *LineCharts* project:

```
public void AddChartStyle(TextBlock tbTitle, TextBlock tbXLabel,
                          TextBlock tbYLabel, DataSeries ds)
{
    ......

    // Create x-axis tick marks:
    for (dx = Xmin; dx < Xmax; dx += xTick)
    {
        pt = NormalizePoint(new Point(dx, Ymin));
        tick = new Line();
        tick.Stroke = Brushes.Black;
        tick.X1 = pt.X;
        tick.Y1 = pt.Y;
        tick.X2 = pt.X;
        tick.Y2 = pt.Y - 5;
        ChartCanvas.Children.Add(tick);

        if (dx >= 0 && dx < ds.DataString.GetLength(1))
        {
            tb = new TextBlock();
            double d0 = DateToDouble(ds.DataString[0, 0]);
            double d1 = DateToDouble(ds.DataString[0, 1]);
            double d = DateToDouble(ds.DataString[0, (int)dx]);
            if(d0 > d1)
                d = DateToDouble(ds.DataString[0,
                        ds.DataString.GetLength(1) - 1 - (int)dx]);
            tb.Text = DoubleToDate(d).ToString("m");
            tb.Measure(new Size(Double.PositiveInfinity, Double.PositiveInfinity));
            size = tb.DesiredSize;
            TextCanvas.Children.Add(tb);
            Canvas.SetLeft(tb, leftOffset + pt.X - size.Width / 2);
            Canvas.SetTop(tb, pt.Y + 2 + size.Height / 2);
        }
    }
    ......
}
```

If you are interested, you can view the complete code listing by opening the *ChartStyle.cs* file in the current project. Add a new class to the project and name it *TextFileReader*. Here is its code listing:

```
using System;
```

```
using System.Collections.Generic;
using System.Windows;
using System.IO;
using System.Data;
using Microsoft.Win32;

namespace StockCharts
{
    public class TextFileReader
    {
        public string[,] LoadFile()
        {
            OpenFileDialog ofd = new OpenFileDialog();
            if (ofd.ShowDialog() == true)
            {
                string filePath = ofd.FileName;
                List<string> sc = new List<string>();
                FileStream fs = new FileStream(filePath, FileMode.Open,
                                              FileAccess.ReadWrite);
                StreamReader sr = new StreamReader(fs);

                // Read file into a string collection:
                int noBytesRead = 0;
                string oneLine;
                while ((oneLine = sr.ReadLine()) != null)
                {
                    noBytesRead += oneLine.Length;
                    sc.Add(oneLine);
                }
                sr.Close();

                // Extract the stock data from the file:
                string[] sa = new string[sc.Count];
                sc.CopyTo(sa, 0);
                char[] splitter = { ' ', ',', ':', '\t' };
                string[] sa1 = sa[0].Split(splitter);
                string[,] result = new string[sa1.Length, sc.Count];

                for (int i = 0; i < sc.Count; i++)
                {
                    sa1 = sa[i].Split(splitter);
                    for (int j = 0; j < sa1.Length; j++)
                        result[j, i] = sa1[j];
                }

                return result;
            }
            else
                return null;
        }
    }
}
```

In this class, the public method *LoadFile* returns a 2D string array. The stock text file should be formatted the same way as shown in Figure 7-1. The figure presents the stock price data for GE from 4-7-2006 to 5-5-2006, which is stored in a tab-delimited text file, *GE.txt*.

```
5-May-06          34.94     35.22     34.87     35.16
4-May-06          34.5      34.94     34.48     34.8
3-May-06          34.22     34.67     34.19     34.4
2-May-06          34.39     34.59     34.1      34.48
1-May-06          34.64     34.72     34.32     34.39
28-Apr-06         34.49     34.78     34.35     34.59
27-Apr-06         33.9      34.68     33.89     34.43
26-Apr-06         34.07     34.44     33.88     34.13
25-Apr-06         34        34.06     33.8      33.97
24-Apr-06         33.81     34        33.8      33.93
21-Apr-06         34.25     34.32     33.68     33.97
20-Apr-06         33.8      34.18     33.63     34.12
19-Apr-06         33.95     33.97     33.5      33.89
18-Apr-06         33.52     33.97     33.21     33.87
17-Apr-06         33.76     33.76     33.07     33.29
13-Apr-06         34.19     34.36     33.61     33.89
12-Apr-06         34.3      34.53     34.17     34.46
11-Apr-06         33.92     34.07     33.63     34.05
10-Apr-06         34.06     34.08     33.8      33.92
7-Apr-06          34.55     34.75     34.01     34.03
```

Figure 7-1. *GE stock data*

In this file, the first column is the date, and the second to fifth columns represent the open, high, low, and close prices of the stock, respectively. Please note that there is no header row in this text file. If you want the stock data file to have a header row or a different format, you must change the *TextFileReader* class correspondingly to take care of the file format change.

DataSeries and *DataCollection* for Stock Charts

You'll need to make some modifications to the *DataSeries* and *DataCollection* classes. Open the *DataSeries.cs* file and add the following one-line code snippet:

```
public string[,] DataString { get; set; }
```

This public property specifies where to store the stock data. The rest of the code of the *DataSeries* class remains the same as that used in the *LineCharts* project.

We'll need to add a new *DataCollection* class to the current project. Here is its code listing:

```
using System;
using System.Windows;
using System.Collections.Generic;
using System.Windows.Media;
using System.Windows.Shapes;

namespace StockCharts
{
    public class DataCollection
```

```
{
    private List<DataSeries> dataList = new List<DataSeries>();
    private StockChartTypeEnum stockChartType =
                            StockChartTypeEnum.HiLoOpenClose;

    public StockChartTypeEnum StockChartType
    {
        get { return stockChartType; }
        set { stockChartType = value; }
    }

    public List<DataSeries> DataList
    {
        get { return dataList; }
        set { dataList = value; }
    }

    public void AddStockChart(ChartStyle cs)
    {
        foreach (DataSeries ds in DataList)
        {
            double barWidth = cs.ChartCanvas.Width /
                            (5 * ds.DataString.GetLength(1));
            double d0 = cs.DateToDouble(ds.DataString[0, 0]);
            double d1 = cs.DateToDouble(ds.DataString[0, 1]);

            double[,] stockData = new double[ds.DataString.GetLength(0),
                                    ds.DataString.GetLength(1)];
            for (int i = 0; i < ds.DataString.GetLength(1); i++)
            {
                for (int j = 1; j < stockData.GetLength(0); j++)
                {
                    if (d0 > d1)
                        stockData[j, i] = Convert.ToDouble(ds.DataString[j,
                                    ds.DataString.GetLength(1) - 1 - i]);
                    else
                        stockData[j, i] = Convert.ToDouble(ds.DataString[j, i]);
                }
            }
            for (int i = 0; i < ds.DataString.GetLength(1); i++)
            {
                Point ptHigh = cs.NormalizePoint(new Point(i, stockData[2, i]));
                Point ptLow = cs.NormalizePoint(new Point(i, stockData[3, i]));
                Point ptOpen = cs.NormalizePoint(new Point(i, stockData[1, i]));
                Point ptClose = cs.NormalizePoint(
                                new Point(i, stockData[4, i]));
                Point ptOpen1 = new Point(ptOpen.X - barWidth, ptOpen.Y);
                Point ptClose1 = new Point(ptClose.X + barWidth, ptClose.Y);
                Point ptOpen2 = new Point(ptOpen.X + barWidth, ptOpen.Y);
                Point ptClose2 = new Point(ptClose.X - barWidth, ptClose.Y);

                switch (StockChartType)
                {
```

```
                    case StockChartTypeEnum.Line:    // Draw Line stock chart:
                        if (i > 0)
                        {
                            Point pt1 = cs.NormalizePoint(
                                        new Point(i - 1, stockData[4, i - 1]));
                            Point pt2 = cs.NormalizePoint(
                                        new Point(i, stockData[4, i]));
                            DrawLine(cs.ChartCanvas, pt1, pt2,
                                        ds.LineColor, ds.LineThickness);
                        }
                        break;
                    // Draw Hi-Lo stock chart:
                    case StockChartTypeEnum.HiLo:
                        DrawLine(cs.ChartCanvas, ptLow, ptHigh,
                                    ds.LineColor, ds.LineThickness);
                        break;
                    // Draw Hi-Lo-Open-Close stock chart:
                    case StockChartTypeEnum.HiLoOpenClose:
                        DrawLine(cs.ChartCanvas, ptLow, ptHigh,
                                    ds.LineColor, ds.LineThickness);
                        DrawLine(cs.ChartCanvas, ptOpen, ptOpen1,
                                    ds.LineColor, ds.LineThickness);
                        DrawLine(cs.ChartCanvas, ptClose, ptClose1,
                                    ds.LineColor, ds.LineThickness);
                        break;
                    // Draw candle stock chart:
                    case StockChartTypeEnum.Candle:
                        DrawLine(cs.ChartCanvas, ptLow, ptHigh,
                                    ds.LineColor, ds.LineThickness);
                        Polygon plg = new Polygon();
                        plg.Stroke = ds.LineColor;
                        plg.StrokeThickness = ds.LineThickness;
                        Brush fillColor = ds.FillColor;
                        if (stockData[1, i] < stockData[4, i])
                            fillColor = Brushes.White;
                        plg.Fill = fillColor;
                        plg.Points.Add(ptOpen1);
                        plg.Points.Add(ptOpen2);
                        plg.Points.Add(ptClose1);
                        plg.Points.Add(ptClose2);
                        cs.ChartCanvas.Children.Add(plg);
                        break;
                }
            }
        }
    }

    private void DrawLine(Canvas canvas, Point pt1, Point pt2,
                    Brush lineColor, double lineThickness)
    {
        Line line = new Line();
        line.Stroke = lineColor;
        line.StrokeThickness = lineThickness;
```

```
                line.X1 = pt1.X;
                line.Y1 = pt1.Y;
                line.X2 = pt2.X;
                line.Y2 = pt2.Y;
                canvas.Children.Add(line);
        }

        public enum StockChartTypeEnum
        {
                HiLo = 0,
                HiLoOpenClose = 1,
                Candle = 2,
                Line = 3
        }
    }
}
```

In this class, we add the *StockChartType* enumeration, from which you can select a special chart from four stock chart types, *HiLo*, *HiLoOpenClose*, *Candle*, and *Line*. The public method, *AddStockChart*, draws the stock data according to the specified stock chart type. Pay special attention to the *Candle* chart type, in which we draw solid polygons when the close price is less than the open price and open polygons (filled with a white brush) otherwise.

Hi-Lo Stock Charts

Now it is time to test our stock chart project. First, we will draw a Hi-Lo stock chart. Add a new WPF Application Window to the current project and name it *StaticStockCharts*. The XAML file for this example is similar to that used in creating line charts. I'll list it here for your reference:

```xml
<Window x:Class="StockCharts.StaticStockCharts"
    xmlns="http://schemas.microsoft.com/winfx/2006/xaml/presentation"
    xmlns:x="http://schemas.microsoft.com/winfx/2006/xaml"
   Title="Static Stock Charts" Height="400" Width="400">

    <Grid Name="grid1" Margin="10">
        <Grid.ColumnDefinitions>
            <ColumnDefinition Width="Auto"/>
            <ColumnDefinition Width="*"/>
        </Grid.ColumnDefinitions>
        <Grid.RowDefinitions>
            <RowDefinition Height="Auto"/>
            <RowDefinition Height="*"/>
            <RowDefinition Height="Auto"/>
            <RowDefinition Height="Auto"/>
            <RowDefinition Height="Auto"/>
        </Grid.RowDefinitions>
        <TextBlock Margin="2" x:Name="tbTitle" Grid.Column="1" Grid.Row="0"
                   RenderTransformOrigin="0.5,0.5" FontSize="14" FontWeight="Bold"
                   HorizontalAlignment="Stretch" VerticalAlignment="Stretch"
                   TextAlignment="Center" Text="Title"/>

        <TextBlock Margin="2" x:Name="tbXLabel" Grid.Column="1" Grid.Row="2"
                   RenderTransformOrigin="0.5,0.5" TextAlignment="Center"
```

```
                             Text="X Axis"/>
        <StackPanel Grid.Column="1" Grid.Row="4" Orientation="Horizontal"
                    HorizontalAlignment="Center">
            <Button Click="LoadFile_Click" Width="120" Height="25"
                    Content="Load Stock File" Margin="5"/>
            <Button Click="Close_Click" Width="120" Height="25"
                    Content="Close" Margin="15,5,5,5"/>
        </StackPanel>
        <StackPanel Grid.Column="1" Grid.Row="3" Orientation="Horizontal"
                    HorizontalAlignment="Center">
            <TextBlock Text="Ymin" Margin="0,5,5,5"/>
            <TextBox x:Name="txYmin" Text="32" Width="50"
                     TextAlignment="Center" Margin="5"/>
            <TextBlock Text="Ymax" Margin="10,5,5,5"/>
            <TextBox x:Name="txYmax" Text="36" Width="50"
                     TextAlignment="Center" Margin="5"/>
            <TextBlock Text="YTick" Margin="10,5,5,5"/>
            <TextBox x:Name="txYTick" Text="1" Width="50"
                     TextAlignment="Center" Margin="5"/>
        </StackPanel>

        <TextBlock Margin="2" Name="tbYLabel" Grid.Column="0" Grid.Row="1"
                   RenderTransformOrigin="0.5,0.5" TextAlignment="Center"
                   Text="Y Axis">
            <TextBlock.LayoutTransform>
                <RotateTransform Angle="-90"/>
            </TextBlock.LayoutTransform>
        </TextBlock>

        <Grid  Margin="0,0,0,0" x:Name ="chartGrid" Grid.Column="1" Grid.Row="1"
               ClipToBounds="False" Background="Transparent"
               SizeChanged="chartGrid_SizeChanged" >
        </Grid>
        <Canvas Margin="2" Name="textCanvas" Grid.Column="1" Grid.Row="1"
                ClipToBounds="True">
            <Canvas Name="chartCanvas" ClipToBounds="True"/>
        </Canvas>
    </Grid>
</Window>
```

In addition to the *textCanvas* and *chartCanvas,* we add some text boxes and two button controls. The text boxes allow you to specify the stock variation range. One button loads stock data from an *OpenFileDialog;* the other closes the application window.

Here is the code-behind file for this example:

```
using System;
using System.IO;
using System.Collections.Generic;
using System.Windows;
using System.Windows.Media;
using System.Windows.Shapes;

namespace StockCharts
{
```

```csharp
public partial class StaticStockCharts : Window
{
    private ChartStyle cs;
    private DataCollection dc;
    private DataSeries ds;
    private TextFileReader tfr;

    public StaticStockCharts()
    {
        InitializeComponent();
        dc = new DataCollection();
        tfr = new TextFileReader();
        cs = new ChartStyle();
    }

    private void chartGrid_SizeChanged(object sender, SizeChangedEventArgs e)
    {
        textCanvas.Width = chartGrid.ActualWidth;
        textCanvas.Height = chartGrid.ActualHeight;
        chartCanvas.Children.Clear();
        textCanvas.Children.RemoveRange(1, textCanvas.Children.Count - 1);

        AddChart();
    }

    private void LoadFile_Click(object sender, RoutedEventArgs e)
    {
        dc.DataList.Clear();
        ds = new DataSeries();
        ds.DataString = tfr.LoadFile();
        ds.LineColor = Brushes.DarkBlue;
        ds.FillColor = Brushes.DarkBlue;
        dc.DataList.Add(ds);
        AddChart();
    }

    private void AddChart()
    {
        if (dc.DataList.Count > 0)
        {
            cs = new ChartStyle();
            cs.ChartCanvas = chartCanvas;
            cs.TextCanvas = textCanvas;
            cs.Xmin = -1;
            cs.Xmax = ds.DataString.GetLength(1);
            cs.XTick = 3;
            cs.Ymin = double.Parse(txYmin.Text);
            cs.Ymax = double.Parse(txYmax.Text);
            cs.YTick = double.Parse(txYTick.Text);
            cs.Title = "Stock Chart";
            cs.AddChartStyle(tbTitle, tbXLabel, tbYLabel, ds);
            dc.StockChartType = DataCollection.StockChartTypeEnum.HiLo;
            dc.AddStockChart(cs);
```

```
            }
        }

        private void Close_Click(object sender, RoutedEventArgs e)
        {
            this.Close();
        }
    }
}
```

Here, in addition to the standard definitions for a chart application, we add the following line of code:

```
dc.StockChartType = DataCollection.StockChartTypeEnum.HiLo;
```

This specifies the stock chart type to be a Hi-Lo plot.

Inside the *AddChart* method, we also create a new instance of the *TextFileReader* and call its public method *LoadFile* to bring up the *OpenFileDialog* window, which allows you to select the stock data file:

```
ds.DataString = tfr.LoadFile();
```

In this example, we add two text files, *GE.txt* and *IBM.txt*, to the Application directory for this project. If you stored your stock data file in a different directory, you need to go to that directory to import the stock data.

Running this project by pressing F5 will first bring up the *OpenFileDialog* window, as shown in Figure 7-2. Select the *GE.txt* file and click Open. This produces the result shown in Figure 7-3. You can click the *Load File* button to import the other set of stock data and display it on the chart.

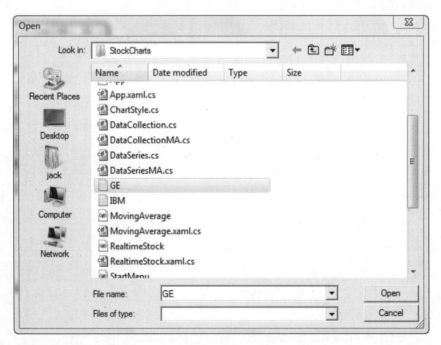

Figure 7-2. OpenFileDialog window used to import the stock data

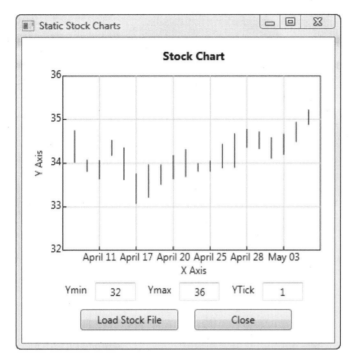

Figure 7-3. A Hi-Lo stock chart

Hi-Lo Open-Close Stock Charts

You can create a Hi-Lo Open-Close stock chart by replacing the *StockChartType* with the following line of code:

```
dc.StockChartType = DataCollection.StockChartTypeEnum.HiLoOpenClose;
```

This generates the output shown in Figure 7-4.

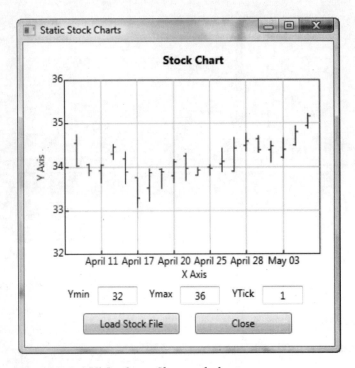

Figure 7-4. *A Hi-Lo-Open-Close stock chart*

Candlestick Stock Charts

You can also obtain a candlestick stock chart by replacing the *StockChartType* with the following code snippet:

```
dc.StockChartType = DataCollection.StockChartTypeEnum.Candle;
```

Running this application produces the result shown in Figure 7-5.

Figure 7-5. *A candlestick stock chart*

Moving Averages

Moving averages are often used in analyzing time series data. They are widely applied in finance, especially in technical analysis. They can also be used as a generic smoothing operation, in which case the data need not be a time series.

A moving-average series can be calculated for any time series. In finance it is most often applied to stock prices, returns, or trading volumes. Moving averages are used to smooth out short-term fluctuations, thus highlighting longer-term trends or cycles. The threshold between short-term and long-term depends on the application, and the parameters of the moving average are set accordingly.

A moving average smooths data by replacing each data point with the average of the neighboring data points defined within the time span. This process is equivalent to low-pass filters used in digital signal processing.

Simple Moving Averages

In this section, we first discuss the simple moving average. A simple moving average (SMA) is the mean value of the previous n data points. For example, a 5-day simple moving average of opening price is the mean of the previous 5 days' opening prices. If those prices are p_0, p_{-1}, p_{-2}, p_{-3}, p_{-4}, then the moving average is described by

$$SMA = \frac{p_0 + p_{-1} + p_{-2} + p_{-3} + p_{-4}}{5}$$

In general, for an n-day moving average, we have

$$SMA = \frac{p_0 + p_{-1} + \cdots + p_{-n+1}}{n} = \frac{1}{n}\sum_{i=0}^{n-1} p_{-i}$$

When calculating successive values, a new value comes into the sum and an old value drops out, meaning a full summation each time is unnecessary:

$$SMA_{today} = MSA_{yesterday} - \frac{p_{-n+1}}{n} + \frac{p_1}{n}$$

In technical analysis, there are various common values for n, such as 10 days, 40 days, and 100 days. The period selected depends on the kind of movement you are concentrating on, such as short, intermediate, or long term. In any case, moving-average levels are interpreted as support in a rising market or as resistance in a falling market.

In all cases, a moving average lags behind the latest data point, simply due to the nature of its smoothing. An SMA can lag to an undesirable extent and can be disproportionately influenced by old data points' dropping out of the average. We can address this issue by giving extra weight to more recent data points, as done in weighted and exponential moving averages, which will be discussed in following sections.

One characteristic of the SMA is that if the data have a periodic fluctuation, then applying an SMA over that period will eliminate that variation.

Implementation

Using the algorithm developed in the previous section, we can implement a simple moving average in WPF. First, we need to modify the *DataSeries* class. Add a new class to the current project and name it *DataSeriesMA*. Here is the code for this class:

```
using System;
using System.Windows;
using System.Windows.Media;
using System.Windows.Shapes;

namespace StockCharts
{
    public class DataSeriesMA : DataSeries
    {
        private int nDays = 5;
        public int NDays
        {
            get { return nDays; }
            set { nDays = value; }
        }

        // Simple Moving Average:
        private Polyline smaLineSeries = new Polyline();
        private Brush smaLineColor = Brushes.Black;
```

```
        private double smaLineThickness = 1;

        public Polyline SMALineSeries
        {
            get { return smaLineSeries; }
            set { smaLineSeries = value; }
        }

        public Brush SMALineColor
        {
            get { return smaLineColor; }
            set { smaLineColor = value; }
        }

        public double SMALineThickness
        {
            get { return smaLineThickness; }
            set { smaLineThickness = value; }
        }

        public double[] SimpleMovingAverage()
        {
            int m = DataString.GetLength(1);
            double[] data = new double[m];
            for (int i = 0; i < m; i++)
                data[i] = Convert.ToDouble(DataString[1, i]);

            double[] sma = new double[m - NDays + 1];
            if (m > NDays)
            {
                double sum = 0.0;
                for (int i = 0; i < NDays; i++)
                {
                    sum += data[i];
                }

                sma[0] = sum / NDays;

                for (int i = 1; i <= m - NDays; i++)
                {
                    sma[i] = sma[i - 1] +
                            (data[NDays + i - 1] - data[i - 1]) / NDays;
                }
            }
            return sma;
        }
    }
}
```

Note here that we redefine the line style specifically for the SMA curve. This is necessary because the line style defined in the original *DataSeries* class specifies the type of stock chart itself, such as Hi-Lo or Candlestick chart. This way, you can use different line styles for the stock chart and the simple moving average curve. The method *SimpleMovingAverage* implements the simple moving average algorithm presented in the previous section.

You'll also need to modify the *DataCollection* class. Add a new class to the current project and name it *DataCollectionMA*. Here is its code listing:

```
using System;
using System.Windows;
using System.Collections.Generic;
using System.Windows.Controls;
using System.Windows.Media;
using System.Windows.Shapes;

namespace StockCharts
{
    public class DataCollectionMA : DataCollection
    {
        public void AddSimpleMovingAverage(ChartStyle cs)
        {
            foreach (DataSeriesMA ds in DataList)
            {
                ds.SMALineSeries.Stroke = ds.SMALineColor;
                ds.SMALineSeries.StrokeThickness = ds.SMALineThickness;
                double[] data = ds.SimpleMovingAverage();
                ds.SMALineSeries.Points.Clear();
                for (int i = 0; i < data.Length; i++)
                {
                    ds.SMALineSeries.Points.Add(cs.NormalizePoint(
                        new Point(i + ds.NDays - 1, data[i])));
                }
                cs.ChartCanvas.Children.Add(ds.SMALineSeries);
            }
        }
    }
}
```

This class contains only one method, *AddSimpleMovingAverage*, which is used to create the SMA curve.

Creating SMA Curves

Here, we'll examine the simple moving average algorithm implemented in the previous section. Add a new WPF Window to the current project and name it *MovingAverage*. The XAML file is the same as that used in the previous example. Here is the C# code-behind file for this example:

```
using System;
using System.IO;
using System.Windows;
using System.Windows.Media;

namespace StockCharts
{
    public partial class MovingAverage : Window
    {
        private ChartStyle cs;
        private DataCollectionMA dc;
```

```
private DataSeriesMA ds;
private TextFileReader tfr;

public MovingAverage()
{
    InitializeComponent();
    dc = new DataCollectionMA();
    tfr = new TextFileReader();
    cs = new ChartStyle();
}

private void chartGrid_SizeChanged(object sender, SizeChangedEventArgs e)
{
    textCanvas.Width = chartGrid.ActualWidth;
    textCanvas.Height = chartGrid.ActualHeight;
    chartCanvas.Children.Clear();
    textCanvas.Children.RemoveRange(1, textCanvas.Children.Count - 1);
    AddChart();
}

private void LoadFile_Click(object sender, RoutedEventArgs e)
{
    dc.DataList.Clear();
    ds = new DataSeriesMA();
    ds.DataString = tfr.LoadFile();
    ds.NDays = 5;
    ds.LineColor = Brushes.Black;
    ds.SMALineColor = Brushes.Red;
    dc.DataList.Add(ds);
    AddChart();
}

private void AddChart()
{
    if (dc.DataList.Count > 0)
    {
        cs = new ChartStyle();
        cs.ChartCanvas = chartCanvas;
        cs.TextCanvas = textCanvas;
        cs.Xmin = -1;
        cs.Xmax = ds.DataString.GetLength(1);
        cs.XTick = 3;
        cs.Ymin = double.Parse(txYmin.Text);
        cs.Ymax = double.Parse(txYmax.Text);
        cs.YTick = double.Parse(txYTick.Text);
        cs.Title = "Stock Chart";
        cs.AddChartStyle(tbTitle, tbXLabel, tbYLabel, ds);
        dc.StockChartType = DataCollection.StockChartTypeEnum.Candle;
        dc.AddStockChart(cs);
        dc.AddSimpleMovingAverage(cs);
        dc.AddWeightedMovingAverage(cs);
        dc.AddExponentialMovingAverage(cs);
    }
```

```
        }

        private void Close_Click(object sender, RoutedEventArgs e)
        {
            this.Close();
        }
    }
}
```

You can see that you can specify the line styles for the stock chart (Candlestick in this case) and the SMA curve independently, from the following code snippet:

```
ds.LineColor = Brushes.Black;
ds.SMALineColor = Brushes.Red;
```

The rest of the code is standard for any chart application. Running this example will create the output shown in Figure 7-6, where the IBM stock data are displayed. Note that there is no simple moving average data for the first four days, since there are not enough data to make the calculations until the fifth day.

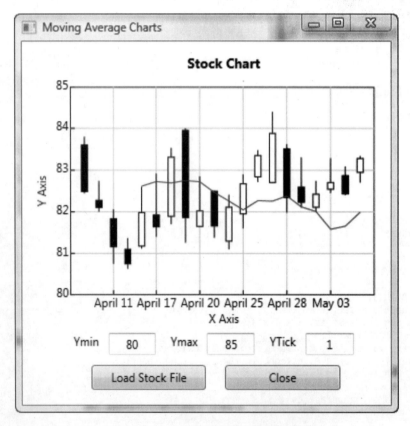

Figure 7-6. A stock chart with five-day simple moving average

For comparison, we plot both the stock data and the five-day simple moving average in Figure 7-6. In practice, longer time periods are typically used for simple moving averages.

Weighted Moving Averages

A weighted average is any average that has multiplying factors to give different weights to different data points. In technical analysis, a weighted moving average (WMA) specifically means weights that decrease arithmetically. In an n-day WMA, the latest day has weight n, the second latest $n - 1$, etc., down to zero:

$$WMA = \frac{np_0 + (n-1)p_{-1} + \cdots + 2p_{-n+2} + p_{-n+1}}{n + (n-1) + \cdots + 2 + 1} = \frac{2}{n(n+1)} \sum_{i=0}^{n-1} (n-i)p_{-i}$$

Note, when calculating the WMA across successive values, that the difference between the numerators of WMA_{+1} and WMA is $np_{+1} - p_0 - \cdots - p_{-n+1}$. If we denote $p_0^{sum} = p_0 + p_{-1} + \cdots + p_{-n+1}$, then we have

$$p_{+1}^{sum} = p_0^{sum} + p_{+1} - p_{-n+1}$$

$$Numerator_{+1} = Numerator_0 + np_{+1} - p_0^{sum}$$

$$WMA_{+1} = \frac{2}{n(n+1)} Numerator_{+1}$$

Implementation

Using the algorithm developed in the previous section, we can implement the weighted moving average in WPF. First, add the following code to the *DataSeriesMA* class:

```
// Weighted Moving Average:
private Polyline wmaLineSeries = new Polyline();
private Brush wmaLineColor = Brushes.Black;
private double wmaLineThickness = 1;

public Polyline WMALineSeries
{
    get { return wmaLineSeries; }
    set { wmaLineSeries = value; }
}

public Brush WMALineColor
{
    get { return wmaLineColor; }
    set { wmaLineColor = value; }
}

public double WMALineThickness
{
    get { return wmaLineThickness; }
    set { wmaLineThickness = value; }
}
```

```
}

public double[] WeightedMovingAverage()
{
    int m = DataString.GetLength(1);
    double[] data = new double[m];
    for (int i = 0; i < m; i++)
        data[i] = Convert.ToDouble(DataString[1, i]);

    double[] wma = new double[m - NDays + 1];
    double psum = 0.0;
    double numerator = 0.0;
    double[] numerator1 = new double[m - NDays + 1];
    double[] psum1 = new double[m - NDays + 1];

    if (m > NDays)
    {
        for (int i = 0; i < NDays; i++)
        {
            psum += data[i];
            numerator += (i + 1) * data[i];
        }
        psum1[0] = psum;
        numerator1[0] = numerator;
        wma[0] = 2 * numerator / NDays / (NDays + 1);

        for (int i = 1; i <= m - NDays; i++)
        {
            numerator1[i] =
            numerator1[i - 1] + NDays * data[i + NDays - 1] - psum1[i - 1];
            psum1[i] = psum1[i - 1] + data[i + NDays - 1] - data[i - 1];
            wma[i] = 2 * numerator1[i] / NDays / (NDays + 1);
        }
    }
    return wma;
}
```

This code is similar to that used in an SMA, except for the *WeightedMovingAverage* method, where the weighted moving average algorithm is implemented. In this method, you can see that each period's price is multiplied by a given weight. The products of the calculation are summed and divided by the total of the weights.

You also need to add a new method, *AddWeightedMovingAverage*, to the *DataCollectionMA* class:

```
public void AddWeightedMovingAverage(ChartStyle cs)
{
    foreach (DataSeriesMA ds in DataList)
    {
        ds.WMALineSeries.Stroke = ds.WMALineColor;
        ds.WMALineSeries.StrokeThickness = ds.WMALineThickness;
        double[] data = ds.WeightedMovingAverage();
        ds.WMALineSeries.Points.Clear();
        for (int i = 0; i < data.Length; i++)
        {
            ds.WMALineSeries.Points.Add(cs.NormalizePoint(
```

```
                    new Point(i + ds.NDays - 1, data[i])));
            }
        cs.ChartCanvas.Children.Add(ds.WMALineSeries);
        }
}
```

Creating WMA Curves

Creating a weighted moving average curve is very simple. Open the *MovingAverage.xaml.cs* file and add the following bolded code snippet to the *LoadFile_Click* and *AddChart* method:

```
private void LoadFile_Click(object sender, RoutedEventArgs e)
{
    dc.DataList.Clear();
    ds = new DataSeriesMA();
    ds.DataString = tfr.LoadFile();
    ds.NDays = 5;
    ds.LineColor = Brushes.Black;
    ds.SMALineColor = Brushes.Red;
    ds.WMALineColor = Brushes.DarkGreen;
    dc.DataList.Add(ds);
    AddChart();
}
private void AddChart()
{
    if (dc.DataList.Count > 0)
    {
        cs = new ChartStyle();
        cs.ChartCanvas = chartCanvas;
        cs.TextCanvas = textCanvas;
        cs.Xmin = -1;
        cs.Xmax = ds.DataString.GetLength(1);
        cs.XTick = 3;
        cs.Ymin = double.Parse(txYmin.Text);
        cs.Ymax = double.Parse(txYmax.Text);
        cs.YTick = double.Parse(txYTick.Text);
        cs.Title = "Stock Chart";
        cs.AddChartStyle(tbTitle, tbXLabel, tbYLabel, ds);
        dc.StockChartType = DataCollection.StockChartTypeEnum.Candle;
        dc.AddStockChart(cs);
        dc.AddSimpleMovingAverage(cs);
        dc.AddWeightedMovingAverage(cs);
    }
}
```

Running this application again produces the results shown in Figure 7-7, where IMB stock data are displayed. Note that there is no weighted moving average data for the first four days, since there are not enough data to make the calculations until the fifth day.

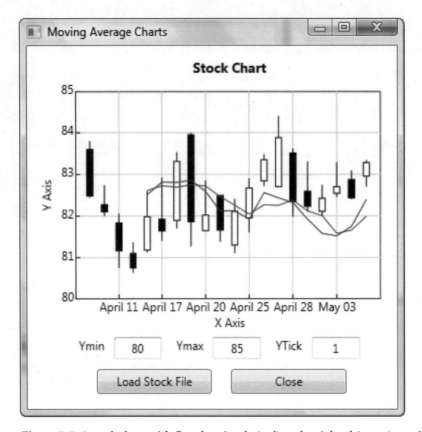

Figure 7-7. A stock chart with five-day simple (red) and weighted (green) moving averages

For comparison, we also plot the stock data and simple moving averages in the figure. You can see that the weighted moving average is closer to the original stock data than the simple moving average is.

Exponential Moving Averages

One drawback of both the simple and weighted moving averages is that they include data for only the number of periods the moving average covers. For example, a five-day simple or weighted moving average uses only five days' worth of data. Data prior to those five days are not included in the calculation of the moving average.

In some situations, however, the prior data are an important reflection of prices and should be included in the moving-average calculation. You can achieve this by using an exponential moving average (EMA).

An EMA uses weight factors that decrease exponentially. The weight for each older data point decreases exponentially, giving much more importance to recent observations while not discarding older observations entirely.

The degree of weight decrease is expressed as a constant smoothing factor α, which is a number between 0 and 1. α may be expressed as a percentage, so a smoothing factor of 10% is equivalent to

$\alpha = 0.1$. Alternatively, α may be expressed in terms of n time periods, where $\alpha = 2/(n+1)$. For example, $n = 19$ is equivalent to $\alpha = 0.1$.

The observation at a time period t is designated Y_t, and the value of the EMA at any time period t is designated S_t. S_1 is undefined. S_2 may be initialized in a number of different ways, most commonly by setting S_2 to Y_1, though other techniques exist, such as setting S_2 to an average of the first four or five observations. The prominence of the S_2 initialization's effect on the resultant moving average depends on α: Smaller α values make the choice of S_2 relatively more important than larger α values, since a higher discounts older observations faster.

The formula for calculating the EMA at time periods $t \geq 2$ is

$$S_t = \alpha Y_{t-1} + (1-\alpha)S_{t-1}$$

This formula can also be expressed in technical analysis terms as follows, showing how the EMA steps toward the latest data point:

$$EMA_{today} = EMA_{yesterday} + \alpha(p_0 - EMA_{yesterday})$$

where p_0 is the current price. Expanding out $EMA_{yesterday}$ each time results in the following power series, showing how the weighting factor on each data point p_1, p_2, etc., decreases exponentially:

$$EMA = \frac{p_{-1} + (1-\alpha)p_{-2} + (1-\alpha)^2 p_{-3} + \cdots}{1 + (1-\alpha) + (1-\alpha)^2 + \cdots} = \frac{\sum_{i=0}^{\infty}(1-\alpha)^i p_{-i-1}}{\sum_{i=0}^{\infty}(1-\alpha)^i} = \alpha \sum_{i=0}^{\infty}(1-\alpha)^i p_{-i-1}$$

Theoretically, this is an infinite sum, but because $1-\alpha$ is less than 1, the terms become smaller and smaller and can be ignored once they are small enough.

The n periods in an n-day EMA only specify the α factor. n is not a stopping point for the calculation in the way it is in an SMA or WMA. The first n data points in an EMA represent about 86% of the total weight in the calculation. As an approximation, we set $\alpha \approx 2/(n+1)$.

Implementation

Using the algorithm developed in the previous section, we can implement the exponential moving average in WPF. First, add the following code to the *DataSeriesMA* class:

```
// Exponential Moving Average:
private Polyline emaLineSeries = new Polyline();
private Brush emaLineColor = Brushes.Black;
private double emaLineThickness = 1;

public Polyline EMALineSeries
{
    get { return emaLineSeries; }
    set { emaLineSeries = value; }
}

public Brush EMALineColor
{
    get { return emaLineColor; }
    set { emaLineColor = value; }
}
```

```
public double EMALineThickness
{
    get { return emaLineThickness; }
    set { emaLineThickness = value; }
}

public double[] ExponentialMovingAverage()
{
    int m = DataString.GetLength(1);
    double[] data = new double[m];
    for (int i = 0; i < m; i++)
        data[i] = Convert.ToDouble(DataString[1, i]);

    double[] ema = new double[m - NDays + 1];
    double psum = 0.0;
    double alpha = 2.0 / NDays;

    if (m > NDays)
    {
        for (int i = 0; i < NDays; i++)
        {
            psum += data[i];
        }
        ema[0] = psum / NDays + alpha * (data[NDays - 1] - psum / NDays);

        for (int i = 1; i <= m - NDays; i++)
        {
            ema[i] = ema[i - 1] + alpha * (data[i + NDays - 1] - ema[i - 1]);
        }
    }
    return ema;
}
```

In this method, before calculating the exponential moving average, we must have an initial moving-average number. To start, here we use an *n*-day simple moving average for the previous day's exponential moving average. Each day we make the following calculation: We subtract the previous day's exponential moving average from the current day's price. We then multiply that difference by the exponential factor α to arrive at a number that we add to the previous day's exponential moving average, resulting in the current day's exponential moving average.

You also need to add a method, *AddExponentialMovingAverage*, to the *DataCollectionMA* class:

```
public void AddExponentialMovingAverage(ChartStyle cs)
{
    foreach (DataSeriesMA ds in DataList)
    {
        ds.EMALineSeries.Stroke = ds.EMALineColor;
        ds.EMALineSeries.StrokeThickness = ds.EMALineThickness;
        double[] data = ds.ExponentialMovingAverage();
        ds.EMALineSeries.Points.Clear();
        for (int i = 0; i < data.Length; i++)
        {
            ds.EMALineSeries.Points.Add(cs.NormalizePoint(
                new Point(i + ds.NDays - 1, data[i])));
        }
```

```
        cs.ChartCanvas.Children.Add(ds.EMALineSeries);
    }
}
```

Creating EMA Curves

Creating an exponential moving average curve is very simple. Open the *MovingAverage.xaml.cs* file and add the following code snippet to the *AddChart* method:

```
ds.EMALineColor = Brushes.Blue;
dc.AddExponentialMovingAverage(cs);
```

Running this application again produces the results shown in Figure 7-8, where IMB stock data are displayed.

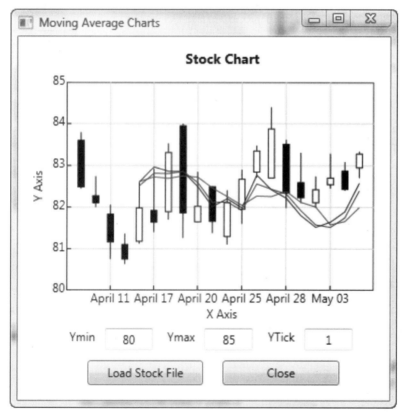

Figure 7-8. A stock chart with five-day simple (red), weighted (green), and exponential (blue) moving averages

Note that there is no exponential moving average data for the first four days, since there are not enough data to make the calculations until the fifth day.

For comparison, we plot the stock data, the five-day exponential, weighted, and simple moving averages together in Figure 7-8.

Using Yahoo Stock Charts in WPF

Nowadays, you can download real-time or time-delayed stock data from the Internet. For example, Yahoo Finance provides 15-minute-delayed stock price history data and stock charts. You can download these data from Yahoo, store them in your database, and process the data for your own applications.

In this section, I'll show you how to embed Yahoo stock charts directly into your WPF applications.

Connecting to Yahoo Stock Charts

In order to download Yahoo stock charts, you need to implement a program to establish an Internet connection to the Yahoo web site. Add a new class to the *StockCharts* project and name it *YahooStock*. Here is the code:

```
using System;
using System.ComponentModel;
using System.Windows.Threading;
using System.Net;
using System.Windows;

namespace StockCharts
{
    public class YahooStock
    {
        private static string chartURI = @"http://ichart.yahoo.com/z?z=m&a=vm";
        private string symbol = "IBM";
        private string chartType = "l";
        private string logScale = "off";
        private string movingAverage = "m50";
        private string stockPeriod = "6m";
        private int updateIntervalInSeconds = 12;

        public int UpdateIntervalInSeconds
        {
            get { return updateIntervalInSeconds; }
            set { updateIntervalInSeconds = value; }
        }

        public string ChartURI
        {
            get
            {
                return chartURI + "&s=" + this.Symbol + "&q=" + this.ChartType +
                    "&l=" + this.LogScale + "&p=" + this.MovingAverage +
                    "&t=" + this.StockPeriod;
            }
        }

        public string Symbol
```

```
{
    get { return symbol; }
    set { symbol = value; }
}
public string StockPeriod
{
    get { return stockPeriod; }
    set { stockPeriod = value; }
}

public string MovingAverage
{
    get { return movingAverage; }
    set { movingAverage = value; }
}

public string ChartType
{
    get { return chartType; }
    set { chartType = value; }
}

public string LogScale
{
    get { return logScale; }
    set { logScale = value; }
}

public bool CheckInternetConnection()
{
    try
    {
        System.Net.Sockets.TcpClient clnt =
            new System.Net.Sockets.TcpClient("www.microsoft.com", 80);
        clnt.Close();
        return true;
    }
    catch (Exception)
    {
        return false;
    }
}
}
}
```

This class provides properties and methods that allow you to establish an Internet connection to the Yahoo stock chart web site. You can select different stock symbols and format for the stock chart. Here, we only specify a few commonly used parameters, including symbol, chart type, log scale, moving average, and stock period. You can have more control over the stock chart by including more parameters. You can check the available parameters on Yahoo's web site.

Creating Yahoo Stock Charts in WPF

You can easily insert Yahoo stock charts into your WPF applications using the *YahooStock* class developed in the previous section. Add a new WPF Window to the current project and name it *YahooStockChart*. Here is the XAML file for this example:

```
<Window x:Class="StockCharts.YahooStockChart"
    xmlns="http://schemas.microsoft.com/winfx/2006/xaml/presentation"
    xmlns:x="http://schemas.microsoft.com/winfx/2006/xaml"
    Title="Yahoo Stock Charts" Height="400" Width="558">
    <StackPanel>
        <Image x:Name="chartImage" Width="512" Height="288" Margin="10"/>
        <StackPanel Orientation="Horizontal" HorizontalAlignment="Center">
            <TextBox Name="txStockSymbol" Text="IBM" Width="75" Height="25"
                    TextAlignment="Center"/>
            <Button Click="Update_Click" Width="100" Height="25"
                    Content="Update" Margin="10"/>
            <Button Click="Close_Click" Width="100" Height="25"
                    Content="Close" Margin="10"/>
        </StackPanel>
    </StackPanel>
</Window>
```

Here, we add an *Image* element to the application, which will host the Yahoo stock chart. The *TextBox* object, *txStockSymbol*, allows the user to enter the stock symbol and update the stock chart by clicking the *Update* button. Here is the corresponding code-behind file for this example:

```
using System;
using System.Windows;
using System.Windows.Input;
using System.Windows.Media;
using System.Windows.Media.Imaging;

namespace StockCharts
{
    public partial class YahooStockChart : Window
    {
        YahooStock ys;

        public YahooStockChart()
        {
            InitializeComponent();
            ys = new YahooStock();
            ys.StockPeriod = "1d";
            ys.ChartType = "c";
            ys.Symbol = txStockSymbol.Text;
            chartImage.Source = new BitmapImage(new Uri(ys.ChartURI));
        }

        private void Close_Click(object sender, RoutedEventArgs e)
        {
            this.Close();
        }
```

```
        private void Update_Click(object sender, RoutedEventArgs e)
        {
            ys.Symbol = txStockSymbol.Text;
            chartImage.Source = new BitmapImage(new Uri(ys.ChartURI));
        }
    }
}
```

Here, we first create a *YahooStock* instance and specify the properties that will format the stock chart. Then we set the *Source* of the *chartImage* using the downloaded Yahoo stock chart. Inside the *Update* button's event handler, we change the *chartImage*'s *Source* to the Yahoo stock chart with the stock symbol specified by the user.

Running this example generates the output shown in Figure 7-9. You can enter a new stock symbol and click the *Update* button to create a new stock chart for that symbol.

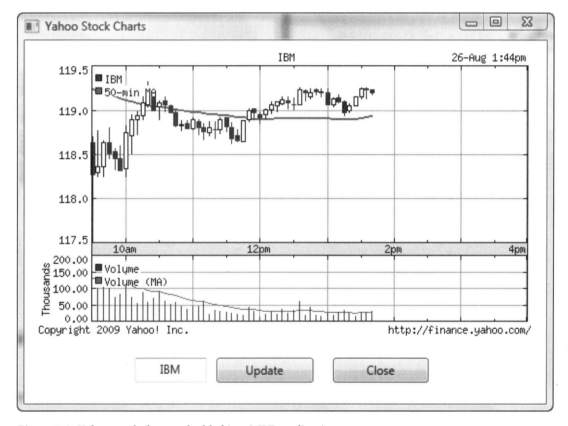

Figure 7-9. *Yahoo stock chart embedded in a WPF application*

CHAPTER 8

■ ■ ■

Interactive 2D Charts

All of the 2D charts discussed in the previous chapters are static in nature, meaning that they do not allow the user to interact directly with them by, for example, mouse-clicking and dragging. In this chapter, I'll discuss interactive 2D charts, which allow the user to interact with them using a mouse to zoom, pan, and retrieve data from the chart.

Automatic Tick Placement

The 2D charts we have discussed so far have one common feature — the user must specify the axis limits and the placement of ticks before these charts are created. The advantage of this manual method for setting the axis limits and positioning the ticks is that you have absolute control over the placement of ticks as well as the tick marks. You can place the ticks arbitrarily over the entire scale of the axis.

However, in interactive chart applications, we require the ticks and tick mark labels to be positioned automatically when the user interacts with the chart using a mouse.

Optimal Tick Spacing

When the user sets the axis limits interactively by mouse-dragging, we need to determine the optimal space for the tick placements. This optimal spacing depends on several factors, such as your computer screen size, application window size, and axis limits. In this section, I'll show you how to implement an optimal tick-spacing method.

Start with a new WPF project and name it *Interactive2DChart*. Add to the current project two classes from the *LineCharts* project, *DataSeries* and *DataCollection*, change their namespaces to *Interactive2DChart*, and comment out the code segment related to the Symbols object. Add another class, *ChartStyle*, from the previous *StockCharts* project and change its namespace to *Interactive2DChart*. Add a new method, *OptimalSpacing*, to the *ChartStyle* class:

```
public double OptimalSpacing(double original)
{
    double[] da = { 1.0, 2.0, 5.0 };
    double multiplier = Math.Pow(10, Math.Floor(Math.Log(original) / Math.Log(10)));
    double dmin = 100 * multiplier;
    double spacing = 0.0;
    double mn = 100;

    foreach (double d in da)
    {
```

```
        double delta = Math.Abs(original - d * multiplier);
        if (delta < dmin)
        {
            dmin = delta;
            spacing = d * multiplier;
        }
        if (d < mn)
        {
            mn = d;
        }
    }

    if (Math.Abs(original - 10 * mn * multiplier) < Math.Abs(original - spacing))
        spacing = 10 * mn * multiplier;
    return spacing;
}
```

You don't need to understand the mathematics behind this method in order to use it in your WPF chart applications. Just remember that for a given original spacing input, this method returns an optimal spacing, which can be used for automatic tick placement. Note that the original spacing must be in the unit of device-independent pixels.

Next, we need to modify the *AddChartStyle* method in the *ChartStyle* class:

```
public void AddChartStyle(TextBlock tbTitle, TextBlock tbXLabel, TextBlock tbYLabel)
{
    Point pt = new Point();
    Line tick = new Line();
    double offset = 0;
    double dx, dy;
    TextBlock tb = new TextBlock();
    double optimalXSpacing = 100;
    double optimalYSpacing = 80;

    //  determine right offset:
    tb.Text = Math.Round(Xmax, 0).ToString();
    tb.Measure(new Size(Double.PositiveInfinity, Double.PositiveInfinity));
    Size size = tb.DesiredSize;
    rightOffset = size.Width / 2 + 2;

    // Determine left offset:
    double xScale = 0.0, yScale = 0.0;
    double xSpacing = 0.0, ySpacing = 0.0;
    double xTick = 0.0, yTick = 0.0;
    int xStart = 0, xEnd = 1;
    int yStart = 0, yEnd = 1;
    double offset0 = 30;

    while (Math.Abs(offset - offset0) > 1)
    {
        if (Xmin != Xmax)
            xScale = (TextCanvas.Width - offset0 - rightOffset - 5) /
                        (Xmax - Xmin);
        if (Ymin != Ymax)
            yScale = TextCanvas.Height / (Ymax - Ymin);
```

```
            xSpacing = optimalXSpacing / xScale;
            xTick = OptimalSpacing(xSpacing);
            ySpacing = optimalYSpacing / yScale;
            yTick = OptimalSpacing(ySpacing);
            xStart = (int)Math.Ceiling(Xmin / xTick);
            xEnd = (int)Math.Floor(Xmax / xTick);
            yStart = (int)Math.Ceiling(Ymin / yTick);
            yEnd = (int)Math.Floor(Ymax / yTick);

            for (int i = yStart; i <= yEnd; i++)
            {
                dy = i * yTick;
                pt = NormalizePoint(new Point(Xmin, dy));
                tb = new TextBlock();
                tb.Text = dy.ToString();
                tb.TextAlignment = TextAlignment.Right;
                tb.Measure(new Size(Double.PositiveInfinity, Double.PositiveInfinity));
                size = tb.DesiredSize;
                if (offset < size.Width)
                    offset = size.Width;
            }
            if (offset0 > offset)
                offset0 -= 0.5;
            else if (offset0 < offset)
                offset0 += 0.5;
}

leftOffset = offset + 5;

Canvas.SetLeft(ChartCanvas, leftOffset);
Canvas.SetBottom(ChartCanvas, bottomOffset);
ChartCanvas.Width = TextCanvas.Width - leftOffset - rightOffset;
ChartCanvas.Height = TextCanvas.Height - bottomOffset - size.Height / 2;
Rectangle chartRect = new Rectangle();
chartRect.Stroke = Brushes.Black;
chartRect.Width = ChartCanvas.Width;
chartRect.Height = ChartCanvas.Height;
ChartCanvas.Children.Add(chartRect);

if (Xmin != Xmax)
    xScale = ChartCanvas.Width / (Xmax - Xmin);
if (Ymin != Ymax)
    yScale = ChartCanvas.Height / (Ymax - Ymin);
xSpacing = optimalXSpacing / xScale;
xTick = OptimalSpacing(xSpacing);
ySpacing = optimalYSpacing / yScale;
yTick = OptimalSpacing(ySpacing);
xStart = (int)Math.Ceiling(Xmin / xTick);
xEnd = (int)Math.Floor(Xmax / xTick);
yStart = (int)Math.Ceiling(Ymin / yTick);
yEnd = (int)Math.Floor(Ymax / yTick);

// Create vertical gridlines and x tick marks:
```

```
    if (IsYGrid == true)
    {
        for (int i = xStart; i <= xEnd; i++)
        {
            gridline = new Line();
            AddLinePattern();
            dx = i * xTick;
            gridline.X1 = NormalizePoint(new Point(dx, Ymin)).X;
            gridline.Y1 = NormalizePoint(new Point(dx, Ymin)).Y;
            gridline.X2 = NormalizePoint(new Point(dx, Ymax)).X;
            gridline.Y2 = NormalizePoint(new Point(dx, Ymax)).Y;
            ChartCanvas.Children.Add(gridline);

            pt = NormalizePoint(new Point(dx, Ymin));
            tick = new Line();
            tick.Stroke = Brushes.Black;
            tick.X1 = pt.X;
            tick.Y1 = pt.Y;
            tick.X2 = pt.X;
            tick.Y2 = pt.Y - 5;
            ChartCanvas.Children.Add(tick);

            tb = new TextBlock();
            tb.Text = dx.ToString();
            tb.Measure(new Size(Double.PositiveInfinity, Double.PositiveInfinity));
            size = tb.DesiredSize;
            TextCanvas.Children.Add(tb);
            Canvas.SetLeft(tb, leftOffset + pt.X - size.Width / 2);
            Canvas.SetTop(tb, pt.Y + 2 + size.Height / 2);
        }
    }

    // Create horizontal gridlines and y tick marks:
    if (IsXGrid == true)
    {
        for (int i = yStart; i <= yEnd; i++)
        {
            gridline = new Line();
            AddLinePattern();
            dy = i * yTick;
            gridline.X1 = NormalizePoint(new Point(Xmin, dy)).X;
            gridline.Y1 = NormalizePoint(new Point(Xmin, dy)).Y;
            gridline.X2 = NormalizePoint(new Point(Xmax, dy)).X;
            gridline.Y2 = NormalizePoint(new Point(Xmax, dy)).Y;
            ChartCanvas.Children.Add(gridline);

            pt = NormalizePoint(new Point(Xmin, dy));
            tick = new Line();
            tick.Stroke = Brushes.Black;
            tick.X1 = pt.X;
            tick.Y1 = pt.Y;
            tick.X2 = pt.X + 5;
            tick.Y2 = pt.Y;
```

```
            ChartCanvas.Children.Add(tick);

            tb = new TextBlock();
            tb.Text = dy.ToString();
            tb.Measure(new Size(Double.PositiveInfinity, Double.PositiveInfinity));
            size = tb.DesiredSize;
            TextCanvas.Children.Add(tb);
            Canvas.SetRight(tb, ChartCanvas.Width + 10);
            Canvas.SetTop(tb, pt.Y);
        }
    }

    // Add title and labels:
    tbTitle.Text = Title;
    tbXLabel.Text = XLabel;
    tbYLabel.Text = YLabel;
    tbXLabel.Margin = new Thickness(leftOffset + 2, 2, 2, 2);
    tbTitle.Margin = new Thickness(leftOffset + 2, 2, 2, 2);
}
```

The corresponding changes are highlighted in bold. Note that the original public properties *XTick* and *YTick* have been removed from the *ChartStyle* class. Instead, we now compute the parameters *xTick* and *yTick* using the *OptimalSpacing* method.

Creating Charts with Automatic Ticks

In this section, we'll test the automatic tick-placement method implemented in the previous section. Add a new WPF Window to the current project and name it *AutomaticTicks*. Here is the XAML file for this example:

```
<Window x:Class="Interactive2DChart.AutomaticTicks"
    xmlns="http://schemas.microsoft.com/winfx/2006/xaml/presentation"
    xmlns:x="http://schemas.microsoft.com/winfx/2006/xaml"
    Title="Automatical Tick Placement" Height="400" Width="400">

    <Grid Margin="10">
        <Grid.ColumnDefinitions>
            <ColumnDefinition Width="Auto"/>
            <ColumnDefinition Width="*"/>
        </Grid.ColumnDefinitions>
        <Grid.RowDefinitions>
            <RowDefinition Height="Auto"/>
            <RowDefinition Height="Auto"/>
            <RowDefinition Height="*"/>
            <RowDefinition Height="Auto"/>
        </Grid.RowDefinitions>
        <TextBlock Margin="2" x:Name="tbTitle" Grid.Column="1" Grid.Row="0"
                RenderTransformOrigin="0.5,0.5" FontSize="14" FontWeight="Bold"
                HorizontalAlignment="Stretch" VerticalAlignment="Stretch"
                TextAlignment="Center" Text="Title"/>

        <TextBlock Margin="2" x:Name="tbDate" Grid.Column="0" Grid.ColumnSpan="2"
                Grid.Row="1" RenderTransformOrigin="0.5,0.5" FontSize="10"
```

```
                          Foreground="Blue" HorizontalAlignment="Stretch"
                          VerticalAlignment="Stretch" TextAlignment="Left" Text="Now"/>

           <TextBlock Margin="2" x:Name="tbResults" Grid.Column="1" Grid.Row="1"
                      RenderTransformOrigin="0.5,0.5" FontSize="10"  Foreground="Blue"
                      HorizontalAlignment="Stretch" VerticalAlignment="Stretch"
                      TextAlignment="Right" Text="Results"/>

           <TextBlock Margin="2" x:Name="tbXLabel" Grid.Column="1" Grid.Row="3"
                      RenderTransformOrigin="0.5,0.5" TextAlignment="Center"
                      Text="X Axis"/>

           <TextBlock Margin="2" Name="tbYLabel" Grid.Column="0" Grid.Row="2"
                      RenderTransformOrigin="0.5,0.5" TextAlignment="Center"
                      Text="Y Axis">
               <TextBlock.LayoutTransform>
                   <RotateTransform Angle="-90"/>
               </TextBlock.LayoutTransform>
           </TextBlock>

           <Grid  Margin="0,0,0,0" x:Name ="chartGrid" Grid.Column="1" Grid.Row="2"
                  ClipToBounds="False" Background="Transparent"
                  SizeChanged="chartGrid_SizeChanged" >
           </Grid>
           <Canvas Margin="2" Name="textCanvas" Grid.Column="1" Grid.Row="2"
                   ClipToBounds="True">
               <Canvas Name="chartCanvas" ClipToBounds="True"/>
           </Canvas>
       </Grid>
</Window>
```

This XAML file is similar to that used in examples from the previous chapters except that we add two additional text blocks, one to display the current time and the other to display the data point value. Here is the corresponding code-behind file for this example:

```
using System;
using System.Windows;
using System.Windows.Media;

namespace Interactive2DChart
{
    public partial class AutomaticTicks : Window
    {
        private ChartStyle cs;
        private DataCollection dc;
        private DataSeries ds;

        public AutomaticTicks()
        {
            InitializeComponent();
        }

        private void AddChart()
        {
```

```
        cs = new ChartStyle();
        dc = new DataCollection();
        ds = new DataSeries();

        cs.ChartCanvas = chartCanvas;
        cs.TextCanvas = textCanvas;
        cs.Title = "Sine and Cosine Chart";
        cs.Xmin = 0;
        cs.Xmax = 7;
        cs.Ymin = -1.1;
        cs.Ymax = 1.1;
        cs.GridlinePattern = ChartStyle.GridlinePatternEnum.Dot;
        cs.GridlineColor = Brushes.Black;
        cs.AddChartStyle(tbTitle, tbXLabel, tbYLabel);

        // Draw Sine-like curve:
        ds.LineColor = Brushes.Blue;
        ds.LineThickness = 2;
        double dx = (cs.Xmax - cs.Xmin) / 100;

        for (double x = cs.Xmin; x <= cs.Xmax + dx; x += dx)
        {
            double y = Math.Exp(-0.3 * Math.Abs(x)) * Math.Sin(x);
            ds.LineSeries.Points.Add(new Point(x, y));
        }
        dc.DataList.Add(ds);

        // Draw Cosine-like curve:
        ds = new DataSeries();
        ds.LineColor = Brushes.Red;
        ds.LinePattern = DataSeries.LinePatternEnum.DashDot;
        ds.LineThickness = 2;

        for (double x = cs.Xmin; x <= cs.Xmax + dx; x += dx)
        {
            double y = Math.Exp(-0.3 * Math.Abs(x)) * Math.Cos(x);
            ds.LineSeries.Points.Add(new Point(x, y));
        }
        dc.DataList.Add(ds);
        dc.AddLines(cs);
    }

    private void chartGrid_SizeChanged(object sender, SizeChangedEventArgs e)
    {
        tbDate.Text = DateTime.Now.ToShortDateString();
        textCanvas.Width = chartGrid.ActualWidth;
        textCanvas.Height = chartGrid.ActualHeight;
        chartCanvas.Children.Clear();
        textCanvas.Children.RemoveRange(1, textCanvas.Children.Count - 1);
        AddChart();
    }
  }
}
```

Again, this code-behind file is similar to that used in previous examples, except you no longer need to specify the tick-related properties.

Running this example by pressing F5 produces the results shown in Figure 8-1. You can see that the chart has ticks and tick labels on both the X and Y axes, whose locations are determined by the *OptimalSpacing* method.

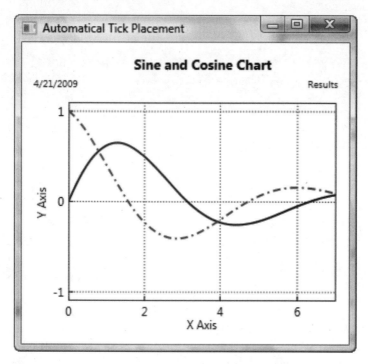

Figure 8-1. *2D chart with automatic tick placement*

The real magic of the program occurs when you resize the chart window — the number of ticks and tick labels will increase or decrease depending on the application window's actual size. Figure 8-2 shows the resized chart. You can see that this enlarged 2D chart has more ticks and tick labels in both the X and Y axes and that all of these ticks and tick labels are placed automatically.

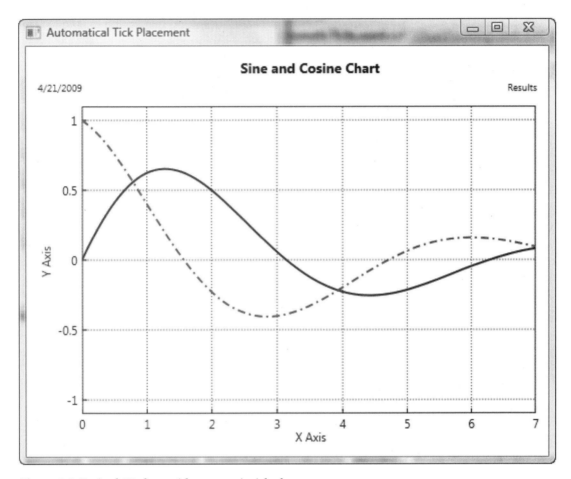

Figure 8-2. *Resized 2D chart with automatic tick placement*

Chart Panning with a Mouse

In Chapter 3, you learned how to move a 2D chart around on a chart canvas by manually changing its axis limits. In this section, I'll show you how to pan a 2D chart interactively using a mouse.

Add a new WPF Window to the current project and name it *ChartPanning*. The XAML file is basically similar to that used in the previous example, except for the addition of a few mouse events to the *chartCanvas*:

```
<Canvas Name="chartCanvas" ClipToBounds="True" Background="Transparent"
        MouseLeftButtonDown="OnMouseLeftButtonDown"
        MouseMove="OnMouseMove"
        MouseLeftButtonUp="OnMouseLeftButtonUp"
        MouseRightButtonDown="OnMouseRightButtonDown">
</Canvas>
```

The code-behind file of this example is listed below:

```
using System;
using System.Windows;
using System.Windows.Input;
using System.Windows.Media;

namespace Interactive2DChart
{
    public partial class ChartPanning : Window
    {
        private Point startPoint = new Point();
        private Point endPoint = new Point();
        private ChartStyle cs;
        private DataCollection dc;
        private DataSeries ds;
        private double xmin0 = 0;
        private double xmax0 = 7;
        private double ymin0 = -1.5;
        private double ymax0 = 1.5;

        public ChartPanning()
        {
            InitializeComponent();
            cs = new ChartStyle();
            cs.Xmin = xmin0;
            cs.Xmax = xmax0;
            cs.Ymin = ymin0;
            cs.Ymax = ymax0;
        }

        private void AddChart(double xmin, double xmax, double ymin, double ymax)
        {
            dc = new DataCollection();
            ds = new DataSeries();
            cs = new ChartStyle();

            cs.ChartCanvas = chartCanvas;
            cs.TextCanvas = textCanvas;
            cs.Title = "My 2D Chart";
            cs.Xmin = xmin;
            cs.Xmax = xmax;
            cs.Ymin = ymin;
            cs.Ymax = ymax;
            cs.GridlinePattern = ChartStyle.GridlinePatternEnum.Dot;
            cs.GridlineColor = Brushes.Black;
            cs.AddChartStyle(tbTitle, tbXLabel, tbYLabel);

            // Draw Sine-like curve:
            ds.LineColor = Brushes.Blue;
            ds.LineThickness = 2;
            double dx = (cs.Xmax - cs.Xmin) / 100;

            for (double x = cs.Xmin; x <= cs.Xmax + dx; x += dx)
```

```
            {
                double y = Math.Exp(-0.3 * Math.Abs(x)) * Math.Sin(x);
                ds.LineSeries.Points.Add(new Point(x, y));
            }
            dc.DataList.Add(ds);

            // Draw Cosine-like curve:
            ds = new DataSeries();
            ds.LineColor = Brushes.Red;
            ds.LinePattern = DataSeries.LinePatternEnum.DashDot;
            ds.LineThickness = 2;

            for (double x = cs.Xmin; x <= cs.Xmax + dx; x += dx)
            {
                double y = Math.Exp(-0.3 * Math.Abs(x)) * Math.Cos(x);
                ds.LineSeries.Points.Add(new Point(x, y));
            }
            dc.DataList.Add(ds);
            dc.AddLines(cs);
        }

        private void chartGrid_SizeChanged(object sender, SizeChangedEventArgs e)
        {
            tbDate.Text = DateTime.Now.ToShortDateString();
            textCanvas.Width = chartGrid.ActualWidth;
            textCanvas.Height = chartGrid.ActualHeight;
            chartCanvas.Children.Clear();
            textCanvas.Children.RemoveRange(1, textCanvas.Children.Count - 1);
            AddChart(cs.Xmin, cs.Xmax, cs.Ymin, cs.Ymax);
        }

        private void OnMouseLeftButtonDown(object sender, MouseButtonEventArgs e)
        {
            if (!chartCanvas.IsMouseCaptured)
            {
                startPoint = e.GetPosition(chartCanvas);
                chartCanvas.CaptureMouse();
            }
        }

        private void OnMouseMove(object sender, MouseEventArgs e)
        {
            if (chartCanvas.IsMouseCaptured)
            {
                endPoint = e.GetPosition(chartCanvas);
                TranslateTransform tt = new TranslateTransform();
                tt.X = endPoint.X - startPoint.X;
                tt.Y = endPoint.Y - startPoint.Y;
                for (int i = 0; i < dc.DataList.Count; i++)
                {
                    dc.DataList[i].LineSeries.RenderTransform = tt;
                }
            }
```

```
    }

    private void OnMouseLeftButtonUp(object sender, MouseButtonEventArgs e)
    {
        double dx = 0;
        double dy = 0;
        double x0 = 0;
        double x1 = 1;
        double y0 = 0;
        double y1 = 1;
        endPoint = e.GetPosition(chartCanvas);
        dx = (cs.Xmax - cs.Xmin) * (endPoint.X - startPoint.X) /
            chartCanvas.Width;
        dy = (cs.Ymax - cs.Ymin) * (endPoint.Y - startPoint.Y) /
            chartCanvas.Height;
        x0 = cs.Xmin + dx;
        x1 = cs.Xmax + dx;
        y0 = cs.Ymin + dy;
        y1 = cs.Ymax + dy;

        chartCanvas.Children.Clear();
        textCanvas.Children.RemoveRange(1, textCanvas.Children.Count - 1);
        AddChart(x0, x1, y0, y1);

        chartCanvas.ReleaseMouseCapture();
        chartCanvas.Cursor = Cursors.Arrow;
    }

    private void OnMouseRightButtonDown(object sender, MouseButtonEventArgs e)
    {
        chartCanvas.Children.Clear();
        textCanvas.Children.RemoveRange(1, textCanvas.Children.Count - 1);
        AddChart(xmin0, xmax0, ymin0, ymax0);
    }
    }
}
```

This example involves several mouse click events that allow the user to interact with the chart. These mouse events perform various operations, including *LeftMouseButtonUp*, *LeftMouseButtonDown*, *RightMouseButtonDown*, and *MouseMove*. The mouse button events provide a *MouseButtonEventArgs* object. The *MouseButtonEventArgs* class derives from the *MouseEventArgs* base class. When you run the program and bring up the chart on your screen, you can click anywhere within the chart area to fire the mouse button events. First, you obtain the position at which the left mouse button is clicked on the *chartCanvas* control. You then set the mouse's capture state. Usually, when an object receives a *mouse button down* event, it will receive a corresponding *mouse button up* event shortly thereafter. However, in this example, you need to hold down the mouse and move it around within the chart area in order to pan the chart. Next, you want to have a notification of the *mouse button up* event. To do so, you need to capture the mouse by calling the *CaptureMouse* method and passing to the *chartCanvas*.

Inside the *MouseMove* event handler, *OnMouseMove*, you convert the mouse movement into a translation transform, which is attached to the line series' *RenderTransform* property. This way, you can pan the curves within the chart area by moving your mouse. When you release the left mouse button, the *LeftMouseButtonUp* event is fired. Within the *OnLeftMouseButtonUp* event handler, you redefine the axis limits by taking into account the translation due to the mouse movement, and the chart is redrawn using these new axis limits. Finally, the *RightMouseButtonDown* event allows you to return the chart to its original axis limits.

In this example, we use four mouse events. There are more mouse events in WPF you can use to develop interactive chart and graphics applications. For example, mouse events can allow you to react when the mouse pointer moves over an element. These events include *MouseEnter* and *MouseLeave*, which provide information about a *MouseEventArgs* object for your program. The *MouseEventArgs* object includes properties that show you the state of the mouse button. If you need more information about mouse events, you can refer to Microsoft online help or tutorial books on the topic.

Running this example generates the result shown in Figure 8-3.

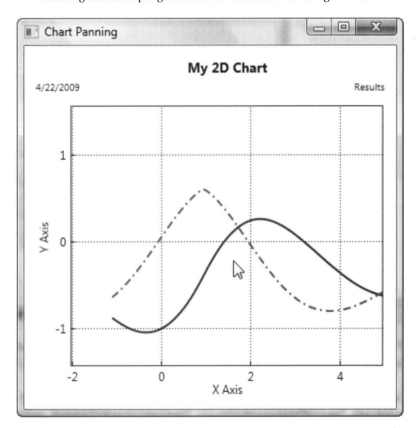

Figure 8-3. Pan a 2D chart using your mouse.

Chart Zooming with a Mouse

In Chapter 3, you learned how to zoom in on a 2D chart on a chart canvas by manually changing its axis limits. In this section, I'll show you how to zoom in or out of a 2D chart interactively using a mouse.

Add a new WPF Window to the current project and name it *ChartZooming*. The XAML is the same as that used in the previous panning example. Here is the code-behind file for this example:

```
using System;
using System.Windows;
using System.Windows.Input;
using System.Windows.Media;
using System.Windows.Shapes;
using System.Windows.Controls;

namespace Interactive2DChart
{
    public partial class ChartZooming : Window
    {
        private Point startPoint = new Point();
        private Point endPoint = new Point();
        private Shape rubberBand = null;
        private ChartStyle cs;
        private DataCollection dc;
        private DataSeries ds;
        private double xmin0 = 0;
        private double xmax0 = 7;
        private double ymin0 = -1.5;
        private double ymax0 = 1.5;

        public ChartZooming()
        {
            InitializeComponent();
            cs = new ChartStyle();
            cs.Xmin = xmin0;
            cs.Xmax = xmax0;
            cs.Ymin = ymin0;
            cs.Ymax = ymax0;
        }

        private void AddChart(double xmin, double xmax, double ymin, double ymax)
        {
            dc = new DataCollection();
            ds = new DataSeries();
            cs = new ChartStyle();

            cs.ChartCanvas = chartCanvas;
            cs.TextCanvas = textCanvas;
            cs.Title = "Sine and Cosine Chart";
            cs.Xmin = xmin;
            cs.Xmax = xmax;
            cs.Ymin = ymin;
            cs.Ymax = ymax;
            cs.GridlinePattern = ChartStyle.GridlinePatternEnum.Dot;
            cs.GridlineColor = Brushes.Black;
            cs.AddChartStyle(tbTitle, tbXLabel, tbYLabel);

            // Draw Sine-like curve:
            ds.LineColor = Brushes.Blue;
            ds.LineThickness = 2;
            double dx = (cs.Xmax - cs.Xmin) / 100;
```

```csharp
    for (double x = cs.Xmin; x <= cs.Xmax + dx; x += dx)
    {
        double y = Math.Exp(-0.3 * Math.Abs(x)) * Math.Sin(x);
        ds.LineSeries.Points.Add(new Point(x, y));
    }
    dc.DataList.Add(ds);

    // Draw Cosine-like curve:
    ds = new DataSeries();
    ds.LineColor = Brushes.Red;
    ds.LinePattern = DataSeries.LinePatternEnum.DashDot;
    ds.LineThickness = 2;

    for (double x = cs.Xmin; x <= cs.Xmax + dx; x += dx)
    {
        double y = Math.Exp(-0.3 * Math.Abs(x)) * Math.Cos(x);
        ds.LineSeries.Points.Add(new Point(x, y));
    }
    dc.DataList.Add(ds);
    dc.AddLines(cs);
}

private void chartGrid_SizeChanged(object sender, SizeChangedEventArgs e)
{
    tbDate.Text = DateTime.Now.ToShortDateString();
    textCanvas.Width = chartGrid.ActualWidth;
    textCanvas.Height = chartGrid.ActualHeight;
    chartCanvas.Children.Clear();
    textCanvas.Children.RemoveRange(1, textCanvas.Children.Count - 1);
    AddChart(cs.Xmin, cs.Xmax, cs.Ymin, cs.Ymax);
}

private void OnMouseLeftButtonDown(object sender, MouseButtonEventArgs e)
{
    if (!chartCanvas.IsMouseCaptured)
    {
        startPoint = e.GetPosition(chartCanvas);
        chartCanvas.CaptureMouse();
    }
}

private void OnMouseMove(object sender, MouseEventArgs e)
{
    if (chartCanvas.IsMouseCaptured)
    {
        endPoint = e.GetPosition(chartCanvas);
        if (rubberBand == null)
        {
            rubberBand = new Rectangle();
            rubberBand.Stroke = Brushes.Red;
            chartCanvas.Children.Add(rubberBand);
        }
```

```
                rubberBand.Width = Math.Abs(startPoint.X - endPoint.X);
                rubberBand.Height = Math.Abs(startPoint.Y - endPoint.Y);
                double left = Math.Min(startPoint.X, endPoint.X);
                double top = Math.Min(startPoint.Y, endPoint.Y);
                Canvas.SetLeft(rubberBand, left);
                Canvas.SetTop(rubberBand, top);
            }
        }

        private void OnMouseLeftButtonUp(object sender, MouseButtonEventArgs e)
        {
            double x0 = 0;
            double x1 = 1;
            double y0 = 0;
            double y1 = 1;
            endPoint = e.GetPosition(chartCanvas);

            if (endPoint.X > startPoint.X)
            {
                x0 = cs.Xmin + (cs.Xmax - cs.Xmin) * startPoint.X /
                    chartCanvas.Width;
                x1 = cs.Xmin + (cs.Xmax - cs.Xmin) * endPoint.X /
                    chartCanvas.Width;
            }
            else if (endPoint.X < startPoint.X)
            {
                x1 = cs.Xmin + (cs.Xmax - cs.Xmin) * startPoint.X /
                    chartCanvas.Width;
                x0 = cs.Xmin + (cs.Xmax - cs.Xmin) * endPoint.X /
                    chartCanvas.Width;
            }

            if (endPoint.Y < startPoint.Y)
            {
                y0 = cs.Ymin + (cs.Ymax - cs.Ymin) * (chartCanvas.Height -
                    startPoint.Y) / chartCanvas.Height;
                y1 = cs.Ymin + (cs.Ymax - cs.Ymin) * (chartCanvas.Height -
                    endPoint.Y) / chartCanvas.Height;
            }
            else if (endPoint.Y > startPoint.Y)
            {
                y1 = cs.Ymin + (cs.Ymax - cs.Ymin) * (chartCanvas.Height -
                    startPoint.Y) / chartCanvas.Height;
                y0 = cs.Ymin + (cs.Ymax - cs.Ymin) * (chartCanvas.Height -
                    endPoint.Y) / chartCanvas.Height;
            }

            chartCanvas.Children.Clear();
            textCanvas.Children.RemoveRange(1, textCanvas.Children.Count - 1);
            AddChart(x0, x1, y0, y1);

            if (rubberBand != null)
            {
```

```
                rubberBand = null;
                chartCanvas.ReleaseMouseCapture();
            }
        }

        private void OnMouseRightButtonDown(object sender, MouseButtonEventArgs e)
        {
            chartCanvas.Children.Clear();
            textCanvas.Children.RemoveRange(1, textCanvas.Children.Count - 1);
            AddChart(xmin0, xmax0, ymin0, ymax0);
        }
    }
}
```

The foregoing code involves four mouse events, which are the same as those used in the previous example. In this case, the mouse event handlers are used to create a zoom area in the chart with the mouse. In particular, the *MouseMove* event creates a rubber band, a common feature in graphics applications. The rubber band provides an outline following the mouse cursor of the area to be zoomed in on, so you can visualize exactly which portion of the chart will be zoomed in on your screen. The *OnRightMouseButtonDown* event handler allows you to return to the original, unzoomed chart.

This example creates the output shown in Figures 8-4 and 8-5.

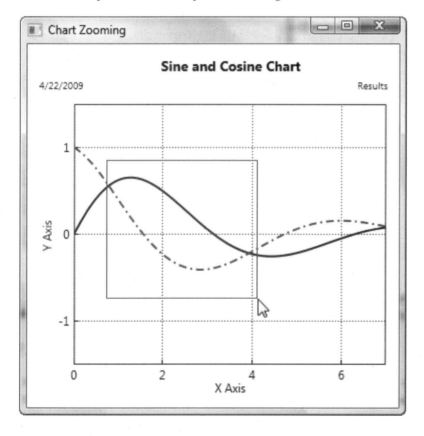

Figure 8-4. Creating a rubber band on a 2D chart using mouse

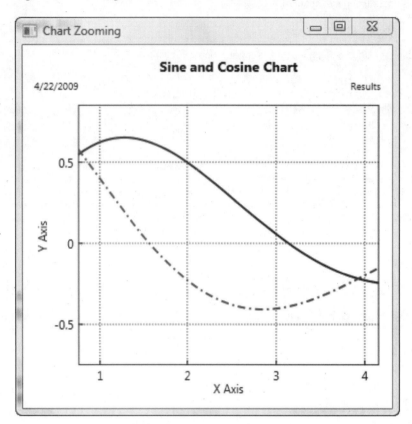

Figure 8-5. The rubber band area in Figure 8-4 occupies the entire application window (zoom-in effect).

You can zoom in to the chart by following these steps. Press your left mouse button, and hold it down, drag the mouse to create a red zoom rectangle (a rubber band). Release the left mouse button, and the chart will be redrawn within the zooming area defined by the rubber band. Press your right mouse button to restore the original unzoomed chart generated using the original axis limits.

Chart Zooming with a Mouse Wheel

In the previous section, I showed you how to zoom in on a 2D chart using mouse button events. You can also use the *MouseWheel* event to zoom in and out, a method more commonly used in interactive applications. In this section, I'll show you how to zoom a 2D chart interactively using the *MouseWheel* event.

Add a new WPF Window to the current project and name it *MouseWheelZooming*. The XAML file is basically similar to that used in the previous example, except for this change in the mouse events attached to the *chartCanvas*:

```
<Canvas Name="chartCanvas" ClipToBounds="True" Background="Transparent"
        MouseWheel="OnMouseWheel"
        MouseRightButtonDown="OnMouseRightButtonDown"/>
```

Here, we create two mouse events, *MouseRightButtonDown* (which restores the original chart) and *MouseWheel* (which zooms in the chart). Here is the corresponding code-behind file for this example:

```csharp
using System;
using System.Windows;
using System.Windows.Controls;
using System.Windows.Input;
using System.Windows.Media;
using System.Windows.Shapes;

namespace Interactive2DChart
{
    public partial class MouseWheelZooming : Window
    {
        private ChartStyle cs;
        private DataCollection dc;
        private DataSeries ds;
        private double xmin0 = 0;
        private double xmax0 = 7;
        private double ymin0 = -1.5;
        private double ymax0 = 1.5;
        private double xIncrement = 5;
        private double yIncrement = 0;

        public MouseWheelZooming()
        {
            InitializeComponent();
            cs = new ChartStyle();
            cs.Xmin = xmin0;
            cs.Xmax = xmax0;
            cs.Ymin = ymin0;
            cs.Ymax = ymax0;
        }

        private void AddChart(double xmin, double xmax, double ymin, double ymax)
        {
            dc = new DataCollection();
            ds = new DataSeries();
            cs = new ChartStyle();

            cs.ChartCanvas = chartCanvas;
            cs.TextCanvas = textCanvas;
            cs.Title = "Sine and Cosine Chart";
            cs.Xmin = xmin;
            cs.Xmax = xmax;
            cs.Ymin = ymin;
            cs.Ymax = ymax;
            cs.GridlinePattern = ChartStyle.GridlinePatternEnum.Dot;
            cs.GridlineColor = Brushes.Black;
```

323

```
        cs.AddChartStyle(tbTitle, tbXLabel, tbYLabel);

        // Draw Sine-like curve:
        ds.LineColor = Brushes.Blue;
        ds.LineThickness = 2;
        double dx = (cs.Xmax - cs.Xmin) / 100;

        for (double x = cs.Xmin; x <= cs.Xmax + dx; x += dx)
        {
            double y = Math.Exp(-0.3 * Math.Abs(x)) * Math.Sin(x);
            ds.LineSeries.Points.Add(new Point(x, y));
        }
        dc.DataList.Add(ds);

        // Draw Cosine-like curve:
        ds = new DataSeries();
        ds.LineColor = Brushes.Red;
        ds.LinePattern = DataSeries.LinePatternEnum.DashDot;
        ds.LineThickness = 2;

        for (double x = cs.Xmin; x <= cs.Xmax + dx; x += dx)
        {
            double y = Math.Exp(-0.3 * Math.Abs(x)) * Math.Cos(x);
            ds.LineSeries.Points.Add(new Point(x, y));
        }
        dc.DataList.Add(ds);
        dc.AddLines(cs);
    }

    private void chartGrid_SizeChanged(object sender, SizeChangedEventArgs e)
    {
        tbDate.Text = DateTime.Now.ToShortDateString();
        textCanvas.Width = chartGrid.ActualWidth;
        textCanvas.Height = chartGrid.ActualHeight;
        chartCanvas.Children.Clear();
        textCanvas.Children.RemoveRange(1, textCanvas.Children.Count - 1);
        AddChart(cs.Xmin, cs.Xmax, cs.Ymin, cs.Ymax);
    }

    private void OnMouseRightButtonDown(object sender, MouseButtonEventArgs e)
    {
        chartCanvas.Children.Clear();
        textCanvas.Children.RemoveRange(1, textCanvas.Children.Count - 1);
        AddChart(xmin0, xmax0, ymin0, ymax0);
    }

    private void OnMouseWheel(object sender, MouseWheelEventArgs e)
    {
        double dx = (e.Delta > 0) ? xIncrement : -xIncrement;
        double dy = (e.Delta > 0) ? yIncrement : -yIncrement;
        double x0 = cs.Xmin + (cs.Xmax - cs.Xmin) * dx / chartCanvas.Width;
        double x1 = cs.Xmax - (cs.Xmax - cs.Xmin) * dx / chartCanvas.Width;
        double y0 = cs.Ymin + (cs.Ymax - cs.Ymin) * dy / chartCanvas.Height;
```

```
            double y1 = cs.Ymax - (cs.Ymax - cs.Ymin) * dy / chartCanvas.Height;

            chartCanvas.Children.Clear();
            textCanvas.Children.RemoveRange(1, textCanvas.Children.Count - 1);
            AddChart(x0, x1, y0, y1);
        }
    }
}
```

There are two field members, *xIncrement* and *yIncrement*, that are used to control the zooming in or out in both the *X* and *Y* directions. You can see that the *yIncrement* is set to zero in this example, meaning there will be no zooming effect in the *Y* direction. Note how we relate these two increment parameters to the mouse wheel's *Delta* property inside the *OnMouseWheel* event handler:

```
double dx = (e.Delta > 0) ? xIncrement : -xIncrement;
double dy = (e.Delta > 0) ? yIncrement : -yIncrement;
```

The sign of *e.Delta* depends on the direction of the mouse wheel's motion: It will be positive if the user scrolls forward and negative if the user scrolls backward, resulting in either a zooming-in or zooming-out effect. Also notice that in order for the chart to capture the *MouseWheel* event, it has to have focus. You can just click the chart or use the *MouseEnter* event to give the chart focus as soon as the mouse enters the chart.

Running this example generates the result shown in Figure 8-6.

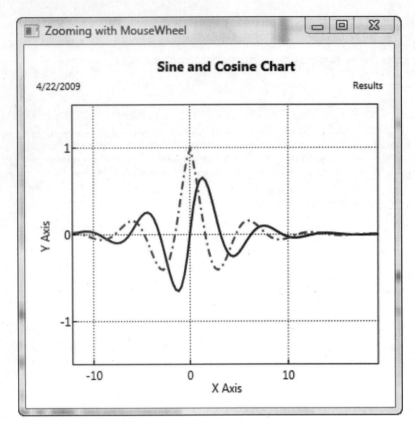

Figure 8-6. Zooming a 2D chart using mouse wheel

Retrieving Chart Data

In some situations, you may want to retrieve data values directly from a chart. You can do this interactively using mouse events. Here, I'll show you how to retrieve data from a 2D chart and display the result directly on the screen.

Add a new WPF Window to the current project and name it *RetrieveChartData*. The XAML file for this example is similar to that used in the previous example, except for the addition of a *StackPanel* object and these three mouse events attached to the *chartCanvas*:

```
<StackPanel Name="resultPanel" Orientation="Horizontal" Grid.Column="1"
        Grid.Row="1" HorizontalAlignment="Right"></StackPanel>

<Canvas Name="chartCanvas" ClipToBounds="True" Background="Transparent"
        MouseLeftButtonDown="OnMouseLeftButtonDown"
        MouseMove="OnMouseMove"
        MouseLeftButtonUp="OnMouseLeftButtonUp"/>
```

Here is the corresponding code-behind file:

```
using System;
using System.Windows;
using System.Collections.Generic;
using System.Windows.Controls;
using System.Windows.Input;
using System.Windows.Media;
using System.Windows.Media.Imaging;
using System.Windows.Shapes;

namespace Interactive2DChart
{
    public partial class RetrieveChartData : Window
    {
        private Point startPoint = new Point();
        private Point endPoint = new Point();
        private ChartStyle cs;
        private DataCollection dc;
        private DataSeries ds;
        private double xmin0 = 0;
        private double xmax0 = 7;
        private double ymin0 = -1.5;
        private double ymax0 = 1.5;
        private List<Ellipse> circles = new List<Ellipse>();
        private List<Ellipse> labelCircles = new List<Ellipse>();
        private List<TextBlock> labelResults = new List<TextBlock>();
        private TextBlock xCoordinate = new TextBlock();

        public RetrieveChartData()
        {
            InitializeComponent();
            cs = new ChartStyle();
            cs.Xmin = xmin0;
            cs.Xmax = xmax0;
            cs.Ymin = ymin0;
            cs.Ymax = ymax0;
        }

        private void AddChart(double xmin, double xmax, double ymin, double ymax)
        {
            dc = new DataCollection();
            ds = new DataSeries();
            cs = new ChartStyle();

            cs.ChartCanvas = chartCanvas;
            cs.TextCanvas = textCanvas;
            cs.Title = "Sine and Cosine Chart";
            cs.Xmin = xmin;
            cs.Xmax = xmax;
            cs.Ymin = ymin;
            cs.Ymax = ymax;
            cs.GridlinePattern = ChartStyle.GridlinePatternEnum.Dot;
            cs.GridlineColor = Brushes.Black;
            cs.AddChartStyle(tbTitle, tbXLabel, tbYLabel);
```

```
// Draw Sine-like curve:
ds.LineColor = Brushes.Blue;
ds.LineThickness = 2;
double dx = (cs.Xmax - cs.Xmin) / 100;

for (double x = cs.Xmin; x <= cs.Xmax + dx; x += dx)
{
    double y = Math.Exp(-0.3 * Math.Abs(x)) * Math.Sin(x);
    ds.LineSeries.Points.Add(new Point(x, y));
}
dc.DataList.Add(ds);
Ellipse circle = new Ellipse();
circle.Width = 8;
circle.Height = 8;
circle.Margin = new Thickness(2);
circle.Fill = ds.LineColor;
labelCircles.Add(circle);
TextBlock tb = new TextBlock();
tb.Text = "Y0 Value";
tb.FontSize = 10;
tb.Margin = new Thickness(2);
labelResults.Add(tb);
circle = new Ellipse();
circle.Width = 8;
circle.Height = 8;
circle.Fill = ds.LineColor;
circle.Visibility = Visibility.Hidden;
circles.Add(circle);

// Draw Cosine-like curve:
ds = new DataSeries();
ds.LineColor = Brushes.Red;
ds.LinePattern = DataSeries.LinePatternEnum.DashDot;
ds.LineThickness = 2;

for (double x = cs.Xmin; x <= cs.Xmax + dx; x += dx)
{
    double y = Math.Exp(-0.3 * Math.Abs(x)) * Math.Cos(x);
    ds.LineSeries.Points.Add(new Point(x, y));
}
dc.DataList.Add(ds);
dc.AddLines(cs);
circle = new Ellipse();
circle.Width = 8;
circle.Height = 8;
circle.Margin = new Thickness(2, 2, 2, 2);
circle.Fill = ds.LineColor;
labelCircles.Add(circle);
tb = new TextBlock();
tb.Text = "Y1 Value";
tb.FontSize = 10;
tb.Margin = new Thickness(2);
```

```
        labelResults.Add(tb);

        circle = new Ellipse();
        circle.Width = 8;
        circle.Height = 8;
        circle.Fill = ds.LineColor;
        circle.Visibility = Visibility.Hidden;
        circles.Add(circle);

        xCoordinate.Text = "X Value";
        xCoordinate.FontSize = 10;
        xCoordinate.Margin = new Thickness(2);
        resultPanel.Children.Add(xCoordinate);

        for (int i = 0; i < dc.DataList.Count; i++)
        {
            chartCanvas.Children.Add(circles[i]);
            Canvas.SetTop(circles[i], 0);
            Canvas.SetLeft(circles[i], 0);
            resultPanel.Children.Add(labelCircles[i]);
            resultPanel.Children.Add(labelResults[i]);
        }
    }

    private void chartGrid_SizeChanged(object sender, SizeChangedEventArgs e)
    {
        tbDate.Text = DateTime.Now.ToShortDateString();
        resultPanel.Children.Clear();
        textCanvas.Width = chartGrid.ActualWidth;
        textCanvas.Height = chartGrid.ActualHeight;
        chartCanvas.Children.Clear();
        textCanvas.Children.RemoveRange(1, textCanvas.Children.Count - 1);
        AddChart(cs.Xmin, cs.Xmax, cs.Ymin, cs.Ymax);
    }

    private void OnMouseLeftButtonDown(object sender, MouseButtonEventArgs e)
    {
        if (!chartCanvas.IsMouseCaptured)
        {
            startPoint = e.GetPosition(chartCanvas);
            chartCanvas.Cursor = Cursors.Cross;
            chartCanvas.CaptureMouse();
            for (int i = 0; i < dc.DataList.Count; i++)
            {
                double x = startPoint.X;
                double y = GetInterpolatedYValue(dc.DataList[i], x);
                Canvas.SetLeft(circles[i], x - circles[i].Width / 2);
                Canvas.SetTop(circles[i], y - circles[i].Height / 2);
            }
        }
    }

    private void OnMouseMove(object sender, MouseEventArgs e)
```

```
    {
        if (chartCanvas.IsMouseCaptured)
        {
            endPoint = e.GetPosition(chartCanvas);
            if (Math.Abs(endPoint.X - startPoint.X) >
                    SystemParameters.MinimumHorizontalDragDistance &&
                Math.Abs(endPoint.Y - startPoint.Y) >
                    SystemParameters.MinimumVerticalDragDistance)
            {
                double x, y;
                for (int i = 0; i < dc.DataList.Count; i++)
                {
                    TranslateTransform tt = new TranslateTransform();
                    tt.X = endPoint.X - startPoint.X;
                    tt.Y = GetInterpolatedYValue(dc.DataList[i], endPoint.X) -
                        GetInterpolatedYValue(dc.DataList[i], startPoint.X);
                    circles[i].RenderTransform = tt;
                    circles[i].Visibility = Visibility.Visible;
                    x = endPoint.X;
                    x = cs.Xmin + x * (cs.Xmax - cs.Xmin) / chartCanvas.Width;
                    y = GetInterpolatedYValue(dc.DataList[i], endPoint.X);
                    y = cs.Ymin + (chartCanvas.Height - y) *
                        (cs.Ymax - cs.Ymin) / chartCanvas.Height;
                    xCoordinate.Text = Math.Round(x, 4).ToString();
                    labelResults[i].Text = Math.Round(y, 4).ToString();
                }
            }
        }
    }

    private void OnMouseLeftButtonUp(object sender, MouseButtonEventArgs e)
    {
        chartCanvas.ReleaseMouseCapture();
        chartCanvas.Cursor = Cursors.Arrow;

        xCoordinate.Text = "X Value";
        for (int i = 0; i < dc.DataList.Count; i++ )
        {
            circles[i].Visibility = Visibility.Hidden;
            labelResults[i].Text = "Y" + i.ToString() + " Value";
        }
    }

    private double GetInterpolatedYValue(DataSeries data, double x)
    {
        double result = double.NaN;
        for (int i = 1; i < data.LineSeries.Points.Count; i++)
        {
            double x1 = data.LineSeries.Points[i - 1].X;
            double x2 = data.LineSeries.Points[i].X;
            if (x >= x1 && x < x2)
            {
                double y1 = data.LineSeries.Points[i - 1].Y;
```

```
            double y2 = data.LineSeries.Points[i].Y;
            result = y1 + (y2 - y1) * (x - x1) / (x2 - x1);
        }
    }
    }
    return result;
    }
  }
}
```

In the foregoing code list, we define two sets of ellipse lists: one for marking the data points associated with your mouse's movement and the other for the legend displaying the results on your screen. You specify the fill color for each of these ellipses using the line color of the corresponding line series. Note how we create these two sets of ellipse lists for each line series inside the *AddChart* method:

```
circle = new Ellipse();
circle.Width = 8;
circle.Height = 8;
circle.Margin = new Thickness(2, 2, 2, 2);
circle.Fill = ds.LineColor;
labelCircles.Add(circle);
… …
circle = new Ellipse();
circle.Width = 8;
circle.Height = 8;
circle.Fill = ds.LineColor;
circle.Visibility = Visibility.Hidden;
circles.Add(circle);
```

The first set of ellipse lists, named *labelCircles*, displays results, and the other set, *circles*, marks the data points. Note also that we initially set the *Visibility* property for all of the ellipses in the *circles* list to *Hidden*, meaning that by default these ellipse objects are invisible on your computer screen. You can trigger this property to *Visible* or *Hidden* using different mouse events.

When you press the left mouse button, you obtain a position (*startPoint*), set the mouse's *Capture* state, and change *chartCanvas' Cursor* property to *Cross*. You then try to retrieve the *Y* data values for each curve on the chart from the *startPoint*'s *X* coordinate. Notice that you cannot obtain the *Y* data from the curve directly because there may be no *Y* data available in the original data sets used to create the curves at the *startPoint* at which you initially clicked your mouse. In order to retrieve the *Y* data in this situation, you must generate corresponding *Y* data values at the position of the mouse pointer using interpolation. In this example, we implement a linear interpolation algorithm inside the *GetInterpolatedYValue* method, which allows you to extract *Y* data values from each curve series at any *X* coordinate where your mouse pointer may be.

The *MouseMove* event performs the data-retrieving task. When you hold down the left mouse button and start to move your mouse, the *MouseMove* event fires. First, for each curve series, you create a translation transform using the mouse movement, and then you attach the transform to the *RenderTransform* property of the corresponding ellipse in the *circles* collection. At the same time, you change the ellipse's *Visibility* property to *Visible*:

```
circles[i].RenderTransform = tt;
circles[i].Visibility = Visibility.Visible;
```

This way, the ellipse objects will move following the corresponding curve series with your mouse. Next, the retrieved data points will be displayed in the legend field on your screen.

Finally, the *MouseLeftButtonUp* event finishes the data-retrieving process and restores the program to its original state, including releasing the mouse's *Capture* state, changing the mouse's cursor to arrow, and setting the ellipses' *Visibility* to *Hidden*.

Running this example generates the result shown in Figure 8-7.

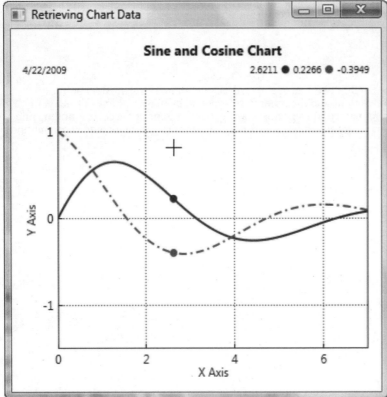

Figure 8-7. Retrieving data from a 2D chart using a mouse

In this chapter, I presented several commonly used techniques for creating interactive WPF applications and discussed them separately, for simplicity. In practice, you may need to combine all of these techniques to create a complex interactive application.

CHAPTER 9

■ ■ ■

2D Chart Controls

In the previous chapters, we implemented the source code for all of the classes in our graphics and chart programs directly. For simple applications, this approach works well. However, if you want to reuse the same code in multiple WPF applications, this method becomes ineffective. The .NET Framework and WPF provide a powerful means, the user control, that solves this problem.

Custom user controls in WPF are just like the simple buttons or text boxes already provided in .NET and WPF. Typically, the controls you design are to be used in multiple windows or to modularize your code. These custom controls can reduce the amount of code you have to type as well as make it easier for you to change the implementation of your program. There is no reason to duplicate code in your applications, because this leaves a lot of room for bugs. Therefore, it is good programming practice to create functionalities specific to the user control in the control's source code, which can reduce code duplication and modularize your code.

Custom user controls are a key theme in WPF and .NET development. They can greatly enhance your programming style by improving encapsulation, simplifying the programming model, and making the user interface more pluggable. Of course, custom controls can also have other benefits, such as giving you the ability to transform a generic window into a state-of-the-art modern interface.

In this chapter, you'll learn how to put the line charts and specialized 2D charts we developed in Chapters 5 and 6 into custom user controls and how to use such controls in your WPF applications. You'll also learn how to make chart controls into first-class WPF citizens and make them available in XAML. This means that you'll need to define dependency properties and routed events for the chart controls in order to get support for essential WPF services, such as data binding, styles, and animation.

Line Chart Control

A *UserControl* in WPF is a content control that can be configured using a design-time surface. Although a user control is basically similar to an ordinary content control, it is typically used when you want to reuse quickly an unchanging block of user interface in more than one application.

Creating a basic chart control based on the line charts developed in Chapter 5 is easy. For simplicity's sake, we will build a line chart control without the second *Y* axis (adding a second *Y* axis to this control is trivial). The layout of the control is the same as that shown in Figure 5-7. The development model for the chart user control is very similar to the model used for application development in WPF.

Now, start with a new WPF project. Instead of a WPF Windows application, you need to select a new WPF User Control Library from templates and name it *LineChartControl*. When you do this, Microsoft Visual Studio creates an XAML markup file and a corresponding custom class to hold your initialization and event-handling code. This is the same as when you create a new WPF Window or Page application — the only difference is that the top-level container is the *UserControl* class. This will generate a default user control named UserControl1. Rename it *LineChartControlLib* by right-clicking on the *UserControl1*.xaml in the solution explorer and selecting Rename. You need also to change the name

UserControl1 to *LineChartControlLib* in both the XAML and the code-behind file for the control. Add to the current project the following classes from the *LineCharts* project presented in Chapter 5: *ChartStyle*, *ChartStyleGridlines*, *DataSeries*, *DataCollection*, *Legend*, and *Symbols*. When we convert the Windows application to a user control, we'll try not to change or modify these classes from the original *LineCharts* project.

Here is the XAML file for the control:

```
<UserControl x:Class="LineChartControl.LineChartControlLib"
    xmlns="http://schemas.microsoft.com/winfx/2006/xaml/presentation"
    xmlns:x="http://schemas.microsoft.com/winfx/2006/xaml"
    Width="400" Height="300">
    <Grid Name="grid1" Margin="10">
        <Grid.ColumnDefinitions>
            <ColumnDefinition Width="Auto"/>
            <ColumnDefinition Width="*"/>
        </Grid.ColumnDefinitions>
        <Grid.RowDefinitions>
            <RowDefinition Height="Auto"/>
            <RowDefinition Height="*"/>
            <RowDefinition Height="Auto"/>
        </Grid.RowDefinitions>
        <TextBlock Margin="2" x:Name="tbTitle" Grid.Column="1" Grid.Row="0"
                   RenderTransformOrigin="0.5,0.5" FontSize="14" FontWeight="Bold"
                   HorizontalAlignment="Stretch" VerticalAlignment="Stretch"
                   TextAlignment="Center" Text="{Binding Path=Title}"/>
        <TextBlock Margin="2" x:Name="tbXLabel" Grid.Column="1" Grid.Row="2"
                   RenderTransformOrigin="0.5,0.5" TextAlignment="Center"
                   Text="{Binding Path=XLabel}"/>
        <TextBlock Margin="2" Name="tbYLabel" Grid.Column="0" Grid.Row="1"
                   RenderTransformOrigin="0.5,0.5" TextAlignment="Center"
                   Text="{Binding Path=YLabel}">
            <TextBlock.LayoutTransform>
                <RotateTransform Angle="-90"/>
            </TextBlock.LayoutTransform>
        </TextBlock>
        <Grid  Margin="0" x:Name ="chartGrid" Grid.Column="1" Grid.Row="1"
               ClipToBounds="True" Background="Transparent"
               SizeChanged="chartGrid_SizeChanged" />
        <Canvas Margin="2" Name="textCanvas" ClipToBounds="True" Grid.Column="1"
               Grid.Row="1">
            <Canvas Name="chartCanvas" ClipToBounds="True">
                <Canvas Name="legendCanvas" Background="Transparent" />
            </Canvas>
        </Canvas>
    </Grid>
</UserControl>
```

This markup is basically the same as that used in creating a WPF Windows application for line charts, except the text boxes for *Title*, *XLabel*, and *YLabel* are now bound to corresponding dependency properties, which are to be defined in the code-behind file. Data binding in WPF provides a way of extracting information from a source object and using it to set a property in a target object. The simplest data binding scenario occurs when the source object is a WPF element and the source property is a dependency property, because dependency properties have a built-in support for change notification. As a result, changing the value of the dependency property in the source object updates the bound property in the target object immediately. That is exactly what you want — and it happens without requiring you to build any additional infrastructure, such as an *INotifyPropertyChanged* interface.

Defining Dependency Properties

Next, you need to design the public interface that the line chart control exposes to the outside world. In other words, it is time to create the properties, methods, and events that the control consumer (the application that uses the control) will rely on to interact with your chart control.

You may want to expose to the outside world most of the properties in the *ChartStyleGridlines* class in the previous example, such as axis limits, title, and labels; at the same time, we'll keep the classes from the original *LineCharts* project unchanged. In order to support WPF features such as data binding, styles, and animation, the control properties are almost always dependency properties.

The first step in creating a dependency property is to define a static field for it, adding the word *Property* to the end of the property name. Add the following dependency properties to the code-behind file:

```
using System;
using System.Collections.Generic;
using System.Windows;
using System.Windows.Controls;
using System.Windows.Media;
using System.Windows.Shapes;
using LineCharts;

namespace LineChartControl
{
    public partial class LineChartControlLib : UserControl
    {
        private ChartStyleGridlines cs;
        private DataCollection dc;
        private DataSeries ds;
        private Legend lg;

        public LineChartControlLib()
        {
            InitializeComponent();
            this.cs = new ChartStyleGridlines();
            this.dc = new DataCollection();
            this.ds = new DataSeries();
            this.lg = new Legend();
            cs.TextCanvas = textCanvas;
            cs.ChartCanvas = chartCanvas;
            lg.LegendCanvas = legendCanvas;
        }

        private void chartGrid_SizeChanged(object sender, SizeChangedEventArgs e)
        {
            textCanvas.Width = chartGrid.ActualWidth;
            textCanvas.Height = chartGrid.ActualHeight;
            legendCanvas.Children.Clear();
            chartCanvas.Children.RemoveRange(1, chartCanvas.Children.Count - 1);
            textCanvas.Children.RemoveRange(1, textCanvas.Children.Count - 1);
```

```
        AddChart();
    }

    private void AddChart()
    {
        cs.AddChartStyle(tbTitle, tbXLabel, tbYLabel);
        if (dc.DataList.Count != 0)
        {
            dc.AddLines(cs);
            Legend.AddLegend(chartCanvas, dc);
        }
    }

    public ChartStyleGridlines ChartStyle
    {
        get { return cs; }
        set { cs = value; }
    }

    public DataCollection DataCollection
    {
        get { return dc; }
        set { dc = value; }
    }

    public DataSeries DataSeries
    {
        get { return ds; }
        set { ds = value; }
    }

    public Legend Legend
    {
        get { return lg; }
        set { lg = value; }
    }

    public static DependencyProperty XminProperty =
                DependencyProperty.Register("Xmin", typeof(double),
                typeof(LineChartControlLib),
                new FrameworkPropertyMetadata(0.0,
                new PropertyChangedCallback(OnPropertyChanged)));

    public double Xmin
    {
        get { return (double)GetValue(XminProperty); }
        set
        {
            SetValue(XminProperty, value);
            cs.Xmin = value;
        }
    }
```

```
public static DependencyProperty XmaxProperty =
            DependencyProperty.Register("Xmax", typeof(double),
            typeof(LineChartControlLib),
            new FrameworkPropertyMetadata(10.0,
            new PropertyChangedCallback(OnPropertyChanged)));

public double Xmax
{
    get { return (double)GetValue(XmaxProperty); }
    set
    {
        SetValue(XmaxProperty, value);
        cs.Xmax = value;
    }
}

public static DependencyProperty YminProperty =
            DependencyProperty.Register("Ymin", typeof(double),
            typeof(LineChartControlLib),
            new FrameworkPropertyMetadata(0.0,
            new PropertyChangedCallback(OnPropertyChanged)));

public double Ymin
{
    get { return (double)GetValue(YminProperty); }
    set
    {
        SetValue(YminProperty, value);
        cs.Ymin = value;
    }
}

public static DependencyProperty YmaxProperty =
            DependencyProperty.Register("Ymax", typeof(double),
            typeof(LineChartControlLib),
            new FrameworkPropertyMetadata(10.0,
            new PropertyChangedCallback(OnPropertyChanged)));

public double Ymax
{
    get { return (double)GetValue(YmaxProperty); }
    set
    {
        SetValue(YmaxProperty, value);
        cs.Ymax = value;
    }
}

public static DependencyProperty XTickProperty =
            DependencyProperty.Register("XTick", typeof(double),
            typeof(LineChartControlLib),
            new FrameworkPropertyMetadata(2.0,
            new PropertyChangedCallback(OnPropertyChanged)));
```

337

```csharp
public double XTick
{
    get { return (double)GetValue(XTickProperty); }
    set
    {
        SetValue(XTickProperty, value);
        cs.XTick = value;
    }
}

public static DependencyProperty YTickProperty =
            DependencyProperty.Register("YTick", typeof(double),
            typeof(LineChartControlLib),
            new FrameworkPropertyMetadata(2.0,
            new PropertyChangedCallback(OnPropertyChanged)));

public double YTick
{
    get { return (double)GetValue(YTickProperty); }
    set
    {
        SetValue(YTickProperty, value);
        cs.YTick = value;
    }
}

public static DependencyProperty XLabelProperty =
            DependencyProperty.Register("XLabel", typeof(string),
            typeof(LineChartControlLib),
            new FrameworkPropertyMetadata("X Axis",
            new PropertyChangedCallback(OnPropertyChanged)));

public string XLabel
{
    get { return (string)GetValue(XLabelProperty); }
    set
    {
        SetValue(XLabelProperty, value);
        cs.XLabel = value;
    }
}

public static DependencyProperty YLabelProperty =
            DependencyProperty.Register("YLabel", typeof(string),
            typeof(LineChartControlLib),
            new FrameworkPropertyMetadata("Y Axis",
            new PropertyChangedCallback(OnPropertyChanged)));

public string YLabel
{
    get { return (string)GetValue(YLabelProperty); }
    set
```

```
        {
            SetValue(YLabelProperty, value);
            cs.YLabel = value;
        }
}

public static DependencyProperty TitleProperty =
            DependencyProperty.Register("Title", typeof(string),
            typeof(LineChartControlLib),
            new FrameworkPropertyMetadata("Title",
            new PropertyChangedCallback(OnPropertyChanged)));

public string Title
{
    get { return (string)GetValue(TitleProperty); }
    set
    {
        SetValue(TitleProperty, value);
        cs.Title = value;
    }
}

public static DependencyProperty IsXGridProperty =
            DependencyProperty.Register("IsXGrid", typeof(bool),
            typeof(LineChartControlLib),
            new FrameworkPropertyMetadata(true,
            new PropertyChangedCallback(OnPropertyChanged)));

public bool IsXGrid
{
    get { return (bool)GetValue(IsXGridProperty); }
    set
    {
        SetValue(IsXGridProperty, value);
        cs.IsXGrid = value;
    }
}

public static DependencyProperty IsYGridProperty =
            DependencyProperty.Register("IsYGrid", typeof(bool),
            typeof(LineChartControlLib),
            new FrameworkPropertyMetadata(true,
            new PropertyChangedCallback(OnPropertyChanged)));

public bool IsYGrid
{
    get { return (bool)GetValue(IsYGridProperty); }
    set
    {
        SetValue(IsYGridProperty, value);
        cs.IsYGrid = value;
    }
}
```

```
public static DependencyProperty GridlineColorProperty =
            DependencyProperty.Register("GridlineColor", typeof(Brush),
            typeof(LineChartControlLib),
            new FrameworkPropertyMetadata(Brushes.Gray,
            new PropertyChangedCallback(OnPropertyChanged)));

public Brush GridlineColor
{
    get { return (Brush)GetValue(GridlineColorProperty); }
    set
    {
        SetValue(GridlineColorProperty, value);
        cs.GridlineColor = value;
    }
}

public static DependencyProperty GridlinePatternProperty =
            DependencyProperty.Register("GridlinePattern",
            typeof(ChartStyleGridlines.GridlinePatternEnum),
            typeof(LineChartControlLib),
            new FrameworkPropertyMetadata(
                ChartStyleGridlines.GridlinePatternEnum.Solid,
              new PropertyChangedCallback(OnPropertyChanged)));

public ChartStyleGridlines.GridlinePatternEnum GridlinePattern
{
    get { return (ChartStyleGridlines.GridlinePatternEnum)
                GetValue(GridlinePatternProperty); }
    set
    {
        SetValue(GridlinePatternProperty, value);
        cs.GridlinePattern = value;
    }
}

public static DependencyProperty IsLegendProperty =
            DependencyProperty.Register("IsLegend", typeof(bool),
            typeof(LineChartControlLib),
            new FrameworkPropertyMetadata(false,
            new PropertyChangedCallback(OnPropertyChanged)));

public bool IsLegend
{
    get { return (bool)GetValue(IsLegendProperty); }
    set
    {
        SetValue(IsLegendProperty, value);
        lg.IsLegend = value;
    }
}

public static DependencyProperty LegendPositionProperty =
```

```
                DependencyProperty.Register("LegendPosition",
                typeof(Legend.LegendPositionEnum),
                typeof(LineChartControlLib),
          new FrameworkPropertyMetadata(Legend.LegendPositionEnum.NorthEast,
          new PropertyChangedCallback(OnPropertyChanged)));

public Legend.LegendPositionEnum LegendPosition
{
    get { return (Legend.LegendPositionEnum)
                GetValue(LegendPositionProperty); }
    set
    {
        SetValue(LegendPositionProperty, value);
        lg.LegendPosition = value;
    }
}

private static void OnPropertyChanged(DependencyObject sender,
                    DependencyPropertyChangedEventArgs e)
{
    LineChartControlLib lcc = sender as LineChartControlLib;
    if (e.Property == XminProperty)
        lcc.Xmin = (double)e.NewValue;
    else if (e.Property == XmaxProperty)
        lcc.Xmax = (double)e.NewValue;
    else if (e.Property == YminProperty)
        lcc.Ymin = (double)e.NewValue;
    else if (e.Property == YmaxProperty)
        lcc.Ymax = (double)e.NewValue;
    else if (e.Property == XTickProperty)
        lcc.XTick = (double)e.NewValue;
    else if (e.Property == YTickProperty)
        lcc.YTick = (double)e.NewValue;
    else if (e.Property == GridlinePatternProperty)
        lcc.GridlinePattern =
            (ChartStyleGridlines.GridlinePatternEnum)e.NewValue;
    else if (e.Property== GridlineColorProperty)
        lcc.GridlineColor = (Brush)e.NewValue;
    else if (e.Property == TitleProperty)
        lcc.Title = (string)e.NewValue;
    else if (e.Property == XLabelProperty)
        lcc.XLabel = (string)e.NewValue;
    else if (e.Property == YLabelProperty)
        lcc.YLabel = (string)e.NewValue;
    else if (e.Property == IsXGridProperty)
        lcc.IsXGrid = (bool)e.NewValue;
    else if (e.Property == IsYGridProperty)
        lcc.IsYGrid = (bool)e.NewValue;
    else if (e.Property == IsLegendProperty)
        lcc.IsLegend = (bool)e.NewValue;
    else if(e.Property== LegendPositionProperty)
        lcc.LegendPosition = (Legend.LegendPositionEnum)e.NewValue;
}
```

```
        }
    }
```

At the beginning of this code-behind file, we add a using statement:

```
using LineCharts;
```

This allows you to access all of the files in the *LineCharts* project without changing the original namespaces of these files to the current project's namespace.

We then define several conventional public properties for the *ChartStyleGridlines, DataSeries, DataCollection*, and *Legend* objects, which will allow you to access the public properties and methods of these objects programmatically when you use the user control in your applications.

Next, we convert most of public properties of the *ChartStyleGridlines* and *Legend* classes into dependency properties. For example, we use the following code snippet to define the dependency property for the *Xmin* property of the *ChartStyleGridlines* class:

```
public static DependencyProperty XminProperty =
            DependencyProperty.Register("Xmin", typeof(double),
            typeof(LineChartControlLib),
            new FrameworkPropertyMetadata(0.0,
            new PropertyChangedCallback(OnPropertyChanged)));

public double Xmin
{
    get { return (double)GetValue(XminProperty); }
    set
    {
        SetValue(XminProperty, value);
        cs.Xmin = value;
    }
}
```

Here, we first define the dependency property of *Xmin*, and then we add standard property wrappers that make the properties easier to access and usable in XAML. The property wrappers should not contain any logic, because properties may be set and retrieved directly using the *SetValue* and *GetValue* methods of the base *DependencyObject* class. For example, the property synchronization logic in this control is implemented using a callback method that fires when the property changes through the property wrapper or a direct *SetValue* call.

Note that in the setter we relate the *Xmin* property in the *ChartStyleGridlines* class directly to the value of the dependency property *XminProperty*. This way, whenever the *XminProperty* in the *LineChartControlLib* class is changed, the property *Xmin* in the *ChartStyleGridlines* class will change correspondingly. We convert all of the other properties into the dependency properties in a similar manner.

The property change callback is responsible for keeping the property values consistent with the corresponding dependency properties. Whenever the property values are changed, the corresponding dependency properties are adjusted accordingly. There are several types of property change callbacks, including callbacks for changes in string, double, bool, and line patterns. Make sure you cast each property correctly when you call the *OnPropertyChanged* callback method.

You can add more dependency properties to the line chart control following the procedure presented earlier if you want to expose more properties from other classes, such as properties from the *DataSeries* and *DataCollection* classes.

Using the Line Chart Control

Now that the 2D line chart control has been completed, you can easily use it in your WPF applications. To use the control in another WPF window, you need to begin by mapping the .NET namespace and assembly to an XML namespace, as shown here:

```
xmlns:local="clr-namespace:LineChartControl;assembly=LineChartControl"
```

If your control is located in the same assembly as your application, you only need to map the namesapce:

```
xmlns:local="clr-namespace:LineChartControl"
```

Using the XML namespace and the user control class name, you can add the user control exactly as you would add any other type of object to the XAML file. You can also set its properties and attach event handlers directly in the control tag, as shown here:

```
<local:LineChartControlLib x:Name="myLineChart"
      Xmin="0" Xmax="7" Ymin="-1.5" Ymax="1.5" Width="350"
      Height="300" Background="LightBlue" Title=" My Chart"
      GridlinePattern="DashDot"/>
```

Notice how you specify the *GridlinePattern* property — you simply choose from the *Solid, Dash, Dot*, or *DashDot* properties defined in the *GridlinePatternEnum* of the chart style class. This is much simpler than using code, in which case you would need to type the full path in order to define the gridlines' line pattern, as shown here:

```
myLineChart.GridlinePattern =
    ChartStyleLineChartControl.GridlinePatternEnum.DashDot;
```

You can also specify other properties standard to WPF elements for the chart control, such as *Width, Height, Canvas.Left, Canvas.Top*, and *Background*. These standard properties allow you to position the control, set the size of the control, or set the background color of the control.

Creating a Simple Line Chart

Here, you'll learn how to use the line chart control to create simple sine and cosine function graphs. Open the *LineChartControl* project in Visual Studio 2008. Click on the File menu and select Add | New project… Select WPF Application from templates and name it *LineChartControlTest*. Now right-click Reference and select Add References… in the new project to bring up the "Add References" window. Click the Projects tab in this window and highlight the *LineChartControl*, as shown in Figure 9-1.

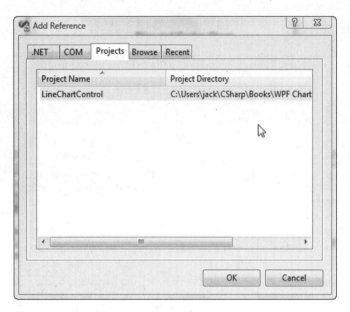

Figure 9-1. *"Add References" Window*

Click OK to add the *LineChartControl* to the current project. This way, you can use the control in your WPF application just like the default elements. Now, in the Solution Explorer, right-click the new project and select Set as StartUp Project.

Add a new WPF Window to the *LineChartControlTest* project and name it *LineChart*. The layout of the example is very simple; you can create it using the following XAML:

```
<Window x:Class="LineChartControlTest.LineChart"
    xmlns="http://schemas.microsoft.com/winfx/2006/xaml/presentation"
    xmlns:x="http://schemas.microsoft.com/winfx/2006/xaml"
    xmlns:local="clr-namespace:LineChartControl;assembly=LineChartControl"
    Title="Window1" Height="350" Width="400">
    <Grid x:Name="rootGrid" SizeChanged="rootGrid_SizeChanged">
        <local:LineChartControlLib x:Name="myLineChart" Xmin="0" Xmax="7"
                XTick="1" Ymin="-1.5" Ymax="1.5" YTick="0.5"
                Title="Sine and Cosine Chart" GridlinePattern="Dash"/>
    </Grid>
</Window>
```

Here, you simply create a line chart control called *myLineChart* exactly as you would create any other type of WPF element. The following is the corresponding code-behind file for this example:

```
using System;
using System.Windows;
using System.Windows.Media;

namespace LineChartControlTest
{
    public partial class LineChart : Window
    {
```

```
public LineChart()
{
    InitializeComponent();
}

private void rootGrid_SizeChanged(object sender, SizeChangedEventArgs e)
{
    myLineChart.Width = rootGrid.ActualWidth;
    myLineChart.Height = rootGrid.ActualHeight;
    AddData();
}

private void AddData()
{
    myLineChart.DataCollection.DataList.Clear();

    // Draw Sine curve:
    LineCharts.DataSeries ds = new LineCharts.DataSeries();
    ds.LineColor = Brushes.Blue;
    ds.LineThickness = 1;
    ds.SeriesName = "Sine";
    ds.Symbols.SymbolType = LineCharts.Symbols.SymbolTypeEnum.Circle;
    ds.Symbols.BorderColor = ds.LineColor;
    for (int i = 0; i < 70; i++)
    {
        double x = i / 5.0;
        double y = Math.Sin(x);
        ds.LineSeries.Points.Add(new Point(x, y));
    }
    myLineChart.DataCollection.DataList.Add(ds);

    // Draw cosine curve:
    ds = new LineCharts.DataSeries();
    ds.LineColor = Brushes.Red;
    ds.SeriesName = "Cosine";
    ds.Symbols.SymbolType = LineCharts.Symbols.SymbolTypeEnum.OpenDiamond;
    ds.Symbols.BorderColor = ds.LineColor;
    ds.LinePattern = LineCharts.DataSeries.LinePatternEnum.DashDot;
    ds.LineThickness = 2;
    for (int i = 0; i < 70; i++)
    {
        double x = i / 5.0;
        double y = Math.Cos(x);
        ds.LineSeries.Points.Add(new Point(x, y));
    }
    myLineChart.DataCollection.DataList.Add(ds);

    myLineChart.IsLegend = true;
    myLineChart.LegendPosition =
        LineCharts.Legend.LegendPositionEnum.NorthEast;
    }
  }
}
```

Just as you did when you created line charts in Chapter 5, you need first to create the data series and then to add them to the chart control's *DataCollection*. It is good programming practice to specify all chart style–related properties in XAML and to create the data series in code. Of course, if you like you can use the code-only approach to create a chart using the line chart control.

Running this example generates the result shown in Figure 9-2.

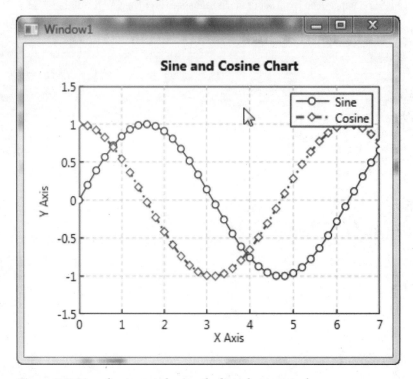

Figure 9-2. Line chart created using the line chart control

Creating Multiple Line Charts

Using the line chart control, you can easily create multiple charts in a single WPF Window. Let's add a new WPF Window to the project *LineChartControlTest* and name it *MultipleLineCharts*. Create a 2 × 2 *Grid* control and add a line chart control to each of the four cells of the *Grid*, which can be done using the following XAML file:

```
<Window x:Class="LineChartControlTest.MultipleLineCharts"
    xmlns="http://schemas.microsoft.com/winfx/2006/xaml/presentation"
    xmlns:x="http://schemas.microsoft.com/winfx/2006/xaml"
    xmlns:local="clr-namespace:LineChartControl;assembly=LineChartControl"
    Title="Multiple Charts" Height="500" Width="500">
    <Grid Margin="10">
        <Grid.ColumnDefinitions>
            <ColumnDefinition/>
            <ColumnDefinition/>
```

```xml
        </Grid.ColumnDefinitions>
        <Grid.RowDefinitions>
            <RowDefinition/>
            <RowDefinition/>
        </Grid.RowDefinitions>

        <Grid x:Name="grid1" SizeChanged="grid1_SizeChanged"
            Grid.Column="0" Grid.Row="0">
            <local:LineChartControlLib x:Name="myLineChart1" Xmin="0"
                Xmax="7" XTick="1" Ymin="-1.5" Ymax="2" YTick="0.5"
                Title="Chart One" GridlinePattern="Dash"
                GridlineColor="LightPink" />
        </Grid>

        <Grid x:Name="grid2" SizeChanged="grid2_SizeChanged"
            Grid.Column="1" Grid.Row="0">
            <local:LineChartControlLib x:Name="myLineChart2" Xmin="0"
                Xmax="7" XTick="1" Ymin="-1.5" Ymax="2" YTick="0.5"
                Title="Chart Two" GridlinePattern="Solid"
                GridlineColor="LightPink" />
        </Grid>

        <Grid x:Name="grid3" SizeChanged="grid3_SizeChanged"
            Grid.Column="0" Grid.Row="1">
            <local:LineChartControlLib x:Name="myLineChart3" Xmin="0"
                Xmax="7" XTick="1" Ymin="-1.5" Ymax="2" YTick="0.5"
                Title="Chart Three" GridlinePattern="Dash"
                GridlineColor="LightBlue" />
        </Grid>

        <Grid x:Name="grid4" SizeChanged="grid4_SizeChanged"
            Grid.Column="1" Grid.Row="1">
            <local:LineChartControlLib x:Name="myLineChart4" Xmin="0"
                Xmax="7" XTick="1" Ymin="-1.5" Ymax="2" YTick="0.5"
                Title="Chart Four" GridlinePattern="Solid"
                GridlineColor="LightBlue" />
        </Grid>
    </Grid>
</Window>
```

Here, you create four line chart controls: *chart1*, *chart2*, *chart3*, and *chart4*. For simplicity, in this example you plot the same sine and cosine functions on each chart. But you set a different gridline property for each chart. In practice, you can plot different math functions on each chart according to your application's requirements. Here is the corresponding code-behind file, which creates the curves on each chart:

```csharp
using System;
using System.Windows;
using System.Windows.Media;

namespace LineChartControlTest
{
    public partial class MultipleLineCharts : Window
    {
```

```
public MultipleLineCharts()
{
    InitializeComponent();
}

private void AddData(LineChartControl.LineChartControlLib myLineChart)
{
    LineCharts.DataSeries ds = new LineCharts.DataSeries();
    myLineChart.DataCollection.DataList.Clear();

    // Draw Sine curve:
    ds.LineColor = Brushes.Blue;
    ds.LineThickness = 1;
    ds.SeriesName = "Sine";
    ds.Symbols.SymbolType = LineCharts.Symbols.SymbolTypeEnum.Circle;
    ds.Symbols.BorderColor = ds.LineColor;
    ds.Symbols.SymbolSize = 6;
    for (int i = 0; i < 15; i++)
    {
        double x = i / 2.0;
        double y = Math.Sin(x);
        ds.LineSeries.Points.Add(new Point(x, y));
    }
    myLineChart.DataCollection.DataList.Add(ds);

    // Draw cosine curve:
    ds = new LineCharts.DataSeries();
    ds.LineColor = Brushes.Red;
    ds.SeriesName = "Cosine";
    ds.Symbols.SymbolType = LineCharts.Symbols.SymbolTypeEnum.OpenDiamond;
    ds.Symbols.BorderColor = ds.LineColor;
    ds.Symbols.SymbolSize = 6;
    for (int i = 0; i < 15; i++)
    {
        double x = i / 2.0;
        double y = Math.Cos(x);
        ds.LineSeries.Points.Add(new Point(x, y));
    }
    myLineChart.DataCollection.DataList.Add(ds);

    myLineChart.IsLegend = true;
    myLineChart.LegendPosition =
        LineCharts.Legend.LegendPositionEnum.NorthEast;

}

private void grid1_SizeChanged(object sender, SizeChangedEventArgs e)
{
    myLineChart1.Width = grid1.ActualWidth;
    myLineChart1.Height = grid1.ActualHeight;
    AddData(myLineChart1);
}
private void grid2_SizeChanged(object sender, SizeChangedEventArgs e)
```

```
        {
            myLineChart2.Width = grid2.ActualWidth;
            myLineChart2.Height = grid2.ActualHeight;
            AddData(myLineChart2);
        }

        private void grid3_SizeChanged(object sender, SizeChangedEventArgs e)
        {
            myLineChart3.Width = grid3.ActualWidth;
            myLineChart3.Height = grid3.ActualHeight;
            AddData(myLineChart3);
        }
        private void grid4_SizeChanged(object sender, SizeChangedEventArgs e)
        {
            myLineChart4.Width = grid4.ActualWidth;
            myLineChart4.Height = grid4.ActualHeight;
            AddData(myLineChart4);
        }
    }
}
```

This class creates four charts that are equivalent to the 2 × 2 subcharts. As with any other WPF built-in element, you can place as many line chart controls as you need in a single WPF Window.

Figure 9-3 shows the results of running this example.

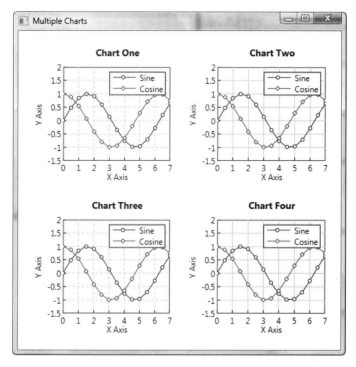

Figure 9-3. *Subcharts created using line chart controls*

Specialized 2D Chart Control

In previous sections, I showed you how to create a simple line chart control and how to use the line chart control in your WPF applications. Following a similar procedure, you can also easily convert the specialized 2D charts presented in Chapter 6 into a user control.

There is some difference between the line chart control and the specialized 2D control. The line chart control uses a single XAML layout file, whereas the XAML layouts for the specialized 2D chart control must be different for different types of charts. Therefore, we need to create a different user control for each type of specialized 2D chart.

Here, we'll use a simplified approach to create specialized chart controls. Namely, we'll not define dependency properties; instead, we'll simply introduce the minimum number of conventional public properties. This means you must create specialized 2D charts programmatically in code when you use specialized chart controls in your WPF applications. The purpose of doing this is simply to show you how easy it is to convert WPF Windows applications for specialized 2D charts into user controls. If you really want to expose properties to the outside world in XAML, you can always follow the procedure for creating the line chart controls presented earlier in this chapter to define corresponding dependency properties.

Bar Chart Control

In this section, I'll show you how to create a bar chart control. Start with a new WPF project. Instead of a WPF Windows application, you need to select a new WPF User Control Library from templates and name it *Specialized2DChartControl*.

Implementation

Add a new WPF User Control to the *Specialized2DChartControl* project and name it *BarControl*. Add to the current project the following classes from the *Specialized2DCharts* project presented in Chapter 6: *ChartStyle*, *ChartStyleGridlines*, *DataSeries*, *DataCollection*, *Symbols*, *DataSeriesBar*, and *DataCollectionBar*. When we convert the Windows application into a user control, we'll try not to change or modify these classes from the original project.

Here is the XAML file for the bar control:

```
<UserControl x:Class="Specialized2DChartControl.BarControl"
    xmlns="http://schemas.microsoft.com/winfx/2006/xaml/presentation"
    xmlns:x="http://schemas.microsoft.com/winfx/2006/xaml"
    Height="400" Width="500">
    <Grid Name="grid1" Margin="10">
        <Grid.ColumnDefinitions>
            <ColumnDefinition Width="Auto"/>
            <ColumnDefinition Name="column1" Width="*"/>
        </Grid.ColumnDefinitions>
        <Grid.RowDefinitions>
            <RowDefinition Height="Auto"/>
            <RowDefinition Name="row1" Height="*"/>
            <RowDefinition Height="Auto"/>
        </Grid.RowDefinitions>
        <TextBlock Margin="2" x:Name="tbTitle" Grid.Column="1" Grid.Row="0"
                   RenderTransformOrigin="0.5,0.5" FontSize="14" FontWeight="Bold"
                   HorizontalAlignment="Stretch" VerticalAlignment="Stretch"
                   TextAlignment="Center" Text="Title"/>
```

```xml
<TextBlock Margin="2" x:Name="tbXLabel" Grid.Column="1" Grid.Row="2"
           RenderTransformOrigin="0.5,0.5" TextAlignment="Center"
           Text="X Axis"/>
<TextBlock Margin="2" Name="tbYLabel" Grid.Column="0" Grid.Row="1"
           RenderTransformOrigin="0.5,0.5" TextAlignment="Center"
           Text="Y Axis">
    <TextBlock.LayoutTransform>
        <RotateTransform Angle="-90"/>
    </TextBlock.LayoutTransform>
</TextBlock>
<Grid  Margin="0" x:Name ="chartGrid" Grid.Column="1" Grid.Row="1"
ClipToBounds="True" Background="Transparent"
       SizeChanged="chartGrid_SizeChanged" />
<Canvas Margin="2" Name="textCanvas" ClipToBounds="True"
       Grid.Column="1" Grid.Row="1">
    <Canvas Name="chartCanvas" ClipToBounds="True">
        <Canvas Name="legendCanvas" Background="Transparent" />
    </Canvas>
</Canvas>
        </Grid>
</UserControl>
```

This markup is basically the same as that used to create WPF Windows applications for bar charts.

Next, we need to design the public interface that the bar chart control exposes to the outside world. Here, we only define the necessary public properties in the control. Add the following code to the code-behind file:

```csharp
using System;
using System.Windows;
using System.Windows.Controls;
using System.Windows.Media;
using Specialized2DCharts;

namespace Specialized2DChartControl
{
    public partial class BarControl : UserControl
    {
        private ChartStyleGridlines cs;
        private DataCollectionBar dc;
        private DataSeriesBar ds;

        public BarControl()
        {
            InitializeComponent();
            this.cs = new ChartStyleGridlines();
            this.dc = new DataCollectionBar();
            this.ds = new DataSeriesBar();
            cs.ChartCanvas = chartCanvas;
            cs.TextCanvas = textCanvas;
        }

        private void chartGrid_SizeChanged(object sender, SizeChangedEventArgs e)
        {
            textCanvas.Width = chartGrid.ActualWidth;
```

```
            textCanvas.Height = chartGrid.ActualHeight;
            legendCanvas.Children.Clear();
            chartCanvas.Children.RemoveRange(1, chartCanvas.Children.Count - 1);
            textCanvas.Children.RemoveRange(1, textCanvas.Children.Count - 1);
            AddChart();
        }

        private void AddChart()
        {
            cs.AddChartStyle(tbTitle, tbXLabel, tbYLabel);
            if (dc.DataList.Count != 0)
                dc.AddBars(cs);
        }

        public ChartStyleGridlines ChartStyle
        {
            get { return cs; }
            set { cs = value; }
        }

        public DataCollectionBar DataCollection
        {
            get { return dc; }
            set { dc = value; }
        }

        public DataSeriesBar DataSeries
        {
            get { return ds; }
            set { ds = value; }
        }
    }
}
```

Note that a *using* statement is added at the beginning of the code:

using Specialized2DCharts;

This allows you to access all of the public classes in the *Specialized2DCharts* project. You can see that we define only three public properties, which are related directly to the *ChartStyleGridlines, DataSeriesBar,* and *DataCollectionBar* objects. These three properties set up an interface between the user control and the original corresponding classes and allow you to access the public properties and methods inside these classes.

Creating Bar Charts

Here, I'll show you how to use the bar chart control to create simple bar charts. Open the *Specialized2DChartControl* solution in Visual Studio 2008. Click on the File menu and select Add | New project... Select WPF Application from templates and name it *Specialized2DChartControlTest*. Now right-click Reference and select Add References... in the Specialized2DChartControlTest project to bring up "Add References." Click the Projects tab in this "Add Reference" window and highlight the *Specialized2DChartControl*. Click OK to add the *Specialize2DChartControl* to the current project. This way, you can use the control in your WPF applications the same way as a default element. Now right-click the new project and select Set as StartUp Project.

Add a new WPF Window to the *Specialized2DChartControlTest* project and name it *BarCharts*. The layout for the example is very simple; you create it using the following XAML:

```
<Window x:Class="Specialized2DChartControlTest.BarCharts"
    xmlns="http://schemas.microsoft.com/winfx/2006/xaml/presentation"
    xmlns:x="http://schemas.microsoft.com/winfx/2006/xaml"
    xmlns:local="clr-namespace:Specialized2DChartControl;
                 assembly=Specialized2DChartControl"
    Title="Bar Charts" Height="350" Width="400">
    <Grid x:Name="rootGrid" SizeChanged="rootGrid_SizeChanged">
        <local:BarControl x:Name="myBarChart"/>
    </Grid>
</Window>
```

And the corresponding code-behind file is given below:

```
using System;
using System.Collections.Generic;
using System.Windows;
using System.Windows.Controls;
using System.Windows.Media;
using System.Windows.Shapes;

namespace Specialized2DChartControlTest
{
    public partial class BarCharts : Window
    {
        public BarCharts()
        {
            InitializeComponent();
        }

        private void rootGrid_SizeChanged(object sender, SizeChangedEventArgs e)
        {
            myBarChart.Height = rootGrid.ActualHeight;
            myBarChart.Width = rootGrid.ActualWidth;
            AddHorizontalGroupBarChart();
        }

        private void AddHorizontalGroupBarChart()
        {
            myBarChart.DataCollection.DataList.Clear();
            Specialized2DCharts.DataSeriesBar ds;
            myBarChart.DataCollection.BarType =
                Specialized2DCharts.DataCollectionBar.BarTypeEnum.HorizontalStack;
            myBarChart.ChartStyle.Title =
                myBarChart.DataCollection.BarType.ToString();
            myBarChart.ChartStyle.Xmin = 0;
            myBarChart.ChartStyle.Xmax = 25;
            myBarChart.ChartStyle.Ymin = 0;
            myBarChart.ChartStyle.Ymax = 5;
            myBarChart.ChartStyle.XTick = 5;
```

```
myBarChart.ChartStyle.YTick = 1;
myBarChart.ChartStyle.GridlinePattern =
    Specialized2DCharts.ChartStyleGridlines.GridlinePatternEnum.Dot;
myBarChart.ChartStyle.GridlineColor = Brushes.Black;

// Add the first bar series:
ds = new Specialized2DCharts.DataSeriesBar();
ds.BorderColor = Brushes.Red;
ds.FillColor = Brushes.Green;
ds.BarWidth = 0.8;

for (int i = 0; i < 5; i++)
{
    double x = i + 1.0;
    double y = 2.0 * x;
    ds.LineSeries.Points.Add(new Point(y, x));
}
myBarChart.DataCollection.DataList.Add(ds);

// Add the second bar series:
ds = new Specialized2DCharts.DataSeriesBar();
ds.BorderColor = Brushes.Red;
ds.FillColor = Brushes.Yellow;
ds.BarWidth = 0.8;

for (int i = 0; i < 5; i++)
{
    double x = i + 1.0;
    double y = 1.5 * x;
    ds.LineSeries.Points.Add(new Point(y, x));
}
myBarChart.DataCollection.DataList.Add(ds);

// Add the third bar series:
ds = new Specialized2DCharts.DataSeriesBar();
ds.BorderColor = Brushes.Red;
ds.FillColor = Brushes.Blue;
ds.BarWidth = 0.8;

for (int i = 0; i < 5; i++)
{
    double x = i + 1.0;
    double y = 1.0 * x;
    ds.LineSeries.Points.Add(new Point(y, x));
}
myBarChart.DataCollection.DataList.Add(ds);
myBarChart.DataCollection.AddBars(myBarChart.ChartStyle);
        }
    }
}
```

This code is very similar to that used in Chapter 6 to create bar charts in code directly. In this example, I demonstrate how to create a horizontal group bar chart. You can modify the preceding code to create various bar charts presented previously in Chapter 6.

Running this example generates the same result as that shown in Figure 6-9.

Creating Multiple Bar Charts

Using the bar chart control, you can easily create multiple bar charts in a single WPF window. Add a new WPF Window to the project *Specialized2DChartControlTest* and name it *MultiplebarCharts*. Create a 2 × 2 *Grid* control and add a line chart control to each of the four cells of the *Grid*, which can be done using the following XAML file:

```
<Window x:Class="Specialized2DChartControlTest.MultipleBarCharts"
    xmlns="http://schemas.microsoft.com/winfx/2006/xaml/presentation"
    xmlns:x="http://schemas.microsoft.com/winfx/2006/xaml"
    xmlns:local="clr-namespace:Specialized2DChartControl;
                assembly=Specialized2DChartControl"
    Title="MultipleBarCharts" Height="500" Width="500">
    <Grid>
        <Grid.RowDefinitions>
            <RowDefinition/>
            <RowDefinition/>
        </Grid.RowDefinitions>
        <Grid.ColumnDefinitions>
            <ColumnDefinition/>
            <ColumnDefinition/>
        </Grid.ColumnDefinitions>

        <Grid x:Name="grid1" SizeChanged="grid1_SizeChanged"
            Grid.Column="0" Grid.Row="0">
            <local:BarControl x:Name="bar1"/>
        </Grid>
        <Grid x:Name="grid2" SizeChanged="grid2_SizeChanged"
            Grid.Column="1" Grid.Row="0">
            <local:BarControl x:Name="bar2"/>
        </Grid>
        <Grid x:Name="grid3" SizeChanged="grid3_SizeChanged"
            Grid.Column="0" Grid.Row="1">
            <local:BarControl x:Name="bar3"/>
        </Grid>
        <Grid x:Name="grid4" SizeChanged="grid4_SizeChanged"
            Grid.Column="1" Grid.Row="1">
            <local:BarControl x:Name="bar4"/>
        </Grid>
    </Grid>
</Window>
```

Here, you create four bar chart controls: *bar1*, *bar2*, *bar3*, and *bar4*. Here is the corresponding code-behind file that draws the bars on each chart:

```
using System;
using System.Collections.Generic;
using System.Windows;
using System.Windows.Controls;
using System.Windows.Media;
using System.Windows.Shapes;
```

```
namespace Specialized2DChartControlTest
{
    public partial class MultipleBarCharts : Window
    {
        public MultipleBarCharts()
        {
            InitializeComponent();
        }

        private void grid1_SizeChanged(object sender, SizeChangedEventArgs e)
        {
            bar1.Height = grid1.ActualHeight;
            bar1.Width = grid1.ActualWidth;
            AddVerticalBarData(bar1);
        }

        private void grid2_SizeChanged(object sender, SizeChangedEventArgs e)
        {
            bar2.Height = grid2.ActualHeight;
            bar2.Width = grid2.ActualWidth;
            AddHorizontalBarChart(bar2);
        }

        private void grid3_SizeChanged(object sender, SizeChangedEventArgs e)
        {
            bar3.Height = grid3.ActualHeight;
            bar3.Width = grid3.ActualWidth;
            AddVerticalGroupBarData(bar3);
        }

        private void grid4_SizeChanged(object sender, SizeChangedEventArgs e)
        {
            bar4.Height = grid4.ActualHeight;
            bar4.Width = grid4.ActualWidth;
            AddHorizontalGroupBarChart(bar4);
        }

        private void AddVerticalBarData(
                Specialized2DChartControl.BarControl myBarChart)
        {
            myBarChart.DataCollection.DataList.Clear();
            Specialized2DCharts.DataSeriesBar ds =
                new Specialized2DCharts.DataSeriesBar();
            myBarChart.DataCollection.BarType =
                Specialized2DCharts.DataCollectionBar.BarTypeEnum.Vertical;
            myBarChart.ChartStyle.Title = "1st Bar Chart";
            myBarChart.ChartStyle.Xmin = 0;
            myBarChart.ChartStyle.Xmax = 5;
            myBarChart.ChartStyle.Ymin = 0;
            myBarChart.ChartStyle.Ymax = 10;
            myBarChart.ChartStyle.XTick = 1;
            myBarChart.ChartStyle.YTick = 2;
```

```
    myBarChart.ChartStyle.GridlinePattern =
        Specialized2DCharts.ChartStyleGridlines.GridlinePatternEnum.Dot;
    myBarChart.ChartStyle.GridlineColor = Brushes.Black;

    // Draw the bar chart:
    ds.BorderColor = Brushes.Red;
    ds.FillColor = Brushes.Green;
    ds.BarWidth = 0.6;

    for (int i = 0; i < 5; i++)
    {
        double x = i + 1.0;
        double y = 2.0 * x;
        ds.LineSeries.Points.Add(new Point(x, y));
    }
    myBarChart.DataCollection.DataList.Add(ds);
    myBarChart.DataCollection.AddBars(myBarChart.ChartStyle);
}

private void AddVerticalGroupBarData(
            Specialized2DChartControl.BarControl myBarChart)
{
    myBarChart.DataCollection.DataList.Clear();
    Specialized2DCharts.DataSeriesBar ds =
        new Specialized2DCharts.DataSeriesBar();
    myBarChart.DataCollection.BarType =
        Specialized2DCharts.DataCollectionBar.BarTypeEnum.Vertical;
    myBarChart.ChartStyle.Title = "3rd Bar Chart";
    myBarChart.ChartStyle.Xmin = 0;
    myBarChart.ChartStyle.Xmax = 5;
    myBarChart.ChartStyle.Ymin = 0;
    myBarChart.ChartStyle.Ymax = 10;
    myBarChart.ChartStyle.XTick = 1;
    myBarChart.ChartStyle.YTick = 2;
    myBarChart.ChartStyle.GridlinePattern =
        Specialized2DCharts.ChartStyleGridlines.GridlinePatternEnum.Dot;
    myBarChart.ChartStyle.GridlineColor = Brushes.Black;

    // Add the first bar series:
    ds = new Specialized2DCharts.DataSeriesBar();
    ds.BorderColor = Brushes.Red;
    ds.FillColor = Brushes.Green;
    ds.BarWidth = 0.9;

    for (int i = 0; i < 5; i++)
    {
        double x = i + 1.0;
        double y = 2.0 * x;
        ds.LineSeries.Points.Add(new Point(x, y));
    }
    myBarChart.DataCollection.DataList.Add(ds);

    // Add the second bar series:
```

```
        ds = new Specialized2DCharts.DataSeriesBar();
        ds.BorderColor = Brushes.Red;
        ds.FillColor = Brushes.Yellow;
        ds.BarWidth = 0.9;

        for (int i = 0; i < 5; i++)
        {
            double x = i + 1.0;
            double y = 1.5 * x;
            ds.LineSeries.Points.Add(new Point(x, y));
        }
        myBarChart.DataCollection.DataList.Add(ds);

        // Add the third bar series:
        ds = new Specialized2DCharts.DataSeriesBar();
        ds.BorderColor = Brushes.Red;
        ds.FillColor = Brushes.Blue;
        ds.BarWidth = 0.9;

        for (int i = 0; i < 5; i++)
        {
            double x = i + 1.0;
            double y = 1.0 * x;
            ds.LineSeries.Points.Add(new Point(x, y));
        }
        myBarChart.DataCollection.DataList.Add(ds);
        myBarChart.DataCollection.AddBars(myBarChart.ChartStyle);
    }

    private void AddHorizontalBarChart(
        Specialized2DChartControl.BarControl myBarChart)
    {
        myBarChart.DataCollection.DataList.Clear();
        Specialized2DCharts.DataSeriesBar ds =
            new Specialized2DCharts.DataSeriesBar();
        myBarChart.DataCollection.BarType =
            Specialized2DCharts.DataCollectionBar.BarTypeEnum.Horizontal;
        myBarChart.ChartStyle.Title = "2nd Bar Chart";
        myBarChart.ChartStyle.Xmin = 0;
        myBarChart.ChartStyle.Xmax = 10;
        myBarChart.ChartStyle.Ymin = 0;
        myBarChart.ChartStyle.Ymax = 5;
        myBarChart.ChartStyle.XTick = 2;
        myBarChart.ChartStyle.YTick = 1;
        myBarChart.ChartStyle.GridlinePattern =
            Specialized2DCharts.ChartStyleGridlines.GridlinePatternEnum.Dot;
        myBarChart.ChartStyle.GridlineColor = Brushes.Black;

        // Draw the bar chart:
        ds = new Specialized2DCharts.DataSeriesBar();
        ds.BorderColor = Brushes.Red;
        ds.FillColor = Brushes.Green;
        ds.BarWidth = 0.6;
```

```
    for (int i = 0; i < 5; i++)
    {
        double x = i + 1.0;
        double y = 2.0 * x;
        ds.LineSeries.Points.Add(new Point(y, x));
    }
    myBarChart.DataCollection.DataList.Add(ds);
    myBarChart.DataCollection.AddBars(myBarChart.ChartStyle);
}


private void AddHorizontalGroupBarChart(
    Specialized2DChartControl.BarControl myBarChart)
{
    myBarChart.DataCollection.DataList.Clear();
    Specialized2DCharts.DataSeriesBar ds =
        new Specialized2DCharts.DataSeriesBar();
    myBarChart.DataCollection.BarType =
        Specialized2DCharts.DataCollectionBar.BarTypeEnum.HorizontalStack;
    myBarChart.ChartStyle.Title = "4th Bar Chart";
    myBarChart.ChartStyle.Xmin = 0;
    myBarChart.ChartStyle.Xmax = 25;
    myBarChart.ChartStyle.Ymin = 0;
    myBarChart.ChartStyle.Ymax = 5;
    myBarChart.ChartStyle.XTick = 5;
    myBarChart.ChartStyle.YTick = 1;
    myBarChart.ChartStyle.GridlinePattern =
        Specialized2DCharts.ChartStyleGridlines.GridlinePatternEnum.Dot;
    myBarChart.ChartStyle.GridlineColor = Brushes.Black;

    // Add the first bar series:
    ds = new Specialized2DCharts.DataSeriesBar();
    ds.BorderColor = Brushes.Red;
    ds.FillColor = Brushes.Green;
    ds.BarWidth = 0.8;

    for (int i = 0; i < 5; i++)
    {
        double x = i + 1.0;
        double y = 2.0 * x;
        ds.LineSeries.Points.Add(new Point(y, x));
    }
    myBarChart.DataCollection.DataList.Add(ds);

    // Add the second bar series:
    ds = new Specialized2DCharts.DataSeriesBar();
    ds.BorderColor = Brushes.Red;
    ds.FillColor = Brushes.Yellow;
    ds.BarWidth = 0.8;

    for (int i = 0; i < 5; i++)
    {
```

```
                double x = i + 1.0;
                double y = 1.5 * x;
                ds.LineSeries.Points.Add(new Point(y, x));
            }
            myBarChart.DataCollection.DataList.Add(ds);

            // Add the third bar series:
            ds = new Specialized2DCharts.DataSeriesBar();
            ds.BorderColor = Brushes.Red;
            ds.FillColor = Brushes.Blue;
            ds.BarWidth = 0.8;

            for (int i = 0; i < 5; i++)
            {
                double x = i + 1.0;
                double y = 1.0 * x;
                ds.LineSeries.Points.Add(new Point(y, x));
            }
            myBarChart.DataCollection.DataList.Add(ds);
            myBarChart.DataCollection.AddBars(myBarChart.ChartStyle);
        }
    }
}
```

This example creates four different bar charts that are equivalent to the 2 X 2 subcharts. As with any other WPF built-in element, you can place as many bar chart controls as you need in a single WPF Window.

Figure 9-4 shows the results of running this example.

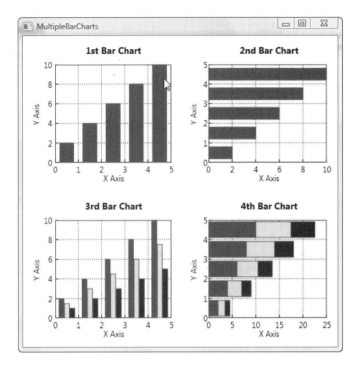

Figure 9-4. Subcharts created using the bar chart controls

Stair-Step Chart Control

In this section, you'll learn how to create a stair-step chart control.

Implementation

Add a new WPF User Control to the *Specialized2DChartControl* project and name it *StairstepControl*. Add to the current project the following classes from the *Specialized2DCharts* project presented in Chapter 6: *DataSeriesStairstep* and *DataCollectionStairstep*. When we convert the Windows application into a user control, we'll try not to change or modify these classes from the original project.

Here is the XAML file for the stair-step control:

```
<UserControl x:Class="Specialized2DChartControl.StairstepControl"
    xmlns="http://schemas.microsoft.com/winfx/2006/xaml/presentation"
    xmlns:x="http://schemas.microsoft.com/winfx/2006/xaml"
    Height="400" Width="500">
    <Grid Name="grid1" Margin="10">
        <Grid.ColumnDefinitions>
            <ColumnDefinition Width="Auto"/>
            <ColumnDefinition Name="column1" Width="*"/>
        </Grid.ColumnDefinitions>
        <Grid.RowDefinitions>
```

```
                <RowDefinition Height="Auto"/>
                <RowDefinition Name="row1" Height="*"/>
                <RowDefinition Height="Auto"/>
            </Grid.RowDefinitions>
            <TextBlock Margin="2" x:Name="tbTitle" Grid.Column="1" Grid.Row="0"
                       RenderTransformOrigin="0.5,0.5" FontSize="14" FontWeight="Bold"
                       HorizontalAlignment="Stretch" VerticalAlignment="Stretch"
                       TextAlignment="Center" Text="Title"/>
            <TextBlock Margin="2" x:Name="tbXLabel" Grid.Column="1" Grid.Row="2"
                       RenderTransformOrigin="0.5,0.5" TextAlignment="Center"
                       Text="X Axis"/>
            <TextBlock Margin="2" Name="tbYLabel" Grid.Column="0" Grid.Row="1"
                       RenderTransformOrigin="0.5,0.5" TextAlignment="Center"
                       Text="Y Axis">
                <TextBlock.LayoutTransform>
                    <RotateTransform Angle="-90"/>
                </TextBlock.LayoutTransform>
            </TextBlock>
            <Grid  Margin="0" x:Name ="chartGrid" Grid.Column="1" Grid.Row="1"
                   ClipToBounds="True" Background="Transparent"
                   SizeChanged="chartGrid_SizeChanged" />
            <Canvas Margin="2" Name="textCanvas" ClipToBounds="True"
                    Grid.Column="1" Grid.Row="1">
                <Canvas Name="chartCanvas" ClipToBounds="True">
                    <Canvas Name="legendCanvas" Background="Transparent" />
                </Canvas>
            </Canvas>
        </Grid>
</UserControl>
```

This XAML file is basically the same as that used in creating the WPF Window Application for stair step charts presented in Chapter 6.

Next, we need to design the public interface that the stair step chart control exposes to the outside world. Here, we only define necessary public properties in the control. Add the following code to the code-behind file:

```
using System;
using System.Collections.Generic;
using System.Windows;
using System.Windows.Controls;
using System.Windows.Media;
using Specialized2DCharts;

namespace Specialized2DChartControl
{
    public partial class StairstepControl : UserControl
    {
        private ChartStyleGridlines cs;
        private DataCollectionStairstep dc;
        private DataSeriesStairstep ds;

        public StairstepControl()
        {
            InitializeComponent();
```

```
            cs = new ChartStyleGridlines();
            dc = new DataCollectionStairstep();
            ds = new DataSeriesStairstep();
            cs.TextCanvas = textCanvas;
            cs.ChartCanvas = chartCanvas;
        }

        private void chartGrid_SizeChanged(object sender, SizeChangedEventArgs e)
        {
            textCanvas.Width = chartGrid.ActualWidth;
            textCanvas.Height = chartGrid.ActualHeight;
            legendCanvas.Children.Clear();
            chartCanvas.Children.RemoveRange(1, chartCanvas.Children.Count - 1);
            textCanvas.Children.RemoveRange(1, textCanvas.Children.Count - 1);
            AddChart();
        }

        private void AddChart()
        {
            cs.AddChartStyle(tbTitle, tbXLabel, tbYLabel);
            if (dc.DataList.Count != 0)
            {
                dc.AddStairstep(cs);
                dc.AddLines(cs);
            }
        }

        public ChartStyleGridlines ChartStyle
        {
            get { return cs; }
            set { cs = value; }
        }

        public DataCollectionStairstep DataCollection
        {
            get { return dc; }
            set { dc = value; }
        }

        public DataSeriesStairstep DataSeries
        {
            get { return ds; }
            set { ds = value; }
        }
    }
}
```

As we did for the previous bar chart control, here we define only three public properties, which are related directly to the *ChartStyleGridlines*, *DataSeriesStairstep*, and *DataCollectionStairstep* objects. These three properties set up an interface between the user control and the original corresponding classes and allow you to access the public properties and methods inside these classes.

Creating Stair-Step Charts

Here, I'll show you how to use the stair-step chart control to create stair-step charts. Open the *Specialized2DChartControl* project. Add a new WPF Window to the *Specialized2DChartControlTest* project and name it *StairstepChart*. The layout of the example is very simple; you create it using the following XAML:

```
<Window x:Class="Specialized2DChartControlTest.StairstepChart"
    xmlns="http://schemas.microsoft.com/winfx/2006/xaml/presentation"
    xmlns:x="http://schemas.microsoft.com/winfx/2006/xaml"
    xmlns:local="clr-namespace:Specialized2DChartControl;
                assembly=Specialized2DChartControl"
    Title="StairstepChart" Height="350" Width="400">
    <Grid x:Name="rootGrid" SizeChanged="rootGrid_SizeChanged">
        <local:StairstepControl x:Name="myStairstepChart"/>
    </Grid>
</Window>
```

And the corresponding code-behind file is given below:

```
using System;
using System.Windows;
using System.Windows.Controls;
using System.Windows.Media;

namespace Specialized2DChartControlTest
{
    public partial class StairstepChart : Window
    {
        public StairstepChart()
        {
            InitializeComponent();
        }

        private void rootGrid_SizeChanged(object sender, SizeChangedEventArgs e)
        {
            myStairstepChart.Height = rootGrid.Height;
            myStairstepChart.Width = rootGrid.Width;
            AddData();
        }

        private void AddData()
        {
            myStairstepChart.DataCollection.DataList.Clear();
            myStairstepChart.ChartStyle.Title = "Stair Step Chart";
            Specialized2DCharts.DataSeriesStairstep ds =
                new Specialized2DCharts.DataSeriesStairstep();
            myStairstepChart.ChartStyle.Xmin = 0;
            myStairstepChart.ChartStyle.Xmax = 8;
            myStairstepChart.ChartStyle.Ymin = -1.5;
            myStairstepChart.ChartStyle.Ymax = 1.5;
            myStairstepChart.ChartStyle.XTick = 1;
            myStairstepChart.ChartStyle.YTick = 0.5;
            myStairstepChart.ChartStyle.GridlinePattern =
```

```
            Specialized2DCharts.ChartStyleGridlines.GridlinePatternEnum.Dot;
        myStairstepChart.ChartStyle.GridlineColor = Brushes.Black;

        // Draw the stair step chart:
        ds.StairstepLineColor = Brushes.Red;
        for (int i = 0; i < 50; i++)
        {
            ds.LineSeries.Points.Add(new Point(0.4 * i, Math.Sin(0.4 * i)));
        }
        ds.LineColor = Brushes.Black;
        ds.LinePattern = Specialized2DCharts.DataSeries.LinePatternEnum.Dash;
        ds.Symbols.SymbolType =
            Specialized2DCharts.Symbols.SymbolTypeEnum.Circle;
        myStairstepChart.DataCollection.DataList.Add(ds);
    }
  }
}
```

This code is very similar to that used in Chapter 6 to create stair step charts in code directly. Running this example produces the same result as that shown in Figure 6-11.

Stem Chart Control

In this section, you'll learn how to create a stem chart control.

Implementation

Add a new WPF User Control to the *Specialized2DChartControl* project and name it *StemControl*. Add to the current project the *DataCollectionStem* class from the *Specialized2DCharts* project presented in Chapter 6. When we convert the Windows application into a user control, we'll try not to change or modify these classes from the original project.

Here is the XAML file for the stem control:

```
<UserControl x:Class="Specialized2DChartControl.StemControl"
    xmlns="http://schemas.microsoft.com/winfx/2006/xaml/presentation"
    xmlns:x="http://schemas.microsoft.com/winfx/2006/xaml"
    Height="400" Width="500">
    <Grid Name="grid1" Margin="10">
        <Grid.ColumnDefinitions>
            <ColumnDefinition Width="Auto"/>
            <ColumnDefinition Name="column1" Width="*"/>
        </Grid.ColumnDefinitions>
        <Grid.RowDefinitions>
            <RowDefinition Height="Auto"/>
            <RowDefinition Name="row1" Height="*"/>
            <RowDefinition Height="Auto"/>
        </Grid.RowDefinitions>
        <TextBlock Margin="2" x:Name="tbTitle" Grid.Column="1" Grid.Row="0"
                RenderTransformOrigin="0.5,0.5" FontSize="14" FontWeight="Bold"
                HorizontalAlignment="Stretch" VerticalAlignment="Stretch"
                TextAlignment="Center" Text="Title"/>
        <TextBlock Margin="2" x:Name="tbXLabel" Grid.Column="1" Grid.Row="2"
```

```
                    RenderTransformOrigin="0.5,0.5" TextAlignment="Center"
                    Text="X Axis"/>
        <TextBlock Margin="2" Name="tbYLabel" Grid.Column="0" Grid.Row="1"
                    RenderTransformOrigin="0.5,0.5" TextAlignment="Center"
                    Text="Y Axis">
            <TextBlock.LayoutTransform>
                <RotateTransform Angle="-90"/>
            </TextBlock.LayoutTransform>
        </TextBlock>
        <Grid  Margin="0" x:Name ="chartGrid" Grid.Column="1" Grid.Row="1"
                ClipToBounds="True" Background="Transparent"
                SizeChanged="chartGrid_SizeChanged" />
        <Canvas Margin="2" Name="textCanvas" ClipToBounds="True"
                Grid.Column="1" Grid.Row="1">
            <Canvas Name="chartCanvas" ClipToBounds="True">
                <Canvas Name="legendCanvas" Background="Transparent"/>
            </Canvas>
        </Canvas>
    </Grid>
</UserControl>
```

This markup is basically the same as that used in creating a WPF Windows application for stem charts.

Next, we need to design the public interface that the bar chart control exposes to the outside world. Here, we only define necessary public properties in the control. Add the following code to the code-behind file:

```
using System;
using System.Windows;
using System.Windows.Controls;
using System.Windows.Media;
using Specialized2DCharts;

namespace Specialized2DChartControl
{
    public partial class StemControl : UserControl
    {
        private ChartStyleGridlines cs;
        private DataCollectionStem dc;
        private DataSeries ds;

        public StemControl()
        {
            InitializeComponent();
            cs = new ChartStyleGridlines();
            dc = new DataCollectionStem();
            ds = new DataSeries();
            cs.TextCanvas = textCanvas;
            cs.ChartCanvas = chartCanvas;
        }

        private void chartGrid_SizeChanged(object sender, SizeChangedEventArgs e)
        {
            textCanvas.Width = chartGrid.ActualWidth;
            textCanvas.Height = chartGrid.ActualHeight;
```

```
            legendCanvas.Children.Clear();
            chartCanvas.Children.RemoveRange(1, chartCanvas.Children.Count - 1);
            textCanvas.Children.RemoveRange(1, textCanvas.Children.Count - 1);
            AddChart();
        }

        private void AddChart()
        {
            cs.AddChartStyle(tbTitle, tbXLabel, tbYLabel);
            if (dc.DataList.Count != 0)
            {
                dc.AddStems(cs);
            }
        }

        public ChartStyleGridlines ChartStyle
        {
            get { return cs; }
            set { cs = value; }
        }

        public DataCollectionStem DataCollection
        {
            get { return dc; }
            set { dc = value; }
        }

        public DataSeries DataSeries
        {
            get { return ds; }
            set { ds = value; }
        }
    }
}
```

Here, as before, we define only three public properties, which are related directly to the *ChartStyleGridlines*, *DataSeriesStem*, and *DataCollectionStem* objects. These three properties set up an interface between the user control and the original corresponding classes and allow you to access the public properties and methods inside these classes.

Creating Stem Charts

Here, I'll show you how to use the stem chart control to create stem charts. Open the *Specialized2DChartControl* project. Add a new WPF Window to the *Specialized2DChartControlTest* project and name it *StemChart*. The layout of the example is very simple; you create it using the following XAML:

```
<Window x:Class="Specialized2DChartControlTest.StemChart"
    xmlns="http://schemas.microsoft.com/winfx/2006/xaml/presentation"
    xmlns:x="http://schemas.microsoft.com/winfx/2006/xaml"
    xmlns:local="clr-namespace:Specialized2DChartControl;
            assembly=Specialized2DChartControl"
    Title="StemChart" Height="350" Width="400">
```

```
    <Grid x:Name="rootGrid" SizeChanged="rootGrid_SizeChanged">
        <local:StemControl x:Name="myStemChart"/>
    </Grid>
</Window>
```

Here is the corresponding code-behind file:

```
using System;
using System.Collections.Generic;
using System.Windows;
using System.Windows.Controls;
using System.Windows.Media;

namespace Specialized2DChartControlTest
{
    public partial class StemChart : Window
    {
        public StemChart()
        {
            InitializeComponent();
        }

        private void rootGrid_SizeChanged(object sender, SizeChangedEventArgs e)
        {
            myStemChart.Height = rootGrid.Height;
            myStemChart.Width = rootGrid.Width;
            AddData();
        }

        private void AddData()
        {
            myStemChart.DataCollection.DataList.Clear();
            Specialized2DCharts.DataSeries ds =
                new Specialized2DCharts.DataSeries();
            myStemChart.ChartStyle.Title = "Stem Chart";
            myStemChart.ChartStyle.Xmin = 0;
            myStemChart.ChartStyle.Xmax = 8;
            myStemChart.ChartStyle.Ymin = -1.5;
            myStemChart.ChartStyle.Ymax = 1.5;
            myStemChart.ChartStyle.XTick = 1;
            myStemChart.ChartStyle.YTick = 0.5;
            myStemChart.ChartStyle.GridlinePattern =
                Specialized2DCharts.ChartStyleGridlines.GridlinePatternEnum.Dot;
            myStemChart.ChartStyle.GridlineColor = Brushes.Black;

            // Draw the stair step chart:
            for (int i = 0; i < 50; i++)
            {
                ds.LineSeries.Points.Add(new Point(0.4 * i, Math.Sin(0.4 * i)));
            }

            ds.LineColor = Brushes.Red;
            ds.Symbols.SymbolType =
                Specialized2DCharts.Symbols.SymbolTypeEnum.Diamond;
```

```
            ds.Symbols.FillColor = Brushes.Yellow;
            ds.Symbols.BorderColor = Brushes.DarkGreen;
            myStemChart.DataCollection.DataList.Add(ds);
        }
    }
}
```

This code is very similar to that used in Chapter 6 to create stem charts in code directly. Running this example produces the same output as that shown in Figure 6-12.

Error Bar Control

In this section, you'll learn how to create an error bar chart control.

Implementation

Add a new WPF User Control to the *Specialized2DChartControl* project and name it *ErrorbarsControl*. Add to the current project the *DataSeriesErrorbar* and *DataCollectionErrorbar* classes from the *Specialized2DCharts* project presented in Chapter 6. When we convert the Windows application into a user control, we'll try not to change or modify these classes from the original project.

Here is the XAML file for the stem control:

```
<UserControl x:Class="Specialized2DChartControl.ErrorbarsControl"
    xmlns="http://schemas.microsoft.com/winfx/2006/xaml/presentation"
    xmlns:x="http://schemas.microsoft.com/winfx/2006/xaml"
    Height="400" Width="500">
    <Grid Name="grid1" Margin="10">
        <Grid.ColumnDefinitions>
            <ColumnDefinition Width="Auto"/>
            <ColumnDefinition Name="column1" Width="*"/>
        </Grid.ColumnDefinitions>
        <Grid.RowDefinitions>
            <RowDefinition Height="Auto"/>
            <RowDefinition Name="row1" Height="*"/>
            <RowDefinition Height="Auto"/>
        </Grid.RowDefinitions>
        <TextBlock Margin="2" x:Name="tbTitle" Grid.Column="1" Grid.Row="0"
                RenderTransformOrigin="0.5,0.5" FontSize="14" FontWeight="Bold"
                HorizontalAlignment="Stretch" VerticalAlignment="Stretch"
                TextAlignment="Center" Text="Title"/>
        <TextBlock Margin="2" x:Name="tbXLabel" Grid.Column="1" Grid.Row="2"
                RenderTransformOrigin="0.5,0.5" TextAlignment="Center"
                Text="X Axis"/>
        <TextBlock Margin="2" Name="tbYLabel" Grid.Column="0" Grid.Row="1"
                RenderTransformOrigin="0.5,0.5" TextAlignment="Center"
                Text="Y Axis">
            <TextBlock.LayoutTransform>
                <RotateTransform Angle="-90"/>
            </TextBlock.LayoutTransform>
        </TextBlock>
        <Grid  Margin="0" x:Name ="chartGrid" Grid.Column="1" Grid.Row="1"
                ClipToBounds="True" Background="Transparent"
```

```
                SizeChanged="chartGrid_SizeChanged" />
        <Canvas Margin="2" Name="textCanvas" ClipToBounds="True"
                Grid.Column="1" Grid.Row="1">
            <Canvas Name="chartCanvas" ClipToBounds="True"/>
        </Canvas>
    </Grid>
</UserControl>
```

This XAML file is basically the same as that used in creating the WPF Window Application for error bar charts presented in Chapter 6.

Next, we need to design the public interface that the error bar chart control exposes to the outside world. Here, we only define necessary public properties in the control. Add the following code to the code-behind file:

```
using System;
using System.Windows;
using System.Windows.Controls;
using System.Windows.Media;
using Specialized2DCharts;

namespace Specialized2DChartControl
{
    public partial class ErrorbarsControl : UserControl
    {
        private ChartStyleGridlines cs;
        private DataCollectionErrorbar dc;
        private DataSeriesErrorbar ds;

        public ErrorbarsControl()
        {
            InitializeComponent();
            cs = new ChartStyleGridlines();
            dc = new DataCollectionErrorbar();
            ds = new DataSeriesErrorbar();
            cs.TextCanvas = textCanvas;
            cs.ChartCanvas = chartCanvas;
        }

        private void chartGrid_SizeChanged(object sender, SizeChangedEventArgs e)
        {
            textCanvas.Width = chartGrid.ActualWidth;
            textCanvas.Height = chartGrid.ActualHeight;
            chartCanvas.Children.Clear();
            textCanvas.Children.RemoveRange(1, textCanvas.Children.Count - 1);
            AddChart();
        }

        private void AddChart()
        {
            cs.AddChartStyle(tbTitle, tbXLabel, tbYLabel);
            if (dc.DataList.Count != 0)
            {
                dc.AddErrorbars(cs);
                dc.AddLines(cs);
```

```
            }
        }

        public ChartStyleGridlines ChartStyle
        {
            get { return cs; }
            set { cs = value; }
        }

        public DataCollectionErrorbar DataCollection
        {
            get { return dc; }
            set { dc = value; }
        }

        public DataSeriesErrorbar DataSeries
        {
            get { return ds; }
            set { ds = value; }
        }
    }
}
```

Here, as before, we define only three public properties, which are related directly to the *ChartStyleGridlines*, *DataSeriesErrorbar*, and *DataCollectionErrorbar* objects. These three properties set up an interface between the user control and the original corresponding classes and allow you to access the public properties and methods inside these classes.

Creating Error Bar Charts

Here, I'll show you how to use the error bar chart control to create charts with error bars. Open the *Specialized2DChartControl* project. Add a new WPF Window to the *Specialized2DChartControlTest* project and name it *ErrorBars*. The layout of the example is very simple; you create it using the following XAML:

```
<Window x:Class="Specialized2DChartControlTest.ErrorBars"
    xmlns="http://schemas.microsoft.com/winfx/2006/xaml/presentation"
    xmlns:x="http://schemas.microsoft.com/winfx/2006/xaml"
    xmlns:local="clr-namespace:Specialized2DChartControl;
                assembly=Specialized2DChartControl"
    Title="ErrorBars" Height="300" Width="300">
    <Grid x:Name="rootGrid" SizeChanged="rootGrid_SizeChanged">
        <local:ErrorbarsControl x:Name="myErrorbar"/>
    </Grid>
</Window>
```

And the corresponding code-behind file is given below:

```
using System;
using System.Windows;
using System.Windows.Controls;
using System.Windows.Media;
```

```
namespace Specialized2DChartControlTest
{
    public partial class ErrorBars : Window
    {
        public ErrorBars()
        {
            InitializeComponent();
        }

        private void rootGrid_SizeChanged(object sender, SizeChangedEventArgs e)
        {
            myErrorbar.Height = rootGrid.ActualHeight;
            myErrorbar.Width = rootGrid.ActualWidth;
            AddData();
        }

        private void AddData()
        {
            myErrorbar.DataCollection.DataList.Clear();
            myErrorbar.DataCollection.ErrorList.Clear();
            Specialized2DCharts.DataSeriesErrorbar ds =
                new Specialized2DCharts.DataSeriesErrorbar();
            myErrorbar.ChartStyle.Title = "Error Bar Chart";
            myErrorbar.ChartStyle.Xmin = 0;
            myErrorbar.ChartStyle.Xmax = 12;
            myErrorbar.ChartStyle.Ymin = -1;
            myErrorbar.ChartStyle.Ymax = 6;
            myErrorbar.ChartStyle.XTick = 2;
            myErrorbar.ChartStyle.YTick = 1;
            myErrorbar.ChartStyle.GridlinePattern=
                Specialized2DCharts.ChartStyleGridlines.GridlinePatternEnum.Dot;
            myErrorbar.ChartStyle.GridlineColor = Brushes.Black;
            ds.LineColor = Brushes.Blue;
            ds.Symbols.SymbolType=
                Specialized2DCharts.Symbols.SymbolTypeEnum.Circle;
            ds.Symbols.BorderColor = Brushes.DarkGreen;
            ds.ErrorLineColor = Brushes.Red;
            for (int i = 2; i < 22; i++)
            {
                ds.LineSeries.Points.Add(
                    new Point(0.5 * i, 10.0 * Math.Exp(-0.5 * i)));
                ds.ErrorLineSeries.Points.Add(new Point(0.5 * i, 3.0 / (0.5 * i)));
            }
            myErrorbar.DataCollection.DataList.Add(ds);
        }
    }
}
```

This code is very similar to that used in creating error bar charts directly in code in Chapter 6. Running this example produces the same result as that shown in Figure 6-13.

Area Chart Control

In this section, we'll discuss how to create an area chart control.

Implementation

Add a new WPF User Control to the *Specialized2DChartControl* project and name it *AreaControl*. Add to the current project the *DataSeriesArea* and *DataCollectionArea* classes from the *Specialized2DCharts* project presented in Chapter 6. When we convert the Window Application into a user control, we'll try not to change or modify these classes from the original project.

Here is the XAML file for the area control:

```xaml
<UserControl x:Class="Specialized2DChartControl.AreaControl"
    xmlns="http://schemas.microsoft.com/winfx/2006/xaml/presentation"
    xmlns:x="http://schemas.microsoft.com/winfx/2006/xaml"
    Height="400" Width="500">
    <Grid Name="grid1" Margin="10">
        <Grid.ColumnDefinitions>
            <ColumnDefinition Width="Auto"/>
            <ColumnDefinition Name="column1" Width="*"/>
        </Grid.ColumnDefinitions>
        <Grid.RowDefinitions>
            <RowDefinition Height="Auto"/>
            <RowDefinition Name="row1" Height="*"/>
            <RowDefinition Height="Auto"/>
        </Grid.RowDefinitions>
        <TextBlock Margin="2" x:Name="tbTitle" Grid.Column="1" Grid.Row="0"
                   RenderTransformOrigin="0.5,0.5" FontSize="14" FontWeight="Bold"
                   HorizontalAlignment="Stretch" VerticalAlignment="Stretch"
                   TextAlignment="Center" Text="Title"/>
        <TextBlock Margin="2" x:Name="tbXLabel" Grid.Column="1" Grid.Row="2"
                   RenderTransformOrigin="0.5,0.5" TextAlignment="Center"
                   Text="X Axis"/>
        <TextBlock Margin="2" Name="tbYLabel" Grid.Column="0" Grid.Row="1"
                   RenderTransformOrigin="0.5,0.5" TextAlignment="Center"
                   Text="Y Axis">
            <TextBlock.LayoutTransform>
                <RotateTransform Angle="-90"/>
            </TextBlock.LayoutTransform>
        </TextBlock>
        <Grid  Margin="0" x:Name ="chartGrid" Grid.Column="1" Grid.Row="1"
               ClipToBounds="True" Background="Transparent"
               SizeChanged="chartGrid_SizeChanged" />
        <Canvas Margin="2" Name="textCanvas" ClipToBounds="True"
                Grid.Column="1" Grid.Row="1">
            <Canvas Name="chartCanvas" ClipToBounds="True">
            </Canvas>
        </Canvas>
    </Grid>
</UserControl>
```

This XAML layout is basically the same as that used in creating a WPF Windows application for area charts.

Next, we need to design the public interface that the bar chart control exposes to the outside world. Here, we only define necessary public properties in the control. Add the following code to the code-behind file:

```
using System;
using System.Windows;
using System.Windows.Controls;
using System.Windows.Media;
using Specialized2DCharts;

namespace Specialized2DChartControl
{
    public partial class AreaControl : UserControl
    {
        private ChartStyleGridlines cs;
        private DataCollectionArea dc;
        private DataSeriesArea area;

        public AreaControl()
        {
            InitializeComponent();
            cs = new ChartStyleGridlines();
            dc = new DataCollectionArea();
            area = new DataSeriesArea();
            cs.ChartCanvas = chartCanvas;
            cs.TextCanvas = textCanvas;
        }

        private void chartGrid_SizeChanged(object sender, SizeChangedEventArgs e)
        {
            textCanvas.Width = chartGrid.ActualWidth;
            textCanvas.Height = chartGrid.ActualHeight;
            chartCanvas.Children.Clear();
            textCanvas.Children.RemoveRange(1, textCanvas.Children.Count - 1);
            AddChart();
        }

        private void AddChart()
        {
            cs.AddChartStyle(tbTitle, tbXLabel, tbYLabel);
            if (dc.AreaList.Count != 0)
            {
                dc.AddAreas(cs);
            }
        }

        public ChartStyleGridlines ChartStyle
        {
            get { return cs; }
            set { cs = value; }
        }

        public DataCollectionArea DataCollection
        {
```

```
            get { return dc; }
            set { dc = value; }
        }

        public DataSeriesArea DataSeries
        {
            get { return area; }
            set { area = value; }
        }
    }
}
```

Here, we also define only three public properties, which are related directly to the *ChartStyleGridlines*, *DataSeriesArea*, and *DataCollectionArea* objects. These three properties set up an interface between the user control and the original corresponding classes and allow you to access the public properties and methods inside these classes.

Creating Area Charts

Here, I'll show you how to use the area chart control to create area charts. Open the *Specialized2DChartControl* project. Add a new WPF Window to the *Specialized2DChartControlTest* project and name it *AreaChart*. The layout of the example is very simple; you create it using the following XAML:

```
<Window x:Class="Specialized2DChartControlTest.AreaChart"
    xmlns="http://schemas.microsoft.com/winfx/2006/xaml/presentation"
    xmlns:x="http://schemas.microsoft.com/winfx/2006/xaml"
        xmlns:local="clr-namespace:Specialized2DChartControl;
                     assembly=Specialized2DChartControl"
    Title="AreaChart" Height="300" Width="300">
    <Grid x:Name="rootGrid" SizeChanged="rootGrid_SizeChanged">
        <local:AreaControl x:Name="myAreaChart"/>
    </Grid>
</Window>
```

Here is the corresponding code-behind file for this example:

```
using System;
using System.Windows;
using System.Windows.Controls;
using System.Windows.Media;

namespace Specialized2DChartControlTest
{
    public partial class AreaChart : Window
    {
        public AreaChart()
        {
            InitializeComponent();
        }
```

```
private void rootGrid_SizeChanged(object sender, SizeChangedEventArgs e)
{
    myAreaChart.Height = rootGrid.Height;
    myAreaChart.Width = rootGrid.ActualWidth;
    AddData();
}

private void AddData()
{
    myAreaChart.DataCollection.AreaList.Clear();
    Specialized2DCharts.DataSeriesArea area =
        new Specialized2DCharts.DataSeriesArea();
    myAreaChart.ChartStyle.Title = "Area Chart";
    myAreaChart.ChartStyle.Xmin = 0;
    myAreaChart.ChartStyle.Xmax = 10;
    myAreaChart.ChartStyle.Ymin = 0;
    myAreaChart.ChartStyle.Ymax = 10;
    myAreaChart.ChartStyle.XTick = 2;
    myAreaChart.ChartStyle.YTick = 2;
    myAreaChart.ChartStyle.GridlinePattern=
        Specialized2DCharts.ChartStyleGridlines.GridlinePatternEnum.Dot;
    myAreaChart.ChartStyle.GridlineColor = Brushes.Black;

    // Add sine data:
    area = new Specialized2DCharts.DataSeriesArea();
    area.BorderColor = Brushes.Black;
    area.FillColor = Brushes.LightPink;
    for (int i = 0; i < 21; i++)
    {
        area.AreaSeries.Points.Add(
            new Point(0.5 * i, 2.0 + Math.Sin(0.5 * i)));
    }
    myAreaChart.DataCollection.AreaList.Add(area);

    // Add cosine data:
    area = new Specialized2DCharts.DataSeriesArea();
    area.BorderColor = Brushes.Black;
    area.FillColor = Brushes.LightBlue;
    for (int i = 0; i < 21; i++)
    {
        area.AreaSeries.Points.Add(
            new Point(0.5 * i, 2.0 + Math.Cos(0.5 * i)));
    }
    myAreaChart.DataCollection.AreaList.Add(area);

    // Add another sine data:
    area = new Specialized2DCharts.DataSeriesArea();
    area.BorderColor = Brushes.Black;
    area.FillColor = Brushes.LightGreen;
    for (int i = 0; i < 21; i++)
    {
        area.AreaSeries.Points.Add(
            new Point(0.5 * i, 3.0 + Math.Sin(0.5 * i)));
```

```
            }
            myAreaChart.DataCollection.AreaList.Add(area);
        }
    }
}
```

This code is very similar to that used in Chapter 6 to create area charts directly in code. Running this example produces the same result as that shown in Figure 6-14.

Polar Chart Control

In this section, I'll show you how to create the polar chart control.

Implementation

Add a new WPF User Control to the *Specialized2DChartControl* project and name it *PolarControl*. Add to the current project the *ChartStylePolar* and *DataCollectionpolar* classes from the *Specialized2DCharts* project presented in Chapter 6. When we convert the Windows application into a user control, we'll try not to change or modify these classes from the original project.

Here is the XAML file for the stem control:

```xaml
<UserControl x:Class="Specialized2DChartControl.PolarControl"
    xmlns="http://schemas.microsoft.com/winfx/2006/xaml/presentation"
    xmlns:x="http://schemas.microsoft.com/winfx/2006/xaml"
    Height="400" Width="500">
    <Grid Name="grid1" Margin="10">
        <Grid.ColumnDefinitions>
            <ColumnDefinition Width="30"/>
            <ColumnDefinition Name="column1" Width="*"/>
            <ColumnDefinition Width="30"/>
        </Grid.ColumnDefinitions>
        <Grid.RowDefinitions>
            <RowDefinition Height="30"/>
            <RowDefinition Name="row1" Height="*"/>
            <RowDefinition Height="30"/>
        </Grid.RowDefinitions>
        <Grid  Margin="0" x:Name ="chartGrid" Grid.Column="1" Grid.Row="1"
            ClipToBounds="False" Background="Transparent"
            SizeChanged="chartGrid_SizeChanged" />
        <Canvas Margin="2" Name="chartCanvas" ClipToBounds="False"
            Grid.Column="1" Grid.Row="1"/>
    </Grid>
</UserControl>
```

This XAML layout is basically the same as that used in creating a WPF Windows application for polar charts.

Next, we need to design the public interface that the bar chart control exposes to the outside world. Here, we only define necessary public properties in the control. Add the following code to the code-behind file:

```
using System;
using System.Windows;
using System.Windows.Controls;
```

377

```
using System.Windows.Media;
using Specialized2DCharts;

namespace Specialized2DChartControl
{
    public partial class PolarControl : UserControl
    {
        private ChartStylePolar cs;
        private DataCollectionPolar dc;
        private DataSeries ds;

        public PolarControl()
        {
            InitializeComponent();
            cs = new ChartStylePolar();
            dc = new DataCollectionPolar();
            ds = new DataSeries();
            cs.ChartCanvas = chartCanvas;
        }

        private void chartGrid_SizeChanged(object sender, SizeChangedEventArgs e)
        {
            double width = chartGrid.ActualWidth;
            double height = chartGrid.ActualHeight;
            double side = width;
            if (width > height)
                side = height;
            chartCanvas.Width = side;
            chartCanvas.Height = side;
            chartCanvas.Children.Clear();
            AddChart();
        }

        private void AddChart()
        {
            cs.SetPolarAxes();
            if (dc.DataList.Count != 0)
            {
                dc.AddPolar(cs);
            }
        }

        public ChartStylePolar ChartStyle
        {
            get { return cs; }
            set { cs = value; }
        }

        public DataCollectionPolar DataCollection
        {
            get { return dc; }
            set { dc = value; }
        }
```

```
        public DataSeries DataSeries
        {
            get { return ds; }
            set { ds = value; }
        }
    }
}
```

Here, we also define only three public properties, which are related directly to the *ChartStylePolar*, *DataSeries*, and *DataCollectionPolar* objects. These three properties set up an interface between the user control and original corresponding classes and allow you to access the public properties and methods inside these classes.

Creating Polar Charts

Here, I'll show you how to use the polar chart control to create polar charts. Open the *Specialized2DChartControl* project. Add a new WPF Window to the *Specialized2DChartControlTest* project and name it *PolarChart*. The layout of the example is very simple; you create it using the following XAML:

```
<Window x:Class="Specialized2DChartControlTest.PolarChart"
    xmlns="http://schemas.microsoft.com/winfx/2006/xaml/presentation"
    xmlns:x="http://schemas.microsoft.com/winfx/2006/xaml"
    xmlns:local="clr-namespace:Specialized2DChartControl;
                 assembly=Specialized2DChartControl"
    Title="PolarChart" Height="300" Width="300">
    <Grid x:Name="rootGrid" SizeChanged="rootGrid_SizeChanged">
        <local:PolarControl x:Name="myPolarChart"/>
    </Grid>
</Window>
```

Here is the corresponding code-behind file:

```
using System;
using System.Windows;
using System.Windows.Controls;
using System.Windows.Media;

namespace Specialized2DChartControlTest
{
    public partial class PolarChart : Window
    {
        public PolarChart()
        {
            InitializeComponent();
        }

        private void rootGrid_SizeChanged(object sender, SizeChangedEventArgs e)
        {
            myPolarChart.Height = rootGrid.ActualHeight;
            myPolarChart.Width = rootGrid.ActualWidth;
            AddData1();
        }
```

```
private void AddData()
{
    myPolarChart.DataCollection.DataList.Clear();
    Specialized2DCharts.DataSeries ds =
        new Specialized2DCharts.DataSeries();
    myPolarChart.ChartStyle.Rmax = 0.5;
    myPolarChart.ChartStyle.Rmin = 0;
    myPolarChart.ChartStyle.NTicks = 4;
    myPolarChart.ChartStyle.AngleStep = 30;
    myPolarChart.ChartStyle.AngleDirection=
    Specialized2DCharts.ChartStylePolar.AngleDirectionEnum.CounterClockWise;
    myPolarChart.ChartStyle.LinePattern=
        Specialized2DCharts.ChartStylePolar.LinePatternEnum.Dot;
    myPolarChart.ChartStyle.LineColor = Brushes.Black;

    ds.LineColor = Brushes.Red;
    for (int i = 0; i < 360; i++)
    {
        double theta = 1.0 * i;
        double r = Math.Abs(Math.Cos(2.0 * theta * Math.PI / 180) *
                   Math.Sin(2.0 * theta * Math.PI / 180));
        ds.LineSeries.Points.Add(new Point(theta, r));
    }
    myPolarChart.DataCollection.DataList.Add(ds);
}

private void AddData1()
{
    myPolarChart.DataCollection.DataList.Clear();
    Specialized2DCharts.DataSeries ds =
        new Specialized2DCharts.DataSeries();

    myPolarChart.ChartStyle.Rmax = 1;
    myPolarChart.ChartStyle.Rmin = -7;
    myPolarChart.ChartStyle.NTicks = 4;
    myPolarChart.ChartStyle.AngleStep = 30;
    myPolarChart.ChartStyle.AngleDirection =
    Specialized2DCharts.ChartStylePolar.AngleDirectionEnum.CounterClockWise;
    myPolarChart.ChartStyle.LinePattern =
        Specialized2DCharts.ChartStylePolar.LinePatternEnum.Dot;
    myPolarChart.ChartStyle.LineColor = Brushes.Black;

    ds= new Specialized2DCharts.DataSeries();
    ds.LineColor = Brushes.Red;
    for (int i = 0; i < 361; i++)
    {
        double theta = 1.0 * i;
        double r = Math.Log(1.001 + Math.Sin(2 * theta * Math.PI / 180));
        ds.LineSeries.Points.Add(new Point(theta, r));
    }
    myPolarChart.DataCollection.DataList.Add(ds);
```

```
        ds = new Specialized2DCharts.DataSeries();
        ds.LineColor = Brushes.Blue;
        for (int i = 0; i < 361; i++)
        {
            double theta = 1.0 * i;
            double r = Math.Log(1.001 + Math.Cos(2 * theta * Math.PI / 180));
            ds.LineSeries.Points.Add(new Point(theta, r));
        }
        myPolarChart.DataCollection.DataList.Add(ds);
    }
  }
}
```

This code is very similar to that used in Chapter 6 to create polar charts in code directly. Running this example produces the result shown in Figure 9-5.

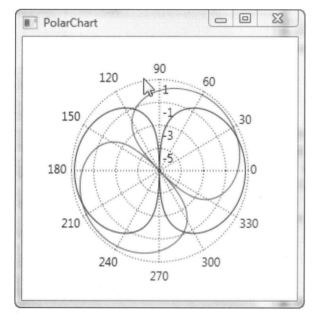

Figure 9-5. *Polar chart created using the PolarControl*

Pie Chart Control

Finally, I'll show you how to create a pie chart control.

Implementation

Add a new WPF User Control to the *Specialized2DChartControl* project and name it *PieControl*. Add to the current project the *PieStyle* and *PieLegend* classes from the *Specialized2DCharts* project presented in

Chapter 6. When we convert the Windows application into a user control, we'll try not to change or modify these classes from the original project.

Here is the XAML file for the pie chart control:

```
<UserControl x:Class="Specialized2DChartControl.PieControl"
    xmlns="http://schemas.microsoft.com/winfx/2006/xaml/presentation"
    xmlns:x="http://schemas.microsoft.com/winfx/2006/xaml"
    Height="400" Width="500">
    <Grid Name="grid1" Margin="10">
        <Grid.ColumnDefinitions>
            <ColumnDefinition Width="30"/>
            <ColumnDefinition Name="column1" Width="*"/>
            <ColumnDefinition Width="auto"/>
            <ColumnDefinition Width="30"/>
        </Grid.ColumnDefinitions>
        <Grid.RowDefinitions>
            <RowDefinition Height="30"/>
            <RowDefinition Name="row1" Height="*"/>
            <RowDefinition Height="30"/>
        </Grid.RowDefinitions>
        <Grid  Margin="0" x:Name ="chartGrid" Grid.Column="1" Grid.Row="1"
                ClipToBounds="False" Background="Transparent"
                SizeChanged="chartGrid_SizeChanged" />
        <Canvas Margin="0,0,0,20" Name="chartCanvas" ClipToBounds="False"
                Grid.Column="1" Grid.Row="1"/>
        <Canvas Margin="2" Name="legendCanvas" Grid.Column="2"
                Grid.Row="1" HorizontalAlignment="Left"/>
    </Grid>
</UserControl>
```

This XAML layout is basically the same as that used in creating a WPF Windows application for pie charts.

Next, we need to design the public interface that the pie chart control exposes to the outside world. Here, we only define necessary public properties in the control. Add the following code to the code-behind file:

```
using System;
using System.Windows;
using System.Windows.Controls;
using Specialized2DCharts;

namespace Specialized2DChartControl
{
    public partial class PieControl : UserControl
    {
        private PieStyle ps;
        private PieLegend pl;

        public PieControl()
        {
            InitializeComponent();
            ps = new PieStyle();
            pl = new PieLegend();
        }
```

```
private void chartGrid_SizeChanged(object sender, SizeChangedEventArgs e)
{
    double width = chartGrid.ActualWidth;
    double height = chartGrid.ActualHeight;
    double side = width;
    if (width > height)
        side = height;
    chartCanvas.Width = side;
    chartCanvas.Height = side;
    chartCanvas.Children.Clear();
    legendCanvas.Children.Clear();
    AddChart();
}

private void AddChart()
{
    if (ps.DataList.Count != 0)
    {
        ps.AddPie(chartCanvas);
        if (pl.IsLegendVisible)
        {
            pl.AddLegend(legendCanvas, ps);
        }
    }
}

public PieStyle PieStyle
{
    get { return ps; }
    set { ps = value; }
}

public PieLegend PieLegend
{
    get { return pl; }
    set { pl = value; }
}
    }
}
```

Here, we also define only two public properties, which are related directly to the *PieStyle* and *PieLegend* objects. These two properties set up an interface between the user control and the original corresponding classes and allow you to access the public properties and methods inside these classes.

Creating Pie Charts

Here, I'll show you how to use the pie chart control to create pie charts. Open the *Specialized2DChartControl* project. Add a new WPF Window to the *Specialized2DChartControlTest* project and name it *PieChart*. The layout of the example is very simple; you create it using the following XAML:

```
<Window x:Class="Specialized2DChartControlTest.PieChart"
```

```xml
    xmlns="http://schemas.microsoft.com/winfx/2006/xaml/presentation"
    xmlns:x="http://schemas.microsoft.com/winfx/2006/xaml"
    xmlns:local="clr-namespace:Specialized2DChartControl;
                 assembly=Specialized2DChartControl"
    Title="PieChart" Height="300" Width="400">
    <Grid x:Name="rootGrid" SizeChanged="rootGrid_SizeChanged">
        <local:PieControl x:Name="myPieChart"/>
    </Grid>
</Window>
```

Here is the corresponding code-behind file:

```csharp
using System;
using System.Collections.Generic;
using System.Windows;
using System.Windows.Controls;

namespace Specialized2DChartControlTest
{
    public partial class PieChart : Window
    {
        public PieChart()
        {
            InitializeComponent();
        }

        private void rootGrid_SizeChanged(object sender, SizeChangedEventArgs e)
        {
            myPieChart.Height = rootGrid.ActualHeight;
            myPieChart.Width = rootGrid.ActualWidth;
            AddData();
        }

        private void AddData()
        {
            myPieChart.PieStyle = new Specialized2DCharts.PieStyle();
            myPieChart.PieLegend = new Specialized2DCharts.PieLegend();
            double[] data = new double[] { 30, 35, 15, 10, 8 };
            int[] explode = new int[] { 20, 0, 20, 0, 0 };
            string[] labels = new string[] { "Soc. Sec. Tax", "Income Tax",
                            "Borrowing", "Corp. Tax", "Misc." };
            for (int i = 0; i < data.Length; i++)
            {
                myPieChart.PieStyle.DataList.Add(data[i]);
                myPieChart.PieStyle.ExplodeList.Add(explode[i]);
                myPieChart.PieStyle.LabelList.Add(labels[i]);
            }
            myPieChart.PieStyle.ColormapBrushes.ColormapBrushType=
                Specialized2DCharts.ColormapBrush.ColormapBrushEnum.Summer;
            myPieChart.PieLegend.IsLegendVisible = true;
        }
    }
}
```

This code is very similar to that used in Chapter 6 to create pie charts directly in code. Running this example generates the output shown in Figure 9-6.

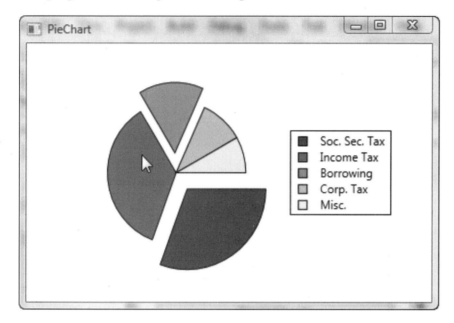

Figure 9-6. Pie chart created using the PieControl

Creating Multiple Charts

In the previous sections, we discussed a variety of specialized chart controls and demonstrated how to use them in WPF applications. In practice, you can also use different chart controls in a single WPF application. Here, I'll show you how to accomplish this.

Open the *Specialized2DChartControl* project. Add a new WPF Window to the *Specialized2DChartControlTest* project and name it *MultipleCharts*. The layout of the example is very simple; you create it using the following XAML:

```
<Window x:Class="Specialized2DChartControlTest.MultipleCharts"
    xmlns="http://schemas.microsoft.com/winfx/2006/xaml/presentation"
    xmlns:x="http://schemas.microsoft.com/winfx/2006/xaml"
    xmlns:local="clr-namespace:Specialized2DChartControl;
            assembly=Specialized2DChartControl"
    Title="MultipleCharts" Height="700" Width="550">
    <Grid>
        <Grid.ColumnDefinitions>
            <ColumnDefinition/>
            <ColumnDefinition/>
        </Grid.ColumnDefinitions>
        <Grid.RowDefinitions>
            <RowDefinition/>
            <RowDefinition/>
```

```
            <RowDefinition/>
        </Grid.RowDefinitions>

        <Grid x:Name="grid1" SizeChanged="grid1_SizeChanged"
              Grid.Column="0" Grid.Row="0">
            <local:StemControl x:Name="chart1"/>
        </Grid>
        <Grid x:Name="grid2" SizeChanged="grid2_SizeChanged"
              Grid.Column="1" Grid.Row="0">
            <local:StairstepControl x:Name="chart2"/>
        </Grid>
        <Grid x:Name="grid3" SizeChanged="grid3_SizeChanged"
              Grid.Column="0" Grid.Row="1">
            <local:AreaControl x:Name="chart3"/>
        </Grid>
        <Grid x:Name="grid4" SizeChanged="grid4_SizeChanged"
              Grid.Column="1" Grid.Row="1">
            <local:ErrorbarsControl x:Name="chart4"/>
        </Grid>
        <Grid x:Name="grid5" SizeChanged="grid5_SizeChanged"
              Grid.Column="0" Grid.Row="2">
            <local:BarControl x:Name="chart5"/>
        </Grid>
        <Grid x:Name="grid6" SizeChanged="grid6_SizeChanged"
              Grid.Column="1" Grid.Row="2">
            <local:PolarControl x:Name="chart6"/>
        </Grid>
    </Grid>
</Window>
```

Here, we create six charts using six different chart controls. Here is the corresponding code-behind file:

```
using System;
using System.Windows;
using System.Windows.Controls;
using System.Windows.Media;

namespace Specialized2DChartControlTest
{
    public partial class MultipleCharts : Window
    {
        public MultipleCharts()
        {
            InitializeComponent();
        }

        private void grid1_SizeChanged(object sender, SizeChangedEventArgs e)
        {
            chart1.Width = grid1.ActualWidth;
            chart1.Height = grid1.ActualHeight;
            AddData1();
        }
```

```
private void grid2_SizeChanged(object sender, SizeChangedEventArgs e)
{
    chart2.Width = grid2.ActualWidth;
    chart2.Height = grid2.ActualHeight;
    AddData2();
}


private void grid3_SizeChanged(object sender, SizeChangedEventArgs e)
{
    chart3.Width = grid3.ActualWidth;
    chart3.Height = grid3.ActualHeight;
    AddData3();
}

private void grid4_SizeChanged(object sender, SizeChangedEventArgs e)
{
    chart4.Width = grid4.ActualWidth;
    chart4.Height = grid4.ActualHeight;
    AddData4();
}

private void grid5_SizeChanged(object sender, SizeChangedEventArgs e)
{
    chart5.Width = grid5.ActualWidth;
    chart5.Height = grid5.ActualHeight;
    AddData5();
}

private void grid6_SizeChanged(object sender, SizeChangedEventArgs e)
{
    chart6.Width = grid6.ActualWidth;
    chart6.Height = grid6.ActualHeight;
    AddData6();
}

 private void AddData1()
{
    chart1.DataCollection.DataList.Clear();
    Specialized2DCharts.DataSeries ds =
        new Specialized2DCharts.DataSeries();
    chart1.ChartStyle.Title = "Stem Chart";
    chart1.ChartStyle.Xmin = 0;
    chart1.ChartStyle.Xmax = 8;
    chart1.ChartStyle.Ymin = -1.5;
    chart1.ChartStyle.Ymax = 1.5;
    chart1.ChartStyle.XTick = 1;
    chart1.ChartStyle.YTick = 0.5;
    chart1.ChartStyle.GridlinePattern =
        Specialized2DCharts.ChartStyleGridlines.GridlinePatternEnum.Dot;
    chart1.ChartStyle.GridlineColor = Brushes.Black;

    // Generate the stair step data:
```

```
        for (int i = 0; i < 50; i++)
        {
            ds.LineSeries.Points.Add(new Point(0.4 * i, Math.Sin(0.4 * i)));
        }
        ds.LineColor = Brushes.Red;
        ds.Symbols.SymbolType =
            Specialized2DCharts.Symbols.SymbolTypeEnum.Diamond;
        ds.Symbols.FillColor = Brushes.Yellow;
        ds.Symbols.BorderColor = Brushes.DarkGreen;
        chart1.DataCollection.DataList.Add(ds);
    }

    private void AddData2()
    {
        chart2.DataCollection.DataList.Clear();
        chart2.ChartStyle.Title = "Stair Step Chart";
        Specialized2DCharts.DataSeriesStairstep ds =
            new Specialized2DCharts.DataSeriesStairstep();
        chart2.ChartStyle.Xmin = 0;
        chart2.ChartStyle.Xmax = 8;
        chart2.ChartStyle.Ymin = -1.5;
        chart2.ChartStyle.Ymax = 1.5;
        chart2.ChartStyle.XTick = 1;
        chart2.ChartStyle.YTick = 0.5;
        chart2.ChartStyle.GridlinePattern =
            Specialized2DCharts.ChartStyleGridlines.GridlinePatternEnum.Dot;
        chart2.ChartStyle.GridlineColor = Brushes.Black;

        // Draw the stair step chart:
        ds.StairstepLineColor = Brushes.Red;
        for (int i = 0; i < 50; i++)
        {
            ds.LineSeries.Points.Add(new Point(0.4 * i, Math.Sin(0.4 * i)));
        }
        ds.LineColor = Brushes.Black;
        ds.LinePattern = Specialized2DCharts.DataSeries.LinePatternEnum.Dash;
        ds.Symbols.SymbolType =
            Specialized2DCharts.Symbols.SymbolTypeEnum.Circle;
        chart2.DataCollection.DataList.Add(ds);
    }

    private void AddData3()
    {
        chart3.DataCollection.AreaList.Clear();
        Specialized2DCharts.DataSeriesArea area =
            new Specialized2DCharts.DataSeriesArea();
        chart3.ChartStyle.Title = "Area Chart";
        chart3.ChartStyle.Xmin = 0;
        chart3.ChartStyle.Xmax = 10;
        chart3.ChartStyle.Ymin = 0;
        chart3.ChartStyle.Ymax = 10;
        chart3.ChartStyle.XTick = 2;
        chart3.ChartStyle.YTick = 2;
```

```
        chart3.ChartStyle.GridlinePattern =
            Specialized2DCharts.ChartStyleGridlines.GridlinePatternEnum.Dot;
        chart3.ChartStyle.GridlineColor = Brushes.Black;

        // Add sine data:
        area = new Specialized2DCharts.DataSeriesArea();
        area.BorderColor = Brushes.Black;
        area.FillColor = Brushes.LightPink;
        for (int i = 0; i < 21; i++)
        {
            area.AreaSeries.Points.Add(
                new Point(0.5 * i, 2.0 + Math.Sin(0.5 * i)));
        }
        chart3.DataCollection.AreaList.Add(area);

        // Add cosine data:
        area = new Specialized2DCharts.DataSeriesArea();
        area.BorderColor = Brushes.Black;
        area.FillColor = Brushes.LightBlue;
        for (int i = 0; i < 21; i++)
        {
            area.AreaSeries.Points.Add(
                new Point(0.5 * i, 2.0 + Math.Cos(0.5 * i)));
        }
        chart3.DataCollection.AreaList.Add(area);

        // Add another sine data:
        area = new Specialized2DCharts.DataSeriesArea();
        area.BorderColor = Brushes.Black;
        area.FillColor = Brushes.LightGreen;
        for (int i = 0; i < 21; i++)
        {
            area.AreaSeries.Points.Add(
                new Point(0.5 * i, 3.0 + Math.Sin(0.5 * i)));
        }
        chart3.DataCollection.AreaList.Add(area);
    }

    private void AddData4()
    {
        chart4.DataCollection.DataList.Clear();
        chart4.DataCollection.ErrorList.Clear();
        Specialized2DCharts.DataSeriesErrorbar ds =
            new Specialized2DCharts.DataSeriesErrorbar();
        chart4.ChartStyle.Title = "Error Bar Chart";
        chart4.ChartStyle.Xmin = 0;
        chart4.ChartStyle.Xmax = 12;
        chart4.ChartStyle.Ymin = -1;
        chart4.ChartStyle.Ymax = 6;
        chart4.ChartStyle.XTick = 2;
        chart4.ChartStyle.YTick = 1;
        chart4.ChartStyle.GridlinePattern =
            Specialized2DCharts.ChartStyleGridlines.GridlinePatternEnum.Dot;
```

```
        chart4.ChartStyle.GridlineColor = Brushes.Black;
        ds.LineColor = Brushes.Blue;
        ds.Symbols.SymbolType =
            Specialized2DCharts.Symbols.SymbolTypeEnum.Circle;
        ds.Symbols.BorderColor = Brushes.DarkGreen;
        ds.ErrorLineColor = Brushes.Red;

        for (int i = 2; i < 22; i++)
        {
            ds.LineSeries.Points.Add(
                new Point(0.5 * i, 10.0 * Math.Exp(-0.5 * i)));
            ds.ErrorLineSeries.Points.Add(new Point(0.5 * i, 3.0 / (0.5 * i)));
        }
        chart4.DataCollection.DataList.Add(ds);
    }

    private void AddData5()
    {
        chart5.DataCollection.DataList.Clear();
        Specialized2DCharts.DataSeriesBar ds =
            new Specialized2DCharts.DataSeriesBar();
        chart5.DataCollection.BarType =
            Specialized2DCharts.DataCollectionBar.BarTypeEnum.Vertical;
        chart5.ChartStyle.Title = "Bar Chart";
        chart5.ChartStyle.Xmin = 0;
        chart5.ChartStyle.Xmax = 5;
        chart5.ChartStyle.Ymin = 0;
        chart5.ChartStyle.Ymax = 10;
        chart5.ChartStyle.XTick = 1;
        chart5.ChartStyle.YTick = 2;
        chart5.ChartStyle.GridlinePattern =
            Specialized2DCharts.ChartStyleGridlines.GridlinePatternEnum.Dot;
        chart5.ChartStyle.GridlineColor = Brushes.Black;

        // Add the first bar series:
        ds = new Specialized2DCharts.DataSeriesBar();
        ds.BorderColor = Brushes.Red;
        ds.FillColor = Brushes.Green;
        ds.BarWidth = 0.9;

        for (int i = 0; i < 5; i++)
        {
            double x = i + 1.0;
            double y = 2.0 * x;
            ds.LineSeries.Points.Add(new Point(x, y));
        }
        chart5.DataCollection.DataList.Add(ds);

        // Add the second bar series:
        ds = new Specialized2DCharts.DataSeriesBar();
        ds.BorderColor = Brushes.Red;
        ds.FillColor = Brushes.Yellow;
        ds.BarWidth = 0.9;
```

```
        for (int i = 0; i < 5; i++)
        {
            double x = i + 1.0;
            double y = 1.5 * x;
            ds.LineSeries.Points.Add(new Point(x, y));
        }
        chart5.DataCollection.DataList.Add(ds);

        // Add the third bar series:
        ds = new Specialized2DCharts.DataSeriesBar();
        ds.BorderColor = Brushes.Red;
        ds.FillColor = Brushes.Blue;
        ds.BarWidth = 0.9;

        for (int i = 0; i < 5; i++)
        {
            double x = i + 1.0;
            double y = 1.0 * x;
            ds.LineSeries.Points.Add(new Point(x, y));
        }
        chart5.DataCollection.DataList.Add(ds);
        chart5.DataCollection.AddBars(chart5.ChartStyle);
    }

    private void AddData6()
    {
        chart6.DataCollection.DataList.Clear();
        Specialized2DCharts.DataSeries ds =
            new Specialized2DCharts.DataSeries();
        chart6.ChartStyle.Rmax = 0.5;
        chart6.ChartStyle.Rmin = 0;
        chart6.ChartStyle.NTicks = 4;
        chart6.ChartStyle.AngleStep = 30;
        chart6.ChartStyle.AngleDirection =
            Specialized2DCharts.ChartStylePolar.
            AngleDirectionEnum.CounterClockWise;
        chart6.ChartStyle.LinePattern =
            Specialized2DCharts.ChartStylePolar.LinePatternEnum.Dot;
        chart6.ChartStyle.LineColor = Brushes.Black;
        ds.LineColor = Brushes.Red;
        for (int i = 0; i < 360; i++)
        {
            double theta = 1.0 * i;
            double r = Math.Abs(Math.Cos(2.0 * theta * Math.PI / 180) *
                       Math.Sin(2.0 * theta * Math.PI / 180));
            ds.LineSeries.Points.Add(new Point(theta, r));
        }
        chart6.DataCollection.DataList.Add(ds);
    }
  }
}
```

You should be familiar with the preceding code because we implemented it earlier when we created each individual chart control. Figure 9-7 shows the results of running this example.

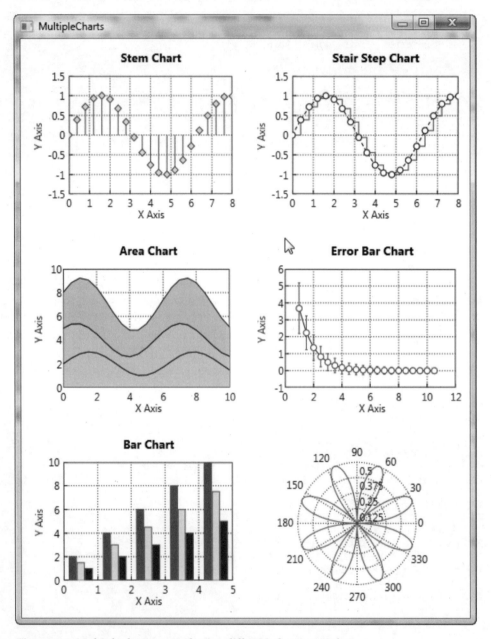

Figure 9-7. Multiple charts created using different chart controls

■ ■ ■

CHAPTER 10

Data Interpolations

In numerical analysis, interpolation is a method of constructing new data points within the range of a discrete set of known data points. In science and engineering, we often will have a number of data points obtained by sampling and experimentation, and we must try to construct a function that closely fits those data points. This process is usually called *curve fitting* or *regression analysis*. Interpolation can be regarded as a special case of curve fitting in which the function must pass exactly through the data points. This implicitly assumes that the given data points in an interpolation are accurate and distinct.

Suppose that a function $y = f(x)$ is given only at discrete points such as (x_0, y_0), (x_1, y_1), ..., (x_n, y_n). The purpose of interpolation is to find the y value at any other point of x besides the ones provided. In this chapter, we will present some popular methods for interpolating the function $y = f(x)$. Most interpolation methods are based on the Taylor series expansion of a function $f(x)$ about a specific value of x_0. Each method manipulates the Taylor series differently to yield the interpolation algorithm.

Linear Interpolation

Linear interpolation is a simple method of curve fitting based on linear polynomials. It is widely used in numerical analysis and computer graphics.

Algorithm

As shown in Figure 10-1, if two known points are given by (x_0, y_0) and (x_1, y_1), the linear interpolation is the straight line between these two points. For any value of x in the range (x_0, x_1), the corresponding y value along the straight line can be found by the following relationship:

$$y = y_0 + (x - x_0)\frac{y_1 - y_0}{x_1 - x_0}$$

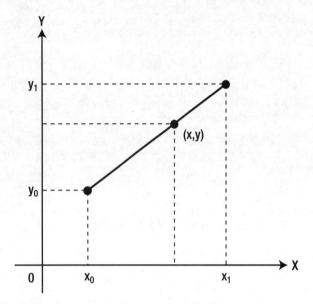

Figure 10-1. *Linear interpolation: Given two points (x_0, y_0) and (x_1, y_1), the line between these two points is the result of the linear interpolation.*

The linear interpolation on a set of data points (x_0, y_0), (x_1, y_1), ..., (x_n, y_n) is defined as the concatenation of linear interpolants between pairs of data points. This results in a continuous curve with a discontinuous derivative.

Implementation

Here, we'll implement the linear interpolation. Start with a new WPF Windows application and name it *Interpolation*. Add a new class, *InterpolationAlgorithms*, to the project. Here is the code listing for this class:

```
using System;
using System.Collections.Generic;

namespace Interpolation
{
    public class InterpolationAlgorithms
    {
        public static double Linear(double[] xarray, double[] yarray, double x)
        {
            double y = double.NaN;
            for (int i = 0; i < xarray.Length - 1; i++)
            {
                if (x >= xarray[i] && x < xarray[i + 1])
                {
                    y = yarray[i] + (x - xarray[i]) * (yarray[i + 1] - yarray[i]) /
                        (xarray[i + 1] - xarray[i]);
```

```
            }
        }
        return y;
    }

    public static double[] Linear(double[] xarray, double[] yarray, double[] x)
    {
        double[] y = new double[x.Length];
        for (int i = 0; i < x.Length; i++)
            y[i] = Linear(xarray, yarray, x[i]);
        return y;
    }
    }
}
```

Here, we implement a static overloaded method, *Linear*. The *xarray* and *yarray* are the sets of *x* and *y* data, which present a set of given data points. The *Linear* method will find a single *y* value or a *y* array at the input *x* (a double value or double array), depending on the input variable *x*.

Testing Linear Interpolation

You can easily perform linear interpolations using the *Linear* method that we implemented in the *InterpolationAlgorithms* class. The results can be displayed using the line chart control presented in the previous chapter. To achieve this, you need to add the line chart control to the current project's References. Right-click References in the Solution Explorer and select Add Reference... to bring up the Add Reference window. Then click the Browse tab to navigate to the directory where the *LineChartControl* project is located. Go to the bin\Debug subdirectory and select *LineChartControl.dll*. This process adds the line chart control to the References of your current project so that you can use the control in your current application.

Add a new WPF Window to the current project and name it *LinearInterpolation*. Here is the XAML layout of this example:

```
<Window x:Class="Interpolation.LinearInterpolation"
    xmlns="http://schemas.microsoft.com/winfx/2006/xaml/presentation"
    xmlns:x="http://schemas.microsoft.com/winfx/2006/xaml"
    xmlns:chart="clr-namespace:LineChartControl;assembly=LineChartControl"
    Title="LinearInterpolation" Height="300" Width="300">
    <Grid x:Name="rootGrid" SizeChanged="rootGrid_SizeChanged">
        <chart:LineChartControlLib x:Name="myChart" Title="Linear Interpolation"
                Xmin="0" Xmax="7" Ymin="-1.5" Ymax="1.5" XTick="1" YTick="0.5"/>
    </Grid>
</Window>
```

This XAML file simply creates a line chart control named *myChart*, which will be used to display the results of the linear interpolation. Here is the corresponding code-behind file:

```
using System;
using System.Windows;
using System.Windows.Controls;
using System.Windows.Media;

namespace Interpolation
{
    public partial class LinearInterpolation : Window
```

```
{
    public LinearInterpolation()
    {
        InitializeComponent();
    }

    private void rootGrid_SizeChanged(object sender, SizeChangedEventArgs e)
    {
        myChart.Width = rootGrid.ActualWidth;
        myChart.Height = rootGrid.ActualHeight;
        AddData();
    }

    private void AddData()
    {
        double[] x0 = new double[8];
        double[] y0 = new double[8];
        double[] x = new double[70];

        for (int i = 0; i < x0.Length; i++)
        {
            x0[i] = 1.0 * i;
            y0[i] = Math.Sin(x0[i]);
        }

        for (int i = 0; i < x.Length; i++)
        {
            x[i] = i / 10.0;
        }

        double[] y = InterpolationAlgorithms.Linear(x0, y0, x);

        myChart.DataCollection.DataList.Clear();

        // plot interpolated data:
        LineCharts.DataSeries ds = new LineCharts.DataSeries();
        ds.LineColor = Brushes.Transparent;
        ds.SeriesName = "Interpolated";
        ds.Symbols.SymbolType = LineCharts.Symbols.SymbolTypeEnum.Dot;
        ds.Symbols.SymbolSize = 3;
        ds.Symbols.BorderColor = Brushes.Red;
        for (int i = 0; i < x.Length; i++)
        {
            ds.LineSeries.Points.Add(new Point(x[i], y[i]));
        }
        myChart.DataCollection.DataList.Add(ds);

        // Plot original data
        ds = new LineCharts.DataSeries();
        ds.LineColor = Brushes.Transparent;
        ds.SeriesName = "Original";
        ds.Symbols.SymbolType = LineCharts.Symbols.SymbolTypeEnum.Diamond;
        ds.Symbols.BorderColor = Brushes.DarkBlue;
```

```
        for (int i = 0; i < xO.Length; i++)
        {
            ds.LineSeries.Points.Add(new Point(xO[i], yO[i]));
        }
        myChart.DataCollection.DataList.Add(ds);
        myChart.IsLegend = true;
        myChart.LegendPosition = LineCharts.Legend.LegendPositionEnum.NorthEast;
    }
  }
}
```

Here, we take eight original data points from a sine function and interpolate 70 data points linearly within the original data points using the following statement:

```
double[] y = InterpolationAlgorithms.Linear(xO, yO, x);
```

Here, you provide the *x* and *y* arrays of the original data and a given *x* array of the data to be interpolated as inputs of the *Linear* method. The method will return the interpolated *y* data array.

Running this example generates the result shown in Figure 10-2. You can see from the figure that the data points interpolated between two adjacent points of the original data form a straight line segment, as expected.

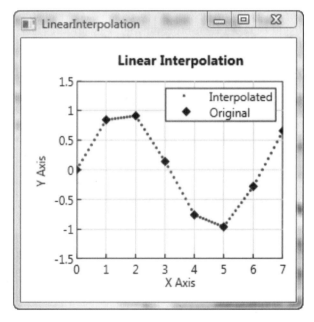

Figure 10-2. Results created using Linear interpolation

Lagrange Interpolation

Lagrange interpolation is a well-known, classic technique for interpolation. Sometimes, Lagrange interpolation is also called *polynomial interpolation*. In the first-order approximation, Lagrange interpolation reduces to linear interpolation, which we discussed in the previous section.

Algorithm

For a given set of $n + 1$ data points (x_0, y_0), (x_1, y_1), ..., (x_n, y_n), where no two x_i are the same, the interpolation polynomial in the Lagrange form is the linear combination

$$y = f(x) = \sum_{i=0}^{n} l_i(x) f(x_i)$$

where

$$l_i(x) = \prod_{j=0, j \neq i}^{n} \frac{x - x_j}{x_i - x_j} = \frac{(x - x_0) \cdots (x - x_{i-1})(x - x_{i+1}) \cdots (x - x_n)}{(x_i - x_0) \cdots (x_i - x_{i-1})(x_i - x_{i+1}) \cdots (x_i - x_n)}$$

From the numerator of this definition, you can see that $l_i(x)$ is an nth-order polynomial with zeros at all of the sample points except the nth.

Implementation

Here, we'll implement the Lagrange interpolation. Add a new public static method, *Lagrangian*, to the *InterpolationAlgorithms* class:

```
public static double Lagrangian(double[] xarray, double[] yarray, double x)
{
    double y = 0.0;
    double product = yarray[0];
    for (int i = 0; i < xarray.Length; i++)
    {
        product = yarray[i];
        for (int j = 0; j < xarray.Length; j++)
        {
            if (i != j)
            {
                product *= (x - xarray[j]) / (xarray[i] - xarray[j]);
            }
        }
        y += product;
    }
    return y;
}

public static double[] Lagrangian(double[] xarray, double[] yarray, double[] x)
{
    double[] y = new double[x.Length];
```

```
for (int i = 0; i < x.Length; i++)
    y[i] = Lagrangian(xarray, yarray, x[i]);
return y;
}
```

Here, we implement a public static overloaded method, *Lagrangian*. The *xarray* and *yarray* are the sets of *x* and *y* data that present a set of given data points. The *Lagrangian* method will find a single *y* value or a *y* array at the input *x* (a double value or double array), depending on the input variable *x*.

Testing Lagrange Interpolation

You can easily perform Lagrange interpolation using the *Lagrange* method implemented in the *InterpolationAlgorithms* class. The results can be displayed using the line chart control presented in the previous chapter.

Add a new WPF Window to the current project and name it *LagrangeInterpolation*. Here is the XAML layout of this example:

```
<Window x:Class="Interpolation.LagrangeInterpolation"
    xmlns="http://schemas.microsoft.com/winfx/2006/xaml/presentation"
    xmlns:x="http://schemas.microsoft.com/winfx/2006/xaml"
    xmlns:chart="clr-namespace:LineChartControl;assembly=LineChartControl"
    Title="LagrangeInterpolation" Height="300" Width="300">
    <Grid x:Name="rootGrid" SizeChanged="rootGrid_SizeChanged">
        <chart:LineChartControlLib x:Name="myChart" Title="Lagrange Interpolation"
                Xmin="0" Xmax="7" Ymin="-1.5" Ymax="1.5" XTick="1" YTick="0.5"/>
    </Grid>
</Window>
```

This XAML file simply creates a line chart control named *myChart*, which will be used to display the results of the Lagrange interpolation. Here is the corresponding code-behind file:

```
using System;
using System.Windows;
using System.Windows.Controls;
using System.Windows.Media;

namespace Interpolation
{
    public partial class LagrangeInterpolation : Window
    {
        public LagrangeInterpolation()
        {
            InitializeComponent();
        }

        private void rootGrid_SizeChanged(object sender, SizeChangedEventArgs e)
        {
            myChart.Width = rootGrid.ActualWidth;
            myChart.Height = rootGrid.ActualHeight;
            AddData();
        }

        private void AddData()
        {
```

```
double[] x0 = new double[8];
double[] y0 = new double[8];
double[] x = new double[70];

for (int i = 0; i < x0.Length; i++)
{
    x0[i] = 1.0 * i;
    y0[i] = Math.Sin(x0[i]);
}

for (int i = 0; i < x.Length; i++)
{
    x[i] = i / 10.0;
}

double[] y = InterpolationAlgorithms.Lagrangian(x0, y0, x);

myChart.DataCollection.DataList.Clear();

// plot interpolated data:
LineCharts.DataSeries ds = new LineCharts.DataSeries();
ds.LineColor = Brushes.Transparent;
ds.SeriesName = "Interpolated";
ds.Symbols.SymbolType = LineCharts.Symbols.SymbolTypeEnum.Dot;
ds.Symbols.SymbolSize = 3;
ds.Symbols.BorderColor = Brushes.Red;
for (int i = 0; i < x.Length; i++)
{
    ds.LineSeries.Points.Add(new Point(x[i], y[i]));
}
myChart.DataCollection.DataList.Add(ds);

// Plot original data
ds = new LineCharts.DataSeries();
ds.LineColor = Brushes.Transparent;
ds.SeriesName = "Original";
ds.Symbols.SymbolType = LineCharts.Symbols.SymbolTypeEnum.Diamond;
ds.Symbols.BorderColor = Brushes.DarkBlue;
for (int i = 0; i < x0.Length; i++)
{
    ds.LineSeries.Points.Add(new Point(x0[i], y0[i]));
}
myChart.DataCollection.DataList.Add(ds);
myChart.IsLegend = true;
myChart.LegendPosition = LineCharts.Legend.LegendPositionEnum.NorthEast;
        }
    }
}
```

This file is similar to that used in the previous example, involving linear interpolation. Here, we also take eight original data points from a sine function and try to interpolate 70 data points within the original data points using the following statement to perform a Lagrange interpolation:

```
double[] y = InterpolationAlgorithms.Lagrangian(x0, y0, x);
```

Here, you provide the *x* and *y* arrays of the original data and a given *x* array of the data to be interpolated as inputs of the *Lagrangian* method, and the method will return the interpolated *y* data array.

Running this example generates the result shown in Figure 10-3. You can see from the figure that compared to linear interpolation, the interpolated result of the *Lagrange* method is much closer to the real sine function.

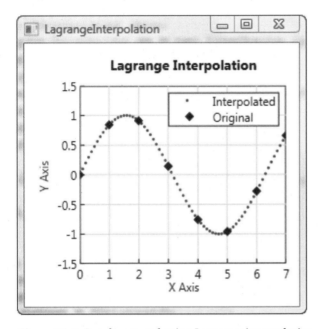

Figure 10-3. Results created using Lagrange interpolation

Barycentric Interpolation

The Lagrange interpolation just discussed requires recomputing all of the terms for each distinct *x* value, meaning this method can be applied only for small-*n* case. There are several shortcomings associated with Lagrange interpolation:

- Each evaluation of $f(x)$ requires $O(n^2)$ additions and multiplications.
- Adding a new data point (x_{n+1}, y_{n+1}) requires a new computation from scratch.
- The computation is numerically unstable.

In order to improve the Lagrange method, we can rearrange the terms in the equation of the Lagrange interpolation by defining weight functions that do not depend on the interpolated value of *x*.

Algorithm

Let's introduce the quantity

$$l(x) = (x - x_0)(x - x_1)\cdots(x - x_n)$$

We can then rearrange the Lagrange basis polynomial as

$$l_i(x) = \frac{l(x)}{x - x_i} \frac{1}{\prod_{j=0, j \ne i}^{n}(x_i - x_j)}$$

We can define the barycentric weight function:

$$w_i = \frac{1}{\prod_{j=0, j \ne i}^{n}(x_i - x_j)}$$

Then, we can simply write

$$l_i(x) = l(x)\frac{w_i}{x - x_i}$$

which is usually referred to as the *barycentric interpolation formula*. The advantage of this representation is that the interpolation polynomial may now be evaluated as

$$y = f(x) = l(x)\sum_{i=0}^{n}\frac{w_i}{x - x_i}f(x_i)$$

Now, if the weight function w_i has been precomputed, the barycentric interpolation method requires only $O(n)$ operations, as opposed to the $O(n^2)$ operations required to evaluate the Lagrange-basis polynomials of $l_i(x)$ individually.

Implementation

Here, we'll implement the barycentric interpolation. Add a new public static method, *Barycentric*, to the *InterpolationAlgorithms* class:

```
public static double Barycentric(double[] xarray, double[] yarray, double x)
{
    double product;
    double dx;
    double c1 = 0;
    double c2 = 0;
    int n = xarray.Length;
    double[] wt = new double[n];
    for (int i = 0; i < n; i++)
    {
        product = 1;
```

```
        for (int j = 0; j < n; j++)
        {
            if (i != j)
            {
                product *= (xarray[i] - xarray[j]);
                wt[i] = 1.0 / product;
            }
        }
    }
    for (int i = 0; i < n; i++)
    {
        dx = wt[i] / (x - xarray[i]);
        c1 += yarray[i] * dx;
        c2 += dx;
    }
    return c1 / c2;
}

public static double[] Barycentric(double[] xarray, double[] yarray, double[] x)
{
    double[] y = new double[x.Length];
    for (int i = 0; i < x.Length; i++)
        y[i] = Barycentric(xarray, yarray, x[i]);
    return y;
}
```

Here, we implement a static overloaded method, *Barycentric*. The *xarray* and *yarray* are the sets of *x* and *y* data that present a set of given data points. The *Barycentric* method returns a single *y* value or a *y* array at the input *x* (a double value or double array), depending on the input variable *x*.

Testing Barycentric interpolation

You can easily perform a barycentric interpolation using the *Barycentric* method implemented in the *InterpolationAlgorithms* class. You can display the results using the line chart control presented in the previous chapter.

Add a new WPF Window to the current project and name it *BarycentricInterpolation*. Here is the XAML layout of this example:

```
<Window x:Class="Interpolation.BarycentricInterpolation"
    xmlns="http://schemas.microsoft.com/winfx/2006/xaml/presentation"
    xmlns:x="http://schemas.microsoft.com/winfx/2006/xaml"
    xmlns:chart="clr-namespace:LineChartControl;assembly=LineChartControl"
    Title="Barycentric Interpolation" Height="300" Width="300">
    <Grid x:Name="rootGrid" SizeChanged="rootGrid_SizeChanged">
        <chart:LineChartControlLib x:Name="myChart"
                Title="Barycentric Interpolation"
                Xmin="-1" Xmax="1" XTick="0.5" Ymin="-3" Ymax="2" YTick="1"/>
    </Grid>
</Window>
```

This XAML simply creates a line chart control named *myChart*, which will be used to display the results of the barycentric interpolation. Here is the corresponding code-behind file:

```
using System;
using System.Windows;
using System.Windows.Controls;
using System.Windows.Media;

namespace Interpolation
{
    public partial class BarycentricInterpolation : Window
    {
        public BarycentricInterpolation()
        {
            InitializeComponent();
        }

        private void rootGrid_SizeChanged(object sender, SizeChangedEventArgs e)
        {
            myChart.Width = rootGrid.ActualWidth;
            myChart.Height = rootGrid.ActualHeight;
            AddData();
        }

        private void AddData()
        {
            double[] x0 = new double[15];
            double[] y0 = new double[15];
            double[] xe = new double[101];
            double[] ye = new double[101];

            double[] x = new double[31];


            for (int i = 0; i < x0.Length; i++)
            {
                x0[i] = Math.Round(-1.2 + i / 5.0, 3);
                y0[i] =
                    Math.Round(Math.Sin(8*x0[i]) + 0.5 * x0[i] - x0[i] * x0[i], 2);
            }

            for (int i = 0; i < xe.Length; i++)
            {
                xe[i] = Math.Round(-1.0 + i / 50.0, 3);
                ye[i] =
                    Math.Round(Math.Sin(8*xe[i]) + 0.5 * xe[i] - xe[i] * xe[i], 2);
            }

            for (int i = 0; i < x.Length; i++)
            {
                x[i] = Math.Round(-1.0 + i / 15.0, 3);
            }

            double[] y = InterpolationAlgorithms.Lagrangian(x0, y0, x);

            myChart.DataCollection.DataList.Clear();
```

```
        LineCharts.DataSeries ds;

        // Plot exact data:
        ds = new LineCharts.DataSeries();
        ds.LineColor = Brushes.DarkGreen;
        ds.SeriesName = "Exact";
        for (int i = 1; i < xe.Length - 1; i++)
        {
            ds.LineSeries.Points.Add(new Point(xe[i], ye[i]));
        }
        myChart.DataCollection.DataList.Add(ds);

        // plot interpolated data:
        ds = new LineCharts.DataSeries();
        ds.LineColor = Brushes.Transparent;
        ds.SeriesName = "Interpolated";
        ds.Symbols.SymbolType = LineCharts.Symbols.SymbolTypeEnum.Circle;
        ds.Symbols.BorderColor = Brushes.Red;
        for (int i = 1; i < x.Length - 1; i++)
        {
            ds.LineSeries.Points.Add(new Point(x[i], y[i]));
        }
        myChart.DataCollection.DataList.Add(ds);

        // Plot original data
        ds = new LineCharts.DataSeries();
        ds.LineColor = Brushes.Transparent;
        ds.SeriesName = "Original";
        ds.Symbols.SymbolType = LineCharts.Symbols.SymbolTypeEnum.Dot;
        ds.Symbols.BorderColor = Brushes.DarkBlue;
        for (int i = 0; i < x0.Length; i++)
        {
            ds.LineSeries.Points.Add(new Point(x0[i], y0[i]));
        }
        myChart.DataCollection.DataList.Add(ds);
        myChart.IsLegend = true;
        myChart.LegendPosition = LineCharts.Legend.LegendPositionEnum.NorthWest;
    }
  }
}
```

Here, we generate three sets of data from a math function, $\sin 8x + x/2 - x^2$. These data sets include the original 15 data points, 100 data points calculated directly from the math function (that is, the exact results), and the 30 data points interpolated from the original 15 data points using barycentric interpolation. All three data sets are plotted in Figure 10-4. You can see from this figure that the interpolated results from the barycentric method are very close to the exact ones.

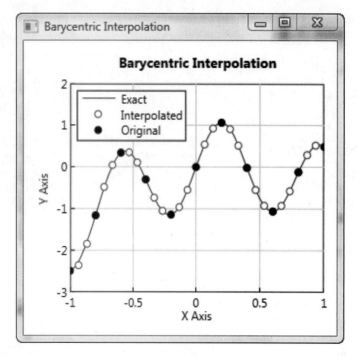

Figure 10-4. *Results created using barycentric interpolation*

Newton Divided-Difference Interpolation

Newton divided-difference interpolation is the interpolation polynomial approximation for a given set of data points in the Newton form. It uses Taylor expansion to perform the interpolation. The divided differences are used to approximate the various derivatives.

Algorithm

Let's first examine the linear and quadratic approximations. Given two data points (x_0, y_0) and (x_1, y_1), the linear interpolation can be expressed in the form

$$f_1(x) = c_0 + c_1(x - x_0) = f(x_0) + \frac{f(x_1) - f(x_0)}{x_1 - x_0}(x - x_0)$$

For a given set of three data points (x_0, y_0), (x_1, y_1), and (x_2, y_2), we can fit a quadratic interpolant through the data:

$$f_2(x) = c_0 + c_1(x - x_0) + c2(x - x_0)(x - x_1)$$

$$= f(x_0) + \frac{f(x_1) - f(x_0)}{x_1 - x_0}(x - x_0) + \frac{\dfrac{f(x_2) - f(x_1)}{x_2 - x_1} - \dfrac{f(x_1) - f(x_0)}{x_1 - x_0}}{x_2 - x_0}(x - x_0)(x - x_1)$$

In these two cases, we see how the linear and quadratic interpolations are derived by the Newton divided-difference polynomial method.

We can rewrite the quadratic polynomial interpolant formula by introducing the notation

$$f[x_0] = f(x_0)$$

$$f[x_1, x_0] = \frac{f(x_1) - f(x_0)}{x_1 - x_0}$$

$$f[x_2, x_1, x_0] = \frac{f[x_2, x_1] - f[x_1, x_0]}{x_2 - x_0}$$

where $f[x_0]$, $f[x_1, x_0]$, and $f[x_2, x_1, x_0]$ are called *bracketed functions* of the variables enclosed in square brackets. Using this notation, we can then write the quadratic interpolant formula as

$$f_2(x) = f[x_0] + f[x_1, x_0](x - x_0) + f[x_2, x_1, x_0](x - x_0)(x - x_1)$$

This leads us to write the general form of the Newton divided-difference polynomial for a given set of $(n + 1)$ data points, (x_0, y_0), (x_1, y_1), ..., (x_n, y_n) as

$$f_n(x) = c_0 + c_1(x - x_0) + \cdots + c_n(x - x_0)(x - x_1)\cdots(x - x_{n-1})$$

where

$$c_0 = f[x_0]$$

$$c_1 = f[x_1, x_0]$$

$$\vdots$$

$$c_n = f[x_n, x_{n-1}, \cdots, x_0]$$

From the foregoing definition, you can see that Newton divided differences are calculated recursively. The divided differences can also be written in the form of a table:

$$x_0 \quad f[x_0]$$
$$f[x_1,x_0]$$
$$x_1 \quad f[x_1] \qquad\qquad f[x_2,x_1,x_0]$$
$$f[x_2,x_1] \qquad\qquad\qquad f[x_3,x_2,x_1,x_0]$$
$$x_2 \quad f[x_2] \qquad\qquad f[x_3,x_2,x_1]$$
$$f[x_3,x_2] \qquad\qquad\qquad\qquad\qquad\vdots \qquad\qquad f[x_n,x_{n-1},\cdots,x_0]$$
$$x_3 \quad f[x_3] \qquad\qquad\qquad\vdots \qquad\qquad f[x_n,x_{n-1},x_{n-2},x_{n-3}]$$
$$\vdots \quad \vdots \qquad\quad \vdots \qquad\quad f[x_n,x_{n-1},x_{n-2}]$$
$$f[x_n,x_{n-1}]$$
$$x_n \quad f[x_n]$$

This difference table is an upper triangular matrix. You can store this kind of matrix in a one-dimensional array to save space.

Implementation

Here, we'll implement the Newton divided-difference interpolation. Add a new public static method, *NewtonDividedDifference*, to the *InterpolationAlgorithms* class:

```
public static double NewtonDividedDifference(double[] xarray,
                                             double[] yarray, double x)
{
    double y;
    int n = xarray.Length;
    double[] temp = new double[n];
    for (int i = 0; i < n; i++)
    {
        temp[i] = yarray[i];
    }
    for (int i = 0; i < n - 1; i++)
    {
        for (int j = n - 1; j > i; j--)
        {
            temp[j] = (temp[j - 1] - temp[j]) / (xarray[j - 1 - i] - xarray[j]);
        }
    }
    y = temp[n - 1];
    for (int i = n - 2; i >= 0; i--)
    {
        y = temp[i] + (x - xarray[i]) * y;
    }
    return y;
}
```

```
public static double[] NewtonDividedDifference(double[] xarray,
                                    double[] yarray, double[] x)
{
    double[] y = new double[x.Length];
    for (int i = 0; i < x.Length; i++)
        y[i] = NewtonDividedDifference(xarray, yarray, x[i]);
    return y;
}
```

Here, we implement an overloaded method, *NewtonDividedDifference*. The *xarray* and *yarray* are the sets of *x* and *y* data that present a set of given data points. This method returns a single *y* value or a *y* array at the input *x* (a double value or double array), depending on the input variable *x*.

Testing Newton Divided-Difference Interpolation

You can easily perform a Newton divided-difference interpolation using the *NewtonDividedDifference* method implemented in the *InterpolationAlgorithms* class. You can display the results using the line chart control presented in the previous chapter.

Add a new WPF Window to the current project and name it *DividedDifferenceInterpolation*. Here is the XAML layout for this example:

```
<Window x:Class="Interpolation.DividedDifferenceInterpolation"
    xmlns="http://schemas.microsoft.com/winfx/2006/xaml/presentation"
    xmlns:x="http://schemas.microsoft.com/winfx/2006/xaml"
    xmlns:chart="clr-namespace:LineChartControl;assembly=LineChartControl"
    Title="DividedDifferenceInterpolation" Height="350" Width="400">
    <Grid x:Name="rootGrid" SizeChanged="rootGrid_SizeChanged">
        <chart:LineChartControlLib x:Name="myChart"
                Title="Newton Divided Difference Interpolation"
                Xmin="1950" Xmax="1990" XTick="10" Ymin="140" Ymax="260"
                YTick="20" XLabel="Year" YLabel="Population (Million)"/>
    </Grid>
</Window>
```

This XAML file simply creates a line chart control named *myChart*, which will be used to display the results of the Newton divided-difference interpolation. Here is the corresponding code-behind file:

```
using System;
using System.Windows;
using System.Windows.Controls;
using System.Windows.Media;

namespace Interpolation
{
    public partial class DividedDifferenceInterpolation : Window
    {
        public DividedDifferenceInterpolation()
        {
            InitializeComponent();
        }

        private void rootGrid_SizeChanged(object sender, SizeChangedEventArgs e)
        {
            myChart.Width = rootGrid.ActualWidth;
```

```
        myChart.Height = rootGrid.ActualHeight;
        AddData();
    }

    private void AddData()
    {
        double[] x0 = new double[] { 1950, 1960, 1970, 1980, 1990 };
        double[] y0 = new double[] { 150.697, 179.323, 203.212,
                                     226.505, 249.633 };
        double[] x = new double[] { 1952, 1955, 1958, 1962, 1965, 1968,
                                    1972, 1975, 1978, 1982, 1985, 1988 };
        double[] y = InterpolationAlgorithms.NewtonDividedDifference(x0, y0, x);
        myChart.DataCollection.DataList.Clear();
        LineCharts.DataSeries ds;

        // plot interpolated data:
        ds = new LineCharts.DataSeries();
        ds.LineColor = Brushes.Transparent;
        ds.SeriesName = "Interpolated";
        ds.Symbols.SymbolType = LineCharts.Symbols.SymbolTypeEnum.Circle;
        ds.Symbols.BorderColor = Brushes.Red;
        for (int i = 0; i < x.Length; i++)
        {
            ds.LineSeries.Points.Add(new Point(x[i], y[i]));
        }
        myChart.DataCollection.DataList.Add(ds);

        // Plot original data
        ds = new LineCharts.DataSeries();
        ds.LineColor = Brushes.DarkGreen;
        ds.SeriesName = "Original";
        ds.Symbols.SymbolType = LineCharts.Symbols.SymbolTypeEnum.Dot;
        ds.Symbols.BorderColor = Brushes.DarkBlue;
        for (int i = 0; i < x0.Length; i++)
        {
            ds.LineSeries.Points.Add(new Point(x0[i], y0[i]));
        }
        myChart.DataCollection.DataList.Add(ds);
        myChart.IsLegend = true;
        myChart.LegendPosition = LineCharts.Legend.LegendPositionEnum.NorthWest;
    }
}
}
```

Here, we first create two initial data arrays, $x0$ and $y0$, which represent the census years from 1950 to 1990 and the corresponding United States population, in millions of people; we then want to use the Newton divided-difference interpolation to interpolate within the census data to estimate the population in other years.

This example generates the result shown in Figure 10-5.

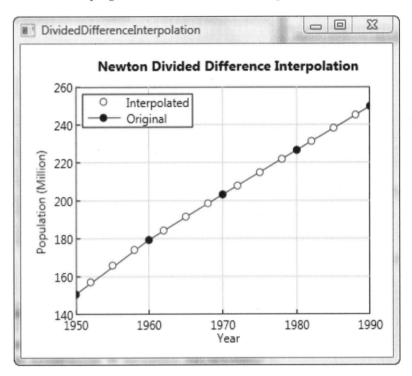

Figure 10-5. *Results created using the Newton divided-difference interpolation*

Cubic Spline Interpolation

In numerical analysis, spline interpolation is a form of interpolation in which the interpolant is a special type of piecewise polynomial called a *spline*. This method provides a great deal of smoothness for interpolations involving data that vary significantly.

Cubic spline interpolation uses weight coefficients on the cubic polynomials to interpolate the data. These coefficients bend the line so that it passes through each of the data points without any erratic behavior or breaks in continuity.

Algorithm

The basic idea of the cubic spline is to fit a piecewise function of the form

$$S(x) = \begin{cases} s_1(x) & \text{if} \quad x_1 \le x < x_2 \\ s_2(x) & \text{if} \quad x_2 \le x < x_3 \\ \vdots \\ s_{n-1}(x) & \text{if} \quad x_{n-1} \le x < x_n \end{cases}$$

where s_i is a third-degree polynomial defined by

$$s_i = a_i(x - x_i)^3 + b_i(x - x_i)^2 + c_i(x - x_i) + d_i, \quad \text{for } i = 1, 2, \cdots, n-1$$

The first and second derivatives of these $n-1$ equations are fundamental to this process, and they are given by

$$s_i'(x) = 3a_i(x - x_i)^2 + 2b_i(x - x_i) + c_i$$
$$s_i''(x) = 6a_i(x - x_i) + 2b_i$$

We require that the piecewise function $S(x)$ be able to interpolate all data points and that its first and second derivatives be continuous in the interval $[x_1, x_n]$. Using these properties, we can compute the coefficients

$$a_i = \frac{M_{i+1} - M_i}{6h}$$

$$b_i = \frac{M_i}{2}$$

$$c_i = \frac{y_{i+1} - y_i}{h} - \left(\frac{M_{i+1} + 2M_i}{6} \right) h$$

$$d_i = y_i$$

where

$$M_i = s_i''(x_i), \quad y_i = S(x_i) = s_i(x_i)$$

Implementation

In order to implement the cubic spline interpolation, we first need to calculate the second derivatives using two private static methods, *SecondDerivative* and *Tridiagonal*. Add these two methods to the *InterpolationAlgorithms* class. Here are code listings for these two methods:

```
private static double[] SecondDerivatives(double[] xarray, double[] yarray)
{
```

```
    int n = xarray.Length;
    double[] c1 = new double[n];
    double[] c2 = new double[n];
    double[] c3 = new double[n];
    double[] dx = new double[n];
    double[] derivative = new double[n];

    for (int i = 1; i < n; i++)
    {
        dx[i] = xarray[i] - xarray[i - 1];
        derivative[i] = (yarray[i] - yarray[i - 1]) / dx[i];
    }
    for (int i = 1; i < n - 1; i++)
    {
        c2[i - 1] = 2;
        c3[i - 1] = dx[i + 1] / (dx[i] + dx[i + 1]);
        c1[i - 1] = 1 - c3[i - 1];
        derivative[i - 1] = 6 * (derivative[i + 1] - derivative[i]) /
                            (dx[i] + dx[i + 1]);
    }
    derivative = Tridiagonal(n - 2, c1, c2, c3, derivative);
    return derivative;
}

private static double[] Tridiagonal(int n, double[] c1, double[] c2,
                                    double[] c3, double[] derivative)
{
    double tol = 1.0e-12;
    bool isSingular = (c2[0] < tol) ? true : false;
    for (int i = 1; i < n && !isSingular; i++)
    {
        c1[i] = c1[i] / c2[i - 1];
        c2[i] = c2[i] - c1[i] * c3[i - 1];
        isSingular = (c2[i] < tol) ? true : false;
        derivative[i] = derivative[i] - c1[i] * derivative[i - 1];
    }

    if (!isSingular)
    {
        derivative[n - 1] = derivative[n - 1] / c2[n - 1];
        for (int i = n - 2; i >= 0; i--)
        {
            derivative[i] = (derivative[i] - c3[i] * derivative[i + 1]) / c2[i];
        }
        return derivative;
    }
    else
        return null;
}
```

Once the derivatives are obtained, we can use them to implement the cubic spline interpolation. Add a new public static method, *Spline*, to the *InterpolationAlgorithms* class:

```
public static double Spline(double[] xarray, double[] yarray, double x)
{
    double[] xa = new double[xarray.Length + 1];
    double[] ya = new double[yarray.Length + 1];
    xa[0] = (1.0 - 1.0e-6) * xarray[0];
    ya[0] = (1.0 - 1.0e-6) * yarray[0];
    for (int i = 0; i < xarray.Length; i++)
    {
        xa[i + 1] = xarray[i];
        ya[i + 1] = yarray[i];
    }
    xarray = xa;
    yarray = ya;
    double d1, d2;
    double y = double.NaN;
    int n = xarray.Length;
    double[] dx = new double[n];
    double[] derivative = SecondDerivatives(xarray, yarray);

    for (int i = 1; i < n; i++)
    {
        dx[i] = xarray[i] - xarray[i - 1];
    }
    for (int i = 1; i < n - 1; i++)
    {
        if (x >= xarray[i] && x < xarray[i + 1])
        {
            d1 = x - xarray[i];
            d2 = xarray[i + 1] - x;
            y = derivative[i - 1] * d2 * d2 * d2 / (6.0 * dx[i + 1]) +
                derivative[i] * d1 * d1 * d1 / (6.0 * dx[i + 1]) +
                (yarray[i + 1] / dx[i + 1] - derivative[i] * dx[i + 1] / 6.0) * d1 +
                (yarray[i] / dx[i + 1] - derivative[i - 1] * dx[i + 1] / 6.0) * d2;
        }
    }
    return y;
}

public static double[] Spline(double[] xarray, double[] yarray, double[] x)
{
    double[] y = new double[x.Length];
    for (int i = 0; i < x.Length; i++)
        y[i] = Spline(xarray, yarray, x[i]);
    return y;
}
```

Here, we implement an overloaded method, *Spline*. The *xarray* and *yarray* are the sets of *x* and *y* data that present a set of given data points. This method returns a single *y* value or a *y* array at the input *x* (a double value or double array), depending on the input variable *x*.

Testing Cubic Spline Interpolation

You can easily perform a cubic spline interpolation using the *Spline* method implemented in the *InterpolationAlgorithms* class. You can display the results using the line chart control presented in the previous chapter.

Add a new WPF Window to the current project and name it *CubicSplineInterpolation*. Here is the XAML layout for this example:

```
<Window x:Class="Interpolation.CubicSplineInterpolation"
    xmlns="http://schemas.microsoft.com/winfx/2006/xaml/presentation"
    xmlns:x="http://schemas.microsoft.com/winfx/2006/xaml"
    xmlns:chart="clr-namespace:LineChartControl;assembly=LineChartControl"
    Title="CubicSplineInterpolation" Height="350" Width="400">
    <Grid x:Name="rootGrid" SizeChanged="rootGrid_SizeChanged">
        <chart:LineChartControlLib x:Name="myChart"
                Title="Cubic Spline Interpolation"
                Xmin="0" Xmax="4" XTick="1" Ymin="0" Ymax="6" YTick="1"/>
    </Grid>
</Window>
```

This XAML file simply creates a line chart control named *myChart*, which will be used to display the results of the cubic spline interpolation. Here is the corresponding code-behind file:

```
using System;
using System.Windows;
using System.Windows.Controls;
using System.Windows.Media;

namespace Interpolation
{
    public partial class CubicSplineInterpolation : Window
    {
        public CubicSplineInterpolation()
        {
            InitializeComponent();
        }

        private void rootGrid_SizeChanged(object sender, SizeChangedEventArgs e)
        {
            myChart.Width = rootGrid.ActualWidth;
            myChart.Height = rootGrid.ActualHeight;
            AddData();
        }

        private void AddData()
        {
            double[] x0 = new double[] { 1, 2, 3};
            double[] y0 = new double[] { 1, 5, 4};
            double[] x = new double[199];
            for (int i = 0; i < x.Length; i++)
            {
                x[i] = 1.01 + i / 100.0;
            }
            double[] y = InterpolationAlgorithms.Spline(x0, y0, x);
```

415

```
myChart.DataCollection.DataList.Clear();
LineCharts.DataSeries ds;

// Plot original data
ds = new LineCharts.DataSeries();
ds.LineColor = Brushes.Transparent;
ds.SeriesName = "Original";
ds.Symbols.SymbolType = LineCharts.Symbols.SymbolTypeEnum.Dot;
ds.Symbols.BorderColor = Brushes.DarkBlue;
for (int i = 0; i < x0.Length; i++)
{
    ds.LineSeries.Points.Add(new Point(x0[i], y0[i]));
}
myChart.DataCollection.DataList.Add(ds);

// plot interpolated data:
ds = new LineCharts.DataSeries();
ds.LineColor = Brushes.DarkGreen;
ds.SeriesName = "Interpolated";
for (int i = 0; i < x.Length; i++)
{
    ds.LineSeries.Points.Add(new Point(x[i], y[i]));
}
myChart.DataCollection.DataList.Add(ds);
myChart.IsLegend = true;
myChart.LegendPosition = LineCharts.Legend.LegendPositionEnum.NorthWest;
        }
    }
}
```

Here, we first create three initial data points represented by the arrays $x0$ and $y0$. We then want to find 200 data points using the cubic spline interpolation method. Running this example generates the result shown in Figure 10-6.

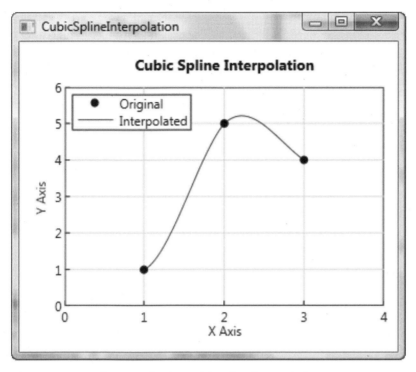

Figure 10-6. *Results created using cubic spline interpolation*

CHAPTER 11

■ ■ ■

Curve Fitting

In science and engineering, the data obtained from experiments usually contain a significant amount of random noise due to measurement errors. The purpose of curve fitting is to find a smooth curve that fits the data points on average. We usually require that this curve have a simple form with a low-order polynomial so that it does not reproduce the random errors of the data.

There is a distinction between interpolation and curve fitting. Interpolation, as discussed in the previous chapter, can be regarded as a special case of curve fitting in which the function must pass exactly through the data points. This implicitly assumes that the given data points in an interpolation are accurate and distinct. Curve fitting is applied to data that contain noise, usually due to measurement errors. It tries to find the best fit to a given set of data. Thus, the curve does not necessarily pass through the given data points.

Linear Algebraic Equations

Curve-fitting techniques often require solving linear algebraic equations. In this section, we review a commonly used method, the Gauss-Jordan elimination, for solving linear equations. Generally, the linear equation system involves multiple variables. General vector and matrix analysis is the basic theory of this linear system.

Note that the vector and matrix structures contained in WPF are designed specifically for transformation operations on various graphics elements, but they are not general enough for applications such as solving linear equation systems. For example, if a linear system consists of 10 equations and 10 unknowns, the vector and matrix involved in this system will be 10-dimensional. The 2D *Vector* and *Matrix* or the 3D *Vector3D* and *Matrix3D* structures in WPF cannot be applied to such a system. Thus, we need to create general n-dimensional vectors and $n \times n$ matrix structures.

In my other book, *Practical Numerical Methods with C#*, I presented detailed instructions on how to create such general vectors and matrices for real and complex variables. Here, I'll use these *VectorR* and *MatrixR* structures for real variables directly without derivations. If you are interested in the implementation of these structures, please refer to *Practical Numerical Methods with C#*.

Here, we'll consider how to solve linear equations containing an arbitrary number of unknowns. A set of linear equations can be written in a matrix form as

$$A \cdot x = b \qquad (11.1)$$

Here, A is a square matrix of coefficients, and both x and b are column vectors representing unknowns and right-hand constants, respectively. In the following sections, I'll present the Gauss-Jordan method for solving linear equations.

Gauss-Jordan Algorithm

Solving sets of linear equations using Gauss-Jordan elimination produces both the solution of the equations and the inverse of the coefficient matrix. The Gauss-Jordan elimination process requires two steps. The first step, called the *forward elimination*, reduces a given system to either triangular or echelon form or results in a degenerate equation indicating that the system has no solution. We accomplish this through the use of elementary operations. The second step, called the *backward elimination*, uses back-substitution to find the solution of the linear equations.

In terms of matrix formalism, the first step reduces a matrix to row-echelon form using elementary operations, and the second step reduces it to row-canonical form.

Gauss-Jordan elimination computes the matrix decomposition using three elementary operations: multiplying rows, switching rows, and adding multiples of rows to other rows. The first part of the algorithm computes the decomposition; the second part writes the original matrix as the product of a uniquely determined invertible matrix and a uniquely determined reduced row-echelon matrix. The Gauss-Jordan method is generally as efficient as other techniques and is very stable.

The simplest method in Gauss-Jordan elimination is to eliminate $x[0]$ in Equation (11.1) from all equations with $i > 0$; $x[1]$ from all the resulting equations with $i > 1$; and, in general, $x[j]$ from all equations with $i > j$. The process, called *Gauss-Jordan elimination*, produces a triangular matrix of coefficients with all zero elements below the principal diagonal.

We must take care when using this elimination method. It may fail if one of the diagonal elements becomes zero or becomes too small in the process of triangulation. We can avoid this problem by interchanging the two sets of equations. The order in which the equations are presented makes no difference to their solutions, but it can have a great impact on how you solve the equations. Thus, we can rearrange the equations to make the diagonal elements as large as possible. We'll use the *Pivot* method to perform this task.

Implementation

Start with a new WPF Windows application and name it *CurveFitting*. First we need to add the structures *VectorR* and *MatrixR* to the current project by right-clicking the *CurveFitting* project, selecting Add | Add Existing Item.... You can view the source code by opening the *VectorR.cs* and *MatrixR.cs* files to see how they are implemented. You can find a detailed explanation of their implementation in *Practical Numerical Methods with C#.* Add a new class to the project and name it *CurveFittingAlgorithms*. Here, we only consider linear systems with real variables. The following is the code listing for this class:

```
using System;
using System.Collections;
namespace CurveFitting
{
    public class CurveFittingAlgorithms
    {
        public static VectorR GaussJordan(MatrixR A, VectorR b)
        {
            Triangulate(A, b);
            int n = b.GetSize();
            VectorR x = new VectorR(n);
            for (int i = n - 1; i >= 0; i--)
            {
                double d = A[i, i];
                if (Math.Abs(d) < 1.0e-500)
                    throw new ArgumentException("Diagonal element is too small!");
                x[i] = (b[i] - VectorR.DotProduct(A.GetRowVector(i), x)) / d;
```

```
        }
        return x;
    }

    private static void Triangulate(MatrixR A, VectorR b)
    {
        int n = A.GetRows();
        VectorR v = new VectorR(n);
        for (int i = 0; i < n - 1; i++)
        {
            double d = Pivot(A, b, i);
            if (Math.Abs(d) < 1.0e-500)
                throw new ArgumentException("Diagonal element is too small!");
            for (int j = i + 1; j < n; j++)
            {
                double dd = A[j, i] / d;
                for (int k = i + 1; k < n; k++)
                {
                    A[j, k] -= dd * A[i, k];
                }
                b[j] -= dd * b[i];
            }
        }
    }

    private static double Pivot(MatrixR A, VectorR b, int q)
    {
        int n = b.GetSize();
        int i = q;
        double d = 0.0;
        for (int j = q; j < n; j++)
        {
            double dd = Math.Abs(A[j, q]);
            if (dd > d)
            {
                d = dd;
                i = j;
            }
        }
        if (i > q)
        {
            A.GetRowSwap(q, i);
            b.GetSwap(q, i);
        }
        return A[q, q];
    }
    }
}
```

This class includes three methods for performing Gauss-Jordan eliminations. The *Pivot* method is intended to return the largest available diagonal element by rearranging the equations. If needed, we interchange the rows for both the matrix of coefficients *A* and the constant vector *b* by using the *Swap* method, defined in the *MatrixR* and *VectorR* classes.

We achieve the triangulation using the *Triangulate* method. In the first loop, instead of using the diagonal element $A[i, i]$ directly, we use the largest possible element from the *Pivot* method.

Finally, we implement the public *GaussJordan* method. In this method, we find the values of the unknowns for triangulated equations by using back-substitution. This process starts with the last equation, which contains a single unknown, meaning we can find its solution immediately. We can substitute this value into the second-to-last equation in order to calculate the next unknown. We repeat this process until we have found all of the unknowns.

Least-Squares Fit

The most popular curve-fitting technique is the least-squares method, which is usually used to solve overdetermined systems. It is often applied in statistics, particularly in regression analysis. The best fit in the least-squares sense is the instance of the model in which the sum of the squared residuals has its smallest value. The residual in the least-squares method is the difference between the observed data value and the value provided by the model.

Suppose that a given data set consists of $n + 1$ data points (x_i, y_i), $i = 0, 1, \ldots, n$, where x_i is an independent variable and y_i is a dependent variable whose value is obtained by observation. The model function can be defined as

$$f(x; \mathbf{a}) = f(x; a_0, a_1, \cdots, a_m)$$

This function is to be fitted to a data set with $n + 1$ data points. The preceding model function contains $m + 1$ variable parameters $a_0, a_1, \ldots, a_m$, where $m < n$. We wish to find those parameter values for which the model best fits the data.

The form of the model function is determined beforehand, usually from the theory associated with the experiment from which the data are obtained. The curve-fitting process involves two steps: choosing the form of the model function, followed by computing the parameters that produce the best fit to the data.

The least-squares method minimizes the sum of squared residuals

$$S(\mathbf{a}) = \sum_{i=0}^{n} r_i^2, \quad r_i = y_i - f(x_i; \mathbf{a})$$

with respect to each parameter a_i. The terms in this equation are called *residuals*, which represent the discrepancy between the data points and the fitting function. Therefore, the optimal values of the parameters are given by the following conditions:

$$\frac{\partial S(\mathbf{a})}{\partial a_i} = 2 \sum_{i=0}^{n} r_i \frac{\partial r_i}{\partial a_i} = -2 \sum_{i=0}^{n} \frac{\partial f(x_i; \mathbf{a})}{\partial a_i} r_i = 0, \quad i = 0, 1, \cdots, m$$

The foregoing equation is generally nonlinear in a_i and may be difficult to solve. This gradient equation applies to all least-squares problems. Each particular problem requires particular expressions for the model function and its partial derivatives. For example, the model function is often chosen as a linear combination of the specified functions $f_i(x)$:

$$f(x; \mathbf{a}) = \sum_{i=0}^{m} a_i f_i(x)$$

In this case, the gradient equation becomes linear. If the model function is a polynomial, we have $f_0(x) = 1, f_1(x) = x, f_2(x) = x^2$, etc.

Straight-Line Fit

The simplest linear regression is the straight-line fit, which attempts to fit a straight line using the least-squares technique. It examines the correlation between an independent variable x and a dependent variable y. In this case, the model function has the following simple form:

$$f(x;\mathbf{a}) = a + bx$$

The sum function of the linear regression to be minimized becomes

$$S(a,b) = \sum_{i=0}^{n} [y_i - f(x_i;\mathbf{a})]^2 = \sum_{i=0}^{n} (y_i - a - bx_i)^2$$

The corresponding gradient equation becomes

$$\frac{\partial S}{\partial a} = -2\sum_{i=0}^{n} (y_i - a - bx_i) = 0$$

$$\frac{\partial S}{\partial b} = -2\sum_{i=0}^{n} (y_i - a - bx_i)x_i = 0$$

We can find a solution for parameters a and b by solving the preceding two equations:

$$a = y_m - x_m b$$

$$b = \frac{\sum_{i=0}^{n} y_i(x_i - x_m)}{\sum_{i=0}^{n} x_i(x_i - x_m)}$$

Here, x_m and y_m are the mean values of the x and y data:

$$x_m = \frac{1}{n+1}\sum_{i=0}^{n} x_i, \quad y_m = \frac{1}{n+1}\sum_{i=0}^{n} y_i$$

The standard deviation σ can be expressed by

$$\sigma = \sqrt{\frac{S}{n-m}}$$

Implementation

Add a new method to the *CurveFittingAlgorithms* class and name it *StraightLineFit*. Here is the code listing for this method:

```
public static double[] StraightLineFit(double[] xarray, double[] yarray)
{
    int n = xarray.Length;
    double xm = 0.0;
    double ym = 0.0;
    double b1 = 0.0;
```

```
        double b2 = 0.0;
        double a = 0.0;
        double b = 0.0;
        double s = 0.0;
        double sigma = 0.0;
        for (int i = 0; i < n; i++)
        {
            xm += xarray[i] / n;
            ym += yarray[i] / n;
        }
        for (int i = 0; i < n; i++)
        {
            b1 += yarray[i] * (xarray[i] - xm);
            b2 += xarray[i] * (xarray[i] - xm);
        }
        b = b1 / b2;
        a = ym - xm * b;
        for (int i = 0; i < n; i++)
        {
            s += (yarray[i] - a - b * xarray[i]) * (yarray[i] - a - b * xarray[i]);
        }
        sigma = Math.Sqrt(s / (n - 2));
        return new double[] {a, b, sigma };
}
```

Here, the *xarray* and *yarray* are the sets of *x* and *y* data that present a set of given data points. This method returns the coefficients *a* and *b* of the model function and the standard deviation, *sigma*.

Testing Straight-Line Fit

You can easily perform a straight-line fit using the method implemented in the previous section. To display the results directly on your screen, you'll need to add the *LineChartControl* to the References for this project, as we did in the previous chapter. Add a new WPF Windows application to the current project and name it *StraightLineFit*. Here is the XAML file for this example:

```
<Window x:Class="CurveFitting.StraightLineFit"
    xmlns="http://schemas.microsoft.com/winfx/2006/xaml/presentation"
    xmlns:x="http://schemas.microsoft.com/winfx/2006/xaml"
    xmlns:chart="clr-namespace:LineChartControl;assembly=LineChartControl"
    Title="StraightLineFit" Height="350" Width="400">
    <Grid x:Name="rootGrid" SizeChanged="rootGrid_SizeChanged">
        <chart:LineChartControlLib x:Name="myChart" Xmin="-1" Xmax="6"
                XTick="1" Ymin="1" Ymax="7" YTick="1" Title="Straight Line Fitting"/>
    </Grid>
</Window>
```

This XAML creates a line chart control named *myChart*, which will be used to display the result of the curve fitting. The corresponding code-behind file is listed below:

```
using System;
using System.Windows;
using System.Windows.Controls;
using System.Windows.Media;
```

```
namespace CurveFitting
{
    public partial class StraightLineFit : Window
    {
        public StraightLineFit()
        {
            InitializeComponent();
        }

        private void rootGrid_SizeChanged(object sender, SizeChangedEventArgs e)
        {
            myChart.Height = rootGrid.ActualHeight;
            myChart.Width = rootGrid.ActualWidth;
            AddData();
        }

        private void AddData()
        {
            double[] x0 = new double[] { 0, 1, 2, 3, 4, 5 };
            double[] y0 = new double[] { 1.9, 2.7, 3.3, 4.4, 5.5, 6.5 };
            double[] results = CurveFittingAlgorithms.StraightLineFit(x0, y0);

            myChart.DataCollection.DataList.Clear();
            LineCharts.DataSeries ds;

            // Plot original data
            ds = new LineCharts.DataSeries();
            ds.LineColor = Brushes.Transparent;
            ds.SeriesName = "Original";
            ds.Symbols.SymbolType = LineCharts.Symbols.SymbolTypeEnum.OpenTriangle;
            ds.Symbols.BorderColor = Brushes.DarkBlue;
            for (int i = 0; i < x0.Length; i++)
            {
                ds.LineSeries.Points.Add(new Point(x0[i], y0[i]));
            }
            myChart.DataCollection.DataList.Add(ds);

            // Curve fitting data:
            ds = new LineCharts.DataSeries();
            ds.LineColor = Brushes.DarkGreen;
            ds.SeriesName = "Curve Fitting";
            for (int i = 0; i < 101; i++)
            {
                double x = i / 20.0;
                double y = results[0] + results[1] * x;
                ds.LineSeries.Points.Add(new Point(x, y));
            }
            myChart.DataCollection.DataList.Add(ds);
            myChart.IsLegend = true;
            myChart.LegendPosition = LineCharts.Legend.LegendPositionEnum.NorthWest;
        }
    }
}
```

Here, we provide the input data points using two double arrays *xarray* and *yarray*, and we use the following statement to calculate the coefficients of the straight-line fit:

```
double[] results = CurveFittingAlgorithms.StraightLineFit(x0, y0);
```

You can view the results using a Message Box by adding the following code snippet to the *AddData* method:

```
MessageBox.Show(results[0].ToString() + ", " +
                results[1].ToString() + ", " +
                results[2].ToString());
```

which should display (1.729, 0.929, 0.191). Therefore, the straight line can be represented by

$$f(x) = 1.729 + 0.929x$$

and the standard deviation is 0.191.

Figure 11-1 shows the results of the straight-line fit to the original data.

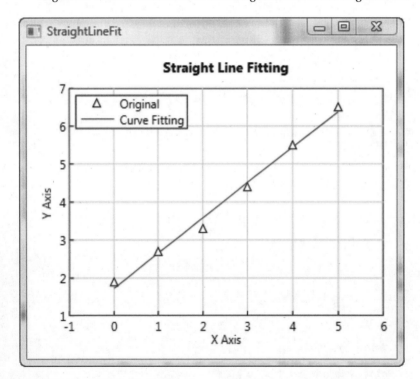

Figure 11-1. Straight-line fit

Linear Regression

Let's first consider the least-squares fit with the linear form

$$f(x;\boldsymbol{\alpha}) = \sum_{i=0}^{m} a_i f_i(x)$$

where $f_i(x)$ is a predetermined function of x, called a *basis function*. In this case, the sum of the residuals is given by

$$S(\boldsymbol{\alpha}) = \sum_{i=0}^{n} \left[y_i - \sum_{j=0}^{m} a_j f_j(x_i) \right]^2$$

The corresponding gradient equation from $\partial S / \partial a_k = 0$ reduces to

$$\sum_{j=0}^{m}\sum_{i=0}^{n} f_j(x_i) f_k(x_i) a_j = \sum_{i=0}^{n} f_k(x_i) y_i, \quad k = 0,1,\cdots,m$$

The preceding equation can be rewritten in matrix form:

$$\mathbf{A\alpha = \beta}, \quad A_{jk} = \sum_{i=0}^{n} f_j(x_i) f_k(x_i), \quad \beta_k = \sum_{i=0}^{n} f_k(x_i) y_i$$

This matrix form is also called the *normal equations of the least-squares fit*, which can be solved via the Gauss-Jordan method previously discussed in this chapter.

Implementation

Using the algorithm developed in the previous section, we can implement the linear regression method. Add a new public static method, *LinearRegression*, to the *CurveFittingAlgorithms* class:

```
public delegate double ModelFunction(double x);
public static VectorR LinearRegression(double[] xarray, double[] yarray,
                                       ModelFunction[] f, out double sigma)
{
    int m = f.Length;
    MatrixR A = new MatrixR(m, m);
    VectorR b = new VectorR(m);
    int n = xarray.Length;

    for (int k = 0; k < m; k++)
    {
        b[k] = 0.0;
        for (int i = 0; i < n; i++)
        {
            b[k] += f[k](xarray[i]) * yarray[i];
        }
    }
```

```
for (int j = 0; j < m; j++)
{
    for (int k = 0; k < m; k++)
    {
        A[j, k] = 0.0;
        for (int i = 0; i < n; i++)
        {
            A[j, k] += f[j](xarray[i]) * f[k](xarray[i]);
        }
    }
}
VectorR coef = GaussJordan(A, b);

// Calculate the standard deviation:
double s = 0.0;
for (int i = 0; i < n; i++)
{
    double s1 = 0.0;
    for (int j = 0; j < m; j++)
    {
        s1 += coef[j] * f[j](xarray[i]);
    }
    s += (yarray[i] - s1) * (yarray[i] - s1);
}
sigma = Math.Sqrt(s / (n - m));
return coef;
}
```

Notice that we first define a delegate function that takes a double variable *x* as its input parameter. Then we implement a public static method, *LinearRegression*, which returns a *VectorR* object with its components as the coefficients of a basis function.

Inside the *LinearRegression* method, we specify the coefficient matrix *A* and vector *b*. We then solve the normal equations via the *GaussJordan* method. Following the solution, we compute the standard deviation. This method returns the coefficients of the polynomial (a *VectorR* object); we specify the standard deviation using the *out* prefix in the *PolynomialFit* method:

```
public static VectorR LinearRegression(double[] xarray, double[] yarray,
                    ModelFunction[] f, out double sigma)
{
    ⋮
}
```

This way, you can obtain multiple output results from a single C# method.

Testing Linear Regression

You can easily perform a linear regression using the method implemented in the previous section. Add a new WPF Windows application to the current project and name it *LinearRegression*. Here is the XAML file for this example:

```
<Window x:Class="CurveFitting.LinearRegression"
    xmlns="http://schemas.microsoft.com/winfx/2006/xaml/presentation"
    xmlns:x="http://schemas.microsoft.com/winfx/2006/xaml"
    xmlns:chart="clr-namespace:LineChartControl;assembly=LineChartControl"
    Title="LinearRegression" Height="400" Width="450">
    <Grid x:Name="rootGrid" SizeChanged="rootGrid_SizeChanged">
        <chart:LineChartControlLib x:Name="myChart" Title="Linear Regression"
                Xmin="-1" Xmax="6" XTick="1" Ymin="0" Ymax="5" YTick="1"/>
    </Grid>
</Window>
```

This XAML file creates a line chart control named *myChart*, which will be used to display the result of the curve fitting. Here is the corresponding code-behind file:

```
using System;
using System.Windows;
using System.Windows.Controls;
using System.Windows.Media;
using System.Windows.Shapes;

namespace CurveFitting
{
    public partial class LinearRegression : Window
    {
        public LinearRegression()
        {
            InitializeComponent();
        }

        private void rootGrid_SizeChanged(object sender, SizeChangedEventArgs e)
        {
            myChart.Width = rootGrid.ActualWidth;
            myChart.Height = rootGrid.ActualHeight;
            AddData();
        }

        private void AddData()
        {
            double[] x0 = new double[] { 0, 1, 2, 3, 4, 5 };
            double[] y0 = new double[] { 2, 1, 4, 4, 3, 2 };

            // First order polynormial (m = 1):
            CurveFittingAlgorithms.ModelFunction[] f =
                new CurveFittingAlgorithms.ModelFunction[] { f0, f1 };
            double sigma = 0.0;
            VectorR results1 = CurveFittingAlgorithms.LinearRegression(x0, y0,
```

```
                                    f, out sigma);

        // Second order polynormial (m = 2):
        f = new CurveFittingAlgorithms.ModelFunction[] { f0, f1, f2 };
        VectorR results2 = CurveFittingAlgorithms.LinearRegression(x0, y0,
                            f, out sigma);

        // Third order polynormial (m = 3):
        f = new CurveFittingAlgorithms.ModelFunction[] { f0, f1, f2, f3 };
        VectorR results3 = CurveFittingAlgorithms.LinearRegression(x0, y0,
                            f, out sigma);

        // Plot results:
        myChart.DataCollection.DataList.Clear();
        LineCharts.DataSeries ds;

        // Plot original data:
        ds = new LineCharts.DataSeries();
        ds.LineColor = Brushes.Transparent;
        ds.SeriesName = "Original";
        ds.Symbols.SymbolType = LineCharts.Symbols.SymbolTypeEnum.Triangle;
        ds.Symbols.BorderColor = Brushes.Black;
        for (int i = 0; i < x0.Length; i++)
        {
            ds.LineSeries.Points.Add(new Point(x0[i], y0[i]));
        }
        myChart.DataCollection.DataList.Add(ds);

        // 1st order fitting data:
        ds = new LineCharts.DataSeries();
        ds.LineColor = Brushes.DarkGreen;
        ds.LineThickness = 2;
        ds.SeriesName = "1st Order Fitting";
        for (int i = 0; i < 141; i++)
        {
            double x = -1.0 + i / 20.0;
            double y = results1[0] + results1[1] * x;
            ds.LineSeries.Points.Add(new Point(x, y));
        }
        myChart.DataCollection.DataList.Add(ds);

        // 2nd order fitting data:
        ds = new LineCharts.DataSeries();
        ds.LineColor = Brushes.Red;
        ds.LineThickness = 2;
        ds.LinePattern = LineCharts.DataSeries.LinePatternEnum.Dash;
        ds.SeriesName = "2nd Order Fitting";
        for (int i = 0; i < 141; i++)
        {
            double x = -1.0 + i / 20.0;
            double y = results2[0] + results2[1] * x + results2[2] * x * x;
            ds.LineSeries.Points.Add(new Point(x, y));
        }
```

```
        myChart.DataCollection.DataList.Add(ds);

        // 3rd order fitting data:
        ds = new LineCharts.DataSeries();
        ds.LineColor = Brushes.DarkBlue;
        ds.LineThickness = 2;
        ds.LinePattern = LineCharts.DataSeries.LinePatternEnum.DashDot;
        ds.SeriesName = "3rd Order Fitting";
        for (int i = 0; i < 141; i++)
        {
            double x = -1.0 + i / 20.0;
            double y = results3[0] + results3[1] * x +
                    results3[2] * x * x + results3[3] * x * x * x;
            ds.LineSeries.Points.Add(new Point(x, y));
        }
        myChart.DataCollection.DataList.Add(ds);
        myChart.IsLegend = true;
        myChart.LegendPosition = LineCharts.Legend.LegendPositionEnum.NorthWest;
    }

    private static double f0(double x)
    {
        return 1.0;
    }

    private static double f1(double x)
    {
        return x;
    }

    private static double f2(double x)
    {
        return x * x;
    }

    private static double f3(double x)
    {
        return x * x * x;
    }
    }
}
```

Here, we fit a polynomial of different orders (from 1 to 3) to the data points. In addition, we define the delegate functions used to compute the results based on the linear regression.

Running this example generates the results shown in Figure 11-2.

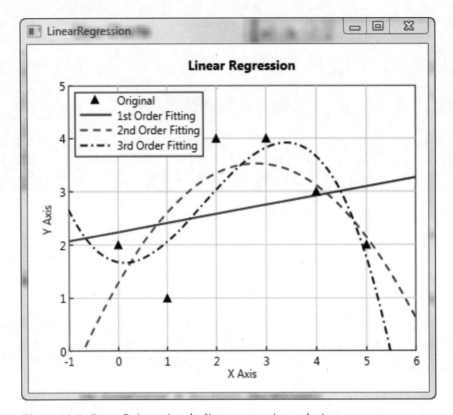

***Figure 11-2.** Curve fitting using the linear regression technique*

From these results we see that the second-order polynomial fitting produces the smallest standard deviation. Thus, it could be considered as the "best" fit to the data. Note, however, that the standard deviation is not a reliable measure of the accuracy of the fit. It is always a good idea to plot the data points and the fitting function $f(x)$ before making the final determination. In Figure 11-2, we plot the data points and the first- to third-order polynomials. From this figure, it is hard to see which polynomial provides a better fit to the data.

The linear regression method is very general. You can use any basis functions $f_j(x)$ you like.

Polynomial Fit

As mentioned earlier, the polynomial fit is a special case of the linear least-squares method. In this case, the basis function becomes

$$f_j(x) = x^j, \quad j = 0, 1, \cdots, m$$

Thus, the matrix and vector in the normal equation become

$$A_{jk} = \sum_{i=0}^{n} x_i^{j+k}, \quad \beta_k = \sum_{i=0}^{n} x_i^k y_i$$

Implementation

Using the algorithm developed in the previous section, we can implement the polynomial curve-fitting method. This method is very similar to the *LinearRegression* method presented earlier, but with the basis functions $f_j(x)$ replaced with x^j. Add a new public static method, *PolynomialFit*, to the *CurveFittingAlgorithms* class:

```
public static VectorR PolynomialFit(double[] xarray, double[] yarray, int m,
                                    out double sigma)
{
    m++;
    MatrixR A = new MatrixR(m, m);
    VectorR b = new VectorR(m);
    int n = xarray.Length;

    for (int k = 0; k < m; k++)
    {
        b[k] = 0.0;
        for (int i = 0; i < n; i++)
        {
            b[k] += Math.Pow(xarray[i], k) * yarray[i];
        }
    }

    for (int j = 0; j < m; j++)
    {
        for (int k = 0; k < m; k++)
        {
            A[j, k] = 0.0;
            for (int i = 0; i < n; i++)
            {
                A[j, k] += Math.Pow(xarray[i], j + k);
            }
        }
    }
    VectorR coef = GaussJordan(A, b);
```

```
    // Calculate the standard deviation:
    double s = 0.0;
    for (int i = 0; i < n; i++)
    {
        double s1 = 0.0;
        for (int j = 0; j < m; j++)
        {
            s1 += coef[j] * Math.Pow(xarray[i], j);
        }
        s += (yarray[i] - s1) * (yarray[i] - s1);
    }
    sigma = Math.Sqrt(s / (n - m));
    return coef;
}
```

Here, we don't need to define the delegate function, since the basis functions are predetermined as polynomials. The method *PolynomialFit* sets up and solves the normal equation for the coefficients of a polynomial of degree *m*. It returns the coefficients of the polynomial.

Testing Polynomial Fit

You can easily perform a polynomial fit using the method implemented in the previous section. Add a new WPF Windows application to the current project and name it *PolynomialFit*. Here is the XAML file for this example:

```
<Window x:Class="CurveFitting.PolynomialFit"
    xmlns="http://schemas.microsoft.com/winfx/2006/xaml/presentation"
    xmlns:x="http://schemas.microsoft.com/winfx/2006/xaml"
    xmlns:chart="clr-namespace:LineChartControl;assembly=LineChartControl"
    Title="PolynomialFit" Height="450" Width="500">
    <Grid x:Name="rootGrid" SizeChanged="rootGrid_SizeChanged">
        <chart:LineChartControlLib x:Name="myChart" Xmin="0" Xmax="6" XTick="1"
                Ymin="-100" Ymax="600" YTick="100" Title="Polynomial Fitting"/>
    </Grid>
</Window>
```

This XAML creates a line chart control named *myChart*, which will be used to display the result of the curve fitting. Here is the corresponding code-behind file:

```
using System;
using System.Windows;
using System.Windows.Controls;
using System.Windows.Media;

namespace CurveFitting
{
    public partial class PolynomialFit : Window
    {
        public PolynomialFit()
        {
            InitializeComponent();
        }
```

```csharp
private void rootGrid_SizeChanged(object sender, SizeChangedEventArgs e)
{
    myChart.Width = rootGrid.ActualWidth;
    myChart.Height = rootGrid.ActualHeight;
    AddData();
}

private void AddData()
{
    double[] x0 = new double[] { 1, 2, 3, 4, 5 };
    double[] y0 = new double[] { 5.5, 43.1, 128, 290.7, 498.4 };

    VectorR[] results = new VectorR[3];

    for (int i = 0; i < results.Length; i++)
    {
        double sigma = 0;
        results[i] = CurveFittingAlgorithms.PolynomialFit(x0, y0,
                    i + 1, out sigma);
    }

    // Plot results:
    myChart.DataCollection.DataList.Clear();
    LineCharts.DataSeries ds;

    // Plot original data:
    ds = new LineCharts.DataSeries();
    ds.LineColor = Brushes.Transparent;
    ds.SeriesName = "Original";
    ds.Symbols.SymbolType = LineCharts.Symbols.SymbolTypeEnum.Triangle;
    ds.Symbols.BorderColor = Brushes.Black;
    for (int i = 0; i < x0.Length; i++)
    {
        ds.LineSeries.Points.Add(new Point(x0[i], y0[i]));
    }
    myChart.DataCollection.DataList.Add(ds);

    // 1st order fitting data:
    ds = new LineCharts.DataSeries();
    ds.LineColor = Brushes.DarkGreen;
    ds.LineThickness = 2;
    ds.SeriesName = "1st Order Fitting";
    for (int i = 0; i < 141; i++)
    {
        double x = -1.0 + i / 20.0;
        double y = results[0][0] + results[0][1] * x;
        ds.LineSeries.Points.Add(new Point(x, y));
    }
    myChart.DataCollection.DataList.Add(ds);

    // 2nd order fitting data:
    ds = new LineCharts.DataSeries();
    ds.LineColor = Brushes.Red;
```

```
        ds.LineThickness = 2;
        ds.LinePattern = LineCharts.DataSeries.LinePatternEnum.Dash;
        ds.SeriesName = "2nd Order Fitting";
        for (int i = 0; i < 141; i++)
        {
            double x = -1.0 + i / 20.0;
            double y = results[1][0] + results[1][1] * x +
                       results[1][2] * x * x;
            ds.LineSeries.Points.Add(new Point(x, y));
        }
        myChart.DataCollection.DataList.Add(ds);

        // 3rd order fitting data:
        ds = new LineCharts.DataSeries();
        ds.LineColor = Brushes.DarkBlue;
        ds.LineThickness = 2;
        ds.LinePattern = LineCharts.DataSeries.LinePatternEnum.DashDot;
        ds.SeriesName = "3rd Order Fitting";
        for (int i = 0; i < 141; i++)
        {
            double x = -1.0 + i / 20.0;
            double y = results[2][0] + results[2][1] * x +
                       results[2][2] * x * x + results[2][3] * x * x * x;
            ds.LineSeries.Points.Add(new Point(x, y));
        }
        myChart.DataCollection.DataList.Add(ds);
        myChart.IsLegend = true;
        myChart.LegendPosition = LineCharts.Legend.LegendPositionEnum.NorthWest;
    }
  }
}
```

Here, we fit a polynomial of different order (from 1 to 3) to the data points. Running this application generates the results shown in Figure 11-3. You can see from the figure that for this specific set of data points, the result from the second-order polynomial fitting is almost identical to that from the third-order polynomial fitting.

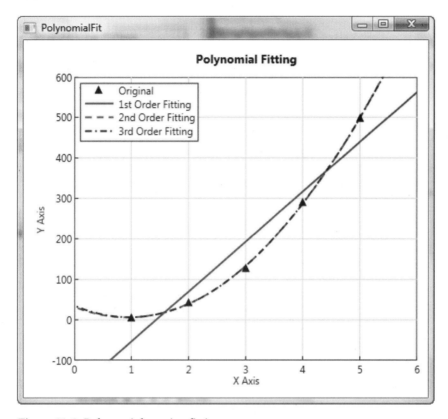

Figure 11-3. *Polynomial curving fitting*

Weighted Linear Regression

As we discussed earlier, linear regression is a useful technique for representing observed data by a model function, which is formulated as a least-squares minimization problem. In the case of the linear least squares, the resulting analysis requires the solution of a set of simultaneous equations using the Gauss-Jordan method. One important assumption in linear regression is that all of the errors have the same significance.

However, there are occasions when the confidence in the accuracy of data varies from point to point. For example, there may be a drift in the precision of the measurements, and some errors may be more or less important than others. In order to take these factors into account, we can introduce a weight factor to each data point and minimize the sum of the squares of the weighted residuals:

$$S(\mathbf{a}) = \sum_{i=0}^{n} r_i^2 = \sum_{i=0}^{n} w_i^2 \left[y_i - f(x_i) \right]^2$$

This procedure forces the fitting function $f(x)$ closer to the data points that have greater weight.

For the simplest linear regression, i.e., the straight-line fit, whose fitting function is given by $f(x) = a + bx$, the preceding equation becomes

437

$$S(a,b) = \sum_{i=0}^{n} w_i^2 \left(y_i - a - bx_i \right)^2$$

From the minimization conditions $\partial S / \partial a = 0$ and $\partial S / \partial b = 0$, we can determine the coefficients a and b:

$$a = y_w - bx_w, \quad b = \frac{\sum_{i=0}^{n} w_i^2 y_i (x_i - x_w)}{\sum_{i=0}^{n} w_i^2 x_i (x_i - x_w)}$$

Here, x_w and y_w are weighted averages:

$$x_w = \frac{\sum_{i=0}^{n} w_i^2 x_i}{\sum_{i=0}^{n} w_i^2}, \quad y_w = \frac{\sum_{i=0}^{n} w_i^2 y_i}{\sum_{i=0}^{n} w_i^2}$$

Implementation

Using the algorithm developed in the previous section, we can implement the weighted linear regression. Add a new public static method, *WeightedLinearRegression*, to the *CurveFittingAlgorithms* class:

```
public static double[] WeightedLinearRegression(double[] xarray, double[] yarray,
                                                double[] warray)
{
    int n = xarray.Length;
    double xw = 0.0;
    double yw = 0.0;
    double b1 = 0.0;
    double b2 = 0.0;
    double a = 0.0;
    double b = 0.0;

    for (int i = 0; i < n; i++)
    {
        xw += xarray[i] / n;
        yw += yarray[i] / n;
    }
    for (int i = 0; i < n; i++)
    {
        b1 += warray[i] * warray[i] * yarray[i] * (xarray[i] - xw);
        b2 += warray[i] * warray[i] * xarray[i] * (xarray[i] - xw);
    }
    b = b1 / b2;
    a = yw - xw * b;
    return new double[] { a, b };
}
```

Here, *xarray* and *yarray* are the sets of x and y data that present a set of given data points. The *warray* is the weight for each data point. This method returns the coefficients a and b of the model function.

Exponential-Function Fit

We can use weighted linear regression to fit various exponential functions to a given set of data points. For example, the model function $f(x)=ae^{bx}$, when used in the least-squares technique, usually leads to nonlinear dependence on the coefficients a and b. However, if we use log y rather than y, the problem is transformed into a linear regression. In this case, the fit function becomes

$$F(x) = \ln f(c) = \ln a + bx$$

Note that the least-squares fit to the logarithm of the data is different from the least-squares fit to the original data. The residuals of the logarithmic fit are given by

$$R_i = \ln y_i - F(x_i) = \ln y_i - \ln a - bx_i$$

and the residuals used in fitting the original data are

$$r_i = y_i - f(x_i) = y_i - ae^{bx_i}$$

We can eliminate this discrepancy by weighting the logarithmic fit. From the preceding equation, we have

$$\ln(r_i - y_i) = \ln(ae^{bx_i}) = \ln a + bx_i$$

So the residuals of the logarithmic fit can be rewritten in the form

$$R_i = \ln y_i - \ln(r_i - y_i) = \ln\left(1 - \frac{r_i}{y_i}\right)$$

In the limit of $r_i \ll y_i$, we can use the approximation $R_i = r_i/y_i$. You can see that by minimizing $\sum_{i=0}^n R_i^2$, we need to introduce the weight factor $1/y_i$. We can do this if we apply the weight $w_i = y_i$ when fitting $F(x)$ to the data points $(x_i, \ln y_i)$. Thus, minimizing

$$S = \sum_{i=0}^n y_i^2 R_i^2$$

will be a good approximation of minimizing $\sum_{i=0}^n r_i^2$.

Suppose we have the following set of data:

```
x = 1,  2 , 3, 4, 5 , 6, 7, 8, 9, 10
y = 1.9398, 2.9836, 5.9890, 10.2, 20.7414, 23.232, 69.5855, 82.5836, 98.1779
    339.3256
```

We want to fit these data with an exponential function $y = ae^{bx}$. We first need to perform a logarithmic transformation log y = log a +bx and then use the *WeightedLinearRegression* method to calculate the coefficients log a and b.

Add a new WPF Windows application to the current project and name it *WeightedLinearRegression*. Here is the XAML file for this example:

```
<Window x:Class="CurveFitting.WeightedLinearRegression"
    xmlns="http://schemas.microsoft.com/winfx/2006/xaml/presentation"
```

```
        xmlns:x="http://schemas.microsoft.com/winfx/2006/xaml"
        xmlns:chart="clr-namespace:LineChartControl;assembly=LineChartControl"
        Title="WeightedLinearRegression" Height="320" Width="600">
    <Grid x:Name="rootGrid" SizeChanged="rootGrid_SizeChanged">
        <StackPanel Orientation="Horizontal">
            <chart:LineChartControlLib x:Name="logChart"
                    Xmin="0" Xmax="11" XTick="1" Title="Log Scale Plot"/>
            <chart:LineChartControlLib x:Name="linearChart"
                    Xmin="0" Xmax="11" XTick="1" Title="Linear Scale Plot"/>
        </StackPanel>
    </Grid>
</Window>
```

Here, we create two line chart controls: one to display the result in log scale and the other to display the result in linear scale. Here is the corresponding code-behind file:

```
using System;
using System.Windows;
using System.Windows.Controls;
using System.Windows.Media;

namespace CurveFitting
{
    public partial class WeightedLinearRegression : Window
    {
        public WeightedLinearRegression()
        {
            InitializeComponent();
        }

        private void rootGrid_SizeChanged(object sender, SizeChangedEventArgs e)
        {
            logChart.Width = rootGrid.ActualWidth / 2;
            logChart.Height = rootGrid.ActualHeight;
            linearChart.Width = rootGrid.ActualWidth / 2;
            linearChart.Height = rootGrid.ActualHeight;
            AddData();
        }

        private void AddData()
        {
            double[] x0 = new double[] { 1, 2, 3, 4, 5, 6, 7, 8, 9, 10 };
            double[] y0 = new double[] { 1.9398, 2.9836, 5.9890, 10.2, 20.7414,
                23.232, 69.5855, 82.5836, 98.1779, 339.3256 };
            double[] ylog = new double[] { 0.6626, 1.0931, 1.7899, 2.3224,
                3.0321, 3.1455, 4.2426, 4.4138, 4.5868, 5.8270 };

            double[] results =
                CurveFittingAlgorithms.WeightedLinearRegression(x0, ylog, y0);

            // Plot linear scale results:
            LinearScale(x0, y0, results);

            // Plot log scale results:
```

```
        LogScale(x0, ylog, results);
}

private void LinearScale(double[] x0, double[] y0, double[] results)
{
    linearChart.DataCollection.DataList.Clear();
    LineCharts.DataSeries ds;

    linearChart.ChartStyle.Ymin = -50;
    linearChart.ChartStyle.Ymax = 350;
    linearChart.ChartStyle.YTick = 50;
    linearChart.ChartStyle.YLabel = "Y";

    // Plot original data:
    ds = new LineCharts.DataSeries();
    ds.LineColor = Brushes.Transparent;
    ds.SeriesName = "Original";
    ds.Symbols.SymbolType = LineCharts.Symbols.SymbolTypeEnum.Triangle;
    ds.Symbols.BorderColor = Brushes.Black;
    for (int i = 0; i < x0.Length; i++)
    {
        ds.LineSeries.Points.Add(new Point(x0[i], y0[i]));
    }
    linearChart.DataCollection.DataList.Add(ds);

    // Plot curve fittin data:
    ds = new LineCharts.DataSeries();
    ds.LineColor = Brushes.DarkGreen;
    ds.LineThickness = 2;
    ds.SeriesName = "Curve Fitting";
    for (int i = 0; i < 111; i++)
    {
        double x = 0.1 + i / 10.0;
        double y = Math.Exp(results[0] + results[1] * x);
        ds.LineSeries.Points.Add(new Point(x, y));
    }
    linearChart.DataCollection.DataList.Add(ds);

    linearChart.Legend.IsLegend = true;
    linearChart.Legend.LegendPosition =
        LineCharts.Legend.LegendPositionEnum.NorthWest;
}

private void LogScale(double[] x0, double[] ylog, double[] results)
{
    logChart.DataCollection.DataList.Clear();
    LineCharts.DataSeries ds;
    logChart.ChartStyle.Ymin = 0;
    logChart.ChartStyle.Ymax = 7;
    logChart.ChartStyle.YTick = 1;
    logChart.ChartStyle.YLabel = "Log(y)";

    // Plot original data:
```

441

```
        ds = new LineCharts.DataSeries();
        ds.LineColor = Brushes.Transparent;
        ds.SeriesName = "Original";
        ds.Symbols.SymbolType = LineCharts.Symbols.SymbolTypeEnum.Triangle;
        ds.Symbols.BorderColor = Brushes.Black;
        for (int i = 0; i < x0.Length; i++)
        {
            ds.LineSeries.Points.Add(new Point(x0[i], ylog[i]));
        }
        logChart.DataCollection.DataList.Add(ds);

        // Plot curve fittin data:
        ds = new LineCharts.DataSeries();
        ds.LineColor = Brushes.DarkGreen;
        ds.LineThickness = 2;
        ds.SeriesName = "Curve Fitting";
        for (int i = 0; i < 111; i++)
        {
            double x = 0.1 + i / 10.0;
            double y = results[0] + results[1] * x;
            ds.LineSeries.Points.Add(new Point(x, y));
        }
        logChart.DataCollection.DataList.Add(ds);
        logChart.Legend.IsLegend = true;
        logChart.Legend.LegendPosition =
            LineCharts.Legend.LegendPositionEnum.NorthWest;
    }
  }
}
```

Inside the *AddData* method, the statement

```
double[] results = CurveFittingAlgorithms.WeightedLinearRegression(x0, ylog, y0);
```

will generate the result (–0.0686983921044781, 0.578232434928087). The first number is the parameter (log a) and the second is the parameter b, which gives

$\ln y \approx -0.0687 + 0.5782x$

$y \approx 0.9336e^{0.5782x}$

We can check how good the fit results are by plotting them graphically (see Figure 11-4). You can see from Figure 11-4 that the weighted linear regression indeed gives a reasonably good fit.

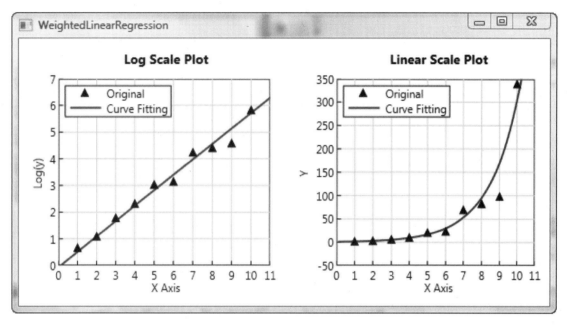

Figure 11-4. Results of the weighted linear regression: log plot (left) and linear plot (right)

CHAPTER 12

■ ■ ■

3D Transformations

In the previous chapters, we discussed 2D charts, graphics, and transformations. This chapter will explain the mathematical basics of 3D transformations, which will be used to perform operations on 3D graphics objects. Most 3D transformations are analogous to the 2D transformations described in Chapter 2. Using homogeneous coordinates and matrix representations similar to the ones used in 2D, I'll show you how to perform basic transformations, including translation, scaling, and rotation, in 3D. This chapter will also describe various projection matrices, which allow you to view 3D graphics objects on a 2D screen. As is the case with 2D, you can combine 3D basic transform matrices to represent complicated transformations with a single transform matrix. This chapter will also show you how WPF defines transform matrices in 3D and how to perform a variety of transformations on 3D objects.

3D Matrices in WPF

Matrix representations play an important role in transformations and operations on graphics objects. A matrix is a multidimensional array. This section explains the basics of 3D matrices and transformations. General 3D transforms are quite complicated. As in the case of 2D transformations, you can build more useful transforms with combinations of simple basic transforms, including translation, scaling, rotation, and projection. The following sections describe these fundamental transformations. Once you understand how to use these basic 3D transformations, you can combine them to create more general 3D transformations.

3D Points and Vectors

WPF defines two 3D Point structures: *Point3D* and *Point4D*. The *Point3D* structure defines the *X*, *Y*, and *Z* coordinates of a point in 3D space. *Point4D* defines the *X*, *Y*, *Z*, and *W* coordinates of a point in a 3D homogeneous coordinate system, which is used to perform transformations with nonaffine 3D matrices. The *Vector3D* structure defines a displacement with components *X*, *Y*, and *Z* in 3D space.

A vector in 3D is represented by a row array with three elements *X*, *Y*, and *Z*. For instance, you can create a 3D vector object using the following code snippet:

```
Vector3D v = new Vector3D(1, 2, 3);
```

Note that a *Vector3D* object and a *Point3D* object in WPF are two different objects. The following statement is invalid:

```
Vector3D v = new Point3D(1, 2, 3);
```

However, you can define a *Vector3D* object using *Point3D*, or vice versa. The following are valid statements:

```
Vector3D v1 = new Point3D(2, 3, 4) - new Point3D(1, 2, 3);
Vector3D v2 = (Vector3D)new Point3D(1, 2, 3);
Point3D pt = (Point3D)new Vector3D(1, 2, 3);
```

A *Vector3D* object has five public properties:

- *Length* – Gets the length of the *Vector3D*.

- *LengthSquared* – Gets the square of the length of the *Vector3D*.

- *X* – Gets or sets the *X* component of the *Vector3D*.

- *Y* – Gets or sets the *Y* component of the *Vector3D*.

- *Z* – Gets or sets the *Z* component of the *Vector3D*.

In addition, there are methods associated with *Vector3D* that allow you to perform various mathematical operations on *Vector3D* objects. Here are some frequently used methods:

- *Add* – Adds a *Vector3D* structure to a *Point3D* or to another *Vector3D*.

- *Subtract* – Subtracts a *Vector3D* structure or a *Point3D* structure from a *Vector3D* structure.

- *Multiply* – Multiplies a *Vector3D* structure by the specified double or *Matrix3D* and returns the result as a *Vector3D*.

- *Divide* – Divides a *Vector3D* structure by a scalar and returns the result as a *Vector3D*.

- *CrossProduct* – Calculates the cross product of two *Vector3D* structures.

- *AngleBetween* – Retrieves the angle required to rotate the first *Vector3D* structure into the second *Vector3D* structure.

- *Normalize* – Normalizes the specified *Vector3D* structure.

For example:

```
Vector3D v1 = new Vector3D(20, 10, 0);
Vector3D v2 = new Vector3D(0, 10, 20);
Vector3D cross = Vector3D.CrossProduct(v1, v2);
double angle = Vector3D.AngleBetween(v1, v2);
v1.Normalize();
double length2 = v1.LengthSquared;
```

This generates the following output: *cross* = (100, –200, 100) and *angle* = 44.42 degrees. The normalized result of *v1* is stored in *v1* again; in this case, *v1* becomes (0.802, 0.535, 0.267), which is confirmed by its length squared: *length2* = 1.

A *Point3D* structure has three public properties:

- X – Gets or sets the *X* coordinate of the *Point3D* structure.

- Y – Gets or sets the *Y* coordinate of the *Point3D* structure.

- Z – Gets or sets the *Z* coordinate of the *Point3D* structure.

In addition, there are methods associated with *Point3D* that allow you to perform various mathematical operations on *Point3D* objects. Here are some frequently used methods:

- *Add* – Adds a *Point3D* structure to a *Vector3D* and returns the results as a *Point3D* structure.

- *Subtract* – Subtracts a *Point3D* structure or a *Vector3D* structure from a *Point3D* structure.

- *Multiply* – Transforms the specified *Point3D* structure by a specified *Matrix3D* structure.

- *Offset* – Changes the *X*, *Y*, and *Z* values of the *Point3D* structure by a specified amount.

The *Point4D* structure represents a 3D point in a homogeneous coordinate system. This structure is specifically designed to perform transforms with nonaffine 3D matrices.

A *Point4D* structure has four public properties:

- *X* – Gets or sets the *X* component of the *Point4D* structure.

- *Y* – Gets or sets the *Y* component of the *Point4D* structure.

- *Z* – Gets or sets the *Z* component of the *Point4D* structure.

- *W* – Gets or sets the *W* component of the *Point4D* structure.

In addition, there are methods associated with *Point4D* that allow you to perform various mathematical operations on *Point4D* objects. The following are some frequently used methods:

- *Add* – Adds a *Point4D* structure to another *Point4D* structure.

- *Subtract* – Subtracts a *Point4D* structure from another *Point4D* structure.

- *Multiply* – Transforms the specified *Point4D* structure by the specified *Matrix3D* structure.

- *Offset* – Changes the *X*, *Y*, *Z*, and *W* values of the *Point4D* structure by a specified amount.

It is possible to cast a *Point3D* object to a *Point4D* object, as shown in the following statement:

```
Point4D pt4 = (Point4D)new Point3D(10, 15, 20);
```

The following code snippet is also valid:

```
Point4D pt4 = (Point4D)(Point3D)new Vector3D(10, 15, 20);
```

where the *Vector3D* object is first cast to a *Point3D* object, which is then cast to a *Point4D* object. In the preceding casting process, the *Point4D* object has the values *pt*4 = (10, 15, 20, 1). The *W* component with a value of 1 is automatically added.

Matrix3D Structure

WPF defines a 3D matrix structure, *Matrix3D*. It is a 4 x 4 matrix in the 3D homogeneous coordinate system and has the following row-vector syntax:

$$
\begin{pmatrix}
M_1 & M_2 & M_3 & M_4 \\
M_2 & M_2 & M_3 & M_3 \\
M_3 & M_3 & M_3 & M_3 \\
OffsetX & OffsetY & OffsetZ & M_4
\end{pmatrix}
$$

Unlike 2D matrices, here the last column is defined and accessible. The *Matrix3D* structure allows you to represent affine as well as nonaffine 3D transformations. Nonaffine transformations with nonzero $M14$, $M24$, or $M34$ values often represent perspective projection transformations.

All 16 of these elements are public properties of a *Matrix3D* structure. In particular, the elements of *OffsetX*, *OffsetY*, and *OffsetZ* get and set values of translation in the X, Y, and Z directions, respectively. In addition to the element properties, there are other public properties associated with the *Matrix3D* structure that are useful in performing matrix operations:

- *Determinant* – Retrieves the determinant of the *Matrix3D* structure.

- *HasInverse* – Gets a value that indicates whether the *Matrix3D* is invertible.

- *Identity* – Changes a *Matrix3D* structure into an identity *Matrix3D*.

- *IsAffine* – Gets a value that indicates whether the Matrix3D structure is affine.

- *IsIdentity* – Determines whether the *Matrix3D* structure is an identity *Matrix3D*.

You can create a *Matrix3D* object in WPF by using overloaded constructors, which take an array of double values as arguments. Please note that before using the *Matrix3D* structure in your applications, you'll need to add a reference to the *System.Windows.Media.Media3D* namespace. The following code snippet creates three *Matrix3D* objects that perform translation, scaling, and rotation around the Z axis by specifying the corresponding matrix elements directly:

```
double dx = 3;
double dy = 2;
double dz = 1.5;
double sx = 0.5;
double sy = 1.5;
double sz = 2.5;
double theta = Math.PI / 4;
double sin = Math.Sin(theta);
double cos = Math.Cos(theta);
Matrix3D tm = new Matrix3D( 1,  0,  0, 0,
                            0,  1,  0, 0,
                            0,  0,  1, 0,
                           dx, dy, dz, 1);
Matrix3D sm = new Matrix3D(sx,  0,  0, 0,
                            0, sy,  0, 0,
                            0,  0, sz, 0,
                            0,  0,  0, 1);
Matrix3D rm = new Matrix3D(cos, sin, 0, 0,
```

```
                          -sin, cos, 0, 0,
                            0,   0, 1, 0,
                            0,   0, 0, 1);
```

The matrix *tm* is a translation matrix that translates an object by 3 units in the *X* direction, by 2 units in the *Y* direction, and by 1.5 units in the *Z* direction. The scaling matrix *sm* scales an object by a factor of 0.5 in the *X* direction, by a factor of 1.5 in the *Y* direction, and by a factor of 2.5 in the *Z* direction. Finally, the matrix *rm* is a rotation matrix that rotates an object about the *Z* axis by 45 degrees.

Matrix3D Operations

The *Matrix3D* structure in WPF provides methods to rotate, scale, and translate objects. It also uses several methods to perform matrix operations. For example, the *Invert* method inverts a *Matrix3D* object if it is invertible. This method takes no parameters. The *Multiply* method multiplies two matrices and returns the result in a new matrix.

You must take care when applying *Matrix3D* to *Point3D*, *Point4D*, and *Vector3D* objects. For standard scaling and rotation, *Matrix3D* takes a form such that the last row and the last column consist of the elements (0, 0, 0, 1). In such cases, there will be no unexpected results. For example:

```
Matrix3D m3 = new Matrix3D(    1, 0.5, 0, 0,
                            -0.5,   1, 0, 0,
                               0,   0, 1, 0,
                               0,   0, 0, 1);
Point3D pt3 = new Point3D(2, 3, 4);
Vector3D v3 = new Vector3D(2, 3, 4);
Point4D pt4 = new Point4D(2, 3, 4, 1);
Point3D pt3t = pt3 * m3;
Vector3D v3t = v3 * m3;
Point4D pt4t = pt4 * m3;
```

This generates the expected results of *pt3t* = (0.5, 4, 4), *v3t* = (0.5, 4, 4), and *pt4t* = (0.5, 4, 4, 1) after the transformation. However, if you add a translation in the *X* direction to *Matrix3D* by changing *m3* to the form

```
Matrix3D m3 = new Matrix3D(    1, 0.5, 0, 0,
                            -0.5,   1, 0, 0,
                               0,   0, 1, 0,
                             100,   0, 0, 1);
```

then recalculating the transformation produces the output *pt3t* = (100.5, 4, 4), *v3t* = (0.5, 4, 4), and *pt4t* = (100.5, 4, 4, 1). You can see that a translation of 100 units in the *X* direction has no effect on the *Vector3D* object. This is because the *Vector3D* object is defined in real 3D space but not in a homogeneous coordinate system. The *Vector3D* object has no *W* component. When you transform a *Vector3D* object using *Matrix3D*, WPF simply uses the first 3 x 3 submatrix of the *Matrix3D* and neglects the last column and the last row.

For a *Point3D* object, even though it is defined using only the three components *X*, *Y*, and *Z*, WPF implicitly adds a *W* = 1 component to the *Point3D* object. That is why both *pt3t* and *pt4t* give correct results.

Now let's change *m3* into a nonaffine matrix by adding a nonzero element of M_{34} = 2:

```
Matrix3D m3 = new Matrix3D(    1, 0.5, 0, 0,
                            -0.5,   1, 0, 0,
                               0,   0, 1, 2,
                             100,   0, 0, 1);
```

449

This corresponds to a transform matrix with a perspective projection. After applying this transformation, you will obtain the following "strange" results:

```
pt3t = (11.167, 0.444, 0.444)
v3t = (0.5, 4, 4)
pt4t = (100.5, 4, 4, 9)
```

What happened here? It is easy to understand the result of $v3t$, since a vector always neglects the last row and the last column of a *Matrix3D*. Thus, $v3t$ will remain the same when you change the elements of the last row or the last column. The result of $pt4t$ is also expected, since it is simply a direct multiplication of $pt4*m3$.

Let's take a look at $pt3t$. This result is obtained in two steps. First, *Matrix3D* and *Point3D* object are directly multiplied with an additional $W = 1$ component, which gives the result of $pt4t$. Then $pt3t$ is obtained by normalizing the X, Y, and Z components of $pt4t$ with its W component:

```
pt3t  = (100.9/9, 4/9, 4/9) = (11.167, 0.444, 0.444)
```

In general, for an arbitrary *Point4D* = (x, y, z, w) in the homogeneous coordinate system, the plane at infinity is usually identified by a set of points with $w = 0$. When points are away from the plane at infinity, you can use $(x/w, y/w, z/w)$ to define the *Point3D*'s X, Y, and Z components. WPF automatically performs the transform on the *Point3D* objects and gives you the normalized results. The discussion presented here simply shows you the mathematical basis used by WPF to perform transforms on *Point3D* objects.

Let's consider an example to show you how to perform 3D matrix operations in WPF. Start with a new WPF Windows application project and call it *Transformation3D*. Add a new WPF Window and name it *StartMenu*. This window will be the main menu window, from which you can access all the examples in this chapter.

Next, add another WPF Window, called *Matrix3DOperation*, to the project. Here is the XAML file for this example:

```
<Window x:Class="Transformation3D.Matrix3DOperation"
    xmlns="http://schemas.microsoft.com/winfx/2006/xaml/presentation"
    xmlns:x="http://schemas.microsoft.com/winfx/2006/xaml"
    Title="Matrix3D Operation" Height="320" Width="260">
    <StackPanel>
        <TextBlock Margin="10,10,5,5" Text="Original Matrix:"/>
        <TextBlock Name="tbOriginal" Margin="20,0,5,5"/>
        <TextBlock Name="tbOriginal1" Margin="20,0,5,5"/>
        <TextBlock Margin="10,0,5,5" Text="Inverted Matrix:"/>
        <TextBlock TextWrapping="Wrap" x:Name="tbInvert" Margin="20,0,5,5"/>
        <TextBlock Margin="10,0,5,5" Text="M * M_Invert:"/>
        <TextBlock TextWrapping="Wrap" x:Name="tbInvert1" Margin="20,0,5,5"/>
        <TextBlock Margin="10,0,5,5" Text="Original Matrices:"/>
        <TextBlock Name="tbM1" Margin="20,0,5,5"/>
        <TextBlock Name="tbM2" Margin="20,0,5,5"/>
        <TextBlock Margin="10,0,5,5" Text="M1 x M2:"/>
        <TextBlock Name="tbM12" Margin="20,0,5,5"/>
        <TextBlock Margin="10,0,5,5" Text="M2 x M1:"/>
        <TextBlock Name="tbM21" Margin="20,0,5,5"/>
    </StackPanel>
</Window>
```

The foregoing code creates the layout, which displays results in text blocks. Here is the corresponding code-behind file for this example:

```
using System;
using System.Windows;
```

```
using System.Windows.Media;
using System.Windows.Media.Media3D;

namespace Transformation3D
{
public partial class Matrix3DOperation : Window
    {
        public Matrix3DOperation()
        {
            InitializeComponent();
            Matrix3D M =  new Matrix3D(1, 2, 3, 4,
                                       2, 1, 0, 0,
                                       0, 0, 1, 0,
                                       1, 2, 3, 1);
            Matrix3D M1 = M;
            Matrix3D M2 = new Matrix3D(1, 2, 0, 0,
                                       2, 1, 0, 3,
                                       0, 0, 1, 2,
                                       1, 2, 3, 1);

            tbOriginal.Text = "M = (" + M.ToString() + ")";
            tbOriginal1.Text = "M1 = M";

            // Invert matrix:
            M.Invert();
            tbInvert.Text = "(" + Utility.Matrix3DRound(M, 3).ToString() + ")";
            tbInvert1.Text = "(" + (M1 * M).ToString() + ")";

            // Matrix multiplication:
            Matrix3D M12 = M1 * M2;
            Matrix3D M21 = M2 * M1;
            tbM1.Text = "M1 = (" + M1.ToString() + ")";
            tbM2.Text = "M2 = (" + M2.ToString() + ")";
            tbM12.Text = "(" + M12.ToString() + ")";
            tbM21.Text = "(" + M21.ToString() + ")";
        }
    }
}
```

Here, you perform matrix inversions and multiplications. Note that this example uses a static method, *Matrix3DRound*, which is implemented in the *Utility* class, to display the results of the *Matrix3D* inversion. For your reference, here is the code snippet for this method:

```
public static Matrix3D Matrix3DRound(Matrix3D m, int n)
{
    m.M11 = Math.Round(m.M11, n);
    m.M12 = Math.Round(m.M12, n);
    m.M13 = Math.Round(m.M13, n);
    m.M14 = Math.Round(m.M14, n);
    m.M21 = Math.Round(m.M21, n);
    m.M22 = Math.Round(m.M22, n);
    m.M23 = Math.Round(m.M23, n);
    m.M24 = Math.Round(m.M24, n);
    m.M31 = Math.Round(m.M31, n);
```

```
    m.M32 = Math.Round(m.M32, n);
    m.M33 = Math.Round(m.M33, n);
    m.M34 = Math.Round(m.M34, n);
    m.OffsetX = Math.Round(m.OffsetX, n);
    m.OffsetY = Math.Round(m.OffsetY, n);
    m.OffsetZ = Math.Round(m.OffsetZ, n);
    m.M44 = Math.Round(m.M44, n);
    return m;
}
```

This method allows you to round the decimals of matrix elements for a *Matrix3D* object. You can see that the results of the matrix multiplications depend on the order of the matrices. By executing the project and selecting *Matrix3DOperation* from the *Start Menu,* you will obtain the output shown in Figure 12-1. First, we examine the matrix *Invert* method, which inverts the matrix (1, 2, 3, 4, 2, 1, 0, 0, 0, 0, 1, 0, 1, 2, 3, 1). The *Matrix3D.Invert* method gives the result shown in the figure. You can confirm this result by directly multiplying *M* and its inverted matrix, which will indeed give you an identity matrix.

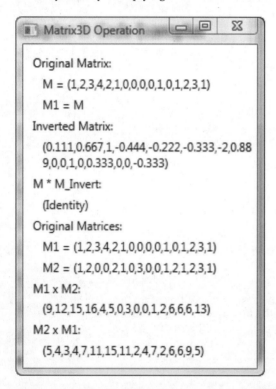

Figure 12-1. Results of Matrix3D operations in WPF

For matrix multiplications, as expected, the result depends on the order of the matrices. The results shown in Figure 12-1 demonstrate that $M1 * M2 \neq M2 * M1$.

Matrix3D Transforms

The *Matrix3D* structure in WPF also provides methods to rotate, scale, and translate matrices. Here are some of the most frequently used methods for *Matrix3D* operations:

- *Scale* – Appends the specified scale *Vector3D* to the *Matrix3D* structure.

- *ScaleAt* – Scales the *Matrix3D* by the specified *Vector3D* about the specified *Point3D*.

- *Translate* – Appends a translation of the specified offsets to the current *Matrix3D* structure.

- *Rotate* – Appends a rotation transformation to the current *Matrix3D*.

- *RotateAt* – Rotates the *Matrix3D* about the specified *Point3D*.

- *Invert* – Inverts the *Matrix3D* structure.

- *Multiply* – Multiplies the specified matrices.

- *Transform* – Transforms the specified *Point3D*, array of *Point3D* objects, *Point4D*, array of *Point4D* objects, *Vector3D*, or array of *Vector3D* objects by the *Matrix3D*.

Please note that there is no *Skew* transform in the *Matrix3D* structure. To perform a *Skew* transformation in 3D, you need to manipulate the elements of the *Matrix3D* object directly. There are corresponding *Prepend* methods associated with the scale, translation, and rotation transformations. The default methods are *Append*. Both *Append* and *Prepend* determine the matrix operation order. *Append* specifies that the new operation be applied after the preceding operation; *Prepend* specifies that the new operation be applied before the preceding operation during cumulative operations.

Let's illustrate the basic *Matrix3D* transforms (translation, scaling, and rotation) in WPF using an example. Add a new WPF Window to the project *Transformation3D*, and call it *Matrix3DTransforms*. The following is the XAML file for this example:

```
<Window x:Class=" Transformation3D.Matrix3DTransforms"
    xmlns="http://schemas.microsoft.com/winfx/2006/xaml/presentation"
    xmlns:x="http://schemas.microsoft.com/winfx/2006/xaml"
    Title="Matrix3D Transformations" Height="450" Width="300">
    <StackPanel>
        <TextBlock Margin="10,10,5,5" Text="Original Matrix:"/>
        <TextBlock Name="tbOriginal" Margin="20,0,5,5"/>
        <TextBlock Margin="10,0,5,5" Text="Scale:"/>
        <TextBlock Name="tbScale" Margin="20,0,5,5"/>
        <TextBlock Margin="10,0,5,5" Text="Scale - Prepend:"/>
        <TextBlock Name="tbScalePrepend" Margin="20,0,5,5"/>
        <TextBlock Margin="10,0,5,5" Text="Translation:"/>
        <TextBlock Name="tbTranslate" Margin="20,0,5,5"/>
        <TextBlock Margin="10,0,5,5" Text="Translation - Prepend:"/>
        <TextBlock Name="tbTranslatePrepend" Margin="20,0,5,5"/>
        <TextBlock Margin="10,0,5,5" Text="Rotation:"/>
        <TextBlock Name="tbRotate" Margin="20,0,5,5" TextWrapping="Wrap"/>
        <TextBlock Margin="10,0,5,5" Text="Rotation - Prepend:"/>
        <TextBlock Name="tbRotatePrepend" Margin="20,0,5,5" TextWrapping="Wrap"/>
        <TextBlock Margin="10,0,5,5" Text="RotationAt:"/>
        <TextBlock Name="tbRotateAt" Margin="20,0,5,5" TextWrapping="Wrap"/>
        <TextBlock Margin="10,0,5,5" Text="RotationAt - Prepend:"/>
        <TextBlock Name="tbRotateAtPrepend" Margin="20,0,5,5" TextWrapping="Wrap"/>
```

```
        </StackPanel>
</Window>
```

The foregoing code creates a layout that displays results using text blocks, which are embedded in a *StackPanel* control. The corresponding code-behind file is given by the following code:

```csharp
using System;
using System.Windows;
using System.Windows.Media;
using System.Windows.Media.Media3D;

namespace Transformation3D
{
public partial class Matrix3DTransforms: Window
    {
        public Matrix3DTransforms()
        {
            InitializeComponent();

            // Original matrix:
            Matrix3D M = new Matrix3D(1, 2, 3, 4,
                                      2, 1, 0, 0,
                                      0, 0, 1, 0,
                                      1, 2, 3, 1);
            Matrix3D M1 = M;
            tbOriginal.Text = "(" + M.ToString() + ")";

            //Scale:
            M.Scale(new Vector3D(0.5, 1.5, 2.5));
            tbScale.Text = "(" + M.ToString() + ")";

            M = M1; // Reset M to the original matrix.
            M.ScalePrepend(new Vector3D(0.5, 1.5, 2.5));
            tbScalePrepend.Text = "(" + M.ToString() + ")";

            //Translation:
            M = M1; // Reset M to the original matrix.
            M.Translate(new Vector3D(100, 150, 200));
            tbTranslate.Text = "(" + M.ToString() + ")";

            // Translation - Prepend:
            M = M1; // Reset M to the original matrix.
            M.TranslatePrepend(new Vector3D(100, 150, 200));
            tbTranslatePrepend.Text = "(" + M.ToString() + ")";

            // Rotation:
            M = M1; // Reset M to the original matrix.
            M.Rotate(new Quaternion(new Vector3D(1, 2, 3), 45));
            tbRotate.Text = "(" + Utility.Matrix3DRound(M, 3).ToString() + ")";

            // Rotation - Prepend:
            M = M1; // Reset M to the original matrix.
            M.RotatePrepend(new Quaternion(new Vector3D(1, 2, 3), 45));
            tbRotatePrepend.Text = "(" +
                        Utility.Matrix3DRound(M, 3).ToString() + ")";
```

```
        //Rotation at (x = 10, y = 20, z = 30):
        M = M1; // Reset M to the original matrix.
        M.RotateAt(new Quaternion(new Vector3D(1, 2, 3), 45),
                        new Point3D(10, 20, 30));
        tbRotateAt.Text = "(" + Utility.Matrix3DRound(M, 3).ToString() + ")";

        // Rotation at (x = 10, y = 20, z = 30) - Prepend:
        M = M1; // Reset M to the original matrix.
        M.RotateAtPrepend(new Quaternion(new Vector3D(1, 2, 3), 45),
                        new Point3D(10, 20, 30));
        tbRotateAtPrepend.Text = "(" +
                    Utility.Matrix3DRound(M, 3).ToString() + ")";
    }
  }
}
```

Building and running this example generates the output shown in Figure 12-2. The original *Matrix3D* object *M* is operated on by various transforms. Next, we'll examine the WPF results using direct matrix computations.

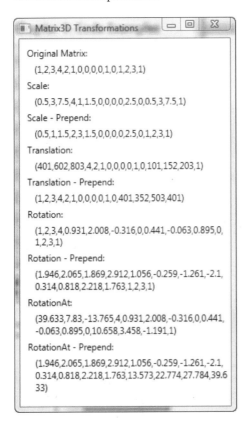

Figure 12-2. Results of the Matrix3D transformations

455

First, let's examine the scale transformation, which sets a scaling factor of 0.5 in the X direction, 1.5 in the Y direction, and 2.5 in the Z direction. You must specify these scale parameters using a *Vector3D* object. For the *Append* scaling (the default setting), we have

$$\begin{pmatrix} 1 & 2 & 3 & 4 \\ 2 & 1 & 0 & 0 \\ 0 & 0 & 1 & 0 \\ 1 & 2 & 3 & 1 \end{pmatrix} \begin{pmatrix} 0.5 & 0 & 0 & 0 \\ 0 & 1.5 & 0 & 0 \\ 0 & 0 & 2.5 & 0 \\ 0 & 0 & 0 & 1 \end{pmatrix} = \begin{pmatrix} 0.5 & 3 & 7.5 & 4 \\ 1 & 1.5 & 0 & 0 \\ 0 & 0 & 2.5 & 0 \\ 0.5 & 3 & 7.5 & 1 \end{pmatrix}$$

This gives the same result seen in Figure 12-2.

On the other hand, for the *Prepend* scaling, we have

$$\begin{pmatrix} 0.5 & 0 & 0 & 0 \\ 0 & 1.5 & 0 & 0 \\ 0 & 0 & 2.5 & 0 \\ 0 & 0 & 0 & 1 \end{pmatrix} \begin{pmatrix} 1 & 2 & 3 & 4 \\ 2 & 1 & 0 & 0 \\ 0 & 0 & 1 & 0 \\ 1 & 2 & 3 & 1 \end{pmatrix} = \begin{pmatrix} 0.5 & 1 & 1.5 & 2 \\ 3 & 1.5 & 0 & 0 \\ 0 & 0 & 2.5 & 0 \\ 1 & 2 & 3 & 1 \end{pmatrix}$$

This confirms the output shown in Figure 12-1.

Next, you translate the matrix M by 100 units in the X direction, 150 units in the Y direction, and 200 units in the Z direction. For the default *Append* translation, you have

$$\begin{pmatrix} 1 & 2 & 3 & 4 \\ 2 & 1 & 0 & 0 \\ 0 & 0 & 1 & 0 \\ 1 & 2 & 3 & 1 \end{pmatrix} \begin{pmatrix} 1 & 0 & 0 & 0 \\ 0 & 1 & 0 & 0 \\ 0 & 0 & 1 & 0 \\ 100 & 150 & 200 & 1 \end{pmatrix} = \begin{pmatrix} 401 & 602 & 803 & 4 \\ 2 & 1 & 0 & 0 \\ 0 & 0 & 1 & 0 \\ 101 & 152 & 203 & 1 \end{pmatrix}$$

This is consistent with the results shown in Figure 12-2.

The *Prepend* translation involves the following transformation:

$$\begin{pmatrix} 1 & 0 & 0 & 0 \\ 0 & 1 & 0 & 0 \\ 0 & 0 & 1 & 0 \\ 100 & 150 & 200 & 1 \end{pmatrix} \begin{pmatrix} 1 & 2 & 3 & 4 \\ 2 & 1 & 0 & 0 \\ 0 & 0 & 1 & 0 \\ 1 & 2 & 3 & 1 \end{pmatrix} = \begin{pmatrix} 1 & 2 & 3 & 4 \\ 2 & 1 & 0 & 0 \\ 0 & 0 & 1 & 0 \\ 401 & 352 & 503 & 401 \end{pmatrix}$$

This is also confirmed by the result shown in Figure 12-2.

Rotation and Quaternion

Rotation is one of the most commonly used transforms in 3D. 3D rotation about an arbitrary axis is also one of the most complex 3D transforms. WPF uses quaternion notation, which can be specified either by a position *Vector3D* object and a rotation angle or by four quaternion components in the form of (x, y, z, w).

You can calculate the quaternion components from a rotation axis vector and rotation angle, but note that the axis vector must be normalized. Suppose that the rotation axis for a 3D rotation is denoted by a unit *Vector3D* object (*ax*, *ay*, *az*) and the rotation angle is θ. You can find the quaternion (*x*, *y*, *z*, *w*) using the following formula:

$$x = ax \cdot \sin(\theta/2)$$
$$y = ay \cdot \sin(\theta/2)$$
$$z = az \cdot \sin(\theta/2) \qquad (12.1)$$
$$w = \cos(\theta/2)$$

For the rotation transform demonstrated in the *Matrix3DTransforms* example, you rotate the original *M* matrix by 45 degrees along the axis specified by a *Vector3D* object (1, 2, 3). The unit rotation axis can be obtained by normalizing this *Vector3D* object:

$$(ax, ay\ az) = (1, 2, 3)/\sqrt{14} = (0.267, 0.535, 0.802)$$

and θ = 45 degrees. You can then easily calculate its quaternion using Equation (12.1):

$$(x, y, z, w) = (0.102, 0.205, 0.307, 0.924)$$

You can see that the preceding quaternion (*x*, *y*, *z*, *w*) is also normalized to unity. Using this quaternion, you can construct the rotation matrix:

$$
\begin{pmatrix}
w^2 + x^2 - y^2 - z^2 & 2xy + 2zw & 2xz - 2yw & 0 \\
2xy - 2zw & w^2 - x^2 + y^2 - z^2 & 2yz + 2xw & 0 \\
2xz + 2yw & 2yz - 2xw & w^2 - x^2 - y^2 + z^2 & 0 \\
0 & 0 & 0 & w^2 + x^2 + y^2 + z^2
\end{pmatrix}
$$

$$
=
\begin{pmatrix}
0.728 & 0.609 & -0.315 & 0 \\
-0.525 & 0.791 & 0.315 & 0 \\
0.441 & -0.063 & 0.895 & 0 \\
0 & 0 & 0 & 1
\end{pmatrix}
$$

From this rotation matrix, you can examine the effect of the rotation on the original *Matrix3D* object *M*. In the case of the Append rotation, we have

$$
\begin{pmatrix}
1 & 2 & 3 & 4 \\
2 & 1 & 0 & 0 \\
0 & 0 & 1 & 0 \\
1 & 2 & 3 & 1
\end{pmatrix}
\begin{pmatrix}
0.728 & 0.609 & -0.315 & 0 \\
-0.525 & 0.791 & 0.315 & 0 \\
0.441 & -0.063 & 0.895 & 0 \\
0 & 0 & 0 & 1
\end{pmatrix}
=
\begin{pmatrix}
1 & 2 & 3 & 4 \\
0.913 & 2 & -0.316 & 0 \\
0.441 & -0.063 & 0.895 & 0 \\
1 & 2 & 3 & 1
\end{pmatrix}
$$

This result is the same as that given in Figure 12-2.

For the *Prepend* rotation, we have

$$\begin{pmatrix} 0.728 & 0.609 & -0.315 & 0 \\ -0.525 & 0.791 & 0.315 & 0 \\ 0.441 & -0.063 & 0.895 & 0 \\ 0 & 0 & 0 & 1 \end{pmatrix} \begin{pmatrix} 1 & 2 & 3 & 4 \\ 2 & 1 & 0 & 0 \\ 0 & 0 & 1 & 0 \\ 1 & 2 & 3 & 1 \end{pmatrix} = \begin{pmatrix} 1.946 & 2.065 & 1.869 & 2.912 \\ 1.056 & -0.259 & -0.1.261 & -2.1 \\ 0.314 & 0.818 & 2.218 & 1.763 \\ 1 & 2 & 3 & 1 \end{pmatrix}$$

This result is also consistent with that given in Figure 12-2.

The *RotateAt* method in 3D is designed for cases in which you need to change the center of rotation. In fact, the *Rotate* method is a special case of *RotateAt*, with the rotation center at (0, 0, 0). The rotation center in 3D is specified by a *Point3D* object. In this example, the matrix is rotated at the point (10, 20, 30). As we've discussed previously, the rotation of an object about an arbitrary point *P*1 must be performed according to the following procedures:

- Translate *P*1 to the origin.

- Rotate the object to the desired angle.

- Translate so that the point at the origin returns to *P*1.

Considering the definition of matrix transforms in WPF, the rotation matrix at the point (10, 30, 20) should be expressed in the following form:

$$T(-dx,-dy,-dz)\cdot R(\theta)\cdot T(dx,dy,dz)$$

$$= \begin{pmatrix} 1 & 0 & 0 & 0 \\ 0 & 1 & 0 & 0 \\ 0 & 0 & 1 & 0 \\ -10 & -30 & -20 & 1 \end{pmatrix} \begin{pmatrix} 0.728 & 0.609 & -0.315 & 0 \\ -0.525 & 0.791 & 0.315 & 0 \\ 0.441 & -0.063 & 0.895 & 0 \\ 0 & 0 & 0 & 1 \end{pmatrix} \begin{pmatrix} 1 & 0 & 0 & 0 \\ 0 & 1 & 0 & 0 \\ 0 & 0 & 1 & 0 \\ 10 & 30 & 20 & 1 \end{pmatrix}$$

$$= \begin{pmatrix} 0.728 & 0.609 & -0.315 & 0 \\ -0.525 & 0.791 & 0.315 & 0 \\ 0.441 & -0.063 & 0.895 & 0 \\ 9.658 & 1.458 & -4.191 & 1 \end{pmatrix}$$

Thus, the *Append* rotation of matrix *M* at point (10, 30, 20) becomes:

$$\begin{pmatrix} 1 & 2 & 3 & 4 \\ 2 & 1 & 0 & 0 \\ 0 & 0 & 1 & 0 \\ 1 & 2 & 3 & 1 \end{pmatrix} \begin{pmatrix} 0.728 & 0.609 & -0.315 & 0 \\ -0.525 & 0.791 & 0.315 & 0 \\ 0.441 & -0.063 & 0.895 & 0 \\ 9.658 & 1.458 & -4.191 & 1 \end{pmatrix} = \begin{pmatrix} 39.633 & 7.83 & -13.765 & 4 \\ 0.931 & 2.008 & -0.316 & 0 \\ 0.441 & -0.063 & 0.895 & 0 \\ 10.658 & 3.458 & -1.191 & 1 \end{pmatrix}$$

This again confirms the result shown in Figure 12-2.

Similarly, the *Prepend* rotation of *Matrix3D* object *M* at point (10, 30, 20) should be

$$\begin{pmatrix} 0.728 & 0.609 & -0.315 & 0 \\ -0.525 & 0.791 & 0.315 & 0 \\ 0.441 & -0.063 & 0.895 & 0 \\ 9.658 & 1.458 & -4.191 & 1 \end{pmatrix} \begin{pmatrix} 1 & 2 & 3 & 4 \\ 2 & 1 & 0 & 0 \\ 0 & 0 & 1 & 0 \\ 1 & 2 & 3 & 1 \end{pmatrix} = \begin{pmatrix} 1.946 & 2.065 & 1.869 & 2.912 \\ 1.056 & -0.259 & -1.261 & -2.1 \\ 0.314 & 0.818 & 2.218 & 1.763 \\ 13.573 & 22.774 & 27.784 & 39.633 \end{pmatrix}$$

This result is also the same as the one given in Figure 12-2.

Here, I have presented detailed explanations of 3D matrix transforms in WPF. This information is useful in understanding the definitions and internal representations of *Matrix3D* in WPF. It is also important in making sure that you are applying matrix transformations correctly to 3D objects in your applications.

Projections

Since the computer screen is two-dimensional, it can't display 3D objects directly. In order to view 3D objects on a 2D screen, you have to project the objects from 3D to 2D.

The most common types of projections are called *planar geometric projections*. These are a distinct class of projections that maintain straight lines when mapping an object onto a viewing surface. In a planar geometric projection, a ray or projector is passed from a center of projection through the points being projected onto a planar viewing surface, called the *view plane*. Figure 12-3 shows the projection of a square object onto a 2D view plane.

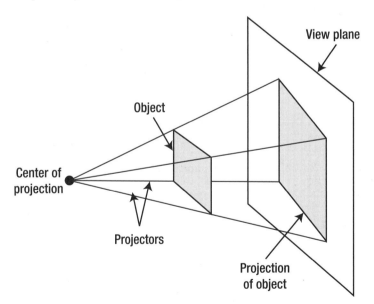

Figure 12-3. Projection of a square object from 3D to a 2D view plane

WPF implements two kinds of projections: orthographic and perspective. I'll discuss these two kinds of projections in the following subsections.

Orthographic Projections

Orthographic projection is kind of parallel projection, meaning that the center of projection is located at an infinite distance from the view plane. By placing the center of projection at an infinite distance from the view plane, the projectors become parallel to the view plane. For a parallel projection, instead of specifying a center of projection, you need to specify a direction of projection. Figure 12-4 shows a parallel projection of a square object onto the view plane.

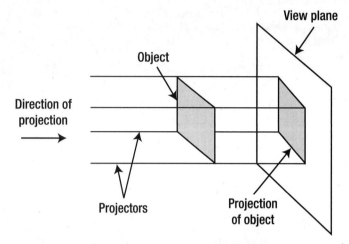

Figure 12-4. *A parallel projection of a square object*

In addition to being parallel, projectors in an orthographic projection are perpendicular to the view plane. Orthographic projections are often used in architectural and mechanical drawings. We can categorize them further as either multiview or axonometric projections, which we describe next.

Multiview Projections

A multiview projection shows a single face of a 3D object. Common choices for viewing a 3D object in 2D include front, side, and top view. Figure 12-5 shows a house object as well as its front, side, and top views.

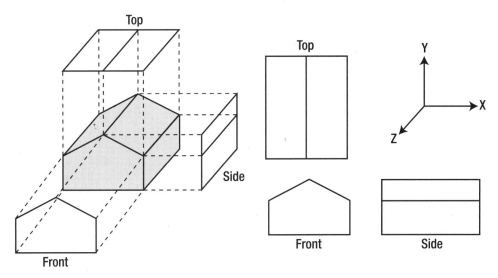

Figure 12-5. *Front, side, and top views of the orthographic projections*

These kinds of projections are very simple. To project a point, simply ignore the point's unneeded third coordinate. In top view, the normal of the view plane is parallel to the positive *Y* axis in a right-handed system, as shown in Figure 12-5. To project the top view of a 3D object, we discard the *Y* coordinates and map the *X* and *Z* coordinates for each point onto the view plane. Repositioning the normal of the view plane to the positive *Z* axis and selecting the *X* and *Y* coordinates for each point projects a front view onto the view plane.

Likewise, we can achieve a side view when we direct the normal of the view plane along the positive *X* axis and project the *Y* and *Z* coordinates of a 3D object onto the view plane. These projections are often used in engineering and architectural drawings. Although they don't show the 3D aspect of an object, multiview projections are useful because they maintain the angles and dimensions of the object.

Axonometric Projections

Multiview projections preserve distances and angles; in other words, you can measure distances and angles directly from the projection of an object. However, it is often difficult to understand the 3D structure of an object by examining only its multiview projections.

To make the 3D nature of an object more apparent, you can use projections that aren't parallel to the *X*, *Y*, or *Z* axes. Such projections include axonometric orthographic projections. Unlike multiview projections, axonometric projections allow you to place the normal of the view plane in any direction so that three adjacent faces of a "cubelike" object are visible. To avoid duplication of the views displayed by multiview projections, we usually do not place the normal of the view plane parallel to a major axis for axonometric views. The increased versatility in the direction of the normal of the view plane should position the view plane so that it intersects at least two of the major axes. Lines on a 3D object that are parallel in the world coordinate system are likewise projected to the view plane as parallel lines. In addition, this maintains the length of a line, or line preservation, for lines parallel to the view plane. Other receding lines maintain only their proportion and are foreshortened equally with lines along the same axes.

We can divide axonometric projections further into three types that depend on the number of major axes foreshortened equally: isometric, dimetric, and trimetric projections.

Isometric Projections

An isometric projection is a commonly used type of axonometric projection. In this kind of projection, all three of the major axes are foreshortened equally, since the normal of the view plane makes equal angles with all three coordinate axes.

Figure 12-6 shows the isometric projection of a cube object. Isometric projection scales lines equally along each axis, which is often useful since we can measure and convert lines along the coordinate axes using the same scale.

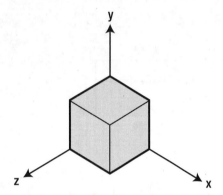

Figure 12-6. *Isometric projection of a cube object*

Dimetric Projections

Dimetric projections differ from isometric projections in the direction of the normal of the view plane. In this case, the view plane is set so that it makes equal angles with two of the coordinate axes.

Figure 12-7 shows a dimetric projection of a cube object. Setting the normal of the view plane so that the view plane is parallel to a major axis maintains line measurements in the projection for lines that are parallel to the chosen axis.

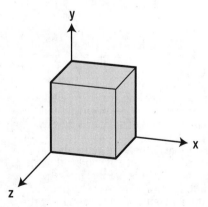

Figure 12-7. *Dimetric projection of a cube object*

Trimetric Projections

In trimetric projection, the normal of the view plane makes different angles with each coordinate axis, since no two components have the same value. As with a dimetric view, a trimetric view can display different orientations when differing amounts of emphasis are placed on the faces. A potential disadvantage of the trimetric projections is that measuring lines along the axes becomes difficult due to the difference in scaling factors.

Figure 12-8 shows a trimetric projection of a cube object. You can see how the unequal-foreshortening characteristic of this type of projection affects line measurements along the different axes. While disadvantageous for maintaining measurements, a trimetric projection, with the correct orientation, can offer a realistic and natural view of an object.

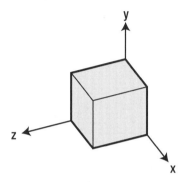

Figure 12-8. Trimetric projection of a cube object

In addition to orthographic projections, parallel projections include oblique projections. Oblique projections are useful because they combine the advantageous qualities of both multiview and axonometric projections. Like axonometric projections, this type of projection emphasizes the 3D features of an object. At the same time, like multiview projections, oblique views display the exact shape of one face. Oblique view uses parallel projectors, but the angle between the projectors and the view plane is no longer orthogonal. Because of these properties, more than one face of the object is visible in an oblique projection. We will not discuss oblique projections further in this book. For more information about these projections and their projection matrices, please refer to my other book, *Practical C# Charts and Graphics*.

Perspective Projections

In a perspective projection, objects of equal size at different distances from the view plane will be projected at different sizes, so nearer objects will appear closer. The projectors pass from a center of projection through each point in the object onto the view plane.

Figure 12-9 shows a perspective projection of two identical square objects. The square that is farther from the center of projection is projected as a smaller image on the view plane.

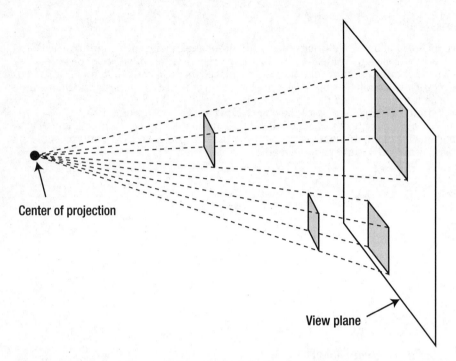

Center of projection

View plane

Figure 12-9. Perspective projections: Objects farther from the center of projection appear smaller than closer objects.

In comparison to parallel projections, perspective projections often provide a more natural and realistic view of a 3D object. If we compare the view plane of a perspective projection with the view seen from the lens of a camera, we can easily understand the underlying principle of perspective projection. Like the view from a camera, lines in a perspective projection that are not parallel to the view plane converge at a distant point (called the *vanishing point*) in the background. When the eye or camera is positioned close to the object, perspective foreshortening occurs, with distant objects appearing smaller in the view plane than closer objects of the same size, as shown in Figure 12-9.

We can classify perspective projections by the number of vanishing points they contain. There are three types of perspective projections: one-point, two-point, and three-point perspective projections. Each type differs in the orientation of the view plane and the number of vanishing points.

One-Point Perspective Projections

In one-point perspective, lines of a 3D object along a coordinate axis converge at a single vanishing point and lines parallel to the other axes remain horizontal or vertical in the view plane. To create a one-point perspective view, we set the view plane parallel to one of the principal planes in the world coordinate system. Figure 12-10 shows a one-point perspective view of a cube. In this projection, we have positioned the view plane in front of the cube and parallel to the X-Y plane.

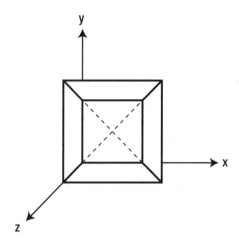

Figure 12-10. *One-point perspective projection*

Two-Point Perspective Projections

Two-point perspective projects an object onto the view plane so that lines parallel to two of the major axes converge at two separate vanishing points. To create a two-point perspective projection, we set the view plane parallel to a coordinate axis rather than to a plane. To satisfy this condition, we must set the normal of the view plane perpendicular to one of the major world coordinate system axes. Figure 12-11 shows a two-point perspective view of a cube. In this figure, lines parallel to the *X* axis converge at a vanishing point and lines parallel to the *Z* axis converge at another vanishing point. Two-point perspective views often provide greater realism in comparison to other projection types; for this reason, they are commonly used in architectural, engineering, and industrial designs.

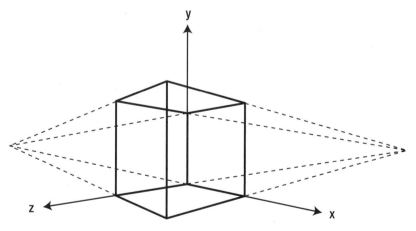

Figure 12-11. *Two-point perspective projection*

Three-Point Perspective Projections

A three-point perspective projection has three vanishing points. In this case, the view plane is not parallel to any of the major axes. To position the view plane, each component of the view plane's normal is set to a nonzero value so that the view plane intersects three major axes. Artists often use three-vanishing-point projection for highlighting features or increasing dramatic effect. Figure 12-12 shows a three-point perspective projection of a cube.

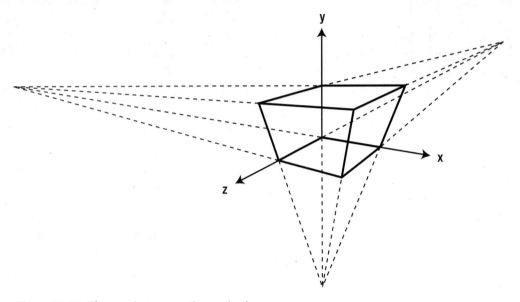

Figure 12-12. Three-point perspective projection

Perspective Projection Matrix

Constructing a general perspective projection matrix is quite complicated. Here, we will only discuss a simple case of perspective projection. This simple perspective view projects onto the X-Y plane when the center of projection lies on the Z axis. Figure 12-13 shows a point $P = (x, y, z)$ being projected onto the point $P1 = (x1, y1, z1)$ in the X-Y plane. The center of projection is located at $(0, 0, d)$, where d is the distance along the Z axis. On the right of Figure 12-13 is a side view of the projection showing the Y and Z axes. The point A is the center of projection, and the point B is the point on the Z axis that has the same Z coordinates as point P.

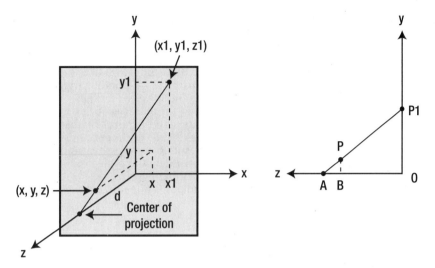

Figure 12-13. *Perspective projection of a point P = (x, y, z)*

From this figure, you can see that $AO = d$, $OP1 = y1$, $BP = y$, and $AB = d - z$. When you solve for $y1$, you get $y1 = d * y/(d - z)$. This gives the Y coordinate of the projected point $P1$. By examining a similar top view that shows the X and Z axes, you can find that $x1 = d * x/(d - z)$. For the projected point on the X-Y plane, $z1$ should equal 0. From this information, you can construct a transform matrix for this perspective projection:

$$(x1 \quad y1 \quad z1 \quad w1) = (x \quad y \quad z \quad 1)\begin{pmatrix} 1 & 0 & 0 & 0 \\ 0 & 1 & 0 & 0 \\ 0 & 0 & 0 & -1/d \\ 0 & 0 & 0 & 1 \end{pmatrix} = (x \quad y \quad 0 \quad 1-z/d)$$

Remember that in homogeneous coordinates, the w-component of a point represents a scaling factor. Normalizing the projected point $P1$ by $w1$, you have

$$(x1/w1 \quad y1/w1 \quad z1/w1 \quad 1) = (x/(1-z/d) \quad y/(1-z/d) \quad 0 \quad 1)$$

This agrees with the information deduced from Figure 12-13.

Views and Projections in WPF

In order to display 3D objects on a 2D screen, we must perform a series of transformations on the 3D objects. WPF uses several transforms to change the 3D model coordinates into device-independent pixels. These transforms include view transforms, projection transforms, and world transforms. Remember that perspective projection in WPF is based on one-point perspective projection.

The world transform controls how model coordinates are transformed into world coordinates. The world transform can include translation, scaling, and rotation. The view transform controls the transition from world coordinates into camera space. It determines the camera position in the world coordinate system. The projection transform changes the geometry of 3D objects from the camera space into the clipping space and applies perspective distortion to the objects. The *clipping space* refers to how the geometry is clipped to the view volume during this transformation. Finally, the geometry in the clipping space is transformed into device-independent pixels (the *screen space*). This transform is controlled by the *Viewport* settings.

WPF provides a variety of classes that allow you to perform various transformations on 3D objects. It also constructs transform matrices for *View* and *Projection* and performs the corresponding transforms behind the scene. For your part, you simply need to specify the *Camera* and *Viewport* settings. Technically, in order to create 3D objects in WPF, you don't need to know the matrices of view and projection transforms. However, understanding the mathematical basics of these transform matrices and knowing how to construct them from *Camera* and *Viewport* settings is still very important in developing professional 3D graphics applications. For example, if you want to customize the *Camera* and *Viewport* settings provided by WPF, you'll have to construct your own view and projection transform matrices.

In the following sections, you'll learn how to construct the view and projection transform matrices that are used in WPF.

View Transform

In order to display 3D objects on a 2D computer screen, you must first decide how you want to position the objects in the scene, and you must choose a vantage point from which to view the scene.

The transformation process used to create the scene for viewing is analogous to taking a photograph with a camera. Using a view transform is analogous to positioning and aligning a camera. A view transform changes the position and orientation of the viewport.

View transforms locate the viewer in world space and transform 3D objects into camera space. In camera space, the camera (or viewer) is at the origin, looking in the negative Z direction. Recall that WPF uses a right-handed coordinate system, so Z is negative in a scene. The view matrix relocates the objects in the world coordinate system around a camera's position — the origin and orientation of the camera.

There are many ways to construct a view matrix. In each case, the camera has a logical position and orientation in world space, which serves as a starting point to create a view matrix. We will apply this view matrix to the models in a scene. The view matrix translates and rotates objects in order to place them in camera space, where the camera is at the origin. One way to construct a view matrix is to combine a translation matrix with rotation matrices for each axis. Here are steps to obtain a view transform:

- Translate a given camera position to the origin.

- Rotate about the Y axis in the world space to bring the camera coordinate's Z axis into the Y-Z plane of world coordinates.

- Rotate about the world coordinate X axis to align the Z axes of both the world and camera systems.

- Rotate about the world coordinate Z axis to align the Y axis in both the world and camera spaces.

Then, the view transform can be written in the form

$$V = T \cdot R(y) \cdot R(x) \cdot R(z)$$

In this formula, V is the view matrix, T is a translation matrix that repositions objects (or the camera) in the world space, and $R(x)$, $R(y)$, and $R(z)$ are rotation matrices that rotate objects along the X, Y, and Z axes, respectively. The translation and rotation matrices are based on the camera's logical position and orientation in world space. So if the camera's logical position in the world is (10, 20, 30), the purpose of the translation matrix is to move objects –10 units along the X axis, –20 units along the Y axis, and –30 units along the Z axis. The rotation matrices in the formula are based on the camera's orientation, in terms of the degree to which we rotate the axes of camera space out of alignment with the world space.

In practice, we specify the relationship between the camera and the object by three sets of arguments: the camera position $P(x, y, z)$, the *look at* vector N, which defines the camera's look-at direction, and the *up* vector U, which indicates which is the up-direction of the camera. Choose the camera position to yield the desired view of the scene, which will typically be somewhere in the middle of the scene. WPF uses these three quantities to set the camera. Here, I'll show you how to construct the view transform matrix using these three parameters.

- Create three vectors in 3D space: *XScale*, *YScale*, and *ZScale*.

- Normalize N and U; i.e., let both N and U be unit vectors.

- Let $ZScale = N$; i.e., set *ZScale* to the look-at direction.

- Compute *YScale* using the formula $YScale = \dfrac{\vec{U} - (\vec{U} \cdot \vec{N})\vec{N}}{\sqrt{1 - (\vec{U} \cdot \vec{N})^2}}$.

- Compute *XScale* using the formula $XScale = \dfrac{\vec{N} \times \vec{U}}{\sqrt{1 - (\vec{U} \cdot \vec{N})^2}}$.

- Construct an M matrix in the 3D homogeneous coordinate system

$$M = \begin{pmatrix} XScale.X & YScale.X & ZScale.X & 0 \\ XScale.Y & YScale.Y & ZScale.Y & 0 \\ XScale.Z & YScale.Z & ZScale.Z & 0 \\ 0 & 0 & 0 & 1 \end{pmatrix} .$$

- Translate the camera position to the origin and reflect it about the Z axis. Thus, the view transform matrix V is given by $V = T(-x, -y, -z) \cdot M \cdot S(1, 1, -1)$, where T is a translation matrix and S is a scaling matrix with a scaling factor of $sz = -1$, which corresponds to a reflection about the Z axis.

You can easily construct a view transform matrix following the foregoing steps. Open the *Transformation3D* project and add a public static method, *SetViewMatrix*, to the *Utility* class:

```
public static Matrix3D SetViewMatrix(Point3D cameraPosition,
                             Vector3D lookDirection, Vector3D upDirection)
{
    // Normalize vectors:
    lookDirection.Normalize();
    upDirection.Normalize();

    // Define vectors, XScale, YScale, and ZScale:
    double denom = Math.Sqrt(1 - Math.Pow(Vector3D.DotProduct(lookDirection,
                        upDirection), 2));
    Vector3D XScale = Vector3D.CrossProduct(lookDirection, upDirection) / denom;
    Vector3D YScale = (upDirection - (Vector3D.DotProduct(upDirection,
                        lookDirection)) * lookDirection) / denom;
    Vector3D ZScale = lookDirection;
```

469

```
// Construct M matrix:
Matrix3D M = new Matrix3D();
M.M11 = XScale.X;
M.M21 = XScale.Y;
M.M31 = XScale.Z;
M.M12 = YScale.X;
M.M22 = YScale.Y;
M.M32 = YScale.Z;
M.M13 = ZScale.X;
M.M23 = ZScale.Y;
M.M33 = ZScale.Z;

// Translate the camera position to the origin:
Matrix3D translateMatrix = new Matrix3D();
translateMatrix.Translate(new Vector3D(-cameraPosition.X,
                          -cameraPosition.Y, -cameraPosition.Z));

// Define reflect matrix about the Z axis:
Matrix3D reflectMatrix = new Matrix3D();
reflectMatrix.M33 = -1;

// Construct the View matrix:
Matrix3D viewMatrix = translateMatrix * M * reflectMatrix;
return viewMatrix;
}
```

Perspective Projection

The preceding section described how to compose the view transform matrix so that you can apply the correct modeling and viewing transform. In this section, I'll explain how to define the desired perspective projection matrix in WPF, which is needed to transform the vertices in your scene.

View Frustum

In earlier sections of this chapter we discussed the projections in a general way, but we didn't consider the effect of the camera and viewport settings on projections. Now we need to consider these factors in order to apply projections in real-world WPF graphics applications.

The purpose of the projection transformation is to define a view volume, called *View Frustum*, which we use in two ways. The frustum determines how an object is projected onto the screen. It also defines which objects or portions of objects are clipped out of the final image.

The key feature of perspective projection is *foreshortening*: The farther an object is from the camera, the smaller it appears on the screen. This occurs because the frustum for a perspective projection is a truncated pyramid whose top has been cut off by a plane parallel to its base. Objects falling within the frustum are projected toward the apex of the pyramid, where the camera is located. Objects that are closer to the camera appear larger because they occupy a proportionately larger amount of the viewing volume than those that are farther away. This method of projection is commonly used in 3D computer graphics and visual simulation, because it is similar to how a camera works.

Remember that the viewing volume is used to clip objects that lie outside of it; the four sides of the frustum, its top, and its base correspond to the six clipping planes of the viewing volume, as shown in Figure 12-14. Objects or parts of objects outside these planes are clipped from the final image.

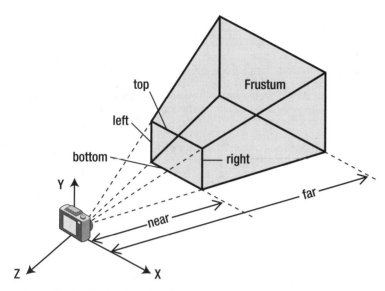

Figure 12-14. *Projective view frustum*

Perspective Transform Matrix

Now our task is to construct the perspective transform matrix used in WPF. A perspective projection maps the X and Y coordinates onto the projection plane while maintaining depth information, which we can achieve by mapping the view frustum onto a cube. This cube is the projection into 3D space of what is called the *clip space*, which is centered at the origin and extends from –1 to 1 on each of the X, Y, and Z axes.

Let $P = (x, y, z, 1)$ be a point in the camera space that lies inside the view frustum. We will try to construct the projection matrix using the parameters of this view frustum. The left edge of the rectangle carved out of the near plane by the four side planes of the view frustum will be at $x = l$, the right edge at $x = r$, the bottom edge at $y = b$, and the top edge at $y = t$.

The near plane and the far plane are located at $z = -zn$ and zf in the right-hand coordinate system. Thus, you can calculate the projected $x1$ and $y1$ coordinates of the point P on the near plane:

$$x1 = -\frac{zn}{z}x, \qquad y1 = -\frac{zn}{z}y \qquad (12.2)$$

Note that $z < 0$ because the camera points in the negative Z direction. We want to map these coordinates into the range [–1, 1], which is needed to fit the view frustum into the clip space. This can be done using the following relationships:

$$x2 = (x1 - l)\frac{2}{r - l} - 1, \qquad y2 = (y1 - b)\frac{2}{t - b} - 1 \qquad (12.3)$$

Substituting $x1$ and $y1$ in Equation (12.3) using Equation (12.1) yields:

$$x2 = \left(-\frac{x}{z}\right)\frac{2 \cdot zn}{r-l} - \frac{r+l}{r-l}, \quad y2 = \left(-\frac{y}{z}\right)\frac{2 \cdot zn}{t-b} - \frac{t+b}{t-b} \quad (12.4)$$

I should point out here that the range used to map the projected Z component is different for different technologies. In the OpenGL platform, this mapping range is from –1 to +1. However, Microsoft uses the mapping range [0, 1] for its Direct3D and WPF frameworks. These two mapping ranges do give slightly different projection matrices; however, they have no effect on the final image displayed on your screen.

Here, we'll use Microsoft convention. That is, we will use the range [0, 1] for mapping the projected Z component. This mapping involves a somewhat more complex computation. Since the point P lies inside the view frustum, its Z component must be within the range [–zf, –zn]. We need to find a function that maps –$zn \rightarrow 0$, –$zf \rightarrow 1$. Assume that the mapping function has the following form:

$$z2 = \frac{C1}{z} + C2 \quad (12.5)$$

You can solve for the coefficients $C1$ and $C2$ by plugging in the known mappings –$zn \rightarrow 0$ and –$zf \rightarrow 1$ to obtain

$$0 = \frac{C1}{-zn} + C2 \quad \text{and} \quad 1 = \frac{C1}{-zf} + C2$$

Solving these equations yields the following results:

$$C1 = \frac{zn \cdot zf}{zf - zn}, \quad C2 = \frac{zf}{zf - zn}$$

Substituting the foregoing equations into Equation (12.5) yields

$$z2 = \left(\frac{1}{z}\right)\left(\frac{zn \cdot zf}{zf - zn}\right) + \frac{zf}{zf - zn} \quad (12.6)$$

You can see from Equations (12.4) and (12.6) that $x2$, $y2$, and $z2$ are all divided by –z, so the 3D point $P2 = (x2, y2, z2)$ is equivalent to the following 4D point in the homogeneous coordinate system:

$$P2 = (-x2 \cdot z, -y2 \cdot z, -z2 \cdot z, -z)$$

From Equations (12.4) and (12.6) we obtain the values of –$x2\ z$, –$y2\ z$, and –$z2\ z$ by means of the following equations:

$$-x2 \cdot z = \frac{2 \cdot zn}{r-l}x + \frac{r+l}{r-l}z$$

$$-y2 \cdot z = \frac{2 \cdot zn}{t-b}y + \frac{t+b}{t-b}z$$

$$-z2 \cdot z = -\frac{zf}{zf - zn}z - \frac{zn \cdot zf}{zf - zn}$$

$$w = -z$$

The foregoing equations can be rewritten in matrix form:

$$P2 = P \cdot M_{perpective} = \begin{pmatrix} x & y & z & 1 \end{pmatrix} \begin{pmatrix} \dfrac{2 \cdot zn}{r-l} & 0 & 0 & 0 \\ 0 & \dfrac{2 \cdot zn}{t-b} & 0 & 0 \\ \dfrac{r+l}{r-l} & \dfrac{t+b}{t-b} & \dfrac{zf}{zn-zf} & -1 \\ 0 & 0 & \dfrac{zn \cdot zf}{zn-zf} & 0 \end{pmatrix} \qquad (12.7)$$

The $M_{perpective}$ in Equation (12.7) is the perspective projection matrix. This matrix is in a general form and applies to the view frustum both if it's symmetric and if it's not.

For a symmetric view frustum, you can specify the width (w) and the height (h) of the near plane and use the following relationships:

$$l = -w/2, \quad r = w/2, \quad b = -h/2, \quad t = h/2$$

Then the perspective matrix in Equation (12.7) reduces to

$$M_{perspective} = \begin{pmatrix} \dfrac{2 \cdot zn}{w} & 0 & 0 & 0 \\ 0 & \dfrac{2 \cdot zn}{h} & 0 & 0 \\ 0 & 0 & \dfrac{zf}{zn-zf} & -1 \\ 0 & 0 & \dfrac{zn \cdot zf}{zn-zf} & 0 \end{pmatrix} \qquad (12.8)$$

Sometimes, it is convenient to specify the view frustum using the field of view (*fov*) in the *Y* direction and the aspect ratio, instead of the width and the height. In this case, we have the following relationships:

$$yscale = \frac{zn}{h/2} = \frac{1}{\tan(f\,ov/2)}, \quad xscale = \frac{yscale}{aspectRatio}$$

Here, *aspectRatio* = w/h. Thus you can express the perspective matrix in terms of the field of view angle:

$$M_{perspective} = \begin{pmatrix} xscale & 0 & 0 & 0 \\ 0 & yscale & 0 & 0 \\ 0 & 0 & \dfrac{zf}{zn-zf} & -1 \\ 0 & 0 & \dfrac{zn \cdot zf}{zn-zf} & 0 \end{pmatrix} \quad (12.9)$$

Implementing Perspective Transforms

WPF has implemented a *PerspectiveCamera* class, which requires a symmetric view frustum with a square near and far plane. It uses the field of view and the distances to the near plane and the far plane as input parameters. Although it is convenient, this class does have many limitations. If you want to customize your perspective transforms, you need to implement your own perspective transform matrix and pass it to the *MatrixCamera* class.

Now you are ready to implement the customized perspective matrices described in Equations (12.7) to (12.9). Open the project *Transformation3D* and add the following three public static methods to the *Utility* class:

```
public static Matrix3D SetPerspectiveOffCenter(double left, double right,
    double bottom, double top, double near, double far)
{
    Matrix3D perspectiveMatrix = new Matrix3D();
    perspectiveMatrix.M11 = 2 * near / (right - left);
    perspectiveMatrix.M22 = 2 * near / (top - bottom);
    perspectiveMatrix.M31 = (right + left) / (right - left);
    perspectiveMatrix.M32 = (top + bottom) / (top - bottom);
    perspectiveMatrix.M33 = far / (near - far);
    perspectiveMatrix.M34 = -1.0;
    perspectiveMatrix.OffsetZ = near * far / (near - far);
    perspectiveMatrix.M44 = 0;
    return perspectiveMatrix;
}

public static Matrix3D SetPerspective(double width, double height,
    double near, double far)
{
    Matrix3D perspectiveMatrix = new Matrix3D();
    perspectiveMatrix.M11 = 2 * near / width;
    perspectiveMatrix.M22 = 2 * near / height;
    perspectiveMatrix.M33 = far / (near - far);
    perspectiveMatrix.M34 = -1.0;
    perspectiveMatrix.OffsetZ = near * far / (near - far);
    perspectiveMatrix.M44 = 0;
    return perspectiveMatrix;
}

public static Matrix3D SetPerspectiveFov(double fov,
    double aspectRatio, double near, double far)
```

```
{
    Matrix3D perspectiveMatrix = new Matrix3D();
    double yscale = 1.0 / Math.Tan(fov * Math.PI / 180 / 2);
    double xscale = yscale / aspectRatio;
    perspectiveMatrix.M11 = xscale;
    perspectiveMatrix.M22 = yscale;
    perspectiveMatrix.M33 = far / (near - far);
    perspectiveMatrix.M34 = -1.0;
    perspectiveMatrix.OffsetZ = near * far / (near - far);
    perspectiveMatrix.M44 = 0;
    return perspectiveMatrix;
}
```

The *SetPerspectiveOffCenter* method returns a general perspective matrix for an asymmetric frustum, which takes as input parameters four sides of the near plane as well as the distances to the near plane and the far plane.

The method *SetPerspetive* is designed for a symmetric-view frustum with four input parameters: the width and height of the near plane and the distances to the near and far planes.

The method *SetPerspectiveFov* is also for a symmetric-view frustum, but with the field of view and aspect ratio, instead of the width and height, as parameters. By setting the aspect ratio to 1, you can compare the results of this custom perspective matrix method with those obtained by using the *PerspectiveCamera* class directly.

Testing Perspective Projections

Using the view transform and perspective projection matrices that we have implemented in the *Utility* class, we can test the perspective projection of a 3D graphics object. To examine the effect of perspective projections, you will first need to create a 3D object. I'll describe in detail the steps of creating various 3D objects in later chapters. Here, we'll simply create a 3D cube for the purpose of testing the perspective effect without getting into the procedure of creating such a cube.

Let's consider an example that applies perspective projection to a 3D cube object. Add a new WPF Window to the project *Transformation3D* and name it *PerspectiveProjection*. Here is the XAML file for this example:

```
<Window x:Class="Transformation3D.PerspectiveProjection"
    xmlns="http://schemas.microsoft.com/winfx/2006/xaml/presentation"
    xmlns:x="http://schemas.microsoft.com/winfx/2006/xaml"
    Title="Perspective Projection" Height="320" Width="400">

    <Window.Resources>
        <MeshGeometry3D x:Key="geometry"
            Positions="-1  1  1, 1  1  1, 1  1 -1,-1  1 -1,
                       -1 -1  1,-1 -1 -1, 1 -1 -1, 1 -1  1,
                       -1  1  1,-1 -1  1, 1 -1  1, 1  1  1,
                        1  1  1, 1 -1  1, 1 -1 -1, 1  1 -1,
                        1  1 -1, 1 -1 -1,-1 -1 -1,-1  1 -1,
                       -1  1 -1,-1 -1 -1,-1 -1  1,-1  1  1"
            TriangleIndices=" 0  1  2, 2  3  0,
                              4  5  6, 6  7  4,
                              8  9 10,10 11  8,
                             12 13 14,14 15 12,
                             16 17 18,18 19 16,
                             20 21 22,22 23 20"/>
```

```
            <DiffuseMaterial x:Key="material" Brush="SteelBlue"/>
    </Window.Resources>

    <Viewbox Stretch="Uniform">
        <Grid Width="430" Height="320" HorizontalAlignment="Left"
              VerticalAlignment="Top" ShowGridLines="False">
            <Grid.ColumnDefinitions>
                <ColumnDefinition Width="100" />
                <ColumnDefinition Width="330" />
            </Grid.ColumnDefinitions>

            <StackPanel Margin="5" Grid.Column="0">
                <TextBlock Text="Camera Position" Margin="2"/>
                <TextBox Name="tbCameraPosition" Margin="2"
                        HorizontalAlignment="Left" Text="3,4,5"/>
                <TextBlock Text="Look Direction" Margin="2"/>
                <TextBox Name="tbLookDirection" Margin="2"
                        HorizontalAlignment="Left" Text="-3,-4,-5"/>
                <TextBlock Text="Up Direction" Margin="2"/>
                <TextBox Name="tbUpDirection" Margin="2"
                        HorizontalAlignment="Left" Text="0,1,0"/>
                <TextBlock Text="Near Plane" Margin="2"/>
                <TextBox Name="tbNearPlane" Margin="2"
                        HorizontalAlignment="Left" Text="1"/>
                <TextBlock Text="Far Plane" Margin="2"/>
                <TextBox Name="tbFarPlane" Margin="2"
                        HorizontalAlignment="Left" Text="100"/>
                <TextBlock Text="Field of View" Margin="2"/>
                <TextBox Name="tbFieldOfView" Margin="2"
                        HorizontalAlignment="Left" Text="60"/>

                <Button Name="btnApply" Margin="2,5,2,2"
                        Click="btnApply_Click">Apply</Button>
            </StackPanel>

            <Border Margin="5" BorderBrush="Black" BorderThickness="1"
                    HorizontalAlignment="Left" Width="320"
                    Height="290" Grid.Column="1">
                <Viewport3D ClipToBounds="True">
                    <!-- Set camera: -->
                    <Viewport3D.Camera>
                        <MatrixCamera x:Name="myCameraMatrix"/>
                    </Viewport3D.Camera>
                    <ContainerUIElement3D>
                        <ModelUIElement3D>
                            <Model3DGroup>

                                <!-- Create a cube: -->
                                <GeometryModel3D
                                    Geometry="{StaticResource geometry}"
                                    Material="{StaticResource material}">
                                    <!-- Set translation: -->
                                    <GeometryModel3D.Transform>
```

```
                            <TranslateTransform3D OffsetZ="1"/>
                        </GeometryModel3D.Transform>
                    </GeometryModel3D>

                    <!-- Create another cube: -->
                    <GeometryModel3D
                        Geometry="{StaticResource geometry}"
                        Material="{StaticResource material}">
                        <!-- Set translation: -->
                        <GeometryModel3D.Transform>
                            <TranslateTransform3D OffsetZ="-2"/>
                        </GeometryModel3D.Transform>
                    </GeometryModel3D>

                    <!-- Create another cube: -->
                    <GeometryModel3D
                        Geometry="{StaticResource geometry}"
                        Material="{StaticResource material}">
                        <!-- Set translation: -->
                        <GeometryModel3D.Transform>
                            <TranslateTransform3D OffsetZ="-5"/>
                        </GeometryModel3D.Transform>
                    </GeometryModel3D>

                    <!-- Set light source: -->
                    <AmbientLight Color="Gray"/>
                    <DirectionalLight Color="Gray"
                        Direction="-1 -2 -3"/>
                </Model3DGroup>
            </ModelUIElement3D>
        </ContainerUIElement3D>
    </Viewport3D>
  </Border>
 </Grid>
</Viewbox>
</Window>
```

Here, we first create a Window Resource, which defines the mesh geometry and material for a 3D cube object. You can easily create multiple cube objects by using this resource. In the XAML file, three cube objects are created at different locations by performing different translation transforms on the original cube geometry defined in *Window.Resources*. This XAML file also creates a user interface that allows you to examine interactively the perspective projection effect on the three cube objects by entering different values in the text boxes. These values include the camera position, the camera look-at direction, the up vector, and the near plane, far plane, and field of view. Notice that the camera is set for the *Viewport3D* using the *MatrixCamera*, indicating that a custom camera setting will be used. This camera setting includes both the view transformation and perspective projection. We will specify both transforms using the transform matrices created in the *Utility* class.

Here is the corresponding code-behind file for this example:

```
using System;
using System.Windows;
using System.Windows.Media;
using System.Windows.Media.Media3D;
```

```
namespace Transformation3D
{
    public partial class PerspectiveProjection : Window
    {

        public PerspectiveProjection()
        {
            InitializeComponent();
            SetMatrixCamera();
        }

        private void btnApply_Click(object sender,
                RoutedEventArgs e)
        {
            SetMatrixCamera();
        }

        private void SetMatrixCamera()
        {
            Point3D cameraPosition =
                Point3D.Parse(tbCameraPosition.Text);
            Vector3D lookDirection =
                Vector3D.Parse(tbLookDirection.Text);
            Vector3D upDirection =
                Vector3D.Parse(tbUpDirection.Text);
            double fov = Double.Parse(tbFieldOfView.Text);
            double zn = Double.Parse(tbNearPlane.Text);
            double zf = Double.Parse(tbFarPlane.Text);
            double aspectRatio = 1.0;

            myCameraMatrix.ViewMatrix =
                Utility.SetViewMatrix(cameraPosition,
                lookDirection, upDirection);
            myCameraMatrix.ProjectionMatrix =
                Utility.SetPerspectiveFov(fov,
                aspectRatio, zn, zf);
        }
    }
}
```

This class implements the *SetMatrixCamera* method, whose parameters are specified by the user's input. Then these parameters are passed to the custom view and perspective projection matrices implemented in the *Utility* class. Finally, these custom matrices are attached to the *ViewMatrix* and *ProjectionMatrix* properties of the *MatrixCamera*, named *myCameraMatrix*.

Building and running this project and selecting *PerspectiveProjection* from the *Start Menu* produces the output shown in Figure 12-15. Note that the physical dimensions of these three cubes are the same. From the figure you can clearly see the foreshortening effect of the perspective projection: The farther the cube is from the camera, the smaller it appears on the screen.

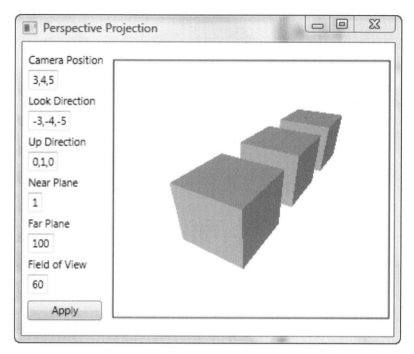

Figure 12-15. *Perspective projection of cube objects*

Of course, you can also use the built-in *PerspectiveCamera* class in WPF to perform a similar perspective projection. When you use the *PerspectiveCamera* class, WPF will create corresponding view and projection transform matrices internally, and it will use them to create the 3D objects on the screen. The purpose of using a custom *MatrixCamera* is to demonstrate how the view transformation and perspective projection matrices are constructed and how they work mathematically.

Orthographic Projection

In WPF, the viewing volume for an orthographic projection is a rectangular parallelepiped, or a box, as shown in Figure 12-16.

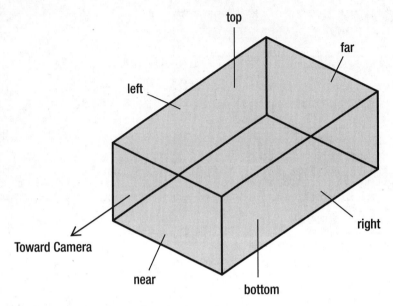

Figure 12-16. Orthographic viewing volume

Unlike perspective projection, the size of the viewing volume doesn't change from one end to the other, so the distance from the camera doesn't affect how large an object appears. Namely, no perspective distortion occurs in orthographic projections. The points in the camera space are always mapped to the projection plane by casting rays that are parallel to the camera's viewing direction. As mentioned previously, this type of projection is usually used in applications for architecture and computer-aided design (CAD), where it is important to maintain the actual sizes of objects and the angles between them as they are projected.

Orthographic Transform Matrix

Orthographic projection corresponds to transforming the viewing volume shown in Figure 12-16 into a box with $-1 \leq x \leq 1$, $-1 \leq y \leq 1$, and $0 \leq z \leq 1$. Again, we use Microsoft's conventions here. In other technologies, such as OpenGL, the range [-1, 1] is used for mapping in the Z direction.

Since there is no perspective distortion, the orthographic projection must be a linear transformation. Therefore, the transform can be written in the following form:

$$x1 = Cx1 \cdot x + Cx2$$
$$y1 = Cy1 \cdot y + Cy2$$
$$z1 = Cz1 \cdot z + Cz2$$

The mapping relations lead to the following results:

$$-1=Cx1 \cdot l + Cx2, \quad +1 = Cx1 \cdot r + Cx2$$
$$-1=Cy1 \cdot b + Cy2, \quad +1 = Cy1 \cdot t + Cy2$$
$$0=Cz1 \cdot zn + Cz2, \quad +1 = Cz2 \cdot zf + Cz2$$

You can obtain the orthographic transform by solving the preceding equations:

$$x1 = \frac{2}{r-l} x - \frac{r+l}{r-l}$$

$$y1 = \frac{2}{t-b} y - \frac{t+b}{t-b}$$

$$z1 = \frac{1}{zf-zn} z - \frac{zn}{zf-zn}$$

You can then get the orthographic projection matrix by rewriting the preceding equations in matrix form:

$$P1 = P \cdot M_{orthographic} = (x,y,z,1) \begin{pmatrix} \dfrac{2}{r-l} & 0 & 0 & 0 \\[2ex] 0 & \dfrac{2}{t-b} & 0 & 0 \\[2ex] 0 & 0 & \dfrac{1}{zf-zn} & 0 \\[2ex] \dfrac{l+r}{l-r} & \dfrac{b+t}{b-t} & \dfrac{zn}{zn-zf} & 1 \end{pmatrix} \qquad (12.10)$$

The matrix $M_{orthographic}$ is the orthographic projection matrix, which is valid for general cases, including for asymmetric viewing volume, or off-center, cases.

For symmetric cases, you can specify the width (w) and height the (h) of the near plane and use the following relations:

$$l = -w/2, \quad r = w/2, \quad b = -h/2, \quad t = h/2$$

The orthographic projection matrix becomes

$$M_{orthographic} = \begin{pmatrix} 2/w & 0 & 0 & 0 \\[2ex] 0 & 2/h & 0 & 0 \\[2ex] 0 & 0 & \dfrac{1}{zn-zf} & 0 \\[2ex] 0 & 0 & \dfrac{zn}{zn-zf} & 1 \end{pmatrix} \qquad (12.11)$$

Implementing Orthographic Transforms

WPF has implemented an *OrthographicCamera* class, which requires a symmetric viewing volume with a square near and far plane. This class takes the width and the distances to the near and far plane as input parameters. Although this class is convenient, it does have many limitations. If you want a customized orthographic transform, you have to implement your own orthographic transform matrix and pass it to the *MatrixCamera* class.

You can implement the customized orthographic matrices given in Equations (12.10) and (12.11). Open the project *Transformation3D* and add two public static methods to the *Utility* class:

```
public static Matrix3D SetOrthographicOffCenter(double left,
        double right, double bottom, double top, double near, double far)
{
    Matrix3D orthographicMatrix = new Matrix3D();
    orthographicMatrix.M11 = 2 / (right - left);
    orthographicMatrix.M22 = 2 / (top - bottom);
    orthographicMatrix.M33 = 1 / (near - far);
    orthographicMatrix.OffsetX = (left + right) / (left - right);
    orthographicMatrix.OffsetY = (bottom + top) / (bottom - top);
    orthographicMatrix.OffsetZ = near / (near - far);
    return orthographicMatrix;
}

public static Matrix3D SetOrthographic(double width, double height,
                                double near, double far)
{
    Matrix3D orthographicMatrix = new Matrix3D();
    orthographicMatrix.M11 = 2 / width;
    orthographicMatrix.M22 = 2 / height;
    orthographicMatrix.M33 = 1 / (near - far);
    orthographicMatrix.OffsetZ = near / (near - far);
    return orthographicMatrix;
}
```

The method *SetOrthographicOffCenter* returns a general orthographic matrix for an asymmetric viewing volume, which takes the four sides of the near plane and the distances to the near and far planes as input parameters.

The method *SetOrthographic* is designed for a symmetric-view frustum with four input parameters: the width and height of the near plane and the distances to the near and far planes. WPF has implemented an *OrthographicCamera* class, that uses squared near and far planes. This means that this class takes only three parameters: the side length (width) of the near plane and the distances to the near and far planes. By setting *height = width* in the *SetOrthographic* method, you can compare the results given by the custom matrix method with those obtained by using the *OrthographicCamera* class directly.

Testing Orthographic Projections

Now you can perform an orthographic projection on a 3D object using the view transform and orthographic projection matrices that we have implemented in the *Utility* class.

Add a new WPF Window to the project *Transformation3D* and name it *OrthographicProjection*. You can use the same XAML file as in the previous example to test perspective projections. The only parameter you need to change is the field of view. Simply change the parameter *fov* to the *width*, which can be done by modifying the code snippet in the previous XAML file:

```
<TextBlock Text="Field of View" Margin="2"/>
<TextBox Name="tbFieldOfView" Margin="2" HorizontalAlignment="Left" Text="60"/>
```

to the following statements:

```
<TextBlock Text="Width" Margin="2"/>
<TextBox Name="tbWidth" Margin="2" HorizontalAlignment="Left" Text="8"/>
```

The code-behind file is also similar to the one we used to test perspective projections. The only change occurs in the *SetMatrixCamera* method:

```
private void SetMatrixCamera()
{
    Point3D cameraPosition = Point3D.Parse(tbCameraPosition.Text);
    Vector3D lookDirection = Vector3D.Parse(tbLookDirection.Text);
    Vector3D upDirection = Vector3D.Parse(tbUpDirection.Text);
    double w = Double.Parse(tbWidth.Text);
    double zn = Double.Parse(tbNearPlane.Text);
    double zf = Double.Parse(tbFarPlane.Text);
    myCameraMatrix.ViewMatrix = Utility.SetViewMatrix(cameraPosition,
                               lookDirection, upDirection);
    myCameraMatrix.ProjectionMatrix = Utility.SetOrthographic(w, w, zn, zf);
}
```

Here, you set the *ProjectionMatrix* property of the *MatrixCamera* to the orthographic matrix defined using the *SetOrthographic* method in the *Utility* class.

Executing this project generates the result shown in Figure 12-17. As you can see, the three cubes have the same view size on your screen regardless of where they are located, indicating that there is no foreshortening effect in an orthographic projection. For comparison, you can perform a similar orthographic projection using the built-in WPF *OrthographicCamera* class.

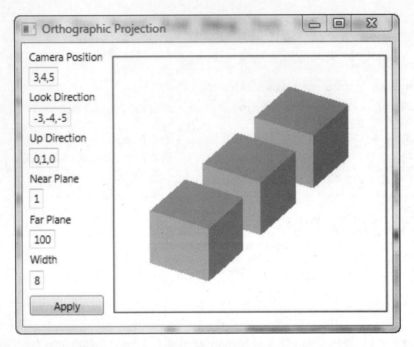

Figure 12-17. Orthographic projection of cube objects

Object Transforms in WPF

Previously, we discussed the *Vector3D* and *Matrix3D* structures as well as their operations in WPF. You can apply the *Matrix3D* structure to a *Point3D* or a *Vector3D* object. However, if you want to apply 3D transforms to objects or coordinate systems, you will need to use the *Transform3D* class. Unlike 2D objects, in order to display a transformed 3D object on your computer screen, you also need to perform projection transforms, as discussed in the previous two sections. WPF has several classes derived from the *Transform3D* class that you can use to perform specific transforms on 3D objects:

- *ScaleTransform3D* – Scales a 3D object in the *X-Y-Z* directions, starting from a defined center. The scaling factors *ScaleX*, *ScaleY*, and *ScaleZ* are defined in the *X*, *Y*, and *Z* directions from this center point.

- *TranslateTransform3D* – Defines a translation along the *X*, *Y*, and *Z* directions. You specify the amount an object is translated using the *OffsetX*, *OffsetY*, and *OffsetZ* properties.

- *RotateTransform3D* – Rotates an object in 3D space by specifying a 3D rotation using the rotation property and a center point specified by the *CenterX*, *CenterY* and *CenterZ* properties. The rotation property can be specified by a *Rotation3D* object. If you want to represent a 3D rotation using a specified angle about a specified rotation axis, you can use the *AxisAngleRotation3D* object to specify the rotation property.

- *MatrixTransform3D* – Creates a 3D transform, specified by a *Matrix3D* object, used to manipulate objects or coordinate systems in 3D space. It is usually used to provide custom transforms not provided by the other *Transform3D* classes. You can multiply custom transform matrices to form any number of linear transforms; for example, you can rotate and scale an object and then translate it.

The structure of the 3D transform matrix is the same as that of the *Matrix3D* in WPF. In the homogeneous coordinate system, the 3D transform matrix has 16 elements defined by M_{ij} (with i, j = 1, 2, 3, 4), except for M_{4j} (with j = 1, 2, 3), where they are replaced by *OffsetX*, *OffsetY*, and *OffsetZ*. These three elements represent a translation in 3D space.

By manipulating matrix values directly via the *MatrixTransform3D* class, you can rotate, scale, move, and even skew a 3D object. For example, if you change the value of *OffsetX* to 10, you move an object 10 units along the *X* axis in the world space. If you change the value in the second column of the second row to 3, you stretch an object to three times its current size in the *Y* direction. If you change both values at the same time, you simultaneously move the object 10 units along the *X* axis and stretch its dimension by a factor of 3 in the *Y* direction.

Although WPF enables you to manipulate matrix values directly in the *MatrixTransform3D* class, it also provides several transform classes that enable you to transform an object without knowing how the underlying matrix structure is configured. For example, the *ScaleTransform3D* class enables you to scale an object by setting its *ScaleX*, *ScaleY,* and *ScaleZ* properties instead of by manipulating an underlying transform matrix. Likewise, the *RotateTransfrom3D* class enables you to rotate an object simply by specifying the angle about a rotation axis through its *Rotation* property. WPF will use the underlying structure of the transform matrix to perform the corresponding operations on objects.

In the following sections, you'll apply various transforms to the 3D cube we used to discuss projections.

ScaleTransform3D Class

The *ScaleTransform3D* class in WPF enables you to scale a 3D object by setting its *ScaleX*, *ScaleY,* and *ScaleZ* properties.

Let's look at an example. Open the *Transformation3D* project, add a new WPF Window, and name it *ScaleTransformation*. The following is the XAML file for this example:

```
<Window x:Class="Transformation3D.ScaleTransformation"
    xmlns="http://schemas.microsoft.com/winfx/2006/xaml/presentation"
    xmlns:x="http://schemas.microsoft.com/winfx/2006/xaml"
    Title="Scale Transformation" Height="310" Width="400">

    <Window.Resources>
        <MeshGeometry3D x:Key="geometry"
            Positions="-1  1  1, 1  1  1, 1  1 -1,-1  1 -1,
                       -1 -1  1,-1 -1 -1, 1 -1 -1, 1 -1  1,
                       -1  1  1,-1 -1  1, 1 -1  1, 1  1  1,
                        1  1  1, 1 -1  1, 1 -1 -1, 1  1 -1,
                        1  1 -1, 1 -1 -1,-1 -1 -1,-1  1 -1,
                       -1  1 -1,-1 -1 -1,-1 -1  1,-1  1  1"
            TriangleIndices=" 0  1  2, 2  3  0,
                              4  5  6, 6  7  4,
                              8  9 10,10 11  8,
                             12 13 14,14 15 12,
                             16 17 18,18 19 16,
                             20 21 22,22 23 20"/>
```

```xml
        <DiffuseMaterial x:Key="material" Brush="SteelBlue"/>
    </Window.Resources>

    <Viewbox Stretch="Uniform">
        <Grid Width="430" Height="300" HorizontalAlignment="Left"
          VerticalAlignment="Top" ShowGridLines="False">
            <Grid.ColumnDefinitions>
                <ColumnDefinition Width="100" />
                <ColumnDefinition Width="330" />
            </Grid.ColumnDefinitions>

            <StackPanel Margin="5" Grid.Column="0">
                <RadioButton x:Name="rbOrthographic" Margin="2"
                         Content="Orthorgriphic" IsChecked="True"/>
                <RadioButton x:Name="rbPerspective" Margin="2"
                         Content="Perspective" IsChecked="False"/>
                <TextBlock Text="ScaleX" Margin="2"/>
                <TextBox Name="tbScaleX" Margin="2"
                         HorizontalAlignment="Left" Text="1"/>
                <TextBlock Text="ScaleY" Margin="2"/>
                <TextBox Name="tbScaleY" Margin="2"
                         HorizontalAlignment="Left" Text="1"/>
                <TextBlock Text="ScaleZ" Margin="2"/>
                <TextBox Name="tbScaleZ" Margin="2"
                         HorizontalAlignment="Left" Text="1"/>
                <TextBlock Text="Scale Center" Margin="2"/>
                <TextBox Name="tbScaleCenter" Margin="2"
                         HorizontalAlignment="Left" Text="0,0,0"/>
                <Button Name="btnApply" Margin="2,5,2,2"
                         Click="btnApply_Click">Apply</Button>
            </StackPanel>

            <Border Margin="5" BorderBrush="Black" BorderThickness="1"
                    HorizontalAlignment="Left" Width="320"
                    Height="290" Grid.Column="1">
                <Viewport3D Name="myViewport" ClipToBounds="True">
                    <Viewport3D.Camera>
                        <MatrixCamera x:Name="myCameraMatrix"/>
                    </Viewport3D.Camera>

                    <ContainerUIElement3D>
                        <ModelUIElement3D>
                            <Model3DGroup>
                                <!-- Create a cube: -->
                                <GeometryModel3D
                                    Geometry="{StaticResource geometry}"
                                    Material="{StaticResource material}">
                                    <!-- Set transform: -->
                                    <GeometryModel3D.Transform>
                                      <ScaleTransform3D x:Name="myTransform"/>
                                    </GeometryModel3D.Transform>
                                </GeometryModel3D>
```

486

```
                    <!-- Set light source: -->
                    <AmbientLight Color="Gray"/>
                    <DirectionalLight Color="Gray"
                            Direction="-1 -2 -3"/>
                </Model3DGroup>
            </ModelUIElement3D>
        </ContainerUIElement3D>
    </Viewport3D>
</Border>
</Grid>
</Viewbox>
</Window>
```

Here, you use the same *Window.Resources* as in the previous example to define the cube geometry and material. This XAML file also creates a user interface that allows you to change the input parameters interactively. Here, you use the *MatrixCamera* class to set the camera by using the customized View and Projection matrices defined in the *Utility* class. Of course, you can instead use the WPF built-in *PerspectiveCamera* class or *OrthographicCamera* class to set the camera. The user interface also allows you to choose either perspective or orthographic projection. The input parameters the user can specify include the scale factors *ScaleX*, *ScaleY*, and *ScaleZ* as well as the scaling center.

The corresponding code-behind file is used to handle the *MatrixCamera* and scale transform:

```
using System;
using System.Windows;
using System.Windows.Media;
using System.Windows.Media.Media3D;

namespace Transformation3D
{
    public partial class ScaleTransformation : Window
    {
        public ScaleTransformation()
        {
            InitializeComponent();
            SetMatrixCamera();
            SetTransform();
        }

        private void btnApply_Click(object sender,
                RoutedEventArgs e)
        {
            SetMatrixCamera();
            SetTransform();
        }

        private void SetTransform()
        {
            Point3D center = Point3D.Parse(tbScaleCenter.Text);
            myTransform.CenterX = center.X;
            myTransform.CenterY = center.Y;
            myTransform.CenterZ = center.Z;
            myTransform.ScaleX = Double.Parse(tbScaleX.Text);
            myTransform.ScaleY = Double.Parse(tbScaleY.Text);
            myTransform.ScaleZ = Double.Parse(tbScaleZ.Text);
```

```
    }

    private void SetMatrixCamera()
    {
        Point3D cameraPosition = new Point3D(3, 3, 3);
        Vector3D lookDirection = new Vector3D(-3, -3, -3);
        Vector3D upDirection = new Vector3D(0, 1, 0);
        double w = 6;
        double zn = 1;
        double zf = 100;
        double fov = 60;
        double aspectRatio = 1.0;
        myCameraMatrix.ViewMatrix = Utility.SetViewMatrix(cameraPosition,
                                    lookDirection, upDirection);

        if (rbOrthographic.IsChecked == true)
        {
            myCameraMatrix.ProjectionMatrix =
                Utility.SetOrthographic(w, w, zn, zf);
        }
        else if (rbPerspective.IsChecked == true)
        {
            myCameraMatrix.ProjectionMatrix = Utility.SetPerspectiveFov(fov,
                                    aspectRatio, zn, zf);
        }
    }
  }
}
```

The *SetMatrixCamera* method sets the camera using either perspective or orthographic projection. You can change the parameters used to set the camera as you like.

The *SetTransform* method in this class performs the scale transform on the cube. You first pass the input parameters to a *Point3D* object and then attach this *Point3D* object and the *ScaleX, ScaleY,* and *ScaleZ* input by the user to the corresponding properties of *myTransform,* defined in the XAML file.

Executing this project generates the result shown in Figure 12-18. You can change any parameter in the user interface and click Apply to examine the scale effect on the cube.

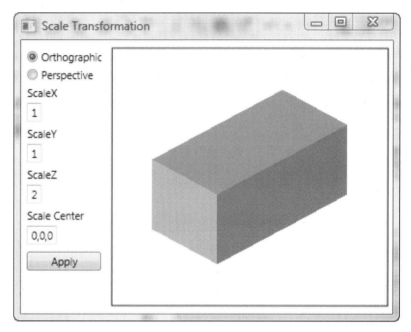

Figure 12-18. Scale transform on a cube

TranslateTransform3D class

The *TranslateTransform3D* class enables you to move a 3D object by setting its *OffsetX*, *OffsetY* and *OffsetZ* properties. This transformation has no center property to set because the translation effect is the same regardless of where it is centered.

Here, let's consider an example that demonstrates a translation on a cube object using a layout and user interface similar to that in the previous example. Open the *Transformation3D* project, add a WPF Window, and call it *TranslateTransformation*. The XAML code is similar to that for the previous *ScaleTransformation* example, except now you need to change the scale transform to a translation transform. Replace the bolded part of the XAML file with the following snippet:

```
<GeometryModel3D.Transform>
    <TranslateTransform3D x:Name="myTransform"/>
</GeometryModel3D.Transform>
```

Also you need to change the corresponding statements related to the scale parameters within the *StackPanel* in the previous XAML file to the following:

```
<StackPanel Margin="5" Grid.Column="0">
    <RadioButton x:Name="rbOrthographic" Margin="2"
                 Content="Orthographic" IsChecked="True"/>
    <RadioButton x:Name="rbPerspective" Margin="2"
                 Content="Perspective" IsChecked="False"/>
    <TextBlock Text="OffsetX" Margin="2"/>
    <TextBox Name="tbOffsetX" Margin="2" HorizontalAlignment="Left" Text="0"/>
    <TextBlock Text="OffsetY" Margin="2"/>
```

489

```
        <TextBox Name="tbOffsetY" Margin="2" HorizontalAlignment="Left" Text="0"/>
        <TextBlock Text="OffsetZ" Margin="2"/>
        <TextBox Name="tbOffsetZ" Margin="2" HorizontalAlignment="Left" Text="0"/>
        <Button Name="btnApply" Margin="2,5,2,2"
                Click="btnApply_Click">Apply</Button>
</StackPanel>
```

The corresponding code-behind file is also similar to that for the previous example, except you need to rewrite the *SetTransform* method:

```
private void SetTransform()
{
    myTransform.OffsetX = Double.Parse(tbOffsetX.Text);
    myTransform.OffsetY = Double.Parse(tbOffsetY.Text);
    myTransform.OffsetZ = Double.Parse(tbOffsetZ.Text);
}
```

Here, you attach the corresponding input parameters to the *OffsetX*, *OffsetY*, and *OffsetZ* properties of *myTransform*, defined in the XAML file.

Running this project produces the result shown in Figure 12-19. You can move the cube around your screen by playing with different parameters for *OffsetX*, *OffsetY*, and *OffsetZ*.

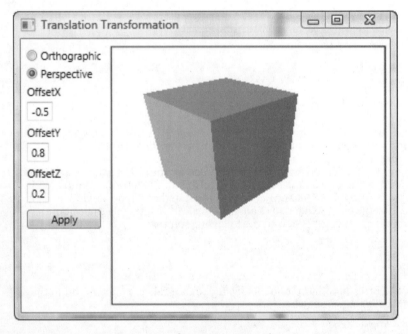

Figure 12-19. Translation transformation on a cube.

490

RotateTransform3D Class

In an earlier section of this chapter, "Rotation and Quaternion," we discussed how to perform a 3D rotation using a quaternion matrix. You can use such a matrix to construct your own custom 3D rotation class; however, there is no need to do so. WPF already provides a 3D rotation class, called *RotateTransform3D*. This class defines a *Rotation* property, which you set to an object of type *Rotation3D*. The *Rotation3D* class is an abstract class. WPF implements two useful classes that derive from *Rotation3D*: *AxisAngleRotation3D* and *QuaternionRotation3D*. You can use either one to perform a 3D rotation. In fact, these two classes use the same mathematical model; both are based on the quaternion technique.

When the 3D object in question is rotated a finite angle about a specified axis, you can use *AxisAngleRotation3D* to perform the rotation. On the other hand, you can also calculate the quaternion of the rotation using Equation (12.1) and then use *QuaternionRotation3D* to perform the same rotation. For example, to rotate an object 90 degrees about the *Y* axis, you can use the following XAML snippet:

```
<RotateTransform3D>
    <RotateTransform3D.Rotation>
        <AxisAngleRotation3D Axis="0 1 0" Angle="90"/>
    </RotateTransform3D.Rotation>
</RotateTransform3D>
```

This rotation can also be performed using *QuaternionRotation3D*:

```
<RotateTransform3D>
    <RotateTransform3D.Rotation>
        <QuaternionRotation3D Quaternion="0 0.707 0 0.707"/>
    </RotateTransform3D.Rotation>
</RotateTransform3D>
```

The *Quaternion* in this XAML snippet is calculated using Equation (12.1). This quaternion describes a rotation of 90 degrees about the *Y* axis. The number 0.707 (the *Y* component) is the Sine of half the angle (or 45 degrees), while the other 0.707 (the *W* component) is the Cosine of 45 degrees. You can use either class to perform 3D rotations. The *AxisAngleRotation3D* class, which is more straightforward, will be used extensively in this book.

Here, let's consider an example that performs a rotation transform on a cube object using the same layout as in the previous example. Open the *Transformation3D* project, add a WPF Window, and call it *RotateTransformation*. You can open the project to look at the complete source code for this example. The XAML file is similar to that used in the previous *ScaleTransformation* example, except you need to change the transform to a rotation. Replace the bolded part of the XAML file with the following snippet:

```
<GeometryModel3D.Transform>
    <RotateTransform3D x:Name="myTransform"/>
</GeometryModel3D.Transform>
```

Also, you need to change the corresponding statements related to the scale parameters within the *StackPanel* in the previous XAML file to the following:

```
<StackPanel Margin="5" Grid.Column="0">
    <RadioButton x:Name="rbOrthographic" Margin="2"
                Content="Orthographic" IsChecked="True"/>
    <RadioButton x:Name="rbPerspective" Margin="2"
                Content="Perspective" IsChecked="False"/>
    <TextBlock Text="Rotation Axis" Margin="2"/>
    <TextBox Name="tbAxis" Margin="2" HorizontalAlignment="Left" Text="0,1,0"/>
    <TextBlock Text="Rotation Angle" Margin="2"/>
```

```
    <TextBox Name="tbAngle" Margin="2" HorizontalAlignment="Left" Text="0"/>
    <TextBlock Text="Rotation Center" Margin="2"/>
    <TextBox Name="tbCenter" Margin="2" HorizontalAlignment="Left" Text="0,0,0"/>
    <Button Name="btnApply" Margin="2,5,2,2" Click="btnApply_Click">Apply</Button>
</StackPanel>
```

The corresponding code-behind file is also similar to that used in the *ScaleTransformation* example, except you need to rewrite the *SetTransform* method:

```
private void SetTransform()
{
    Point3D rotateCenter = Point3D.Parse(tbCenter.Text);
    Vector3D rotateAxis = Vector3D.Parse(tbAxis.Text);
    double rotateAngle = Double.Parse(tbAngle.Text);
    myTransform.CenterX = rotateCenter.X;
    myTransform.CenterY = rotateCenter.Y;
    myTransform.CenterZ = rotateCenter.Z;
    myTransform.Rotation = new AxisAngleRotation3D(rotateAxis, rotateAngle);
}
```

Here, you define the *rotateCenter*, *rotateAxis*, and *rotateAngle* with the user's input parameters. Then you attach the *rotateCenter* to the *CenterX*, *CenterY*, and *CenterZ* properties of the *RotateTransform3D* object, *myTransform*, defined in the XAML file. Then you create a new *AxisAngleRotation3D* object using the *rotateAxis* and *rotateAngle* properties and attach it to the *Rotation* property of *myTransform*.

Executing this project produces the result shown in Figure 12-20. You can play around with this example by changing the rotation center, angle, and axis and then clicking Apply to see the effect on the cube. You can select the Perspective or Orthographic radio button to examine the different projection effects, as well.

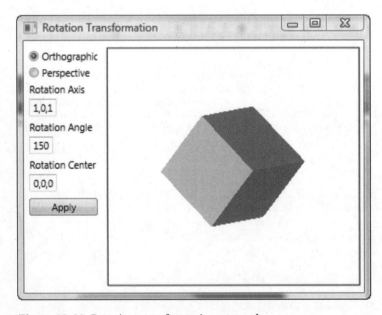

Figure 12-20. Rotation transformation on a cube

MatrixTransform3D Class

In the previous sections, we discussed basic 3D transforms on graphics objects. These transforms include scale, translation, and rotation. However, if you want to perform a 3D transform that isn't provided by the basic *Transform3D* classes (for example, a 3D skew transform), you can create a custom 3D transform using the *MatrixTransform3D* class.

Here, I'll use an example to illustrate how to perform 3D custom transforms directly on a cube object using the *MatrixTransform3D* class. Add a new WPF Window to the project *Transformation3D* and name it *MatrixTransformation*. The XAML file for the *MatrixTransformation* and its layout are similar to those in the previous *ScaleTransformaion* example. The interface allows you to change all 16 elements of the transform matrix and to view the transformed cube on the screen interactively. In the XAML file, you need to make the following change to the 3D transform:

```
<GeometryModel3D.Transform>
    <MatrixTransform3D x:Name="myTransform"/>
</GeometryModel3D.Transform>
```

Here, the name *myTransform* represents the *MatrixTransform3D* object. Also you need to change the corresponding statements related to the scale parameters within the original *StackPanel* in the previous XAML file to the following code snippet within a *Grid* control:

```
<Grid Width="Auto">
    <Grid.ColumnDefinitions>
        <ColumnDefinition Width="Auto"/>
        <ColumnDefinition Width="Auto"/>
        <ColumnDefinition Width="Auto"/>
        <ColumnDefinition Width="Auto"/>
    </Grid.ColumnDefinitions>
    <Grid.RowDefinitions>
        <RowDefinition Height="Auto"/>
        <RowDefinition Height="Auto"/>
        <RowDefinition Height="Auto"/>
        <RowDefinition Height="Auto"/>
        <RowDefinition Height="Auto"/>
        <RowDefinition Height="Auto"/>
        <RowDefinition Height="Auto"/>
        <RowDefinition Height="Auto"/>
        <RowDefinition Height="Auto"/>
        <RowDefinition Height="Auto"/>
        <RowDefinition Height="Auto"/>
    </Grid.RowDefinitions>
    <TextBlock Grid.Column="0" Grid.Row="0" Text="M11" Margin="2,5,2,2"/>
    <TextBlock Grid.Column="0" Grid.Row="1" Text="M21" Margin="2"/>
    <TextBlock Grid.Column="0" Grid.Row="2" Text="M31" Margin="2"/>
    <TextBlock Grid.Column="0" Grid.Row="3" Text="M41" Margin="2"/>
    <TextBlock Grid.Column="0" Grid.Row="4" Text="M12" Margin="2"/>
    <TextBlock Grid.Column="0" Grid.Row="5" Text="M22" Margin="2"/>
    <TextBlock Grid.Column="0" Grid.Row="6" Text="M32" Margin="2"/>
    <TextBlock Grid.Column="0" Grid.Row="7" Text="M42" Margin="2"/>

    <TextBox Name="tbM11" Grid.Column="1" Grid.Row="0" Margin="2,5,2,2"
            HorizontalAlignment="Left" Text="1"/>
    <TextBox Name="tbM21" Grid.Column="1" Grid.Row="1" Margin="2"
            HorizontalAlignment="Left" Text="0"/>
```

```xml
        <TextBox Name="tbM31" Grid.Column="1" Grid.Row="2" Margin="2"
                HorizontalAlignment="Left" Text="0"/>
        <TextBox Name="tbM41" Grid.Column="1" Grid.Row="3" Margin="2"
                HorizontalAlignment="Left" Text="0"/>
        <TextBox Name="tbM12" Grid.Column="1" Grid.Row="4" Margin="2"
                HorizontalAlignment="Left" Text="0"/>
        <TextBox Name="tbM22" Grid.Column="1" Grid.Row="5" Margin="2"
                HorizontalAlignment="Left" Text="1"/>
        <TextBox Name="tbM32" Grid.Column="1" Grid.Row="6" Margin="2"
                HorizontalAlignment="Left" Text="0"/>
        <TextBox Name="tbM42" Grid.Column="1" Grid.Row="7" Margin="2"
                HorizontalAlignment="Left" Text="0"/>

        <TextBlock Grid.Column="2" Grid.Row="0" Text="M13" Margin="2,5,2,2"/>
        <TextBlock Grid.Column="2" Grid.Row="1" Text="M23" Margin="2"/>
        <TextBlock Grid.Column="2" Grid.Row="2" Text="M33" Margin="2"/>
        <TextBlock Grid.Column="2" Grid.Row="3" Text="M43" Margin="2"/>
        <TextBlock Grid.Column="2" Grid.Row="4" Text="M14" Margin="2"/>
        <TextBlock Grid.Column="2" Grid.Row="5" Text="M24" Margin="2"/>
        <TextBlock Grid.Column="2" Grid.Row="6" Text="M34" Margin="2"/>
        <TextBlock Grid.Column="2" Grid.Row="7" Text="M44" Margin="2"/>

        <TextBox Name="tbM13" Grid.Column="3" Grid.Row="0" Margin="2,5,2,2"
                HorizontalAlignment="Left" Text="0"/>
        <TextBox Name="tbM23" Grid.Column="3" Grid.Row="1" Margin="2"
                HorizontalAlignment="Left" Text="0"/>
        <TextBox Name="tbM33" Grid.Column="3" Grid.Row="2" Margin="2"
                HorizontalAlignment="Left" Text="1"/>
        <TextBox Name="tbM43" Grid.Column="3" Grid.Row="3" Margin="2"
                HorizontalAlignment="Left" Text="0"/>
        <TextBox Name="tbM14" Grid.Column="3" Grid.Row="4" Margin="2"
                HorizontalAlignment="Left" Text="0"/>
        <TextBox Name="tbM24" Grid.Column="3" Grid.Row="5" Margin="2"
                HorizontalAlignment="Left" Text="0"/>
        <TextBox Name="tbM34" Grid.Column="3" Grid.Row="6" Margin="2"
                HorizontalAlignment="Left" Text="0"/>
        <TextBox Name="tbM44" Grid.Column="3" Grid.Row="7" Margin="2"
                HorizontalAlignment="Left" Text="1"/>

        <RadioButton x:Name="rbOrthographic" Margin="2,10,2,2"
                Grid.Column="0" Grid.ColumnSpan="4" Grid.Row="8"
                Content="Orthographic" IsChecked="True"/>
        <RadioButton x:Name="rbPerspective" Margin="2"
                Grid.Column="0" Grid.ColumnSpan="4" Grid.Row="9"
                Content="Perspective" IsChecked="False"/>

        <Button Name="btnApply" Margin="2,10,2,2" Grid.Column="0"
                Grid.Row="10" Grid.ColumnSpan="4"
                Click="btnApply_Click">Apply</Button>
    </Grid>
```

The corresponding code-behind file is also similar to that used in the *ScaleTransformation* example, except you need to rewrite the *SetTransform* method:

```
private void SetTransform()
{
    Matrix3D m3 = new Matrix3D();
    m3.M11 = Double.Parse(tbM11.Text);
    m3.M21 = Double.Parse(tbM21.Text);
    m3.M31 = Double.Parse(tbM31.Text);
    m3.OffsetX = Double.Parse(tbM41.Text);
    m3.M12 = Double.Parse(tbM12.Text);
    m3.M22 = Double.Parse(tbM22.Text);
    m3.M32 = Double.Parse(tbM32.Text);
    m3.OffsetY = Double.Parse(tbM42.Text);
    m3.M13 = Double.Parse(tbM13.Text);
    m3.M23 = Double.Parse(tbM23.Text);
    m3.M33 = Double.Parse(tbM33.Text);
    m3.OffsetZ = Double.Parse(tbM43.Text);
    m3.M14 = Double.Parse(tbM14.Text);
    m3.M24 = Double.Parse(tbM24.Text);
    m3.M34 = Double.Parse(tbM34.Text);
    m3.M44 = Double.Parse(tbM44.Text);
    myTransform.Matrix = m3;
}
```

You can see that the *SetTransform* method creates a custom transform matrix *m3* by taking the input parameters as its elements. This matrix is then attached to the *Matrix* property of the *MatrixTransform3D* object *myTransform*, defined in the XAML file.

Executing this project produces the output shown in Figure 12-21. You obtain this result by setting the elements M13 and M23 to 2, producing a shearing effect on the cube. You must create this 3D shearing effect by means of a custom transform matrix, because WPF doesn't provide a *SkewTransform3D* class. You can use the *MatrixTransform3D* class to create any 3D transform you desire by manipulating its corresponding elements directly.

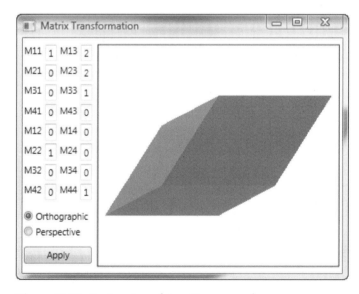

Figure 12-21. Custom transformation on a cube

495

Combining Transforms

The *Transform3DGroup* class is useful when you want to create a combining transformation consisting of any number of *Transform3D* children in its *Transform3D* collection.

Here, I'll present an example to illustrate how to use the *Transform3DGroup* class in a WPF application. In this example, we'll consider a combining transformation that contains a scale transformation and a rotation transformation. We will apply this combining transformation to a cube object.

Open the *Transformation3D* project, add a new WPF Window, and name it *CombineTransformation*. The layout for this example is also similar to that used in the previous *ScaleTransformation* example. Here, I'll only show you the key steps for performing the combining transform. You can view the complete source code for this example by opening its XAML and code-behind files in Visual Studio. In the XAML file for this example, you need to make the following changes to the 3D transform definition:

```
<GeometryModel3D.Transform>
    <Transform3DGroup>
        <ScaleTransform3D x:Name="scaleTransform"/>
        <RotateTransform3D x:Name="rotateTransform"/>
    </Transform3DGroup>
</GeometryModel3D.Transform>
```

Here, you create a *Transform3DGroup* object that includes two transforms: a *ScaleTransform3D* called *scaleTransform* and a *RotateTransform3D* called *rotateTransform*. A *Transform3DGroup* object can contain any number of *Transform3D* objects. Thus, you can easily create complex 3D composite transforms using the *Transform3DGroup*.

You also need to change the *SetTransform* method in the corresponding code-behind file:

```
private void SetTransform()
{
    // Scale transformation:
    scaleTransform.ScaleX = Double.Parse(tbScaleX.Text);
    scaleTransform.ScaleY = Double.Parse(tbScaleY.Text);
    scaleTransform.ScaleZ = Double.Parse(tbScaleZ.Text);

    // Rotation Transformation:
    Vector3D rotateAxis = Vector3D.Parse(tbAxis.Text);
    double rotateAngle = Double.Parse(tbAngle.Text);
    rotateTransform.Rotation = new AxisAngleRotation3D(rotateAxis, rotateAngle);
}
```

Here, you first perform a scale transform, followed by a rotation transform. You specify these transforms by attaching the user's input parameters to the corresponding properties of the 3D transform, *scaleTransform* and *rotateTransform*.

Executing this project produces the results shown in Figure 12-22.

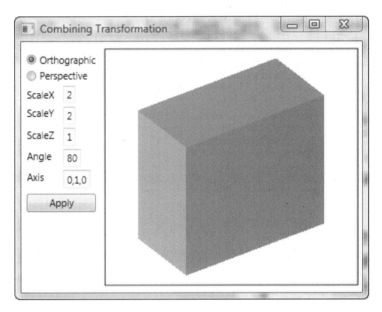

Figure 12-22. Combining transformation on a cube

CHAPTER 13

WPF Graphics Basics in 3D

In the previous chapter, you learned the mathematical basics of 3D transformations and how these transformations are implemented in WPF. In this chapter, you'll learn how to create basic 3D shapes in WPF.

WPF introduces an extensive 3D model that allows you to draw, transform, and animate 3D graphics objects in both markup and code-behind files, using the same capabilities the platform offers for 2D graphics objects. This makes WPF 3D graphics suitable for everything from eye-catching effects in simple games to 3D charts and data visualization in business applications.

Please remember that 3D support in WPF isn't designed to provide a full-featured real-time game development platform. If you are planning to build a complex real-time game application, you will be much better off using the raw power of DirectX or OpenGL.

Even though WPF's 3D model is similar to its 2D counterpart, implementing rich 3D graphics in WPF is still difficult. Creating any meaningful 3D graphics besides trivial 3D scenes using XAML or code-behind files is far more involved than the 2D equivalent of creating an XAML or C# code vector image. This chapter covers 3D graphics basics in WPF, including *Viewport3D*, geometry and mesh, light source, camera setting, and creating basic 3D shapes.

3D Graphics Basics

Even creating the simplest 3D graphics object in WPF, such as a triangle, involves several basic steps:

- Specifying a *Viewport3D* object to host the 3D content.

- Defining the 3D object, which derives from either *ModelVisual3D* or *ModelUIElement3D*.

- Specifying a light source that illuminates a part of or the entire 3D scene.

- Applying materials to the 3D model, which determine the appearance characteristics of the 3D model's surface.

- Setting a camera that projects the 3D object onto a 2D representation, from which you can view the 3D scene.

This list includes only the basic steps for creating 3D objects in WPF. In a practical 3D WPF application, you may require additional procedures, such as transforms and animation. A practical application may also contain multiple graphics objects, multiple light sources, and different materials. These basic ingredients, however, provide a good starting point.

To a new WPF 3D programmer, some of the basic steps just listed may seem unnecessary, especially when compared to the process of creating 2D graphics. You might assume that WPF 3D classes are just a simple means of creating an object with a 3D appearance. In some situations, such as for simple 3D applications, you can construct a graphics object using 2D drawing classes, shapes, and transformations that appears to be 3D. In fact, this approach is usually easier than working with WPF's 3D classes.

However, there are some advantages to using the 3D support offered in WPF. First, you can create effects that would otherwise be extremely complex to calculate using a simulated 3D model. For instance, the lighting effects for an application with multiple light sources and a variety of materials become very involved if you try constructing it using 2D graphics and ray tracing. The other advantage to using the WPF 3D model is that it allows you to interact with your graphics as a set of 3D objects. This greatly extends what you can do programmatically. For example, once you build your desired 3D scene, it becomes almost trivial to rotate your object or to rotate the camera around your object. Doing the same work with 2D programming would require an avalanche of code and math.

In the following sections, you'll learn some basic concepts of 3D graphics in WPF.

Viewport3D

3D graphics content in WPF is encapsulated in the *Viewport3D* class. The graphics object treats *Viewport3D* as a 2D visual element similar to many others in WPF, meaning it can be placed anywhere you can place a normal element. *Viewport3D* functions as a window — a viewport — into a 3D scene. More accurately, it is the surface on which a 3D scene is projected.

The *Viewport3D* class has only two properties, *Camera* and *Children*. The *Camera* property defines your viewpoint into the 3D scene; the *Children* property holds all the 3D objects you want to place in the scene. The light source that illuminates your 3D scene is itself an object in the viewport.

3D Objects in WPF

The *Viewport3D* element can host any 3D object that derives from the *Visual3D* class. However, you need to perform a bit more work than you might expect to create a 3D graphics object. In .NET 3.0 and 3.5, the WPF library lacks a collection of 3D shape primitives. If you want a basic 3D shape such as a cube to be displayed on your screen, you need to build it yourself.

Model3D is an abstract base class that represents a generic 3D object. To build a 3D scene, you need objects to view that derive from *Model3D*. WPF supports modeling Geometries with *GeometryModel3D*. The *Geometry* property of this model takes a mesh primitive.

In .NET 3.0, *Visual3D* is the base class for all 3D objects. As with the Visual class in the 2D world, you could use the *Visual3D* class to derive 3D shapes or to create more complex 3D controls to provide a richer set of events and framework services. WPF includes only one class that derives from *Visual3D*: the all-purpose *ModelVisual3D*.

.NET 3.5 adds some new features to the WPF 3D model. One of these features is the *UIElement3D* class. As you already know, in the 2D world, *UIElement* adds layout, input, focus, and events to the *Visual* class. *UIElement3D* brings these same things to the *Visual3D* class. This means that the standard events and means of adding event handlers in 2D using *UIElement*, with which you are already familiar, now apply to the 3D world with *UIElement3D*.

UIElement3D itself is an abstract class that derives from the *Visual3D* class. To make it so that you don't have to derive from *UIElement3D* yourself, WPF provides two new classes, *ModelUIElement3D* and *ContainerUIElement3D*. The latter is a container for other *Visual3D* objects. It has one main property, *Children*, which you use to add and remove 3D objects. The *ContainerUIElement3D* class doesn't have a visual representation itself; rather, it is simply a collection of other 3D objects. The *ModelUIElement3D* class has one property, *Model*, which is the *Model3D* displayed to represent the *UIElement3D* objects. It has no children itself, and in some ways you can think of *ModelUIElement3D* as a *Shape* object in the 2D world.

If you are familiar with the *ModelVisual3D* class often used in .NET 3.0, then the *ContainerUIElement3D* and *ModelUIElement3D* classes should look very familiar. The difference is that WPF splits the functionality of *ModelVisual3D* (i.e., a model and its children) into two separate classes, one holding the model and the other holding the children.

With these classes, making use of layout, focus, and events in 3D is very easy. For instance, if you want to create a 3D object that responds to mouse events, you can simply use the following statement:

```
<ModelUIElement3D MouseDown="OnMouseDown"/>
```

You can then implement the *OnMouseDown* event handler in the code-behind file, a process identical to that used to add event handlers in the 2D world. Thus, with the addition of *UIElement3D*, you can get in the 3D world all of the functionality that *UIElement* provides to 2D.

From the foregoing discussion, you can see that building a 3D graphics object involves a two-step process. First, you need to define the shapes (which derive from either *ModelVisual3D* or *UIElement3D*) that you want to utilize and then use them with a visual. You can employ this approach for 2D drawing, but it is entirely optional. However, it is mandatory for 3D drawing because there are no built-in 3D shape classes in WPF.

The two-step process is also important because 3D models are much more complex than 2D models. For instance, when you create a *Geometry3D* object, you specify not only the vertices of the shape but also the material out of which it is composed. Different materials have different properties for reflecting and absorbing light.

Geometry and Mesh

To build a 3D object, you begin by building a shape primitive, or *mesh*. A 3D primitive is a collection of vertices that form a single 3D entity. Most 3D systems provide primitives modeled on the simplest closed figure: a triangle defined by three vertices. Since the three points of a triangle are coplanar, you can continue adding triangles to model more complex shapes, called *meshes*.

Currently, WPF's 3D model provides the *MeshGeometry3D* class, which allows you to specify any geometry. If you have ever dealt with 3D drawings or 3D finite-element CAD packages before, you may already know the concept of the mesh. Understanding how a mesh is defined is one of the first keys to 3D programming. If you examine the *MeshGeometry3D* class carefully, you'll find that it adds the following four properties:

- *Positions* — Contains a collection of all the points that define the mesh. Each vertex is specified as a *Point3D* object. Depending on its geometry, the mesh might be composed of many triangles, some of which share the same corners (vertices), meaning that one point will become the vertex of several triangles. You may choose to define the same shared vertex multiple times so that you can better control the way individual triangles are shaded with the *Normals* property.

- *TriangleIndices* — Defines the triangles. Each entry in this collection represents a single triangle by referring to three points from the *Positions* collection. This property specifies the order in which the points in the *Positions* list will determine a triangle.

- *Normals* — Provides a vector for each vertex. To render the surface of the model, the graphics system needs information about the direction the surface is facing at any given triangle. It uses this *Normals* property to make lighting calculations for the model: Surfaces that face directly toward a light source appear brighter than those angled away from the light. WPF can determine default normal vectors by using the position coordinates; you can also specify normal vectors to approximate the appearance of curved surfaces.

- *TextureCoordinates* — Specifies a point collection that tells the graphics system how to map the coordinates, which will determine how a texture is drawn to vertices of the mesh. *TextureCoordinates* are specified as a value between zero and 1. As in the *Normals* property, WPF can calculate default texture coordinates, but you may choose to set different texture coordinates to control the mapping of a texture that, for example, includes part of a repeating pattern.

Let's look at the simplest possible mesh, which consists of a single triangle. The units you use to create the 3D model aren't important because you can always move the camera closer or farther away, and you can change the size or location of individual 3D objects by means of transformations. What's important is the coordinate system, which is shown in Figure 13-1. As you can see, the *X* and *Y* axes have the same orientation as in 2D drawing. What's new is the *Z* axis. As the *Z* axis value decreases, the point moves farther away; as it increases, the point moves closer.

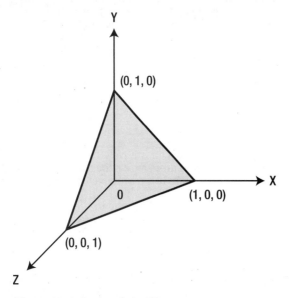

Figure 13-1. *A triangle in 3D space*

You can use *MeshGeometry3D* to define this mesh shape inside a 3D visual. The *MeshGeometry3D* object in this example doesn't require us to specify the *Normals* property or the *TextureCoordinates* property (the default values will be used for these two properties) because the shape is simple and will be painted with a *SolidColorBrush*:

```
<MeshGeometry3D Positions="1,0,0 0,1,0 0,0,1" TriangleIndices="0,1,2"/>
```

Here, there are just three points, which are listed one after another in the *Positions* property. The order you put points in the *Positions* property is important because a position's index value in a mesh's position collection is used when adding the triangle indices. For example, let's say you have a surface composed of four positions {*p0*, *p1*, *p2*, *p3*}. If you want to define a triangle from *p0*, *p2*, and *p3*, you would add triangle indices with index values 0, 2, and 3. If the positions were given in a different order, for instance, {*p3*, *p1*, *p0*, *p2*}, and you want to create a triangle made of the same positions, you would add triangle indices with the values 2, 3, 0.

The mesh positions alone can't describe the mesh triangles. After you have added the *Positions* property, you need to define which positions make up which triangles. The order in which you add triangle indices is also important. When you define a triangle, you are basically defining the points in either a clockwise or a counterclockwise direction, depending on the side of the triangle you are on. This is important because it affects which side of the triangle is visible.

In this example, the *TriangleIndices* property states that there is a single triangle made of points #0, #1, and #2. In other words, the *TriangleIndices* property tells WPF to draw the triangle by drawing a line from (1, 0, 0) to (0, 1, 0) and then to (0, 0, 1).

WPF's 3D model uses a right-hand coordinate system. When defining a shape, you must list the points in counterclockwise order around the *Z* axis. This example follows that rule. However, you could easily violate the rule by changing the *TriangleIndices* to 0, 2, 1. In this case, you would still define the same triangle, but the triangle will be backwards. In other words, if you look at it down the *Z* axis, you will actually be looking at the back of the triangle.

The difference between the back of a 3D shape and the front is not trivial. In some cases, you may paint both sides with a different brush. You may also choose not to paint the back at all in order to avoid using resources for a part of the scene that you will never see.

GeometryModel3D and Surfaces

Once you have a properly configured *MeshGeometry3D*, you need to wrap it in a *GeometryModel3D*. The *GeometryModel3D* class has three properties: *Geometry*, *Material*, and *BackMaterial*. The *Geometry* property takes the *MeshGeometry3D* object that defines the shape of your 3D object. The *Material* and *BackMaterial* properties define the surface out of which your shape is composed.

For a mesh to look like a 3D object, it must have an applied texture that covers the surface defined by its vertices and triangles so that it can be lit and projected by the camera. In 2D, you use the *Brush* class to apply colors, patterns, gradients, or other visual content to areas of the screen. The appearance of 3D objects, however, is a function of the lighting model, not just of the color or pattern applied to objects. Real-world objects reflect light differently depending on the quality of their surfaces. The surface defines the color of the object and how that material responds to light.

To define the characteristics of a 3D model's surface, WPF uses the *Material* abstract class. The concrete subclasses of *Material* determine some of the appearance characteristics of the model's surface, and each subclass provides a *Brush* property to which you can pass a *SolidColorBrush*, *TileBrush*, or *VisualBrush*.

WPF includes four subclasses of *Material*, all of which derive from the abstract *Material* class:

- *DiffuseMaterial* — Specifies that the brush will be applied to the model as though the model is lit diffusely. Using *DiffuseMaterial* resembles using brushes directly on 2D models. The model surfaces do not appear shiny because they don't reflect light.

- *SpecularMaterial* — Specifies that the brush will be applied to the model as though the model's surface is hard or shiny and capable of reflecting highlights. You can use this to create glossy and highlighted effects. It reflects light back directly, like a mirror.

- *EmissiveMaterial* — Specifies that texture will be applied so that the model looks like it is emitting light equal to the color of the brush. It creates a glowing look.

- *MaterialGroup* — Allows you to combine more than one material. To achieve certain surface qualities, such as glowing or reflective effects, you may want to apply several different brushes to a model in succession.

Let's look at a sample XAML code snippet that shows us how to paint a triangle surface with a solid color brush:

```
<GeometryModel3D>
    // Create geometry:
    <GoemetryModel3D.Goemetry>
        <MeshGeometry3D Positions="1,0,0 0,1,0 0,0,1" TriangleIndices="0,1,2"/>
     </GeometryModel3D.Geometry>
    // Set materials:
    <GeometryModel3D.Material>
        <DiffuseMaterial Brush="LightBlue"/>
    </GeometryModel3D.Material>
    <GoemtryModel3D.BackMaterial>
        <DiffuseMaterial Brush = "LightCoral"/>
    </GeometryModel3D.BackMaterial>
</GeometryModel3D>
```

In this example, the *BackMaterial* property is also specified, so the triangle is differently colored if viewed from behind.

Our next step is to use this *GeometryModel3D* to set the *Content* property of a *ModelVisual3D* or *ModelUIElement3D* inside a *ContainerUIElement3D* and to place that *ModelVisual3D* or *ContainerUIElement3D* in a viewport. However, in order to see your object, you will need to specify a light source and set a camera.

Illuminating the Scene

In order to create real-world shaded 3D graphics objects, WPF uses a lighting model that adds one or more light sources to your 3D scene. Your objects are then illuminated based on the type of light you specify, its position, its direction, and its power. Lights determine which portion of a scene will be included in the projection. Light objects in WPF create a variety of light and shadow effects and are modeled after the behavior of various real-world lights. You must specify at least one light source in your 3D scene, or no objects will be visible.

WPF provides four light classes that derive from the base class, *Light*:

- *AmbientLight* — Provides ambient lighting that illuminates all objects uniformly regardless of their location or orientation.

- *DirectionalLight* — Illuminates like a distant light source with parallel rays of light. Directional lights have a direction specified as a *Vector3D* but no specified location.

- *PointLight* — Illuminates like a nearby light source that radiates light in all directions from a single point in 3D space. A *PointLight* has a position and casts light from that position. Objects in the scene are illuminated depending on their position and distance with respect to the light. *PointLightBase* exposes a *Range* property, which determines a distance beyond which models will not be illuminated by light. *PointLight* also exposes attenuation properties that determine how the light's intensity diminishes with distance. You can specify constant, linear, or quadratic interpolations for the light's attenuation.

- *SpotLight* — Inherits from *PointLight*. It illuminates like *PointLight* and has both a position and direction. It projects light in a cone-shaped area set by the *InnerConeAngle* and *OuterConeAngle* properties, specified in degrees.

Here, we define a white *DirectionalLight* to illuminate the triangle you created in the previous section using the following statement:

```
<DirectionalLight Color="White" Direction="-1,-1,-1"/>
```

where the vector that determines the path of the light starts at the origin (0, 0, 0) and goes to (–1, –1, –1). This means that each ray of light is a straight line that travels from the top-right front toward the bottom-left back. This makes sense in this example because the front surface of the triangle shown in Figure 13-1 lines up exactly with the direction of the light.

Camera Position

In Chapter 12, you learned how to construct a projection matrix and set up a camera using the *MatrixCamera* class. When you create a 3D scene, it is important to remember that you are really creating a 2D representation of 3D objects through projection. Since a 3D scene looks different depending on the point of view, you must specify your point of view using the *Camera* class in WPF. This means that in order to see a 3D object, you must set a camera at the correct position and orient it in the correct direction. You achieve this by specifying the *Viewport3D.Camera* property with a *Camera* object.

Basically, as discussed in Chapter 12, the camera determines how a 3D scene is represented on the 2D viewing surface of a viewport. WPF introduces three camera classes: *PerspectiveCamera*, *OrthographicCamera*, and *MatrixCamera*. All of these camera classes and their corresponding matrices were discussed in great detail in Chapter 12. The *PerspectiveCamera* specifies a projection that foreshortens the scene. In other words, the *PerspectiveCamera* renders the scene so that objects that are farther away appear smaller; i.e., it provides a vanishing-point perspective projection. You can specify the position of the camera in the coordinate space of the scene, the camera's direction and its field of view, and a vector that defines the direction of "up" in the scene.

As you learned in Chapter 12 when we discussed the view frustum, the *NearPlaneDistance* and *FarPlaneDistance* properties of the *ProjectionCamera* limit the range of the camera's projection. Because you can locate cameras anywhere in the scene, it is possible to position the camera inside of a model or very near a model, making it hard to distinguish objects properly. *NearPlaneDistance* allows you to specify a minimum distance from the camera within which objects will not be drawn. Conversely, *FarPlaneDistance* lets you specify a distance from the camera beyond which objects will not be drawn, which ensures that objects too far away to be recognizable will not be included in the scene.

The *OrthographicCamera* flattens 3D objects so that the exact scale is preserved, no matter where a shape is positioned, which is useful for some types of visualization tools, such as 3D chart and technical drawing applications. Like other cameras, it specifies a position, viewing direction, and "upward" direction.

Finally, the *MatrixCamera* allows you to specify a matrix that is used to transform the 3D scene into a 2D view. This is an advanced tool intended for highly specialized effects and for porting code from other frameworks that use this type of camera, such as DirectX and OpenGL. In Chapter 12, you used the *MatrixCamera* extensively to view a simple cube object.

Selecting the right camera is relatively easy, but placing and configuring it is a bit trickier. First you need to specify a point in 2D space at which the camera will be positioned by setting its *Position* property. The second step is to set a *Vector3D* object for the *LookDirection* property, which indicates how the camera is oriented. To make sure the camera is correctly oriented, pick a point — the center point of interest — you want to see from your camera. You can then calculate the *LookDirection* using this formula:

```
CameraLookDirection = CenterPointOfInterest - CameraPosition
```

In the triangle example, you can place the camera at the position (2, 2, 2), i.e., right on top of the front surface of the triangle. Assuming you want to focus on the origin (0, 0, 0), you would use the following look direction:

```
CameraLookDirection = (0, 0, 0) - (2, 2, 2) = (-2, -2, -2)
```

This is equivalent to the normalized vector (–1, –1, –1) because the direction it describes is the same. Once you have set the *Position* and *LookDirection* properties, you also need to set the *UpDirection* property. The *UpDirection* determines how the camera is tilted. Generally, the *UpDirection* is set to (0, 1, 0), which means the up-direction is lined up with the positive *Y* axis.

With these details in mind, you can define a *PerspectiveCamera* for this simple triangle example:

```
<Viewport3D.Camera>
    <PerspectiveCamera Position="2,2,2"
                       LookDirection="-2,-2,-2"
                       UpDirection="0,1,0"/>
</Viewport3D.Camera>
```

Simple Triangle in 3D

Now it is time to put all the pieces of our triangle example together. Start a new WPF project and name it *GraphicsBasics3D*. Add a new WPF Window to the project and name it *SimpleTriangle*. The following is the complete XAML file for this example:

```
<Window x:Class="GraphicsBasics3D.SimpleTriangle"
    xmlns="http://schemas.microsoft.com/winfx/2006/xaml/presentation"
    xmlns:x="http://schemas.microsoft.com/winfx/2006/xaml"
    Title="Simple Triangle Example" Height="300" Width="300">
    <Grid Margin="5">
        <Grid.RowDefinitions>
            <RowDefinition/>
            <RowDefinition Height="Auto"/>
        </Grid.RowDefinitions>
        <Border BorderBrush="Gray" BorderThickness="1" Grid.Row="0">
            <Viewport3D>
                <Viewport3D.Camera>
                    <PerspectiveCamera Position="2,2,2" LookDirection="-2,-2,-2"
                                       UpDirection="0,1,0"/>
                </Viewport3D.Camera>
                <ContainerUIElement3D>
                    <ModelUIElement3D>
                        <Model3DGroup>
                            <!-- Set light source: -->
                            <DirectionalLight Color="White" Direction="-1,-1,-1" />
                            <!-- Add triangle: -->
                            <GeometryModel3D>
                                <GeometryModel3D.Geometry>
                                    <MeshGeometry3D Positions="1,0,0 0,1,0 0,0,1"
                                                    TriangleIndices="0,1,2" />
                                </GeometryModel3D.Geometry>
                                <!-- Set material: -->
                                <GeometryModel3D.Material>
                                    <DiffuseMaterial Brush="Blue" />
                                </GeometryModel3D.Material>
                                <GeometryModel3D.BackMaterial>
                                    <DiffuseMaterial Brush="Red" />
                                </GeometryModel3D.BackMaterial>
```

```
                        <!-- Set rotation: -->
                        <GeometryModel3D.Transform>
                            <RotateTransform3D>
                                <RotateTransform3D.Rotation>
                                    <AxisAngleRotation3D x:Name="myRotate"
                                        Axis="-0.707,1,-0.707"/>
                                </RotateTransform3D.Rotation>
                            </RotateTransform3D>
                        </GeometryModel3D.Transform>
                    </GeometryModel3D>
                </Model3DGroup>
            </ModelUIElement3D>
        </ContainerUIElement3D>
    </Viewport3D>
</Border>
<Slider Margin="10,20,10,10" Grid.Row="1" Minimum="0" Maximum="360"
        Orientation="Horizontal"
        Value="{Binding ElementName=myRotate, Path=Angle}"/>
    </Grid>
</Window>
```

Here we add the light source and the *Model3DGroup* contained inside the *ModelUIElement3D*. If you are working in the .NET 3.0 framework, you can replace *ModelUIElement3D* and *ContainerUIElement3D* with *ModelVisual3D.Content* and *ModelVisual3D*, respectively.

We also add a rotation transform to the triangle, which allows you to examine the front and back surfaces of the triangle so that you can see that they are painted with brushes of different colors. Using this rotation, called *myRotate*, you create a data-bound *Slider* that allows you to use your mouse to rotate the triangle interactively around the axis you specify.

Figure 13-2 shows the result of running this example. You can move the slider with your mouse to see how the color changes as the triangle rotates.

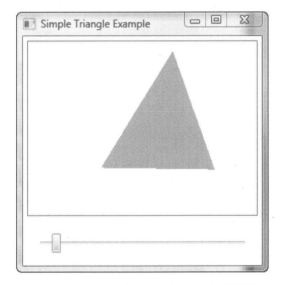

Figure 13-2. *A triangle created using the WPF 3D model*

Basic 3D Shapes

In this section, you'll learn how to create some basic 3D shapes in WPF, including coordinate axes, simple wireframes, cubes, cylinders, cones, spheres, and toruses.

Coordinate Axes and Wireframe

In WPF, everything in 3D is considered a triangle. If you want to draw a 3D line, you have to somehow create it using triangles. It is surprising that WPF doesn't contain a 3D line class, since a 3D line object is so fundamental.

Fortunately, the WPF 3D team at Microsoft has created a 3D tools library that contains several classes designed to make WPF 3D programming easier. One of these classes is the *ScreenSpaceLines3D* class. You can download the *3DTools* library from `http://www.codeplex.com/3DTools`. The DLL library was originally built for the .NET 3.0 framework. I have rebuilt it for NET 3.5 and Visual Studio 2008. This newly built DLL library is included in the References for the *GraphicsBasics3D* project. If you're working on the .NET 3.0 platform, you should use the original DLL from codeplex; if you're working on the .NET 3.5 platform, use newly built DLL.

If you carefully examine the source code of the *ScreenSpaceLines3D* class, you'll find that this class inherits from the *ModelVisual3D* base class. The line event handler is attached to *CompositionTarget.Rendering*, just as it is for a Per-Frame animation. This handy feature of WPF allows you to register a callback function that gets called whenever something is being rendered. However, this callback may get called too often — in fact, it gets called every frame, about 60 times per second! — which may lead to serious memory leaks for complex 3D wireframes you produce using *ScreenSpaceLines3D* objects.

Here, I still want to use this *3DTools* library, because it has already become popular in the WPF 3D community. The *ScreenSpaceLines3D* class allows you to draw straight lines of invariant width in 3D space. In other words, these lines stay fixed at the thickness you specify, no matter where you place the camera. This makes these lines useful for creating coordinate axes and wireframes.

Because the *ScreenSpaceLines3D* object is a *ModelVisual3D* object, you can add this object directly to the Viewport3D, as shown in the following XAML snippet:

```
...
xmlns:tool3d="clr-namespace:_3DTools;assembly=3DTools"
...
<Viewport3D>
    <tool3d:ScreenSpaceLines3D Points="0,0,0 0,2,0" Color="Black" Thickness="2"/>
</Viewport3D>
...
```

Here, to use this class, you first need to register the namespace and assembly in XAML. Then you can create a 3D line object by specifying its points, color, and thickness properties. You can draw multiple line segments by adding a points collection. Please note that the points in the collection must be paired, with each pair of points determining one line segment. For instance, if you have a point collection {p0, p1, p2, p3}, the *ScreenSpaceLines3D* class will draw two line segments, one from p0 to p1 and the other from p2 to p3. Notice that there is no line segment drawn from p1 to p2. If you want to draw a continuous line, you need to set a point collection in the form {p0, p1, p1, p2, p2, p3}.

Let's create a simple triangle wireframe with coordinate axes. Add a new WPF Window to the *GraphicsBasics3D* project and name it *Wireframe*. The following is the XAML code for this example:

```
<Window x:Class="GraphicsBasics3D.Wireframe"
    xmlns="http://schemas.microsoft.com/winfx/2006/xaml/presentation"
    xmlns:x="http://schemas.microsoft.com/winfx/2006/xaml"
```

```
xmlns:tool3d="clr-namespace:_3DTools;assembly=3DTools"
Title="Simple Triangle Example" Height="350" Width="300">

<Window.Resources>
    <RotateTransform3D x:Key="rotate">
        <RotateTransform3D.Rotation>
            <AxisAngleRotation3D Axis="0,1,0"
                Angle="{Binding ElementName=slider, Path=Value, Mode=TwoWay}" />
        </RotateTransform3D.Rotation>
    </RotateTransform3D>
</Window.Resources>

<Grid Margin="5">
    <Grid.RowDefinitions>
        <RowDefinition/>
        <RowDefinition Height="Auto"/>
    </Grid.RowDefinitions>
    <Border BorderBrush="Gray" BorderThickness="1" Grid.Row="0">
        <Viewport3D>
            <Viewport3D.Camera>
                <PerspectiveCamera Position="1,3,3"
                    LookDirection="-1,-3,-3"
                    UpDirection="0,1,0"/>
            </Viewport3D.Camera>

            <!-- Add coordinate axes: -->
            <tool3d:ScreenSpaceLines3D
                Points="0,0,0 1.5,0,0" Color="Red"
                Transform="{StaticResource rotate}"/>
            <tool3d:ScreenSpaceLines3D
                Points="0,0,0 0,1.5,0" Color="Green"
                Transform="{StaticResource rotate}"/>
            <tool3d:ScreenSpaceLines3D
                Points="0,0,0 0,0,1.5" Color="Blue"
                Transform="{StaticResource rotate}"/>


            <!-- Add triangle wireframe -->
            <tool3d:ScreenSpaceLines3D
                Points="1,0,0 0,1,0 0,1,0 0,0,1 0,0,1 1,0,0"
                Thickness="3" Color="Black"
                Transform="{StaticResource rotate}"/>
        </Viewport3D>
    </Border>

    <Slider Name="slider" Margin="10,20,10,10" Grid.Row="1" Minimum="0"
            Maximum="360" Orientation="Horizontal"/>
</Grid>
</Window>
```

Here, the code first creates a Window resource that defines a *RotateTransform3D* object. The *Angle* property of this rotation is controlled by a slider's *Value* property. You then draw three lines for the coordinate axes, using different colors: red for the *X* axis, green for the *Y* axis, and blue for the *Z* axis. Next, you create a triangular wireframe using *ScreenSpaceLines3D*. We also perform a rotation transform on the coordinate axes and triangle wireframe by attaching a *RotateTransform3D* object, called "rotate," defined in the *Window.Resources*, to the *Transform* property of the *ScreenSpaceLines3D* objects. Notice that we only need to define a camera to view the line objects. There is no need to specify the light source and material if all you want to display on your screen are line objects.

Figure 13-3 illustrates the results of running this example. If you move the slider with your mouse, the coordinate axes and triangular wireframe will rotate together accordingly.

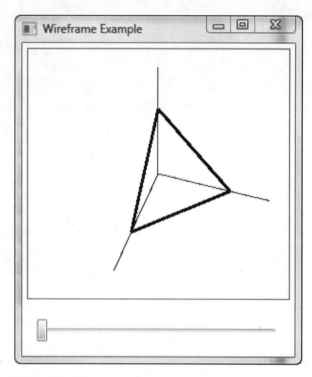

Figure 13-3. *Triangle wireframe and coordinate axes*

Creating a Cube

In this section, you will create a cube shape in WPF. In the previous chapter, we created such a cube in an XAML file by using *Window.Resources* directly . Here, we'll add more features to the cube object, such as painting different faces with different colors and adding a wireframe, from which you can clearly see how the triangular meshes are generated. To add these new features, we'll create the cube object in a code-behind file. A cube object is simply an extension of creating a triangle. The cube consists of six faces, each of which can be constructed with two triangles. Remember to follow the right-hand rule and to follow a counterclockwise direction when you create the triangles.

Let's consider an example of creating a cube in code. Add a new class to the project *GraphicsBasics3D* and name it *Utility*. Add a *CreateTriangleFace* method to the *Utility* class. Here is the code for this class:

```
using System;
using System.Windows;
```

```
using System.Windows.Media;
using System.Windows.Media.Media3D;
using System.Windows.Controls;
using _3DTools;

namespace GraphicsBasics3D
{
    public class Utility
    {
        public static void CreateTriangleFace(
            Point3D p0, Point3D p1, Point3D p2,
            Color color, bool isWireframe,
            Viewport3D viewport)
        {
            MeshGeometry3D mesh = new MeshGeometry3D();
            mesh.Positions.Add(p0);
            mesh.Positions.Add(p1);
            mesh.Positions.Add(p2);
            mesh.TriangleIndices.Add(0);
            mesh.TriangleIndices.Add(1);
            mesh.TriangleIndices.Add(2);
            SolidColorBrush brush = new SolidColorBrush();
            brush.Color = color;
            Material material = new DiffuseMaterial(brush);
            GeometryModel3D geometry = new GeometryModel3D(mesh, material);
            ModelUIElement3D model = new ModelUIElement3D();
            model.Model = geometry;
            viewport.Children.Add(model);

            if (isWireframe == true)
            {
                ScreenSpaceLines3D ssl = new ScreenSpaceLines3D();
                ssl.Points.Add(p0);
                ssl.Points.Add(p1);
                ssl.Points.Add(p1);
                ssl.Points.Add(p2);
                ssl.Points.Add(p2);
                ssl.Points.Add(p0);
                ssl.Color = Colors.Black;
                ssl.Thickness = 2;
                viewport.Children.Add(ssl);
            }
        }
    }
}
```

Note that a using statement

```
using _3DTools;
```

is added to this class so that we can use the *ScreenSpaceLines3D* object directly. The *CreateTriangleFace* method creates a single triangle model, which includes a triangle face and a wireframe if the *isWireframe* field is set to true. The triangle face is created as a *UIElement3D* object that defines the geometry mesh and the material. You then add both the triangle face and the wireframe directly to the *Viewport3D*.

Thus, each triangle is treated as an individual 3D model. From a programmer's point of view, this approach doesn't seem very efficient. For greater efficiency, you may want to use another method, such as putting all of the triangles into a *Model3DGroup* collection and then adding this *Model3DGroup* to the *Viewport3D*. However, the approach based on the individual triangle model does provide some advantages. For example, it is easier to implement, and it provides the flexibility to paint each triangle face with a different material. In addition, since the *ScreenSpaceLines3D* class derives from *ModelVisual3D*, you can't put the wireframe for each triangle into a *Model3DGroup* collection, meaning you need to add it directly to *Viewport3D*. So for illustration purposes, here we'll create a cube object with a wireframe using the individual triangle model.

Now add a new WPF Window to the project *GraphicsBasics3D* and name it *Cube*. In the layout, you'll set the camera and light source and add the coordinate axes using the *ScreenSpaceLines3D* objects. Here is the XAML file for this example:

```
<Window x:Class=" GraphicsBasics3D.Cube"
    xmlns="http://schemas.microsoft.com/winfx/2006/xaml/presentation"
    xmlns:x="http://schemas.microsoft.com/winfx/2006/xaml"
    xmlns:tool3d="clr-namespace:_3DTools;assembly=3DTools"
    Title="Cube" Height="350" Width="300">

    <Grid Margin="5">
        <Border BorderBrush="Gray" BorderThickness="1">
            <Viewport3D Name="myViewport">
                <Viewport3D.Camera>
                    <PerspectiveCamera Position="4,5,6" LookDirection="-4,-5,-6"
                                       UpDirection="0,1,0"/>
                </Viewport3D.Camera>

                <!-- Set light source: -->
                <ModelUIElement3D>
                    <DirectionalLight Color="White" Direction="-1,-1,-1" />
                </ModelUIElement3D>

                <!-- Add coordinate axes: -->
                <tool3d:ScreenSpaceLines3D Points="-4,0,0 3,0,0" Color="Red"/>
                <tool3d:ScreenSpaceLines3D Points="0,-5,0 0,3,0" Color="Green"/>
                <tool3d:ScreenSpaceLines3D Points="0,0,-10 0,0,3" Color="Blue"/>
            </Viewport3D>
        </Border>
    </Grid>
</Window>
```

The corresponding code-behind file shows the detailed procedure of creating a cube shape in WPF:

```
using System;
using System.Windows;
using System.Windows.Controls;
using System.Windows.Media;
using System.Windows.Media.Media3D;

namespace GraphicsBasics3D
{
    public partial class Cube : Window
    {
        public Cube()
```

```
{
    InitializeComponent();

    // Create a cube:
    CreateCube(new Point3D(0, 0, 0), 2, true);

    // Create another cube:
    CreateCube(new Point3D(0, 0, -4), 2, false);
}

public void CreateCube(Point3D center, double side, bool isWireframe)
{
    double a = side / 2.0;
    Point3D[] p = new Point3D[8];
    p[0] = new Point3D(-a,  a,  a);
    p[1] = new Point3D( a,  a,  a);
    p[2] = new Point3D( a,  a, -a);
    p[3] = new Point3D(-a,  a, -a);
    p[4] = new Point3D(-a, -a,  a);
    p[5] = new Point3D( a, -a,  a);
    p[6] = new Point3D( a, -a, -a);
    p[7] = new Point3D(-a, -a, -a);

    // Redefine the center of the cube:
    for (int i = 0; i < 8; i++)
        p[i] += (Vector3D)center;

    // Surface 1 (0,1,2,3):
    Utility.CreateTriangleFace(p[0], p[1], p[2], Colors.LightGray,
                              isWireframe, myViewport);
    Utility.CreateTriangleFace(p[2], p[3], p[0], Colors.LightGray,
                              isWireframe, myViewport);

    // Surface 2 (4,7,6,5):
    Utility.CreateTriangleFace(p[4], p[7], p[6], Colors.Black,
                              isWireframe, myViewport);
    Utility.CreateTriangleFace(p[6], p[5], p[4], Colors.Black,
                              isWireframe, myViewport);

    // Surface 3 (0,4,5,1):
    Utility.CreateTriangleFace(p[0], p[4], p[5], Colors.Red,
                              isWireframe, myViewport);
    Utility.CreateTriangleFace(p[5], p[1], p[0], Colors.Red,
                              isWireframe, myViewport);

    // Surface 4 (1,5,6,2):
    Utility.CreateTriangleFace(p[1], p[5], p[6], Colors.Green,
                              isWireframe, myViewport);
    Utility.CreateTriangleFace(p[6], p[2], p[1], Colors.Green,
                              isWireframe, myViewport);

    // Surface 5 (2,6,7,3):
    Utility.CreateTriangleFace(p[2], p[6], p[7], Colors.Blue,
```

```
                                    isWireframe, myViewport);
        Utility.CreateTriangleFace(p[7], p[3], p[2], Colors.Blue,
                                    isWireframe, myViewport);

        // Surface 2 (0,3,7,4):
        Utility.CreateTriangleFace(p[0], p[3], p[7], Colors.Black,
                                    isWireframe, myViewport);
        Utility.CreateTriangleFace(p[7], p[4], p[0], Colors.Black,
                                    isWireframe, myViewport);
    }
  }
}
```

The *CreateCube* method in this class creates the cube object. It first defines a point array object that contains eight vertices, which specify the coordinates of the cube in the 3D space. Then we create the trangle models, with different colors for the different surfaces of the cube, by calling the static *CreateTriangleFace* method in the *Utility* class. This way, you have the flexibility to specify a different material and wireframe for each individual triangle.

Finally, we create two cube objects at different locations using the *CreateCube* method, one cube with the wireframe and the other without it.

Figure 13-4 illustrates the results of running this application.

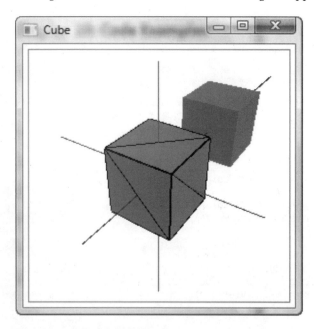

Figure 13-4. *Cubes in WPF*

You can add more features to this example, such as normals and texture coordinates. For example, it is easy to create normals inside the *CreateTriangleFace* method in the *Utility* class by adding the following few lines of code:

```
Vector3D v1 = new Vector3D(p1.X - p0.X, p1.Y - p0.Y, p1.Z - p0.Z);
Vector3D v2 = new Vector3D(p2.X - p1.X, p2.Y - p1.Y, p2.Z - p1.Z);
Vector3D normal = Vector3D.CrossProduct(v1, v2);
mesh.Normals.Add(normal);
```

Creating a Sphere

In this section, you'll create a sphere shape in WPF. To do this, you need to be familiar with the spherical coordinate system. A point in the spherical coordinate system is specified by r, θ, and φ. Here, r is the distance from the point to the origin, θ is the polar angle, and ϕ is the azimuthal angle in the X-Z plane from the X axis. In this notation, you also alternate the conventional Y and Z axes so that the coordinate system is consistent with that used in WPF. Figure 13-5 shows a point in this coordinate system. From this figure, you can easily obtain the following relationships:

$$x = r\sin\theta\cos\phi$$
$$y = r\cos\theta$$
$$z = -r\sin\theta\sin\phi$$

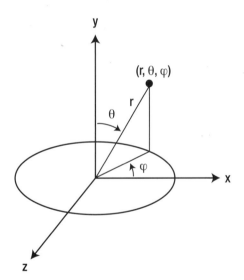

Figure 13-5. *Spherical coordinate system*

In order to create a sphere shape in WPF using these relations, you can start with the familiar concepts of longitude and latitude (sometimes also called the *UV*-sphere method). The standard *UV*-sphere method is made out of u segments and v rings, as shown in Figure 13-6. It can be seen that the u and v lines form grids on the surface of the sphere. In order to create triangles for this surface, it is enough to consider just one unit grid, as shown on the right of Figure 13-6. You can divide this unit grid into two triangles. If you run over all of the grids, you can triangulate the entire surface of the sphere.

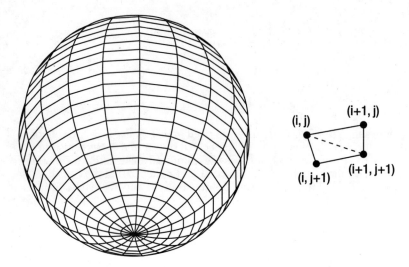

Figure 13-6. A UV-sphere model and a unit grid used to create triangles

Let's start off with an example illustrating how to create a sphere. Add a new WPF Window to the project *GraphicsBasics3D* and name it *Sphere*. The XAML code is the same as that used in the previous example. The XAML file creates the layout, sets the camera and light source, and adds the coordinate axes using the *ScreenSpaceLines3D* class. Here is the corresponding code-behind file, which creates the sphere:

```
using System;
using System.Windows;
using System.Windows.Controls;
using System.Windows.Media;
using System.Windows.Media.Media3D;

namespace GraphicsBasics3D
{
    public partial class Sphere : Window
    {
        public Sphere()
        {
            InitializeComponent();

            // Add a sphere:
            CreateSphere(new Point3D(0, 0, 0), 1.5, 20, 15, Colors.LightBlue, true);

            // Add another sphere:
            CreateSphere(new Point3D(0, 0, -4), 1.5, 20, 15,
                        Colors.LightCoral, false);
        }

        private Point3D GetPosition(double radius, double theta, double phi)
        {
            Point3D pt = new Point3D();
```

```
            double snt = Math.Sin(theta * Math.PI / 180);
            double cnt = Math.Cos(theta * Math.PI / 180);
            double snp = Math.Sin(phi * Math.PI / 180);
            double cnp = Math.Cos(phi * Math.PI / 180);
            pt.X = radius * snt * cnp;
            pt.Y = radius * cnt;
            pt.Z = -radius * snt * snp;
            return pt;
        }

        private void CreateSphere(Point3D center, double radius, int u, int v,
                            Color color, bool isWireframe)
        {
            if (u < 2 || v < 2)
                return;

            Point3D[,] pts = new Point3D[u, v];
            for (int i = 0; i < u; i++)
            {
                for (int j = 0; j < v; j++)
                {
                    pts[i, j] =
                        GetPosition(radius, i * 180 / (u - 1), j * 360 / (v - 1));
                    pts[i, j] += (Vector3D)center;
                }
            }

            Point3D[] p = new Point3D[4];
            for (int i = 0; i < u - 1; i++)
            {
                for (int j = 0; j < v - 1; j++)
                {
                    p[0] = pts[i, j];
                    p[1] = pts[i + 1, j];
                    p[2] = pts[i + 1, j + 1];
                    p[3] = pts[i, j + 1];
                    Utility.CreateTriangleFace(p[0], p[1], p[2], color,
                                            isWireframe, myViewport);
                    Utility.CreateTriangleFace(p[2], p[3], p[0], color,
                                            isWireframe, myViewport);
                }
            }
        }
    }
}
```

Here, you construct triangle meshes by dividing the sphere surface into segments and rings. You can specify the number of segments and rings using two integers, *u* and *v*. This application also allows you to specify the radius and position (the center location) of the sphere. The *GetPosition* method returns the points on the sphere surface by specifying their radius, longitude, and latitude.

Notice how you perform the triangulation for the unit grid inside the *CreateSphere* method, in which the four vertex points that define the unit grid are specified, and two triangles are defined using these four vertices within two for-loops. The triangle is created by calling the *CreateTriangleFace* method in the *Utility* class, which is the same as that used in the previous example.

Finally, you create two sphere objects at different locations using the *CreateSphere* method, one with the wireframe and the other without it.

Figure 13-7 shows the results of running this example.

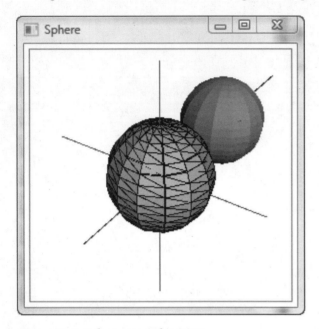

Figure 13-7. *Spheres created in WPF*

Creating a Cylinder

In this section, I'll show you how to create a cylinder shape in WPF. Here, we'll create a general cylinder shape that will allow you to specify its inner and outer radii. By setting a nonzero inner radius, you can create a cylindrical tube shape.

As you probably know, in a cylindrical coordinate system, a point is specified by three parameters, r, θ, and y, which are a bit different from the conventional definition of the system using r, θ, and z. The notation we use here is only for convenience, since the computer screen can always be described using the X-Y plane. Here, r is the distance of a projected point on the X-Z plane from the origin, and θ is the azimuthal angle.

Figure 13-8 shows a point in the cylindrical coordinate system. From this figure you have

$$x = r\cos\theta$$
$$z = -r\sin\theta$$
$$y = y$$

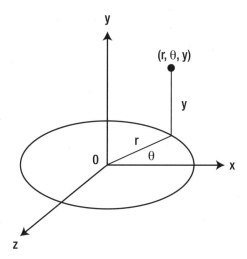

Figure 13-8. *Cylindrical coordinate system*

By using the cylindrical coordinate system, you can easily create cylindrical objects in WPF. First, we need to make slices on the surface of the cylinder. As shown in Figure 13-9, the cylinder surface is divided into *n* slices, and a unit cell is formed by the *i*th and (*i* + 1)th slice lines. You can see that each unit contains eight vertices and four surfaces, which need to be triangulated. Furthermore, each surface can be represented using two triangles.

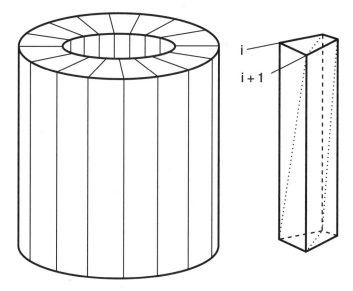

Figure 13-9. *A cylinder and a unit cell*

With this background information, it is now time to consider an example in which we create a cylinder shape in WPF. Add a new WPF Window to the project *GraphicsBasics3D* and name it *Cylinder*. The XAML code is the same as that used in the previous example. The following is the code-behind file for this example:

```
using System;
using System.Windows;
using System.Windows.Media;
using System.Windows.Media.Media3D;

namespace GraphicsBasics3D
{
    public partial class Cylinder : Window
    {
        public Cylinder()
        {
            InitializeComponent();
            //AddCylinder();

            // Create a cylinder:
            CreateCylinder(new Point3D(0, 0, 0), 0, 1.2, 2, 20,
                        Colors.LightBlue, true);

            // Create the other cylinder:
            CreateCylinder(new Point3D(0, 0, -4), 0.8, 1.2, 0.5, 20,
                        Colors.LightCoral, true);

            // Create the other cylinder:
            CreateCylinder(new Point3D(-3, 0, 0), 1, 1.2, 0.5, 40,
                        Colors.Red, false);
        }

        private Point3D GetPosition(double radius, double theta, double y)
        {
            Point3D pt = new Point3D();
            double sn = Math.Sin(theta * Math.PI / 180);
            double cn = Math.Cos(theta * Math.PI / 180);
            pt.X = radius * cn;
            pt.Y = y;
            pt.Z = -radius * sn;
            return pt;
        }

        private void CreateCylinder(Point3D center, double rin, double rout,
                    double height, int n, Color color, bool isWireframe)
        {
            if (n < 2 || rin == rout)
                return;

            double radius = rin;
            if (rin > rout)
            {
                rin = rout;
                rout = radius;
```

```
}

double h = height / 2;
Model3DGroup cylinder = new Model3DGroup();
Point3D[,] pts = new Point3D[n, 4];

for (int i = 0; i < n; i++)
{
    pts[i, 0] = GetPosition(rout, i * 360 / (n - 1), h);
    pts[i, 1] = GetPosition(rout, i * 360 / (n - 1), -h);
    pts[i, 2] = GetPosition(rin, i * 360 / (n - 1), -h);
    pts[i, 3] = GetPosition(rin, i * 360 / (n - 1), h);
}
for (int i = 0; i < n; i++)
{
    for (int j = 0; j < 4; j++)
        pts[i, j] += (Vector3D)center;
}

Point3D[] p = new Point3D[8];
for (int i = 0; i < n - 1; i++)
{
    p[0] = pts[i, 0];
    p[1] = pts[i, 1];
    p[2] = pts[i, 2];
    p[3] = pts[i, 3];
    p[4] = pts[i + 1, 0];
    p[5] = pts[i + 1, 1];
    p[6] = pts[i + 1, 2];
    p[7] = pts[i + 1, 3];

    // Top surface:
    Utility.CreateTriangleFace(p[0], p[4], p[3], color,
                              isWireframe, myViewport);
    Utility.CreateTriangleFace(p[4], p[7], p[3], color,
                              isWireframe, myViewport);

    // Bottom surface:
    Utility.CreateTriangleFace(p[1], p[5], p[2], color,
                              isWireframe, myViewport);
    Utility.CreateTriangleFace(p[5], p[6], p[2], color,
                              isWireframe, myViewport);

    // Outer surface:
    Utility.CreateTriangleFace(p[0], p[1], p[4], color,
                              isWireframe, myViewport);
    Utility.CreateTriangleFace(p[1], p[5], p[4], color,
                              isWireframe, myViewport);

    // Inner surface:
    Utility.CreateTriangleFace(p[2], p[7], p[6], color,
                              isWireframe, myViewport);
    Utility.CreateTriangleFace(p[2], p[3], p[7], color,
```

```
                                        isWireframe, myViewport);
                }
            }
        }
    }
```

This code-behind file allows you to specify the inner and outer radii, the height, the azimuthal angle, and position of the cylinder. The *GetPosition* method creates a point on the cylinder surface using the cylindrical coordinates.

Inside the *CreateCylinder* method, we construct eight vertices for a unit cell (see Figure 13-9) and then perform the triangulation for the four surfaces of this unit cell, including the top, bottom, inner, and outer surfaces. We need to create two triangles for each surface separately by calling the static *CreateTriangleFace* method defined in the *Utility* class, which is identical to that used in the previous examples.

Finally, we create three different cylindrical objects at different locations by calling the *CreateCylinder* method. The parameter *n*, the number of slices, affects the surface smoothness of the cylindrical objects.

Figure 13-10 shows the results of running this application. You can see from this figure that this program can generate not only cylinders but ring objects as well.

Figure 13-10. *Cylinder and rings created in WPF*

Creating a Cone

You can also create cone shapes using the cylindrical coordinate system. Here we want to create a general cone shape whose top radius, bottom radius, and height can all be specified. Figure 13-11 illustrates how slices are made on the surface of the cone and how a unit cell is defined. This unit cell has three surfaces that need to be triangulated, including a top, bottom, and outer surface. The top and bottom surfaces are already triangular shapes, and the outer surface can be represented with two triangles.

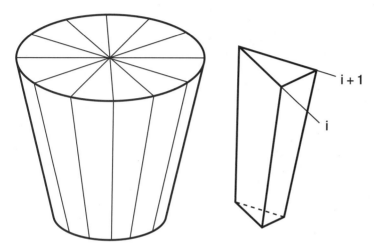

Figure 13-11. *A cone shape and a unit cell*

With this background knowledge, we can now create a cone shape in WPF. Let's consider an example: Add a new WPF Windows application to the project *GraphicsBasics3D* and name it *Cone*. Again, we can use the same XAML code as in the previous examples. Here is the C# code that generates the cone shape:

```
using System;
using System.Windows;
using System.Windows.Media;
using System.Windows.Media.Media3D;

namespace GraphicsBasics3D
{
    public partial class Cone : Window
    {
        public Cone()
        {
            InitializeComponent();

            // Create a cone:
            CreateCone(new Point3D(0, 0, 0), 0, 1.2, 2, 20, Colors.LightBlue, true);

            // Create another cone:
```

```
    CreateCone(new Point3D(0, 0, -3), 0.6, 1.2, 1, 20,
            Colors.LightCoral, false);

    // Create another cone:
    CreateCone(new Point3D(0, 0, -6), 1.2, 0.4, 2, 20,
            Colors.LightGreen, false);

    // Create another cone:
    CreateCone(new Point3D(0, 0, 3), 0.5, 1.2, 1.2, 4,
            Colors.Goldenrod, false);

    // Create another cone:
    CreateCone(new Point3D(-3, 0, 0), 0.8, 0.8, 1.5, 20, Colors.Red, true);

    // Create another cone:
    CreateCone(new Point3D(3, 0, 0), 0, 0.8, 1.5, 5,
            Colors.SteelBlue, false);
}

private Point3D GetPosition(double radius, double theta, double y)
{
    Point3D pt = new Point3D();
    double sn = Math.Sin(theta * Math.PI / 180);
    double cn = Math.Cos(theta * Math.PI / 180);
    pt.X = radius * cn;
    pt.Y = y;
    pt.Z = -radius * sn;
    return pt;
}

private void CreateCone(Point3D center, double rtop, double rbottom,
    double height, int n, Color color, bool isWireframe)
{
    if (n < 2)
        return;

    double h = height / 2;
    Model3DGroup cone = new Model3DGroup();
    Point3D[,] pts = new Point3D[n + 1, 4];


    for (int i = 0; i < n + 1; i++)
    {
        pts[i, 0] = GetPosition(rtop, i * 360 / (n - 1), h);
        pts[i, 1] = GetPosition(rbottom, i * 360 / (n - 1), -h);
        pts[i, 2] = GetPosition(0, i * 360 / (n - 1), -h);
        pts[i, 3] = GetPosition(0, i * 360 / (n - 1), h);
    }
    for (int i = 0; i < n + 1; i++)
    {
        for (int j = 0; j < 4; j++)
            pts[i, j] += (Vector3D)center;
    }
```

```
Point3D[] p = new Point3D[6];
for (int i = 0; i < n; i++)
{
    p[0] = pts[i, 0];
    p[1] = pts[i, 1];
    p[2] = pts[i, 2];
    p[3] = pts[i, 3];
    p[4] = pts[i + 1, 0];
    p[5] = pts[i + 1, 1];

    // Top surface:
    Utility.CreateTriangleFace(p[0], p[4], p[3], color,
                               isWireframe, myViewport);

    // Bottom surface:
    Utility.CreateTriangleFace(p[1], p[5], p[2], color,
                               isWireframe, myViewport);

    // Side surface:
    Utility.CreateTriangleFace(p[0], p[1], p[5], color,
                               isWireframe, myViewport);
    Utility.CreateTriangleFace(p[0], p[5], p[4], color,
                               isWireframe, myViewport);
    }
  }
 }
}
```

Note that the *CreateCone* method, like the *CreateCylinder* method in the previous example, still uses the *GetPosition* method, which returns a point represented in the cylindrical coordinate system, to specify the positions of the vertices of the unit cell. Within a for-loop, the corresponding triangles for each of the three surfaces are constructed from these vertices by calling the *CreateTriangleFace* method in the *Utility* class. Finally, we create several different cone objects using the *CreateCone* method by specifying the top and bottom radii, the height, and the number of slices.

Figure 13-12 shows the results of running this example. You can see that this application can create various cone shapes, including a cylinder (by setting the top and bottom radii to be equal), a cone (by setting one of the radii to zero), a truncated cone (by setting both radii to be finite), and even a pyramid (by setting the number of slices to a small integer).

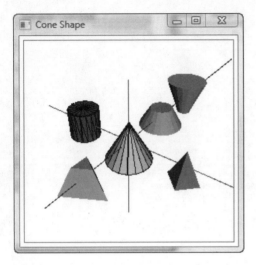

Figure 13-12. *Various cone shapes in WPF*

Creating a Torus

Another popular 3D shape is the torus. A *torus* is a surface of revolution generated by revolving a circle in 3D space about an axis. It can be defined using the following parameterized equations:

$$x = (R + r \cos v) \cos u$$

$$y = r \sin v$$

$$z = -(R + r \cos v) \sin u$$

where u and v are angles defined in the range of [0, 2], R is the distance from the center of the tube to the center of the torus, and r is the radius of the torus.

In order to triangulate a torus, you will need to divide its surface using tube rings and torus rings, as shown in Figure 13-13, which will form grids similar to those used to create a sphere shape (see Figure 13-6). You can use a unit cell (or unit grid) containing four vertices, like the one shown to the right of the figure. This unit cell can be represented with two triangles. When you run over all of the grids using two for-loops, you'll be able to triangulate the entire surface of the torus.

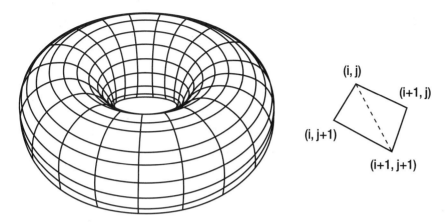

Figure 13-13. A torus and a unit cell

Let's create the torus shape in WPF using an example. Add a new WPF Window to the project *GraphicsBasics3D* and name it *Torus*. Again, you can use the same XAML code as in the previous examples. The following is the corresponding code-behind file:

```
using System;
using System.Windows;
using System.Windows.Media;
using System.Windows.Media.Media3D;

namespace GraphicsBasics3D
{
    public partial class Torus : Window
    {
        public Torus()
        {
            InitializeComponent();

            // Create a torus:
            CreateTorus(new Point3D(0, 0, 0), 1, 0.3, 20, 15,
                    Colors.LightBlue, true);

            // Create another torus:
            CreateTorus(new Point3D(0, 0, -3), 0.5, 0.5, 20, 15,
                    Colors.LightCoral, false);

            // Create another torus:
            CreateTorus(new Point3D(0, 0, -6), 0.3, 0.5, 20, 15,
                    Colors.LightGreen, true);

            // Create another torus:
            CreateTorus(new Point3D(-3, 0, 0), 0.0, 0.8, 20, 25,
                    Colors.SteelBlue, false);

            // Create another torus:
            CreateTorus(new Point3D(3, 0, 0), 0.0, 0.8, 20, 25,
```

```
                    Colors.Goldenrod, false);
        }

        private Point3D GetPosition(double R, double r, double u, double v)
        {
            Point3D pt = new Point3D();
            double snu = Math.Sin(u * Math.PI / 180);
            double cnu = Math.Cos(u * Math.PI / 180);
            double snv = Math.Sin(v * Math.PI / 180);
            double cnv = Math.Cos(v * Math.PI / 180);
            pt.X = (R + r * cnv) * cnu;
            pt.Y = r * snv;
            pt.Z = -(R + r * cnv) * snu;
            return pt;
        }

        private void CreateTorus(Point3D center, double R, double r, int N,
                              int n, Color color, bool isWireframe)
        {
            if (n < 2 || N < 2)
                return;
            Model3DGroup torus = new Model3DGroup();
            Point3D[,] pts = new Point3D[N, n];

            for (int i = 0; i < N; i++)
            {
                for (int j = 0; j < n; j++)
                {
                    pts[i, j] =
                        GetPosition(R, r, i * 360 / (N - 1), j * 360 / (n - 1));
                    pts[i, j] += (Vector3D)center;
                }
            }

            Point3D[] p = new Point3D[4];
            for (int i = 0; i < N - 1; i++)
            {
                for (int j = 0; j < n - 1; j++)
                {
                    p[0] = pts[i, j];
                    p[1] = pts[i + 1, j];
                    p[2] = pts[i + 1, j + 1];
                    p[3] = pts[i, j + 1];
                    Utility.CreateTriangleFace(p[0], p[1], p[2], color,
                                            isWireframe, myViewport);
                    Utility.CreateTriangleFace(p[2], p[3], p[0], color,
                                            isWireframe, myViewport);
                }
            }
        }
    }
}
```

The *GetPosition* method in the foregoing code returns a point on the torus surface. The *CreateTorus* method uses the *GetPosition* method to define the four vertices of the unit cell. The two triangles are constructed from these four vertices within two for-loops by calling the static *CreateTriangleFace* method in the *Utility* class. Finally, we use the *CreateTorus* method to create several different torus shapes with different sets of parameters at different locations.

Figure 13-14 shows the results of running this application. You can see that as the distance to the axis of revolution decreases, the ring torus becomes a spindle torus and finally degenerates into a sphere when the distance goes to zero.

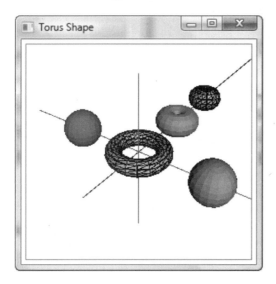

Figure 13-14. *Torus shapes in WPF*

In this chapter, you learned how to create various 3D shapes directly in WPF. This approach is easy to follow and gives you the flexibility to specify a different material for each individual triangle.

CHAPTER 14

3D Charts with the WPF 3D Engine

In the previous two chapters, we discussed 3D transformations and 3D graphics basics in WPF. In this chapter, I'll show you how to create various surface charts in 3D space. Surfaces play an important role in various applications, including computer graphics, virtual reality, computer games, and 3D data visualizations. This chapter begins by describing data structures and the algorithm you use to manipulate and display simple surfaces. With this technique, you can create a variety of simple surfaces, including surfaces containing random data.

The chapter then covers several specialized techniques by which you can create all sorts of complex surface charts, including parametric, extruded, and rotated surfaces.

Simple Surfaces

Mathematically, a surface draws a Z function on a surface for each X and Y coordinate in a region of interest. For each X and Y value, a simple surface can have at most one Z value. Complex surfaces can have multiple Z values for each pair of X and Y values; these will be discussed later in this chapter.

The coordinate system in WPF is oriented so that the Y axis is the "up" direction. To be consistent with WPF notation, we'll consider surfaces defined by functions that return a Y value (instead of a Z value) for each X and Z coordinate in a region of interest. In order to translate a function from a system that gives Z as a function of X and Y, you simply reverse the roles of the Y and Z axes.

You can define a simple surface by the Y coordinates of points above a rectangular grid in the X-Z plane. The surface is formed by joining adjacent points using straight lines. Simple surfaces are useful for visualizing 2D data arrays (matrices) that are too large to display in numerical form and for graphing functions of two variables.

Typically, a surface is formed using rectangular meshes. However, WPF only provides triangles as a basic unit to represent any surface in 3D. In order to represent a surface using the traditional rectangles, you need to write your own class and methods.

Rectangular Meshes

In this section, you'll learn how to write your own class and methods, which will allow you to create rectangular meshes. Since this class provides a technique for generating rectangular meshes that can be used not only in simple surfaces but in complex surfaces as well, you'll implement it in a general *Utility* class.

Start with a new WPF project and name it *Chart3DWithWPFEngine*. Add a new class to this project and call it *Utility*. You'll also need to add Microsoft's *3DTools* to the References. Here is the code listing for this class:

```csharp
using System;
using System.Collections.Generic;
using System.Windows;
using System.Windows.Media;
using System.Windows.Media.Media3D;
using System.Windows.Controls;
using _3DTools;

namespace Chart3DWithWPFEngine
{
    public class Utility
    {
        public static void CreateRectangleFace(Point3D p0, Point3D p1, Point3D p2,
            Point3D p3, Color surfaceColor, Viewport3D viewport)
        {
            MeshGeometry3D mesh = new MeshGeometry3D();
            mesh.Positions.Add(p0);
            mesh.Positions.Add(p1);
            mesh.Positions.Add(p2);
            mesh.Positions.Add(p3);
            mesh.TriangleIndices.Add(0);
            mesh.TriangleIndices.Add(1);
            mesh.TriangleIndices.Add(2);
            mesh.TriangleIndices.Add(2);
            mesh.TriangleIndices.Add(3);
            mesh.TriangleIndices.Add(0);
            SolidColorBrush brush = new SolidColorBrush();
            brush.Color = surfaceColor;
            Material material = new DiffuseMaterial(brush);
            GeometryModel3D geometry = new GeometryModel3D(mesh, material);
            ModelVisual3D model = new ModelVisual3D();
            model.Content = geometry;
            viewport.Children.Add(model);
        }

        public static void CreateWireframe(Point3D p0, Point3D p1, Point3D p2,
            Point3D p3, Color lineColor, Viewport3D viewport)
        {
            ScreenSpaceLines3D ssl = new ScreenSpaceLines3D();
            ssl.Points.Add(p0);
            ssl.Points.Add(p1);
            ssl.Points.Add(p1);
            ssl.Points.Add(p2);
            ssl.Points.Add(p2);
            ssl.Points.Add(p3);
            ssl.Points.Add(p3);
            ssl.Points.Add(p0);
            ssl.Color = lineColor;
            ssl.Thickness = 2;
            viewport.Children.Add(ssl);
        }

        public static Point3D GetNormalize(Point3D pt, double xmin, double xmax,
```

```
        double ymin, double ymax, double zmin, double zmax)
    {
        pt.X = -1 + 2 * (pt.X - xmin) / (xmax - xmin);
        pt.Y = -1 + 2 * (pt.Y - ymin) / (ymax - ymin);
        pt.Z = -1 + 2 * (pt.Z - zmin) / (zmax - zmin);
        return pt;
    }
}
}
```

This class includes three static public methods. The *CreateRectangleFace* method takes four vertex points as its inputs. Inside this method, the rectangular face is constructed using two triangles. You can specify the color of the rectangular face and the *Viewport3D* in which it resides.

The *CreateWireframe* method also takes four vertices as its inputs. Here, you draw a rectangular mesh directly instead of a triangular one. When this method is called, it will create a rectangular wireframe for your surfaces.

The *GetNormalize* method maps the region of your surface into a region of [–1, 1], which gives you a better view on your screen.

SimpleSurface Class

The simplest way to store surface data is to use a 2D array. For each point (*X, Z*) in the region defined for the surface, the (*X, Z*) entry in the array gives the *Y* coordinate of the corresponding point on the surface.

Creating simple surfaces is easy. Add a new class called *SimpleSurface* to the project *Chart3DWithWPFEngine*. Here is the code listing for this class:

```
using System;
using System.Collections.Generic;
using System.Windows;
using System.Windows.Media;
using System.Windows.Media.Media3D;
using System.Windows.Controls;

namespace Chapter13
{
    public class SimpleSurface
    {
        public delegate Point3D Function(double x, double z);
        private double xmin = -3;
        private double xmax = 3;
        private double ymin = -8;
        private double ymax = 8;
        private double zmin = -3;
        private double zmax = 3;
        private int nx = 30;
        private int nz = 30;
        private Color lineColor = Colors.Black;
        private Color surfaceColor = Colors.White;
        private Point3D center = new Point3D();
        private bool isHiddenLine = false;
        private bool isWireframe = true;
        private Viewport3D viewport3d = new Viewport3D();
```

```csharp
public bool IsWireframe
{
    get { return isWireframe; }
    set { isWireframe = value; }
}

public bool IsHiddenLine
{
    get { return isHiddenLine; }
    set { isHiddenLine = value; }
}

public Color LineColor
{
    get { return lineColor; }
    set { lineColor = value; }
}

public Color SurfaceColor
{
    get { return surfaceColor; }
    set { surfaceColor = value; }
}

public double Xmin
{
    get { return xmin; }
    set { xmin = value; }
}

public double Xmax
{
    get { return xmax; }
    set { xmax = value; }
}

public double Ymin
{
    get { return ymin; }
    set { ymin = value; }
}

public double Ymax
{
    get { return ymax; }
    set { ymax = value; }
}

public double Zmin
{
    get { return zmin; }
    set { zmin = value; }
}
```

```csharp
public double Zmax
{
    get { return zmax; }
    set { zmax = value; }
}

public int Nx
{
    get { return nx; }
    set { nx = value; }
}

public int Nz
{
    get { return nz; }
    set { nz = value; }
}

public Point3D Center
{
    get { return center; }
    set { center = value; }
}

public Viewport3D Viewport3d
{
    get { return viewport3d; }
    set { viewport3d = value; }
}

public void CreateSurface(Function f)
{
    double dx = (Xmax - Xmin) / Nx;
    double dz = (Zmax - Zmin) / Nz;
    if (Nx < 2 || Nz < 2)
        return;

    Point3D[,] pts = new Point3D[Nx, Nz];
    for (int i = 0; i < Nx; i++)
    {
        double x = Xmin + i * dx;
        for (int j = 0; j < Nz; j++)
        {
            double z = Zmin + j * dz;
            pts[i, j] = f(x, z);
            pts[i, j] += (Vector3D)Center;
            pts[i, j] = Utility.GetNormalize(pts[i, j], Xmin, Xmax,
                                             Ymin, Ymax, Zmin, Zmax);
        }
    }

    Point3D[] p = new Point3D[4];
```

```
for (int i = 0; i < Nx - 1; i++)
{
    for (int j = 0; j < Nz - 1; j++)
    {
        p[0] = pts[i, j];
        p[1] = pts[i, j + 1];
        p[2] = pts[i + 1, j + 1];
        p[3] = pts[i + 1, j];

        //Create rectangular face:
        if (IsHiddenLine == false)
            Utility.CreateRectangleFace(p[0], p[1], p[2], p[3],
                                        SurfaceColor, Viewport3d);

        // Create wireframe:
        if (IsWireframe == true)
            Utility.CreateWireframe(p[0], p[1], p[2], p[3],
                                    LineColor, Viewport3d);
    }
}
}
}
}
```

First, you define a public delegate function that allows users to import their own functions or data, which will be used to draw the surface. Then you define several fields and their corresponding public properties. The *Nx* and *Nz* properties define the 2D data grid in the *X-Z* plane. Two bool properties, *IsHiddenLine* and *IsWireframe*, control whether or not the hidden lines and wireframes appear on your surface. The default value is false for *IsHiddenLine* (without hidden lines) and true for *IsWireframe* (with wireframes).

Inside the *CreateSurface* method, you first populate a 2D point array with the delegate function $f(x, z)$ on the 2D data grid and then normalize the data of this array into the region [–1, 1] by calling the *GetNormalize* method from the *Utility* class. Next, you define a rectangular mesh using four adjacent vertex points and then call the *CreateRectangleFace* and *CreateWireframe* methods from the *Utility* class to create the rectangular mesh. The entire surface is then created when you run over all the grid points.

Creating Simple Surfaces

Here, you'll create some simple surfaces using the *SimpleSurface* class presented in the previous section. Add a new WPF Windows application to the project *Chart3DWithWPFEngine* and name it *SimpleSurfaceTest*. Here is the XAML file for this example:

```
<Window x:Class="Chart3DWithWPFEngine.SimpleSurfaceTest"
    xmlns="http://schemas.microsoft.com/winfx/2006/xaml/presentation"
    xmlns:x="http://schemas.microsoft.com/winfx/2006/xaml"
    Title="Simple Surface Test" Height="300" Width="600">
    <Grid>
        <Grid.ColumnDefinitions>
            <ColumnDefinition/>
            <ColumnDefinition/>
        </Grid.ColumnDefinitions>
        <Viewport3D Name="viewport1" Grid.Column="0">
            <Viewport3D.Camera>
```

```
                <PerspectiveCamera Position="3,3,2" LookDirection="-3,-3,-2"
                                   UpDirection="0,1,0"/>
            </Viewport3D.Camera>
            <ModelVisual3D>
                <ModelVisual3D.Content>
                    <Model3DGroup>
                        <AmbientLight Color="White"/>
                    </Model3DGroup>
                </ModelVisual3D.Content>
            </ModelVisual3D>
        </Viewport3D>
        <Viewport3D Name="viewport2" Grid.Column="1">
            <Viewport3D.Camera>
                <PerspectiveCamera Position="3,3,2" LookDirection="-3,-3,-2"
                                   UpDirection="0,1,0"/>
            </Viewport3D.Camera>
            <ModelVisual3D>
                <ModelVisual3D.Content>
                    <Model3DGroup>
                        <AmbientLight Color="White"/>
                    </Model3DGroup>
                </ModelVisual3D.Content>
            </ModelVisual3D>
        </Viewport3D>
    </Grid>
</Window>
```

This file defines the camera and light source inside the *Viewport3D*, named *viewport*1 and *viewport*2. Notice that an *AmbientLight* source, which shows the object's original color, is used here. You can play with different light sources to see how they affect the appearance of your surface.

The simple surfaces are created in the code-behind file:

```
using System;
using System.Windows;
using System.Windows.Input;
using System.Windows.Controls;
using System.Windows.Media;
using System.Windows.Media.Media3D;

namespace Chart3DWithWPFEngine
{
    public partial class SimpleSurfaceTest : Window
    {
        private SimpleSurface ss1 = new SimpleSurface();
        private SimpleSurface ss2 = new SimpleSurface();

        public SimpleSurfaceTest()
        {
            InitializeComponent();
            ss1.IsHiddenLine = true;
            ss1.Viewport3d = viewport1;
            ss2.IsHiddenLine = false;
            ss2.Viewport3d = viewport2;
            AddSinc(ss1);
```

```
            AddSinc(ss2);
        }

        private void AddSinc(SimpleSurface ss)
        {
            ss.Xmin = -8;
            ss.Xmax = 8;
            ss.Zmin = -8;
            ss.Zmax = 8;
            ss.Ymin = -1;
            ss.Ymax = 1;
            ss.CreateSurface(Sinc);
        }

        private Point3D Sinc(double x, double z)
        {
            double r = Math.Sqrt(x * x + z * z) + 0.00001;
            double y = Math.Sin(r) / r;
            return new Point3D(x, y, z);
        }
    }
}
```

Here, you first create two *SimpleSurface* instances, *ss*1 and *ss*2 and then specify the *Viewport3D* property of these instances as the *viewport1* and *viewport2* defined in the XAML file. Next, you define a *Sinc* function, which is called directly by the *CreateSurface* method. Inside the *AddSinc* method, you also specify the data range of interest.

Figure 14-1 shows the results of running this application.

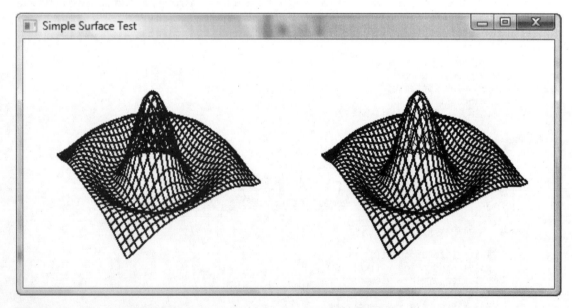

Figure 14-1. *Simple surfaces with (left) and without (right) hidden lines*

You can easily create simple surfaces using other functions. For example, you can create a peak surface using a peak function:

```
private void AddPeaks(SimpleSurface ss)
{
    ss.Xmin = -3;
    ss.Xmax = 3;
    ss.Zmin = -3;
    ss.Zmax = 3;
    ss.Ymin = -8;
    ss.Ymax = 8;
    ss.CreateSurface(Peaks);
}

private Point3D Peaks(double x, double z)
{
    double y = 3 * Math.Pow((1 - x), 2) * Math.Exp(-x * x - (z + 1) * (z + 1)) -
        10 * (0.2 * x - Math.Pow(x, 3) - Math.Pow(z, 5)) * Math.Exp(-x * x - z * z)
        - 1 / 3 * Math.Exp(-(x + 1) * (x + 1) - z * z);
    return new Point3D(x, y, z);
}
```

This function generates the surfaces shown in Figure 14-2.

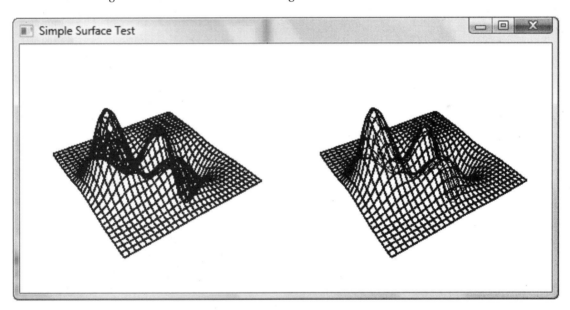

Figure 14-2. Peak surfaces with (left) and without (right) hidden lines

You can even create a surface using a *Random* function:

```
private void AddRandomSurface(SimpleSurface ss)
{
    ss.Xmin = -8;
    ss.Xmax = 8;
    ss.Zmin = -8;
    ss.Zmax = 8;
    ss.Ymin = -1;
    ss.Ymax = 1;
    ss.CreateSurface(RandomSurface);
}

private Random rand = new Random();
private Point3D RandomSurface(double x, double z)
{
    double r = Math.Sqrt(x * x + z * z) + 0.00001;
    double y = Math.Sin(r) / r  + 0.2 * rand.NextDouble();
    return new Point3D(x, y, z);
}
```

This function produces the surfaces shown in Figure 14-3.

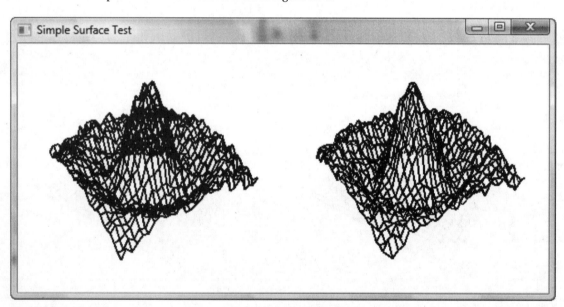

Figure 14-3. *Random surfaces with (left) and without (right) hidden lines*

Parametric Surfaces

In the previous section, you learned how to create simple surfaces. A key feature of this type of surface is that there is at most one *Y* value for each pair of *X* and *Z* values. However, sometimes you may want to create a complex surface of a certain shape. This kind of complex surface can't be represented by a simple function. For certain values of *X* and *Z*, this type of surface has more than one *Y* value. This means that you can't use the approach discussed in the previous sections to store and display the data.

One way to represent such a surface is to use a set of parametric equations. These equations define the *X*, *Y*, and *Z* coordinates of points on the surface in terms of the parametric variables *u* and *v*. Many complex surfaces can be represented using parametric equations. For example, the sphere, the torus, and quadric surfaces are all parametric surfaces.

ParametricSurface Class

In this section, you'll write a *ParametricSurface* class that can create parametric surfaces. Add a new class called *ParametricSurface* to the project *Chart3DWithWPFEngine*. Here is the code listing for this class:

```
using System;
using System.Collections.Generic;
using System.Windows;
using System.Windows.Media;
using System.Windows.Media.Media3D;
using System.Windows.Controls;

namespace Chart3DWithWPFEngine
{
    public class ParametricSurface
    {
        public delegate Point3D Function(double u, double v);

        private int nu = 30;
        private int nv = 30;
        private double umin = -3;
        private double umax = 3;
        private double vmin = -8;
        private double vmax = 8;
        private double xmin = -1;
        private double xmax = 1;
        private double ymin = -1;
        private double ymax = 1;
        private double zmin = -1;
        private double zmax = 1;
        private Color lineColor = Colors.Black;
        private Color surfaceColor = Colors.White;
        private Point3D center = new Point3D();
        private bool isHiddenLine = false;
        private bool isWireframe = true;
        private Viewport3D viewport3d = new Viewport3D();

        public bool IsWireframe
```

```
{
    get { return isWireframe; }
    set { isWireframe = value; }
}

public bool IsHiddenLine
{
    get { return isHiddenLine; }
    set { isHiddenLine = value; }
}

public Color LineColor
{
    get { return lineColor; }
    set { lineColor = value; }
}

public Color SurfaceColor
{
    get { return surfaceColor; }
    set { surfaceColor = value; }
}

public double Umin
{
    get { return umin; }
    set { umin = value; }
}

public double Umax
{
    get { return umax; }
    set { umax = value; }
}

public double Vmin
{
    get { return vmin; }
    set { vmin = value; }
}

public double Vmax
{
    get { return vmax; }
    set { vmax = value; }
}

public int Nu
{
    get { return nu; }
    set { nu = value; }
}
```

```csharp
public int Nv
{
    get { return nv; }
    set { nv = value; }
}

public double Xmin
{
    get { return xmin; }
    set { xmin = value; }
}

public double Xmax
{
    get { return xmax; }
    set { xmax = value; }
}

public double Ymin
{
    get { return ymin; }
    set { ymin = value; }
}

public double Ymax
{
    get { return ymax; }
    set { ymax = value; }
}

public double Zmin
{
    get { return zmin; }
    set { zmin = value; }
}

public double Zmax
{
    get { return zmax; }
    set { zmax = value; }
}

public Point3D Center
{
    get { return center; }
    set { center = value; }
}

public Viewport3D Viewport3d
{
    get { return viewport3d; }
    set { viewport3d = value; }
}
```

```
public void CreateSurface(Function f)
{
    double du = (Umax - Umin) / (Nu - 1);
    double dv = (Vmax - Vmin) / (Nv - 1);
    if (Nu < 2 || Nv < 2)
        return;

    Point3D[,] pts = new Point3D[Nu, Nv];
    for (int i = 0; i < Nu; i++)
    {
        double u = Umin + i * du;
        for (int j = 0; j < Nv; j++)
        {
            double v = Vmin + j * dv;
            pts[i, j] = f(u, v);
            pts[i, j] += (Vector3D)Center;
            pts[i, j] = Utility.GetNormalize(pts[i, j], Xmin, Xmax,
                Ymin, Ymax, Zmin, Zmax);
        }
    }

    Point3D[] p = new Point3D[4];
    for (int i = 0; i < Nu - 1; i++)
    {
        for (int j = 0; j < Nv - 1; j++)
        {
            p[0] = pts[i, j];
            p[1] = pts[i, j + 1];
            p[2] = pts[i + 1, j + 1];
            p[3] = pts[i + 1, j];

            //Create rectangular face:
            if (IsHiddenLine == false)
                Utility.CreateRectangleFace(p[0], p[1], p[2], p[3],
                    SurfaceColor, Viewport3d);

            // Create wireframe:
            if (IsWireframe == true)
                Utility.CreateWireframe(p[0], p[1], p[2], p[3],
                    LineColor, Viewport3d);
        }
    }
}
```

The structure of this class is basically similar to that of the *SimpleSurface* class, except you define the delegate function using the parametric variables u and v instead of x and z. You also define the *umin*, *umax*, *vmin*, and *vmax* fields and their corresponding properties to specify the parametric region of interest. This means that in the parametric u-v space, you create a constant u-v grid (with equal spacing in the u and v directions). The delegate function $f(u, v)$ in this space has at most one value for each pair of u and v values. Thus, you actually create a simple surface in the u-v space using an approach similar to the one for creating simple surfaces. The trick to creating a parametric surface is to map the simple surface in the *u-v* space back to the *X-Y-Z* coordinate system. This mapping is governed by the parametric equations. The resulting surface in the real-world space can be very different than the surface in the parametric space.

Creating Parametric Surfaces

Here, I'll demonstrate how to create common parametric surfaces using the *ParametricSurface* class implemented in the previous section. Add a new WPF Window to the project *Chart3DWithWPFEngine* and name it *ParametricSurfaceTest*. The XAML file for this example is very simple:

```
<Window x:Class="Chart3DWithWPFEngine.ParametricSurfaceTest"
    xmlns="http://schemas.microsoft.com/winfx/2006/xaml/presentation"
    xmlns:x="http://schemas.microsoft.com/winfx/2006/xaml"
    Title="Parametric Surface Test" Height="300" Width="300">
    <Grid>
        <Viewport3D Name="viewport">
            <Viewport3D.Camera>
                <PerspectiveCamera Position="3,2,2" LookDirection="-3,-2,-2"
                                   UpDirection="0,1,0"/>
            </Viewport3D.Camera>
            <ModelVisual3D>
                <ModelVisual3D.Content>
                    <Model3DGroup>
                        <AmbientLight Color="White"/>
                    </Model3DGroup>
                </ModelVisual3D.Content>
            </ModelVisual3D>
        </Viewport3D>
    </Grid>
</Window>
```

This XAML file defines the camera and light source inside the *Viewport3D*, named *viewport*. Notice that we use here an *AmbientLight* source, which shows the object's original color. You can play with different light sources to see how they affect the appearance of your surface. In the following sections, we'll create several parametric surfaces in code.

Helicoid Surface

A helicoid is a trace of a line. For any point on the surface, there is a line on the surface passing through it. Helicoids are shaped like screws and can be described in the Cartesian coordinate system by the following parametric equations:

$$x = u \cos v$$

$$y = v$$

$$z = u \sin v$$

You can easily create a helicoid surface in code using the *ParametricSurface* class:

```
using System;
using System.Windows;
using System.Windows.Input;
```

545

```
using System.Windows.Controls;
using System.Windows.Media;
using System.Windows.Media.Media3D;

namespace Chart3DWithWPFEngine
{
    public partial class ParametricSurfaceTest : Window
    {
        private ParametricSurface ps = new ParametricSurface();

        public ParametricSurfaceTest()
        {
            InitializeComponent();
            ps.IsHiddenLine = false;
            ps.Viewport3d = viewport;
            AddHelicoid();
        }

        private void AddHelicoid()
        {
            ps.Umin = 0;
            ps.Umax = 1;
            ps.Vmin = -3 * Math.PI;
            ps.Vmax = 3 * Math.PI;
            ps.Nv = 100;
            ps.Nu = 10;
            ps.Ymin = ps.Vmin;
            ps.Ymax = ps.Vmax;
            ps.CreateSurface(Helicoid);
        }

        private Point3D Helicoid(double u, double v)
        {
            double x = u * Math.Cos(v);
            double z = u * Math.Sin(v);
            double y = v;
            return new Point3D(x, y, z);
        }
    }
}
```

The *Helicoid* method defines a delegate function in terms of the parameters u and v and returns a *Point3D* object in *X-Y-Z* coordinates. Inside the *AddHelicoid* method, you specify the parameter region and call the *CreateSurface* method using the *Helicoid* function to create the parametric surface.

Figure 14-4 shows the result of running this example.

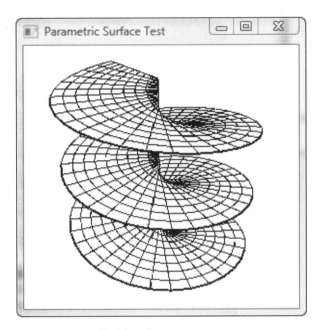

Figure 14-4. Helicoid surface

Sphere Surface

You can also create a sphere surface using the *ParametricSurface* class. This can be done by simply replacing the *Helicoid* and *AddHelicoid* methods in the previous code listing with the following two code snippets:

```
private void AddSphere()
{
    ps.Umin = 0;
    ps.Umax = 2 * Math.PI;
    ps.Vmin = -0.5 * Math.PI;
    ps.Vmax = 0.5 * Math.PI;
    ps.Nu = 20;
    ps.Nv = 20;
    ps.CreateSurface(Sphere);
}

private Point3D Sphere(double u, double v)
{
    double x = Math.Cos(v) * Math.Cos(u);
    double z = Math.Cos(v) * Math.Sin(u);
    double y = Math.Sin(v);
    return new Point3D(x, y, z);
}
```

This generates the results shown in Figure 14-5. You can see that these results provide a better surface appearance than the sphere we created using triangular meshes in the previous chapter.

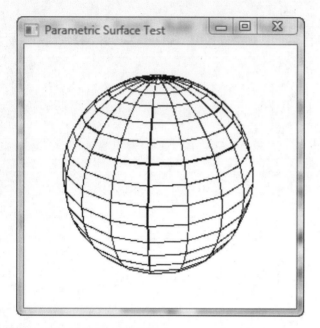

Figure 14-5. *Sphere surface*

Torus Surface

You can also use the *ParametricSurface* class to create a torus surface, using the following methods:

```
private void AddTorus()
{
    ps.Umin = 0;
    ps.Umax = 2 * Math.PI;
    ps.Vmin = 0;
    ps.Vmax = 2 * Math.PI;
    ps.Nu = 50;
    ps.Nv = 20;
    ps.CreateSurface(Torus);
}

private Point3D Torus(double u, double v)
{
    double x = (1 + 0.3 * Math.Cos(v)) * Math.Cos(u);
    double z = (1 + 0.3 * Math.Cos(v)) * Math.Sin(u);
    double y = 0.3 * Math.Sin(v);
    return new Point3D(x, y, z);
}
```

This gives the result shown in Figure 14-6.

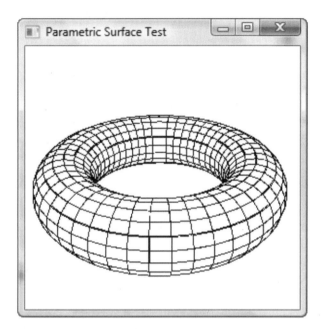

Figure 14-6. *Torus surface*

Quadric Surfaces

You can also easily create various quadric surfaces using the *ParametricSurface* class. For example, consider the following four irreducible quadrics:

- Hyperboloid — described by these parametric equations:

$$x = a \cos u \cosh v$$

- $$y = b \sinh v$$

$$z = c \sin u \cosh v$$

- Paraboloid — described by these parametric equations:

$$x = av \cosh u$$

$$y = v^2$$

$$z = bv \sinh u$$

- Elliptic cone — described by these parametric equations:

$$x = av \cos u$$

$$y = bv$$

$$z = cv \sin u$$

- Elliptic cylinder — described by these parametric equations:

$$x = a \cos u$$

$$y = v$$

$$z = b \sin u$$

Here, a, b, and c are constants. You can easily implement the corresponding methods for each of these quadrics using the preceding parametric equations. You can view the complete source code by opening the file *ParametricSurfaceTest.xaml.cs*.

Figure 14-7 shows the results of creating these quadric surfaces using the *ParametricSurface* class.

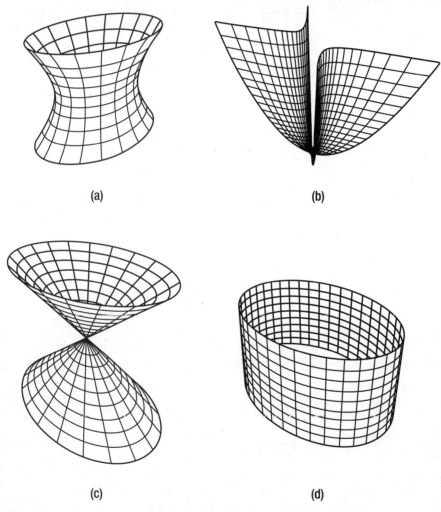

(a)　　　　　　　　　　　　　　(b)

(c)　　　　　　　　　　　　　　(d)

Figure 14-7. Quadric surfaces: (a) hyperboloid, (b) paraboloid, (c) elliptic cone, and (d) elliptic cylinder

Extruded Surfaces

In 3D graphics, you can perform an extrusion by moving a base curve through space along a generating path, sweeping out a 3D surface. This type of surface is called an *extruded surface*. The cross sections of the surface look like the base curve that you are moving. For example, if you move a line segment in the direction perpendicular to it, you'll sweep out a rectangle. In this case, the cross sections of the surface are line segments.

The generating path is not limited to being a straight line. It can also be a longer path or a curved path. The base curve can be any kind of curve. Extruded surfaces have several interesting features. For example, each of the areas that make up the surface is a parallelogram. Each time the base curve is moved along the generating path, the points along the curve are moved a fixed distance and direction determined by the generating path. Since the distance and direction are the same for any two adjacent points along the curve, the line segments connecting the points' new and old positions are parallel. Because these segments are also the same length, connecting any two of these segments results in a parallelogram.

Another interesting feature of extruded surfaces is that you can create the same surface both by moving the base curve along the generating path and by moving the generating path along the base curve. You can create extruded surfaces using either approach.

Like the simple surfaces described earlier in this chapter, you generate extruded surfaces from a set of data points. As you did when you created simple surfaces, you can implement an *ExtrudeSurface* class that stores, manipulates, and displays extruded surfaces.

ExtrudeSurface Class

In order to create the *ExtrudeSurface* class, you need two sets of data points: One set of data points is created along the base curve, and the other is created along the generating path. You can define these two sets of data points using two *List* objects, which allow the user to specify the base curve and the generating path.

Add a new *ExtrudeSurface* class to the project *Chart3DWithWPFEngine*. Here is the code listing for this class:

```
using System;
using System.Collections.Generic;
using System.Windows;
using System.Windows.Media;
using System.Windows.Media.Media3D;
using System.Windows.Controls;
using _3DTools;

namespace Chart3DWithWPFEngine
{
    public class ExtrudeSurface
    {
        private List<Point3D> curvePoints = new List<Point3D>();
        private List<Point3D> pathPoints = new List<Point3D>();
        private double xmin = -1;
        private double xmax = 1;
        private double ymin = -1;
        private double ymax = 1;
        private double zmin = -1;
        private double zmax = 1;
        private Color lineColor = Colors.Black;
```

```csharp
private Color surfaceColor = Colors.White;
private Point3D center = new Point3D();
private bool isHiddenLine = false;
private bool isWireframe = true;
private Viewport3D viewport3d = new Viewport3D();

public bool IsWireframe
{
    get { return isWireframe; }
    set { isWireframe = value; }
}

public bool IsHiddenLine
{
    get { return isHiddenLine; }
    set { isHiddenLine = value; }
}

public Color LineColor
{
    get { return lineColor; }
    set { lineColor = value; }
}

public Color SurfaceColor
{
    get { return surfaceColor; }
    set { surfaceColor = value; }
}

public List<Point3D> CurvePoints
{
    get { return curvePoints; }
    set { curvePoints = value; }
}

public List<Point3D> PathPoints
{
    get { return pathPoints; }
    set { pathPoints = value; }
}

public double Xmin
{
    get { return xmin; }
    set { xmin = value; }
}

public double Xmax
{
    get { return xmax; }
    set { xmax = value; }
}
```

```csharp
public double Ymin
{
    get { return ymin; }
    set { ymin = value; }
}

public double Ymax
{
    get { return ymax; }
    set { ymax = value; }
}

public double Zmin
{
    get { return zmin; }
    set { zmin = value; }
}

public double Zmax
{
    get { return zmax; }
    set { zmax = value; }
}

public Point3D Center
{
    get { return center; }
    set { center = value; }
}

public Viewport3D Viewport3d
{
    get { return viewport3d; }
    set { viewport3d = value; }
}

public void CreateSurface()
{
    double dx, dy, dz;

    // create all points used to create extruded surface:
    Point3D[,] pts = new Point3D[PathPoints.Count, CurvePoints.Count];
    for (int i = 0; i < PathPoints.Count; i++)
    {
        // Calculate offsets for path points:
        dx = PathPoints[i].X - PathPoints[0].X;
        dy = PathPoints[i].Y - PathPoints[0].Y;
        dz = PathPoints[i].Z - PathPoints[0].Z;

        for (int j = 0; j < CurvePoints.Count; j++)
        {
            pts[i, j].X = CurvePoints[j].X + dx;
```

```
                    pts[i, j].Y = CurvePoints[j].Y + dy;
                    pts[i, j].Z = CurvePoints[j].Z + dz;
                    pts[i, j] += (Vector3D)Center;
                    pts[i, j] = Utility.GetNormalize(pts[i, j],
                        Xmin, Xmax, Ymin, Ymax, Zmin, Zmax);
                }
            }

        Point3D[] p = new Point3D[4];
        for (int i = 0; i < PathPoints.Count - 1; i++)
        {
            for (int j = 0; j < CurvePoints.Count - 1; j++)
            {
                p[0] = pts[i, j];
                p[1] = pts[i + 1, j];
                p[2] = pts[i + 1, j + 1];
                p[3] = pts[i, j + 1];

                //Create rectangular face:
                if (IsHiddenLine == false)
                    Utility.CreateRectangleFace(p[0], p[1], p[2], p[3],
                        SurfaceColor, Viewport3d);

                // Create wireframe:
                if (IsWireframe == true)
                    Utility.CreateWireframe(p[0], p[1], p[2], p[3],
                        LineColor, Viewport3d);
            }
        }
    }
}
```

This class begins by defining two *Point3D* lists, *curvePoints* and *pathPoints*, which will be used to define the base curve and the generating path. The other fields and their corresponding properties are similar to those used in creating simple surfaces.

Inside the *CreateSurface* method, you compute the positions of the points on the surface using the *CurvePoints* and *PathPoints* objects. As long as you obtain all of the points on the surface, you can process them the same way you did when you created simple surfaces.

Creating Extruded Surfaces

It is easy to create extruded surfaces using the *ExtrudeSurface* class. Add a new WPF Window application to the project *Chart3DWithWPFEngine* and name it *ExtrudeSurfaceTest*. The XAML file for this example is similar to that used to create simple surfaces, except for the changes in creating the Viewport3D and Camera. The following is the code-behind file for this example:

```
using System;
using System.Windows;
using System.Windows.Input;
using System.Windows.Controls;
using System.Windows.Media;
using System.Windows.Media.Media3D;
```

```
namespace Chart3DWithWPFEngine
{
    public partial class ExtrudeSurfaceTest : Window
    {
        private ExtrudeSurface es = new ExtrudeSurface();

        public ExtrudeSurfaceTest()
        {
            InitializeComponent();

            es.Viewport3d = viewport;
            es.IsHiddenLine = false;
            AddExtrudeSurface1();
            //AddExtrudeSurface2();
        }

        // Extruded surface:
        private void AddExtrudeSurface1()
        {
            for (int i = 0; i < 17; i++)
            {
                double angle = i * Math.PI / 16 + 3 * Math.PI / 2;
                es.CurvePoints.Add(new Point3D(Math.Cos(angle),
                    0, Math.Sin(angle)));
            }

            for (int i = 0; i < 33; i++)
            {
                es.PathPoints.Add(new Point3D(Math.Cos(i * Math.PI / 12),
                    i * Math.PI / 12, 0));
            }
            es.Xmin = -3;
            es.Xmax = 3;
            es.Ymin = 5;
            es.Ymax = 20;
            es.Zmin = -3;
            es.Zmax = 5;
            es.CreateSurface();
        }

        // Another Extruded surface:
        private void AddExtrudeSurface2()
        {
            for (int i = 0; i < 17; i++)
            {
                double angle = i * Math.PI / 8;
                es.CurvePoints.Add(new Point3D(1 + 0.3 * Math.Cos(angle), 0,
                    0.3 * Math.Sin(angle)));
            }

            for (int i = 0; i < 45; i++)
            {
```

```
        double angle = i * Math.PI / 16;
        es.PathPoints.Add(new Point3D(1.3*Math.Cos(angle), angle,
            1.3*Math.Sin(angle)));
    }
    es.Xmin = -3;
    es.Xmax = 3;
    es.Ymin = 5;
    es.Ymax = 30;
    es.Zmin = -3;
    es.Zmax = 3;
    es.CreateSurface();
        }
    }
}
```

Here, you create two extruded surfaces. The first surface is generated by moving a semicircle (the base curve) along a cosine path (the generating path). The other surface is created by moving a circle (the base curve) along a helix path (the generating path).

Figure 14-8 shows the results of running this example.

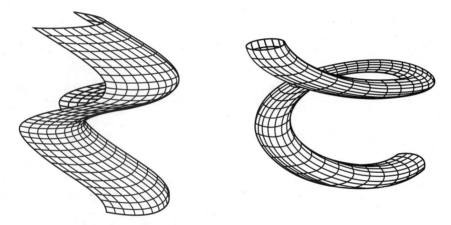

Figure 14-8. *Extruded surfaces in WPF*

Surfaces of Revolution

When you create an extruded surface, you move a base curve along a generating path. To create a surface of revolution, on the other hand, you rotate a base curve around an axis of rotation. Figure 14-9 shows a surface of revolution, with the base curve drawn in heavy lines. To create this surface, you rotate the base curve around the Y axis.

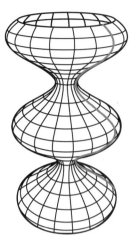

Figure 14-9. *A surface of revolution created by rotating a base curve (heavy lines) around the Y axis*

Creating a surface of revolution is similar to creating an extruded surface. In both cases, you take a base curve and repeatedly transform it. You can produce a surface of revolution by rotating the base curve around any axis in 3D space.

In practice, however, it is much easier to rotate the base curve around the coordinate axes. If you want to rotate a curve around some other axis, you first apply translations and rotations until the axis you specify coincides with a coordinate axis. After you perform the rotation of the base curve around the coordinate axis, you then simply translate and rotate the axis back to its original position. These transform operations are described in detail in Chapter 12.

RotateSurface Class

In this section, you'll implement a *RotateSurface* class, which you can use to create surfaces of revolution. Add a new class called *RotateSurface* to the project *Chart3DWithWPFEngine*. Here is the code listing for this class:

```
using System;
using System.Collections.Generic;
using System.Windows;
using System.Windows.Media;
using System.Windows.Media.Media3D;
using System.Windows.Controls;
using _3DTools;

namespace Chart3DWithWPFEngine
{
    public class RorateSurface
    {
        private List<Point3D> curvePoints = new List<Point3D>();
        private int thetaDiv = 20;
        private double xmin = -1;
        private double xmax = 1;
        private double ymin = -1;
```

```csharp
        private double ymax = 1;
        private double zmin = -1;
        private double zmax = 1;
        private Color lineColor = Colors.Black;
        private Color surfaceColor = Colors.White;
        private Point3D center = new Point3D();
        private bool isHiddenLine = false;
        private bool isWireframe = true;
        private Viewport3D viewport3d = new Viewport3D();

        public bool IsWireframe
        {
            get { return isWireframe; }
            set { isWireframe = value; }
        }

        public int ThetaDiv
        {
            get { return thetaDiv; }
            set { thetaDiv = value; }
        }

        public bool IsHiddenLine
        {
            get { return isHiddenLine; }
            set { isHiddenLine = value; }
        }

        public Color LineColor
        {
            get { return lineColor; }
            set { lineColor = value; }
        }

        public Color SurfaceColor
        {
            get { return surfaceColor; }
            set { surfaceColor = value; }
        }

        public List<Point3D> CurvePoints
        {
            get { return curvePoints; }
            set { curvePoints = value; }
        }

        public double Xmin
        {
            get { return xmin; }
            set { xmin = value; }
        }

        public double Xmax
```

```
{
    get { return xmax; }
    set { xmax = value; }
}

public double Ymin
{
    get { return ymin; }
    set { ymin = value; }
}

public double Ymax
{
    get { return ymax; }
    set { ymax = value; }
}

public double Zmin
{
    get { return zmin; }
    set { zmin = value; }
}

public double Zmax
{
    get { return zmax; }
    set { zmax = value; }
}

public Point3D Center
{
    get { return center; }
    set { center = value; }
}

public Viewport3D Viewport3d
{
    get { return viewport3d; }
    set { viewport3d = value; }
}

private Point3D GetPosition(double r,
    double y, double theta)
{
    double x = r * Math.Cos(theta);
    double z = -r * Math.Sin(theta);
    return new Point3D(x, y, z);
}

public void CreateSurface()
{
    // create all points used to create surfaces of revolution around
    // the Y axis:
```

```
Point3D[,] pts = new Point3D[ThetaDiv, CurvePoints.Count];
for (int i = 0; i < ThetaDiv; i++)
{
    double theta = i * 2 * Math.PI / (ThetaDiv - 1);
    for (int j = 0; j < CurvePoints.Count; j++)
    {
        double x = CurvePoints[j].X;
        double z = CurvePoints[j].Z;
        double r = Math.Sqrt(x * x + z * z);

        pts[i, j] = GetPosition(r, CurvePoints[j].Y, theta);
        pts[i, j] += (Vector3D)Center;
        pts[i, j] = Utility.GetNormalize(pts[i, j],
            Xmin, Xmax, Ymin, Ymax, Zmin, Zmax);
    }
}

Point3D[] p = new Point3D[4];
for (int i = 0; i < ThetaDiv - 1; i++)
{
    for (int j = 0; j < CurvePoints.Count - 1; j++)
    {
        p[0] = pts[i, j];
        p[1] = pts[i + 1, j];
        p[2] = pts[i + 1, j + 1];
        p[3] = pts[i, j + 1];

        //Create rectangular face:
        if (IsHiddenLine == false)
            Utility.CreateRectangleFace(p[0], p[1], p[2], p[3],
                SurfaceColor, Viewport3d);

        // Create wireframe:
        if (IsWireframe == true)
            Utility.CreateWireframe(p[0], p[1], p[2], p[3],
            LineColor, Viewport3d);
    }
}
}
}
```

This class begins by defining a *Point3D* list object called *curvePoints*, which will be used to create the base curve. The other fields and their corresponding properties are similar to those used in creating simple surfaces.

Inside the *CreateSurface* method, you compute the positions of the points on the surface using the *CurvePoints* and *GetPostion* methods. The *GetPosition* method computes the positions of the points on the surface when the base curve is rotated around the *Y* axis. As long as all of the points on the surface are obtained, you can process them the same way you processed simple surfaces.

Creating Surfaces of Revolution

It is easy to create surfaces of revolution using the *RotateSurface* class. Add a new WPF Window to the project *Chart3DWithWPFEngine* and name it *RotateSurfaceTest*. The XAML file for this example is similar to that used to create simple surfaces, except for the changes in defining *Viewport3D* and *Camera*. The following is the code-behind file for this example:

```
using System;
using System.Windows;
using System.Windows.Input;
using System.Windows.Controls;
using System.Windows.Media;
using System.Windows.Media.Media3D;

namespace Chart3DWithWPFEngine
{
    public partial class RotateSurfaceTest : Window
    {
        private RorateSurface rs = new RorateSurface();

        public RotateSurfaceTest()
        {
            InitializeComponent();

            rs.Viewport3d = viewport;
            rs.IsHiddenLine = false;
            AddRotateSurface();
            //AddSphereSurface();
            //AddTorusSurface();
        }

        // Rotated surface:
        private void AddRotateSurface()
        {
            for (int i = 0; i < 33; i++)
            {
                double y = i * Math.PI / 12;
                double siny = Math.Sin(y);
                rs.CurvePoints.Add(new Point3D(0.2 + siny * siny, y, 0));
            }
            rs.Xmin = -3;
            rs.Xmax = 3;
            rs.Ymin = 5;
            rs.Ymax = 15;
            rs.Zmin = -3;
            rs.Zmax = 3;
            rs.CreateSurface();
        }

        // Sphere surface:
        private void AddSphereSurface()
        {
            for (int i = 0; i < 11; i++)
```

```
        {
            double theta = -Math.PI / 2 + i * Math.PI / 10;
            rs.CurvePoints.Add(new Point3D(Math.Cos(theta),
                Math.Sin(theta), 0));
        }
        rs.Xmin = -2;
        rs.Xmax = 2;
        rs.Ymin = 0;
        rs.Ymax = 4;
        rs.Zmin = -2;
        rs.Zmax = 2;
        rs.CreateSurface();
    }

    // Torus surface:
    private void AddTorusSurface()
    {
        for (int i = 0; i < 21; i++)
        {
            double theta = i * Math.PI / 10;
            Point3D pt = new Point3D(0.3 * Math.Cos(theta),
                0.3 * Math.Sin(theta), 0);
            pt += new Vector3D(1, 0, 0);
            rs.CurvePoints.Add(pt);
        }
        rs.Xmin = -2;
        rs.Xmax = 2;
        rs.Ymin = 0;
        rs.Ymax = 4;
        rs.Zmin = -2;
        rs.Zmax = 2;
        rs.CreateSurface();
    }
}
}
```

This code creates three surfaces of revolution. The first surface is created by rotating a sine-squared function around the Y axis, which I already showed in Figure 14-9. The second surface represents a sphere, which you create by rotating a semicircle around the Y axis. The third surface represents a torus, which you produce by rotating a circle around the Y axis.

The sphere and torus surfaces generated by means of this approach are shown in Figure 14-10. As you can see, you can produce sphere and torus surfaces by several different methods, providing flexibility when you need to create these surfaces — you can choose the approach most suitable for your application.

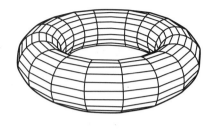

Figure 14-10. Sphere and torus created using the RotateSurface class

Surface Shading

In the previous sections, we created surfaces using rectangular mesh lines. In some applications, however, you may want to paint your surfaces with color and shading effects. In this section, you'll learn how to paint surfaces with different color, shading, and lighting effects. Here, when you are considering surface shading, you won't draw mesh lines on the surfaces.

SurfaceShading Class

In this section, you'll write a *SurfaceShading* class, which can create surfaces with lighting and shading effects. Add a new class called *SurfaceShading* to the project *Chart3DWithWPFEngine*. Here is the code listing for this class:

```
using System;
using System.Collections.Generic;
using System.Windows;
using System.Windows.Media;
using System.Windows.Media.Media3D;
using System.Windows.Controls;

namespace Chart3DWithWPFEngine
{
    public class SurfaceShading
    {
        public delegate Point3D Function(double u, double v);

        private MaterialGroup materialGroup = new MaterialGroup();
        private Material backMaterial = new DiffuseMaterial();
        private int nu = 30;
        private int nv = 30;
        private double umin = -3;
        private double umax = 3;
        private double vmin = -8;
        private double vmax = 8;
        private double xmin = -1;
        private double xmax = 1;
        private double ymin = -1;
```

```csharp
        private double ymax = 1;
        private double zmin = -1;
        private double zmax = 1;
        private Point3D center = new Point3D();
        private Viewport3D viewport3d = new Viewport3D();

        public Material BackMaterial
        {
            get { return backMaterial; }
            set { backMaterial = value; }
        }

        public MaterialGroup MaterialGroup
        {
            get { return materialGroup; }
            set { materialGroup = value; }
        }

        public double Umin
        {
            get { return umin; }
            set { umin = value; }
        }

        public double Umax
        {
            get { return umax; }
            set { umax = value; }
        }

        public double Vmin
        {
            get { return vmin; }
            set { vmin = value; }
        }

        public double Vmax
        {
            get { return vmax; }
            set { vmax = value; }
        }

        public int Nu
        {
            get { return nu; }
            set { nu = value; }
        }

        public int Nv
        {
            get { return nv; }
            set { nv = value; }
        }
```

```
public double Xmin
{
    get { return xmin; }
    set { xmin = value; }
}

public double Xmax
{
    get { return xmax; }
    set { xmax = value; }
}

public double Ymin
{
    get { return ymin; }
    set { ymin = value; }
}

public double Ymax
{
    get { return ymax; }
    set { ymax = value; }
}

public double Zmin
{
    get { return zmin; }
    set { zmin = value; }
}

public double Zmax
{
    get { return zmax; }
    set { zmax = value; }
}

public Point3D Center
{
    get { return center; }
    set { center = value; }
}

public Viewport3D Viewport3d
{
    get { return viewport3d; }
    set { viewport3d = value; }
}

public void CreateSurface(Function f)
{
    double du = (Umax - Umin) / (Nu - 1);
    double dv = (Vmax - Vmin) / (Nv - 1);
```

```
        if (Nu < 2 || Nv < 2)
            return;

        Point3D[,] pts = new Point3D[Nu, Nv];
        for (int i = 0; i < Nu; i++)
        {
            double u = Umin + i * du;
            for (int j = 0; j < Nv; j++)
            {
                double v = Vmin + j * dv;
                pts[i, j] = f(u, v);
                pts[i, j] += (Vector3D)Center;
                pts[i, j] = GetNormalize(pts[i, j]);
            }
        }

        Point3D[] p = new Point3D[4];
        for (int i = 0; i < Nu - 1; i++)
        {
            for (int j = 0; j < Nv - 1; j++)
            {
                p[0] = pts[i, j];
                p[1] = pts[i, j + 1];
                p[2] = pts[i + 1, j + 1];
                p[3] = pts[i + 1, j];

                CreateRectangleFace(p[0], p[1], p[2], p[3]);
            }
        }
    }

    public void CreateRectangleFace(Point3D p0, Point3D p1,
                                    Point3D p2, Point3D p3)
    {
        MeshGeometry3D mesh = new MeshGeometry3D();
        mesh.Positions.Add(p0);
        mesh.Positions.Add(p1);
        mesh.Positions.Add(p2);
        mesh.Positions.Add(p3);
        mesh.TriangleIndices.Add(0);
        mesh.TriangleIndices.Add(1);
        mesh.TriangleIndices.Add(2);
        mesh.TriangleIndices.Add(2);
        mesh.TriangleIndices.Add(3);
        mesh.TriangleIndices.Add(0);

        GeometryModel3D geometry = new GeometryModel3D(mesh, MaterialGroup);
        geometry.BackMaterial = BackMaterial;
        ModelVisual3D model = new ModelVisual3D();
        model.Content = geometry;
        Viewport3d.Children.Add(model);
    }
```

```
        public Point3D GetNormalize(Point3D pt)
        {
            pt.X = -1 + 2 * (pt.X - Xmin) / (Xmax - Xmin);
            pt.Y = -1 + 2 * (pt.Y - Ymin) / (Ymax - Ymin);
            pt.Z = -1 + 2 * (pt.Z - Zmin) / (Zmax - Zmin);
            return pt;
        }
    }
}
```

This class creates surfaces based on the parametric approach discussed earlier. In order to obtain better color and lighting effects, you use a *MaterialGroup* to specify the *Material* property of the surfaces. The *MaterialGroup* can contain multiple materials. You also define a *BackMaterial* property for the surface, because parametric surfaces usually are not closed surfaces. In order to see the back side of your surface, you need to specify the *BackMaterial* property of the surface.

Creating Shaded Surfaces

It is easy to create surfaces with shading effects using the *SurfaceShading* class. Add a new WPF Windows application to the project *Chart3DWithWPFEngine* and name it *SurfaceShadingTest*. Here is the XAML file for this example:

```xml
<Window x:Class=" Chart3DWithWPFEngine.SurfaceShadingTest"
    xmlns="http://schemas.microsoft.com/winfx/2006/xaml/presentation"
    xmlns:x="http://schemas.microsoft.com/winfx/2006/xaml"
    Title="Surface Shading" Height="300" Width="300">

    <Grid>
        <Viewport3D Name="viewport">
            <Viewport3D.Camera>
                <PerspectiveCamera Position="6,4,4" LookDirection="-6,-4,-4"
                                   UpDirection="0,1,0"/>
            </Viewport3D.Camera>
            <ModelUIElement3D>
                <Model3DGroup>
                    <AmbientLight Color="Gray"/>
                    <DirectionalLight Color="Gray" Direction="-1,0,-1"/>
                    <DirectionalLight Color="Gray" Direction="1,-1,-1"/>
                </Model3DGroup>
            </ModelUIElement3D>
        </Viewport3D>
    </Grid>
</Window>
```

This XAML file sets the camera and light sources. Note that three light sources are used to illuminate the surfaces in order to get a better lighting effect. The following is the code-behind file for this example:

```
using System;
using System.Windows;
using System.Windows.Input;
using System.Windows.Controls;
using System.Windows.Media;
using System.Windows.Media.Media3D;
```

```
namespace Chart3DWithWPFEngine
{
    public partial class SurfaceShadingTest : Window
    {
        private SurfaceShading ss;

        public SurfaceShadingTest()
        {
            InitializeComponent();
            AddHyperboloid();
            AddEllipticCone();
            AddEllipticCylinder();
        }

        // Hyperboloid surface:
        private void AddHyperboloid()
        {
            ss = new SurfaceShading();

            Material material = new DiffuseMaterial(Brushes.Red);
            ss.MaterialGroup.Children.Add(material);
            material = new SpecularMaterial(Brushes.Yellow, 60);
            ss.MaterialGroup.Children.Add(material);
            material = new DiffuseMaterial(Brushes.SteelBlue);
            ss.BackMaterial = material;

            ss.Viewport3d = viewport;
            ss.Center = new Point3D(0, 0, 2);
            ss.Umin = 0;
            ss.Umax = 2 * Math.PI;
            ss.Vmin = -1;
            ss.Vmax = 1;
            ss.Nu = 30;
            ss.Nv = 30;
            ss.CreateSurface(Hyperboloid);
        }
        private Point3D Hyperboloid(double u, double v)
        {
            double x = 0.3 * Math.Cos(u) * Math.Cosh(v);
            double z = 0.5 * Math.Sin(u) * Math.Cosh(v);
            double y = Math.Sinh(v);
            return new Point3D(x, y, z);
        }

        //Elliptic cone:
        private void AddEllipticCone()
        {
            ss = new SurfaceShading();

            Material material = new DiffuseMaterial(Brushes.Green);
            ss.MaterialGroup.Children.Add(material);
            material = new SpecularMaterial(Brushes.LightGreen, 60);
            ss.MaterialGroup.Children.Add(material);
```

```
        material = new DiffuseMaterial(Brushes.SteelBlue);
        ss.BackMaterial = material;

        ss.Viewport3d = viewport;
        ss.Center = new Point3D(0, 0, 0);
        ss.Umin = 0;
        ss.Umax = 2 * Math.PI;
        ss.Vmin = -1;
        ss.Vmax = 1;
        ss.Nu = 30;
        ss.Nv = 30;
        ss.CreateSurface(EllipticCone);
    }
    private Point3D EllipticCone(double u, double v)
    {
        double x = 1.2 * v * Math.Cos(u);
        double z = 0.8 * v * Math.Sin(u);
        double y = 0.9 * v;
        return new Point3D(x, y, z);
    }

    //Elliptic cylinder:
    private void AddEllipticCylinder()
    {
        ss = new SurfaceShading();

        Material material = new DiffuseMaterial(Brushes.Goldenrod);
        ss.MaterialGroup.Children.Add(material);
        material = new SpecularMaterial(Brushes.LightGoldenrodYellow, 60);
        ss.MaterialGroup.Children.Add(material);
        material = new DiffuseMaterial(Brushes.SteelBlue);
        ss.BackMaterial = material;

        ss.Viewport3d = viewport;
        ss.Center = new Point3D(0, 1, -2);
        ss.Umin = 0;
        ss.Umax = 2 * Math.PI;
        ss.Vmin = -0.5;
        ss.Vmax = 0.5;
        ss.Nu = 40;
        ss.Nv = 10;
        ss.CreateSurface(EllipticCylinder);
    }

    private Point3D EllipticCylinder(double u, double v)
    {
        ss.Viewport3d = viewport;
        double x = 1.2 * Math.Cos(u);
        double z = 0.8 * Math.Sin(u);
        double y = 2 * v;
        return new Point3D(x, y, z);
    }
  }
}
```

In this class, you create three surfaces using different materials. These three surfaces are a hyperboloid, an elliptic cone, and an elliptic cylinder.

Figure 14-11 shows the results of running this application.

Figure 14-11. Shaded surfaces in WPF

In this chapter, we emphasized the algorithm used to create various surfaces, leaving some important topics untouched. For example, you may want your surfaces to have a colormap scaled with the *Y* values and a colorbar. This will be the topic of the next chapter, where you'll find an in-depth discussion of surface colormaps, colorbars, and various surface charts that don't use the WPF 3D engine.

We did not discuss two kinds of parametric surfaces: Bezier and B-spline surfaces. These surfaces are the 3D counterparts to 2D Bezier curves and B-splines. Following the procedures presented here, you should be able to create these two particular kinds of surfaces without any difficulty.

CHAPTER 15

3D Charts Without the WPF 3D Engine

In the previous chapter, I demonstrated how to create a variety of 3D surface charts using the WPF 3D engine. However, it is difficult to implement professional 3D charts based on the default WPF 3D framework. In this chapter, you'll learn how to use a direct projection approach, without using the WPF 3D engine, to create more sophisticated 3D charts with more features, including colormaps and colorbars. I'll start with a description of the coordinate system used for 3D charts and show you how to create 3D coordinate axes, tick marks, axis labels, and gridlines. The 3D coordinate system used in 3D charts is the most fundamental part of creating 3D chart applications because it involves almost all of the matrix operations and transformations used to create 3D charts.

This chapter will then show you how to create various 3D chart applications, including 3D line charts, 3D meshes, and surface charts. The example programs in this chapter provide basic solutions for 3D chart applications. Based on this example code, with or without modifications, you can easily create your own professional and advanced 3D charts in your WPF applications.

3D Coordinate System

Here, I'll show you how to create a 3D coordinate system using a direct projection method, disregarding the WPF 3D engine. Creating 3D coordinate axes on a 2D screen is more involved than creating 2D coordinates. Here, we'll use the azimuth and elevation view to control the orientation of the 3D charts and graphics objects displayed in the coordinate axes.

Azimuth and Elevation View

Specifying the viewpoint in terms of azimuth and elevation is conceptually simple. The 3D charts that will be represented in the following sections will use this azimuth and elevation view to display various 3D plots on a 2D computer screen. There are some limitations to this view setting, however. Azimuth and elevation view does not allow you to specify the actual position of the viewpoint — just its direction — and the Z axis is always pointing up. In addition, it does not allow you to zoom in and out of the scene or perform arbitrary rotations and translations. Even with these limitations, this view setting is good enough for most 3D chart and graphics applications.

In this view setting, the conventional Cartesian coordinate system is used. The azimuth angle is a polar angle in the X-Y plane, with positive angles indicating a counterclockwise rotation of the viewpoint. Elevation is the angle above (positive angle) or below (negative angle) the X-Y plane, as shown in Figure 15-1.

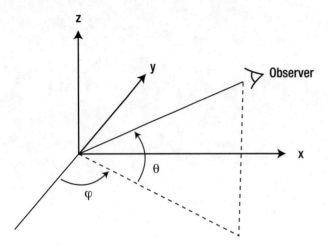

Figure 15-1. *Azimuth and elevation view system*

We can construct the transformation matrix for this view system by considering two successive 2D rotations. First, we rotate the original coordinate system by an angle $-\phi$ about the Z axis; then we rotate the newly generated coordinate system by $\theta - \pi/2$ about the X axis. We can then obtain the combined effect of these two 2D rotations:

$$R_z(-\phi)R_x(\theta - \pi/2) = \begin{pmatrix} \cos\phi & -\sin\phi & 0 & 0 \\ \sin\phi & \cos\phi & 0 & 0 \\ 0 & 0 & 1 & 0 \\ 0 & 0 & 0 & 1 \end{pmatrix} \begin{pmatrix} 1 & 0 & 0 & 0 \\ 0 & \sin\theta & -\cos\theta & 0 \\ 0 & \cos\theta & \sin\theta & 0 \\ 0 & 0 & 0 & 1 \end{pmatrix}$$

$$= \begin{pmatrix} \cos\phi & -\sin\phi\sin\theta & \sin\phi\cos\theta & 0 \\ \sin\phi & \cos\phi\sin\theta & -\cos\phi\cos\theta & 0 \\ 0 & \cos\theta & \sin\theta & 0 \\ 0 & 0 & 0 & 1 \end{pmatrix}$$

You can easily implement this azimuth and elevation view matrix in WPF. Start with a new WPF Windows application and name it *Chart3DNoWPFEngine*. Add a new *Utility* class to the project. Here is the code listing for the *Utility* class:

```
using System;
using System.Windows;
using System.Windows.Media;
using System.Windows.Media.Media3D;

namespace Chart3DNoWPFEngine
{
    public class Utility
    {
        public static Matrix3D AzimuthElevation(double elevation, double azimuth)
```

```
    {
        // Make sure elevation is in the range of [-90, 90]:
        if (elevation > 90)
            elevation = 90;
        else if (elevation < -90)
            elevation = -90;

        // Make sure azimuth is in the range of [-180, 180]:
        if (azimuth > 180)
            azimuth = 180;
        else if (azimuth < -180)
            azimuth = -180;

        elevation = elevation * Math.PI / 180;
        azimuth = azimuth * Math.PI / 180;
        double sne = Math.Sin(elevation);
        double cne = Math.Cos(elevation);
        double sna = Math.Sin(azimuth);
        double cna = Math.Cos(azimuth);

        Matrix3D result = new Matrix3D(cna, -sne * sna,  cne * sna, 0,
                                       sna,  sne * cna, -cne * cna, 0,
                                         0,        cne,        sne, 0,
                                         0,          0,          0, 1);

        return result;
    }
  }
}
```

This method takes elevation and azimuth angles as input parameters. In real-world 3D chart applications, we usually use parallel projection instead of perspective projection. This means that we can use the preceding azimuth and elevation view matrix to perform a 3D parallel projection on a 2D screen.

Creating a Cube

Here, I'll show you how to create a simple 3D cube object using the azimuth and elevation view matrix presented in the previous section. Add a new WPF Windows application to the project *Chart3DNoWPFEngine* and name it *Cube*. Here is the XAML file for this example:

```
<Window x:Class="Chart3DNoWPFEngine.Cube"
    xmlns="http://schemas.microsoft.com/winfx/2006/xaml/presentation"
    xmlns:x="http://schemas.microsoft.com/winfx/2006/xaml"
    Title="Cube" Height="350" Width="450">
    <Grid x:Name="LayoutRoot" Background="White">
        <Border BorderBrush="Gray" BorderThickness="1"
                CornerRadius="10" Margin="10">
            <StackPanel Orientation="Horizontal">
                <StackPanel Margin="5" Grid.Column="0">
                    <TextBlock Text="Elevation" Margin="2" FontSize="12"/>
                    <TextBox Name="tbElevation" Margin="2" Text="30"
                            FontSize="12" Width="70" Height="20"
```

```
                                      TextAlignment="Center"/>
                    <TextBlock Text="Azimuth" Margin="2" FontSize="12"/>
                    <TextBox Name="tbAzimuth" Margin="2" Text="-30"
                             FontSize="12" Width="70" Height="20"
                             TextAlignment="Center"/>
                    <Button Margin="2,30,2,2" Click="Apply_Click"
                            Content="Apply" Width="70" Height="22"/>
                </StackPanel>
                <Border BorderBrush="Gray" BorderThickness="1" Margin="10">
                    <Canvas x:Name="canvas1" Width="300" Height="305">
                        <Canvas.Clip>
                            <RectangleGeometry Rect="0 0 300 305"/>
                        </Canvas.Clip>
                    </Canvas>
                </Border>
            </StackPanel>
        </Border>
    </Grid>
</Window>
```

This XAML file creates an interface that allows the user to change the azimuth and elevation angles interactively. The cube object will be created on the *canvas*1 control in code. Here is the code-behind file for this example:

```
using System;
using System.Windows;
using System.Windows.Controls;
using System.Windows.Media;
using System.Windows.Media.Media3D;
using System.Windows.Shapes;

namespace Chart3DNoWPFEngine
{
    public partial class Cube : Window
    {
        private double side = 50;
        private Point center;
        private Point3D[] vertices0;
        private Point3D[] vertices;
        private Face[] faces;
        private bool isVisible;

        public Cube()
        {
            InitializeComponent();
            center = new Point(canvas1.Width / 2, canvas1.Height / 2);
            center = new Point(canvas1.Width / 2, canvas1.Height / 2);
            vertices0 = new Point3D[] { new Point3D(-side,-side,-side),
                                        new Point3D( side,-side,-side),
                                        new Point3D( side, side,-side),
                                        new Point3D(-side, side,-side),
                                        new Point3D(-side, side, side),
                                        new Point3D( side, side, side),
                                        new Point3D( side,-side, side),
```

```
                                 new Point3D(-side,-side, side)};
     faces = new Face[] {new Face(0,1,2,3), new Face(4,5,6,7),
                         new Face(3,4,7,0), new Face(2,1,6,5),
                         new Face(5,4,3,2), new Face(0,7,6,1)};
     AddCube();
}

public void AddCube()
{
    double elevation = double.Parse(tbElevation.Text);
    double azimuth = double.Parse(tbAzimuth.Text);
    Matrix3D transformMatrix =
        Utility.AzimuthElevation(elevation, azimuth);
    vertices = new Point3D[8];
    for (int i = 0; i < vertices0.Length; i++)
    {
        vertices[i] = Point3D.Multiply(vertices0[i], transformMatrix);
    }
    canvas1.Children.Clear();
    int ii = 0;
    foreach (Face face in this.faces)
    {
        ii++;
        Point3D va = vertices[face.VertexA];
        Point3D vb = vertices[face.VertexB];
        Point3D vc = vertices[face.VertexC];
        Point3D vd = vertices[face.VertexD];
        Vector3D normal = Utility.NormalVector(va, vb, vc);
        Vector3D viewDirection = new Vector3D();
        viewDirection = new Vector3D(0, 0, -1);
        double mixProduct = Vector3D.DotProduct(normal, viewDirection);
        isVisible = mixProduct > 0;
        if (isVisible)
        {
            byte red = 0;
            byte green = 0;
            byte blue = 0;
            if (ii == 1)
            {
                red = 255;
                green = 0;
                blue = 0;
            }
            else if (ii == 2)
            {
                red = 0;
                green = 255;
                blue = 0;
            }
            else if (ii == 3)
            {
                red = 0;
                green = 0;
```

```
                    blue = 255;
                }
                else if (ii == 4)
                {
                    red = 255;
                    green = 0;
                    blue = 255;
                }
                else if (ii == 5)
                {
                    red = 255;
                    green = 255;
                    blue = 0;
                }
                else if (ii == 6)
                {
                    red = 0;
                    green = 255;
                    blue = 255;
                }
                Polygon polygon = new Polygon();
                PointCollection collection = new PointCollection();
                collection.Add(new Point(va.X, va.Y));
                collection.Add(new Point(vb.X, vb.Y));
                collection.Add(new Point(vc.X, vc.Y));
                collection.Add(new Point(vd.X, vd.Y));
                polygon.Points = collection;
                polygon.Fill =
                    new SolidColorBrush(Color.FromArgb(255, red, green, blue));
                TranslateTransform tt = new TranslateTransform();
                tt.X = center.X;
                tt.Y = center.Y;
                polygon.RenderTransform = tt;
                canvas1.Children.Add(polygon);
            }
        }
    }

    private void Apply_Click(object sender, RoutedEventArgs e)
    {
        AddCube();
    }
}

public class Face
{
    public int VertexA, VertexB, VertexC, VertexD;
    public Face(int vertexA, int vertexB, int vertexC, int vertexD)
    {
        this.VertexA = vertexA;
        this.VertexB = vertexB;
        this.VertexC = vertexC;
        this.VertexD = vertexD;
```

```
        }
    }
}
```

Note that we implement a new class, *Face*, which contains four vertex indices. For a cube object, there are six faces, each with four vertices. The *Face* class allows you to create the cube faces easily.

Inside the constructor of the *Cube* class, we define a vertex point array and a face object array, which are used to create the cube object. The *AddCube* method first converts the user's inputs into azimuth and elevation angles; then it creates a transform matrix using the azimuth and elevation view defined in the *Utility* class. Next, we perform the projection transformation on the vertex points. This way, we project the 3D point objects on a 2D screen.

In order to distinguish the faces of the cube, we paint each face with a different color. Depending on the viewing direction, not all six faces will be visible at one time. We need to implement a technique that removes the back faces. Here, we use the sign of the dot product of the face's normal and the view direction to identify whether the face is a back or front face. If this dot product is less than or equal to zero, then the surface is a back face and we don't need to draw it on the computer screen.

Mathematically, we can represent a face in 3D using three points. We add a new method, *NormalVector*, to the *Utility* class. This method takes three points, representing a face in 3D, as inputs and returns a vector object that represents the normal of the face:

```
public static Vector3D NormalVector(Point3D pt1, Point3D pt2, Point3D pt3)
{
    Vector3D v1 = new Vector3D();
    Vector3D v2 = new Vector3D();
    v1.X = pt2.X - pt1.X;
    v1.Y = pt2.Y - pt1.Y;
    v1.Z = pt2.Z - pt1.Z;
    v2.X = pt3.X - pt2.X;
    v2.Y = pt3.Y - pt2.Y;
    v2.Z = pt3.Z - pt1.Z;
    return Vector3D.CrossProduct(v1, v2);
}
```

Finally, we use the projected point collection to draw a 2D polygon for each front face.

Running this example generates the output of Figure 15-2. You can see that the cube object in the figure corresponds to an orthogonal projection with an elevation angle of 30 degrees and an azimuth angle of –30 degrees. You can rotate the cube by entering different elevation and azimuth angles. Pay special attention to how the back faces are automatically removed when you rotate the cube.

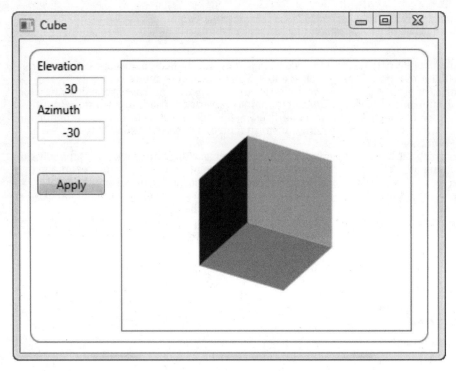

Figure 15-2. A cube object created directly using azimuth and elevation view

Chart Style in 3D

The chart style used in 3D charts is similar to that in 2D. Add a new class, *ChartStyle*, to the current project. The following code snippet shows its member fields and corresponding public properties:

```
using System;
using System.Collections.Generic;
using System.Windows;
using System.Windows.Controls;
using System.Windows.Media;
using System.Windows.Media.Media3D;
using System.Windows.Shapes;

namespace Chart3DNoWPFEngine
{
    public class ChartStyle
    {
        private Canvas chartCanvas;
        private double xmin = -5;
        private double xmax = 5;
        private double ymin = -3;
        private double ymax = 3;
```

```csharp
private double zmin = -6;
private double zmax = 6;
private double xtick = 1;
private double ytick = 1;
private double ztick = 3;
private FontFamily tickFont = new FontFamily("Arial Narrow");
private double tickFontSize =
    (double)new FontSizeConverter().ConvertFrom("8pt");
private Brush tickColor = Brushes.Black;
private string title = "My 3D Chart";
private FontFamily titleFont = new FontFamily("Arial Narrow");
private double titleFontSize =
    (double)new FontSizeConverter().ConvertFrom("14pt");
private Brush titleColor = Brushes.Black;
private string xLabel = "X Axis";
private string yLabel = "Y Axis";
private string zLabel = "Z Axis";
private FontFamily labelFont = new FontFamily("Arial Narrow");
private double labelFontSize =
    (double)new FontSizeConverter().ConvertFrom("10pt");
private Brush labelColor = Brushes.Black;
private double elevation = 30;
private double azimuth = -37.5;
private bool isXGrid = true;
private bool isYGrid = true;
private bool isZGrid = true;
private bool isColorBar = false;
private Line gridline = new Line();
private Brush gridlineColor = Brushes.LightGray;
private double gridlineThickness = 1;
private GridlinePatternEnum gridlinePattern = GridlinePatternEnum.Dash;
private Line axisLine = new Line();
private Brush axisColor = Brushes.Black;
private AxisPatternEnum axisPattern = AxisPatternEnum.Solid;
private double axisThickness = 1;

public Canvas ChartCanvas
{
    get { return chartCanvas; }
    set { chartCanvas = value; }
}

public bool IsColorBar
{
    get { return isColorBar; }
    set { isColorBar = value; }
}

public Brush AxisColor
{
    get { return axisColor; }
    set { axisColor = value; }
}
```

579

```
public AxisPatternEnum AxisPattern
{
    get { return axisPattern; }
    set { axisPattern = value; }
}

public double AxisThickness
{
    get { return axisThickness; }
    set { axisThickness = value; }
}

public Brush GridlineColor
{
    get { return gridlineColor; }
    set { gridlineColor = value; }
}

public GridlinePatternEnum GridlinePattern
{
    get { return gridlinePattern; }
    set { gridlinePattern = value; }
}

public double GridlineThickness
{
    get { return gridlineThickness; }
    set { gridlineThickness = value; }
}

public FontFamily LabelFont
{
    get { return labelFont; }
    set { labelFont = value; }
}

public Brush LabelColor
{
    get { return labelColor; }
    set { labelColor = value; }
}

public double LabelFontSize
{
    get { return labelFontSize; }
    set { labelFontSize = value; }
}

public FontFamily TitleFont
{
    get { return titleFont; }
    set { titleFont = value; }
```

```
    }

    public Brush TitleColor
    {
        get { return titleColor; }
        set { titleColor = value; }
    }

    public double TitleFontSize
    {
        get { return titleFontSize; }
        set { titleFontSize = value; }
    }

    public FontFamily TickFont
    {
        get { return tickFont; }
        set { tickFont = value; }
    }

    public Brush TickColor
    {
        get { return tickColor; }
        set { tickColor = value; }
    }

    public double TickFontSize
    {
        get { return tickFontSize; }
        set { tickFontSize = value; }
    }

    public bool IsXGrid
    {
        get { return isXGrid; }
        set { isXGrid = value; }
    }

    public bool IsYGrid
    {
        get { return isYGrid; }
        set { isYGrid = value; }
    }

    public bool IsZGrid
    {
        get { return isZGrid; }
        set { isZGrid = value; }
    }

    public string Title
    {
        get { return title; }
```

```csharp
        set { title = value; }
    }

    public string XLabel
    {
        get { return xLabel; }
        set { xLabel = value; }
    }

    public string YLabel
    {
        get { return yLabel; }
        set { yLabel = value; }
    }

    public string ZLabel
    {
        get { return zLabel; }
        set { zLabel = value; }
    }

    public double Elevation
    {
        get { return elevation; }
        set
        {
            elevation = value; }
    }

    public double Azimuth
    {
        get { return azimuth; }
        set { azimuth = value; }
    }

    public double Xmax
    {
        get { return xmax; }
        set { xmax = value; }
    }

    public double Xmin
    {
        get { return xmin; }
        set { xmin = value; }
    }

    public double Ymax
    {
        get { return ymax; }
        set { ymax = value; }
    }
```

```csharp
public double Ymin
{
    get { return ymin; }
    set { ymin = value; }
}

public double Zmax
{
    get { return zmax; }
    set { zmax = value; }
}

public double Zmin
{
    get { return zmin; }
    set { zmin = value; }
}

public double XTick
{
    get { return xtick; }
    set { xtick = value; }
}

public double YTick
{
    get { return ytick; }
    set { ytick = value; }
}

public double ZTick
{
    get { return ztick; }
    set { ztick = value; }
}

public enum GridlinePatternEnum
{
    Solid = 1,
    Dash = 2,
    Dot = 3,
    DashDot = 4
}

public enum AxisPatternEnum
{
    Solid = 1,
    Dash = 2,
    Dot = 3,
    DashDot = 4
}
......    }
}
```

You can specify and change the chart style for a 3D chart using the foregoing properties. If you need more features to control the appearance of your 3D charts, you can easily add your own member fields and corresponding properties to this class.

Another basic class you will need in 3D charts is *DataSeries*, which we discuss in the following example projects. You don't need the *DataCollection* class in 3D charts because most 3D charts display only one set of data.

3D Coordinate Axes

Correctly creating 3D coordinate axes is critical for 3D chart applications. First, we need to create the coordinates of the chart box, as shown in Figure 15-3. In 3D charts, all data are plotted within the chart box defined by [*xMin, xMax, yMin, yMax, zMin, zMax*] in the world coordinate system. The coordinate axes are represented by the bold lines in the figure. The *Z* axis is the vertical bold line, which can be independent of the elevation and azimuth angles. The *X* and *Y* axes, on the other hand, cannot be predefined. Which edge of the chart box represents the *X* or *Y* axis depends on both the elevation and azimuth angles.

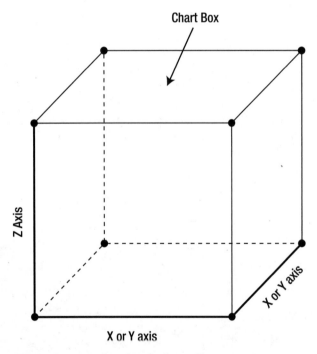

Figure 15-3. *3D chart box and coordinate axes*

In order to create such a coordinate system in WPF, we first need to create the eight-point coordinates of the chart box; then we select four of the points to define three coordinate axes. Add the following method, *CoordinatesOfChartBox*, to the *ChartStyle* class:

```
private Point3D[] CoordinatesOfChartBox()
{
    Point3D[] pta = new Point3D[8];
    pta[0] = new Point3D(Xmax, Ymin, Zmin);
    pta[1] = new Point3D(Xmin, Ymin, Zmin);
    pta[2] = new Point3D(Xmin, Ymax, Zmin);
    pta[3] = new Point3D(Xmin, Ymax, Zmax);
    pta[4] = new Point3D(Xmin, Ymin, Zmax);
    pta[5] = new Point3D(Xmax, Ymin, Zmax);
    pta[6] = new Point3D(Xmax, Ymax, Zmax);
    pta[7] = new Point3D(Xmax, Ymax, Zmin);
    Point3D[] pts = new Point3D[4];
    int[] npts = new int[4] { 0, 1, 2, 3 };

    if (elevation >= 0)
    {
        if (azimuth >= -180 && azimuth < -90)
            npts = new int[4] { 1, 2, 7, 6 };
        else if (azimuth >= -90 && azimuth < 0)
            npts = new int[4] { 0, 1, 2, 3 };
        else if (azimuth >= 0 && azimuth < 90)
            npts = new int[4] { 7, 0, 1, 4 };
        else if (azimuth >= 90 && azimuth <= 180)
            npts = new int[4] { 2, 7, 0, 5 };
    }
    else if (elevation < 0)
    {
        if (azimuth >= -180 && azimuth < -90)
            npts = new int[4] { 1, 0, 7, 6 };
        else if (azimuth >= -90 && azimuth < 0)
            npts = new int[4] { 0, 7, 2, 3 };
        else if (azimuth >= 0 && azimuth < 90)
            npts = new int[4] { 7, 2, 1, 4 };
        else if (azimuth >= 90 && azimuth <= 180)
            npts = new int[4] { 2, 1, 0, 5 };
    }
    for (int i = 0; i < 4; i++)
        pts[i] = pta[npts[i]];
    return pts;
}
```

In this method, we use a trial-and-error approach to select a different four-point array every time the azimuth and elevation angles change. Calling this method creates a point array of four points, which determines the *X*, *Y*, and *Z* axes for arbitrary elevation and azimuth angles. Now we can create the coordinate axes by adding the following two methods, *AddAxes* and *Normalize3D*, to the *ChartStyle* class:

```
private void AddAxes()
{
    Matrix3D m = Utility.AzimuthElevation(Elevation, Azimuth);
    Point3D[] pts = CoordinatesOfChartBox();
    for (int i = 0; i < pts.Length; i++)
    {
```

```
        pts[i] = Normalize3D(m, pts[i]);
    }
    DrawAxisLine(pts[0], pts[1]);
    DrawAxisLine(pts[1], pts[2]);
    DrawAxisLine(pts[2], pts[3]);
}
public Point3D Normalize3D(Matrix3D m, Point3D pt)
{
    Point3D result = new Point3D();

    // Normalize the point:
    double x1 = (pt.X - Xmin) / (Xmax - Xmin) - 0.5;
    double y1 = (pt.Y - Ymin) / (Ymax - Ymin) - 0.5;
    double z1 = (pt.Z - Zmin) / (Zmax - zmin) - 0.5;

    // Perform transformation on the point using matrix m:
    result.X = m.Transform(new Point3D(x1, y1, z1)).X;
    result.Y = m.Transform(new Point3D(x1, y1, z1)).Y;

    // Coordinate transformation from World to Device system:
    double xShift = 1.05;
    double xScale = 1;
    double yShift = 1.05;
    double yScale = 0.9;
    if (Title == "No Title")
    {
        yShift = 0.95;
        yScale = 1;
    }
    if (IsColorBar)
    {
        xShift = 0.95;
        xScale = 0.9;
    }
    result.X = (xShift + xScale * result.X) * ChartCanvas.Width / 2;
    result.Y = (yShift - yScale * result.Y) * ChartCanvas.Height / 2;
    return result;
}
```

The *Normalize3D* method is very similar to the *NormalizePoint* method previously used in 2D. It takes the transform matrix and a *Point3D* object as inputs. In this method, we first normalize the X, Y, and Z data ranges into a unit cube so that the transformations that are performed on the point within this unit cube are independent of the real data ranges. Then we transform the normalized point using the transform matrix. Finally, we carry out the coordinate transformation from the world coordinate system to the device coordinate system. This method performs all of the transformations necessary for a point to be displayed on a 2D screen, which will greatly simplify the programming procedure for 3D chart applications.

You might notice that in this method, only the X and Y components of the point undergo the transformations, whereas the Z and W components retain their original values. You can see this from the following code snippet:

```
// Perform transformation on the point using matrix m:
result.X = m.Transform(new Point3D(x1, y1, z1)).X;
result.Y = m.Transform(new Point3D(x1, y1, z1)).Y;
```

The *Z* and *W* components retain their original information; otherwise, after the orthogonal transformations, the *Z* component might end up a combination of the original *X*, *Y*, and *Z* values, which destroys the original *Z* coordinate information, meaning that you cannot use the *Z* component to compare the points' *Z* values. In 3D charts, we often do need the original *Z* coordinate information, such as when we apply color maps to a 3D chart.

In the *AddAxes* method, we first get the coordinates of the three coordinate axes by calling the *CoordinatesOfChartBox* method. Then we perform the transformation and normalization on these four points using the elevation and azimuth matrix and the *Normalize3D* method. Finally, we use the *X* and *Y* components of the transformed points to draw the coordinate axes. Although the *AddAxes* method creates three coordinate axes, we still do not know which axis is the *X* or *Y* axis. The program will automatically tell you when you place labels on the coordinate axes.

The following *AddTicks* method in the *ChartStyle* class creates tick marks on the coordinate axes:

```
private void AddTicks()
{
    Matrix3D m = Utility.AzimuthElevation(Elevation, Azimuth);
    Point3D[] pta = new Point3D[2];
    Point3D[] pts = CoordinatesOfChartBox();

    // Add x ticks:
    double offset = (Ymax - Ymin) / 30.0;
    double ticklength = offset;
    for (double x = Xmin; x <= Xmax; x = x + XTick)
    {
        if (Elevation >= 0)
        {
            if (Azimuth >= -90 && Azimuth < 90)
                ticklength = -offset;
        }
        else if (Elevation < 0)
        {
            if ((Azimuth >= -180 && Azimuth < -90) ||
                 Azimuth >= 90 && Azimuth <= 180)
                ticklength = -(Ymax - Ymin) / 30;
        }
        pta[0] = new Point3D(x, pts[1].Y + ticklength, pts[1].Z);
        pta[1] = new Point3D(x, pts[1].Y, pts[1].Z);
        for (int i = 0; i < pta.Length; i++)
        {
            pta[i] = Normalize3D(m, pta[i]);
        }
        AddTickLine(pta[0], pta[1]);
    }

    // Add y ticks:
    offset = (Xmax - Xmin) / 30.0;
    ticklength = offset;
    for (double y = Ymin; y <= Ymax; y = y + YTick)
    {
        pts = CoordinatesOfChartBox();
        if (Elevation >= 0)
        {
            if (Azimuth >= -180 && Azimuth < 0)
                ticklength = -offset;
```

```
    }
    else if (Elevation < 0)
    {
        if (Azimuth >= 0 && Azimuth < 180)
            ticklength = -offset;
    }
    pta[0] = new Point3D(pts[1].X + ticklength, y, pts[1].Z);
    pta[1] = new Point3D(pts[1].X, y, pts[1].Z);
    for (int i = 0; i < pta.Length; i++)
    {
        pta[i] = Normalize3D(m, pta[i]);
    }
    AddTickLine(pta[0], pta[1]);
}

// Add z ticks:
double xoffset = (Xmax - Xmin) / 45.0f;
double yoffset = (Ymax - Ymin) / 20.0f;
double xticklength = xoffset;
double yticklength = yoffset;
for (double z = Zmin; z <= Zmax; z = z + ZTick)
{
    if (Elevation >= 0)
    {
        if (Azimuth >= -180 && Azimuth < -90)
        {
            xticklength = 0;
            yticklength = yoffset;
        }
        else if (Azimuth >= -90 && Azimuth < 0)
        {
            xticklength = xoffset;
            yticklength = 0;
        }
        else if (Azimuth >= 0 && Azimuth < 90)
        {
            xticklength = 0;
            yticklength = -yoffset;
        }
        else if (Azimuth >= 90 && Azimuth <= 180)
        {
            xticklength = -xoffset;
            yticklength = 0;
        }
    }
    else if (Elevation < 0)
    {
        if (Azimuth >= -180 && Azimuth < -90)
        {
            yticklength = 0;
            xticklength = xoffset;
        }
        else if (Azimuth >= -90 && Azimuth < 0)
```

```
        {
            yticklength = -yoffset;
            xticklength = 0;
        }
        else if (Azimuth >= 0 && Azimuth < 90)
        {
            yticklength = 0;
            xticklength = -xoffset;
        }
        else if (Azimuth >= 90 && Azimuth <= 180)
        {
            yticklength = yoffset;
            xticklength = 0;
        }
    }
    pta[0] = new Point3D(pts[2].X, pts[2].Y, z);
    pta[1] = new Point3D(pts[2].X + yticklength, pts[2].Y + xticklength, z);
    for (int i = 0; i < pta.Length; i++)
    {
        pta[i] = Normalize3D(m, pta[i]);
    }
    AddTickLine(pta[0], pta[1]);
    }
}

private void AddTickLine(Point3D pt1, Point3D pt2)
{
    Line line = new Line();
    line.Stroke = AxisColor;
    line.X1 = pt1.X;
    line.Y1 = pt1.Y;
    line.X2 = pt2.X;
    line.Y2 = pt2.Y;
    ChartCanvas.Children.Add(line);
}
```

In this method, we define the length of the ticks in terms of the axis limit instead of a fixed length in the device coordinate system. This keeps the ticks distributed proportionally when the chart is resized. Please note how we place the tick markers in their proper positions on the coordinate axes when the elevation and azimuth angles are changed.

Gridlines

As in 2D charts, gridlines in 3D charts can help you to get a better view of the data ranges. In the case of 3D, we want to place gridlines on three faces located behind your data curves or surfaces. These three faces (or planes) must be properly selected according to the variation of the elevation and azimuth angles. The following *AddGrids* method in the *ChartStyle* class creates gridlines on the proper faces:

```
private void AddGridlines()
{
    Matrix3D m = Utility.AzimuthElevation(Elevation, Azimuth);
    Point3D[] pta = new Point3D[3];
    Point3D[] pts = CoordinatesOfChartBox();
```

```
// Draw x gridlines:
if (IsXGrid)
{
    for (double x = Xmin; x <= Xmax; x = x + XTick)
    {
        pts = CoordinatesOfChartBox();
        pta[0] = new Point3D(x, pts[1].Y, pts[1].Z);
        if (Elevation >= 0)
        {
            if ((Azimuth >= -180 && Azimuth < -90) ||
                (Azimuth >= 0 && Azimuth < 90))
            {
                pta[1] = new Point3D(x, pts[0].Y, pts[1].Z);
                pta[2] = new Point3D(x, pts[0].Y, pts[3].Z);
            }
            else
            {
                pta[1] = new Point3D(x, pts[2].Y, pts[1].Z);
                pta[2] = new Point3D(x, pts[2].Y, pts[3].Z);
            }
        }
        else if (Elevation < 0)
        {
            if ((Azimuth >= -180 && Azimuth < -90) ||
                (Azimuth >= 0 && Azimuth < 90))
            {
                pta[1] = new Point3D(x, pts[2].Y, pts[1].Z);
                pta[2] = new Point3D(x, pts[2].Y, pts[3].Z);
            }
            else
            {
                pta[1] = new Point3D(x, pts[0].Y, pts[1].Z);
                pta[2] = new Point3D(x, pts[0].Y, pts[3].Z);
            }
        }
        for (int i = 0; i < pta.Length; i++)
        {
            pta[i] = Normalize3D(m, pta[i]);
        }
        DrawGridline(pta[0], pta[1]);
        DrawGridline(pta[1], pta[2]);
    }
}

// Draw y gridlines:
if (IsYGrid)
{
    for (double y = Ymin; y <= Ymax; y = y + YTick)
    {
        pts = CoordinatesOfChartBox();
        pta[0] = new Point3D(pts[1].X, y, pts[1].Z);
        if (Elevation >= 0)
        {
```

```
            if ((Azimuth >= -180 && Azimuth < -90) ||
                (Azimuth >= 0 && Azimuth < 90))
            {
                pta[1] = new Point3D(pts[2].X, y, pts[1].Z);
                pta[2] = new Point3D(pts[2].X, y, pts[3].Z);
            }
            else
            {
                pta[1] = new Point3D(pts[0].X, y, pts[1].Z);
                pta[2] = new Point3D(pts[0].X, y, pts[3].Z);
            }
        }
        if (elevation < 0)
        {
            if ((Azimuth >= -180 && Azimuth < -90) ||
                (Azimuth >= 0 && Azimuth < 90))
            {
                pta[1] = new Point3D(pts[0].X, y, pts[1].Z);
                pta[2] = new Point3D(pts[0].X, y, pts[3].Z);
            }
            else
            {
                pta[1] = new Point3D(pts[2].X, y, pts[1].Z);
                pta[2] = new Point3D(pts[2].X, y, pts[3].Z);
            }
        }
        for (int i = 0; i < pta.Length; i++)
        {
            pta[i] = Normalize3D(m, pta[i]);
        }
        DrawGridline(pta[0], pta[1]);
        DrawGridline(pta[1], pta[2]);
    }
}

// Draw Z gridlines:
if (IsZGrid)
{
    for (double z = Zmin; z <= Zmax; z = z + ZTick)
    {
        pts = CoordinatesOfChartBox();
        pta[0] = new Point3D(pts[2].X, pts[2].Y, z);
        if (Elevation >= 0)
        {
            if ((Azimuth >= -180 && Azimuth < -90) ||
                (Azimuth >= 0 && Azimuth < 90))
            {
                pta[1] = new Point3D(pts[2].X, pts[0].Y, z);
                pta[2] = new Point3D(pts[0].X, pts[0].Y, z);
            }
            else
            {
                pta[1] = new Point3D(pts[0].X, pts[2].Y, z);
```

```
                    pta[2] = new Point3D(pts[0].X, pts[1].Y, z);
                }
            }
            if (Elevation < 0)
            {
                if ((Azimuth >= -180 && Azimuth < -90) ||
                    (Azimuth >= 0 && Azimuth < 90))
                {
                    pta[1] = new Point3D(pts[0].X, pts[2].Y, z);
                    pta[2] = new Point3D(pts[0].X, pts[0].Y, z);
                }
                else
                {
                    pta[1] = new Point3D(pts[2].X, pts[0].Y, z);
                    pta[2] = new Point3D(pts[0].X, pts[0].Y, z);
                }
            }
            for (int i = 0; i < pta.Length; i++)
            {
                pta[i] = Normalize3D(m, pta[i]);
            }
            DrawGridline(pta[0], pta[1]);
            DrawGridline(pta[1], pta[2]);
        }
    }
}

private void DrawGridline(Point3D pt1, Point3D pt2)
{
    gridline = new Line();
    gridline.Stroke = GridlineColor;
    gridline.StrokeThickness = GridlineThickness;
    AddGridlinePattern();
    gridline.X1 = pt1.X;
    gridline.Y1 = pt1.Y;
    gridline.X2 = pt2.X;
    gridline.Y2 = pt2.Y;
    ChartCanvas.Children.Add(gridline);
}
```

In the *AddGridlines* method, we create the *X*, *Y*, and *Z* gridlines on different faces, depending on values of the elevation and azimuth angles, ensuring that the gridlines are drawn on the right faces when the 3D chart is rotated.

Labels

3D labels include three parts: the title, the tick labels, and the labels for the coordinate axes. Creating a title label in 3D is similar to doing so in 2D. However, the tick labels and axis labels in 3D charts are much more complicated than those in 2D charts. First, we need to properly position these labels by considering the variation of the elevation and azimuth angles. Then we need to rotate them to be parallel to the coordinate axes when the elevation and azimuth angles are changed. Finally, we want these labels to be properly spaced from the coordinate axes.

The following *AddLabels* method in the *ChartStyle* class creates labels in a 3D chart:

```
private void AddLabels()
{
    Matrix3D m = Utility.AzimuthElevation(Elevation, Azimuth);
    Point3D pt = new Point3D();
    Point3D[] pts = CoordinatesOfChartBox();
    TextBlock tb = new TextBlock();

    // Add x tick labels:
    double offset = (Ymax - Ymin) / 20;
    double labelSpace = offset;
    for (double x = Xmin; x <= Xmax; x = x + XTick)
    {
        if (Elevation >= 0)
        {
            if (Azimuth >= -90 && Azimuth < 90)
                labelSpace = -offset;
        }
        else if (Elevation < 0)
        {
            if ((Azimuth >= -180 && Azimuth < -90) ||
                 Azimuth >= 90 && Azimuth <= 180)
                labelSpace = -offset;
        }
        pt = new Point3D(x, pts[1].Y + labelSpace, pts[1].Z);
        pt = Normalize3D(m, pt);
        tb = new TextBlock();
        tb.Text = x.ToString();
        tb.Foreground = TickColor;
        tb.FontFamily = TickFont;
        tb.FontSize = TickFontSize;
        tb.TextAlignment = TextAlignment.Center;
        ChartCanvas.Children.Add(tb);
        Canvas.SetLeft(tb, pt.X);
        Canvas.SetTop(tb, pt.Y);
    }

    // Add y tick labels:
    offset = (Xmax - Xmin) / 20;
    labelSpace = offset;
    for (double y = Ymin; y <= Ymax; y = y + YTick)
    {
        pts = CoordinatesOfChartBox();
        if (elevation >= 0)
        {
            if (azimuth >= -180 && azimuth < 0)
                labelSpace = -offset;
        }
        else if (elevation < 0)
        {
            if (azimuth >= 0 && azimuth < 180)
                labelSpace = -offset;
        }
```

```
        pt = new Point3D(pts[1].X + labelSpace, y, pts[1].Z);
        pt = Normalize3D(m, pt);
        tb = new TextBlock();
        tb.Text = y.ToString();
        tb.Foreground = TickColor;
        tb.FontFamily = TickFont;
        tb.FontSize = TickFontSize;
        tb.Measure(new Size(Double.PositiveInfinity, Double.PositiveInfinity));
        Size ytickSize = tb.DesiredSize;
        ChartCanvas.Children.Add(tb);
        Canvas.SetLeft(tb, pt.X - ytickSize.Width / 2);
        Canvas.SetTop(tb, pt.Y);
    }

    // Add z tick labels:
    double xoffset = (Xmax - Xmin) / 30.0;
    double yoffset = (Ymax - Ymin) / 15.0;
    double xlabelSpace = xoffset;
    double ylabelSpace = yoffset;
    tb = new TextBlock();
    tb.Text = "A";
    tb.Measure(new Size(Double.PositiveInfinity, Double.PositiveInfinity));
    Size size = tb.DesiredSize;
    for (double z = Zmin; z <= Zmax; z = z + ZTick)
    {
        pts = CoordinatesOfChartBox();
        if (Elevation >= 0)
        {
            if (Azimuth >= -180 && Azimuth < -90)
            {
                xlabelSpace = 0;
                ylabelSpace = yoffset;
            }
            else if (Azimuth >= -90 && Azimuth < 0)
            {
                xlabelSpace = xoffset;
                ylabelSpace = 0;
            }
            else if (Azimuth >= 0 && Azimuth < 90)
            {
                xlabelSpace = 0;
                ylabelSpace = -yoffset;
            }
            else if (Azimuth >= 90 && Azimuth <= 180)
            {
                xlabelSpace = -xoffset;
                ylabelSpace = 0;
            }
        }
        else if (Elevation < 0)
        {
            if (Azimuth >= -180 && Azimuth < -90)
            {
```

```
                ylabelSpace = 0;
                xlabelSpace = xoffset;
            }
            else if (Azimuth >= -90 && Azimuth < 0)
            {
                ylabelSpace = -yoffset;
                xlabelSpace = 0;
            }
            else if (Azimuth >= 0 && Azimuth < 90)
            {
                ylabelSpace = 0;
                xlabelSpace = -xoffset;
            }
            else if (Azimuth >= 90 && Azimuth <= 180)
            {
                ylabelSpace = yoffset;
                xlabelSpace = 0;
            }
        }
        pt = new Point3D(pts[2].X + ylabelSpace, pts[2].Y + xlabelSpace, z);
        pt = Normalize3D(m, pt);
        tb = new TextBlock();
        tb.Text = z.ToString();
        tb.Foreground = TickColor;
        tb.FontFamily = TickFont;
        tb.FontSize = TickFontSize;
        tb.Measure(new Size(Double.PositiveInfinity, Double.PositiveInfinity));
        Size ztickSize = tb.DesiredSize;
        ChartCanvas.Children.Add(tb);
        Canvas.SetLeft(tb, pt.X - ztickSize.Width - 1);
        Canvas.SetTop(tb, pt.Y - ztickSize.Height / 2);
    }
}

// Add Title:
tb = new TextBlock();
tb.Text = Title;
tb.Foreground = TitleColor;
tb.FontSize = TitleFontSize;
tb.FontFamily = TitleFont;
tb.Measure(new Size(Double.PositiveInfinity, Double.PositiveInfinity));
Size titleSize = tb.DesiredSize;
if (tb.Text != "No Title")
{
    ChartCanvas.Children.Add(tb);
    Canvas.SetLeft(tb, ChartCanvas.Width / 2 - titleSize.Width / 2);
    Canvas.SetTop(tb, ChartCanvas.Height / 30);
}

// Add x axis label:
offset = (Ymax - Ymin) / 3;
labelSpace = offset;
double offset1 = (Xmax - Xmin) / 10;
double xc = offset1;
```

```
    if (Elevation >= 0)
    {
        if (Azimuth >= -90 && Azimuth < 90)
            labelSpace = -offset;
        if (Azimuth >= 0 && Azimuth <= 180)
            xc = -offset1;
    }
    else if (Elevation < 0)
    {
        if ((Azimuth >= -180 && Azimuth < -90) ||
             Azimuth >= 90 && Azimuth <= 180)
            labelSpace = -offset;
        if (Azimuth >= -180 && Azimuth <= 0)
            xc = -offset1;
    }
    Point3D[] pta = new Point3D[2];
    pta[0] = new Point3D(Xmin, pts[1].Y + labelSpace, pts[1].Z);
    pta[1] = new Point3D((Xmin + Xmax) / 2 - xc, pts[1].Y + labelSpace, pts[1].Z);
    pta[0] = Normalize3D(m, pta[0]);
    pta[1] = Normalize3D(m, pta[1]);
    double theta = Math.Atan((pta[1].Y - pta[0].Y) / (pta[1].X - pta[0].X));
    theta = theta * 180 / Math.PI;
    tb = new TextBlock();
    tb.Text = XLabel;
    tb.Foreground = LabelColor;
    tb.FontFamily = LabelFont;
    tb.FontSize = LabelFontSize;
    tb.Measure(new Size(Double.PositiveInfinity, Double.PositiveInfinity));
    Size xLabelSize = tb.DesiredSize;
    TransformGroup tg = new TransformGroup();
    RotateTransform rt = new RotateTransform(theta, 0.5, 0.5);
    TranslateTransform tt = new TranslateTransform(pta[1].X +
        xLabelSize.Width / 2, pta[1].Y - xLabelSize.Height / 2);
    tg.Children.Add(rt);
    tg.Children.Add(tt);
    tb.RenderTransform = tg;
    ChartCanvas.Children.Add(tb);

    // Add y axis label:
    offset = (Xmax - Xmin) / 3;
    offset1 = (Ymax - Ymin) / 5;
    labelSpace = offset;
    double yc = YTick;
    if (Elevation >= 0)
    {
        if (Azimuth >= -180 && Azimuth < 0)
            labelSpace = -offset;
        if (Azimuth >= -90 && Azimuth <= 90)
            yc = -offset1;
    }
    else if (Elevation < 0)
    {
        yc = -offset1;
```

```
        if (Azimuth >= 0 && Azimuth < 180)
            labelSpace = -offset;
        if (Azimuth >= -90 && Azimuth <= 90)
            yc = offset1;
}
pta[0] = new Point3D(pts[1].X + labelSpace, Ymin, pts[1].Z);
pta[1] = new Point3D(pts[1].X + labelSpace, (Ymin + Ymax) / 2 + yc, pts[1].Z);
pta[0] = Normalize3D(m, pta[0]);
pta[1] = Normalize3D(m, pta[1]);
theta = (double)Math.Atan((pta[1].Y - pta[0].Y) / (pta[1].X - pta[0].X));
theta = theta * 180 / (double)Math.PI;
tb = new TextBlock();
tb.Text = YLabel;
tb.Foreground = LabelColor;
tb.FontFamily = LabelFont;
tb.FontSize = LabelFontSize;
tb.Measure(new Size(Double.PositiveInfinity, Double.PositiveInfinity));
Size yLabelSize = tb.DesiredSize;
tg = new TransformGroup();
tt = new TranslateTransform(pta[1].X - yLabelSize.Width / 2,
    pta[1].Y - yLabelSize.Height / 2);
rt = new RotateTransform(theta, 0.5, 0.5);
tg.Children.Add(rt);
tg.Children.Add(tt);
tb.RenderTransform = tg;
ChartCanvas.Children.Add(tb);

// Add z axis labels:
double zticklength = 10;
labelSpace = -1.3f * offset;
offset1 = (Zmax - Zmin) / 8;
double zc = -offset1;
for (double z = Zmin; z < Zmax; z = z + ZTick)
{
    tb = new TextBlock();
    tb.Text = z.ToString();
    tb.Measure(new Size(Double.PositiveInfinity, Double.PositiveInfinity));
    Size size1 = tb.DesiredSize;
    if (zticklength < size1.Width)
        zticklength = size1.Width;
}
double zlength = -zticklength;
if (Elevation >= 0)
{
    if (Azimuth >= -180 && Azimuth < -90)
    {
        zlength = -zticklength;
        labelSpace = -1.3f * offset;
        zc = -offset1;
    }
    else if (Azimuth >= -90 && Azimuth < 0)
    {
        zlength = zticklength;
```

```
                    labelSpace = 2 * offset / 3;
                    zc = offset1;
                }
                else if (Azimuth >= 0 && Azimuth < 90)
                {
                    zlength = zticklength;
                    labelSpace = 2 * offset / 3;
                    zc = -offset1;
                }
                else if (Azimuth >= 90 && Azimuth <= 180)
                {
                    zlength = -zticklength;
                    labelSpace = -1.3f * offset;
                    zc = offset1;
                }
            }
            else if (Elevation < 0)
            {
                if (Azimuth >= -180 && Azimuth < -90)
                {
                    zlength = -zticklength;
                    labelSpace = -1.3f * offset;
                    zc = offset1;
                }
                else if (Azimuth >= -90 && Azimuth < 0)
                {
                    zlength = zticklength;
                    labelSpace = 2 * offset / 3;
                    zc = -offset1;
                }
                else if (Azimuth >= 0 && Azimuth < 90)
                {
                    zlength = zticklength;
                    labelSpace = 2 * offset / 3;
                    zc = offset1;
                }
                else if (Azimuth >= 90 && Azimuth <= 180)
                {
                    zlength = -zticklength;
                    labelSpace = -1.3f * offset;
                    zc = -offset1;
                }
            }
            pta[0] = new Point3D(pts[2].X - labelSpace, pts[2].Y, (Zmin + Zmax) / 2 + zc);
            pta[0] = Normalize3D(m, pta[0]);
            tb = new TextBlock();
            tb.Text = ZLabel;
            tb.Foreground = LabelColor;
            tb.FontFamily = LabelFont;
            tb.FontSize = LabelFontSize;
            tb.Measure(new Size(Double.PositiveInfinity, Double.PositiveInfinity));
            Size zLabelSize = tb.DesiredSize;
            tg = new TransformGroup();
```

```
    tt = new TranslateTransform(pta[0].X - zlength,
        pta[0].Y + zLabelSize.Width / 2);
    rt = new RotateTransform(270, 0.5, 0.5);
    tg.Children.Add(rt);
    tg.Children.Add(tt);
    tb.RenderTransform = tg;
    ChartCanvas.Children.Add(tb);
}
```

The *AddLabels* method may seem complicated, due to the fact that we need to adjust the positions of the labels according to the values of the elevation and azimuth angles.

Finally, in order to simplify the process of adding chart styles to our charts, we need to add a new public method, *AddChartStyle*, to the *ChartStyle* class:

```
public void AddChartStyle()
{
    AddTicks();
    AddGridlines();
    AddAxes();
    AddLabels();
}
```

Testing the Project

Now we can put together all of the code created in the previous sections in a new WPF project. Add a new WPF window and name it *Coordinates3D*. Here is the XAML file for this example:

```
<Window x:Class="Chart3DNoWPFEngine.Coordinates3D"
    xmlns="http://schemas.microsoft.com/winfx/2006/xaml/presentation"
    xmlns:x="http://schemas.microsoft.com/winfx/2006/xaml"
    Title="Coordinates3D" Height="400" Width="520">
    <Grid>
        <Grid.ColumnDefinitions>
            <ColumnDefinition Width="100"/>
            <ColumnDefinition Width="*"/>
        </Grid.ColumnDefinitions>
        <StackPanel Margin="10 10 0 0">
            <TextBlock Margin="0,0,0,5" Text="Elevation:"/>
            <TextBox x:Name="tbElevation" Text="30" Margin="0,0,0,5"
                    TextAlignment="Center" Width="75"/>
            <TextBlock Margin="0,0,0,5" Text="Azimuth:"/>
            <TextBox x:Name="tbAzimuth" Text="-37" Margin="0,0,0,5"
                    TextAlignment="Center" Width="75"/>
            <Button x:Name="Apply" Content="Apply" Click="Apply_Click"
                    Margin="0 20,0,0" Width="75"/>
        </StackPanel>
        <Grid x:Name="chartGrid" SizeChanged="chartGrid_SizeChanged"
                Margin="10" Grid.Row="0" Grid.Column="1">
            <Border BorderBrush="Gray" BorderThickness="1">
                <Canvas x:Name="chartCanvas" Background="Transparent"
                        ClipToBounds="True"/>
            </Border>
        </Grid>
    </Grid>
```

```
    </Grid>
</Window>
```

This XAML file creates a resizable *Canvas,* named *chartCanvas*, on which you'll draw graphics objects. It also sets up an interface that allows the user to change the values of the elevation and azimuth angles interactively. Here is the corresponding code-behind file:

```
using System;
using System.Windows;
using System.Windows.Controls;
using System.Windows.Media;
using System.Windows.Media.Imaging;

namespace Chart3DNoWPFEngine
{
    public partial class Coordinates3D : Window
    {
        ChartStyle cs;
        public Coordinates3D()
        {
            InitializeComponent();
        }

        private void chartGrid_SizeChanged(object sender, SizeChangedEventArgs e)
        {
            chartCanvas.Width = chartGrid.ActualWidth;
            chartCanvas.Height = chartGrid.ActualHeight;
            AddCoordinateAxes();
        }

        private void AddCoordinateAxes()
        {
            chartCanvas.Children.Clear();
            cs = new ChartStyle();
            cs.ChartCanvas = this.chartCanvas;
            cs.GridlinePattern = ChartStyle.GridlinePatternEnum.Solid;
            cs.Elevation = double.Parse(tbElevation.Text);
            cs.Azimuth = double.Parse(tbAzimuth.Text);
            cs.AddChartStyle();
        }

        private void Apply_Click(object sender, RoutedEventArgs e)
        {
            AddCoordinateAxes();
        }
    }
}
```

This code-behind file is very simple. Inside the *AddCoordinateAxes* method, we specify the elevation and azimuth angles by taking the user's inputs directly from the corresponding text boxes, and then we call the *AddChartStyle* method.

Running this example produces the output of Figure 15-4. You can see how the coordinate axes, gridlines, and labels respond to changes in the elevation and azimuth angles.

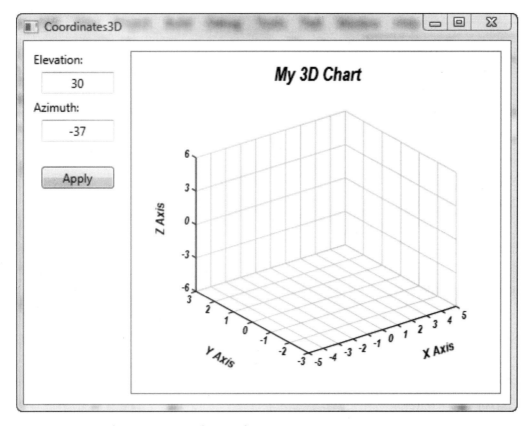

Figure 15-4. Coordinate system used in 3D charts

3D Line Charts

In the previous section, we implemented the basic coordinate system for 3D charts in WPF without using the WPF 3D engine, a process that seems quite involved. However, once you have finished this framework, you can use it without any modification for a wide variety of 3D chart applications. Here, I will show you how easy it is to create a 3D line chart based on this basic framework. The 3D line chart displays a 3D plot of a set of data points. It is similar to a 2D line chart, except it uses an additional Z component to provide data for the third dimension.

Implementation

Add a new *DataSeriesLine3D* class to the current project. This class is very similar to the *DataSeries* class used extensively in 2D charts, except the *PointList* in this class must hold 3D points. The following is its code listing:

```
using System;
using System.Collections.Generic;
```

```csharp
using System.Windows;
using System.Windows.Media;
using System.Windows.Media.Media3D;
using System.Windows.Shapes;

namespace Chart3DNoWPFEngine
{
    public class DataSeriesLine3D
    {
        private Polyline lineSeries = new Polyline();
        private Brush lineColor;
        private double lineThickness = 1;
        private LinePatternEnum linePattern;
        private List<Point3D> point3DList = new List<Point3D>();

        public List<Point3D> Point3DList
        {
            get { return point3DList; }
            set { point3DList = value; }
        }

        public Brush LineColor
        {
            get { return lineColor; }
            set { lineColor = value; }
        }

        public Polyline LineSeries
        {
            get { return lineSeries; }
            set { lineSeries = value; }
        }

        public double LineThickness
        {
            get { return lineThickness; }
            set { lineThickness = value; }
        }

        public LinePatternEnum LinePattern
        {
            get { return linePattern; }
            set { linePattern = value; }
        }

        public void AddLinePattern()
        {
            LineSeries.Stroke = LineColor;
            LineSeries.StrokeThickness = LineThickness;

            switch (LinePattern)
            {
                case LinePatternEnum.Dash:
```

```
                LineSeries.StrokeDashArray =
                    new DoubleCollection(new double[2] { 4, 3 });
                break;
            case LinePatternEnum.Dot:
                LineSeries.StrokeDashArray =
                    new DoubleCollection(new double[2] { 1, 2 });
                break;
            case LinePatternEnum.DashDot:
                LineSeries.StrokeDashArray =
                    new DoubleCollection(new double[4] { 4, 2, 1, 2 });
                break;
            case LinePatternEnum.None:
                LineSeries.Stroke = Brushes.Transparent;
                break;
        }
    }

    public enum LinePatternEnum
    {
        Solid = 1,
        Dash = 2,
        Dot = 3,
        DashDot = 4,
        None = 5
    }

    public void AddLine3D(ChartStyle cs)
    {
        Matrix3D m = Utility.AzimuthElevation(cs.Elevation, cs.Azimuth);
        Point3D[] pts = new Point3D[Point3DList.Count];
        for (int i = 0; i < Point3DList.Count; i++)
        {
            pts[i] = cs.Normalize3D(m, Point3DList[i]);
            LineSeries.Points.Add(new Point(pts[i].X, pts[i].Y));
        }
        AddLinePattern();
        cs.ChartCanvas.Children.Add(LineSeries);
    }
}
}
```

You can see that this class is basically similar to that used in 2D chart applications. However, unlike 2D charts, here you do not need a *DataCollection* class, because in a 3D chart you typically allow only one set of data points to be drawn. Drawing multiple sets of data points in a 3D chart becomes more confusing than in 2D. If you do want to have this capability, you can easily add it to your applications using the *DataCollection* class the same way you do in 2D charts. To simplify our discussion, we'll only consider 3D charts containing one set of data points.

Thus, we implement an *AddLine3D* method in the *DataSeriesLine3D* class instead of a *DataCollection* class. Inside the *AddLine3D* method, we first perform the necessary transformations on the 3D data points by calling the *Normalize3D* method, using the *AzimuthElevation* orthogonal projection matrix. Then we draw the line chart using the *X* and *Y* components of the projected 3D data points.

Testing the Project

You can test the 3D line chart in WPF applications. Add a new WPF window to the current project and name it *Line3D*. The XAML file for this example is the same as that used in the previous *Coordinates3D* example; here is the code-behind file:

```
using System;
using System.Collections.Generic;
using System.Windows;
using System.Windows.Controls;
using System.Windows.Media;
using System.Windows.Media.Media3D;

namespace Chart3DNoWPFEngine
{
    public partial class Line3D : Window
    {
        private ChartStyle cs;
        private DataSeriesLine3D ds;
        public Line3D()
        {
            InitializeComponent();
        }

        private void chartGrid_SizeChanged(object sender, SizeChangedEventArgs e)
        {
            chartCanvas.Width = chartGrid.ActualWidth;
            chartCanvas.Height = chartGrid.ActualHeight;
            AddChart();
        }

        private void AddChart()
        {
            chartCanvas.Children.Clear();
            cs = new ChartStyle();
            ds = new DataSeriesLine3D();
            cs.ChartCanvas = this.chartCanvas;
            cs.GridlinePattern = ChartStyle.GridlinePatternEnum.Solid;
            cs.Elevation = double.Parse(tbElevation.Text);
            cs.Azimuth = double.Parse(tbAzimuth.Text);
            cs.Xmin = -1;
            cs.Xmax = 1;
            cs.Ymin = -1;
            cs.Ymax = 1;
            cs.Zmin = 0;
            cs.Zmax = 30;
            cs.XTick = 0.5;
            cs.YTick = 0.5;
            cs.ZTick = 5;
            cs.Title = "No Title";
            cs.AddChartStyle();
            ds.LineColor = Brushes.Red;
            for (int i = 0; i < 300; i++)
```

```
            {
                double t = 0.1 * i;
                double x = Math.Exp(-t / 30) * Math.Cos(t);
                double y = Math.Exp(-t / 30) * Math.Sin(t);
                double z = t;
                ds.Point3DList.Add(new Point3D(x, y, z));
            }
            ds.AddLine3D(cs);
        }

        private void Apply_Click(object sender, RoutedEventArgs e)
        {
            AddChart();
        }
    }
}
```

Please note how we add the 3D data points to the *Point3DList* in the *AddChart* method.

This project generates the result of Figure 15-5. As with 2D line charts, here you can specify the line color, dash style, and thickness. You can also look at the line chart from different viewpoints by changing the elevation and azimuth angles.

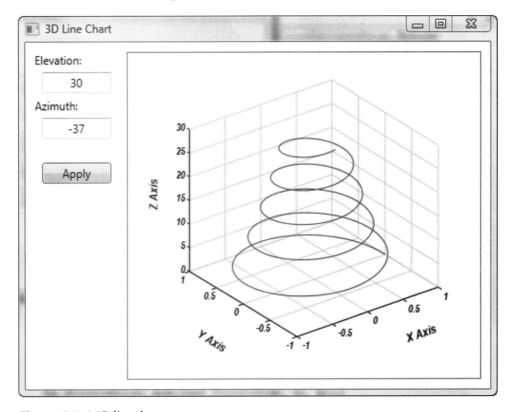

Figure 15-5. *A 3D line chart*

3D Surface Charts

As we mentioned in Chapter 14, a surface chart draws a Z function on a surface for each X and Y coordinate in a region of interest. In this chapter, we will discuss only simple types of surface charts. For each X and Y value, a simple surface can have at most one Z value. Complicated surfaces with multiple Z values for each pair of X and Y values were discussed in Chapter 14.

We now define a surface by the Z coordinates of points above a rectangular grid in the X-Y plane. The surface chart is formed by joining adjacent points with straight lines. Surface charts are useful for visualizing 2D data arrays (i.e., matrices) that are too large to display in numerical form and for graphing functions of two variables.

In this section, I will show you how to create different forms of surface charts. Mesh charts are special cases of surface charts. They are basically wireframe surfaces that draw only the lines connecting the defining points. On the other hand, surface charts display both the connecting lines and the faces of the surface in color. I will implement the following specific methods in WPF to create various surface charts:

- *AddMesh* — Creates a mesh chart with or without hidden lines.
- *AddMeshZ* — Creates a mesh chart with a curtain (reference plane).
- *AddWaterfall* — Creates a chart similar to *MeshZ* but without lines from the Y data.
- *AddSurface* — Creates a surface chart with or without a colormap.

Implementation

The simplest way to store surface data is in a 2D array. For each point (X, Y) in the region defined for the surface, the (X, Y) entry in the array gives the Z coordinate of the corresponding point on the surface.

DataSeries Class

To make managing the surface easier, we can create a data structure specifically for surface charts in the *DataSeries* class. This class should contain variables to describe the data it holds, including the minimum X and Y data values, the spacing between the rows of data in the X and Y directions, and the number of data points in the X and Y directions. Add a new class to the current project and name it *DataSeriesSurface*. The following is the code listing for this class:

```
using System;
using System.Collections.Generic;
using System.Windows;
using System.Windows.Media;
using System.Windows.Media.Media3D;
using System.Windows.Shapes;

namespace Chart3DNoWPFEngine
{
    public class DataSeriesSurface : DataSeriesLine3D
    {
        private double xLimitMin = -5;
        private double yLimitMin = 5;
        private double zLimitMin = -5;
```

```csharp
private double xSpacing = 1;
private double ySpacing = 1;
private double zSpacing = 1;
private int xNumber = 10;
private int yNumber = 10;
private int zNumber = 10;

public Point3D[,] PointArray { get; set; }

public double XLimitMin
{
    get { return xLimitMin; }
    set { xLimitMin = value; }
}

public double YLimitMin
{
    get { return yLimitMin; }
    set { yLimitMin = value; }
}

public double ZLimitMin
{
    get { return zLimitMin; }
    set { zLimitMin = value; }
}

public double XSpacing
{
    get { return xSpacing; }
    set { xSpacing = value; }
}

public double YSpacing
{
    get { return ySpacing; }
    set { ySpacing = value; }
}

public double ZSpacing
{
    get { return zSpacing; }
    set { zSpacing = value; }
}

public int XNumber
{
    get { return xNumber; }
    set { xNumber = value; }
}

public int YNumber
{
```

```
        get { return yNumber; }
        set { yNumber = value; }
    }

    public int ZNumber
    {
        get { return zNumber; }
        set { zNumber = value; }
    }

    public double ZDataMin()
    {
        double zmin = 0;
        for (int i = 0; i < PointArray.GetLength(0); i++)
        {
            for (int j = 0; j < PointArray.GetLength(1); j++)
            {
                zmin = Math.Min(zmin, PointArray[i, j].Z);
            }
        }
        return zmin;
    }

    public double ZDataMax()
    {
        double zmax = 0;
        for (int i = 0; i < PointArray.GetLength(0); i++)
        {
            for (int j = 0; j < PointArray.GetLength(1); j++)
            {
                zmax = Math.Max(zmax, PointArray[i, j].Z);
            }
        }
        return zmax;
    }
    }
}
```

This class inherits from the *DataSeriesLine3D* class and sets the data range for the *X, Y,* and *Z* axes. It also contains a couple of public methods that compute the minimum and maximum of the data set.

Chart Functions

When we are testing our 3D surface charts, we'll use two 3D math functions, *Peak3D* and *Sinc3D*, and put them together into the *Utility* class:

```
public static void Peak3D(ChartStyle cs, DataSeriesSurface ds)
{
    cs.Xmin = -3;
    cs.Xmax = 3;
    cs.Ymin = -3;
    cs.Ymax = 3;
    cs.Zmin = -8;
```

```
        cs.Zmax = 8;
        cs.XTick = 1;
        cs.YTick = 1;
        cs.ZTick = 4;
        ds.XLimitMin = cs.Xmin;
        ds.YLimitMin = cs.Ymin;
        ds.XSpacing = 0.2;
        ds.YSpacing = 0.2;
        ds.XNumber = Convert.ToInt16((cs.Xmax - cs.Xmin) / ds.XSpacing) + 1;
        ds.YNumber = Convert.ToInt16((cs.Ymax - cs.Ymin) / ds.YSpacing) + 1;

        Point3D[,] pts = new Point3D[ds.XNumber, ds.YNumber];
        for (int i = 0; i < ds.XNumber; i++)
        {
            for (int j = 0; j < ds.YNumber; j++)
            {
                double x = ds.XLimitMin + i * ds.XSpacing;
                double y = ds.YLimitMin + j * ds.YSpacing;
                double z = 3 * Math.Pow((1 - x), 2) *
                    Math.Exp(-x * x - (y + 1) * (y + 1)) - 10 *
                    (0.2 * x - Math.Pow(x, 3) - Math.Pow(y, 5)) *
                    Math.Exp(-x * x - y * y) - 1 / 3 *
                    Math.Exp(-(x + 1) * (x + 1) - y * y);
                pts[i, j] = new Point3D(x, y, z);
            }
        }
        ds.PointArray = pts;
}

public static void Sinc3D(ChartStyle cs, DataSeriesSurface ds)
{
        cs.Xmin = -8;
        cs.Xmax = 8;
        cs.Ymin = -8;
        cs.Ymax = 8;
        cs.Zmin = -0.5f;
        cs.Zmax = 1;
        cs.XTick = 4;
        cs.YTick = 4;
        cs.ZTick = 0.5f;
        ds.XLimitMin = cs.Xmin;
        ds.YLimitMin = cs.Ymin;
        ds.XSpacing = 0.5;
        ds.YSpacing = 0.5;
        ds.XNumber = Convert.ToInt16((cs.Xmax - cs.Xmin) / ds.XSpacing) + 1;
        ds.YNumber = Convert.ToInt16((cs.Ymax - cs.Ymin) / ds.YSpacing) + 1;

        Point3D[,] pts = new Point3D[ds.XNumber, ds.YNumber];
        for (int i = 0; i < ds.XNumber; i++)
        {
            for (int j = 0; j < ds.YNumber; j++)
            {
                double x = ds.XLimitMin + i * ds.XSpacing;
```

609

```
            double y = ds.YLimitMin + j * ds.YSpacing;
            double r = Math.Sqrt(x * x + y * y) + 0.000001;
            double z = Math.Sin(r) / r;
            pts[i, j] = new Point3D(x, y, z);
        }
    }
    ds.PointArray = pts;
}
```

Both the *Peak3D* and *Sinc3D* methods generate data for testing mesh and surface charts.

DrawSurfaceChart Class

Now add to the current project the class *ColormapBrush* from the *ColorsAndBrushes* project in Chapter 4, and change its namespace to *Chart3DNoWPFEngine*. We'll need this class when we create surface charts and colorbars. Add another new class to the current project and name it *DrawSurfaceChart*. Here is the code listing for this class:

```
using System;
using System.Collections.Generic;
using System.Windows;
using System.Windows.Controls;
using System.Windows.Media;
using System.Windows.Media.Media3D;
using System.Windows.Shapes;

namespace Chart3DNoWPFEngine
{
    public class DrawSurfaceChart
    {
        private SurfaceChartTypeEnum surfaceChartType = SurfaceChartTypeEnum.Mesh;
        private bool isColormap = true;
        private bool isHiddenLine = false;
        private bool isInterp = false;
        private int numberInterp = 2;
        private ColormapBrush colormap = new ColormapBrush();

        public ColormapBrush Colormap
        {
            get { return colormap; }
            set { colormap = value; }
        }

        public SurfaceChartTypeEnum SurfaceChartType
        {
            get { return surfaceChartType; }
            set { surfaceChartType = value; }
        }

        public bool IsColormap
        {
            get { return isColormap; }
            set { isColormap = value; }
```

```
}

public bool IsHiddenLine
{
    get { return isHiddenLine; }
    set { isHiddenLine = value; }
}

public bool IsInterp
{
    get { return isInterp; }
    set { isInterp = value; }
}

public int NumberInterp
{
    get { return numberInterp; }
    set { numberInterp = value; }
}

public enum SurfaceChartTypeEnum
{
    Surface = 1,
    Mesh = 2,
    MeshZ = 3,
    Waterfall =4
}

public void AddSurfaceChart(ChartStyle cs, DataSeriesSurface ds)
{
    switch (SurfaceChartType)
    {
        case SurfaceChartTypeEnum.Mesh:
            AddMesh(cs, ds);
            //AddColorBar(cs, ds);
            break;
        case SurfaceChartTypeEnum.MeshZ:
            AddMeshZ(cs, ds);
            break;
        case SurfaceChartTypeEnum.Waterfall:
            AddWaterfall(cs, ds);
            break;
        case SurfaceChartTypeEnum.Surface:
            AddSurface(cs, ds);
            break;
    }
}

public void AddColorBar(ChartStyle cs, DataSeriesSurface ds,
                        double zmin, double zmax)
{
    TextBlock tb;
    tb = new TextBlock();
```

```
tb.Text = "A";
tb.FontFamily = cs.TickFont;
tb.FontSize = cs.TickFontSize;
tb.Measure(new Size(Double.PositiveInfinity, Double.PositiveInfinity));
Size tickSize = tb.DesiredSize;

double x = 6 * cs.ChartCanvas.Width / 7;
double y = cs.ChartCanvas.Height / 10;
double width = cs.ChartCanvas.Width / 25;
double height = 8 * cs.ChartCanvas.Height / 10;
Point3D[] pts = new Point3D[64];
double dz = (zmax - zmin) / 63;

// Create the color bar:
Polygon plg;
for (int i = 0; i < 64; i++)
{
    pts[i] = new Point3D(x, y, zmin + i * dz);
}
for (int i = 0; i < 63; i++)
{
    SolidColorBrush brush = GetBrush(pts[i].Z, zmin, zmax);
    double y1 = y + height - (pts[i].Z - zmin) * height / (zmax - zmin);
    double y2 = y + height -
        (pts[i + 1].Z - zmin) * height / (zmax - zmin);
    plg = new Polygon();
    plg.Points.Add(new Point(x, y2));
    plg.Points.Add(new Point(x + width, y2));
    plg.Points.Add(new Point(x + width, y1));
    plg.Points.Add(new Point(x, y1));
    plg.Fill = brush;
    plg.Stroke = brush;
    cs.ChartCanvas.Children.Add(plg);
}
Rectangle rect = new Rectangle();
rect.Width = width + 2;
rect.Height = height + 2;
rect.Stroke = Brushes.Black;
Canvas.SetLeft(rect, x - 1);
Canvas.SetTop(rect, y - 1);
cs.ChartCanvas.Children.Add(rect);

// Add ticks and labels to the color bar:
double tickLength = 0.15 * width;
for (double z = zmin; z <= zmax; z = z + (zmax - zmin) / 6)
{
    double yy = y + height - (z - zmin) * height / (zmax - zmin);
    AddTickLine(cs, new Point(x, yy), new Point(x + tickLength, yy));
    AddTickLine(cs, new Point(x + width, yy),
                new Point(x + width - tickLength, yy));
    tb = new TextBlock();
    tb.Text = (Math.Round(z, 2)).ToString();
    tb.FontFamily = cs.TickFont;
```

```
            tb.FontSize = cs.TickFontSize;
            cs.ChartCanvas.Children.Add(tb);
            Canvas.SetLeft(tb, x + width + 5);
            Canvas.SetTop(tb, yy - tickSize.Height / 2);
        }
    }

    private void AddTickLine(ChartStyle cs, Point pt1, Point pt2)
    {
        Line line = new Line();
        line.X1 = pt1.X;
        line.Y1 = pt1.Y;
        line.X2 = pt2.X;
        line.Y2 = pt2.Y;
        line.Stroke = Brushes.Black;
        cs.ChartCanvas.Children.Add(line);
    }

    private SolidColorBrush GetBrush(double z, double zmin, double zmax)
    {
        SolidColorBrush brush = new SolidColorBrush();
        Colormap.Ydivisions =
            (int)((zmax - zmin) / (Colormap.ColormapLength - 1));
        Colormap.Ymin = zmin;
        Colormap.Ymax = zmax;
        Colormap.Ydivisions = 64;
        int colorIndex = (int)((((Colormap.ColormapLength - 1) * (z - zmin) +
                          zmax - z) / (zmax - zmin)));
        if (colorIndex < 0)
            colorIndex = 0;
        if (colorIndex >= Colormap.ColormapLength)
            colorIndex = Colormap.ColormapLength - 1;
        brush = Colormap.ColormapBrushes()[colorIndex];
        return brush;
    }
    private void AddMesh(ChartStyle cs, DataSeriesSurface ds)
    {
     … …
    }
    private void AddMeshZ(ChartStyle cs, DataSeriesSurface ds)
    {
     … …
    }
    private void AddWaterfall(ChartStyle cs, DataSeriesSurface ds)
    {
     … …
    }
    private void AddSurface(ChartStyle cs, DataSeriesSurface ds)
    {
     … …
    }
    }
}
```

In this class, the field members and their corresponding public properties are used to control the appearance of various 3D charts. You can create a specific 3D chart by selecting the *SurfaceChartType* from the enumeration *SurfaceChartTypeEnum*. You can see that four different chart types are available to select from in this enumeration. You can add more chart types to this enumeration and create their corresponding 3D charts the same way we do here.

The *ColormapBrush* property is used to create the colormap for a specified 3D chart type. The colormap is associated with the *Z* value. The *AddColorBar* method creates a colorbar on the right side of a 3D chart. This colorbar, much like the legend in a 2D chart, indicates the data values for different colors in the colormap.

In the following few sections, I'll present the detailed procedures for creating various 3D charts.

Mesh Charts

To create mesh charts, we'll add an *AddMesh* method to the *DrawSurfaceChart* class. The following is the code listing for this method:

```
private void AddMesh(ChartStyle cs, DataSeriesSurface ds)
{
    Matrix3D m = Utility.AzimuthElevation(cs.Elevation, cs.Azimuth);
    Polygon plg = new Polygon();
    Point3D[,] pts = ds.PointArray;
    double[,] zValues = new double[pts.GetLength(0), pts.GetLength(1)];
    double zmin = ds.ZDataMin();
    double zmax = ds.ZDataMax();

    for (int i = 0; i < pts.GetLength(0); i++)
    {
        for (int j = 0; j < pts.GetLength(1); j++)
        {
            zValues[i, j] = pts[i, j].Z;
            pts[i, j] = cs.Normalize3D(m, pts[i, j]);
        }
    }

    // Draw mesh chart:
    for (int i = 0; i < pts.GetLength(0) - 1; i++)
    {
        int ii = i;
        if (cs.Elevation >= 0)
        {
            ii = i;
            if (cs.Azimuth >= -180 && cs.Azimuth < 0)
                ii = pts.GetLength(0) - 2 - i;
        }
        else
        {
            ii = pts.GetLength(0) - 2 - i;
            if (cs.Azimuth >= -180 && cs.Azimuth < 0)
                ii = i;
        }
        for (int j = 0; j < pts.GetLength(1) - 1; j++)
        {
            int jj = j;
```

```
            if (cs.Elevation < 0)
                jj = pts.GetLength(1) - 2 - j;
            plg = new Polygon();
            plg.Points.Add(new Point(pts[ii, jj].X, pts[ii, jj].Y));
            plg.Points.Add(new Point(pts[ii, jj + 1].X, pts[ii, jj + 1].Y));
            plg.Points.Add(new Point(pts[ii + 1, jj + 1].X, pts[ii + 1, jj + 1].Y));
            plg.Points.Add(new Point(pts[ii + 1, jj].X, pts[ii + 1, jj].Y));
            plg.Stroke = Brushes.Black;
            plg.StrokeThickness = ds.LineThickness;
            plg.Fill = Brushes.White;
            if (IsHiddenLine)
                plg.Fill = Brushes.Transparent;
            if (IsColormap)
                plg.Stroke = GetBrush(zValues[ii, jj], zmin, zmax);
            cs.ChartCanvas.Children.Add(plg);
        }
    }
    if (cs.IsColorBar && IsColormap)
        AddColorBar(cs, ds, zmin, zmax);
}
```

You can select the *Mesh* chart type using the following code snippet:

```
DrawSurfaceChart dsc = new DrawSurfaceChart();
dsc.ChartType = DrawChart.ChartTypeEnum.Mesh;
```

This way, you can create a 3D mesh chart with or without hidden lines. You can also produce a mesh chart with a single color or with a complete scaled colormap. We use the *Z*-order algorithm to remove hidden lines in a mesh plot. The *Z*-order algorithm draws polygons from back to front. A polygon drawn in this order can obscure only the polygon drawn before it. Filling the polygon with a white color (or the background color of the plot area) covers up any lines that should be obscured. Notice that when the elevation and azimuth angles change, we change the order of drawing the polygons, ensuring that the program always draws the polygons from back to front.

Here, I'll show you how to create a mesh chart in a WPF application. Add a new WPF window and name it *SurfaceChart*. Here is the XAML file for this example:

```
<Window x:Class="Chart3DNoWPFEngine.SurfaceChart"
    xmlns="http://schemas.microsoft.com/winfx/2006/xaml/presentation"
    xmlns:x="http://schemas.microsoft.com/winfx/2006/xaml"
    Title="Surface Chart" Height="400" Width="500">
    <Grid>
        <Grid.ColumnDefinitions>
            <ColumnDefinition Width="*"/>
            <ColumnDefinition Width="auto"/>
        </Grid.ColumnDefinitions>
        <Grid x:Name="chartGrid" SizeChanged="chartGrid_SizeChanged"
            Margin="10 10 0 10" Grid.Row="0" Grid.Column="0">
            <Canvas x:Name="chartCanvas" Background="Transparent"
                ClipToBounds="True"/>
        </Grid>
        <Grid x:Name="colorbarGrid" Margin="0 10 10 10"
            Grid.Row="0" Grid.Column="1">
        </Grid>
    </Grid>
</Window>
```

This XAML file creates a resizable chart canvas, on which we'll draw the mesh chart.

Here is the corresponding code-behind file for this example:

```
using System;
using System.Collections.Generic;
using System.Windows;
using System.Windows.Controls;
using System.Windows.Media;
using System.Windows.Media.Media3D;
using System.Windows.Shapes;

namespace Chart3DNoWPFEngine
{
    public partial class SurfaceChart : Window
    {
        private ChartStyle cs;
        private DataSeriesSurface ds;
        private DrawSurfaceChart dsc;

        public SurfaceChart()
        {
            InitializeComponent();
        }


        private void chartGrid_SizeChanged(object sender, SizeChangedEventArgs e)
        {
            chartCanvas.Width = chartGrid.ActualWidth;
            chartCanvas.Height = chartGrid.ActualHeight;
            AddChart();
        }

        private void AddChart()
        {
            chartCanvas.Children.Clear();
            cs = new ChartStyle();
            cs.ChartCanvas = this.chartCanvas;
            cs.GridlinePattern = ChartStyle.GridlinePatternEnum.Solid;
            cs.Elevation = 30;
            cs.Azimuth = -37;
            cs.Title = "No Title";
            cs.AddChartStyle();

            ds = new DataSeriesSurface();
            ds.LineColor = Brushes.Black;
            Utility.Peak3D(cs, ds);
            dsc = new DrawSurfaceChart();
            dsc.SurfaceChartType = DrawSurfaceChart.SurfaceChartTypeEnum.Mesh;
            dsc.IsColormap = false;
            dsc.IsHiddenLine = true;
            dsc.AddSurfaceChart(cs, ds);
        }
    }
}
```

By building and running this project, you'll create a mesh chart with hidden lines, as shown in Figure 15-6.

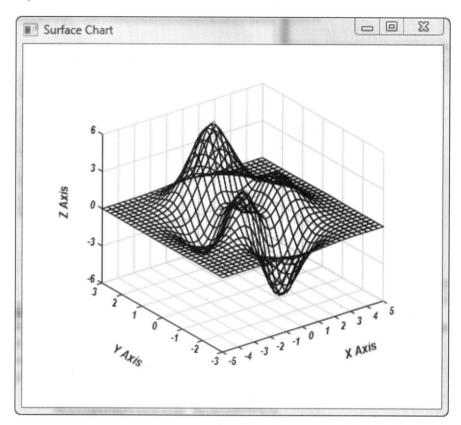

Figure 15-6. *Mesh chart with hidden lines*

You can just as easily create a mesh chart without hidden lines by changing one line of code:

```
dsc.IsHiddenLine = false;
```

The bool parameter *IsHiddenLine* is set to false, meaning that you do not want to show the hidden lines in your mesh plot. This produces the results of Figure 15-7.

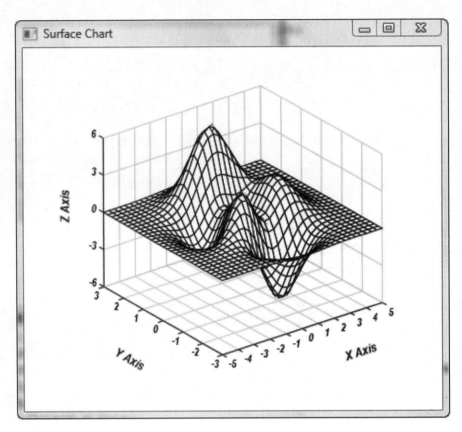

Figure 15-7. Mesh chart without hidden lines

You can also create a colormapped mesh chart with a colorbar using the following code snippet:

```
cs.IsColorBar = true;
dsc.IsColormap = true;
```

This tells the program to draw the mesh plot using a colormapped brush and to add a colorbar to the chart. The result is shown in Figure 15-8.

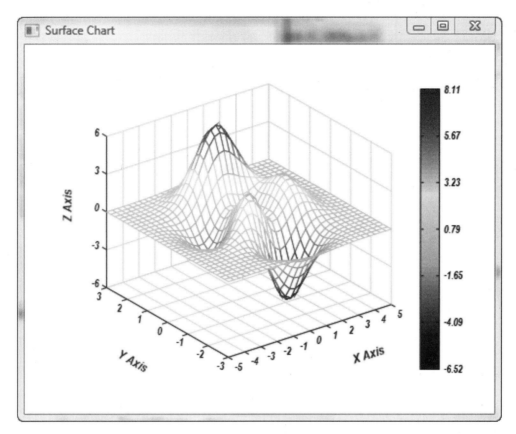

Figure 15-8. *Mesh chart with a colormap and a colorbar*

Curtain Charts

The chart type *MeshZ* creates a curtain plot from a reference plane around the mesh chart. The curtain is drawn by dropping lines down from the edge of the surface to the plane parallel to the *X-Y* plane, at a height equal to the lowest point on the surface.

We can create a curtain chart using the following *AddMeshZ* method in the *DrawSurfaceChart* class:

```
private void AddMeshZ(ChartStyle cs, DataSeriesSurface ds)
{
    Matrix3D m = Utility.AzimuthElevation(cs.Elevation, cs.Azimuth);
    Polygon plg = new Polygon();
    Point3D[,] pts = ds.PointArray;
    Point3D[,] pts1 = new Point3D[pts.GetLength(0), pts.GetLength(1)];
    double[,] zValues = new double[pts.GetLength(0), pts.GetLength(1)];
    double zmin = ds.ZDataMin();
    double zmax = ds.ZDataMax();

    for (int i = 0; i < pts.GetLength(0); i++)
```

```
    {
        for (int j = 0; j < pts.GetLength(1); j++)
        {
            zValues[i, j] = pts[i, j].Z;
            pts1[i, j] = new Point3D(pts[i, j].X, pts[i, j].Y, pts[i, j].Z);
            pts[i, j] = cs.Normalize3D(m, pts[i, j]);
        }
    }

    // Draw mesh using the z-order method:
    for (int i = 0; i < pts.GetLength(0) - 1; i++)
    {
        int ii = i;
        if (cs.Elevation >= 0)
        {
            ii = i;
            if (cs.Azimuth >= -180 && cs.Azimuth < 0)
                ii = pts.GetLength(0) - 2 - i;
        }
        else
        {
            ii = pts.GetLength(0) - 2 - i;
            if (cs.Azimuth >= -180 && cs.Azimuth < 0)
                ii = i;
        }
        for (int j = 0; j < pts.GetLength(1) - 1; j++)
        {
            int jj = j;
            if (cs.Elevation < 0)
                jj = pts.GetLength(1) - 2 - j;
            plg = new Polygon();
            plg.Points.Add(new Point(pts[ii, jj].X, pts[ii, jj].Y));
            plg.Points.Add(new Point(pts[ii, jj + 1].X, pts[ii, jj + 1].Y));
            plg.Points.Add(new Point(pts[ii + 1, jj + 1].X, pts[ii + 1, jj + 1].Y));
            plg.Points.Add(new Point(pts[ii + 1, jj].X, pts[ii + 1, jj].Y));
            plg.Stroke = Brushes.Black;
            plg.StrokeThickness = ds.LineThickness;
            plg.Fill = Brushes.White;
            if (!IsHiddenLine)
                plg.Fill = Brushes.Transparent;
            if (IsColormap)
                plg.Stroke = GetBrush(zValues[ii, jj], zmin, zmax);
            cs.ChartCanvas.Children.Add(plg);
        }
    }

    //Draw curtain lines:
    Point3D[] pta = new Point3D[4];
    for (int i = 0; i < pts1.GetLength(0); i++)
    {
        int jj = pts1.GetLength(0) - 1;
        if (cs.Elevation >= 0)
        {
```

```
        if (cs.Azimuth >= -90 && cs.Azimuth <= 90)
            jj = 0;
    }
    else if (cs.Elevation < 0)
    {
        jj = 0;
        if (cs.Azimuth >= -90 && cs.Azimuth <= 90)
            jj = pts1.GetLength(0) - 1;
    }
    if (i < pts1.GetLength(0) - 1)
    {
        pta[0] = new Point3D(pts1[i, jj].X, pts1[i, jj].Y, pts1[i, jj].Z);
        pta[1] = new Point3D(pts1[i + 1, jj].X,
                    pts1[i + 1, jj].Y, pts1[i + 1, jj].Z);
        pta[2] = new Point3D(pts1[i + 1, jj].X, pts1[i + 1, jj].Y, cs.Zmin);
        pta[3] = new Point3D(pts1[i, jj].X, pts1[i, jj].Y, cs.Zmin);
        for (int k = 0; k < 4; k++)
            pta[k] = cs.Normalize3D(m, pta[k]);
        plg = new Polygon();
        plg.Stroke = Brushes.Black;
        plg.StrokeThickness = ds.LineThickness;
        plg.Fill = Brushes.White;
        plg.Points.Add(new Point(pta[0].X, pta[0].Y));
        plg.Points.Add(new Point(pta[1].X, pta[1].Y));
        plg.Points.Add(new Point(pta[2].X, pta[2].Y));
        plg.Points.Add(new Point(pta[3].X, pta[3].Y));
        if (!IsHiddenLine)
            plg.Fill = Brushes.Transparent;
        if (IsColormap)
            plg.Stroke = GetBrush(pts1[i,jj].Z, zmin, zmax);
        cs.ChartCanvas.Children.Add(plg);
    }
}

for (int j = 0; j < pts1.GetLength(1); j++)
{
    int ii = 0;
    if (cs.Elevation >= 0)
    {
        if (cs.Azimuth >= 0 && cs.Azimuth <= 180)
            ii = pts1.GetLength(1) - 1;
    }
    else if (cs.Elevation < 0)
    {
        if (cs.Azimuth >= -180 && cs.Azimuth <= 0)
            ii = pts1.GetLength(1) - 1;
    }
    if (j < pts1.GetLength(1) - 1)
    {
        pta[0] = new Point3D(pts1[ii, j].X, pts1[ii, j].Y, pts1[ii, j].Z);
        pta[1] = new Point3D(pts1[ii, j + 1].X,
                    pts1[ii, j + 1].Y, pts1[ii, j + 1].Z);
        pta[2] = new Point3D(pts1[ii, j + 1].X, pts1[ii, j + 1].Y, cs.Zmin);
```

621

```
            pta[3] = new Point3D(pts1[ii, j].X, pts1[ii, j].Y, cs.Zmin);
            for (int k = 0; k < 4; k++)
                pta[k] = cs.Normalize3D(m, pta[k]);
            plg = new Polygon();
            plg.Stroke = Brushes.Black;
            plg.StrokeThickness = ds.LineThickness;
            plg.Fill = Brushes.White;
            plg.Points.Add(new Point(pta[0].X, pta[0].Y));
            plg.Points.Add(new Point(pta[1].X, pta[1].Y));
            plg.Points.Add(new Point(pta[2].X, pta[2].Y));
            plg.Points.Add(new Point(pta[3].X, pta[3].Y));
            if (IsHiddenLine)
                plg.Fill = Brushes.Transparent;
            if (IsColormap)
                plg.Stroke = GetBrush(pts1[ii, j].Z, zmin, zmax);
            cs.ChartCanvas.Children.Add(plg);
        }
    }
    if (cs.IsColorBar && IsColormap)
        AddColorBar(cs, ds, zmin, zmax);
}
```

In this method, we first create a mesh plot, and then we add the curtain to it. The curtain lines must be drawn on the appropriate surface when the elevation and azimuth angles are changed.

We can test the curtain chart using the same code we used to test mesh charts, except for a change in the following line:

```
dsc.SurfaceChartType = DrawSurfaceChart.SurfaceChartTypeEnum.MeshZ;
```

You can also change the chart function to *Sinc3D* and the colormap matrix to *Cool*:

```
Utility.Sinc3D(cs, ds);
dsc.IsColormap = true;
dsc.IsHiddenLine = false;
dsc.Colormap.ColormapBrushType = ColormapBrush.ColormapBrushEnum.Cool;
```

This produces the output of Figure 15-9.

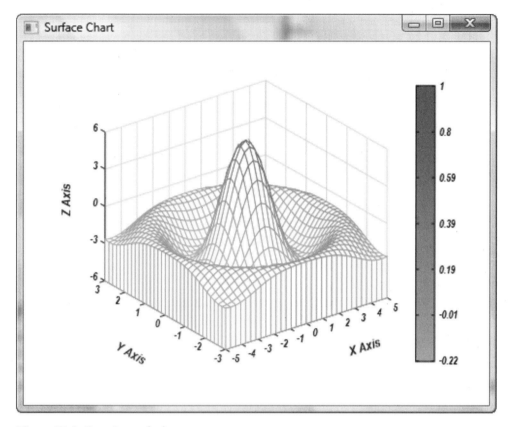

Figure 15-9. *Curtain mesh chart*

Waterfall Charts

A waterfall chart draws a mesh plot similar to a curtain chart, but it does not generate vertical lines from the *X* component of the data. This produces a "waterfall" effect.

You can create a waterfall chart using the following *AddWaterfall* method in the *DrawSurfaceChart* class:

```
private void AddWaterfall(ChartStyle cs, DataSeriesSurface ds)
{
    Matrix3D m = Utility.AzimuthElevation(cs.Elevation, cs.Azimuth);
    Polygon plg = new Polygon();
    Point3D[,] pts = ds.PointArray;
    Point3D[] pt3 = new Point3D[pts.GetLength(0) + 2];
    double[] zValues = new double[pts.Length];
    Point[] pta = new Point[pts.GetLength(0) + 2];
    double zmin = ds.ZDataMin();
    double zmax = ds.ZDataMax();
```

```
    for (int j = 0; j < pts.GetLength(1); j++)
    {
        int jj = j;
        if (cs.Elevation >= 0)
        {
            if (cs.Azimuth >= -90 && cs.Azimuth < 90)
                jj = pts.GetLength(1) - 1 - j;
        }
        else if (cs.Elevation < 0)
        {
            jj = pts.GetLength(1) - 1 - j;
            if (cs.Azimuth >= -90 && cs.Azimuth < 90)
                jj = j;
        }
        for (int i = 0; i < pts.GetLength(0); i++)
        {
            pt3[i + 1] = pts[i, jj];
            if (i == 0)
                pt3[0] = new Point3D(pt3[i + 1].X, pt3[i + 1].Y, cs.Zmin);
            if (i == pts.GetLength(0) - 1)
            {
                pt3[pts.GetLength(0) + 1] =
                    new Point3D(pt3[i + 1].X, pt3[i + 1].Y, cs.Zmin);
            }
        }
        plg = new Polygon();
        for (int i = 0; i < pt3.Length; i++)
        {
            zValues[i] = pt3[i].Z;
            pt3[i] = cs.Normalize3D(m, pt3[i]);
            pta[i] = new Point(pt3[i].X, pt3[i].Y);
            plg.Points.Add(new Point(pt3[i].X, pt3[i].Y));
        }
        plg.Stroke = Brushes.Transparent;
        plg.StrokeThickness = ds.LineThickness;
        plg.Fill = Brushes.White;
        cs.ChartCanvas.Children.Add(plg);
        for (int i = 1; i < pt3.Length; i++)
        {
            Line line = new Line();
            line.Stroke = Brushes.Black;
            line.StrokeThickness = ds.LineThickness;
            if (IsColormap)
            {
                if (i < pt3.Length - 1)
                    line.Stroke = GetBrush(zValues[i], zmin, zmax);
                else
                    line.Stroke = GetBrush(zValues[i - 1], zmin, zmax);
            }
            line.X1 = pta[i - 1].X;
            line.Y1 = pta[i - 1].Y;
            line.X2 = pta[i].X;
            line.Y2 = pta[i].Y;
```

```
            cs.ChartCanvas.Children.Add(line);
        }
    }
    if (cs.IsColorBar && IsColormap)
        AddColorBar(cs, ds, zmin, zmax);
}
```

In this method, we first create the mesh plot, and then we add the vertical lines from the *Y* component of the data, producing the waterfall effect. The vertical lines must be drawn on the appropriate surface when the elevation and azimuth angles change.

We can test the waterfall chart using the same code we used to test curtain charts, except for a change in the following line:

```
dsc.SurfaceChartType = DrawSurfaceChart.SurfaceChartTypeEnum.Waterfall;
```

This generates the output of Figure 15-10.

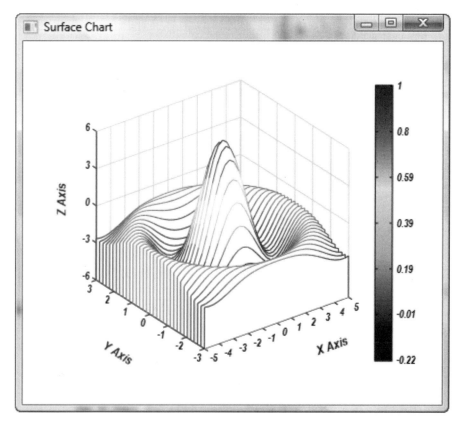

Figure 15-10. *Waterfall chart*

Surface Charts

Surface charts are similar to mesh charts, in that both display data as a shaded surface. The difference between surface and mesh charts is that a surface chart creates colored quadrilaterals and black mesh lines, whereas a mesh plot creates only mesh lines, which can be black or colored.

We can create a surface chart using the following *AddSurface* method in the *DrawSurfaceChart* class:

```
private void AddSurface(ChartStyle cs, DataSeriesSurface ds)
{
    Matrix3D m = Utility.AzimuthElevation(cs.Elevation, cs.Azimuth);
    Polygon plg = new Polygon();
    Point3D[,] pts = ds.PointArray;
    Point3D[,] pts1 = new Point3D[pts.GetLength(0), pts.GetLength(1)];
    double zmin = ds.ZDataMin();
    double zmax = ds.ZDataMax();

    for (int i = 0; i < pts.GetLength(0); i++)
    {
        for (int j = 0; j < pts.GetLength(1); j++)
        {
            pts1[i, j] = pts[i, j];
            pts[i, j] = cs.Normalize3D(m, pts[i, j]);
        }
    }

    // Draw surface chart:
    if (!IsInterp)
    {
        for (int i = 0; i < pts.GetLength(0) - 1; i++)
        {
            int ii = i;
            if (cs.Elevation >= 0)
            {
                ii = i;
                if (cs.Azimuth >= -180 && cs.Azimuth < 0)
                    ii = pts.GetLength(0) - 2 - i;
            }
            else
            {
                ii = pts.GetLength(0) - 2 - i;
                if (cs.Azimuth >= -180 && cs.Azimuth < 0)
                    ii = i;
            }
            for (int j = 0; j < pts.GetLength(1) - 1; j++)
            {
                int jj = j;
                if (cs.Elevation < 0)
                    jj = pts.GetLength(1) - 2 - j;
                plg = new Polygon();
                plg.Points.Add(new Point(pts[ii, jj].X, pts[ii, jj].Y));
                plg.Points.Add(new Point(pts[ii, jj + 1].X, pts[ii, jj + 1].Y));
                plg.Points.Add(new Point(pts[ii + 1, jj + 1].X,
```

```
                                    pts[ii + 1, jj + 1].Y));
                    plg.Points.Add(new Point(pts[ii + 1, jj].X, pts[ii + 1, jj].Y));
                    plg.StrokeThickness = ds.LineThickness;
                    plg.Stroke = ds.LineColor;
                    plg.Fill = GetBrush(pts1[ii,jj].Z, zmin, zmax);
                    cs.ChartCanvas.Children.Add(plg);
                }
            }
            if (cs.IsColorBar && IsColormap)
                AddColorBar(cs, ds, zmin, zmax);
        }
        else if (IsInterp)
        {
            for (int i = 0; i < pts.GetLength(0) - 1; i++)
            {
                int ii = i;
                if (cs.Elevation >= 0)
                {
                    ii = i;
                    if (cs.Azimuth >= -180 && cs.Azimuth < 0)
                        ii = pts.GetLength(0) - 2 - i;
                }
                else
                {
                    ii = pts.GetLength(0) - 2 - i;
                    if (cs.Azimuth >= -180 && cs.Azimuth < 0)
                        ii = i;
                }
                for (int j = 0; j < pts.GetLength(1) - 1; j++)
                {
                    int jj = j;
                    if (cs.Elevation < 0)
                        jj = pts.GetLength(1) - 2 - j;
                    Point3D[] points = new Point3D[4];
                    points[0] = pts1[ii, j];
                    points[1] = pts1[ii, j + 1];
                    points[2] = pts1[ii + 1, j + 1];
                    points[3] = pts1[ii + 1, j];
                    Interp(cs, m, points, zmin, zmax);
                    plg = new Polygon();
                    plg.Stroke = ds.LineColor;
                    plg.Points.Add(new Point(pts[ii, j].X, pts[ii, j].Y));
                    plg.Points.Add(new Point(pts[ii, j+1].X, pts[ii, j+1].Y));
                    plg.Points.Add(new Point(pts[ii+1, j+1].X, pts[ii+1, j+1].Y));
                    plg.Points.Add(new Point(pts[ii+1, j].X, pts[ii+1, j].Y));
                }
            }
        }
        if (cs.IsColorBar && IsColormap)
            AddColorBar(cs, ds, zmin, zmax);
    }
```

In this method, we draw surface charts using two different approaches: One is similar to the approach used to create mesh charts; the other applies interpolated shading to the surface plot by calling the following *Interp* method:

```
private void Interp(ChartStyle cs, Matrix3D m, Point3D[] pta,
                    double zmin, double zmax)
{
    Polygon plg = new Polygon();
    Point[] points = new Point[4];
    int npoints = NumberInterp;
    Point3D[,] pts = new Point3D[npoints + 1, npoints + 1];
    Point3D[,] pts1 = new Point3D[npoints + 1, npoints + 1];
    double x0 = pta[0].X;
    double y0 = pta[0].Y;
    double x1 = pta[2].X;
    double y1 = pta[2].Y;
    double dx = (x1 - x0) / npoints;
    double dy = (y1 - y0) / npoints;
    double c00 = pta[0].Z;
    double c10 = pta[3].Z;
    double c11 = pta[2].Z;
    double c01 = pta[1].Z;
    double x, y, c;

    for (int i = 0; i <= npoints; i++)
    {
        x = x0 + i * dx;
        for (int j = 0; j <= npoints; j++)
        {
            y = y0 + j * dy;
            c = (y1 - y) * ((x1 - x) * c00 +
                (x - x0) * c10) / (x1 - x0) / (y1 - y0) +
                (y - y0) * ((x1 - x) * c01 +
                (x - x0) * c11) / (x1 - x0) / (y1 - y0);
            pts[i, j] = new Point3D(x, y, c);
            pts1[i, j] = new Point3D(x, y, c);
            pts[i, j] = cs.Normalize3D(m, pts[i, j]);
        }
    }
    for (int i = 0; i < npoints; i++)
    {
        for (int j = 0; j < npoints; j++)
        {
            plg = new Polygon();
            Brush brush = GetBrush(pts1[i, j].Z, zmin, zmax);
            plg.Fill = brush;
            plg.StrokeThickness = 0.1;
            plg.Stroke = brush;
            plg.Points.Add(new Point(pts[i, j].X, pts[i, j].Y));
            plg.Points.Add(new Point(pts[i + 1, j].X, pts[i + 1, j].Y));
            plg.Points.Add(new Point(pts[i + 1, j + 1].X, pts[i + 1, j + 1].Y));
            plg.Points.Add(new Point(pts[i, j + 1].X, pts[i, j + 1].Y));
            cs.ChartCanvas.Children.Add(plg);
```

```
            }
        }
}
```

This interpolation method forces the color within each polygon of a surface chart to vary bilinearly, producing the effect of smooth color variation across the surface. You can control the fineness of the interpolated surface by changing the *NumberInterp* property.

We can test the surface chart using the same code we used to test mesh charts, except for a change in the following line:

```
dsc.SurfaceChartType = DrawSurfaceChart.SurfaceChartTypeEnum.Surface;
```

You can also change the chart function to *Peak3D* and the colormap matrix to *Jet*:

```
Utility.Peak3D(cs, ds);
dsc.Colormap.ColormapBrushType = ColormapBrush.ColormapBrushEnum.Jet;
```

This produces the output of Figure 15-11.

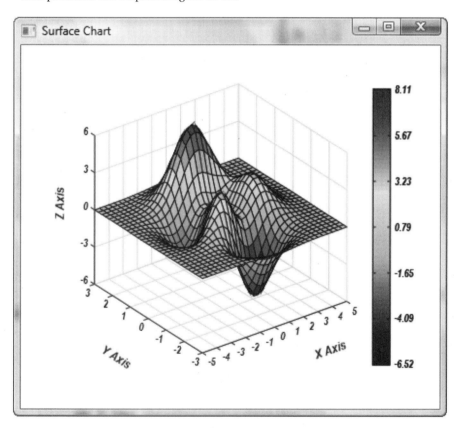

Figure 15-11. A standard surface chart

You can also create a shaded surface chart without mesh lines by adding the following line of code:

```
ds.LineColor = Brushes.Transparent;
```

This produces the results shown in Figure 15-12, in which the mesh lines are no longer visible.

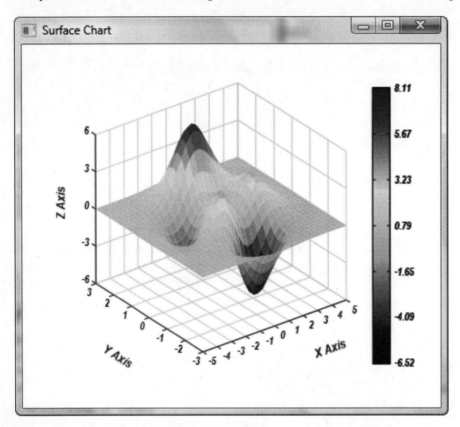

Figure 15-12. A surface chart without mesh lines

As you can see from Figure 15-12, the colormap is still coarse, and a single color is clearly visible for each polygon on the surface. You can obtain a surface chart with a much better colormap by applying interpolated shading using the following code snippet:

```
dsc.IsInterp = true;
dsc.NumberInterp = 3;
```

This creates the surface chart shown in Figure 15-13, which has a much smoother color across its whole surface.

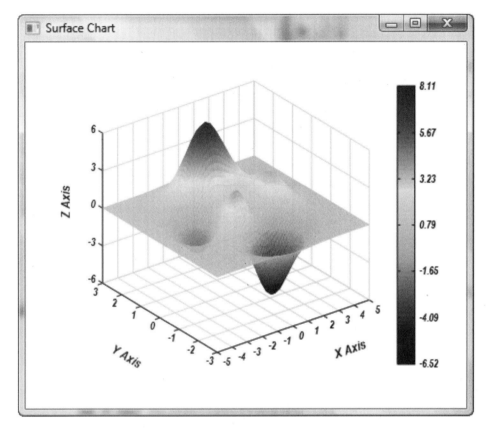

Figure 15-13. *A surface chart with interpolated shading*

CHAPTER 16

Specialized 3D Charts

In the previous chapter, I showed you how to create simple 3D surface charts without using the WPF 3D engine. This approach allows you to create professional 3D chart applications in WPF that include more advanced features, including colormaps and colorbars. In this chapter, I'll show you how to create a variety of specialized 3D charts, such as contour charts and 3D bar charts, among others, using the same framework discussed in Chapter 15. Based on these example projects, with or without modifications, you can easily create your own professional and sophisticated 3D charts in your WPF applications.

Implementation

Since all of the different specialized 3D charts share a similar framework, instead of creating a separate program for each type of 3D chart, here we'll implement a unified program, which integrates several types of specialized 3D charts. With this program as a basis, you can easily create your own professional 3D chart applications.

2D Chart Style

Some 3D specialized charts are actually projections of 3D charts on a 2D X-Y plane. For example, a contour chart helps visualize 3D surfaces on a 2D screen. In this case, data values are plotted as a function of mesh grid points in the X-Y plane. Thus, these projected specialized 3D charts require a 2D-like chart style, similar to that used to create 2D charts in Chapters 5 and 6. However, this 2D-like chart style must also inherit some 3D features from the original 3D chart style used in the previous chapter, because the X and Y coordinates must be the projected coordinates in 3D space. Here, for your reference, I'll list the source code of this 2D-like chart style.

Start with a new WPF Windows application and name it *Specialized3DChart*. Add to the current project the classes *DataSeriesLine3D*, *DataSeriesSurface*, *ChartStyle*, *ColormapBrush*, *DrawSurfaceChart*, and *Utility* as well as the WPF project *SurfaceChart* from the *Chart3DNoWPFEngine* project in Chapter 15, and change their corresponding namespace to *Specialized3DChart*. Add a new class to the current project and name it *ChartStyle2D*. This class is inherited from the original 3D *ChartStyle* class:

```
using System;
using System.Windows.Controls;
using System.Windows;
using System.Windows.Media;
using System.Windows.Media.Media3D;
using System.Windows.Shapes;
```

```
namespace Specialized3DChart
{
    public class ChartStyle2D : ChartStyle
    {
        private double leftOffset = 20;
        private double bottomOffset = 40;
        private double rightOffset = 10;
        private Canvas chart2dCanvas = new Canvas();
        Border chart2dBorder;
        double colorbarWidth;
        Line gridline = new Line();

        public Canvas Chart2dCanvas
        {
            get { return chart2dCanvas; }
        }

        public ChartStyle2D()
        {
            chart2dBorder = new Border();
            chart2dBorder.BorderBrush = Brushes.Black;
            chart2dBorder.BorderThickness = new Thickness(1);
            chart2dBorder.Child = chart2dCanvas;
        }

        public void AddChartStyle2D(DrawSurfaceChart dsc)
        {
            colorbarWidth = ChartCanvas.Width / 7;
            ChartCanvas.Children.Clear();
            ChartCanvas.Children.Add(chart2dBorder);
            Point pt = new Point();
            Line tick = new Line();
            double offset = 0;
            double dx, dy;
            TextBlock tb = new TextBlock();

            //  determine right offset:
            tb.Text = Xmax.ToString();
            tb.Measure(new Size(Double.PositiveInfinity, Double.PositiveInfinity));
            Size size = tb.DesiredSize;
            rightOffset = size.Width / 2 + 2;

            // Determine left offset:
            for (dy = Ymin; dy <= Ymax; dy += YTick)
            {
                pt = NormalizePoint(new Point(Xmin, dy));
                tb = new TextBlock();
                tb.Text = dy.ToString();
                tb.TextAlignment = TextAlignment.Right;
                tb.Measure(new Size(Double.PositiveInfinity,
                                    Double.PositiveInfinity));
                size = tb.DesiredSize;
                if (offset < size.Width)
```

```
            offset = size.Width;
    }
    leftOffset = offset + 5 + 30;

    Canvas.SetLeft(chart2dBorder, leftOffset);
    Canvas.SetBottom(chart2dBorder, bottomOffset);
    if (!IsColorBar)
        colorbarWidth = 0;
    chart2dCanvas.Width =
        ChartCanvas.Width - leftOffset - rightOffset - colorbarWidth;
    chart2dCanvas.Height =
        ChartCanvas.Height - bottomOffset - size.Height / 2;

    // Create vertical gridlines:
    if (IsYGrid == true)
    {
        for (dx = Xmin + XTick; dx < Xmax; dx += XTick)
        {
            gridline = new Line();
            gridline.Stroke = GridlineColor;
            gridline.StrokeThickness = GridlineThickness;
            gridline.X1 = NormalizePoint(new Point(dx, Ymin)).X;
            gridline.Y1 = NormalizePoint(new Point(dx, Ymin)).Y;
            gridline.X2 = NormalizePoint(new Point(dx, Ymax)).X;
            gridline.Y2 = NormalizePoint(new Point(dx, Ymax)).Y;
            chart2dCanvas.Children.Add(gridline);
        }
    }

    // Create horizontal gridlines:
    if (IsXGrid == true)
    {
        for (dy = Ymin + YTick; dy < Ymax; dy += YTick)
        {
            gridline = new Line();
            gridline.Stroke = GridlineColor;
            gridline.StrokeThickness = GridlineThickness;
            gridline.X1 = NormalizePoint(new Point(Xmin, dy)).X;
            gridline.Y1 = NormalizePoint(new Point(Xmin, dy)).Y;
            gridline.X2 = NormalizePoint(new Point(Xmax, dy)).X;
            gridline.Y2 = NormalizePoint(new Point(Xmax, dy)).Y;
            chart2dCanvas.Children.Add(gridline);
        }
    }

    // Create x-axis tick marks:
    for (dx = Xmin; dx <= Xmax; dx += XTick)
    {
        pt = NormalizePoint(new Point(dx, Ymin));
        tick = new Line();
        tick.Stroke = Brushes.Black;
        tick.X1 = pt.X;
        tick.Y1 = pt.Y;
```

```
        tick.X2 = pt.X;
        tick.Y2 = pt.Y - 5;
        chart2dCanvas.Children.Add(tick);
        tb = new TextBlock();
        tb.Text = dx.ToString();
        tb.Measure(new Size(Double.PositiveInfinity,
                            Double.PositiveInfinity));
        size = tb.DesiredSize;
        ChartCanvas.Children.Add(tb);
        Canvas.SetLeft(tb, leftOffset + pt.X - size.Width / 2);
        Canvas.SetTop(tb, pt.Y + 2 + size.Height / 2);
    }

    // Create y-axis tick marks:
    for (dy = Ymin; dy <= Ymax; dy += YTick)
    {
        pt = NormalizePoint(new Point(Xmin, dy));
        tick = new Line();
        tick.Stroke = Brushes.Black;
        tick.X1 = pt.X;
        tick.Y1 = pt.Y;
        tick.X2 = pt.X + 5;
        tick.Y2 = pt.Y;
        chart2dCanvas.Children.Add(tick);

        tb = new TextBlock();
        tb.Text = dy.ToString();
        tb.Measure(new Size(Double.PositiveInfinity,
                            Double.PositiveInfinity));
        size = tb.DesiredSize;
        ChartCanvas.Children.Add(tb);
        Canvas.SetRight(tb, chart2dCanvas.Width + 10 + colorbarWidth);
        Canvas.SetTop(tb, pt.Y);
    }

    tb = new TextBlock();
    tb.Text = XLabel;
    tb.FontFamily = LabelFont;
    tb.FontSize = LabelFontSize;
    tb.Foreground = LabelColor;
    tb.Measure(new Size(Double.PositiveInfinity, Double.PositiveInfinity));
    size = tb.DesiredSize;
    ChartCanvas.Children.Add(tb);
    Canvas.SetBottom(tb, bottomOffset / 10);
    Canvas.SetLeft(tb, leftOffset +
                    chart2dCanvas.Width / 2 - size.Width / 2);

    tb = new TextBlock();
    tb.Text = YLabel;
    tb.FontFamily = LabelFont;
    tb.FontSize = LabelFontSize;
    tb.Foreground = LabelColor;
    tb.RenderTransform = new RotateTransform(-90, 0.5, 0.5);
```

636

```
        tb.Measure(new Size(Double.PositiveInfinity, Double.PositiveInfinity));
        size = tb.DesiredSize;
        ChartCanvas.Children.Add(tb);
        Canvas.SetBottom(tb, chart2dCanvas.Height / 2 + size.Width / 3);
        Canvas.SetLeft(tb, leftOffset / 10);
    }

    public Point NormalizePoint(Point pt)
    {
        if (chart2dCanvas.Width.ToString() == "NaN")
            chart2dCanvas.Width = 270;
        if (chart2dCanvas.Height.ToString() == "NaN")
            chart2dCanvas.Height = 250;
        Point result = new Point();
        result.X = (pt.X - Xmin) * chart2dCanvas.Width / (Xmax - Xmin);
        result.Y = chart2dCanvas.Height -
                    (pt.Y - Ymin) * chart2dCanvas.Height / (Ymax - Ymin);
        return result;
    }


    public void AddColorBar2D(ChartStyle2D cs, DataSeriesSurface ds,
                              Draw3DChart dsc, double zmin, double zmax)
    {
        TextBlock tb;
        tb = new TextBlock();
        tb.Text = "A";
        tb.FontFamily = cs.TickFont;
        tb.FontSize = cs.TickFontSize;
        tb.Measure(new Size(Double.PositiveInfinity, Double.PositiveInfinity));
        Size tickSize = tb.DesiredSize;
        double x = 8 * cs.ChartCanvas.Width / 9;
        double y = 7;
        double width = cs.ChartCanvas.Width / 25;
        double height = chart2dCanvas.Height;
        Point3D[] pts = new Point3D[64];
        double dz = (zmax - zmin) / 63;

        // Create the color bar:
        Polygon plg;
        for (int i = 0; i < 64; i++)
        {
            pts[i] = new Point3D(x, y, zmin + i * dz);
        }
        for (int i = 0; i < 63; i++)
        {
            SolidColorBrush brush = dsc.GetBrush(pts[i].Z, zmin, zmax);
            double y1 = y + height - (pts[i].Z - zmin) * height / (zmax - zmin);
            double y2 = y + height -
                        (pts[i + 1].Z - zmin) * height / (zmax - zmin);
            plg = new Polygon();
            plg.Points.Add(new Point(x, y2));
            plg.Points.Add(new Point(x + width, y2));
```

637

```
            plg.Points.Add(new Point(x + width, y1));
            plg.Points.Add(new Point(x, y1));
            plg.Fill = brush;
            plg.Stroke = brush;
            cs.ChartCanvas.Children.Add(plg);
        }
        Rectangle rect = new Rectangle();
        rect.Width = width + 2;
        rect.Height = height + 2;
        rect.Stroke = Brushes.Black;
        Canvas.SetLeft(rect, x - 1);
        Canvas.SetTop(rect, y - 1);
        cs.ChartCanvas.Children.Add(rect);

        // Add ticks and labels to the color bar:
        double tickLength = 0.15 * width;
        for (double z = zmin; z <= zmax; z = z + (zmax - zmin) / 6)
        {
            double yy = y + height - (z - zmin) * height / (zmax - zmin);
            dsc.AddTickLine(cs, new Point(x, yy),
                            new Point(x + tickLength, yy));
            dsc.AddTickLine(cs, new Point(x + width, yy),
                            new Point(x + width - tickLength, yy));
            tb = new TextBlock();
            tb.Text = (Math.Round(z, 2)).ToString();
            tb.FontFamily = cs.TickFont;
            tb.FontSize = cs.TickFontSize;
            cs.ChartCanvas.Children.Add(tb);
            Canvas.SetLeft(tb, x + width + 5);
            Canvas.SetTop(tb, yy - tickSize.Height / 2);
        }
    }
  }
}
```

This class is basically similar to that used to create 2D charts in Chapters 5 and 6, except here we implement a colorbar on the right side.

Draw3DChart Class

In this section, we'll implement all chart-drawing-related code in the *Draw3DChart* class. This class derives from the *DrawSurfaceChart* class implemented in the previous chapter. Here is the code listing for this class:

```
using System;
using System.Collections.Generic;
using System.Windows;
using System.Windows.Controls;
using System.Windows.Media;
using System.Windows.Media.Media3D;
using System.Windows.Shapes;
```

```
namespace Specialized3DChart
{
    public class Draw3DChart : DrawSurfaceChart
    {
        private int numberContours = 10;
        private bool isBarSingleColor = true;
        private bool isLineColorMatch = false;
        private ChartTypeEnum chartType = ChartTypeEnum.XYColor;
        private Polygon plg = new Polygon();

        public ChartTypeEnum ChartType
        {
            get { return chartType; }
            set { chartType = value; }
        }

        public int NumberContours
        {
            get { return numberContours; }
            set { numberContours = value; }
        }

        public bool IsBarSingleColor
        {
            get { return isBarSingleColor; }
            set { isBarSingleColor = value; }
        }

        public bool IsLineColorMatch
        {
            get { return isLineColorMatch; }
            set { isLineColorMatch = value; }
        }

        public enum ChartTypeEnum
        {
            XYColor = 1,
            Contour = 2,
            FillContour = 3,
            XYColor3D = 4,
            MeshContour3D = 5,
            SurfaceContour3D = 6,
            SurfaceFillContour3D = 7,
            BarChart3D = 8
        }

        public void AddChart(ChartStyle2D cs, DataSeriesSurface ds)
        {
            switch (ChartType)
            {
                case ChartTypeEnum.XYColor:
                    cs.AddChartStyle2D(this);
                    if (cs.IsColorBar && IsColormap)
```

```
            {
                cs.AddColorBar2D(cs, ds, this, ds.ZDataMin(),
                                 ds.ZDataMax());
            }
            AddXYColor(cs, ds);
            break;

        case ChartTypeEnum.Contour:
            cs.AddChartStyle2D(this);
            if (cs.IsColorBar && IsColormap)
            {
                cs.AddColorBar2D(cs, ds, this, ds.ZDataMin(),
                                 ds.ZDataMax());
            }
            AddContour(cs, ds);
            break;

        case ChartTypeEnum.FillContour:
            cs.AddChartStyle2D(this);
            if (cs.IsColorBar && IsColormap)
            {
                cs.AddColorBar2D(cs, ds, this, ds.ZDataMin(),
                                 ds.ZDataMax());
            }
            AddXYColor(cs, ds);
            AddContour(cs, ds);
            break;

        case ChartTypeEnum.MeshContour3D:
            cs.AddChartStyle();
            AddContour3D(cs, ds);
            AddMesh(cs, ds);
            break;

        case ChartTypeEnum.SurfaceContour3D:
            cs.AddChartStyle();
            AddContour3D(cs, ds);
            AddSurface(cs, ds);
            break;

        case ChartTypeEnum.SurfaceFillContour3D:
            cs.AddChartStyle();
            AddXYColor3D(cs, ds);
            AddContour3D(cs, ds);
            AddSurface(cs, ds);
            break;
    }
}

private void AddXYColor(ChartStyle2D cs2d, DataSeriesSurface ds)
{
    ......
}
```

```
        private void AddContour(ChartStyle2D cs2d, DataSeriesSurface ds)
        {
            ......
        }

        private void AddXYColor3D(ChartStyle cs, DataSeriesSurface ds)
        {
            ......
        }

        private void AddContour3D(ChartStyle cs, DataSeriesSurface ds)
        {
            ......
        }

        public void AddBar3D(ChartStyle2D cs, Bar3DStyle bs)
        {
            ......           }
    }
}
```

In this class, the field members and their corresponding public properties are used to control the appearance of specialized 3D charts. You can create a specific 3D chart by selecting the *ChartType* from the enumeration, *ChartTypeEnum*. You can see that there are eight different chart types to select in this enumeration. Some of them are a combination of a few different chart types. You can add more chart types to this enumeration and create their corresponding 3D charts in the same manner as we do here.

You may notice that several methods in the *Draw3DChart* class have only a signature. In the following few sections, I'll present detailed implementation of these methods.

Color Charts on the *X-Y* Plane

The *X-Y* color chart can be considered a projected surface chart on the *X-Y* plane. In fact, it is a rectangle mesh grid in the *X-Y* plane with colors determined by the data values at the grid points. Here, we create the *X-Y* color chart using each set of four adjacent points to define the polygon. Each polygon is shaded in a single color. As with surface charts, *X-Y* color charts can have the interpolated shading, in which each polygon is colored by bilinear interpolation of the colors at its four vertices using all elements of the data values. The minimum and maximum elements of data values at grid points are assigned the first and last colors in the colormap. Colors for the remaining elements in the data values are determined by a linear mapping from value to colormap element.

Implementation

In this section, we'll implement the *X-Y* color chart. Add a new public method, *AddXYColor*, to the *Draw3DChart* class:

```
private void AddXYColor(ChartStyle2D cs2d, DataSeriesSurface ds)
{
    Point3D[,] pts = ds.PointArray;
    double zmin = ds.ZDataMin();
    double zmax = ds.ZDataMax();
```

```
// Draw surface on the XY plane:
if (!IsInterp)
{
    for (int i = 0; i < pts.GetLength(0) - 1; i++)
    {
        for (int j = 0; j < pts.GetLength(1) - 1; j++)
        {
            plg = new Polygon();
            plg.Stroke = ds.LineColor;
            plg.StrokeThickness = ds.LineThickness;
            plg.Fill = GetBrush(pts[i, j].Z, zmin, zmax);
            if(IsLineColorMatch)
            plg.Stroke = GetBrush(pts[i, j].Z, zmin, zmax);
            plg.Points.Add(cs2d.NormalizePoint(new Point(pts[i, j].X,
                                                pts[i, j].Y)));
            plg.Points.Add(cs2d.NormalizePoint(new Point(pts[i, j + 1].X,
                                                pts[i, j + 1].Y)));
            plg.Points.Add(cs2d.NormalizePoint(new Point(pts[i + 1, j + 1].X,
                                                pts[i + 1, j + 1].Y)));
            plg.Points.Add(cs2d.NormalizePoint(new Point(pts[i + 1, j].X,
                                                pts[i + 1, j].Y)));

            cs2d.Chart2dCanvas.Children.Add(plg);
        }
    }
}
else if (IsInterp)
{
    for (int i = 0; i < pts.GetLength(0) - 1; i++)
    {
        for (int j = 0; j < pts.GetLength(1) - 1; j++)
        {
            Point3D[] points = new Point3D[4];
            points[0] = pts[i, j];
            points[1] = pts[i, j + 1];
            points[2] = pts[i + 1, j + 1];
            points[3] = pts[i + 1, j];
            Interp2D(cs2d, points, zmin, zmax);
            plg = new Polygon();
            plg.Stroke = ds.LineColor;
            if (IsLineColorMatch)
                plg.Stroke = GetBrush(pts[i, j].Z, zmin, zmax);
            plg.StrokeThickness = ds.LineThickness;
            plg.Fill = Brushes.Transparent;
            plg.Points.Add(cs2d.NormalizePoint(new Point(pts[i, j].X,
                                                pts[i, j].Y)));
            plg.Points.Add(cs2d.NormalizePoint(new Point(pts[i, j + 1].X,
                                                pts[i, j + 1].Y)));
            plg.Points.Add(cs2d.NormalizePoint(new Point(pts[i + 1, j + 1].X,
                                                pts[i + 1, j + 1].Y)));
            plg.Points.Add(cs2d.NormalizePoint(new Point(pts[i + 1, j].X,
                                                pts[i + 1, j].Y)));

            cs2d.Chart2dCanvas.Children.Add(plg);
```

```
                }
            }
        }
    }

    private void Interp2D(ChartStyle2D cs2d, Point3D[] pta, double zmin, double zmax)
    {
        Polygon plg = new Polygon();
        Point[] points = new Point[4];
        int npoints = NumberInterp;
        Point3D[,] pts = new Point3D[npoints + 1, npoints + 1];
        double x0 = pta[0].X;
        double y0 = pta[0].Y;
        double x1 = pta[2].X;
        double y1 = pta[2].Y;
        double dx = (x1 - x0) / npoints;
        double dy = (y1 - y0) / npoints;
        double c00 = pta[0].Z;
        double c10 = pta[3].Z;
        double c11 = pta[2].Z;
        double c01 = pta[1].Z;
        double x, y, c;

        for (int i = 0; i <= npoints; i++)
        {
            x = x0 + i * dx;
            for (int j = 0; j <= npoints; j++)
            {
                y = y0 + j * dy;
                c = (y1 - y) * ((x1 - x) * c00 +
                    (x - x0) * c10) / (x1 - x0) / (y1 - y0) +
                    (y - y0) * ((x1 - x) * c01 +
                    (x - x0) * c11) / (x1 - x0) / (y1 - y0);
                pts[i, j] = new Point3D(x, y, c);
            }
        }
        for (int i = 0; i < npoints; i++)
        {
            for (int j = 0; j < npoints; j++)
            {
                plg = new Polygon();
                Brush brush = GetBrush(pts[i, j].Z, zmin, zmax);
                plg.Fill = brush;
                plg.Stroke = brush;
                plg.Points.Add(cs2d.NormalizePoint(new Point(pts[i, j].X,
                                                   pts[i, j].Y)));
                plg.Points.Add(cs2d.NormalizePoint(new Point(pts[i, j + 1].X,
                                                   pts[i, j + 1].Y)));
                plg.Points.Add(cs2d.NormalizePoint(new Point(pts[i + 1, j + 1].X,
                                                   pts[i + 1, j + 1].Y)));
                plg.Points.Add(cs2d.NormalizePoint(new Point(pts[i + 1, j].X,
                                                   pts[i + 1, j].Y)));
                cs2d.Chart2dCanvas.Children.Add(plg);
```

```
                }
            }
        }
```

In this method, we draw the *X-Y* color chart via two different approaches: One is the standard single-shaded approach; the other applies interpolated shading to the plot by calling the following *Interp2D* method. This interpolation method forces the color within each polygon to vary bilinearly, producing the effect of a smooth color variation across the chart. You can control the fineness of the interpolated surface by changing the *NumberInterp* property.

Testing *X-Y* Color Charts

Here, I'll show you how to create an *X-Y* color chart using the method implemented in the previous section. Add a new WPF window and name it *XYColor*. The XAML file for this example is very simple:

```xml
<Window x:Class="Specialized3DChart.XYColor"
    xmlns="http://schemas.microsoft.com/winfx/2006/xaml/presentation"
    xmlns:x="http://schemas.microsoft.com/winfx/2006/xaml"
    Title="XY Color Chart" Height="400" Width="500">
    <Grid>
        <Grid.ColumnDefinitions>
            <ColumnDefinition Width="*"/>
            <ColumnDefinition Width="auto"/>
        </Grid.ColumnDefinitions>
        <Grid x:Name="chartGrid" SizeChanged="chartGrid_SizeChanged" Margin="20"
            Grid.Row="0" Grid.Column="0">
            <Canvas x:Name="chartCanvas" Background="Transparent"
                ClipToBounds="True"/>
        </Grid>
    </Grid>
</Window>
```

Here is the corresponding code-behind file:

```csharp
using System;
using System.Windows;
using System.Windows.Controls;
using System.Windows.Media;
using System.Windows.Media.Imaging;

namespace Specialized3DChart
{
    public partial class XYColor : Window
    {
        private ChartStyle2D cs;
        private DataSeriesSurface ds;
        private Draw3DChart d3c;

        public XYColor()
        {
            InitializeComponent();
        }

        private void chartGrid_SizeChanged(object sender, SizeChangedEventArgs e)
```

```
        {
            chartCanvas.Width = chartGrid.ActualWidth;
            chartCanvas.Height = chartGrid.ActualHeight;
            AddChart();
        }

        private void AddChart()
        {
            chartCanvas.Children.Clear();
            cs = new ChartStyle2D();
            cs.ChartCanvas = this.chartCanvas;
            cs.GridlinePattern = ChartStyle.GridlinePatternEnum.Solid;
            cs.Elevation = 30;
            cs.Azimuth = -37;
            cs.Title = "No Title";
            cs.IsColorBar = true;
            ds = new DataSeriesSurface();
            ds.LineColor = Brushes.Black;
            Utility.Peak3D(cs, ds);

            d3c = new Draw3DChart();
            d3c.ChartType = Draw3DChart.ChartTypeEnum.XYColor;
            cs.AddChartStyle2D(d3c);
            d3c.IsInterp = false;
            d3c.NumberInterp = 0;
            d3c.AddChart(cs, ds);
        }
    }
}
```

Running this example produces the output shown in Figure 16-1.

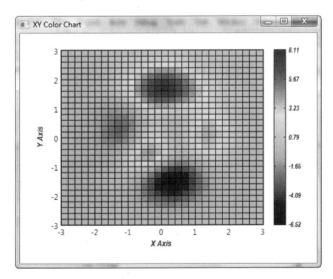

Figure 16-1. *An X-Y color chart with mesh lines*

You can remove the mesh lines from the *X-Y* color chart by changing the *LineColor* property from *Black* to *Transparent*:

```
ds.LineColor = Brushes.Transparent;
```

This generates the result shown in Figure 16-2.

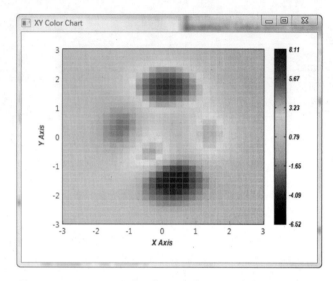

Figure 16-2. *An X-Y color chart without mesh lines*

You can see from the Figure 16-2 that each polygon on the *X-Y* color chart is shaded in a single color. You can obtain an *X-Y* color chart with a much better colormap by applying interpolated shading using the following modified code snippet:

```
d3c.IsInterp = true;
d3c.NumberInterp = 5;
```

This produces the interpolated *X-Y* color chart shown in Figure 16-3.

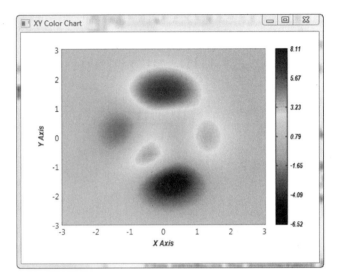

Figure 16-3. An X-Y color chart with an interpolated color shading

Contour Charts

Contour charts help the visualizing of 3D surfaces on a 2D computer screen. In this case, data values are plotted as a function of mesh grid points in the *X-Y* plane. In order to do contouring in a WPF application, you need to describe the data surface and the contour levels you want to draw. Given this information, the program must call an algorithm that calculates the line segments that make up a contour curve and then plot these line segments on your computer screen.

In order to satisfy the foregoing requirements, here we'll use an algorithm that is relatively simple to implement and very reliable and that does not require sophisticated programming techniques or a high level of mathematics to understand how it works.

Algorithm

Suppose that 3D surface data are stored in a 2D array to form a rectangular grid in the *X-Y* plane. We consider four grid points at a time: the rectangular cell (i, j), $(i + 1, j)$, $(i, j + 1)$, and $(i + 1, j + 1)$. This rectangular grid cell is further divided into two triangular grid cells, as shown in Figure 16-4. The contouring is drawn by systematically examining each triangular cell. Intersection points, if any, between each edge of the cell and a given contour-level curve are computed using bilinear interpolation. Line segments are plotted between intersection points of a contour-level curve, with each of the two edges belonging to the cell. Note that if any edges belonging to a triangular cell are intersected by a given-level curve, then exactly two edges are intersected.

647

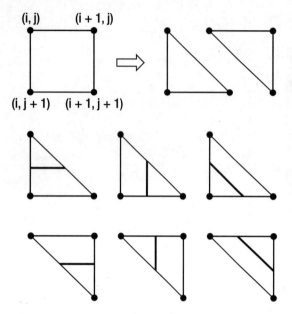

Figure 16-4. *A rectangular grid cell is further divided into two triangular cells. Each triangular cell has three possible cases that draw different contouring line segments.*

You can see from the figure that there are three cases for each triangular grid cell in which certain types of contouring line segments are drawn, depending on the contour level with respect to the data values at the grid points of a triangular cell. Thus, by examining all of the left and right triangular cells and adding together all of the possible contouring line segments, we can obtain a contour chart for any function or data set defined on a rectangular grid in the *X-Y* plane.

Implementation

Using the algorithm discussed in the previous section, we can easily create contour charts in WPF. Add a public method, *AddContour*, and a private method, *DrawLine*, to the *Draw3DChart* class:

```
private void AddContour(ChartStyle2D cs2d, DataSeriesSurface ds)
{
    Point[] pta = new Point[2];
    SolidColorBrush brush = Brushes.Black;
    Line line = new Line();
    Point3D[,] pts = ds.PointArray;
    double zmin = ds.ZDataMin();
    double zmax = ds.ZDataMax();
    double[] zlevels = new double[NumberContours];

    for (int i = 0; i < NumberContours; i++)
        zlevels[i] = zmin + i * (zmax - zmin) / (NumberContours - 1);
    int i0, i1, i2, j0, j1, j2;
    double zratio = 1;
```

```
// Draw contour on the XY plane:
for (int i = 0; i < pts.GetLength(0) - 1; i++)
{
    for (int j = 0; j < pts.GetLength(1) - 1; j++)
    {
        if (IsColormap && ChartType != ChartTypeEnum.FillContour)
            brush = GetBrush(pts[i, j].Z, zmin, zmax);
        for (int k = 0; k < NumberContours; k++)
        {
            // Left triangle:
            i0 = i;
            j0 = j;
            i1 = i;
            j1 = j + 1;
            i2 = i + 1;
            j2 = j + 1;
            if ((zlevels[k] >= pts[i0, j0].Z &&
                zlevels[k] <  pts[i1, j1].Z ||
                zlevels[k] <  pts[i0, j0].Z &&
                zlevels[k] >= pts[i1, j1].Z) &&
                (zlevels[k] >= pts[i1, j1].Z &&
                zlevels[k] <  pts[i2, j2].Z ||
                zlevels[k] <  pts[i1, j1].Z &&
                zlevels[k] >= pts[i2, j2].Z))
            {
                zratio = (zlevels[k] - pts[i0, j0].Z) /
                        (pts[i1, j1].Z - pts[i0, j0].Z);
                pta[0] = cs2d.NormalizePoint(new Point(pts[i0, j0].X,
                        (1 - zratio) * pts[i0, j0].Y +
                        zratio * pts[i1, j1].Y));
                zratio = (zlevels[k] - pts[i1, j1].Z) /
                        (pts[i2, j2].Z - pts[i1, j1].Z);
                pta[1] = cs2d.NormalizePoint(new Point((1 - zratio) *
                        pts[i1, j1].X + zratio * pts[i2, j2].X,
                        pts[i1, j1].Y));
                DrawLine(cs2d, ds, brush, pta[0], pta[1]);
            }
            else if ((zlevels[k] >= pts[i0, j0].Z &&
                    zlevels[k] <  pts[i2, j2].Z ||
                    zlevels[k] <  pts[i0, j0].Z &&
                    zlevels[k] >= pts[i2, j2].Z) &&
                    (zlevels[k] >= pts[i1, j1].Z &&
                    zlevels[k] <  pts[i2, j2].Z ||
                    zlevels[k] <  pts[i1, j1].Z &&
                    zlevels[k] >= pts[i2, j2].Z))
                {
                zratio = (zlevels[k] - pts[i0, j0].Z) /
                        (pts[i2, j2].Z - pts[i0, j0].Z);
                pta[0] = cs2d.NormalizePoint(new Point((1 - zratio) *
                        pts[i0, j0].X + zratio * pts[i2, j2].X,
                        (1 - zratio) * pts[i0, j0].Y +
                        zratio * pts[i2, j2].Y));
```

```
            zratio = (zlevels[k] - pts[i1, j1].Z) /
                    (pts[i2, j2].Z - pts[i1, j1].Z);
        pta[1] = cs2d.NormalizePoint(new Point((1 - zratio) *
                    pts[i1, j1].X + zratio * pts[i2, j2].X,
                    pts[i1, j1].Y));
        DrawLine(cs2d, ds, brush, pta[0], pta[1]);
    }
    else if ((zlevels[k] >= pts[i0, j0].Z &&
            zlevels[k] <  pts[i1, j1].Z ||
            zlevels[k] <  pts[i0, j0].Z &&
            zlevels[k] >= pts[i1, j1].Z) &&
            (zlevels[k] >= pts[i0, j0].Z &&
            zlevels[k] <  pts[i2, j2].Z ||
            zlevels[k] < pts[i0, j0].Z &&
            zlevels[k] >= pts[i2, j2].Z))
    {
        zratio = (zlevels[k] - pts[i0, j0].Z) /
                (pts[i1, j1].Z - pts[i0, j0].Z);
        pta[0] = cs2d.NormalizePoint(new Point(pts[i0, j0].X,
                (1 - zratio) * pts[i0, j0].Y +
                zratio * pts[i1, j1].Y));
        zratio = (zlevels[k] - pts[i0, j0].Z) /
                (pts[i2, j2].Z - pts[i0, j0].Z);
        pta[1] = cs2d.NormalizePoint(new Point(pts[i0, j0].X *
                (1 - zratio) + pts[i2, j2].X * zratio,
                pts[i0, j0].Y * (1 - zratio) +
                pts[i2, j2].Y * zratio));
        DrawLine(cs2d, ds, brush, pta[0], pta[1]);
    }

    // right triangle:
    i0 = i;
    j0 = j;
    i1 = i + 1;
    j1 = j;
    i2 = i + 1;
    j2 = j + 1;
    if ((zlevels[k] >= pts[i0, j0].Z &&
        zlevels[k] <  pts[i1, j1].Z ||
        zlevels[k] <  pts[i0, j0].Z &&
        zlevels[k] >= pts[i1, j1].Z) &&
        (zlevels[k] >= pts[i1, j1].Z &&
        zlevels[k] <  pts[i2, j2].Z ||
        zlevels[k] <  pts[i1, j1].Z &&
        zlevels[k] >= pts[i2, j2].Z))
    {
        zratio = (zlevels[k] - pts[i0, j0].Z) /
                (pts[i1, j1].Z - pts[i0, j0].Z);
        pta[0] = cs2d.NormalizePoint(new Point(pts[i0, j0].X *
                (1 - zratio) + pts[i1, j1].X * zratio, pts[i0, j0].Y));
        zratio = (zlevels[k] - pts[i1, j1].Z) /
                (pts[i2, j2].Z - pts[i1, j1].Z);
        pta[1] = cs2d.NormalizePoint(new Point(pts[i1, j1].X,
```

```
                    pts[i1, j1].Y * (1 - zratio) +
                    pts[i2, j2].Y * zratio));
                DrawLine(cs2d, ds, brush, pta[0], pta[1]);
        }
        else if ((zlevels[k] >= pts[i0, j0].Z &&
                zlevels[k] <  pts[i2, j2].Z ||
                zlevels[k] <  pts[i0, j0].Z &&
                zlevels[k] >= pts[i2, j2].Z) &&
               (zlevels[k] >= pts[i1, j1].Z &&
                zlevels[k] <  pts[i2, j2].Z ||
                zlevels[k] <  pts[i1, j1].Z &&
                zlevels[k] >= pts[i2, j2].Z))
        {
            zratio = (zlevels[k] - pts[i0, j0].Z) /
                    (pts[i2, j2].Z - pts[i0, j0].Z);
            pta[0] = cs2d.NormalizePoint(new Point(pts[i0, j0].X *
                    (1 - zratio) + pts[i2, j2].X * zratio,
                    pts[i0, j0].Y * (1 - zratio) +
                    pts[i2, j2].Y * zratio));
            zratio = (zlevels[k] - pts[i1, j1].Z) /
                    (pts[i2, j2].Z - pts[i1, j1].Z);
            pta[1] = cs2d.NormalizePoint(new Point(pts[i1, j1].X,
                    pts[i1, j1].Y * (1 - zratio) +
                    pts[i2, j2].Y * zratio));
            DrawLine(cs2d, ds, brush, pta[0], pta[1]);
        }
        else if ((zlevels[k] >= pts[i0, j0].Z &&
                zlevels[k] <  pts[i1, j1].Z ||
                zlevels[k] <  pts[i0, j0].Z &&
                zlevels[k] >= pts[i1, j1].Z) &&
               (zlevels[k] >= pts[i0, j0].Z &&
                zlevels[k] <  pts[i2, j2].Z ||
                zlevels[k] <  pts[i0, j0].Z &&
                zlevels[k] >= pts[i2, j2].Z))
        {
            zratio = (zlevels[k] - pts[i0, j0].Z) /
                    (pts[i1, j1].Z - pts[i0, j0].Z);
            pta[0] = cs2d.NormalizePoint(new Point(pts[i0, j0].X *
                    (1 - zratio) + pts[i1, j1].X * zratio, pts[i0, j0].Y));
            zratio = (zlevels[k] - pts[i0, j0].Z) /
                    (pts[i2, j2].Z - pts[i0, j0].Z);
            pta[1] = cs2d.NormalizePoint(new Point(pts[i0, j0].X *
                    (1 - zratio) + pts[i2, j2].X * zratio,
                    pts[i0, j0].Y * (1 - zratio) +
                    pts[i2, j2].Y * zratio));
            DrawLine(cs2d, ds, brush, pta[0], pta[1]);
        }
    }
  }
 }
}

private void DrawLine(ChartStyle2D cs2d, DataSeriesSurface ds,
```

```
                    SolidColorBrush brush, Point pt0, Point pt1)
{
    Line line = new Line();
    if (IsLineColorMatch)
        line.Stroke = brush;
    else
        line.Stroke = ds.LineColor;
    line.StrokeThickness = ds.LineThickness;
    line.X1 = pt0.X;
    line.Y1 = pt0.Y;
    line.X2 = pt1.X;
    line.Y2 = pt1.Y;
    cs2d.Chart2dCanvas.Children.Add(line);
}
```

In this method, there are several parameters that can be used to control the appearance of the contour chart. The most important parameter is the *NumberContours* property, which determines how many contour lines will be drawn. You can also specify the *IsLineColorMatch* property to determine the kind of color that will be used to draw the contour lines. If this property is set to be false, a single color (specified by the *LineColor* property) is used to draw the contour. On the other hand, if this property is set to be true, a colormapped color is used, depending on the values of the contour levels.

Testing Contour Charts

Add a new WPF window to the project and name it *Contour*. The XAML file is the same as that used earlier in testing the *X-Y* color chart. The only difference is the *AddChart* method in the code-behind file:

```
private void AddChart()
{
    chartCanvas.Children.Clear();
    cs = new ChartStyle2D();
    cs.ChartCanvas = this.chartCanvas;
    cs.GridlinePattern = ChartStyle.GridlinePatternEnum.Solid;
    cs.IsColorBar = false;
    cs.Title = "No Title";
    ds = new DataSeriesSurface();
    ds.LineColor = Brushes.Black;
    Utility.Peak3D(cs, ds);

    d3c = new Draw3DChart();
    d3c.Colormap.ColormapBrushType = ColormapBrush.ColormapBrushEnum.Jet;
    d3c.ChartType = Draw3DChart.ChartTypeEnum.Contour;
    d3c.IsLineColorMatch = false;
    d3c.NumberContours = 15;
    d3c.AddChart(cs, ds);
}
```

Running this example generates the result shown in Figure 16-5.

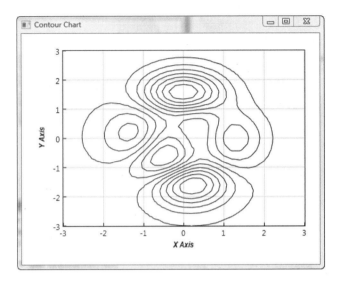

Figure 16-5. A contour chart

You can also easily create a contour chart with colormapped contouring lines by changing the following code snippet:

```
cs.IsColorBar = true;
d3c.IsLineColorMatch = true;
```

This produces the colormapped contour chart shown in Figure 16-6.

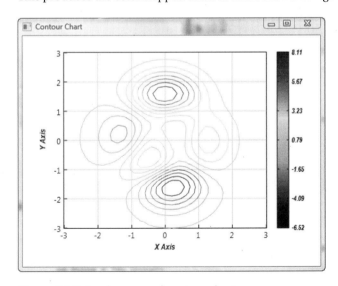

Figure 16-6. A colormapped contour chart

653

Combination Charts

Combination charts are a useful way to exploit the informative properties of various types of graphics charting methods. In this section, we'll show you a few examples of typical combination charts, including filled contour, mesh contour, surface contour, and surface-filled contour charts. By using a similar approach, you can create your own combination charts.

Notice that when we discussed *X-Y* color charts and contour charts in previous sections, we drew these charts directly on the 2D computer screen. However, in order to combine a contour or *X-Y* color chart with a 3D surface chart, we must modify the original 2D *X-Y* color chart and contour chart to be consistent with the 3D coordinate system the surface chart uses.

X-Y Charts in 3D

In creating original 2D *X-Y* charts, we transform the world coordinates to device coordinates by using the *X* and *Y* components of the data points directly and neglecting the *Z* component. In order to add the 3D feature to *X-Y* color charts, you must perform an orthogonal projection transformation on the *X* and *Y* components of the data points at a constant *Z* value (the projection plane where the *X-Y* color chart is drawn) using the transformation matrix defined in the *Utility* class. The *AddXYColor3D* method in the *Draw3DChart* class is implemented in this manner:

```
private void AddXYColor3D(ChartStyle cs, DataSeriesSurface ds)
{
    Point3D[,] pts = ds.PointArray;
    Point3D[,] pts1 = new Point3D[pts.GetLength(0), pts.GetLength(1)];
    Matrix3D m = Utility.AzimuthElevation(cs.Elevation, cs.Azimuth);
    Polygon plg = new Polygon();

    // Find the minumum and maximum z values:
    double zmin = ds.ZDataMin();
    double zmax = ds.ZDataMax();

    // Perform transformation on points:
    for (int i = 0; i < pts.GetLength(0); i++)
    {
        for (int j = 0; j < pts.GetLength(1); j++)
        {
            pts1[i, j] = new Point3D(pts[i, j].X, pts[i, j].Y, cs.Zmin);
            pts1[i, j] = cs.Normalize3D(m, pts1[i, j]);
        }
    }

    // Draw surface on the XY plane:
    for (int i = 0; i < pts.GetLength(0) - 1; i++)
    {
        for (int j = 0; j < pts.GetLength(1) - 1; j++)
        {
            plg = new Polygon();
            plg.Points.Add(new Point(pts1[i, j].X, pts1[i, j].Y));
            plg.Points.Add(new Point(pts1[i, j + 1].X, pts1[i, j + 1].Y));
            plg.Points.Add(new Point(pts1[i + 1, j + 1].X, pts1[i + 1, j + 1].Y));
            plg.Points.Add(new Point(pts1[i + 1, j].X, pts1[i + 1, j].Y));
            plg.StrokeThickness = ds.LineThickness;
```

```
            plg.Fill = GetBrush(pts[i, j].Z, zmin, zmax);
            plg.Stroke = GetBrush(pts[i, j].Z, zmin, zmax);
            cs.ChartCanvas.Children.Add(plg);
        }
    }
}
```

You can see that the transformation is indeed performed on the data points at a constant $Z = zmin$ using the elevation-azimuth transform matrix. This indicates that we'll draw the X-Y color chart on the $Z = zmin$ plane.

Contour Charts in 3D

Similarly, in order to combine the contour chart with 3D surface charts, you must create a contour chart consistent with the 3D coordinate system. The following listing is for the *AddContour3D* method in the *Draw3DChart* class:

```
private void AddContour3D(ChartStyle cs, DataSeriesSurface ds)
{
    Point3D[] pta = new Point3D[2];
    Point3D[,] pts = ds.PointArray;
    Matrix3D m = Utility.AzimuthElevation(cs.Elevation, cs.Azimuth);
    SolidColorBrush brush = Brushes.Black;

    // Find the minumum and maximum z values:
    double zmin = ds.ZDataMin();
    double zmax = ds.ZDataMax();
    double[] zlevels = new Double[NumberContours];
    for (int i = 0; i < NumberContours; i++)
        zlevels[i] = zmin + i * (zmax - zmin) / (NumberContours - 1);
    int i0, i1, i2, j0, j1, j2;
    double zratio = 1;

    // Draw contour on the XY plane:
    for (int i = 0; i < pts.GetLength(0) - 1; i++)
    {
        for (int j = 0; j < pts.GetLength(1) - 1; j++)
        {
            if (IsColormap && ChartType != ChartTypeEnum.FillContour)
                brush = GetBrush(pts[i, j].Z, zmin, zmax);
            for (int k = 0; k < numberContours; k++)
            {
                // Left triangle:
                i0 = i;
                j0 = j;
                i1 = i;
                j1 = j + 1;
                i2 = i + 1;
                j2 = j + 1;
                if ((zlevels[k] >= pts[i0, j0].Z &&
                        zlevels[k] <  pts[i1, j1].Z ||
                        zlevels[k] <  pts[i0, j0].Z &&
                        zlevels[k] >= pts[i1, j1].Z) &&
```

```
                (zlevels[k] >= pts[i1, j1].Z &&
                 zlevels[k] <  pts[i2, j2].Z ||
                 zlevels[k] <  pts[i1, j1].Z &&
                 zlevels[k] >= pts[i2, j2].Z))
            {
                zratio = (zlevels[k] - pts[i0, j0].Z) /
                        (pts[i1, j1].Z - pts[i0, j0].Z);
                pta[0] = new Point3D(pts[i0, j0].X, (1 - zratio) * pts[i0, j0].Y
                        + zratio * pts[i1, j1].Y, cs.Zmin);
                zratio = (zlevels[k] - pts[i1, j1].Z) /
                        (pts[i2, j2].Z - pts[i1, j1].Z);
                pta[1] = new Point3D((1 - zratio) * pts[i1, j1].X +
                        zratio * pts[i2, j2].X, pts[i1, j1].Y, cs.Zmin);
                pta[0] = cs.Normalize3D(m, pta[0]);
                pta[1] = cs.Normalize3D(m, pta[1]);
                DrawLine3D(cs, ds, brush, new Point(pta[0].X, pta[0].Y),
                        new Point(pta[1].X, pta[1].Y));
            }
            else if ((zlevels[k] >= pts[i0, j0].Z &&
                     zlevels[k] <  pts[i2, j2].Z ||
                     zlevels[k] <  pts[i0, j0].Z &&
                     zlevels[k] >= pts[i2, j2].Z) &&
                    (zlevels[k] >= pts[i1, j1].Z &&
                     zlevels[k] <  pts[i2, j2].Z ||
                     zlevels[k] <  pts[i1, j1].Z &&
                     zlevels[k] >= pts[i2, j2].Z))
            {
                zratio = (zlevels[k] - pts[i0, j0].Z) /
                        (pts[i2, j2].Z - pts[i0, j0].Z);
                pta[0] = new Point3D((1 - zratio) * pts[i0, j0].X +
                        zratio * pts[i2, j2].X, (1 - zratio) * pts[i0, j0].Y +
                        zratio * pts[i2, j2].Y, cs.Zmin);
                zratio = (zlevels[k] - pts[i1, j1].Z) /
                        (pts[i2, j2].Z - pts[i1, j1].Z);
                pta[1] = new Point3D((1 - zratio) * pts[i1, j1].X +
                        zratio * pts[i2, j2].X, pts[i1, j1].Y, cs.Zmin);
                pta[0] = cs.Normalize3D(m, pta[0]);
                pta[1] = cs.Normalize3D(m, pta[1]);
                DrawLine3D(cs, ds, brush, new Point(pta[0].X, pta[0].Y),
                        new Point(pta[1].X, pta[1].Y));
            }
            else if ((zlevels[k] >= pts[i0, j0].Z &&
                     zlevels[k] <  pts[i1, j1].Z ||
                     zlevels[k] <  pts[i0, j0].Z &&
                     zlevels[k] >= pts[i1, j1].Z) &&
                    (zlevels[k] >= pts[i0, j0].Z &&
                     zlevels[k] <  pts[i2, j2].Z ||
                     zlevels[k] <  pts[i0, j0].Z &&
                     zlevels[k] >= pts[i2, j2].Z))
            {
                zratio = (zlevels[k] - pts[i0, j0].Z) /
                        (pts[i1, j1].Z - pts[i0, j0].Z);
                pta[0] = new Point3D(pts[i0, j0].X, (1 - zratio) * pts[i0, j0].Y
```

```
                              + zratio * pts[i1, j1].Y, cs.Zmin);
            zratio = (zlevels[k] - pts[i0, j0].Z) /
                        (pts[i2, j2].Z - pts[i0, j0].Z);
            pta[1] = new Point3D(pts[i0, j0].X * (1 - zratio) +
                        pts[i2, j2].X * zratio,
            pts[i0, j0].Y * (1 - zratio) + pts[i2, j2].Y * zratio, cs.Zmin);
            pta[0] = cs.Normalize3D(m, pta[0]);
            pta[1] = cs.Normalize3D(m, pta[1]);
            DrawLine3D(cs, ds, brush, new Point(pta[0].X, pta[0].Y),
                        new Point(pta[1].X, pta[1].Y));
    }

    // right triangle:
    i0 = i;
    j0 = j;
    i1 = i + 1;
    j1 = j;
    i2 = i + 1;
    j2 = j + 1;
    if ((zlevels[k] >= pts[i0, j0].Z &&
         zlevels[k] <  pts[i1, j1].Z ||
         zlevels[k] <  pts[i0, j0].Z &&
         zlevels[k] >= pts[i1, j1].Z) &&
        (zlevels[k] >= pts[i1, j1].Z &&
         zlevels[k] <  pts[i2, j2].Z ||
         zlevels[k] <  pts[i1, j1].Z &&
         zlevels[k] >= pts[i2, j2].Z))
    {
        zratio = (zlevels[k] - pts[i0, j0].Z) /
                    (pts[i1, j1].Z - pts[i0, j0].Z);
        pta[0] = new Point3D(pts[i0, j0].X * (1 - zratio) +
                    pts[i1, j1].X * zratio, pts[i0, j0].Y, cs.Zmin);
        zratio = (zlevels[k] - pts[i1, j1].Z) /
                    (pts[i2, j2].Z - pts[i1, j1].Z);
        pta[1] = new Point3D(pts[i1, j1].X, pts[i1, j1].Y * (1 - zratio)
                    + pts[i2, j2].Y * zratio, cs.Zmin);
        pta[0] = cs.Normalize3D(m, pta[0]);
        pta[1] = cs.Normalize3D(m, pta[1]);
        DrawLine3D(cs, ds, brush, new Point(pta[0].X, pta[0].Y),
                    new Point(pta[1].X, pta[1].Y));
    }
    else if ((zlevels[k] >= pts[i0, j0].Z &&
              zlevels[k] <  pts[i2, j2].Z ||
              zlevels[k] <  pts[i0, j0].Z &&
              zlevels[k] >= pts[i2, j2].Z) &&
             (zlevels[k] >= pts[i1, j1].Z &&
              zlevels[k] <  pts[i2, j2].Z ||
              zlevels[k] <  pts[i1, j1].Z &&
              zlevels[k] >= pts[i2, j2].Z))
    {
        zratio = (zlevels[k] - pts[i0, j0].Z) /
                    (pts[i2, j2].Z - pts[i0, j0].Z);
        pta[0] = new Point3D(pts[i0, j0].X * (1 - zratio) +
```

```
                            pts[i2, j2].X * zratio, pts[i0, j0].Y * (1 - zratio) +
                            pts[i2, j2].Y * zratio, cs.Zmin);
                    zratio = (zlevels[k] - pts[i1, j1].Z) /
                            (pts[i2, j2].Z - pts[i1, j1].Z);
                    pta[1] = new Point3D(pts[i1, j1].X, pts[i1, j1].Y * (1 - zratio)
                            + pts[i2, j2].Y * zratio, cs.Zmin);
                    pta[0] = cs.Normalize3D(m, pta[0]);
                    pta[1] = cs.Normalize3D(m, pta[1]);
                    DrawLine3D(cs, ds, brush, new Point(pta[0].X, pta[0].Y),
                            new Point(pta[1].X, pta[1].Y));
                }
                else if ((zlevels[k] >= pts[i0, j0].Z &&
                        zlevels[k] <  pts[i1, j1].Z ||
                        zlevels[k] <  pts[i0, j0].Z &&
                        zlevels[k] >= pts[i1, j1].Z) &&
                       (zlevels[k] >= pts[i0, j0].Z &&
                        zlevels[k] <  pts[i2, j2].Z ||
                        zlevels[k] <  pts[i0, j0].Z &&
                        zlevels[k] >= pts[i2, j2].Z))
                {
                    zratio = (zlevels[k] - pts[i0, j0].Z) /
                            (pts[i1, j1].Z - pts[i0, j0].Z);
                    pta[0] = new Point3D(pts[i0, j0].X * (1 - zratio) +
                            pts[i1, j1].X * zratio, pts[i0, j0].Y, cs.Zmin);
                    zratio = (zlevels[k] - pts[i0, j0].Z) /
                            (pts[i2, j2].Z - pts[i0, j0].Z);
                    pta[1] = new Point3D(pts[i0, j0].X * (1 - zratio) +
                            pts[i2, j2].X * zratio, pts[i0, j0].Y * (1 - zratio) +
                            pts[i2, j2].Y * zratio, cs.Zmin);
                    pta[0] = cs.Normalize3D(m, pta[0]);
                    pta[1] = cs.Normalize3D(m, pta[1]);
                    DrawLine3D(cs, ds, brush, new Point(pta[0].X, pta[0].Y),
                            new Point(pta[1].X, pta[1].Y));
                }
            }
        }
    }
}

private void DrawLine3D(ChartStyle cs, DataSeriesSurface ds,
                    SolidColorBrush brush, Point pt0, Point pt1)
{
    Line line = new Line();
    line.Stroke = ds.LineColor;
    if (IsLineColorMatch)
        line.Stroke = brush;
    line.StrokeThickness = ds.LineThickness;
    line.X1 = pt0.X;
    line.Y1 = pt0.Y;
    line.X2 = pt1.X;
    line.Y2 = pt1.Y;
    cs.ChartCanvas.Children.Add(line);
}
```

This method draws the contour chart on the $Z = zmin$ plane.

Filled Contour Charts

Here, I'll show you how to create a simple filled contour chart by combining a contour chart with an *X-Y* color chart, as implemented previously in the *AddChart* method of the *Draw3DChart* class:

```
case ChartTypeEnum.FillContour:
    cs.AddChartStyle2D(this);
    if (cs.IsColorBar && IsColormap)
        cs.AddColorBar2D(cs, ds, this, ds.ZDataMin(), ds.ZDataMax());
    AddXYColor(cs, ds);
    AddContour(cs, ds);
    break;
```

You can see from this code snippet that we draw first an *X-Y* color chart and then a contour chart. You can test this by adding a new WPF Windows application, named *FilledContour*, to the project. The XAML file is the same as that used to test the *X-Y* color chart. Here is the code-behind files:

```
using System;
using System.Windows;
using System.Windows.Controls;
using System.Windows.Media;
using System.Windows.Media.Imaging;

namespace Specialized3DChart
{
    public partial class FilledContour : Window
    {
        private ChartStyle2D cs;
        private DataSeriesSurface ds;
        private Draw3DChart d3c;

        public FilledContour()
        {
            InitializeComponent();
        }

        private void chartGrid_SizeChanged(object sender, SizeChangedEventArgs e)
        {
            chartCanvas.Width = chartGrid.ActualWidth;
            chartCanvas.Height = chartGrid.ActualHeight;
            AddChart();
        }

        private void AddChart()
        {
            chartCanvas.Children.Clear();
            cs = new ChartStyle2D();
            cs.ChartCanvas = this.chartCanvas;
            cs.GridlinePattern = ChartStyle.GridlinePatternEnum.Solid;
            cs.IsColorBar = true;
            cs.Title = "No Title";
```

```
            ds = new DataSeriesSurface();
            ds.LineColor = Brushes.Transparent;
            Utility.Peak3D(cs, ds);

            d3c = new Draw3DChart();
            d3c.Colormap.ColormapBrushType = ColormapBrush.ColormapBrushEnum.Jet;
            d3c.ChartType = Draw3DChart.ChartTypeEnum.FillContour;
            d3c.IsLineColorMatch = true;
            d3c.NumberContours = 15;
            d3c.IsInterp = true;
            d3c.NumberInterp = 3;
            d3c.AddChart(cs, ds);
        }
    }
}
```

Here, we set the chart type to *FillContour* and use interpolated color shading to draw the *X-Y* color chart. Running this project should yield the output of Figure 16-7.

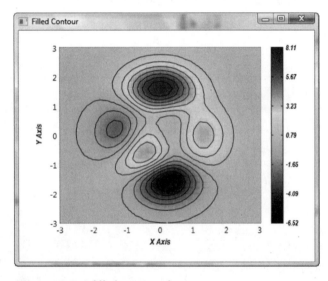

Figure 16-7. *A filled contour chart*

Mesh Contour Charts

It is easy to create a mesh contour combination chart by using the *AddContour3D* and *AddMesh* methods successively. Add a new WPF Windows application to the project and name it *MeshContour*. The XAML file is the same as that in the previous example. Here is the code-behind file:

```
using System;
using System.Windows;
using System.Windows.Controls;
using System.Windows.Media;
using System.Windows.Media.Imaging;
```

```
namespace Specialized3DChart
{
    public partial class MeshContour : Window
    {
        private ChartStyle2D cs;
        private DataSeriesSurface ds;
        private Draw3DChart d3c;

        public MeshContour()
        {
            InitializeComponent();
        }

        private void chartGrid_SizeChanged(object sender, SizeChangedEventArgs e)
        {
            chartCanvas.Width = chartGrid.ActualWidth;
            chartCanvas.Height = chartGrid.ActualHeight;
            AddChart();
        }

        private void AddChart()
        {
            chartCanvas.Children.Clear();
            cs = new ChartStyle2D();
            cs.ChartCanvas = this.chartCanvas;
            cs.GridlinePattern = ChartStyle.GridlinePatternEnum.Solid;
            cs.IsColorBar = true;
            cs.Title = "No Title";
            ds = new DataSeriesSurface();
            Utility.Peak3D(cs, ds);

            d3c = new Draw3DChart();
            d3c.Colormap.ColormapBrushType = ColormapBrush.ColormapBrushEnum.Jet;
            d3c.ChartType = Draw3DChart.ChartTypeEnum.MeshContour3D;
            d3c.IsLineColorMatch = true;
            d3c.NumberContours = 15;
            d3c.AddChart(cs, ds);
        }
    }
}
```

Running this application produces Figure 16-8.

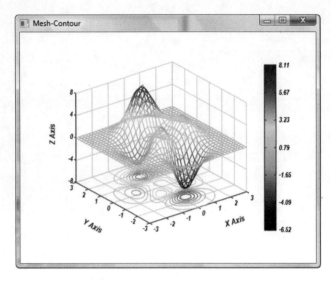

Figure 16-8. *A mesh contour chart*

Surface Contour Charts

Similarly, you can easily create a surface contour chart. You can use the same XAML and code-behind code as in the previous example, except you must set the chart type to *SurfaceContour3D*:

```
d3c.ChartType = Draw3DChart.ChartTypeEnum.SurfaceContour3D;
```

This creates the result shown in Figure 16-9.

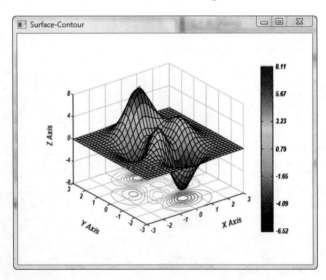

Figure 16-9. *A surface contour chart*

Surface-Filled Contour Charts

You can create a surface-filled contour chart by combining a surface chart with an *X-Y* color chart and a 3D contour chart. You can use the same XAML and code-behind code as in the previous example, except now you set the chart type to *SurfaceFillContour3D*:

```
d3c.ChartType = Draw3DChart.ChartTypeEnum.SurfaceFillContour3D;
```

This creates the result shown in Figure 16-10.

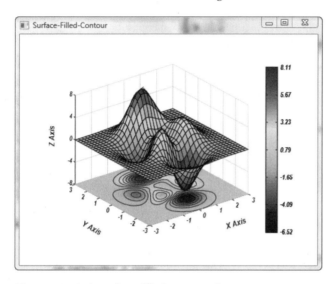

Figure 16-10. A surface-filled contour chart

3D Bar Charts

Using the same data series as when we created the mesh and surface charts, we can also create 3D bar charts. A 3D bar can be constructed in 3D space, as shown in Figure 16-11.

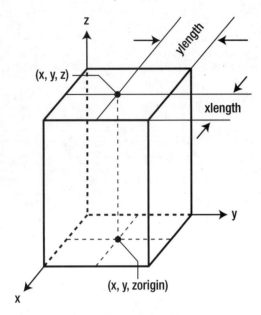

Figure 16-11. *A 3D bar defined in 3D space*

Suppose there is a data point (*x, y, z*) in 3D space. We can define a 3D bar around this point by specifying three parameters: *zorigin*, *xlength*, and *ylength*. The parameter *zorigin* defines the *Z = zorigin* plane from which the 3D bar is filled; the two other parameters set the size of the 3D bar in the *X* and *Y* directions. These length parameters are measured as a percentage of the total amount of space available. In this book, we set these parameters to be in the range [0.1, 0.5]. If you set *xlength* = *ylength* = 0.5, you'll obtain the so-called histogram bar chart; namely, each bar fills the space up to its adjoining bars.

Implementation

First we need to add a *Bar3DStyle* class to the current project:

```
using System;
using System.Collections.Generic;
using System.Windows;
using System.Windows.Controls;
using System.Windows.Media;
using System.Windows.Media.Media3D;
using System.Windows.Shapes;

namespace Specialized3DChart
{
    public class Bar3DStyle : DataSeriesSurface
    {
        private double xLength = 0.5;
        private double yLength = 0.5;
        private double zOrigin = 0;
        private bool isBarSingleColor = true;
```

```
public bool IsBarSingleColor
{
    get { return isBarSingleColor; }
    set { isBarSingleColor = value; }
}

public double ZOrigin
{
    get { return zOrigin; }
    set { zOrigin = value; }
}

public double YLength
{
    get { return yLength; }
    set { yLength = value; }
}

public double XLength
{
    get { return xLength; }
    set { xLength = value; }
}
    }
}
```

This class is very simple. We first define the field members and their corresponding public properties, which allow you to control the appearance and size of the 3D bars. The *bool* property *IsBarSingleColor* lets you specify whether the bars are drawn using a single color or a colormap. Next, we need to create an *AddBar3D* method in the *Draw3DChart* class:

```
public void AddBar3D(ChartStyle2D cs, Bar3DStyle bs)
{
    Matrix3D m = Utility.AzimuthElevation(cs.Elevation, cs.Azimuth);
    Point[] pta = new Point[4];
    Point3D[,] pts = bs.PointArray;

    // Find the minumum and maximum z values:
    double zmin = bs.ZDataMin();
    double zmax = bs.ZDataMax();

    // Check parameters:
    double xlength = bs.XLength;
    if (xlength <= 0)
        xlength = 0.1 * bs.XSpacing;
    else if (xlength > 0.5)
        xlength = 0.5 * bs.XSpacing;
    else
        xlength = bs.XLength * bs.XSpacing;
    double ylength = bs.YLength;
    if (ylength <= 0)
        ylength = 0.1 * bs.YSpacing;
```

```
    else if (ylength > 0.5)
        ylength = 0.5 * bs.YSpacing;
    else
        ylength = bs.YLength * bs.YSpacing;
    double zorigin = bs.ZOrigin;

    // Draw 3D bars:
    for (int i = 0; i < pts.GetLength(0) - 1; i++)
    {
        for (int j = 0; j < pts.GetLength(1) - 1; j++)
        {
            int ii = i;
            int jj = j;
            if (cs.Azimuth >= -180 && cs.Azimuth < -90)
            {
                ii = pts.GetLength(0) - 2 - i;
                jj = j;
            }
            else if (cs.Azimuth >= -90 && cs.Azimuth < 0)
            {
                ii = pts.GetLength(0) - 2 - i;
                jj = pts.GetLength(1) - 2 - j;
            }
            else if (cs.Azimuth >= 0 && cs.Azimuth < 90)
            {
                ii = i;
                jj = pts.GetLength(1) - 2 - j;
            }
            else if (cs.Azimuth >= 90 && cs.Azimuth <= 180)
            {
                ii = i;
                jj = j;
            }
            DrawBar(cs, bs, m, pts[ii, jj], xlength, ylength, zorigin, zmax, zmin);
        }
    }
    if (cs.IsColorBar && IsColormap)
    {
        AddColorBar(cs, bs, zmin, zmax);
    }
}
```

In this method, we first examine whether the parameters provided by the user are in the right ranges. Then we examine the order of drawing the bars according to the variations of the elevation and azimuth angles, making sure that we always draw the bars in back-to-front order (the *Z*-order approach). As mentioned previously, when drawn in this order, a bar can obscure only the bars that have been drawn before it. When the program draws a bar, it fills it so that it covers up any bars that it should obscure. Finally, this method calls another method, *DrawBar*, which performs the actual bar-drawing task:

```
private void DrawBar(ChartStyle2D cs, Bar3DStyle bs, Matrix3D m,
                     Point3D pt, double xlength, double ylength,
                     double zorign, double zmax, double zmin)
{
```

```
SolidColorBrush lineBrush = (SolidColorBrush)bs.LineColor;
SolidColorBrush fillBrush = GetBrush(pt.Z, zmin, zmax);
Point3D[] pts = new Point3D[8];
Point3D[] pts1 = new Point3D[8];
Point3D[] pt3 = new Point3D[4];
Point[] pta = new Point[4];
pts[0] = new Point3D(pt.X - xlength, pt.Y - ylength, zorign);
pts[1] = new Point3D(pt.X - xlength, pt.Y + ylength, zorign);
pts[2] = new Point3D(pt.X + xlength, pt.Y + ylength, zorign);
pts[3] = new Point3D(pt.X + xlength, pt.Y - ylength, zorign);
pts[4] = new Point3D(pt.X + xlength, pt.Y - ylength, pt.Z);
pts[5] = new Point3D(pt.X + xlength, pt.Y + ylength, pt.Z);
pts[6] = new Point3D(pt.X - xlength, pt.Y + ylength, pt.Z);
pts[7] = new Point3D(pt.X - xlength, pt.Y - ylength, pt.Z);

for (int i = 0; i < pts.Length; i++)
{
    pts1[i] = new Point3D(pts[i].X, pts[i].Y, pts[i].Z);
    pts[i] = cs.Normalize3D(m, pts[i]);
}

int[] nconfigs = new int[8];
if (IsBarSingleColor)
{
    pta[0] = new Point(pts[4].X, pts[4].Y);
    pta[1] = new Point(pts[5].X, pts[5].Y);
    pta[2] = new Point(pts[6].X, pts[6].Y);
    pta[3] = new Point(pts[7].X, pts[7].Y);
    DrawPolygon(cs, bs, pta, fillBrush,lineBrush);

    if (cs.Azimuth >= -180 && cs.Azimuth < -90)
        nconfigs = new int[8] { 1, 2, 5, 6, 1, 0, 7, 6 };
    else if (cs.Azimuth >= -90 && cs.Azimuth < 0)
        nconfigs = new int[8] { 1, 0, 7, 6, 0, 3, 4, 7 };
    else if (cs.Azimuth >= 0 && cs.Azimuth < 90)
        nconfigs = new int[8] { 0, 3, 4, 7, 2, 3, 4, 5 };
    else if (cs.Azimuth >= 90 && cs.Azimuth < 180)
        nconfigs = new int[8] { 2, 3, 4, 5, 1, 2, 5, 6 };
    pta[0] = new Point(pts[nconfigs[0]].X, pts[nconfigs[0]].Y);
    pta[1] = new Point(pts[nconfigs[1]].X, pts[nconfigs[1]].Y);
    pta[2] = new Point(pts[nconfigs[2]].X, pts[nconfigs[2]].Y);
    pta[3] = new Point(pts[nconfigs[3]].X, pts[nconfigs[3]].Y);
    DrawPolygon(cs, bs, pta, fillBrush, lineBrush);

    pta[0] = new Point(pts[nconfigs[4]].X, pts[nconfigs[4]].Y);
    pta[1] = new Point(pts[nconfigs[5]].X, pts[nconfigs[5]].Y);
    pta[2] = new Point(pts[nconfigs[6]].X, pts[nconfigs[6]].Y);
    pta[3] = new Point(pts[nconfigs[7]].X, pts[nconfigs[7]].Y);
    DrawPolygon(cs, bs, pta, fillBrush, lineBrush);
}
else if (!IsBarSingleColor && IsColormap)
{
    pta[0] = new Point(pts[4].X, pts[4].Y);
```

```
    pta[1] = new Point(pts[5].X, pts[5].Y);
    pta[2] = new Point(pts[6].X, pts[6].Y);
    pta[3] = new Point(pts[7].X, pts[7].Y);
    DrawPolygon(cs, bs, pta, fillBrush, lineBrush);
    pta[0] = new Point(pts[0].X, pts[0].Y);
    pta[1] = new Point(pts[1].X, pts[1].Y);
    pta[2] = new Point(pts[2].X, pts[2].Y);
    pta[3] = new Point(pts[3].X, pts[3].Y);
    fillBrush = GetBrush(pts1[0].Z, zmin, zmax);
    DrawPolygon(cs, bs, pta, fillBrush, lineBrush);

    double dz = (zmax - zmin) / 63;
    if (pt.Z < zorign)
        dz = -dz;
    int nz = (int)((pt.Z - zorign) / dz) + 1;
    if (nz < 1)
        nz = 1;
    double z = zorign;
    if (cs.Azimuth >= -180 && cs.Azimuth < -90)
        nconfigs = new int[4] { 1, 2, 1, 0 };
    else if (cs.Azimuth >= -90 && cs.Azimuth < 0)
        nconfigs = new int[4] { 1, 0, 0, 3 };
    else if (cs.Azimuth >= 0 && cs.Azimuth < 90)
        nconfigs = new int[4] { 0, 3, 2, 3 };
    else if (cs.Azimuth >= 90 && cs.Azimuth <= 180)
        nconfigs = new int[4] { 2, 3, 1, 2 };

    for (int i = 0; i < nz; i++)
    {
        z = zorign + i * dz;
        pt3[0] = new Point3D(pts1[nconfigs[0]].X, pts1[nconfigs[0]].Y, z);
        pt3[1] = new Point3D(pts1[nconfigs[1]].X, pts1[nconfigs[1]].Y, z);
        pt3[2] = new Point3D(pts1[nconfigs[1]].X, pts1[nconfigs[1]].Y, z + dz);
        pt3[3] = new Point3D(pts1[nconfigs[0]].X, pts1[nconfigs[0]].Y, z + dz);
        for (int j = 0; j < pt3.Length; j++)
            pt3[j] = cs.Normalize3D(m, pt3[j]);
        pta[0] = new Point(pt3[0].X, pt3[0].Y);
        pta[1] = new Point(pt3[1].X, pt3[1].Y);
        pta[2] = new Point(pt3[2].X, pt3[2].Y);
        pta[3] = new Point(pt3[3].X, pt3[3].Y);
        fillBrush = GetBrush(z, zmin, zmax);
        DrawPolygon(cs, bs, pta, fillBrush, fillBrush);
    }
    pt3[0] = new Point3D(pts1[nconfigs[0]].X, pts1[nconfigs[0]].Y, zorign);
    pt3[1] = new Point3D(pts1[nconfigs[1]].X, pts1[nconfigs[1]].Y, zorign);
    pt3[2] = new Point3D(pts1[nconfigs[1]].X, pts1[nconfigs[1]].Y, pt.Z);
    pt3[3] = new Point3D(pts1[nconfigs[0]].X, pts1[nconfigs[0]].Y, pt.Z);
    for (int j = 0; j < pt3.Length; j++)
        pt3[j] = cs.Normalize3D(m, pt3[j]);
    pta[0] = new Point(pt3[0].X, pt3[0].Y);
    pta[1] = new Point(pt3[1].X, pt3[1].Y);
    pta[2] = new Point(pt3[2].X, pt3[2].Y);
    pta[3] = new Point(pt3[3].X, pt3[3].Y);
```

```
        fillBrush = Brushes.Transparent;
        DrawPolygon(cs, bs, pta, fillBrush, lineBrush);

        for (int i = 0; i < nz; i++)
        {
            z = zorign + i * dz;
            pt3[0] = new Point3D(pts1[nconfigs[2]].X, pts1[nconfigs[2]].Y, z);
            pt3[1] = new Point3D(pts1[nconfigs[3]].X, pts1[nconfigs[3]].Y, z);
            pt3[2] = new Point3D(pts1[nconfigs[3]].X, pts1[nconfigs[3]].Y, z + dz);
            pt3[3] = new Point3D(pts1[nconfigs[2]].X, pts1[nconfigs[2]].Y, z + dz);
            for (int j = 0; j < pt3.Length; j++)
                pt3[j] = cs.Normalize3D(m, pt3[j]);
            pta[0] = new Point(pt3[0].X, pt3[0].Y);
            pta[1] = new Point(pt3[1].X, pt3[1].Y);
            pta[2] = new Point(pt3[2].X, pt3[2].Y);
            pta[3] = new Point(pt3[3].X, pt3[3].Y);
            fillBrush = GetBrush(z, zmin, zmax);
            DrawPolygon(cs, bs, pta, fillBrush, fillBrush);
        }
        pt3[0] = new Point3D(pts1[nconfigs[2]].X, pts1[nconfigs[2]].Y, zorign);
        pt3[1] = new Point3D(pts1[nconfigs[3]].X, pts1[nconfigs[3]].Y, zorign);
        pt3[2] = new Point3D(pts1[nconfigs[3]].X, pts1[nconfigs[3]].Y, pt.Z);
        pt3[3] = new Point3D(pts1[nconfigs[2]].X, pts1[nconfigs[2]].Y, pt.Z);
        for (int j = 0; j < pt3.Length; j++)
            pt3[j] = cs.Normalize3D(m, pt3[j]);
        pta[0] = new Point(pt3[0].X, pt3[0].Y);
        pta[1] = new Point(pt3[1].X, pt3[1].Y);
        pta[2] = new Point(pt3[2].X, pt3[2].Y);
        pta[3] = new Point(pt3[3].X, pt3[3].Y);
        fillBrush = Brushes.Transparent;
        DrawPolygon(cs, bs, pta, fillBrush, lineBrush);
    }
}

private void DrawPolygon(ChartStyle2D cs, Bar3DStyle bs, Point[] pts,
                         SolidColorBrush fillBrush, SolidColorBrush lineBrush)
{
    Polygon plg = new Polygon();
    plg.Stroke = lineBrush;
    plg.StrokeThickness = bs.LineThickness;
    plg.Fill = fillBrush;
    for (int i = 0; i < pts.Length; i++)
        plg.Points.Add(pts[i]);
    cs.ChartCanvas.Children.Add(plg);
}
```

In the *DrawBar* method, we first create eight vertices of a 3D bar using a data point and the *xlength*, *ylength*, and *zorign* parameters. We then perform an orthogonal projection transformation on these vertices using the azimuth-elevation matrix. Next, we consider two cases separately: drawing bars using a single color or a colormap. For each case, we examine which faces should be drawn, depending on the elevation and azimuth angles. In the case of single-color shading, the color of a bar is determined by the *Z* value of the input point; in the case of a colormap, each bar is colormapped linearly from the *zorign* to the *Z* value of its input point.

Testing 3D Bar Charts

In this section, I'll show how to create a 3D bar chart using the code implemented in the previous section. Add a new WPF window to the current project and name it *BarChart3D*. The XAML file is similar to that used in creating the contour chart, except for changing the window title from "Contour Chart" to "3D Bar Chart." Here is the code-behind file:

```
using System;
using System.Windows;
using System.Windows.Controls;
using System.Windows.Media;
using System.Windows.Media.Imaging;

namespace Specialized3DChart
{
    public partial class BarChart3D : Window
    {
        private ChartStyle2D cs;
        private Bar3DStyle ds;
        private Draw3DChart d3c;

        public BarChart3D()
        {
            InitializeComponent();
        }

        private void chartGrid_SizeChanged(object sender, SizeChangedEventArgs e)
        {
            chartCanvas.Width = chartGrid.ActualWidth;
            chartCanvas.Height = chartGrid.ActualHeight;
            AddChart();
        }

        private void AddChart()
        {
            chartCanvas.Children.Clear();
            cs = new ChartStyle2D();
            cs.ChartCanvas = this.chartCanvas;
            cs.GridlinePattern = ChartStyle.GridlinePatternEnum.Solid;
            cs.IsColorBar = true;
            cs.Title = "No Title";
            ds = new Bar3DStyle();
            ds.LineColor = Brushes.Black;
            ds.ZOrigin = cs.Zmin;
            ds.XLength = 0.6;
            ds.YLength = 0.6;
            Utility.Peak3D(cs, ds);
            d3c = new Draw3DChart();
            d3c.Colormap.ColormapBrushType = ColormapBrush.ColormapBrushEnum.Jet;
            d3c.IsBarSingleColor = true;
            d3c.IsColormap = true;
            cs.AddChartStyle();
            d3c.AddBar3D(cs, ds);
```

```
        }
    }
}
```

Here, we set *ZOrigin = cs.Zmin*. The bars are drawn in a single color because we set the parameter *IsBarSingleColor* to *true*. This produces the output of Figure 16-12.

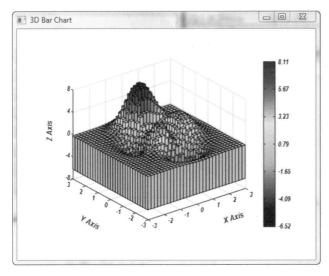

Figure 16-12. *A single-colored 3D bar chart*

If we set the property *IsBarSingleColor* to *false*:

d3c.IsBarSingleColor = false;

we'll obtain a colormapped 3D bar chart, as shown in Figure 16-13.

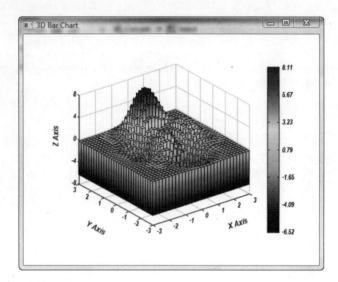

Figure 16-13. *A colormapped 3D bar chart*

You can also change the *ZOrigin* property. Figure 16-14 is created by setting the *ZOrigin* property to zero.

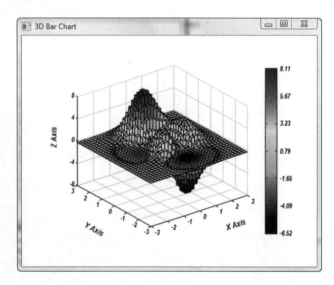

Figure 16-14. *A single-colored 3D bar chart with ZOrigin = 0*

In this chapter, I demonstrated how to create a variety of 3D specialized charts. Following the same procedures we used to create the 2D chart control, you can easily create a 3D chart control. You can then use this 3D chart control in your own WPF applications.

Index

■ ■ ■

You Need the Companion eBook

Your purchase of this book entitles you to buy the companion PDF-version eBook for only $10. Take the weightless companion with you anywhere.

We believe this Apress title will prove so indispensable that you'll want to carry it with you everywhere, which is why we are offering the companion eBook (in PDF format) for $10 to customers who purchase this book now. Convenient and fully searchable, the PDF version of any content-rich, page-heavy Apress book makes a valuable addition to your programming library. You can easily find and copy code—or perform examples by quickly toggling between instructions and the application. Even simultaneously tackling a donut, diet soda, and complex code becomes simplified with hands-free eBooks!

Once you purchase your book, getting the $10 companion eBook is simple:

❶ Visit **www.apress.com/promo/tendollars/**.

❷ Complete a basic registration form to receive a randomly generated question about this title.

❸ Answer the question correctly in 60 seconds, and you will receive a promotional code to redeem for the $10.00 eBook.

eBookshop

233 Spring Street, New York, NY 10013

Offer valid through 4/10.